THE PRIME MINISTERS

THE PRIME MINISTERS

FROM SIR ROBERT WALPOLE TO EDWARD HEATH

EDITED BY HERBERT VAN THAL

STEIN AND DAY/*Publishers*/New York

First published in the United States of America in 1975
Copyright © 1974 by George Allen & Unwin Ltd
All rights reserved
Printed in the United States of America
Stein and Day/*Publishers*/Scarborough House,
Briarcliff Manor, N.Y. 10510

Library of Congress Cataloging in Publication Data

Van Thal, Herbert Maurice, 1904–
The Prime Ministers.

Includes bibliographies.
CONTENTS: Sir Robert Walpole to Sir Robert
Peel.—From Lord John Russell to Edward Heath.
1.   Prime ministers—Great Britain—Biography.
I.   Title.
DA28.4.V36   942'.00992 [B]   74-26983
ISBN 0-8128-1738-9

CONTENTS

PART ONE

PART TWO

ILLUSTRATIONS

—————

PART ONE

PART TWO

All portraits except those listed below are from the National Portrait Gallery, with whose permission they are published in this volume.

The portraits on pages 94, 116, 522, and 610 are from the Mansell Collection. The one on page 200 is from the Radio Times Picture Library. The photographs on pages 676, 704, 722, 742, 754, and 776 were supplied by the photographer Vivienne.

PART ONE

THE PRIME MINISTERS

SIR ROBERT WALPOLE TO SIR ROBERT PEEL

INTRODUCTION BY G. W. JONES

THE OFFICE OF PRIME MINISTER

THE OFFICE OF PRIME MINISTER

There is really in law no office of prime minister. No statute grants him powers. Only in 1905 did the prime minister even become known to the law, when by royal warrant he was declared as having precedence next after the Archbishop of York. Statutes occasionally mention him, as in 1937 when the Ministers of the Crown Act referred to the salary to be paid to the 'Prime Minister and First Lord of the Treasury'. Even the name came into official use only from 1878 when, in the Treaty of Berlin, the Earl of Beaconsfield was called 'First Lord of the Treasury and Prime Minister of Her Britannic Majesty'. The office of prime minister has been based on convention, and has been shaped by personal and political factors. It is often noted that the office is what the holder makes of it, and that is why a sensible way to study the development of the office is by biographies of its holders.

Some prime ministers have been assertive, keen to stamp their ideas on the whole government and frequently interfering in the departments of their ministers, taking initiatives and revelling in the shaping of specific policies, above all in foreign affairs, the area most susceptible to prime ministerial involvement. Others have been passive, content to preside over a team of prima donnas and to arbitrate in disputes between them. The office of prime minister is sufficiently unstructured for different men with different personalities to make entirely different use of it, and in this respect there has been little change over the years, certainly no progression from the passive to the assertive. The indolent Melbourne merely presided, while Peel engaged himself in the work of every department. Lloyd George was the most powerful prime minister of any, but he was followed by Bonar Law, the unknown prime minister, and the even more retiring Baldwin, who was in turn succeeded by the dynamic Chamberlain. To arrive at the top, and to stay, demands assertion and ambition, but the drive to become prime minister does not necessarily manifest itself later in a desire to dominate what cabinet colleagues are doing. Further, those who have been responsible for choosing prime ministers have not always picked the most assertive. At times the conciliator and healer of party wounds has been selected, at other times a harsher character. The fussy Eden was followed by the subtle Macmillan; and the bland Sir Alec Douglas-Home was replaced by the abrasive Edward Heath.

In addition to the temperaments of prime ministers and the way they have conceived their role, the office has been much affected by the political circumstances of the time and by the cabinet colleagues prime ministers have faced. Some prime ministers reach office in a very strong position, often after winning an election, and can select their ministers and shape policies with little challenge. Later, however, troubles mount up, public support is eroded, criticism from the party grows and rivals manoeuvre to unseat them. Much of a prime minister's time, his most precious resource, may have to be expended simply on retaining his position. Others may take over in difficult circumstances, surmount the problems, win public applause and then decline, battered by events over which they have little control, like foreign affairs, the performance of the economy or personal scandals. It might be expected that war raises up prime ministers, like Lloyd George and Churchill, but it has destroyed the careers of as many as it has elevated, like Asquith and Chamberlain. A prime minister faces not only a changing situation but also a group of colleagues between whom the balance of power is constantly shifting. They are far from being his subordinates, and their ambitions and fortunes rise and fall, at times to support and at others to undermine his authority.

Despite all these variables certain general political forces and developments have contributed to shape the office of prime minister from Walpole's time onwards: the waning of the influence of the Crown, for example, the extension of the franchise, the rise of political parties, the decline of the House of Lords and the growth in the functions of government and its full-time officials. Changes in the Constitution emerged by fits and starts; the development was not even. With hindsight it is all too easy to see certain isolated incidents as establishing some new convention, whereas they were really the result of temporary personal and political factors. One has to be wary of dating certain practices before the basic political forces had begun to operate. For example, it is sometimes suggested that the doctrine of collective responsibility can be identified from 1746, when the King forced out the Pelhams and replaced them with Granville and Bath. Forty-five of the Pelham administration resigned too and the King, finding that he could not secure a stable administration with a firm majority in the Commons, dismissed Granville and took back the Pelhams. This episode, however, was unique at the time and marked no major change in the Constitution. In 1782, although North and most of his ministers resigned, the King's favourite, Thurlow, remained as Lord Chancellor, and a year later George III was able to dismiss the Fox–North Coalition and by royal favour alone sustain Pitt in office, despite a number of Commons defeats, until his eventual triumph at the general election. Governments of the eighteenth century rarely came and went as a body: collective responsibility was slow to develop.

The office of prime minister was itself slow to develop before the eighteenth century, because kings were their own prime ministers. The monarch directed his Government, initiating and formulating its policies and watching over their implementation. He selected and dismissed his ministers, who were truly royal servants dependent on his favour. His closest advisers were those who possessed particular talents he valued, such as military prowess, diplomatic skill, administrative capacity and political acumen. They were a loose group of individuals, bound together only by a common allegiance to the Crown. He consulted them individually whenever he felt the need of their advice or else met them together in sessions of his Privy Council and its committees. Occasionally one minister might come to exercise a preponderant influence, and the King would for a time follow his suggestions on a wide range of issues. Opponents of the minister and his policies would depict him as an overmighty subject holding the King in thrall. As long as he retained the confidence of the King, however, he was secure. But once the King withdrew his support, the minister faced exclusion from the court, disgrace, exile and sometimes the block. Precursors of the prime minister might be found in Henry VII's Morton, Henry VIII's Wolsey or Cromwell, Elizabeth's Burghley, James I's Cecil and Charles I's Buckingham and Strafford. Most came to a sorry end, although some were more circumspect and survived and indeed prospered.

During Elizabeth's reign, Parliament was at times very critical of her Government's measures, and a major task of some of her ministers, therefore, became the management of Parliament, especially the Commons. On its front bench sat a few of her Privy Councillors to argue the Queen's cause. James I and especially Charles I, finding that words were not enough to persuade Parliament, tried to rule without it, but the Civil War established Parliament as a permanent part of the Constitution. Charles II, determined never again to endure exile, tried to produce an amenable Parliament, remodelling the borough corporations which sent representatives to the Commons. In his reign his chief ministers, Clarendon and later Danby, began the first systematic attempts to build a block of loyal government adherents in the Commons through a careful distribution of patronage, pensions and preferment. Their attempts failed and Charles II sought to dispense with Parliament. His brother James II also found Parliament impossible to control, and his efforts to tamper with the justices of the peace, who played a major part in electing country representatives to the Commons, helped provoke the Glorious Revolution. From 1689 annual sessions of Parliament were necessary to provide the King with the money he needed, especially for his wars.

Now that the King could no longer ignore Parliament one skill became increasingly necessary for his ministers: the ability to win its support. A figure like Sunderland, who could take over and elaborate the methods of Clarendon and Danby, soon became a leading minister. Between 1689 and 1714 such a broker would undertake to act as an intermediary between the Crown and the parties in Parliament, forming alliances amongst selected peers who were prominent in the Lords and controlled some nominations in the Commons. Patronage was dispensed to create ties of loyalty, and to the aristocratic dependants in the Commons would be added those MPs from constituencies controlled by the Crown. But because the latter group was so small and party loyalties were so strong, the Crown could never be certain of Parliamentary support which could be eroded by incompetence, disasters or demands for heavy taxes. William III relied heavily on his parliamentary manager, but he never allowed one man to engross his ear on the policies of his Government. Anne, however, because of her poor health and inferior abilities, let her parliamentary managers, notably Godolphin and Harley, supervise the Government generally, although she was no figurehead. So great was the influence of Godolphin and Harley that they were called 'prime ministers', a term first used for the chief ministers of the King of France.

In 1721 Walpole emerged as the single most important minister. His pre-eminence was to last for twenty-one years and to earn him in popular estimation the title of Britain's first prime minister. Before Walpole, the King's chief ministers had invariably been members of the House of Lords and had exercised their influence from a variety of the great offices of state: as Lord Chancellor, Secretary of State or, most commonly, Lord Treasurer. Walpole was the first chief minister to operate from the Commons, and he began the association of the King's first minister with the position of First Lord of the Treasury. In this department, the centre for the distribution of patronage, especially government jobs, Walpole was able to form his alliances, win elections and build a block of supporters in Parliament. In this department, too, he was strategically placed to shape and then pilot through the Commons the Government's annual money bills, its main legislation. For this reason, also, Walpole held the office of Chancellor of the Exchequer.

Walpole's dominance depended above all on royal favour. The King was still the major force in government decision-making. His closet was where the main decisions were taken and where Walpole courted him, even using the Queen to further his policies. Walpole also depended on the House of Commons, which could obstruct the King's legislative proposals and bring down his ministers, for patronage could tie many to the Government but was never enough to bind a sure majority. Walpole wooed the Commons, paying attention to its moods, deploying his debating skill to allay its anxieties, and winning its support by argument and by adopting policies of which it approved. The independent country gentry who could not be bought were especially cultivated by Walpole, who loved to display himself as at heart really one of them. Management of the Commons was Walpole's *forte*. The King's support alone could not sustain Walpole when he lost his majority in the Commons due to mismanagement of the war. The confidence of both the Court and the Commons was essential to keep him in office.

There was strictly no office of prime minister. Indeed the term was used as one of opprobrium against Walpole who in fact denied that he was prime minister. Later in the century both George Grenville and Lord North disavowed the expression as applied to them. The King was the head of his Government and dealt with each minister individually about departmental matters without the interposition of a chief minister, or a Cabinet. The Commons, too, opposed the development of the office of prime minister, since it wanted to hold each minister responsible to it, and any sole or prime minister would blur that line of direct responsibility. Walpole was prime minister because of his personal sway, not because he held a particular office.

The Hanoverians only rarely attended Cabinet, thus leaving the chairman, the prime minister, the most important member except for the rare occasions when he was overshadowed by more powerful colleagues as happened to the Earl of Wilmington, 1742-3, or the Duke of Portland, 1783. But kings were still decisive. They selected all the ministers, each one of whom enjoyed direct access to the Crown. The King expected the Cabinet to discuss only matters he had referred to it and to give advice only when he asked it to. He kept control over major policy, and at times had to intervene in detail more than he desired, like George III coping with the indecisiveness of Lord North. The withdrawal of the King from the Cabinet did help it attain some sense of unity from regularly working together, and this was strengthened by bonds of patronage, family connection and a broad adherence to party principles. But because the discipline and ideology of the modern mass party were as yet absent, faction leaders were ready to break away, hoping for royal favour and advancement. This prevented the prime minister from heading a united team, and he still needed the assistance of the Crown to help him win elections. An eighteenth-century prime minister was not prime minister because he won an election; he won the election because the King had made him prime minister.

The decline in the influence of the Crown was the most important factor shaping the rise of prime ministerial power. Pitt, installed in office by royal injunction alone, was the prime minister who did most to weaken the Crown. Although Rockingham's economical reforms had eradicated some of the positions with which the Crown might reward its supporters, Pitt's administrative reforms, which sought to make government cheaper and more efficient, eliminated still more. Pitt also reduced the crown's power by insisting that his Cabinet consist only of men loyal to him – he forced the ejection of Thurlow in 1792 – and also that it should discuss any matter it liked and give advice to the King unasked. The King, however, had confidence in Pitt, and would never have tolerated his main rival, Fox, as chief minister. Pitt's longevity in office, 1783-1801 and 1804-6, further enhanced his personal authority, as did the King's insanity, beginning in 1788, which left more and more business in the hands of his ministers, especially the prime minister. The war, too, raised Pitt's stature, since he appeared as the national leader against revolution and the French. Yet Pitt was not prepared to press Catholic emancipation against the King's wishes: on some policies the King was still decisive. Although Pitt disclaimed the title of prime minister, he admitted that a principal minister was needed. In the first decade of the nineteenth century the title became acceptable, and Perceval used the term quite comfortably.

The incompetence of George IV and William IV, and the political immaturity of Victoria in her early years, further diminished the power of the Crown, while Liverpool's fifteen-years term as prime minister, even serving George IV who disliked him, strengthened the hold of the King's ministers. The rise of new political issues, the growing public interest and participation in politics, stimulated by the expansion of literacy and the provincial press, and the emergence of a variety of pressure groups, lobbying for numerous causes, all helped to focus more authority on the Cabinet and its chairman, and less on the monarch who seemed increasingly out of touch with the new popular politics.

The Parliamentary Reform Act of 1832, sweeping away rotten and nomination boroughs, finally shattered the capacity of the Crown to win elections. In 1834-5 the King's weakness was starkly revealed. William IV dismissed Melbourne and appointed Peel. At the ensuing general election royal influence was not enough to secure Peel a majority. In six weeks he was defeated six times by the new Commons. The King recognised that he had to return to Melbourne. In 1839 Melbourne's Government met a number of defeats in the Commons, and Victoria reluctantly asked Peel to try to form an administration. He refused when she rejected his request to dismiss some Whig ladies from her bedchamber as a gesture of her good faith, and so Melbourne continued with his minority Government. Peel had thought that a sign of royal confidence was necessary for him to serve as prime minister. In 1841 Victoria's support of Melbourne at the general election failed to bring him a majority in the Commons, where his Government was defeated. He then resigned and the Queen sent for Peel. He formed an administration and insisted on the removal of the Whigs from the Queen's bedchamber. The Commons had imposed a prime minister on the Queen and he had imposed on her his views as to who should be her intimate advisers. The precedent had been established that the Commons not the Crown determined the fate of governments.

Between 1832 and 1867 the power of Parliament to make and un-make prime ministers was at its peak. Royal and aristocratic 'influence' had not yet been replaced by 'party' as the device to bind followers and leaders. Elections in these years produced Parliaments made up of loose groupings with unstable attachments. Governments rarely had a clear majority, and suffered frequent defeats, but only resigned when the votes indicated a clear discrediting of the administration. This fluidity enabled the Crown to play a role as an intermediary in the negotiations that led to the choice of a prime minister. It had to select one who was able to win the support of enough leaders of the shifting groups to ensure a majority, or at least enough votes to carry on. The individual preference of the monarch could be important in this situation. A prime minister in the mid-years of the century emerged from a mixture of royal favour, support from the leaders of the groups in the Commons, backing from the peers, and popular acclaim – in varying proportions at different times. Once in office the main task of the prime minister was not so much retaining the support of the Crown as retaining the support of his colleagues and leaders of groups in the Commons.

The widening of the franchise in 1867 and 1884, the rough equalisation of electoral divisions in 1885, the secret ballot of 1872 and the limitations on election expenses in 1883 finally put paid to the exercise of patronage or influence as the means by which monarchs and peers could manipulate elections to the Commons. The verdict of the electorate was now decisive in the choice of a prime minister. After Disraeli's defeat at the general election of 1868 he resigned before meeting the Commons, as did Gladstone in 1874. A clear majority for one party and its leader precluded any independent judgement by the Crown, or by the Commons. The Crown's personal preference could be influential only if no party had a clear majority or if a party with a clear majority had no obvious leader, as when a prime minister died in office. Victoria had, reluctantly, to appoint Gladstone in 1892, but she was able to select Rosebery in 1894 after Gladstone's resignation left a void in the leadership. And in the twentieth century the Crown's influence on the choice of prime minister was significant only in 1923 and 1931, and possibly in 1957 and 1963. Now that both parties have laid down clearly that their parliamentary parties will elect their leaders, the freedom of the Crown has been so circumscribed that it can be decisive only when no one party has a clear majority in the Commons.

Nor is the choice of a prime minister limited by the title Deputy Prime Minister, which has been used informally and infrequently since 1942 to describe the minister who performs prime ministerial functions in Cabinet and Parliament if the prime minister is absent or indisposed. However, there is strictly no such position, since it would seem to limit the Crown and the parliamentary party by putting into the hands of the existing prime minister the power to choose his successor. The title

First Secretary of State has sometimes been used since 1962 for the minister to whom the prime minister deputes his duties when absent.

To win the newly enfranchised voters after 1867 the parliamentary parties began to create highly organised central machines linked to local parties. And outside Parliament emerged the Labour Party with a disciplined organisation, seeking to win elections, achieve power and carry out a distinctive programme. The rise of new political issues which polarised opinions, and the more passionate intensity with which politics was conducted, strengthened attachments to the party organisations. Members of the Commons were now elected because of the party label they bore and the leader they championed. In the House they were obliged to support him, unless some exceptional issue justified rebellion and the bringing down of their own government. The influence of the prime minister was thus enhanced now that he was sustained by the votes of the electorate, the party organisation and a normally reliable majority in the Commons.

With these resources he could by the 1870s select whom he wanted for his ministers. The Queen might try to influence his choice, objecting to some, urging the claims of others and suggesting reallocations of responsibilities, but her views amounted to advice only. The Crown's influence over the Cabinet was limited to advising, encouraging and warning. The Queen had the right to be consulted but could not prevail against a united Cabinet with a firm majority in the Commons. The prime minister was the only channel of communication between the Cabinet and the monarch; at his discretion he might inform her of the different views expressed, but rarely who held them so that she could not intrigue behind the scenes to shape Cabinet policy. Besides some little scope in the choice of prime minister, the only important power left to the Crown was to grant or refuse a prime minister's request for a dissolution of Parliament. But this power seems very limited, and there is no British precedent for refusing a request to dissolve. Thus by the twentieth century the powers of the Crown had been narrowly confined. In 1936 the prime minister and Cabinet were able even to compel the abdication of the King.

The prime minister's power over his colleagues increased too. His ability to dismiss them emerged later than his ability to appoint them. Even at the end of the nineteenth century Salisbury felt that he could remove a minister from office only for some clear and palpable failure. Asquith, however, claimed that a prime minister had to be a good butcher, and Lloyd George wielded the axe with dexterity. In the latter part of the nineteenth century it became established that only the prime minister could call cabinet meetings, and since 1918 the decision to request a dissolution is no longer made by the Cabinet, but by the prime minister alone, although most prime ministers usually discuss possible dates with their leading colleagues.

As the franchise was widened the prime minister needed to appeal increasingly to the mass electorate. Although Chatham and Grey had earlier been the darlings of the mob, and although Peel's Tamworth Manifesto might be seen as an early popular appeal, Gladstone's demagogic pilgrimages, typified by his Midlothian campaign of 1879–80, inaugurated the new era. Previously, the public's participation in politics was limited to sporadic bouts of rioting in protest against some enormity. Now they selected the Government and prime minister; they may not have appreciated the significance of the issues being debated but at least they understood the clash of the gladiatorial party leaders. This personalisation of politics, accelerated by Gladstone and Disraeli, increased the stature of the prime minister, and influenced the qualities that were regarded as necessary in the model prime minister. The new mass media of communications of the twentieth century, especially television, made it even more vital for a prime minister to be adept at projecting an attractive public image.

The extension of the franchise and the growing public involvement in politics raised the importance of the House of Commons at the expense of the House of Lords. Of the 22 men who were prime ministers between 1721 and 1834, 14 were in the Lords and 8 in the Commons. Of the 11 between 1834 and 1902, 8 were in the Lords and 5 in the Commons (Russell and Disraeli are counted twice because they headed administrations as commoners and as peers). Since 1902 all 15 have been from the Commons. It was clear that the Commons was the main arena of politics: here the life of the Government was at stake, and its measures, especially financial Bills, could succeed or fail; and here too, in the twentieth century, was the Opposition. When Lord Curzon was not made prime minister in 1923 one reason advanced was that a prime minister should sit in the Commons to be able to reply to the attacks of the Opposition. In the nineteenth century when prime ministers had been peers difficulties had frequently arisen between themselves and the Leaders in the House of Commons. The answer was to have a prime minister in the more important chamber. In 1963 when Lord Home was asked to try to form a government he renounced his peerage and sought election to the Commons.

The reduction of aristocratic participation in Cabinets to around two or three has had the effect, it is sometimes argued, of strengthening the control of the prime minister over his Cabinet. Members of the Commons are said to be more ambitious for office than peers, and to be more likely to defer to prime ministerial views in the hope of promotion or to avoid dismissal. However, the eighteenth and nineteenth centuries show scant evidence that political and personal ambitions, and desire for office, were absent from the aristocratic temperament.

In their allocation of duties all prime ministers since Walpole have held the office of First Lord of the Treasury, except Salisbury during most of his premierships. Until the time of Peel all prime ministers in the Commons were also Chancellors of the Exchequer. After Peel the position of Chancellor of the Exchequer was usually held by another minister, save when Gladstone and Baldwin held it for brief periods. Occasionally a prime minister held some other office in which he was especially concerned, like Wellington, Salisbury and MacDonald, who were also Foreign Secretaries, or Churchill, who was also Minister of Defence. Some have for a short time held non-departmental posts like Lord Privy Seal or Lord President of the Council. But in the twentieth century prime ministers have generally regarded holding offices other than that of prime minister and First Lord of the Treasury as too great a burden. Before 1942 prime ministers in the Commons had acted as Leaders of the House of Commons, but Churchill felt the task too onerous with his other duties and so a separate responsibility was created. A prime minister, however, is normally close to his Leader of the Commons and above all to the Chief Whip, since he wants to keep his finger on the pulse of the Commons. Indeed when Parliament is sitting he normally has daily chats with his Chief Whip about the state of the party in Parliament. Thus some of the functions, especially the details, once performed by the prime minister have been transferred to other ministers in order to reduce his workload.

The great increase in the scope and complexity of government activities in the twentieth century has considerably altered the position of the prime minister, adding to his resources in some ways but constraining him in others. Peel broke his health with the strain of trying to oversee the work of all departments, and in this century no one man can control all that government does. Public expenditure has soared, the number of civil servants grown and the departments of state have become huge administrative empires. At the head of these departments are ministers with statutory powers, and they are the main components of the Cabinet. If the prime minister wants to achieve anything in government, he must work with and through them. They have at their disposal their departments to back and brief them, while the prime minister lacks comparable administrative support and the time to master issues with equal thoroughness. He may have chosen his ministers, and could dismiss them, but usually some of them command so much political support within the party and among the public that he could not exclude them without seriously undermining his Government. His Cabinet ministers are his colleagues, not his subordinates; with them he is engaged in constant negotiations and consultation. He is the most important member of the Cabinet, responsible for drawing up its agenda, for guiding its discussions and for summing up its decisions, and therefore his backing is eagerly sought by ministers for their proposals. But he could not impose his own view on a reluctant Cabinet: he is only as strong as the Cabinet lets him be.

His personal staff is small: now half a dozen civil servants in his private office, separated from a few cronies and political assistants at No. 10 Downing Street, like Harold Wilson's Marcia Williams or Edward Heath's Douglas Hurd. His staff, and its size, is not very different from what was available at the start of the nineteenth century, except that the private office contains about three more people and consists wholly of civil servants. Only in wartime have prime ministers established something akin to a prime minister's department. Lloyd George formed a secretariat, the 'garden suburb', under Professor Adams, and Winston Churchill set up a statistical section under Professor Lindemann. Both units provided their prime ministers with a stream of advice about proposals coming up from the departments. Such prime ministerial personal staff aroused the enmity of other ministers and their civil servants and seemed to undermine Cabinet government. After the wars they were disbanded, and prime ministers have subsequently been punctilious about not having their own department to oversee the work of their colleagues and have stressed that Britain has a Cabinet and not a presidential form of government.

Prime ministers have been able to find some of the administrative assistance they require, while staying within the constraints of the British Constitution, by using the Cabinet Office. First set up in 1916 to serve the War Cabinet, it helps the prime minister to draw up the Cabinet agenda, processes departmental submissions, records Cabinet decisions, circulates them to departments and tries to ensure they are obeyed. It is a general co-ordinator of government, servicing the vast network of Cabinet committees. It provides briefs on topics relating to more than one department. It is the home for a number of special agencies like the Central Statistical Office, the Chief Scientific Adviser and his staff and the Central Policy Review Staff set up in 1970 for strategic policy analysis. During the 1960s the Cabinet Office greatly increased in size and in its range of interests, and its official head, the Cabinet Secretary, is a key adviser of the prime minister. But this important nerve centre of government is not simply at the disposal of the prime minister. It serves the Cabinet as a whole, although the prime minister as chairman of the Cabinet and co-ordinator-in-chief of governmental activities makes most use of it, and directs it.

The prime minister has been depicted as at the apex of the civil service. Since 1920 his approval has been necessary for the leading permanent positions in the departments: permanent secretary, deputy secretary and principal finance and establishment officers. The official head of the home civil service has been a particularly close adviser of the prime minister, and since 1968 the prime minister has been Minister for the Civil Service. However, he does not spend much time on the internal problems of the civil service. He leaves the running of the department to other ministers, and ratifies choices for the top official appointments which come from the consensus of the foremost civil servants themselves. The prime minister does not control the civil service: it largely controls itself.

It is also often said that the prime minister is in a position of impregnable power. At the apex of his party he is depicted as commanding the loyalty of its members both inside and outside Parliament. His Government is never toppled, it is argued, since his majority, however small, will always hold because of party discipline and loyalty. But Asquith in 1916 and Lloyd George in 1922 showed that prime ministers of coalitions are particularly vulnerable to a loss of support from their partners, while MacDonald in 1931 and Chamberlain in 1940 showed that prime ministers can lose enough of their own party's support to make continuing in office an impossibility. In any case all prime ministers have constantly battled against plots and rumours of plots to unseat them. Their office has never been secure.

Although the prime minister is the single most important member of the Cabinet, power has not yet become concentrated in him. He is constrained by two principles of the British Constitution, which still operate. The doctrine of 'individual ministerial responsibility' puts authority into the hands of his ministers, who in addition are buttressed by the administrative resources of their departments and the political resources of their supporters in the party. The doctrine of 'collective Cabinet responsibility' ensures that the Cabinet is still the place where the politically controversial and most important decisions are taken. Britain's executive is genuinely collective. And responsibility to Parliament is still meaningful. Politicians become prime ministers chiefly because they have impressed their parliamentary colleagues by their performances in the Commons, and they retain their positions by demonstrating their continuing parliamentary versatility. Once their hold over the House, in debate or at question time, falters, criticism rises and speculation is rife about the need to change the leader. Prime ministers take great pains to prevent the occurrence that could pull them down – the conjunction of backbench disaffection with the emergence of a single rival around whom the disaffected and the most weighty Cabinet colleagues could coalesce. The resources of the prime minister are great, but so are the constraints on his use of the resources. The Cabinet, his ministers and his party in Parliament cannot be overruled.

FURTHER READING

Carter, Byrum E., *The Office of Prime Minister* (London, 1956)
Crossman, R. H. S., Introduction to Walter Bagehot, *The English Constitution* (London, 1963)
Jennings, Sir Ivor, *Cabinet Government* (Cambridge, 3rd edition, 1959)
King, Anthony (ed.) *The British Prime Minister* (London, 1969)
Mackintosh, John P., *The British Cabinet* (London, 2nd edition, 1968)
Walker, Patrick Gordon, *The Cabinet* (London, 2nd edition, 1972)

SIR ROBERT WALPOLE

BY

GEOFFREY HOLMES

Robert Walpole, born 26 August 1671, third but first surviving son of Robert Walpole, MP, of Houghton, Norfolk, and Mary, daughter of Sir Jeffrey Burwell. Educated at Eton and King's College, Cambridge. Married (1) 1700 Catherine, daughter of John Shorter, Baltic merchant, three sons (Robert, later Lord Walpole, Edward and Horace) and two daughters. (2) 1737 Maria, daughter of Thomas Skerrett, two illegitimate daughters. Whig MP for Castle Rising 1701–2, King's Lynn 1702–Jan. 1712 (expelled from the House for alleged corruption), Feb.–Mar. 1712 (election void) and 1713–42. Member of Prince George's Admiralty Council 1705–8; Secretary-at-War 1708–10 (Acting Secretary Jan.–Sept. 1710); Treasurer of the Navy 1710–11 (dismissed); Paymaster of the Forces 1714–15; Chancellor of the Exchequer and First Lord of the Treasury 1715–17 (resigned); Paymaster of the Forces 1720–1; Chancellor of the Exchequer and First Lord of the Treasury 1721–42 (resigned). KB 1725; KG 1726; created Earl of Orford 1742. Died 1745.

Robert Walpole, 1st Earl of Orford. Studio of J. B. van Loo

SIR ROBERT WALPOLE

Sir Robert Walpole[1] is traditionally considered the first British prime minister; and traditions, however capriciously and illogically their seeds are planted, are notoriously difficult to uproot. In this case tradition will serve as usefully as anything else to mark one of the major watersheds in Britain's political and constitutional development. For how does one define a 'prime minister' in an age when no such office was legally recognised and the term itself, more often than not, was used pejoratively? The criteria are so variable that we would do well to recognise that a cast-iron definition of the indefinable is impossible.

There were many respects in which even Walpole cannot be compared with a modern prime minister. He was not carried to power on the tide of a party electoral victory: that was not how the political system worked in the eighteenth century. What is more, for twenty years Walpole led a government which was never certain, in the twentieth-century sense, of commanding a majority in the House of Commons. He was never asked by either of the two kings he served, George I and George II, 'to form a ministry'; and in the early years of his supremacy he had to share office with some very uncomfortable bedfellows. There were many of his party, the Whigs, to whom he became anathema, who rejected his primacy and who opposed him venomously.

On the other hand he was by no means the first English politician to be labelled 'prime minister' by his contemporaries. A macabre opposition pamphlet of 1733, entitled *A Short History of Prime Ministers in Great Britain*, found abundance of historical material for its cautionary tales. More reputably, there were several seventeenth-century precedents, especially Danby in the 1670s; and two far stronger ones in the early eighteenth century, Lord Godolphin and Robert Harley, Earl of Oxford, who presided over the Treasury in succession from 1702 to 1714. It was after the Revolution of 1688, when Parliament finally came to stay, with automatic yearly sessions of four to six months' duration, that the Treasury took on a new political dimension. Since 'govern-

[1] The name is often spelt 'Walpool' in contemporary correspondence, which suggests that this is how it was pronounced.

ment business' and 'financial business' were largely synonymous, and the Treasury was the most obvious channel of official patronage, it was always easier after the Revolution for the effective head of the Treasury to undertake with more success than any other minister the maintenance of a regular working partnership between the executive and the legislature. And the long wars against Louis XIV's France made this new task crucial.

Under William III royal control remained too firm to allow a 'prime minister' to emerge. But under the invalid and far less able Anne both Godolphin and Harley wielded a good deal of the power, and enjoyed much of the status, that Walpole made his own as First Lord of the Treasury from 1721[2] to 1742. They also experienced – as Walpole did – some of the limitations attendant on any minister's authority at a time when the royal prerogative still carried meaning and when possessing the sovereign's full confidence was an essential ingredient in political mastery. There were, however, important differences. Walpole, for instance, was every inch a party man, serving the national interest as he saw it but wearing his Whiggery as proudly as he wore his Garter ribbon and star. Godolphin and Harley, under whom the young Walpole had served, were birds of a different feather. Though forced to work within the existing two-party framework, each was fundamentally anti-party, concerned as the Queen's 'Manager' or 'Undertaker' with harnessing the power of the dominant party to the working needs of government, while keeping at bay as far as possible its most violent partisans.

This led to two further differences of significance between their primacy and Walpole's. The Cabinets over which they effectively presided, under the Queen, were generally less homogeneous than those of the later era and invariably more difficult for the chief minister to dominate (though the solidarity even of Walpole's Cabinets can be exaggerated); while the discipline which Walpole at his peak was able to impose on *all* office-holders was far more rigorous than anything Godolphin or Harley could achieve. In this respect, perhaps more than any other, Sir Robert's long ministry saw the emergence of a prime ministerial authority without precedent and, as it seemed to many contemporaries, unconstitutional.

[2] Space does not permit discussion of the controversial question of how far Walpole was, in effect, prime minister in his first year at the Treasury, and whether he could have triumphed over his chief rival, Sunderland, had not the latter been prematurely removed from contention by death in April 1722.

Finally, although Godolphin was a competent parliamentarian and
Harley a skilful one, their position rested more on the trust of the monarch than on the approbation of Parliament. Walpole's rested equally on
both; and his personal dominance over Parliament was certainly more
complete. A basic factor here was his realisation that in order to be in
the best position to control Parliament the King's leading minister must
sit, and continue to sit, in the Commons. It cannot be overstressed how
much Walpole was an innovator in this respect; how far he defied convention when in 1723 he accepted a peerage for his son, Robert, instead
of for himself; and how important in the long term his innovation was
– even if not all his successors followed his pattern. And for Walpole
mere presence in the Commons, and periodic participation in key
debates, was not enough. Until 1733 he was the only Commoner in the
Cabinet; and both before and after that he acted as the day-to-day
leader of the House, piloting it through its business with the aid of a
handful of loyal subalterns and, from 1727 onwards, of his invaluable
'Governor', Speaker Onslow. Considering also the 'incredible . . .
variety and quantity of business he dispatched',[3] one can fairly say that
in terms of sheer burden of work he could comfortably stand comparison with any modern peacetime prime minister.

Rarely, if ever, have two decades of British history seemed to
historians so overshadowed by the figure of one man – other than a
king or queen – as the 1720s and 1730s seem to be by Walpole. This is
altogether natural. To contemporaries the presence of 'the great man'
(George II's *gros homme*) was just as engulfing. Not since Burghley had
there been such an epic period of continuous high office. And in length
there has been no equal since 1742. It has a mesmeric quality which can
easily tempt the unwary into assuming that all these twenty-one years,
save the last two or three, saw Walpole's power at much the same pitch
of unquestioned supremacy. This was not so. A graph of his authority
in the ministry and at Court, for instance, would start relatively low;
would begin to rise quite steeply in April 1722, when the Earl of Sunderland died, and sharply again after the defeat of a younger rival, Lord
Carteret, in 1724; but would only reach the highest plateau in 1730,
when Townshend resigned. And from 1737, the year Walpole's position
was damaged by the Prince of Wales's quarrel with his parents and by
the death of Queen Caroline, the year too that loyal Cabinet colleagues

[3] John, Lord Hervey, *Some Materials Towards Memoirs of the Reign of King George II*,
ed. Romney Sedgwick (London, 1931), i, 17.

such as Newcastle and Hardwicke first began to kick over the traces, the line would fall progressively. Even in Parliament, throughout his career from 1721 to the election of 1741 there were peaks and troughs. The Excise crisis is well known. But there were other near-disasters. Only through the abstention of forty Tories did Walpole escape defeat over the emotive issue of the Prince's allowance in February 1737. Twelve months later an Opposition motion to reduce the Army only failed by fifteen votes in a crowded House of 518. The Walpole 'machine' was no automaton.

In certain respects Walpole left his stamp on eighteenth-century England less by what he did than by how he did it. His methods, for good or ill, provided the blueprint for the next two generations of Whigs. This is not to say the positive achievements of his regime were negligible. In some fields they were very far from that. But (in spite of his massive personal authority) it is not easy in every case to assess just how far Walpole himself was responsible for them.

This is true even of the most conspicuous legacy of the 1720s and 1730s, the legacy of political stability. For close on a century prior to the Revolution of 1688 the Constitution had been in a state of acute imbalance. The natural governing class of the country, the aristocracy and landed gentry, had been for much of this time divided in interest and loyalty. Religion and politics had been mutually embroiled. After 1689 the more serious constitutional problems were slowly resolved, but the division of both the political and the religious nations into two contesting parties, ideologically at odds, persisted. Relatively little of the social order remained untouched by the violence of Whig–Tory conflict, and in particular great bitterness was engendered between the landed interest of the country, the overtaxed, economically struggling 'mere gentry', and the rising power of High Finance, which as Henry St John wrote in 1709 was 'a new interest . . . a sort of property which was not known twenty years ago'.[4] An uncertain or insecure succession to the throne and two unpopular foreign rulers stimulated Jacobite intrigue; and although the 1715 rebellion did much to discredit the Tory party and open the way to an unchallengeable Whig supremacy, fear of conspiracy persisted. Also the Whigs in their hour of victory fell prey to fratricidal struggles; and in 1720 – the year Walpole returned to office for the third time as Paymaster-General – the whole political

4 Bodleian Library MS Eng. Misc. e.180, f. 4: to Lord Orrery, 9 July 1709 (copy).

world was convulsed by a major scandal, the South Sea Bubble. By 1721 nine Englishmen in every ten must have seriously doubted whether even under their 'Revolution Constitution' a strong, stable government, commanding widespread support in the country and based on a tranquil social order, would ever be attainable.

The next twenty years were to prove that it was attainable. And clearly it would be absurd to minimise Walpole's personal contribution to a political edifice whose strength and durability long outlived him.[5] The pursuit of tranquillity and stability, social as well as political, had been an overriding concern of his administration. He saw them both as ends eminently desirable in themselves and as prerequisites for the preservation of security; and this – the security of the Hanoverian dynasty and the security of the new United Kingdom of Great Britain from Jacobite activity and foreign threats – was with Walpole a persistent, almost obsessive, preoccupation. By the late 1730s Walpole could point to twenty-five years without major war, to substantial though not universal economic prosperity, low taxation, the repair of the social fabric by the reconciliation of the landed and moneyed interests, and a marked lowering of the political temperature – all part of the climate that made stability possible and all traceable, to a greater or lesser degree, to his specific policies.

And yet the achievement of political calm under the first two Hanoverians was far from being a one-man miracle. Even in the turbulent atmosphere of Anne's reign important lessons had been learnt, especially about the manipulation of patronage and the techniques of imposing effective executive control on the legislature. Between 1714 and 1721, too, there were strong favourable currents running which Walpole was later able to channel, and without which the most outstanding political talent must have been powerless. One such current was steadily bearing away much of the ideological debris of Stuart England, in particular its more violent religious emotions: one has only to compare the electoral issues and propaganda of, say, 1710 with those of 1722 to appreciate this. Another current was carrying along the electorate itself, so volatile and unmanageable since the late 1670s, towards certain captivation. The crucial event here was the Septennial Act of 1716.

By establishing the convention that Parliaments should last for their

[5] See J. H. Plumb, *The Growth of Political Stability in England 1675–1725* (London, 1967), especially the masterly final chapter.

statutory maximum of seven years, except when interrupted (as in 1727) by the death of a monarch, this Act exposed Walpole to only three general elections in nineteen years after 1722. Had he been forced to fight ten elections in just over twenty years, as his predecessors had under the Triennial Act between 1695 and 1715, it is hard to imagine that either he or the stable political system he created could have survived as long as they did. While it is true that large sums of money had been staked on the roulette wheel of electoral fortunes during the fierce Whig–Tory conflict of 1690–1715, the obviously enhanced value of parliamentary seats after the passing of the Septennial Act encouraged still heavier investment in the constituencies, by the great landed magnates and also by the Treasury. As these investments became more secure, so contests became fewer. In the process the contribution to Walpole's remarkably successful electoral organisation of the 'government boroughs', which could return thirty to forty members, of the big local overlords, such as Edgecumbe and Newcastle, and of such large-scale borough owners as Bubb Dodington, was made possible.[6]

Walpole reaped a further harvest from the Septennial Act. The patronage of the Crown appreciated in value no less than the parliamentary seat. When the recipient of an office early in the lifetime of a Parliament could look forward – provided he behaved with reasonable discretion – to at least a six- or seven-year tenancy, the Government's purchasing power could hardly fail to benefit. The contribution of Walpole's patronage system both to political stability and to the solidity of his own regime is now a historical commonplace. The truth is, however, that the total fund of patronage was not as great as it had been under Anne (there had of necessity been some contraction of the inflated wartime administration, and Walpole was apt to complain that there was 'not enough grass for the beasts to feed on'); but the scope of the patronage directly at Walpole's disposal as First Lord, together with the patronage of other departments which he voraciously engrossed, was certainly wider than any previous minister had enjoyed. The key to his position at the heart of the web is a factor often overlooked. The position was one which the great party chieftains of 1689–1714 would have dearly prized; but it was always denied them by the prejudices of the the Crown and the interposition of the Crown's 'Managers'. It was only when the post-Revolution generation of

[6] cf. the situation from 1701 to 1715 in W. A. Speck, *Tory and Whig: The Struggle in the Constituencies* (London, 1970).

Managers finally died out in 1714, with the fall of Oxford and the resignation of Shrewsbury, England's last Lord High Treasurer, that for the first time since the Revolution a political party found itself in direct control of the administration. And for almost seven years before Walpole became prime minister his party used this control to eliminate its opponents from all positions of influence, great and small. The way was thus prepared for him not merely to concentrate this power, uniquely, in one pair of hands, but to turn it in time as ruthlessly against rival or dissident Whigs as against Tories.

In one other respect Walpole found himself rowing with a powerful tide after 1721. He belonged to a generation which from youth to mature manhood had experienced the two most ambitious and costly wars that Englishmen had ever known. The Utrecht peace settlement of 1713 was born of mutual exhaustion. Although war had yielded Britain rich dividends, it had bled the gentry white by its financial demands, had seriously burdened other sections of the community, had added new ferocity to party conflict and had imposed heavy strains on society. Even the Whigs who had supported the struggle against France and the Bourbons most eagerly had been satiated by 1713; and Walpole himself shared in this universal reaction and repugnance scarcely less than the most xenophobic Tory squire. Peace alone did something to repair the damage to the body politic in the eight years after Utrecht. But the Fifteen rebellion, and the South Sea crisis five years later, followed inside two more years by the uncovering of the Atterbury plot, all seemed to emphasise how sick the patient still was; and they made it the more receptive thereafter to the tranquillising medicine that Walpole prescribed.

Most directly the post-war reaction ensured a strong body of support at almost all times until the late thirties for the foreign policy of the Walpole administration. This had a constant aim – to secure the dynasty and the Protestant succession and to maintain the European balance of power by diplomatic negotiation and combination – but varying emphases, resulting in the main from Walpole's own profound ignorance of Europe in 1721. He had no linguistic ability and at 44 had never set foot on continental soil. To earn and keep the confidence of a German monarch, as well as to make a respectable showing in the House of Commons, he had perforce to improve his grasp of European issues and take a stronger interest in them. But as long as his brother-in-law Lord Townshend, Secretary of State for the North, conducted foreign policy in broad accord with the prime minister's priorities, the First Lord interfered as little as possible. After the eruption of a major European crisis in 1725–6, however, Townshend began to develop in Walpole's eyes a rather alarming capacity for brinkmanship, not to mention a disturbing disregard both for the traditional Whig friendship with the Habsburg Emperor[7] and for the financial implications of an over-ambitious policy. This is why from 1728 onwards Britain's foreign policy began increasingly to bear the Prime Minister's own more conciliatory, conservative and pacific stamp. And from 1730, when Townshend resigned in disgust, until 1738, Walpole dominated the country's European relations, through two compliant Secretaries of State,[8] just as thoroughly as he dominated every other field.

In the early years of his activity he claimed two important diplomatic *coups*, the Treaty of Seville with Spain (1729) and the second Treaty of Vienna with the Emperor Charles VI (1731), which seemed at first blush to have settled the outstanding problems of these two powers not merely with Britain but with each other. Of both treaties Walpole was inordinately proud, and they gave him a quite misplaced confidence in his own talent and far-sightedness as a diplomat, a confidence he unwisely backed to the hilt in the Polish Succession crisis of 1733–5. In this crisis he used his now titanic authority to overbear the judgement of George II, Queen Caroline and most of his colleagues in order to preserve Britain's neutrality.

Walpole always remained unrepentant about this crucial decision. But in the light of subsequent events his foreign policy after 1733 is hard to defend with conviction. By 1735 Britain was more isolated than she had been for almost twenty years. Her *entente* with her old enemy, France,[9] which had been the cornerstone of both Townshend's and Walpole's diplomacy, was in ruins, though Walpole perversely refused to recognise the fact. Charles VI was alienated; and Spain, which had commercial and colonial differences with Britain, was encouraged to pursue them in the assurance that Walpole would never resort to force. Nor would he have done so even in 1739, when he reluctantly embarked on the so-called 'War of Jenkins's Ear', if his parliamentary support, his hold over the King and above all his authority over his long-docile fellow ministers had not threatened to crumble as a result of his attitude. 'It is your war,' he acidly told the Duke of Newcastle, 'and I wish you joy of it.'

[7] Since 1711, Charles VI.   [8] Newcastle and Harrington.   [9] Dating from 1716.

The peace Walpole had kept in the 1730s had not been peace with honour. But neither had it been peace at any price. He always maintained, and reiterated in a great speech to the Commons in 1739, that in both Britain's economic interests – 'the interests of a trading nation' – and those of her Protestant dynasty, a policy of neutrality and negotiation was profitable and right. His opponents sneered at his argument that war would provide the Jacobites with an opportunity they could never hope for in peacetime; the Jacobite bogy, they insisted, was just a convenient screen for Walpole to hide behind; but in the end the Forty-five rebellion was to prove him right. The economic argument was more controversial. So far as we can tell from statistics of somewhat questionable validity, some important branches of trade and many industries did make mildly accelerated progress during the years of 'business as usual' in the thirties; and the merchant shipping fleet, notoriously vulnerable in wartime, unquestionably expanded. On the other hand the aggressive mercantilist war against Spain which more and more of the Government's Whig opponents were demanding in the late 1730s, and even such a war undertaken as early as 1733 against France and Spain combined, might *if vigorously and efficiently conducted* (and this was both the crux of the matter and the great imponderable) have paid off more handsomely in terms of colonial gains and valuable future markets.

Walpole, for his part, could justifiably claim that his pacifism had at least been in the interests of the landed classes, that it had kept the Land Tax low and helped to cement the social harmony he had consciously sought since the start of his ministry. But to argue, as he did in his 1739 speech, that it had also preserved 'the balance of Europe' was self-delusion. On the contrary, the scales had been decisively tilted in favour of the Bourbon powers, by then in close alliance; Britain's international prestige was probably at its lowest ebb since the 1680s; and the pathetic failure of Walpole as a war minister in the years 1739–42 reflected in some measure the deflation of national morale as well as his own patent lack of stomach for the job in hand. If France had not been deterred from entering the colonial war by the death of Charles VI, Walpole's political career might have ended not merely in disappointment but in humiliating defeat.

It would be unjust, however, to assess him as a prime minister on his record in foreign policy. Walpole, after all, was First Lord of the Treasury. It was his reputation as the leading Whig financial expert which enabled him to lay claim to this office in the first place. It is primarily on his record as a finance minister, and on the success of his superintending interest over the whole field of the economy, that history must judge him.

It is significant that three of the most important and imaginative of Walpole's financial achievements predated his premiership: they were the fruits of earlier spells of office. His financial blueprint for untangling the ravelled affairs of the South Sea Company in the winter of 1720–1 helped to restore public confidence and government credit, so badly shaken by the Bubble crisis. The decisive first step in his plan to reduce the interest payable on most segments of the long-term National Debt had been taken earlier still, in 1717;[10] and in that same year one of his few genuine innovations, the 'Sinking Fund', devised as a mechanism for progressively paying off the capital of the £40 million War Debt (which then seemed a ruinous burden) had been launched by Stanhope soon after Walpole's resignation from the ministry.[11] These two measures, dating from the first and more adventurous half of a parliamentary career of forty-four years, proved the twin keys to the effectiveness of much of his financial policy as prime minister, and were primarily responsible for his remarkable success in keeping peacetime taxation so low. For by persisting with the Sinking Fund to the very end of his ministry, long after anxiety about the size of the National Debt had become a thing of the past, he was able to cream off into the ordinary revenue the Fund's handsome surplus, accruing from successive interest reductions.

Thanks to the success (as he saw it) of his foreign policy, Walpole was never faced with the necessity of raising the huge sums that had annually confronted Godolphin and Harley. With a modest annual budget varying between 2 and 3½ millions, the need for loans was limited, and when it did arise Walpole had at his disposal the techniques of loan management perfected by Montagu and Godolphin. He was the fortunate heir of the 'Financial Revolution'; though he could thank his own fostering of credit and assiduous cultivation of the City and

[10] His scheme to consolidate the whole Debt in the first instance at 5 per cent, despite being truncated after he left office in 1717, was of great importance. It was later taken further, with a three-stage conversion to 4 per cent in the years 1727–30.
[11] The Fund was fed mainly from the appropriated taxes 'released' by the reduction of interest payments. The best treatment of Walpole and the National Debt is in P. G. M. Dickson, *The Financial Revolution in England* (London, 1967).

financial corporations for the fact that he was able to raise a £1 million loan in 1727 at an astonishing 3 per cent. Such circumstances, it might be thought, offered a glorious opportunity for a minister of Walpole's ability and authority, particularly one with his enviable faculty for making financial complexities intelligible to the most doltish back-bencher, to effect the basic reforms in the fiscal system which his hard-pressed predecessors had not had time to conceive or carry through.

Walpole's *forte*, however, lay not in striking originality but in making the existing system work more efficiently and in rationalising it – as with his radical simplification of Customs duties in 1722[12] – where rationalisation did not reduce the amount of 'grass' available for 'the beasts'. By demanding higher standards from revenue officials and extending the authority of the Customs Commissioners to Scotland, that home-from-home for smugglers, he did what he could – though it was for the most part a losing battle – to reduce the staggering amount of duty evasion. But his celebrated Excise scheme of 1733 was the nearest Walpole came to a truly courageous fiscal reform. This scheme, which involved the relief of imported colonial tobacco, and later of imported wine, from all but nominal customs, and their subjection instead to a bonded ware-house system and an internal excise duty, was far more than an anti-smuggling device to save £500,000 a year. It was the culmination of a long-term strategy for shifting the incidence of taxation away from land and property and on to consumable commodities: ultimately, Walpole seems to have hoped, there would be no direct taxation at all except in time of emergency and war. A pilot scheme in 1724 had proved a striking minor success,[13] and by 1731 the Land Tax had been reduced to one shilling in the pound. The 1733 Excise scheme would have brought this process to its logical conclusion. The case for it on financial grounds was unanswerable. But it was abandoned in the face of an exceptional display of popular hostility, incited by opposition charges that the Government was planning a General Excise and a massive invasion of personal liberty by its inquisitorial officials.

The abortive Excise project does demonstrate, however, that Walpole's policies at the Treasury had social and political as well as financial ends. In addition to a sound and efficient revenue system, he also sought

12 See below.
13 Applying the excise to tea, coffee and cocoa, it had increased revenue on these goods by about £120,000 a year.

an *acceptable* system – one that would be sufficiently fair to conciliate all the important social interests in the country, as well as weaning the squirarchy from its natural Tory allegiance.

Whether Walpole's fiscal measures were part of an overall economic strategy as well is a question on which not all modern historians are agreed.[14] Some would argue that not until the Younger Pitt, at the earliest, did Britain have a prime minister or a Treasury minister who envisaged an organic connection between the raising of money and the regulation of the national economy, or who even recognised a responsibility to pursue a coherent 'economic policy'. It has certainly been shown beyond much doubt[15] that the so-called 'system' of protective tariffs, so marked a feature of Hanoverian England until the 1780s, developed fortuitously as a result of the desperate revenue problems of the governments of the war years 1689–1712, not of a planned ministerial initiative or as a response to contemporary economic dogma. So that Walpole's highly important tariff reforms of the early 1720s, with their emphasis on the deterring of foreign manufactures and the encouragement of domestic industry, should be seen largely as an attempt to impose some order on a haphazard and irrational state of affairs, with a particular eye to satisfying those struggling native industries, such as linen, silk and paper-making, which had benefited from their adventitious tariff cocoon in the previous thirty years. In addition, one can point to measures later in the ministry's life which clearly reflect the lobbying of politically influential pressure groups, the West India interest and others, rather than the implementation of any national policy for the good of the economy at large;[16] while parliamentary historians have revealed that several notable economic measures commonly attributed to Walpole, for example the South Carolina Bill of 1730, were in fact the result of backbench initiatives of which the Prime Minister did not always approve.

These examples of pragmatism dent the traditional picture of Walpole as the watchful economic overlord with a master-plan. But they do not necessarily destroy it. Walpole's rueful reference to the Carolina Act – 'that he was always against repealing old laws, made for the

[14] Argument is inhibited by the fact that much economic groundwork for a close analysis of Walpole's administration still remains to be done.
[15] By Professor Ralph Davis. See 'The Rise of Protection in England', *Economic History Review*, xix (1966).
[16] Of these measures the Molasses Act of 1733 is but the best-known instance.

benefit of trade, and *breaking into the Navigation Act*'[17] – illustrates one element of underlying consistency. And there can be no question that his Government remained faithful to the pledge given in the Speech from the Throne of October 1721: '. . . to make the exportation of our own commodities and the importation of the commodities used in the manufacturing of them as practicable and as easy as may be; by this means, the balance of trade may be preserved in our favour, [and] our navigation greatly increased. . . .' The cosseting of the re-export trade in colonial goods (its encouragement was to have been a major bonus of the Tobacco Excise Bill of 1733), and the crucial link in Walpole's mind between a pacific policy and economic progress, confirm an impression of overall coherence.

What is less certain, because of the different interpretation that can be put on the available statistics, is how far the effects of Walpole's policies answered their intentions. Historical orthodoxy long identified his regime with prosperity and economic growth. It is now apparent that there were important limits to what Walpole's or indeed any eighteenth-century government could achieve in the face of adverse circumstances of market fluctuation, or the natural rise and fall of certain branches of trade, or the discrimination of foreign governments against British goods. Thus Walpole could not possibly have sustained the extraordinary rate of progress the woollen cloth industry had achieved in the seventeenth century; nor could he prevent the relative decline of the sugar trade in the face of increasing French competition after 1720. Yet he still presided over the most prosperous economy in Europe. He had certainly by 1738 achieved his aim of a substantially healthier balance of trade; he had seen English shipping steadily though not spectacularly increase since 1723;[18] and he could point to the slow if painful advance of most of the heavily protected industries. Perhaps, as with so much else, he could have done more had he not been so preoccupied for much of the thirties with his political position and become less and less susceptible to new ideas or bold initiatives.

It is odd that two decades as important as the years 1720–40 in the evolution of the prime minister's office and power should have been in some ways retrogressive in the development of the Constitution. There

---

[17] Historical Manuscripts Commission, *Egmont Diary*, i, 173. Author's italics.
[18] See Ralph Davis, *The Rise of the English Shipping Industry* (London, 1962), especially pp. 27–8.

was one highly important exception. After 1733, when for the first time his administration had to fight for its life in both Houses, Walpole established the principle that *everyone* who held office or commission under the Crown, however petty, was expected politically to dance to the tune of the First Lord of the Treasury, or risk dismissal. Admittedly this principle had been foreshadowed under some of Walpole's immediate predecessors; but minor placemen had rarely been subject to more than occasional, limited purges, and Harley had held in 1706 that as long as an office-holder supported the ministry on votes of supply he should be allowed considerable latitude on other matters.[19] So the change in the 1730s was of great moment.

But what was an advance in terms of the growth of party discipline and executive control over the legislature was a setback in the development of what has been called 'the non-political civil service'. The Managers of the post-Revolution period had done much to ensure that in certain government departments[20] a solid core of experienced 'professionals' would be permitted continuity of office, regardless of the party seesaw. Walpole did not abandon this policy entirely. But even in the case of offices from which MPs were barred (and there were thousands, especially in the revenue field), he showed more political discrimination and paid less regard to professional competence or reputation. In Cabinet government, too, the newly established conventions of the post-Revolution period – regular, minuted meetings of a Cabinet of about a dozen leading ministers at which major policy issues were debated in the royal presence – were rudely disturbed by Walpole's preference for working behind the scenes with a smaller inner group of four or five. The change made for smoother policy-making; but it created suspicion and added to the reputation of the Walpole regime for autocracy and highhandedness.

In this, as in so much else, however, Walpole was a realist and not a theorist. In all his years in office there was never a time when he hankered after perfection, or let preconceived notions or ideal considerations disturb his clear-headed sense of what was attainable, or of what in political terms was necessary, merely desirable or frankly irrelevant. Much of his (in many ways misleading) reputation for 'letting sleeping dogs lie' is simply a reflection of this realism.

[19] Historical Manuscripts Commission, *Bath MSS*, i, 110–11.
[20] Most notably the Treasury, the Navy Office, the Post Office and most of the revenue departments.

In view of the host of abuses and institutions crying out for remedy in early Hanoverian England – social injustices by our standards appalling, religious discrimination, a demoralised state Church, a scandalous penal system, an administrative structure still plagued in many parts with sinecurists and enmeshed in antiquated procedures – Walpole's record of positive legislation over two decades may seem pitifully meagre.[21] But it is significant that in the 1720s and 1730s Walpole, freely slandered for so much else, was rarely criticised for this. He was observing the conventions of his day: that the prime business of government was to *govern* rather than to legislate or reform. And he could make the confession, 'I am no saint, no Spartan, no reformer' without a qualm; for he was at one with the bulk of his contemporaries in believing that government intervention to remedy most social abuses was either irrelevant or unwise at a period when society at large seemed to have rediscovered stability.

Even the historian must concede that since the years of Walpole's premiership were also years of relatively static population and prices, of a lull in the industrial advance made during the war years, and of urbanisation (outside London) at a gentle pace, the need for active paternalism was not urgent. In so far as Walpole had a 'social policy' it might appear to have been a largely oppressive one: he certainly believed in low wages on economic grounds, promoted laws against workers' 'combinations' (nascent unions), and had no hesitation in endorsing increased severity in dealing with crimes against property (it was in 1726 that the notorious 'Waltham Black Act' passed into law). And yet occasional stirrings of a social conscience can be detected. Relief of the poor was sometimes recommended to Parliament's attention (for instance in the King's Speech of 1730); though Walpole usually thought it proper to let the legislature decide how best it should be achieved, and firmly believed that, except in emergencies, the proper initiatives in such matters should be local, private or institutional. Where the Poor Law machinery or the private philanthropy of landlords and businessmen fell short there was the contribution of the Churches – the new Charity Schools, for instance, and the many

---

[21] Almost half the 600 government-sponsored Bills introduced into the Commons between 1715 and 1754 were regular supply Bills or annual mutiny Bills; and only a very small proportion of the remainder could be considered, in any meaningful sense, 'reform legislation'. See R. Sedgwick, *History of Parliament: The House of Commons 1715–54* (London, 1970), i, 5.

Societies for Reformation of Manners which had sprung up after 1688.

Walpole's attitude towards both the Church of England and Dissent was likewise pragmatic. In his apprentice years from 1701–14 he absorbed something of the anti-clericalism of the Augustan Whigs, exposed as they were to the electoral hostility of the High Churchmen, among them 80 per cent of the parish clergy; and his Commons speeches of this period also reflect his party's sympathy with Protestant nonconformity. But the Sacheverell affair of 1710, in which he was a leading prosecutor, taught him a lesson he was never to forget;[22] so too did the vital support given by the Low Church bishops to the Whig Opposition in the House of Lords in its darkest days from 1711–14. By 1721, although the Tory Occasional Conformity and Schism Acts had been repealed, the Test and Corporation Acts of Charles II's reign still remained on the Statute Book, subjecting the dissenters to continuing civil disabilities. Stanhope's attempt to neutralise these Acts in 1719 had failed, no small thanks to Walpole, who then and ever after was adamant that full civil rights for dissenters, as re-urged in the 1730s, could not be granted without offending the bishops and risking a flare-up of the ugly High Church passions of 1710. The farthest he would go in the cause of further toleration was an Annual Indemnity Bill, first passed in 1727. And since this was not always annual, and the indemnification it gave seems to have been uncertain, it left the Whigs' dissenting allies unsatisfied.

The state Church itself had little to thank Walpole for, except the retention of the Test. Politically the Church leadership gave his regime invaluable support; for the celebrated partnership of the years 1723–36 between the Prime Minister and Bishop Gibson of London, made possible by the monastic habits and infirmities of Archbishop Wake, ensured that all but a handful of bishoprics, deaneries and Crown livings in that period were filled by sound Whigs and pro-Walpoleans. Yet in return for this political support, much of it vastly time-consuming, Walpole gave Gibson no official backing for the latter's ambitious and far-reaching reform programme, including a radical administrative reorganisation; and without such encouragement the Bishop's plans withered on the vine. Walpole and his colleagues could not, of course, be entirely blamed for the Church's palpable decline in the twenties and thirties. But their cynicism assuredly did nothing to arrest it.

[22] See Geoffrey Holmes, *The Trial of Doctor Sacheverell* (London, 1973).

Britain, therefore, had some cause to rue, as well as good cause to bless, the long supremacy of Sir Robert Walpole. As well as the criticisms that can be made of specific fields of policy, it is also undeniable that the tone of politics declined between 1721 and 1742. By contrast with some of his recent predecessors Walpole's personal example was hardly edifying. Corruption and a blatantly materialistic view of politics manifestly increased during his period of office. And yet if we judge Walpole's premiership as an exhibition of the political art, in the widest sense, it would be grudging not to bestow on it the accolade.

Although he had been trained in a very different arena, he proved superbly adaptable to a new ambience in which the electrifying issues of Queen Anne's day had been defused and in which politics had become more intimate and personal than at any time since the sixteenth century. Walpole stood head and shoulders above all his contemporaries on such a scene, partly because he was so adept at balancing the major interests within the victorious party oligarchy, and partly because he was himself such a consummate master of personal relationships.[23] Above all he was one of the greatest parliamentarians who have ever lived. Patronage and discipline combined may have held together 'the Court and Treasury party', the core of his majorities in each Parliament, 1722–7, 1727–34, 1734–41. But his true calibre was shown in his peerless handling of the Independents, the 150–200 backbenchers, mostly country gentlemen, who were tied by interest neither to the Court nor to the power politicians of the Opposition. These men could in the last resort make or break any ministry. Indeed, in the end Walpole fell essentially because his foreign policy and his ineffectual war policy disenchanted too many of the country members whom he had successfully wooed for so long. For at least seventeen years, however, he had commanded their confidence and for the most part their support; commanded it by his highly effective debating skills, trenchant and direct; by his techniques of communication, to which he devoted enormous pains; by the genuine respect he showed for the House of Commons, whose 'approbation' he once declared[24] was 'preferable to all that

[23] Though as a matter of sober fact, because of the unfortunate gaps in his surviving correspondence, we know a good deal less about this aspect of his primacy than we should like to do – except as regards his relations with a number of fellow ministers, like Newcastle, and of course as regards the Court, where he hardly put a foot wrong until 1737.

[24] In the House of Commons, February 1739.

power, or even Majesty itself, can bestow'; and not least by his success in cultivating the image of himself, despite his vast fortune and princely style of living,[25] as just such another homespun, earthy, hearty, fox-hunting squire as the average backbencher.

In short, what set Robert Walpole apart from any other prime minister of the eighteenth century, save the Younger Pitt, was his capacity to achieve the maximum conceivable measure of influence and dominance *within the existing political system*. He accepted, and trimmed his sails to meet, all the rough weather which challenged the ambitious politician in early Hanoverian England: the fragmentation of the ruling one-party oligarchy; the uncertain favour of kings and courtiers; above all the crucial fact that because of the power of the independent member, the prime minister and his government never controlled an absolute majority of the Commons. Playing to perfection the dual role of 'minister with the King in the House of Commons' and 'minister for the House of Commons in the closet', Walpole mastered all the inherent difficulties of the political world in which he lived; and not only that, he turned them into positive and long-term assets. No politician can do more.

BIBLIOGRAPHY

The character of both Walpole and his age have been unforgettably captured in the first two volumes of J. H. Plumb's trilogy *Sir Robert Walpole* (London, 1956, 1960). The third volume, which will take the story from 1734 to 1745 is in active preparation. Meanwhile Archdeacon W. Coxe, *Memoirs of the Life and Administration of Sir Robert Walpole*, vol. i (London, 1798) remains a valuable storehouse of information. A brief single-volume study of outstanding merit is H. T. Dickinson, *Robert Walpole and the Whig Supremacy* (Teach Yourself History series, London, 1973). Through the author's kindness I was able to read the book in typescript while preparing this essay, to my great profit.

On particular aspects of Walpole's premiership the following works can be strongly recommended: C. B. Realey, *The Early Opposition to Sir Robert Walpole, 1720–1727* (Philadelphia, 1931); P. G. M. Dickson, *The Financial Revolution in England* (London, 1967); J. B. Owen, *The Rise of the Pelhams* (London, 1957).

[25] See J. H. Plumb, *Sir Robert Walpole: The King's Minister* (London, 1960), pp. 81–91 and *passim*.

THE EARL OF WILMINGTON
and the Carteret Administration
under Wilmington

BY

HERBERT VAN THAL

Spencer Compton, born 1673; third son of the second wife of the 3rd Earl of Northampton. Educated at St Paul's School and Trinity College, Oxford. Unmarried. Chairman of the Committee of Privileges 1705; Treasurer to Prince George of Denmark 1707; with Walpole in the committee for Sacheverell's impeachment 1709; elected member for the Borough of East Grinstead 1713; MP for the County of Sussex 1714; Privy Councillor 1716; Speaker of the House of Commons 1721; Paymaster-General 1722; KB 1725; Lord Privy Seal and Lord President of the Council 1733; First Lord of the Treasury 1742. Died 1743.

The Earl of Wilmington, by Sir Godfrey Kneller

THE EARL OF WILMINGTON

Spencer Compton was born in 1673, the youngest of the three sons of Mary Noel, the second wife of James, third Earl of Northampton. The Comptons had long been supporters of the Crown, one of Spencer's uncles having been made Bishop of London by Charles II. Spencer was educated at St Paul's and then took his degree at Trinity College, Oxford. For a while he practised at the bar in the Middle Temple. In 1698 he travelled abroad, and was elected Tory Member for Eye in Suffolk, but shortly afterwards changed his allegiance to the Whigs, a not uncommon procedure in eighteenth-century politics. He applied himself assiduously to detail work in Parliament, and by 1705 was Chairman of the Committee of Privileges; two years later he became Treasurer to Queen Anne's consort, Prince George of Denmark.

During these years he had kept up a friendship with Walpole, and in 1709 he was nominated with him to draw up the articles of impeachment against Dr Sacheverell.[1]

In 1710 Compton lost his seat in Parliament, and it was not until the new Parliament of 1713 that he was re-elected for the borough of East Grinstead. On the accession of George I in 1714, with the new election, he was nominated for both the borough of East Grinstead and the county of Sussex. He chose to represent the county, and when the new Parliament assembled he was chosen Speaker, though he declared that he had 'neither memory to retain, judgement to collect nor skill to guide their debates'. The King, however, declared he was perfectly well satisfied, and confirmed the choice of the House. When the Prince of Wales came over from Hanover and set up his own household, Compton was appointed Treasurer; his tact in this post would have served him well later if he had had the ability to use his political powers. On 6 July 1716 he became a Privy Counsellor.

When George I died in Hanover in 1727 on his way to Osnabrück, it was natural that speculation was rife as to the future, and the fact that there had been little love lost between the late King and his son boded

[1] *Journals of the House of Commons*, xvii, 241.

ill for members of Walpole's administration. Sir Robert immediately set out to see the new King, George II, at Richmond. When he arrived, Hervey relates,

'. . . the Prince was laid to sleep (as his custom had been for many years after dinner), and the Princess was in the bedchamber with him, when the Duchess of Dorset, the lady-in-waiting, went in to let them know Sir Robert was there, who was immediately brought in. All he [Walpole] said was, 'I am come to acquaint Your Majesty with the death of your father.'

The King seemed extremely surprised, but not enough to forget his resentment to Sir Robert one moment; neither his confusion, nor his joy at this great change, nor the benevolence so naturally felt by almost everybody towards the messenger of such good news, softened his voice or his countenance in one word or look. Whatever questions Sir Robert asked him with regard to the council being summoned, his being proclaimed, or other things necessary immediately to be provided, the King gave him no other answer than 'Go to Chiswick and take your directions from Sir Spencer Compton.'[2]

So Sir Robert made his way to Chiswick, while the King and Queen prepared for their journey to London. At Chiswick, Walpole told Spencer Compton:

'The King, Sir, has sent me to you in such a manner as he declares he intends you for his minister, and has commanded me to receive all my instructions from your mouth. It is what I as well as the rest of the world expected would be whenever this accident happened. You have been the Prince's Treasurer ever since he came to England; it is a natural promotion to continue you upon his being King: your services entitle you to that mark of his favour, and your abilities and experience in business will both enable you to support the employment and justify him in bestowing it. Everything is in your hands; I neither could shake your power if I would, nor would I if I could. My time has been, yours is beginning; but as we all must depend in some degree upon our successors, and that it is always prudent for these successors by way of example to have some regard for their predecessors, that with the measure they mete it may be measured to them again, for this reason I put myself

[2] John, Lord Hervey, *Memoirs*, ed. Sedgwick, i, 22.

under your protection, and for this reason I expect you will give it. I desire no share of power or business; one of your white sticks, or any employment of that sort, is all I ask as a mark from the Crown that I am not abandoned to the enmity of those whose envy is the only source of their hate, and who consequently will wish you no better than they have done me the moment you are vested with those honours and that authority, the possession of which they will always covet, and the possessor of which, of course, they will always hate.'[3]

Naturally, the 'plodding' Compton was highly gratified at Walpole's address to him, and promised him 'his protection, and asked in return the assistance of Sir Robert'.

Together they went to see the Lord President of the Council, the Duke of Devonshire, who was laid up with gout. At a meeting of the Privy Council, only the Lord Chancellor, Lord Trevor, the Privy Seal and Sir Paul Methuen were present. It was after the meeting that Compton told Walpole that he was unable to draft the King's speech and prevailed upon him to do so. Walpole at first, only too naturally, refused, but Compton 'insisted' and 'Walpole took up the employment immediately retiring to another room, and naturally slipped in a charming and appreciative tribute to the ability of the late ministry'.[4]

When Compton made his way to Leicester Fields he found it jammed with the multitudes, while the King's house was thronged, and he had to force his way to the King's closet, where his appointment was confirmed. On returning to Devonshire House, Compton found his speech written by Walpole, which he assiduously copied, and returned to Leicester Fields with Walpole. The King carefully read the speech, though he asked for a passage in the Declaration to be altered. This matter greatly embarrassed Compton, who went to Walpole to ask him if he would not persuade the King to allow it to remain as it was, in which Walpole succeeded.

How was Compton going to form his administration? Of the principal ministers of state, it was known that the King had little regard for them. He thought Walpole's brother Horace, Ambassador to France, 'a scoundrel and fool', while he detested the Duke of Newcastle. As to his other minister of state, Lord Townshend, 'the King looked upon him as

[3] Hervey, op. cit., i, 23.
[4] J. Plumb, *Walpole*, ii, 165.

no more than an able minister, and "scanty genius"'.[5] Even Walpole's son-in-law was dismissed his post as Master of the Robes. However, the first matter that would come up to Parliament would be the Civil List, and already the King had had a long talk with Walpole on 15 June which considerably raised that minister's hopes. Some shrewd moves immediately took place. Thus Horace Walpole went forthwith to Versailles to see Cardinal Fleury and secured a letter of full assurance from the Cardinal of France's fidelity to George II, whereupon he immediately set forth for England and arrived at Kensington, where the Court now was, on 19 June. At first the King was angry at seeing him, but he was appreciative of his splendid activities, while his ministers became very active over the Civil List at the public's expense. Pulteney, who, strangely enough, had never wanted the responsibility of First Lord, offered the King over £800,000 a year. It was pretty obvious that Compton was not going to stand up to this intrigue. Hervey, who has detailed the whole story for us, now took it upon himself to tell Walpole that he really need not worry. Queen Caroline had not forgotten her old friend. She had at once discerned that Compton's capabilities were quite unequal to the task that the King had thought he could do. It was the Queen who was to be his Court influence, and she had no intention of allowing her husband to appoint anyone other than Walpole.

Walpole had in 1721 and 1725 carried votes for the discharge of the debts of the Civil List amounting in the aggregate to over £1,000,000, but in 1727 there was again a debt of £600,000, as well as the jointure to be provided for, and when Compton suggested £50,000 for the Queen, Walpole simply undertook to double it.[6] Any hesitations the King may have had over Walpole were now overcome. Thus ended Compton's first hope of the Premiership. As compensation Walpole recommended the King to make Compton a baron, with the result that he became Lord Wilmington. On this occasion, said Hervey,

'I think he might have said, like Agrippina, the mother of Nero, in Racine's *Britannicus*,

> "*Tous ces présents, hélas! irritent mon dépit,*
> *Je vois mes honneurs croître, et tomber mon crédit.*"

But Wilmington did not seem to feel the ridicule or the contemptible-

[5] Hervey, op. cit., p. 29.
[6] I. S. Leadman, *Political History of England*, xi, 334.

ness of his situation. That snowball level of his, which had opened and that gathered so fast, melted away at as quick a pace; his visionary prospects of authority and grandeur vanished into air, and yet he seemed to be just as well satisfied to be bowing and grinning in the antechamber, possessed of a lucrative employment without credit, and dishonoured by a title which was the mark of his disgrace, as if he had been dictating in the closet, sole fountain of Court favour at home, and regulator of all national transactions abroad.'[7]

When the new Parliament was opened by George II on 23 January 1728, Wilmington held the lucrative post of Paymaster-General of the Forces, and in May 1730 he succeeded Lord Trevor as Lord Privy Seal. In December of that year he was created Viscount Pevensey, and Earl of Wilmington. Three years later he was installed a Knight of the Garter.

In 1739 the Cabinet was divided on the question of the war with Spain. The mob was being fanned for war over 'Jenkins's ear', and Walpole, the great peace minister, was having to deal with a King who too was urging war; and far worse for Walpole, Queen Caroline had died on 20 November 1737. The intrigues against Walpole were considerable. Despite the past, despite Wilmington's own assertions of his own limited capabilities, together with the help he had received from Walpole, new ambitions now began to stir within him, urging him into seeking high office again. Walpole had not the control in the Lords that he had in his own House. Although the Duke of Newcastle was a member of Walpole's Cabinet, he had joined the war party. Likewise Carteret had made a most powerful speech attacking the Spanish right to search British ships for contraband goods. The Opposition opinion was consolidated in the belief that it would be entirely to our advantage to have a maritime war with Spain. However, it was not until 1742 that Walpole fell. The final onslaughts began on 21 January, when Pulteney delivered his attack by moving to refer to a secret committee papers relating to the war. Walpole was not defeated upon this issue, but over a comparatively minor question on the 28th, relating to the Chippenham election, when the Government was in a minority of one. On 2 February the petition was decided against the Government by 241 to 225. Walpole decided to resign. 'All cry out,' wrote Horace Walpole, 'that he is

[7] op. cit., i, 39ff.

still minister behind the curtain.'[8] He was created Earl of Orford, and recommended that the King should send for Pulteney, and a place be found for Carteret. Newcastle had little chance in view of the King's hatred of him, while the Tories were 'political pariahs'.[9] Pulteney explained that his answer must be guided by the rest of the party, adding dramatically that the 'heads of parties are like the heads of snakes, carried on by their tails'.[10] Years before, Pulteney had sworn in a moment of pique with Walpole never to take office again. Now, with his nerve about to desert him, he conveniently recollected this rash vow and replied that consideration for his own reputation would not allow him to go back on his word.[11] Pulteney told the King that he would prefer to go to the Lords. He was created Earl of Bath. Walpole welcomed him saying, 'You and I are now two as insignificant men in England.' The King sent for his old crony Wilmington who was the true King's man. He and his friend, the Duke of Dorset, along with Dodington, were then a small clique. But their abilities were not great enough – the true head of the administration was Carteret.

THE CARTERET ADMINISTRATION UNDER WILMINGTON

Save to historians and those who have studied the political history of the period, Carteret's qualities are not extensively remembered.

Born of a good family, which in the eighteenth century was of essential value, 'he left no diary, no intimate journal, scarcely a private letter, nor for all his immense erudition, any writings beyond his official correspondence'. Of his contemporaries, Smollett said, 'There was no minister in this nation worth the meal that whitened his periwig.' Lord Chesterfield, who, on the contrary, bore him no love, declared, 'When he dies, the ablest head in England dies too.' While Horace Walpole, who admired none but himself, confessed that of the five great men whom he had known during his lifetime, Carteret was 'most a genius of the five'.[12]

Carteret was born at Hawnes, his father's seat in Bedfordshire, on 22

---

[8] Turberville, *The House of Lords in the Eighteenth Century*, p. 247.
[9] Pemberton, *Carteret*, p. 184.
[10] ibid., p. 184.
[11] ibid., p. 185.
[12] Baring Pemberton, *Carteret*, p. 4.

April 1690. He went to Westminster and at the age of fifteen to Christ Church, Oxford, where he matriculated in January 1706. The only degree he took was that of Doctor of Civil Law. He was successfully married to Frances, daughter of Sir Robert Worsley, Bt, and had four daughters but no heir. All his daughters made brilliant matches. Carteret's career began in the reign of Queen Anne.

Although he was born of a Tory family, and his friends at Oxford were of the same party, after the death of Queen Anne Carteret joined the Whigs, and was a confirmed supporter of the Hanoverian Succession. His learning and knowledge of languages were to serve him well, since he was able to converse freely with both George I and George II in German. Yet at the accession of George I he received no better appointment than that of a Lord of the Bedchamber, with which he seemed satisfied. During the time of the great Whig schism, Carteret's benefactor was Stanhope, and he soon made a very considerable mark in European diplomacy. Especially brilliant was his success at the Court of Sweden, to which he was accredited in his twenty-ninth year, in persuading that country to agree to terms with her adversaries. But the years of Carteret's diplomatic triumphs do not concern us here, save to emphasise that he was far more successful abroad than at home, except during his short appointment as Lord Lieutenant of Ireland when he so adroitly handled the issue that was caused over 'Woods's Copper Coinage'. Yet this urbane man, whose love of Homer and wine, whose brilliance and learning would take him far, never ruled this country as was thought he would. Whilst it is probably true that Carteret possessed a greater degree of genius than any of his contemporaries, it must be admitted that genius was not what England required in the third and fourth decades of the eighteenth century so much as matter-of-fact business acumen.

Carteret, after he left office as Lord Lieutenant of Ireland, found himself in the wilderness, and in 1731 joined the Opposition. But the whole position within the parties was to be altered with the tragic death of Queen Caroline. It was the signal for the decline of Walpole himself. Two years later the great minister was to give way to the clamour of war with Spain. Carteret was now to see events moving quickly in Europe. The death of the Emperor Charles VI was to bring the Pragmatic Sanction into force, whereby his daughter the Empress Maria Theresa succeeded to his dominions, and at the same time a flute-loving King ascended the throne of Prussia, who was quickly to play the bully to the young Queen of Hungary, and in December 1740 to seize Silesia. It came to Carteret to advise her to accept the terms of the Treaty of Breslau and cede Silesia to the King. Twenty years later, when Frederick was writing the history of his times, he recognised the skill of Carteret, and wrote, *'Le Lord Carteret fut le principal promoteur de cet ouvrage.'*

The only Act of Parliament that was passed under Wilmington was the Place Bill,[13] limiting the number of offices tenable by Members of Parliament. The new administration consisted of two distinct strands – of Carteret's small personal following and of Walpole's old henchmen, Newcastle and Hardwicke with the Duke of Devonshire.[14] Carteret did not even bother to cultivate his two most powerful followers, Chesterfield and Argyll, and this was to limit his administration painfully.

In the year 1743 England entered the War of Austrian Succession, and the French were defeated at Dettingen, when the King himself bravely led his troops, and where he narrowly escaped death. Carteret was there too. He sat in a coach and six well out of cannon shot, wearing an anxious expression on his face and immersed throughout the action in the solution of a new problem, raised by events of the preceding four weeks. But the French had to withdraw from Germany.

The following month Wilmington died, and on his death Henry Pelham, brother of the Duke of Newcastle, became Prime Minister, while Carteret was out in the wilderness again. He was created Earl of Granville.

Of Wilmington, Hervey composed a ballad:

> The Countess of Wilmington, excellent muse,
> I'll trust with the Treasury, not with the purse,
> For nothing by her I've resolved shall be done:
> She shall sit at that board as you sit on the throne.[15]

Hanbury Williams was even less complimentary:

> See you dull important lord
> Who at the longed for money board

[13] The Place Bill had been formerly introduced in 1740 and defeated.
[14] Turbeville, *History of the House of Lords in the Eighteenth Century*, p. 250.
[15] Bingham, *Prime Ministers*, 'Wilmington'.

Sits first but does not lead,
His younger brethren all things make,
So that the Treasury's like a snake,
And the tail moves the head.[16]

Of all our First Lords of the Treasury, Wilmington was the most shadowy figure. He was a stop-gap. Yet, as Mersey has observed, 'he filled for nearly thirty years the four highest places in the State to which laymen can aspire.'[17] He was, in short, an uninspired, slogging Parliamentarian, not without occasional wit. He spoke slowly and with clarity, and he was able to control the House of Commons when he was Speaker. He died a wealthy man. He never married and his wealth passed to his nephew, the fifth Earl of Northampton, and eventually to the Cavendishes.

As to Granville, he had great parts, and a most uncommon share of learning. He was one of the best speakers in the House of Lords, in both the declamatory and the argumentative way. He had a wonderful quickness and precision in seizing the stress of a question, which no art, no sophistry, could disguise from him.

BIBLIOGRAPHY

Baring, Pemberton, *Carteret* (1936)
Bingham, Clive, *Prime Ministers of England* (1922)
Compton, William, 6th Marquis of Northampton, *History of the Comptons of Compton Tyngates* (1930)
Feiling, Keith, *History of the Tory Party 1714–1832* (1938)
Ilchester, Earl of, *Lord Hervey and his Friends 1726–38* (1950)
Leadham, I. S., *Political History of England 1702–60* (1909)
Lucas, R. L., *George II and His Ministers* (1910)
Plumb, J., *Sir Robert Walpole* (2 vols, 1956)
Sedgwick, Romney (ed.), *Some Materials Towards Memoirs of the Reign of King George II* by John, Lord Hervey (3 vols, 1931)
Torrens, William, *History of Cabinets* (2 vols, 1894)
Turberville, A. S., *The House of Lords in the Eighteenth Century* (1927)
Williams, Basil, *The Whig Supremacy 1714–16* (1939)
Williams, Sir Charles Hanbury, *Works* (3 vols, 1822)

[16] ibid.
[17] ibid.

HENRY PELHAM

BY

AUBREY NEWMAN

*Henry Pelham, born c. January 1696, second son of Thomas, 1st
Baron Pelham, and Lady Grace Holles, daughter of Gilbert, 3rd
Earl of Clare. Educated at Westminster School and Hart Hall,
Oxford. Married 1726, Lady Katherine Manners, daughter of John,
2nd Duke of Rutland. Two sons (Thomas and Henry) died 1739;
six daughters, of whom Catherine married Henry, 9th Earl of
Lincoln, and Grace married Lewis Watson, later 1st Baron Sondes.
MP for Seaford 1717–22 and Sussex 1722–54; Treasurer of the
Chamber 1720–22; Lord of the Treasury 1721–4; Secretary-at-
War 1724–30; Paymaster-General 1730–43; First Lord of the
Treasury, August 1743–54; Chancellor of the Exchequer December
1743–54. Died 6 March 1754.*

Henry Pelham, by William Hoare

HENRY PELHAM

Henry Pelham's career illustrates the basic principles making for equilibrium in eighteenth-century politics. The career of Sir Robert Walpole had, to some extent, clouded these principles, for his success had been seen in terms of his own personality rather than in the political compromises that he personified. It took time for contemporaries to realise that political stability was secured not through formal office but through the gaining of confidence in the holder of office among two different sources of political authority, the King and the leading 'party' in the House of Commons, and that it would inevitably take time for each of these factors in the political equation to recognise the emergence of a new dominant personality, the prime minister. Accordingly it was not immediately evident to contemporaries that Walpole's true successor was neither Wilmington nor Carteret but rather a comparatively insignificant scion of one of the great Whig families, dependent on his brother not merely for an income but also for his very seat in the House of Commons.

Henry Pelham was the second son of a Sussex landowner who had risen in the social and political scale as a result of several fortunate marriages. His elder brother, Thomas, Duke of Newcastle, inherited most of the family wealth and power, so that Henry's political future depended in the first instance on the support that his brother could give him. There was little direct competition between them; both went to Westminster, but while Thomas went to Cambridge Henry went to Oxford, and a contemporary poetaster in a lampoon against the two commented:

> Harry, meanwhile consider'd that
> His means were slender, small his 'State;
> And therefore to make good the Ballance,
> Resolves he will improve his Tallents.
>
> Closely to Study he applies,
> In hopes by this in time to rise,

By dint of merit to a station,
To be the wonder of the Nation.[1]

In the 1715 rising he served as a volunteer and was present in that capacity at the Battle of Preston. Very soon after he came of age his brother had a vacancy in Parliament created for him in his quasi-family constituency of Seaford, and in the following general election secured his return for the county of Sussex. Election by a county was normally considered to be the most prestigious of the ways of entering the House of Commons, but usually was a great handicap to a rising politician. The progression from one office to another, normally regarded as the regular pattern of a career, involved at each stage a fresh election to the House, and a county was usually an expensive and bothersome constituency in this respect. Speaker Onslow, for example, was warned by Sir Robert Walpole of the inconveniences that ensued from sitting for a county: 'What! Will you take a county upon you? Consider what that is with regard to re-election; and should any accident happen to prevent your being chosen Speaker, you will, I suppose, be not unwilling to come into other offices and trusts, perhaps frequent elections may not be so practicable in a county as in a borough.'[2]

Pelham therefore was almost unique among eighteenth-century politicians in sitting for a county seat and yet being able to rely on a re-election at need. In fact the county of Sussex was virtually a pocket borough of the Duke of Newcastle, who prided himself on retaining control over it and on ensuring that his brother was elected. So far indeed did he control the county that in 1722 he was able to breach a long-standing convention of a division in the representation between the east and west of the county, foisting two 'easterners' on the electorate, one of them being his yet unknown and politically inexperienced younger brother. Newcastle's regard for the career of his younger brother and heir presumptive was further illustrated at the time of Pelham's marriage. Half of the Pelham estates were granted to him and he was then assured of an independent and substantial income.

Provided with a secure political base, Henry's political career depended however upon his own talents as a political leader and as a manager in the House of Commons. His first political appointment had

[1] Quoted in S. H. Nulle, *Thomas Pelham-Holles* . . ., pp. 172 and 174.
[2] Onslow MSS, Historical Manuscripts Commission, 14th Report, app. part ix (1895), p. 517.

been to a place in the gift of his brother as Lord Chamberlain, and his first recorded speech on a motion on the Civil List debts which he himself, as Treasurer of the Chamber, proposed, and which Robert Walpole seconded. But when Walpole moved to the Treasury Henry Pelham moved with him, and gradually showed his mastery not merely of financial matters and procedures but, more importantly, of the relationships between government finance and the procedures of the House of Commons. His successive appointments as Secretary-at-War and Paymaster-General involved him in considerable activity in the Commons, so that Walpole seems increasingly to have relied upon him for the proper execution of the albeit limited range of government business there. As Carteret later angrily commented: 'He was only a chief clerk to Sir Robert Walpole, and why he should expect to be more under me I can't imagine. He did his drudgery and he shall do mine.'[3] A different picture is however presented by Lord Hervey in his *Memoirs*:

'Mr Pelham . . . was strongly attached to Sir Robert Walpole, and more personally beloved by him than any man in England. He was a gentleman-like sort of man, of very good character, with moderate parts, in the secret of every transaction, which, added to long practice, made him at last, though not a bright speaker, often a useful one; and by the means of a general affability he had fewer enemies than commonly falls to the share of one so high a rank.'[4]

After Walpole's fall, Pelham was his obvious heir as leader of the 'Old Whigs' in the House of Commons; his close connection with Sir Robert and his abilities as a 'man of business' which earlier had made him Walpole's virtual deputy pointed him out as the successor. There were however three obstacles – rivalry among the other ministers, suspicions among the 'party' in the Commons that he could not adequately defend its interests, and the need to gain the fullest confidence of the King – and until these could be overcome his position could hardly be held as assured. In the meantime he continued as Paymaster-General, and after the elevation of Walpole's main rival, William Pulteney, to the House of Lords became the effective 'leader' of the Commons. As

[3] *Diary of the First Earl of Egmont*, Historical Manuscripts Commission (1923 ff.) iii, 187.
[4] John, Lord Hervey, *Some Materials Towards Memoirs of the Reign of King George II*, ed. Romney Sedgwick (London, 1931), 120.

such Pelham was responsible during the session of 1742–3 for the conduct of essential governmental business, including presiding over the regular meeting of government supporters before the opening of the parliamentary session, and the allocation of House of Commons business among various supporters or potential supporters of the administration. His activities were so successful, and his abilities were so marked, that after the end of that session it was generally agreed that 'at the beginning of the next sessions . . . Lord Wilmington . . . was to have changed his employment. For it was well understood that Mr Pelham was not to go into the House of Commons any more but as head of the Treasury.'[5] Before that date however Wilmington died, and although there was an attempt among the other ministers to have Pulteney appointed as First Lord of the Treasury, Pelham's interest, in alliance with that of Walpole and a substantial part of the coalition, was sufficient to secure his appointment as First Lord of the Treasury and then to add to that the post of Chancellor of the Exchequer.

This was however merely the first step in establishing his ascendancy over his fellow ministers, while his authority among the 'Old Whigs' was as yet far from clear. Moreover, the true lead in the closet was still in the hands of his principal ministerial rival, John, Lord Carteret. The process by which Pelham demonstrated his superiority took a further three years, and was eased as much by Carteret's own neglect of elementary rules of parliamentary tactics and his inability to court and conciliate possible followers in the Commons as by Pelham's skill in emphasising to George II his own indispensability for the smooth running of the King's business in the Commons and for the maintenance of a Whig majority. A letter from Walpole to Pelham in 1743 not only gave sound advice but showed how clearly Walpole himself had understood the process by which he had retained power for so many years.

'The King must, with tenderness and management, be shewn, what he may with reason depend upon, and what, he will be deceived and lost, if he places any confidence and reliance in. The King saw last year, what part the Whigs acted; and, I should hope, he may be convinced, that the Whig party will stand by him, as they have done, through his whole reign, if his majesty does not surrender himself into hands, that mean and wish nothing but his destruction, and want to be armed with his

[5] Henry Fox to the Duke of Marlborough, 26 April 1743. J. B. Owen, *The Rise of the Pelhams*, pp. 159–60.

authority and power only to nail up his cannon, and turn it against himself. . . .

Address and management are the weapons you must fight and defend with: plain truths will not be relished at first; in opposition to prejudices, conceived and infused in favour of his own partialities; and you must dress up all you offer, with the appearance of no other view or tendency, but to promote his service in his own way, to the utmost of your power. And the more you can make any thing appear to be his own, and agreeable to his declaration and orders, given to you before he went, the better you will be heard: as, the power to treat with such persons, as should be necessary to carry on his service in your hands; the encouragement and hopes to be given to the Whigs, by you, as arising from himself. Hint, at first, the danger he will run, in deviating from his own rule; shew him the unavoidable necessity there will be, of dissolving this parliament, if he departs from the body of the Whigs; and let him see the consequences of going to a new election, in the height of the war, which will certainly end in a rank Tory Parliament, that will at once put a stop to all the measures that are now in practice, and for ever defeat all his views and desires, which are made the pretences to him, of hazarding the change.'[6]

The process by which Pelham managed to gain the confidence of both Commons and King extended over the period from 1743 till 1746; it was marked firstly by Carteret's dismissal from office in 1744, much against the King's will, and then, more significantly still, by the removal of Carteret and his associates from any private influence over the King in the spring of 1746. The first step had to be the achievement of some degree of ascendancy in the Commons, if only to persuade the King that Pelham alone was capable of 'doing the King's business'. A judicious combination of bargaining with various opposition groups that might be brought over to support the administration and firmly defending the essential interests of individual members of the 'Old Whigs' went far towards convincing the latter that Pelham could be relied on and thus establishing his general position in the House of Commons. It took time, and there was a considerable period of suspicion of him. But by early 1745 the opposition elements in the House had been for practical purposes reduced to groups of individual backbenchers with little or no organisation or leadership; virtually all the ablest speakers

[6] 20 Oct. 1743. Owen, op. cit., pp. 188–9.

had been added to the ministry in some way or other, and without leaders what was left was politically negligible. Even so the King was reluctant to give the Pelhams his fullest support, preferring to consult in private the erstwhile ministers whom he could not see in public; the danger remained that Carteret might be able to gain back former supporters who had earlier deserted him but who could now see in him a surer channel to royal favour than the Pelhams. For his part Pelham could not be sure that his own position was secure until he knew that he possessed the absolute confidence of the King and an assurance of royal consultation with him on all major issues and appointments. The relationship was therefore unstable. Horace Walpole wrote: 'It is not easy to say where power resides at present: it is plain that it resides not in the King; and yet he has enough to hinder anybody else from having it. His new governors have no interest with him – scarce any converse with him.'[7]

The King's dilemma was that he was unwilling to lose Carteret as his principal adviser, but if Carteret were unsuitable he did not really mind having the Pelhams instead. What he did strongly object to was giving an impression of having driven out Carteret for the sake of the Pelhams. Thus he continued to consult Carteret unofficially and to make himself as disagreeable as he could to the Pelhams without openly breaking with them. Various minutes of conversation between the King and one or other of the Pelham group show this clearly. On 9 April 1745, for instance, Newcastle wrote to Lord Hardwicke, his close friend and Lord Chancellor: 'My brother goes to Court on Thursday with the seals in his pocket to give, as he finds things. I shall do the same.'[8] And on the eve of the King's visit to Hanover that year Newcastle wrote to the King's second son, the Duke of Cumberland: 'We . . . here, my Lord Chancellor, my brother, and myself, represented, in the most dutiful manner, the impossibility of *our* opening another session of Parliament, if His Majesty, at his return, should not have a more favourable opinion of us, and our endeavour for his service, than he has, at present.'[9]

Only the strains of the military situation abroad and at home – this was the year of the 1745 rebellion – prevented the Pelhams from offering their resignations. The beginning of 1746 seemed to offer to the King an opportunity to reshape his ministry and drive out the Pelhams,

[7] Letter to Horace Mann, 24 Dec. 1744, *Correspondence*, ed. W. S. Lewis, xviii, 552.
[8] British Museum Additional MS 35870, f. 95.
[9] 3 May 1745. BM Add. MS 32704, f. 194.

while they for their part determined on making a stand, using their desire to appoint William Pitt to office as the main issue. On 10 and 11 February 1746 the leading ministers resigned. Their surrender of office lasted for two days, for within that time it became clear that Carteret and his connections had no chance of controlling the Commons, while even the City financiers demonstrated their opinion of the King's alternative ministers by withdrawing from arrangements already made for financing the war: 'No Pelhams, no money.' It was not however that the Pelhams were the only possible ministers, or that these particular Whigs had 'the King in chains'. Rather it was that the Commons had declared quite clearly their opinion of Carteret. Had the King been prepared to turn to any other of the Whig leaders, the Commons – and even for the moment the Pelhams themselves – would have acquiesced. But if George could not have Carteret he was prepared to turn back again to the Pelhams, even though they went so far as to make 'conditions':

'Out of duty to the King, and regard to the public it is apprehended that His Majesty's late servants cannot return into his service, without being honoured, with that degree of authority, confidence, and credit from His Majesty, which the ministers of the Crown have usually enjoy'd in this country, and which is absolutely necessary for carrying on his service. That His Majesty will be pleased entirely to withdraw his confidence and countenance from those persons, who of late have, behind the curtain, suggested private councills, with the view of creating difficulties to his servants, who are responsible for everything, whilst those persons are responsible for nothing.'[10]

A year later Pelham consolidated his position by a snap election; this caught a new opposition group completely unprepared. Thereafter his authority was virtually unshaken. New opposition groups emerged, as had occurred under Walpole, and inevitably they attracted the malcontents. The leader of these was the Prince of Wales, Frederick Louis. Pelham always recognised the difficulties that a Prince could make for any administration: 'The House of Commons is a great unwieldy body, which requires great Art and some Cordials to keep it loyal; we have not many of the latter in our power; the Opposition is headed by the Prince, who has much to give in present as we have, and more in

[10] BM Add. MS 35870, f. 117.

Reversion. This makes my task an hard one, and if it were not for that I should sleep in quiet.'[11]

Despite any anxieties that might have come from this quarter, however, the threat was ended in 1751 with Frederick's death and the speed with which nearly all of the Prince's group, the Leicester House faction, precipitated themselves into the Pelham circle. Pelham had still to be careful in his management of the Commons and its various elements, and he had still to be careful in his management of the King's whims and fancies, but he had no serious political rival to contend with. This indeed is the principal feature of Pelham's ministry. No great issues emerged after 1747, such as had bedevilled Walpole, while there were no other leading politicians to compete with him. All who had any ability had been bought off, and Pelham had achieved in effect that great ambition of eighteenth-century ministries, a 'broad-bottom'. To manage to include in office both Pitt and Henry Fox, and not merely to secure their nominal services but to use their debating talents as well, was an achievement no other minister could parallel, and illustrates clearly Pelham's gift of political conciliation, particularly important when he came to concentrate on those changes of policy that he wished to implement.

Pelham's interests were largely domestic. Walpole had tried to insinuate his influences into every aspect of policy, but Pelham, sensing the strength perhaps of Newcastle and Hardwicke, the other members of the 'triumvirate', gave the impression of being uninterested in matters of foreign policy. Those he left largely to his elder brother, Newcastle, save when they impinged on domestic and particularly financial issues. An example of his assiduity in financial matters is illustrated by his record at the Treasury. Between 1743 and 1754 there were over 500 meetings of the Board of the Treasury of which Pelham missed only four. He had a clear policy for the finances. As early as 1748 he wrote to Newcastle:

'You know, I have had very little comfort in the great scene of business, I have long been engaged in. I have no court ambition, and very little interested views; but I was in hopes, by a peace being soon made, and by a proper economy in the administration of the government, afterwards, to have been the author of such a plan, as might, in time to come, have relieved this nation from the vast load of debt, it now labours

[11] Pelham to Newcastle, 18 May 1750. BM Add. MS 32720, f. 348.

under; and, even in my own time, had the satisfaction of demonstrating to the knowing part of the world, that the thing was not impossible. Here, I own, lay my ambition.'[12]

His ambition was to lower the rates of interest on government debts and reduce strictly government expenditure. Walpole had made an attempt at the former but had failed, fearing to lose support in the City of London. Pelham however had a broader base of support in the City, and indeed the events of 1746 had shown the confidence reposed in him by the City brokers. Above all, he had earlier secured the influential support of Sir John Barnard who had been the spokesman in 1737 of the City opposition. Pelham was therefore able in 1749 to propose that interest rates be reduced almost immediately from 4 per cent to $3\frac{1}{2}$ per cent and later to 3 per cent. It was this reduction of interest rates and consolidation of debt into two major categories that was to make possible the large-scale floating of loans and raising of taxes which marked the financing of the Seven Years War.

Pelham's management of the ordinary finances of the Crown was equally striking, even though in this he was often brought into conflict with Newcastle and the King. Their foreign policy involved large payments to various foreign princes, and although Pelham was prepared to acquiesce in its main lines he objected strongly to a continual paying out of subsidies, not only because it involved raising large sums of money but also because it offered opportunities for charges in Parliament that the ministers were following 'Hanoverian' measures. When Newcastle pressed him hard in 1750 on subsidy treaties with Bavaria and Saxony Pelham replied:

'The Civil List, you know, is much in debt . . . I have endeavoured to lessen the expenses at home as much as possible, and have succeeded as far as relates to my own Office, but a long series of uninterrupted extravagance to call it by no worse name, having got into all the great offices of the Kingdom, makes it very difficult, if not impracticable for the best intentioned to get the better of habit and custom.'[13]

Although he was prepared to spend money when it was needed – he never for example cut the Navy and Army expenditures to the low

[12] 4 Aug. 1748. BM Add. MS 32716, f. 13.
[13] 13 July 1750. BM Add. MS 32720, f. 355.

levels that Walpole permitted – Pelham insisted none the less on economy and reforms of procedures. His prudence, and his mastery of the Commons, were welcomed by George II, who in conversation with Newcastle compared Pelham's management of the finances very favourably with that of Sir Robert Walpole, who had 'managed the money matters very ill: he did not indeed give money abroad, but he gave it away liberally at home . . . with regard to money matters . . . your brother does that, understands that, much better.'[14]

Pelham's major difficulties came largely from the jealousies felt by his brother; Newcastle was reluctant to cede to him the premier place in the King's affairs, and particularly reluctant to leave entirely to Pelham detailed domestic affairs or election arrangements. Newcastle wrote to Hardwicke: 'He will do everything himself – he consults none of his friends – he neither has time or patience to give it all the attention, *alone*, that such a great undertaking does require, and things arise which he did not expect.'[15] There were indeed many differences between the two and not only on political issues. In 1744, for instance, Newcastle wrote angrily to Hardwicke of his brother's 'cruel behaviour' and threatened that he would 'break off all correspondence with my brother and his family'; this was at a time when the two were trying to oust Carteret from office. There were occasions when the only communication between the two was through Hardwicke, whose son later commented, 'I have heard him say – he was tired with carrying water between the br[other]s.'[16] On the other hand, despite all their differences, they realised the essential need to retain a unity of purpose and there was obviously very great affection between them. Any illness in one precipitated very anxious inquiries from the other, and Newcastle took tremendous pride in his brother's family. His substantial endowment of them has already been mentioned, and later he had his title re-created for the benefit of Pelham's eldest son-in-law.

Pelham's death came on the eve of the general election of 1754. His health had not been good during the previous winter, and he had gone to Scarborough to recuperate, but even so his death on 6 March 1754 came as a surprise to all and as a severe shock to Newcastle, who was sunk for several days in violent grief, unable and unwilling to attend to

[14] Newcastle to Pelham, 1 July 1752. Owen, *The Rise of the Pelhams*, pp. 319–20.
[15] 17 Oct. 1753. BM Add. MS 32733, f. 81.
[16] 14 Oct. 1744. Quoted in Philip C. Yorke, *The Life and Correspondence of Philip Yorke, Earl of Hardwicke* (Cambridge, 1913), i, 362–3.

any business at all. There were many comments on Pelham by contemporaries, almost all of whom pointed to his integrity in both public and private life. Horace Walpole, in words that have often been quoted, wrote that 'he lived without abusing his power, and died poor',[17] while Lord Chesterfield commented:

'Mr Pelham had good sense, without either shining parts or any degree of literature. He had by no means an elevated or enterprizing genius, but had a more manly and steady resolution than his brother the Duke of Newcastle. . . .

He was a very inelegant speaker in Parliament, but spoke with a certain candour and openness that made him well heard, and generally believed.

He wished well to the public, and managed the finances with great care and personal purity. He . . . had many domestic Virtues and no Vices. If his place, and the power that accompanies it, made him some public enemies, his behaviour in both secured him from personal and rancorous ones. Those who wished him worst, only wished themselves in his place.'[18]

But the most heartfelt comment came from the one man who had originally shown himself opposed to him. George II, who had gone to great lengths to keep Carteret instead of Pelham, lamented, 'Now I shall have no more peace.'[19] The truth of that was to become evident in his relations with Pelham's successors.

BIBLIOGRAPHY

Coxe, William, *Memoirs of the Administration of the Right Honourable Henry Pelham* (2 vols, London, 1829)

Nulle, S. H., *Thomas Pelham-Holles, Duke of Newcastle: His Early Political Career, 1693–1724* (Philadelphia, 1931)

Owen, J. B., *The Rise of the Pelhams* (London, 1957)

Walpole, Horace, *Memoirs of the Last Ten Years of the Reign of George II*, ed. Henry Fox, 3rd Lord Holland (2 vols, London, 1822; 2nd edn, 3 vols, London, 1847)

Wilkes, J. W., *A Whig in Power: The Political Career of Henry Pelham* (Northwestern University Press, 1964)

[17] Horace Walpole, *Memoirs of the Reign of George II*, i, 371.
[18] *Characters by Lord Chesterfield* . . . (London, 1778), pp. 39–40.
[19] H. Walpole, op. cit., i, 378.

THE DUKE OF NEWCASTLE

BY

H. T. DICKINSON

Thomas Pelham-Holles, born 21 July 1693, elder son of Thomas, 1st Baron Pelham, and Lady Grace Holles, sister of John Holles, Duke of Newcastle. Educated at Westminster School and Cambridge University. In 1711 added the name of Holles to that of Pelham on succeeding to the bulk of the estates of his uncle, the Duke of Newcastle. Created Earl of Clare on the accession of George I, and Duke of Newcastle in 1715 after raising a troop for service against the Pretender. Lord Chamberlain in the Stanhope–Sunderland administration 1717; Secretary of State 1724–54 under Walpole and Pelham; succeeded his younger brother as First Lord of the Treasury 1754–6 and also 1757–62; returned to office as Lord Privy Seal July 1765–August 1766. Died 17 November 1768. Married Lady Henrietta Godolphin. No issue.

Thomas Pelham Holles, 1st Duke of Newcastle (right, with the Earl of Lincoln), by Sir Godfrey Knelle

THE DUKE OF NEWCASTLE

No eighteenth-century politician has left behind him such a wealth of detail about his career as the Duke of Newcastle and yet surprisingly little has so far been written about him. The sheer mass of his correspondence in the Newcastle and Hardwicke papers in the British Museum has no doubt daunted many would-be biographers, but it is also likely that many historians have been reluctant to spend years of their lives wading through the voluminous correspondence of a man who has become notorious for his fussiness and fretfulness, for his petty jealousy and his unwillingness to assume responsibility for any policy, and for his inability to pursue any political objective to his own satisfaction or to the nation's profit. Indeed, many of his contemporaries and most historians describe Newcastle as the epitome of unredeemed mediocrity, as a veritable buffoon in office. Horace Walpole, for example, condemned him for his excessive love of power when he lacked the ability to put such power to any constructive use: 'He was a Secretary of State without intelligence, a Duke without money, a man of infinite intrigue, without secrecy or policy, and a Minister despised and hated by his master, by all parties and Ministers, without being turned out by any !'[1] Lord Hervey was equally contemptuous of Newcastle's irresolution and dismissive of his weak understanding,[2] while Lord Waldegrave concluded: 'Talk with him concerning public or private business, of a nice or delicate nature, he will be found confused, irresolute, continually rambling from the subject, contradicting himself almost every instant.'[3]

The memoirs of Horace Walpole, Lord Hervey and Lord Waldegrave are among the most valuable and stimulating sources we have for the political events and characters of Newcastle's day. Their opinions have certainly influenced all later historians writing about this period.

[1] Horace Walpole, *Memoirs of the Reign of King George II*, ed. Lord Holland (1846), i, 166.
[2] John, Lord Hervey, *Some Materials Towards Memoirs of the Reign of King George II*, ed. Romney Sedgwick (1931), i, 209; ii, 344–5, 518; iii, 654–5, 949–50.
[3] James, Earl Waldegrave, *Memoirs from 1754 to 1758* (1821), p. 12.

The popular view of Newcastle is, in fact, largely based on the contemptuous opinions of him expressed by these three writers. There are, however, two important reasons why these sources should be handled with some caution. In the first place, all three of these writers were motivated by strong personal prejudice against Newcastle. And secondly, if their opinions are accepted without reservation, it becomes impossible to understand how Newcastle ever achieved high office let alone stayed in power for nearly forty years.

Horace Walpole bore a grudge against Newcastle because he was convinced that, when Secretary of State, he had betrayed his father, Sir Robert Walpole, and had helped to push him out of office. Lord Hervey hated Newcastle because he knew that in the 1730s he had opposed his own promotion to the office of Lord Privy Seal. Lord Waldegrave's political career had also been blighted by Newcastle. In 1757 Waldegrave was all set to rescue George II from the Devonshire-Pitt administration by agreeing to accept appointment as First Lord of the Treasury, but this scheme collapsed when Newcastle agreed to co-operate with William Pitt in a new administration and to fill this office himself. While these three political commentators were certainly motivated by personal antipathy towards Newcastle, it was probably not prejudice alone that blinded them to Newcastle's merits. He certainly betrayed many of the characteristics they lampooned so effectively, but they were not perceptive enough to see that Newcastle's irresolution, his hypochondria, his nervous twittering, and his inability to express himself with either clarity or conviction, obscured mundane, but genuine, talents.

Without such talents Newcastle would not have held office for so long. He was clearly not just an incompetent neurotic or simply a figure of fun. High offices were not given to him merely because he was a duke with a huge rent roll or because he was the patron of innumerable pocket boroughs. Wealth he certainly possessed, and he spent lavishly to further his political career, but money alone could not have bought him office and his personal electoral influence has usually been grossly exaggerated. Sir Lewis Namier has calculated that he could only nominate members for about twelve seats and even some of these had to be carefully nursed.[4] Much more important than Newcastle's personal electoral influence was his willingness to act as patronage manager

[4] Sir Lewis Namier, *The Structure of Politics at the Accession of George III*, 2nd edn. (1957), p. 9.

for the whole government interest. His untiring and single-minded devotion to tedious and even dirty electoral business made him unique among important ministers of state. Newcastle was prepared to spend his time, his nervous energy, and his own fortune on the kind of work that other magnates and other ministers shirked. Sir Robert Walpole and Henry Pelham both relied upon him to put the Government's patronage to its best use in producing Parliaments amenable to their policies.

This steady application, rather than his persistent political intrigue at Court, is the most important explanation of Newcastle's success. His voluminous correspondence provides ample, though hardly eloquent, testimony to his sleepless, indefatigable attempts to make friends and influence people. Not content with the myriad tasks of a government election manager, he sought to engross other forms of patronage. As Secretary of State for twenty years and later as First Lord of the Treasury he controlled many appointments to minor offices. From the late 1730s he was also the most influential voice in ecclesiastical promotions and, in 1748, he secured his own election as Chancellor of Cambridge University so that he would have a few other rewards at his disposal. Most of the patronage Newcastle dispensed was, of course, the Crown's. His sovereign never gave him an entirely free hand, but, in the 1740s and 1750s, Newcastle was the chief link in the patronage system and the main channel through which preferments flowed. Anyone anxious to secure political or ecclesiastical preferment for himself, his relations or his dependants, knew that he must address his appeals to Newcastle.[5]

In part, Newcastle undertook such herculean drudgery because he hated to offend a possible supporter and because he constantly needed to be reassured that he was important and influential. But his labours also repaid handsome political dividends. He made himself indispensable

[5] For Newcastle's patronage system, see S. H. Nulle, 'The Duke of Newcastle and the Election of 1727', *Journal of Modern History*, ix (1937), 1–22; Basil Williams, 'The Duke of Newcastle and the Election of 1734', *English Historical Review*, xii (1897), 448–88; Mary Bateson, 'Clerical Preferment under the Duke of Newcastle,' ibid., vii (1892), 685–96; Norman Sykes, 'The Duke of Newcastle as Ecclesiastical Minister', ibid., lvii (1942), 59–84; Norman Sykes, *Church and State in England in the Eighteenth Century* (Cambridge, 1934); D. A. Winstanley, *The University of Cambridge in the Eighteenth Century* (Cambridge, 1922); Philip Haffenden, 'Colonial Appointments and Patronage under the Duke of Newcastle, 1724–39', *English Historical Review*, lxxviii (1963), 417–35.

to any ministry that desired a stable majority in Parliament. Robert Walpole, Henry Pelham and William Pitt all had greater talents and pursued more constructive policies, but they all came to recognise the value of Newcastle's assistance. Newcastle's critics, with their greater intelligence and superior wit, easily underrated him. They laughed at the fuss and bustle, and nicknamed him 'hubble bubble', but they overlooked the patient hours of labour that he devoted to politics. Lord Chesterfield was one of the few men of fashion who appreciated the key to Newcastle's success. He said of him: 'The public put him below his level: for though he had no superior parts, or eminent talents, he had a most indefatigable industry, a perseverance, a Court craft, and a servile compliance with the will of his sovereign for the time being.'[6]

Newcastle's main claim to fame was as a hardworking electioneer and manipulator of personal and political allegiances, but he was also a competent, if undistinguished, Secretary of State for thirty years. Though held in contempt by some men of wit and fashion, he was honest, generous and shrewd. His capacity for work and his ample store of sound common sense enabled him to bear his heavy official burdens with greater success than his harsh critics would allow. He was not only conscientious in the performance of his official duties; his grasp of what was essential to Britain's interests was quite sound. He fully realised that Britain's most important rival was France and that Britain needed a European ally to engage the larger French armies. This acceptance of a continental role for Britain was not just to safeguard Hanover and so win favour at Court, though Newcastle recognised that this was politically advisable. He was also aware that France could not exert her full power in a contest with Britain for naval and colonial supremacy if a considerable proportion of her forces were engaged in a European war. It must be admitted that, in seeking a counter-weight to France in Europe, Newcastle may have been too ready to spend lavishly to secure the dubious support of petty German princes and he may have adopted the wrong measures to re-establish friendly relations with Austria, but his basic objective was far from foolish. Indeed, it could be argued that Newcastle was a better Secretary of State than any of the politicians who held the other secretaryship in the 1730s and 1740s. Carteret's foreign policy was more brilliant, but it was also widely regarded in Parliament as being more dangerous and

[6] Cited by Sir Lewis Namier, *England in the Age of the American Revolution*, 2nd edn (1961), p. 67.

expensive. Newcastle's chief mistake, in fact, was to concentrate too exclusively on protecting British interests. He therefore failed to appreciate how the other major powers viewed the European situation. Nevertheless, William Pitt, the greatest critic of his foreign policy, eventually admitted the wisdom of fighting France in Europe in order to distract her from the war in the colonies. The two men shared the same objective, but Newcastle lacked Pitt's consummate ability in pursuing it.[7]

While seeking to defend Newcastle from some of the indiscriminate criticisms that have been levelled against him, and while recognising that Newcastle's long tenure as Secretary of State was not undeserved, it must be acknowledged that Newcastle lacked the essential requirements of an able Prime Minister. He was an able subordinate to a first minister with the abilities of Robert Walpole, Henry Pelham or William Pitt, but he was incapable of leading a ministry himself, particularly in times of stress and war. His talents were essentially second-rate. He was prepared to devote his life to trifling details, but he could rarely devise or implement a coherent political strategy. Throughout his political career he relied on the strength and advice of abler men. After more than forty years in office he still sought the advice of his great friend and confidant, the Earl of Hardwicke, on how to reply to the Town Clerk of Bristol when the freedom of that city was bestowed on him in 1760.[8] It was this kind of constant demand for help, advice and reassurance that made him appear a fool to many of his contemporaries. It led Lord Waldegrave, this time fairly, to observe: 'Upon the whole, he seems tolerably well qualified to act a second part, but wants both spirit and capacity to be first in command: neither has he the smallest particle of that elevation of mind, or of that dignity of behaviour, which command respect, and characterise the great statesman.'[9] Thus, by a lifetime of hard work and intrigue, Newcastle eventually rose to a post, that of Prime Minister, for which he was eminently unsuited by temperament or ability. Nor was he happy in the role until he had handed over

[7] For a defence of Newcastle's foreign policy, see Reed Browning, 'The Duke of Newcastle and the Imperial Election Plan, 1749–54', *Journal of British Studies*, vii (1967), 28–47, and the introduction to *British Diplomatic Instructions*, vol. vii, 'France', part iv, '1745–89', ed. L. G. Wickham Legg (Camden Society, 1934), vol. xlix.

[8] Namier, op. cit., p. 71.

[9] James, Earl Waldegrave, *Memoirs*, p. 14.

real responsibility to his masterful Secretary of State, William Pitt.

For some thirty years, from 1724 to 1754, Newcastle held high office without having to assume responsibility for the ministry's policies and without having to map out a coherent political strategy. During these years Robert Walpole and Henry Pelham strove, not with complete success since Newcastle was jealous of power and was not above conspiring against his mentor or his brother, to restrict Newcastle to his vital but subordinate role in the Government. It was not until after Henry Pelham's death, on 6 March 1754, that Newcastle was in a position to lead the ministry. His conduct on the death of his brother was a mixture of pathetic, even comical, grief[10] and a ruthless determination to outmanoeuvre his rivals in the scramble to fill the vacant post of First Lord of the Treasury. After the long careers of Walpole and Pelham, who had made it appear essential for the Prime Minister to sit in the Commons in order to manage votes of supply and win general approval for the Government's policies, many commentators expected that the post of First Lord of the Treasury would be filled by one of the three leading men in the lower house – Henry Fox, the Secretary at War, William Pitt, the Paymaster-General, or William Murray, the Solicitor-General. All three candidates, however, laboured under serious handicaps. Henry Fox was hated by Lord Chancellor Hardwicke, because of his earlier hostility to the latter's famous Marriage Act, and disliked by the Scottish members and the Leicester House faction because of his connection with the Duke of Cumberland. An able debater and an experienced politician, Fox was, nevertheless, widely distrusted by the independent backbenchers because of his lack of political principles and his unconcealed desire to line his own pockets. William Pitt was an even greater orator and had a greater capacity for carrying through a difficult undertaking. He was also more honest and more popular on the back benches, but he suffered from bad health which frequently kept him away from the Commons, he lacked the backing of a major Whig connection and, worst of all, he was hated by George II for his frequent disparaging remarks about Hanover, which he had once described as 'that despicable little Electorate'. William Murray, the third candidate, was an able debater and a first-class lawyer, but he was a Scotsman, suspected by some of harbouring Jacobite sympathies, and he lacked the determination and political cou-

[10] See *The Letters of Horace Walpole*, ed. Mrs Paget Toynbee (Oxford, 1903), iii, 220: to Richard Bentley, 17 Mar. 1754.

rage to bear the heat of constant parliamentary battles. Since none of these three candidates had an overwhelming claim to succeed Henry Pelham and each of them was ready to oppose the advancement of one of the others, Newcastle hoped to secure the support of all three while keeping them all in subordinate positions within the ministry.[11]

Within a week of his brother's death Newcastle had outmanoeuvred his rivals within the ministry. He and Hardwicke were able to persuade the King to appoint him to the vacant post of First Lord of the Treasury, the most important office in the Government. While his appointment shows that George II preferred him to any of the other candidates for this office, it did not mean that Newcastle enjoyed the full confidence of the King. George II was used to Newcastle and feared him less than he did Pitt or Fox, but he did not hold him in high esteem. Newcastle's position at Court was not as secure as Walpole's and Pelham's had been. In the Commons, it was much weaker. He was sufficiently well versed in the realities of eighteenth-century politics, however, to realise that it would not be easy to lead the ministry from the Lords. He recognised that, unlike Walpole or Pelham before him, he would need not only a Chancellor of the Exchequer to steer his financial measures through the Commons, but a 'Leader of the House' to manage both the Court and Treasury party and the independent backbenchers. Since various colonial disputes with France were threatening to erupt into a full-scale war, the task of managing the Commons could only be performed by a consummate politician. It was to prove impossible to find a man of such outstanding gifts, who was prepared to play second fiddle to the Duke of Newcastle.

The task of explaining to the Commons the technical details of Treasury affairs was entrusted to Henry Bilson Legge, a competent, if uninspired, Chancellor of the Exchequer, but Newcastle could not find an able, yet docile, Leader of the House. He first approached Henry Fox with the offer of the post of Secretary of State and the responsibility of managing the Commons. Despite making these concessions, he insisted on reserving to himself the sole dispensation of secret service money, which was already being lavishly spent on the forthcoming general election. Fox was at first willing to accept this arrangement, but

---

[11] ibid., iii, 216–17: to Horace Mann, 7 Mar. 1754; H. Walpole, *Memoirs of the Reign of King George II*, i, 381–7; and P. C. Yorke, *The Life and Correspondence of Philip Yorke, Earl of Hardwicke* (Cambridge, 1913), ii, 206–8: Hardwicke to the Archbishop of Canterbury, 11 Mar. 1754.

he soon broke off negotiations when he discovered that Newcastle intended to manage the general election himself and to control all nominations to places in the reconstructed administration.[12] If Newcastle retained full control of all this Crown patronage and refused to let Fox have some say in how it should be dispensed, then the latter would appear to be the Leader of the Commons in name only. Fox would bear the most important responsibility within the ministry without controlling the means to gratify those he might need to win over to the ministry's side by the judicious award of a place, pension or favour. Newcastle evidently wanted his services without being ready to pay the market price for them.

Fox was naturally dissatisfied with Newcastle's behaviour, but he remained Secretary at War. Pitt, on the other hand, was furious at the way in which he had been passed over in the promotion stakes in favour of men of inferior ability. After Fox had refused the post of Secretary of State, Newcastle turned to Sir Thomas Robinson, a diplomat of little talent and a politician of negligible importance. Newcastle took refuge in the not unreasonable excuse that the King refused to countenance the appointment of Pitt to a position that would bring him into constant attendance at Court, but Pitt complained that Newcastle had not tried hard enough to remove George II's prejudice against him. Thus Newcastle found himself opposed in the Commons by its two most able members, Pitt and Fox, though they both continued to hold minor offices in the administration. Within days of assuming the office of Prime Minister, Newcastle found himself unable to impose his authority on his ministerial colleagues and saw his decisions challenged by his own subordinates. To answer their criticisms, particularly of his foreign policy, Newcastle had to rely on Legge, Robinson and William Murray, who was promoted to Attorney-General. Even when acting in concert these three were not a match for the combined talents of Pitt and Fox. While Newcastle monopolised Crown patronage and yet failed to pursue a clear policy, his subordinates, bereft of power and direction, gradually lost control of the Commons.

In exceptionally favourable circumstances Newcastle's ministry might have limped along for some time without coming to grief, especially as the general election of 1754 returned a Parliament to Newcastle's satisfaction. It was, after all, never easy, even for politicians with the talents of Pitt and Fox, to persuade the independent back-

[12] *The Letters of Horace Walpole*, iii, 219–20: to Richard Bentley, 17 Mar. 1754.

benchers to defeat a ministry that enjoyed the confidence of the King. In 1754, however, it was clear to all that Britain was drifting close to war with France, both in India and North America, while all the major powers of Europe were desperately seeking reliable allies in case of a general conflagration. News of the French victory over Washington on the Ohio, in July 1754, forced the Government to consider sending reinforcements to the American colonies. Newcastle feared to take strong retaliatory action because he dreaded assuming responsibility for provoking France, but he was not strong enough to resist the demands at home that he should respond to the French threat. His half-hearted measures failed to deter France or to satisfy opinion at home. He failed to urge the fleet under Admiral Boscawen to make every effort to destroy the French reinforcements ordered to Canada, and he supplied General Braddock with an inadequate expeditionary force to push back the French forces on the Ohio. As a result, Admiral Boscawen only managed to intercept two French frigates, while the impetuous General Braddock was defeated and killed by the French in April 1755.[13]

There is some justification for Newcastle's hesitant and ambiguous orders to Boscawen, and later to Hawke, for he feared being irrevocably committed to a war with France until he had built up a powerful network of alliances in Europe. His basic aim was sound. He wanted to deter France from attacking Hanover and to persuade her to fight a colonial war, where she would be at some disadvantage because of Britain's naval superiority, or, if France waged a continental war, to have enough support in Europe to tie down a great part of the French army. Newcastle proved incapable, however, of building up a strong system of continental alliances. The Dutch were anxious to avoid war at all costs, while the Austrians were hoping to effect a *rapprochement* with France in order to concentrate their attentions on Prussia. Newcastle was able to negotiate expensive subsidy treaties with Bavaria, Saxony and Hesse, but he needed the support of a more powerful ally. In September 1755 he arranged a treaty with Russia, whereby 55,000 Russian troops were to be held in readiness in case Hanover was attacked. Then, quite illogically, he began to negotiate with Prussia for the neutralisation of Germany, which would have prevented the Russians marching to the aid of Hanover if she were in fact attacked. Thus, by trying to hold too many cards at once, Newcastle helped to

[13] T. W. Riker, 'The Politics behind Braddock's Expedition', *American Historical Review*, xiii (1907–8), 742–52.

set in train the diplomatic revolution by which Austria and France were driven together and Britain was eventually forced to accept the offer of Prussian support.[14]

Newcastle's fear of provoking France and his failure to build up a continental alliance system which would deter her, drew increasing criticism upon his administration and exposed the weakness of its leadership in the Commons. He was soon forced to admit that he could not afford to continue without the full support of either Pitt or Fox. As early as January 1755 Fox had been partially accommodated by the offer of a seat on the Cabinet council, but Newcastle was well aware that Pitt was the more dangerous critic of his policies and that he had greater influence with the independent backbenchers. His renewed negotiations with Pitt broke down, however, when it became clear that the King was still opposed to his promotion to Cabinet office and Pitt refused to support policies that he had no hand in shaping. Newcastle could only have made terms with Pitt if he had risked his influence at Court by bullying the King into submission, and had also agreed to give up some of his power so that Pitt could influence the ministry's policies and act as its leader in the Commons. He was not prepared to do either until worsening circumstances really did force his hand.

It was only when Legge, the Chancellor of the Exchequer, embarrassed his ministerial colleagues by opposing the Hessian subsidy as wasteful, and Pitt attacked the Government's whole system of subsidy treaties, that Newcastle conceded that he must strengthen the ministry in the Commons. Since Fox was now prepared to be satisfied with Cabinet office and a degree of influence over the dispensation of Crown patronage, whereas Pitt wanted to dictate the Government's policies, Newcastle at last came to terms with the former. In November 1755 he agreed to make Fox both Secretary of State, in place of Sir Thomas Robinson, and Leader of the Commons. On 20 November both Pitt and Legge were dismissed from office. This decision freed Pitt from any inhibition about attacking the ministry's policies. He lashed the subsidy treaties as designed entirely for the preservation of Hanover and as an impracticable and desperate project which would ruin the country. The

---

[14] For Newcastle's foreign policy in these years, see Basil Williams, *Carteret and Newcastle* (Cambridge, 1943), chap. 10; and D. B. Horn, 'The Diplomatic Revolution', in *Cambridge Modern History* (Cambridge, 1957), vii, 440–64, and 'The Duke of Newcastle and the Origins of the Diplomatic Revolution', in *The Diversity of History*, ed. J. H. Elliott and H. G. Koenigsberger (1970), pp. 247–68.

fierceness of this attack alarmed and intimidated most of the ministerial spokesmen in the Commons. Fox had the courage to stand up to him, but he could not frame a policy that would answer Pitt's criticisms.[15]

Newcastle had not conceded enough power to Fox for the latter to control the Government's policy and he himself still failed to give a clear lead to his subordinates. Far from heeding Pitt's advice to concentrate his attention solely on the developing colonial conflict with France, he continued to worry about the safety of Hanover. In January 1756 he negotiated an agreement with Prussia to keep all foreign troops out of Germany. Newcastle believed that this would secure Hanover against French aggression and free Britain from the need to fight on the Continent, but this piece of improvisation soon recoiled on his head. The Russians believed that it ran counter to the aims of the subsidy treaty negotiated in 1755, while the Austrians and French were encouraged to sink their long-standing differences in the face of Anglo-Prussian friendship. Newcastle's plan for a vast system of continental allies against France completely collapsed and he was left only with the chance of forging a more effective treaty with Frederick II of Prussia.

A major colonial confrontation with France had meanwhile become ever more likely, but Newcastle still feared to take the responsibility for declaring war, despite Fox's suggestion that Britain should strike the first telling blow. When Newcastle did finally agree to declare war, in May 1756, he had still not ensured that adequate preparations were made for the conflict. Instead, fearing that France might launch a sudden invasion, Newcastle humiliated the nation by hurrying over Hessian and Hanoverian troops because the country was not in a position to defend itself. France was then given the opportunity to take advantage of Britain's preoccupation with the threat of invasion to send an expedition against Minorca. When Admiral Byng, sent out rather belatedly to relieve Minorca, failed to save the island, an angry and alarmed public rallied to Pitt and condemned the Newcastle administration. The loss of Oswego in North America, the alliance signed by the

---

[15] For the failure to win over Pitt and Pitt's criticisms of Newcastle's foreign policy, see Yorke, *The Life and Correspondence of Philip Yorke, Earl of Hardwicke*, ii, 230–2, 237–42: Hardwicke to Newcastle, 9 Aug. 1755 and Newcastle to Hardwicke, 3 Sept. 1755; and *The Letters of Horace Walpole*, ed. Mrs Paget Toynbee, iii, 365–67: to Henry Seymour Conway, 15 Nov. 1755.

French and Austrians, and the Prussian invasion of Saxony which precipitated a vast continental war, threw the Government into a mood of despair and confusion.

Newcastle sought to escape responsibility for these disasters. When a deputation from the City of London made representations to him about Admiral Byng's failure to save Minorca, the Prime Minister apparently blurted out: 'Oh! indeed he shall be tried immediately – he shall be hanged directly.'[16] Byng was, in fact, subsequently executed for dereliction of duty, but the public as much as Newcastle desired to see him sacrificed. Nevertheless, Newcastle's attempts to avoid, or at least to share, the blame for recent disasters only encouraged his subordinate ministers to push the responsibility back onto his shoulders. With some justification, they believed that Newcastle should take the blame for these failures since, for the last two years, he had sought to avoid sharing power with his ministerial colleagues. Ministers who had been unable to shape government policy were not now prepared to face the violent public reaction to recent events and a House of Commons which was demanding searching inquiries into the whole conduct of the war. In October 1756 William Murray, seeing his chance to escape the savage criticisms of Pitt, insisted on being promoted to the vacant post of Lord Chief Justice, thus removing himself to the Lords as Earl of Mansfield. At the same time Fox deserted the ministry altogether and resigned as Secretary of State. Without able defenders in the Commons and now fully exposed to public and parliamentary censure, Newcastle's nerve cracked. On 26 October 1756 he too resigned. His fall was not due to the loss of his majority in the Commons, but to the absence of able supporters to answer the criticisms of Pitt and to deflect the wrath of the public.

Newcastle's two years as Prime Minister showed that he lacked the capacity to devise and implement effective policies to meet a crisis situation or to delegate power and responsibility to ministerial colleagues who might have been able to perform such tasks. The very office of prime minister suffered from Newcastle's brief tenure of supreme power. Not only was he himself unable to take over the role and mantle of Robert Walpole and Henry Pelham, but he made sure that no other politician could assume such power. Pitt at last became Secretary of State when Newcastle resigned in 1756, under the nominal

16 H. Walpole, *Memoirs of the Reign of King George II*, ii, 231.

leadership of the Duke of Devonshire, but he was unable to construct a stable ministry capable of winning the war. It was widely recognised that the King would prefer the return of a Newcastle administration. Without favour at Court and with most ambitious politicians and placemen still looking to Newcastle as the chief source of Crown patronage, Pitt therefore could not count upon the backing of the Court and Treasury party. Since the war was still going badly, Pitt was not in a position to rally enough independent backbenchers to him either. Only after Pitt reluctantly agreed to join forces with Newcastle, in June 1757, did he find acceptance at Court and a secure majority in Parliament.

In this new administration Newcastle was once more First Lord of the Treasury and so, perhaps, nominally Prime Minister. In reality, however, he did not wield such power. There can be no doubt that William Pitt was the guiding force in the Government. He alone relished responsibility, had a clear idea of how he wished to conduct the war against France, and had the energy and capacity to push through his plans. Nevertheless, it would be unfair to regard Newcastle as a mere cypher in this great war administration which led Britain to victory over France. His task was not merely to manage elections and to dispense Crown patronage, as his critics have too often asserted. The Seven Years War was, after all, the most expensive conflict Britain had yet experienced. As First Lord of the Treasury Newcastle, with the assistance of Henry Legge, who served once more as his Chancellor of the Exchequer, had to provide the vast sums needed to finance Pitt's world-wide campaigns. In 1757 the Government had only to raise about £8½ million, but by 1759 this had increased to £12¾ million and, two years later, to a staggering £19½ million. Such huge sums could not be raised by taxation alone, although the major sources of supply – the Land Tax, the Malt Tax, and a variety of customs and excise duties – were all increased. Newcastle feared the political reaction to more radical proposals to increase taxation and so he resorted to large-scale borrowing instead. As a result, the National Debt more than doubled during the war. To borrow such huge sums the Treasury had to be on excellent terms with the financial interest in the City of London. It was in this sphere that Newcastle showed his great value to the Government. He had always followed his brother's practice of forging a close association with the moneyed interest without alienating the important commercial interest. Without Newcastle, Pitt might have had considerable difficulty in finding the money to finance his military and naval operations.[17]

Newcastle could have exploited his political power as First Lord of the Treasury more effectively, especially as he still retained greater influence with George II than Pitt, but he allowed himself to be over-ruled by Pitt in most conflicts of opinion. Even then, it would be an over-simplification to regard Pitt as the sole mind and voice of the administration. His was certainly the most influential voice in all deliberations upon strategy, but the Government was guided by an inner Cabinet composed of Newcastle, Hardwicke and Holderness, besides Pitt himself. Pitt did manage to reduce Holderness, the other Secretary of State, to a subordinate position, but he could not control his other Cabinet colleagues or dictate to the various heads of departments. Hardwicke still drafted the King's Speech for the opening of each session[18] and he and other lawyers helped to defeat Pitt's projected Habeas Corpus Bill. Pitt certainly bullied the timorous Newcastle and, on occasion, interfered with his running of Treasury business,[19] but most of the time he was content to let Newcastle run his own department in his own way. It has also been shown that Pitt was never able to dictate to the Admiralty and overrule Admiral Anson, the First Lord.[20] It therefore seems that there was no real prime minister in these years and little in the way of Cabinet government. Each department was directly responsible to the King and there was relatively little interference by any ministers, even Pitt, in the day-to-day running of other departments. At times, in fact, there was no effective liaison between ministers and many messages had to be carried by Count de Viry, the Sardinian minister at the Court of St James.[21] It must be admitted, however, that Pitt drew up the magnificent war plans and did most to put

[17] For Newcastle's financial policy, see Reed Browning, 'The Duke of Newcastle and the Financial Management of the Seven Years War in Germany', *Journal of the Society of Army Historical Research*, xlix (1971), 20–35; and Lucy Sutherland, 'The City of London and the Devonshire-Pitt Administration, 1756–7', *Proceedings of the British Academy*, xlvi (1960), 164 and 171–3.
[18] *Correspondence of William Pitt, Earl of Chatham*, ed. W. S. Taylor and J. H. Pringle (1838), i, 448: Newcastle to Pitt, 3 Nov. 1759.
[19] ibid., i, 305–8: Pitt to Newcastle, 4 April 1758, and Newcastle's reply, 5 April 1758.
[20] Richard Middleton, 'Pitt, Anson and the Admiralty, 1756–61', *History*, lv (1970), 199–206.
[21] Namier, *England in the Age of the American Revolution*, p. 81.

them into effect. Nevertheless, he depended more on his ministerial colleagues, particularly Newcastle, than has generally been recognised. Newcastle was once more at his best, playing a vital subordinate role to a great minister.

Thus, whether he liked it or not, Newcastle had to be content to play second fiddle to Pitt in the last years of George II's reign. On the accession of George III, in 1760, he found that his political influence was curtailed even further. George III had been convinced for some years that Newcastle was nothing but a knave and he was anxious to remove him and most of the 'Old Whigs' from office as soon as possible. He had no desire to be bullied by Pitt either, and so he planned to replace him as the leading voice in the ministry by his favourite, the Earl of Bute, as soon as a suitable opportunity should present itself. His plan to purge his ministry of his grandfather's advisers had to hang fire, however, until the war had been clearly won. It would be difficult to remove such a successful team of ministers until it was clear that they had become dispensable. In the meantime, George III took Crown patronage out of Newcastle's hands and appointed Bute as Pitt's fellow Secretary of State. Both he and Bute also skilfully played upon the petty jealousies and disputes of Newcastle and Pitt so that they would not unite in opposition to their plans for the piecemeal reconstruction of the administration. This policy worked only too well, particularly as Newcastle and Pitt began to disagree about the future conduct of the war. Pitt was anxious to expand the war in order to attack Spain before she could ally with France, whereas Newcastle, alarmed at the enormous and spiralling cost of the war, was anxious to negotiate peace as soon as possible. When Pitt resigned on this issue, in October 1761, Bute replaced him with the Earl of Egremont and chose George Grenville as Leader of the Commons. Newcastle was now virtually isolated in the Cabinet and was treated with scant respect by both the King and his ministerial colleagues. Bute was now the real head of the ministry, though Newcastle remained First Lord of the Treasury with the unenviable task of continuing to raise huge sums of money. He could not even count upon the support of his own subordinates at the Treasury. These men recognised that Newcastle could no longer further their careers and so they deserted him to worship the rising sun at Court. Newcastle still clung pathetically to office until he at last discovered this treachery and acknowledged that he had lost all influence at Court and in the Cabinet. When he failed to persuade the Cabinet to continue paying the annual subsidy to Prussia, he finally resigned, on 26 May 1762.[22]

Newcastle had enjoyed a political career of unprecedented length and, in recent years, he had experienced many weary battles with his ministerial colleagues, but he was still reluctant to retire from active politics. He continued to entertain hopes of returning to power, either in alliance with Pitt or with the support of the younger Whigs who resented the ascendancy of Bute. His only weapon against Bute's Court influence, however, was the dubious support of his former political allies who were still in office. When, in November 1762, he asked them to resign so that he could demonstrate his power to the Government, he found that half of those he approached would not desert the Court in order to follow him into the political wilderness. Just in case Newcastle did not now appreciate his lack of power and influence, the ministry decided, in December 1762, to dismiss from office all those friends and dependants of Newcastle who could not be trusted to support the Government's peace negotiations. Newcastle was now to learn that the patronage he had dispensed for decades was not his to control. The real source of patronage was the Crown and yet Newcastle had expected men still in office and place to look to him for direction and not to the Court. Now he discovered that the Court was prepared to dismiss even minor office holders in the revenue service simply because they owed their first appointment to Newcastle's influence. This 'Massacre of the Pelhamite Innocents' finally convinced the political world that Newcastle's day was over and that a new power reigned at Court. Newcastle had witnessed, and, in part, had assisted in, the destruction of the prime minister's office as it had existed in the days of Robert Walpole and Henry Pelham. Now his opponents were dismantling the patronage system he had created with such loving care.

BIBLIOGRAPHY

(The place of publication is London unless otherwise stated.)

The nearest approach to a biography is Basil Williams, *Carteret and Newcastle* (Cambridge 1943). Newcastle's early life is covered by Stebelton H. Nulle, *Thomas Pelham-Holles, Duke of Newcastle: His Early Political Career, 1693–1724* (Philadelphia 1931). There are a number of articles covering certain aspects of Newcastle's career, including Philip Haffenden, 'Colonial Appointments and Patronage

[22] For a study of Newcastle's relations with Bute, 1760-2, see Namier, op. cit., chapters 2 and 5.

under the Duke of Newcastle, 1724–39', *English Historical Review* (1963); S. H. Nulle, 'The Duke of Newcastle and the Election of 1727', *Journal of Modern History* (1937); Basil Williams, 'The Duke of Newcastle and the Election of 1734', *English Historical Review* (1897); Mary Bateson, 'Clerical Preferment under the Duke of Newcastle', EHR (1892); Norman Sykes, 'The Duke of Newcastle as Ecclesiastical Minister', EHR (1942); Reed Browning, 'The Duke of Newcastle and the Imperial Election Plan, 1749–54', *Journal of British Studies* (1967); D. B. Horn, 'The Duke of Newcastle and the Origins of the Diplomatic Revolution', in *The Diversity of History*, ed. J. H. Elliott and H. G. Koenigsberger (1970); T. W. Riker, 'The Politics behind Braddock's Expedition', *American Historical Review* (1907–8); Reed Browning, 'The Duke of Newcastle and the Financial Management of the Seven Years War in Germany', *Journal of the Society of Army Historical Research* (1971); and Reed Browning, 'The Duke of Newcastle and the Financing of the Seven Years War', *Journal of Economic History* (1971). There is a detailed study of one aspect of Newcastle's career in James Henretta, *Salutary Neglect: Colonial Administration under the Duke of Newcastle* (Princeton 1972) and of the Duke's personal finances in Ray A. Kelch, *Newcastle: A Duke without money* (1974).

The hundreds of volumes of Newcastle letters among the Newcastle and Hardwicke papers in the British Museum have never been exhaustively quarried by any student of the Duke. These letters have been extensively used and much quoted, however, in William Coxe, *Memoirs of the Life and Administration of Sir Robert Walpole* (3 vols, 1798); William Coxe, *Memoirs of the Administration of Henry Pelham* (2 vols, 1829); John B. Owen, *The Rise of the Pelhams* (1957); Philip C. Yorke, *The Life and Correspondence of Philip Yorke, Earl of Hardwicke* (3 vols, Cambridge 1913); and in Sir Lewis Namier's two brilliant studies, *The Structure of Politics at the Accession of George III* (2nd edn, 1957), and *England in the Age of the American Revolution* (2nd edn, 1961).

There are a number of biographies of Newcastle's major contemporaries, including J. H. Plumb, *Sir Robert Walpole* (2 vols, 1956, 1960); H. T. Dickinson, *Walpole and the Whig Supremacy* (1973); John W. Wilkes, *A Whig in Power*, a biography of Henry Pelham (Northwestern University Press 1964); Basil Williams, *The Life of William Pitt, Earl of Chatham* (2 vols, 1913); Brian Tunstall, *William Pitt, Earl of Chatham* (1938); and T. W. Riker, *Henry Fox, First Lord Holland* (2 vols, Oxford 1911).

There is a great deal about Newcastle in the major printed primary sources for this period. Particularly worth mentioning are *Some Materials Towards Memoirs of the Reign of King George II*, by John, Lord Hervey, ed. Romney Sedgwick (3 vols, 1931); *Memoirs of the Reign of King George II*, by Horace Walpole, ed. Lord Holland (3 vols, 1846); Horace Walpole, *Memoirs of the Reign of King George III*, ed. Sir Denis Le Marchant (4 vols, 1845); *The Letters of Horace Walpole*, ed. Mrs Paget Toynbee (16 vols, Oxford 1903); *Memoirs from 1754 to 1758*, by James, Earl Waldegrave (1821); *The Political Journal of George Bubb Dodington*, ed. John Carswell and L. A. Dralle (Oxford 1965); *Letters from George III to Lord Bute, 1756–66*, ed. Romney Sedgwick (1939); *Correspondence of William Pitt, Earl of Chatham*, ed. W. S. Taylor and J. H. Pringle (4 vols, 1838); *Correspondence of John, Fourth Duke of Bedford*, ed. Lord John Russell (3 vols, 1842–6); and *The Grenville Papers*, ed. W. J. Smith (4 vols, 1852–3).

THE DUKE OF DEVONSHIRE

BY

G. M. D. HOWAT

William Cavendish, born 1720, eldest son of William Cavendish, 3rd Duke of Devonshire, and Catherine Hoskins, daughter of John Hoskins. Known as the Marquis of Hartington until his father's death in 1755. Married 1748 Charlotte Boyle, Baroness Clifford (died 1754). Four children, the eldest of whom, William (1748–1811) became the 5th Duke. Whig MP for Derbyshire 1741–51; summoned to the House of Lords in his father's barony of Cavendish June 1751; PC; Lord Lieutenant of Ireland 1755–Oct. 1756; First Lord of the Treasury, Nov. 1756–July 1757; Lord Chamberlain 1757–62; Lord High Treasurer of Ireland until his death on 3 October 1764. KG 1756.

William Cavendish, 4th Duke of Devonshire, by Sir Joshua Reynolds

THE DUKE OF DEVONSHIRE

Devonshire was a man whose personal character won universal approval from his contemporaries, and whose political qualities secured modest approval from most of them. To Horace Walpole he was a fashionable model of goodness, to Lord Hardwicke a worthy man, to the Duke of Newcastle an honest gentleman, to George II a very good man. Lord Waldegrave, after suggesting he was better qualified for a court than politics, saw him as possessing the virtues of punctuality and diligence. The only stinging criticism came from Horace Walpole, who went on to say he had 'an impatience to do everything, a fear to do anything, always in a hurry to do nothing'.[1] Walpole had his own reasons for being less than fair to a supporter of the Duke of Newcastle, and Devonshire's career scarcely justifies the jibe. Historians, pausing for a moment to comment on Devonshire, have found him of 'stainless private character',[2] 'an honest neutral',[3] 'the honest broker'[4] and 'distinguished by unsullied uprighteousness and honour'.[5] These were nineteenth-century judgements. Modern historians have seen no reason to depart from them: 'an amiable, straightforward man of no particular parts'[6] and 'notable for common sense rather than statesmanship'.[7]

By background and connection William Cavendish could have been expected to make his career in politics. His family were constantly reminding the Hanoverians that they had conferred the Crown upon their ancestors – in common with other great eighteenth-century households. Cavendish's entry into the House of Commons, as Lord Hartington, on attaining his majority, was in accordance with the customs of the age. That entry coincided with the closing months of Sir Robert Walpole's tenure of office. The young man gave his support to the elder

[1] H. Walpole, *Memoirs of the Reign of King George II*, i, 170.
[2] See Lord Macaulay, *Essays*, v, 401 (1865 edn).
[3] F. Harrison, *Chatham*, p. 80.
[4] Lord Rosebery, *Chatham: His Early Life and Connections*, p. 343.
[5] See Sir Denis Le Marchant's editorial comment in H. Walpole, *Memoirs of the Reign of King George III*, ii, 21.
[6] Brian Tunstall, *William Pitt, Earl of Chatham*, p. 262.
[7] G. A. Sherrard, *Lord Chatham: Pitt and the Seven Years War*, p. 143.

statesman, canvassing for him in his last administration, and rebuking those 'shabby fellows' who were absent from the House when they might have been lending support.[8] Once Walpole had fallen, Hartington transferred his loyalties to the men who dominated politics in the last twenty years of George II's reign. Henry Pelham confided to the third Duke of Devonshire that his son was 'our mainstay among the young ones, of themselves liable to wander'.[9]

During the ten years in which he represented the 4,000 voters of Derbyshire, Hartington remained extremely loyal to the Pelhams, becoming a 'bigot to their faction',[10] and sharing with them the view that 'party' mattered in politics, an opinion that made relations with the rising William Pitt difficult. Hartington's opposition to Pitt in 1751 on the issue of whether or not to reduce the number of seamen was designed to indicate that Pitt could not expect Hartington's support if he deserted Pelham.

Just before Hartington left the Commons to enter the House of Lords in his father's barony of Cavendish, he had been offered – but declined – the post of tutor to the future George III. He took his seat in the Lords in June 1751, having already enhanced his political importance by the estates in Yorkshire, Derbyshire and Ireland which his marriage had brought him. The Irish connection, and his friendship with the Duke of Newcastle whom he strongly supported for the office of First Lord of the Treasury on the death of Henry Pelham in March 1754, led to his appointment to the lord-lieutenancy of Ireland in 1755. There his personal qualities made him popular at a time when the administration of his predecessor, the Duke of Dorset, had brought about a period of violence and dissension largely due to the claims of the Irish Parliament to dispose of its surplus money as it wished.

In Ireland, he was a good administrator. At the same time, he kept in touch with affairs in England through his correspondence with Henry Fox[11] and Newcastle.[12] It was the crisis in those affairs that brought him back to England in October 1756 to a nation hostile at Newcastle's conduct of the Seven Years War. He came as head of a great Whig

[8] W. Coxe, *Walpole*, i, 590.
[9] Quoted in Romney Sedgwick, *History of Parliament: the Commons, 1715-54*, p. 538.
[10] H. Walpole, *Memoirs of the Reign of King George II*, i, 160.
[11] Lord Waldegrave, *Memoirs*, p. 146ff.
[12] See Sir Lewis Namier, *England in the Age of the American Revolution*, p. 113.

family: his father had died on 5 December 1755. He found the Government shaken by events abroad and at home. Abroad, Frederick the Great had been successful in Saxony, and Minorca had been lost. On the colonial front Montcalm had captured Fort Oswego, and the French threatened the whole North American interest. From India had come news of the loss of Calcutta. At home, ministerial dissension was acute, and Newcastle himself came in for major criticism. Since he had been reluctant to confide in his colleagues in the opening months of the war, they abandoned him to the wrath of the House of Commons and, in particular, that of Pitt. Pitt, excluded from senior office in 1754, and dismissed from the paymastership in 1755, flayed the minister who had paid little attention to his views.

This, coupled with Fox's resignation from the secretaryship and public hostility, brought about Newcastle's resignation on 26 October 1756. Within two days George II had approached Fox, who was unable to form a ministry without Pitt's co-operation. On 28 October, the King saw Devonshire, while keeping the options open by seeing Pitt the same day. Five days later Devonshire commented that the King's manner grew softer, which only made 'the matter harder'.[13] Pitt's own ineligibility stemmed from several factors: his lack of influence, his opposition to Newcastle and the distaste in which he was held by George II. For the King, the problem lay in giving office to a politician of comparative experience, yet with the backing of a great family, in the face of strong men of ability who found it difficult to accept each other. In this perplexity he 'ordered the Duke of Devonshire to try to compose some ministry for him'.[14] Pitt himself commended the Duke for office,[15] and agreed to serve as Secretary of State. Devonshire, informing George that he felt at liberty to resign if he 'disliked the employment',[16] set about constructing a government. In practice, it was Pitt's word that counted: those who were advanced, advanced on his nomination. Thus, the appointment of Henry Legge as Chancellor of the Exchequer – when Devonshire preferred Fox – indicated Pitt's authority.

Nevertheless, Devonshire was now First Lord of the Treasury, the politician appointed to this office who was, at that moment, most likely

[13] W. S. Taylor and J. H. Pringle (eds), *Correspondence of William Pitt, Earl of Chatham*, i, 181.

[14] H. Walpole, *Memoirs of the Reign of King George II*, ii, 154.

[15] Lord Hardwicke, *Correspondence*, ii, 376.   [16] Waldegrave, op. cit., p. 86.

to be able to form an administration. Rosebery quaintly calls him 'prime minister under Pitt'.[17] He was in three senses 'prime minister': he was closest to the closet in November 1756, he commanded support from prospective members of the Government, he could manage Parliament.[18] This was the theory. In practice, Pitt, as everyone knew, would dictate policies. Yet Devonshire was no bad choice. Absence in Ireland absolved him from identification with the disasters of recent months, and he was ready to see himself as an intermediary with no grand ambitions for extended office. He was prepared to work with Pitt and make Pitt's ultimate accession to power the more possible. If only on grounds of age, Devonshire was to be reckoned with. He was thirty-six – the youngest man in the Government. Pitt was twelve years his senior. Men like Newcastle and Hardwicke, temporarily in the wilderness, were more than thirty years older.

Within three weeks the new Government had declared its policy in the war. Pitt's speech in the Commons thanked the King for his Hanoverian troops, a matter of concern and surprise to some of his colleagues. Devonshire's speech in the Lords echoed similar sentiments. Government policy over the war was vigorous. Increased Supply was obtained, troops sent to America and a Militia Bill passed.[19] Pitt and Devonshire were frequently in consultation, yet it would be absurd to doubt the realities of the situation. It was Pitt who summoned a Cabinet on 16 December to discuss the sending of troops to America. It was Pitt who wrote over eighty letters of importance on government affairs.[20] When Louisburg was captured by Amherst in July 1758, it was the culmination of plans laid by Pitt in the spring of 1757.

With one *cause célèbre* the Devonshire ministry was closely involved. Admiral Byng's failure to save Minorca had been contributory to Newcastle's fall. Byng was court-martialled in February 1757 and, under a recent change in the Articles of War, sentenced to death. It was a sordid affair involving too closely politics and the armed forces. Pitt sought in vain to save Byng's life. Devonshire, the nominal head of the ministry, was content to let events take their course.[21] It was Pitt's advocacy of

[17] Lord Rosebery, *Chatham: His Early Life and Connections*, p. 289.
[18] See J. P. Mackintosh, *The British Cabinet*, p. 54.
[19] For general comments on these events, see B. Williams, *Life of William Pitt*, i, 283ff.; Tunstall, *William Pitt*, pp. 161ff.
[20] Williams, op. cit., i, 314.
[21] H. Walpole, *Memoirs of the Reign of King George II*, ii, 179.

Byng's cause that contributed to his own resignation in April 1757. It had not improved his relations with George II and he was content to go – knowing he would soon be back. It left Devonshire leading 'a mutilated, enfeebled, half-formed system'.[22] He realised the time had come to leave office himself, acting in the handsomest manner in a disagreeable situation. He recognised that Pitt was the hero of the hour, on whom eighteen towns conferred their freedom. In May Devonshire helped Newcastle towards securing permission from George II to negotiate the forming of a new ministry. In June he was urging Lord Hardwicke, in letters on two consecutive days, to assist in setting up an administration 'to prevent king and country being undone' in the confusion.[23] In July, he resigned. The Pitt-Newcastle administration was reluctantly formed, charged with the business of winning the war.

There can be little doubt that Devonshire's tenure of the Treasury was a makeshift device. Great things had never been expected of him.[24] The ministry was handicapped by George II's relations with Pitt, then by Pitt's departure and, marginally, by Pitt's ill health before he left. To Walpole, the very cement seemed disjunctive: Devonshire was bound to offend one of two great men, Fox or Pitt. Devonshire lacked the influential patronage of Newcastle, if only by comparison with that wielded by the elder duke.[25] This affected the confidence he could command in the City.[26] He was far more than the 'baby politician' that Walpole labelled him in April 1757. But he was far less than the circumstances of the nation's policies demanded. He had been assiduous in attendance at the Lords while in office, and a busy committee man. They were insufficient qualifications.

Devonshire became Lord Chamberlain and so remained until 1762. The office itself cast him as a political supernumerary. Henceforth his political influence lay in his family standing and in his relations with Newcastle, which remained close for the rest of his life. With the death of George II in October 1760 both men moved into the category of the proud dukes of whom the new King was suspicious. Devonshire

[22] Hardwicke, *Correspondence*, ii, 407.   [23] Ibid., ii, 401.
[24] Waldegrave, *Memoirs*, p. 141.
[25] See Namier, *England in the Age of the American Revolution, passim* for comments on the political patronage of the period.
[26] See Lucy Sutherland, 'The City of London and the Devonshire-Pitt Administration', in *Proceedings of the British Academy*, xlvi (1960).

persuaded Newcastle not to resign despite the growing influence of the Earl of Bute who, by March 1761, had become Secretary of State. When political relations between Newcastle and Pitt were threatened later in the summer Devonshire did his best to act as intermediary.[27] By now he desperately wanted the war to end, hoping, as he wrote to Newcastle, some expedient might be found to prevent its continuance. His views changed somewhat when Pitt resigned in October 1761. He was disturbed at the failure of Bute and Newcastle to get on with each another, and he had doubts about the peace terms being considered by Bute in whose abilities he had little confidence. While he had concurred in the need for Pitt's resignation – over Spain – he was not optimistic about the alternatives.

But gradually Devonshire was to become a more isolated figure. When Newcastle at last left office, on 26 May 1762, on the issue of the Prussian subsidy, Devonshire (with Hardwicke) alone supported him. Five months later he himself ceased to be Lord Chamberlain and a Privy Councillor.

The circumstances of his dismissal were these: Devonshire had indicated after Newcastle's resignation that he would seldom or never attend Bute's Councils. In October George III wished him to attend a Cabinet Council to discuss the final terms of the peace, and Devonshire refused on the grounds that he was insufficiently informed on the subject. Shortly afterwards the King's coach overtook Devonshire's on the way to London. George assumed the Duke was coming 'to cabal against' him[28] and to resign office as a protest against the Government. Thus when Devonshire came to Court to take leave before going north to Chatsworth, George refused to see him, and dismissed him. A few days later, on 3 November, he himself erased Devonshire's name from the list of Privy Councillors.

The affair was blown up by George's critics. Newcastle told Hardwicke it was an affront upon one of rank,[29] and told the Marquis of Rockingham it was 'the most extraordinary thing' that had happened in any court in Europe.[30] In the King's defence it may be said that Devonshire was in a false position by retaining office and yet withdrawing from Councils. The King, always suspicious of faction, had a right to his advice. But the manner of Devonshire's dismissal indicated George III's sensitivity where the Whigs were concerned. The King's latest

[27] Hardwicke, op. cit., iii, 274.   [28] ibid., iii, 429.   [29] ibid., iii, 428.
[30] Lord Rockingham, *Memoirs*, i, 135.

biographer considers that no incident in his reign showed George in such a poor light.[31]

Subsequently Devonshire relinquished his lord-lieutenancy of Derbyshire in sympathy with Newcastle and Rockingham whom the King dismissed from theirs. He made one last major political gesture when his house in London was the scene of a dinner-party to plan the opposition to the Government's Cider Tax. This brought Devonshire and Pitt together, and contributed to Bute's resignation in April 1763. Thereafter, Devonshire withdrew from active politics, becoming the recipient of long letters from Newcastle. His last months were spent at Spa in Germany, in indifferent health. He died in October 1764, aged only forty-four.

Devonshire had been a moderate among men of great political passion. If scarcely a spectator in the play of events, he had never bestrode the stage. His death, coming just after those of Hardwicke and Legge, deprived the Whigs of three material men.[32] Given health, he might have returned to office in the Crown's restless pursuit of ministers up to 1770. He had been a man with a concern for king and country. He died the acknowledged leader of the Whigs.[33]

BIBLIOGRAPHY

The Duke of Devonshire is frequently mentioned in the printed primary sources for the eighteenth century. These include:

Correspondence of the 4th Duke of Bedford ed. Lord John Russell (3 vols, London, 1842–6)
Letters from George III to Lord Bute, ed. R. Sedgwick (London, 1939)
The Life and Correspondence of Philip Yorke, Earl of Hardwicke, ed. P. C. Yorke (3 vols, Cambridge, 1913)
Correspondence of William Pitt, Earl of Chatham, ed. W. S. Taylor and J. H. Pringle (4 vols, London, 1838)
Marquis of Rockingham's Memoirs, ed. Lord Albemarle (2 vols, London, 1852)
Memoirs of Earl Waldegrave, 1754–8 (London, 1821)
Memoirs of the Reign of King George II by Horace Walpole, ed. Lord Holland (3 vols, London, 1846)
Memoirs of the Reign of King George III by Horace Walpole, ed. Sir Denis Le Marchant (4 vols, London, 1845).

[31] John Brooke, King George III, p. 97.
[32] H. Walpole, Memoirs of the Reign of King George III, ii, 21.
[33] H. Walpole, op. cit., ii, 21; Rockingham, op. cit., i, 176.

Devonshire has been the subject of no biography but these biographies on William Pitt are useful in understanding his career:

Ruville, A. Von, *William Pitt, Earl of Chatham* (3 vols, London, 1907)
Sherrard, O. A., *Pitt and the Seven Years War* (London, 1955)
Tunstall, Brian, *William Pitt, Earl of Chatham* (London, 1938)
Williams, Basil, *The Life of William Pitt, Earl of Chatham* (2 vols, London, 1913)

The constitutional and political aspects of the period may be pursued in:

Christie, I. R., *Myth and Reality in Late Eighteenth-Century Politics* (London, 1970)
Foord A. S., *His Majesty's Opposition, 1714-1830* (Oxford, 1964)
Namier, Sir Lewis, *The Structure of Politics at the Accession of George III* (London, 1957 edn)
Namier, Sir Lewis, *England in the Age of the American Revolution*, 2nd edn (London, 1961 edn)
Pares, Richard, *King George III and the Politicians* (Oxford, 1953)

There is a brief summary of Devonshire's House of Commons career in:

Sedgwick, Romney, *History of Parliament: The Commons, 1715-54* (London, 1970)

The manuscript diary of the 4th Duke of Devonshire and his correspondence are in the Chatsworth collection.

THE EARL OF BUTE

BY

JOHN BREWER

John Stuart, 3rd Earl of Bute, born 25 May 1713, elder son of 2nd Earl of Bute and Lady Anne Campbell, daughter of 1st Duke of Argyll. Educated at Eton. Married Mary, daughter of the Hon. Edward Montague. Elected representative peer for Scotland 1737; admitted to the Privy Council 1760; Secretary of State 1761; First Lord of the Treasury 1762; KG 1762. Resigned office 1763. Died 10 March 1792.

John Stuart, 3rd Earl of Bute, by Sir Joshua Reynolds

THE EARL OF BUTE

John Stuart, third Earl of Bute (1713–92), held the post of First Lord of the Treasury for a mere eleven months. From 26 May 1762 until 8 April 1763 he was Prime Minister both in form and substance. Yet before as well as after his tenure of the highest political office, he could justly claim to have been the effective leader of the Government. The significance, therefore, of Bute's contribution to eighteenth-century political and constitutional development cannot be discerned simply by an examination of his brief and troubled administration. Rather the few months in which he officially led the nation have to be placed in the context of his entire political career.

Bute can best be described as a well-connected Scottish aristocrat. His family with its sound pedigree had long been allied both by marriage and in politics to the Whig overlords of Scotland, the Dukes of Argyll. Indeed with the death of the third Duke in April 1761, he inherited the Scottish patronage of the Argylls. Temperamentally Bute was not gifted with the qualities that make a successful politician. His early ally and subsequent opponent, Lord Shelburne, remarked of him:

'His bottom was that of any Scotch nobleman, proud, aristocratical, pompous, imposing. . . . He was insolent and cowardly, at least the greatest political coward I ever knew. He was rash and timid, accustom'd to take advice of different persons, but had not sense and sagacity to distinguish and digest, with a perpetual apprehension of being govern'd. . . . He was always on stilts. . . . He felt all the pleasure of power to consist either in punishing or astonishing.'[1]

This uncharitable description bears a semblance of truth. Bute, as Allan Ramsay's portrait of him so tellingly reveals, was both vain and aloof. Yet these qualities stemmed not from arrogance, but from the shyness of a man who had lived as a recluse, and who considered himself (with some justice) to be a scholar and an intellectual. Bute was

[1] Quoted in Sir Lewis Namier, *England in the Age of the American Revolution*, 2nd edn (London, 1961), p. 131.

always far happier classifying his botanical collection, patronising Scottish *literati*, or corresponding with antiquarians about the flora, fauna and economic development of his native Isle of Bute, than he was when he paced the corridors of power. (Throughout his political career he suffered from a gastric malady that was much more intimately connected with the workings of politics than with the workings of his own physiology.) The subtleties of political intrigue, the process of distributing 'loaves and fishes', and the rigours of attending to the 'eternal round of clashing business',[2] were all regarded with equal distaste by this stiff and mannered man. He was born to be a courtier, not a politician. The *bon mot* of his first patron, Frederick, Prince of Wales, captures Bute perfectly: 'Bute, you would make an excellent ambassador in some proud little Court where there is nothing to do.'[3]

Granted the personal indisposition of Bute towards high political office (an indisposition that he frequently admitted),[4] the question arises of how he came to assume such an exalted political station. His road to power was to some extent an unusual one. He rose not because of his political experience, his ability to command a personal following, nor because of his connection with the great Whig families, much less because of his skill in parliamentary debate. He achieved political honour through the Court and through personal favour. In this respect few careers better emphasise the potency of personal considerations in eighteenth-century politics.

In 1747, during a shower at Egham races, the fortuitous absence of a fourth player at cards drew Bute into the orbit of Frederick, Prince of Wales. For the next thirteen years Bute's career focused on the Court of the heir to the throne. After Frederick's untimely death in 1751, he became the confidant of the royal widow, Princess Augusta. This friendship (an intimacy that was subsequently elevated by Bute's enemies into a *mésalliance d'amour*) led in turn to Bute's unofficial appointment as the moral and intellectual preceptor of the young Prince of Wales, the future George III.

Bute very rapidly became much more than George's teacher: he became, to use the young Prince's own words, his 'dearest friend'. To a

[2] Bute to Campbell (16 June 1762 ?), Bute MSS, Mount Stuart. I wish to acknowledge the gracious permission of the Marquess of Bute to cite from these manuscripts.
[3] Horace Walpole, *Memoirs of the Reign of King George III*, ed. Sir Denis Le Marchant (4 vols, London, 1845), i, pp. 299–300.
[4] See, for instance, Bute to Campbell, 30 January 1763, Bute MSS.

quite remarkable degree Bute established a hold over the impressionable George. The Prince corresponded almost daily with his mentor, he was constantly in Bute's company, and imbibed his personal ideals and political principles from the Scottish Earl. Indeed, so great was Bute's influence in shaping the young man's mind that from about 1757 to 1763 it is almost (though not completely) impossible to distinguish the political views of George and his favourite.[5]

The political attitudes that Bute nourished in the young King can best be seen as an amalgam of the political views and analyses of Leicester House (the opposition Court of George II's reign) and the precepts of 'country party ideology'. In the field of foreign policy this composite political creed was to some degree isolationist and pusillanimous. Bute opposed Britain's involvement with continental connections during the Seven Years War, and condemned the influence of George II's beloved Hanover on the formulation of foreign policy. Bute aspired to end European conflict with a just and equitable peace, and to sever all alliances with the major political powers of Europe. He also sought (with complete success) to convince the future King that Hanover should play little or no part in the making of foreign policy.

As far as domestic politics were concerned, Bute was strongly opposed to those who had established Whig hegemony under George II. He reprobated the establishment by Walpole, Newcastle and Pelham of a political system based on the use of patronage, the retention of party distinctions, and the constraint of the *personal* powers of the monarch. His own formulation of politics envisaged a regime of strict economy in which places and pensions were reduced, and political corruption cut to a minimum. He had no truck with party which he saw as a means of maintaining oligarchical control of government, and of constraining the 'independency' of the Crown. In sum he desired a ruler who would rescue 'Monarchy from the inveterate Usurpation of Oligarchy',[6] and act the role of the Patriot King as envisaged by Bolingbroke.

[5] The development of this relationship can be followed in Romney Sedgwick (ed.), *Letters from George III to Bute 1756–66* (London, 1939), *passim*.
[6] Dodington to Bute, 22 December 1760, Bute MSS 1760/206, printed in John Carswell and L. A. Dralle (eds), *The Political Journal of George Bubb Dodington* (Oxford, 1965), p. 407. For a summary of Bute's political views see John Brewer, 'The Misfortunes of Lord Bute: A Case Study in Eighteenth-Century Political Argument and Public Opinion', *Historical Journal* xvi, i (1973).

These attitudes were customarily held by country gentlemen and backbench Members of Parliament. Rarely were they the creed of a courtier, let alone that of a royal favourite. As opposition ideology they were commonplace, but employed by those who held or were to hold power they represented a major political *volte-face*. Moreover they threatened the position as well as the attitudes of the nation's traditional political leaders. It was obvious to the likes of the Duke of Newcastle and the Elder Pitt that once the Prince of Wales ascended the throne Bute's political influence would become paramount and that they, as supporters of the war and continental alliances, as well as those who were *de facto* responsible for constraining the Crown, would become expendable.

Their fears were not unfounded. From the first days of George's reign it was apparent that Bute was effectively the King's chief adviser. Access to the monarch could only be procured via the favourite. As George told Newcastle: '*My Lord Bute is your good Friend, He will tell you my Thoughts at large.*'[7] Not even Devonshire, who as Lord Chamberlain ought to have had ready access to the King, could establish direct contact with George. No measure was concerted without Bute's consultation, and on the occasions when the King appeared in public, the favourite was almost always at his side.

Both Bute and the King were eager to give institutional recognition to the favourite's *de facto* power. Only Pitt's opposition (and a certain amount of chickenheartedness) prevented Bute's appointment as First Lord of the Treasury on the first day of the reign. As it was, he received immediate nomination to the Privy Council. During March of 1761 he was squeezed into the ministry as Secretary of State, and in May 1762 he finally laid hold of the office for which he was predestined, becoming First Lord of the Treasury.[8]

His rise can only be described as meteoric. At George III's accession Bute was not even a member of the legislature, much less the holder of a public office. (He was simply the Groom of the Stole in the Prince of Wales's Household.) His only parliamentary experience had been acquired in the years 1737–41 when he had sat in the House of Lords as a

[7] Newcastle to Hardwicke, 26 October 1760, British Museum Add. MSS 32, 999 f.106, printed in George Harris, *The Life of Lord Chancellor Hardwicke* (3 vols, London, 1847), III, p. 215.
[8] These events may be followed in detail in Namier, *England in the Age of the American Revolution*, pp. 120–70, 283–326.

Scottish representative peer. Yet, within the space of two years, he had become the nation's political leader by virtue of being the personal favourite of the King.

Bute's rapid elevation and assumption of office displeased many. Indeed there can rarely have been a prime minister who was more publicly abused, maligned and manhandled. He was attacked by the mob, threatened with assassination, burnt in effigy on both sides of the Atlantic, and vilified in pamphlets, prints, newspapers, songs, plays and handbills. In order to escape public insult he frequently travelled in disguise, or at least incognito. His rapid rise made him vulnerable to the accusation that he was simply a favourite or 'overmighty subject' who, because of his ideas on monarchy and the end of (Whig) single-party rule, could be seen as 'Tory' and even despotic. Indeed, as the exemplar of the philosophy of royal personal rule, he was readily portrayed as denying the notion of 'responsible government'. His nationality, his paternal name of Stuart, and his putative affair with Augusta, the Princess Dowager, were all added to the indictment against him. At every level of society, from the drawing-rooms of St James's to the gutters of Billingsgate, Bute's name was anathema. Despite his employment of coffee-house spies and newspaper propagandists, the royal favourite was unable to win popular support.[9]

Nevertheless, with the power and favour of the Crown behind him, Bute's parliamentary position was strong. And, once in office, he set about realising his chief political aspirations. The first and most important of these was the successful termination of the Seven Years War and the pursuit of a policy of diplomatic disengagement in Europe. This process of withdrawal had begun before Bute's premiership. Negotiations to end the war had been opened with France in 1761, though these had proved unsuccessful. More significantly, in April 1762 a Cabinet dominated by Bute's supporters had determined not to renew the subsidy that Britain had been paying to Frederick the Great of Prussia. They had also ensured, in a manoeuvre which had been responsible for Newcastle's resignation, that no more money could be invested in a continental war.[10] At the head of the Government Bute accelerated this policy of disengagement. Using the Sardinian ambassadors in London and Paris as a means of exchanging views, he reopened peace

[9] For a detailed substantiation of this paragraph see Brewer, 'The Misfortunes of Lord Bute', *Historical Journal* (1973).
[10] Namier, op. cit., pp. 302–26.

negotiations with France. These negotiations were tortuous and fraught with difficulty. On three important issues – the fate of the island of St Lucia, the negotiation of a peace that did not include Spain, and the question of compensation for Havana – Bute faced a revolt amongst his Cabinet colleagues. In the autumn of 1762, however, the Duke of Bedford was dispatched to Paris as special plenipotentiary, Cabinet difficulties were overcome, and the preliminaries of peace were signed in November. The Peace of Paris finally completed in February 1763 was undoubtedly the greatest achievement of Bute's administration. Although attacked in the press, unpopular in London, and condemned by some sections of the merchant community, it produced an honourable settlement at the end of (to use George III's own words) 'a bloody and expensive war'. Britain held or made substantial gains in Canada, the West Indies – notably St Vincent, Dominica, Tobago – and in India, whilst conceding comparatively little imperial ground to France. The final treaty also saw the triumph of Bute's policy of disengagement from Europe.[11]

Parallel with his diplomatic achievements were Bute's activities on the domestic front. He and the King had always been averse to the political hegemony of the so-called 'Old Corps' of Whigs – a loose-knit coalition of the great Whig factions that had dominated governmental politics since the fall of Walpole. The opposition mounted against Bute's peace by those sections of the Old Corps loyal to Newcastle provided the favourite with the opportunity to destroy the power of the old coalition. Even at the very beginning of the reign Bute and George had begun to undermine Old Corps hegemony, notably by the appointment of a number of Tories to offices in the royal bedchamber.[12] But the confrontation over the peace enabled Bute to make far more sweeping changes. Urged on by Henry Fox, whom Bute had had appointed as the new leader of the majority in the House of Commons, the favourite implemented a thorough removal of the office-holders who had voted in Parliament against the peace preliminaries, together with their allies and dependants. Even the most insignificant local office-holders were dismissed. This 'Massacre of the Pelhamite Innocents' not only undermined the patronage system that Newcastle had so skilfully cultivated,

[11] There is a useful summary of the negotiations and the final terms of the treaty in Lawrence Henry Gipson, *The Great War for Empire, the Culmination, 1760–3* (New York, 1954), pp. 299–311.
[12] Walpole, *Memoirs of . . . George III*, i, pp. 29–30.

it also struck a considerable psychological blow. The end of the dominance of the Old Corps was there for all to see.[13]

By early 1763, therefore, it seemed as if Bute had gone some way towards achieving his chief political aspirations. The nation was at peace, the direction of its foreign policy had changed, and it appeared as if the old political machine had been destroyed, guaranteeing the monarch fuller political powers. But these achievements had cost Bute much. In attacking Newcastle and the Old Corps, the favourite had perforce to use the instruments of patronage, the very gravy-train that he condemned. Bute may have undermined one system of 'corruption', but he had also, as he himself lamented,[14] failed to create a purer politics. Moreover, as a *parvenu* and favourite who had in some sense sought to alter the direction of politics, he had successfully alienated many of the nation's politicians. In this respect he made the politicians more determined than they ever had been to constrain the Crown, for it was only by constraining the King that they could remove the influence of Bute. Bute's transitory success, therefore, was the harbinger of the political conflict between the King and the politicians that was to continue for the next generation. He helped create the spirit of mutual distrust that continued to mar politics until the French Revolution, and which was in part responsible for the political instability of the period.[15] Yet the greatest cost Bute paid for his success was personal: he hated the vituperation that he suffered at the hands of the mob and in the newspapers, the distrust that his friends and colleagues showed towards him, and the sordid jobbery of day-to-day politics. He was scarcely in office than he wanted to resign, and as soon as it was clear that peace would be concluded he made preparations for his retirement. His departure was only delayed by the problem of forming a new administration.

Appropriately enough it was just at the moment when he was determined to resign that his opponents united most strongly against him. His Chancellor of the Exchequer, Sir Francis Dashwood, had proposed a tax on cider, the collection and enforcement of which might have necessitated the entry of excise officers into private dwellings. This measure was seized upon by Bute's opponents and portrayed as part of a scheme to introduce a 'general excise' on the lines that Walpole was

[13] Namier, op. cit., pp. 403–15.
[14] Bute to Campbell, 27 November 1763, Bute MSS.
[15] The best discussion of this problem is in Richard Pares, *George III and the Politicians* (Oxford, 1953), pp. 100–9.

said to have proposed in 1733. When Bute left office, therefore, on 8 April 1763, he resigned in the wake of yet another wave of popular hostility which many felt was responsible for his retirement.

Yet if Bute could do without politics, the King could not do without Bute. George continued to consult the favourite fairly regularly for the next two years, as well as on the specific occasions of the Stamp Act crisis and the negotiation with the Opposition in 1767.[16] Naturally this did not endear the favourite to the incumbent ministers, and after September 1763 every administration insisted that the King cease to consult Bute. By 1766, however, the King's infatuation with his dearest friend had waned, and thereafter Bute's influence declined rapidly. He was abroad for much of 1768-9, and by 1770 his power over the King was negligible.

But Bute continued to be attacked although effectively in political retirement. The activities of his former allies, now the 'King's Friends', and the persistent failure of the politicians to establish an understanding with the King, were both taken as signs of Bute's continued activity as 'minister behind the curtain'. In this respect he served after his retirement as a scapegoat for the errors and misunderstandings of others. Throughout the 1770s his prime political concern seems to have been to avoid the calumny and controversy that dominated his earlier career.[17]

As a Prime Minister Bute was not a success. His sole substantial achievement lay in the treaty of the Peace of Paris. He was unable to reform domestic politics in the way that he wished. Indeed, he succeeded in strengthening rather than weakening party feeling, and increasing rather than dissipating hostility between the Crown and the politicians. The failure of his political career is at once indicative of the naivety of his political aspirations, and of the barriers that existed even in the 1760s to obstruct the success of a premier who held office solely by virtue of personal favour. According to one interpretation of the British Constitution George III was legitimately entitled to appoint Bute to the highest office, but in the light of the political circumstances of the second half of the eighteenth century such a move can only be

[16] This claim is less contentious than it sounds. (See 'Journal of a Late Conference', August 1767, National Library of Scotland, Minto MSS M II/56; 'To the King from Ld Egmont relating what passed with Mr Norton upon his Commission', 11 February 1766, British Museum Add. MSS 47012, f. 22.)

[17] Brewer, 'The Faces of Lord Bute: A Visual Contribution to Anglo-American Political Ideology', *Perspectives in American History*, vi (1972), pp. 113–14.

described as politically injudicious. Perhaps if Bute had been psychologically more predisposed to governing, he would have proved a greater success. But it is doubtful if he would therefore have been the progenitor of less political conflict.

BIBLIOGRAPHY

There is no satisfactory modern biography of Bute. Less than adequate, although it serves as a lightweight introduction, is J. Lovat-Fraser, *John Stuart, Earl of Bute* (London, 1912). There is also a fair amount of information on family matters in Hon. Mrs E. Stuart Wortley (ed.), *A Prime Minister and his Son. From the Correspondence of the 3rd Earl of Bute and of Lt-General the Hon. Sir Charles Stuart, KB* (London, 1925). Much the best book on Bute is Romney Sedgwick's edition of *Letters from George III to Lord Bute 1756–66* (London, 1939), the introduction of which discusses the relationship between the King and his favourite. Scholars should be warned, however, that Sedgwick's edition of the letters is not definitive. There are 400 items of communication between George and Bute in the Bute manuscripts at the Cardiff City Library which were undiscovered when Sedgwick wrote. Sedgwick's analysis is best supplemented by the discussion of Bute in Sir Lewis Namier, *England in the Age of the American Revolution* (2nd edn, London, 1961), and Richard Pares, *George III and the Politicians* (Oxford, 1953). Two articles that touch on the issues that Bute's career raised are: John Brewer, 'The Faces of Lord Bute: A Visual Contribution to Anglo-American Political Ideology', *Perspectives in American History*, vi (1972), and John Brewer, 'The Misfortunes of Lord Bute: a Case Study of Eighteenth-Century Political Argument and Public Opinion', *Historical Journal*, xvi, 1 (1973). For want of a better reference work, the entry on Bute in the *Dictionary of National Biography* is thorough, though it does not include recent interpretation. Bute's manuscripts are to be found in three locations: the bulk of his surviving papers are at Mount Stuart, Isle of Bute, the family seat; there is a substantial collection of papers in the City Library at Cardiff; and there are a few items in the British Museum, including a letter book that duplicates much of the material at Mount Stuart.

GEORGE GRENVILLE

BY

PETER D. G. THOMAS

George Grenville, born 14 October 1712, second son of Richard Grenville, MP, of Wotton, Bucks., and Hester, daughter of Sir Richard Temple, 3rd Bt., MP, of Stowe, Bucks. Educated at Eton and Christ Church, Oxford. Inner Temple 1729; called 1735; bencher 1763; Lincoln's Inn 1734. Married 1749 Elizabeth, daughter of Sir William Wyndham, 3rd Bt., MP, and sister of Charles, 2nd Earl of Egremont; four sons (of whom the third, William, was Prime Minister 1806-7 as Lord Grenville, q.v.); five daughters. MP for Buckingham Borough 1741-70; Admiralty Board 1744-7; Treasury Board 1747-54; PC 1754; Treasurer of Navy 1754-55, 1756-57, 1757-62; Leader of the House of Commons 1761-2; Secretary of State May-October 1762; First Lord of Admiralty 1762-3; First Lord of the Treasury and Chancellor of Exchequer 1763-5. Died 13 November 1770. His sister Hester married William Pitt, later 1st Earl of Chatham, q.v., in 1754, and his brother became 2nd Earl Temple in 1752.

George Grenville, by William Hoare

GEORGE GRENVILLE

In the earlier eighteenth century the Grenvilles were the leading Whig family in Buckinghamshire, untitled squires but predestined to be Parliament men. George's father made the family fortune by marrying the favourite sister of Lord Cobham of Stowe, who settled his vast estate on the eldest Grenville boy, Richard. After Richard inherited Stowe and became Lord Temple in 1752 he allowed George to have the old family home at Wotton. George must have been glad of the house, for in 1749 he had married Elizabeth, daughter of the former Tory leader Sir William Wyndham: he was then thirty-six and she was twenty-nine but, according to Lady Bolingbroke, looked more like forty-nine, for smallpox had marred her looks. This was a fortunate marriage to a devoted wife, who bore him nine children and took such a keen interest in her husband's career that she kept a political diary long attributed to him. 'She was the first prize in the marriage lottery of our century,' wrote one of Grenville's friends to another in 1765.[1]

This background of what seems to have been a happy family life contrasts with Grenville's historical reputation as a cold public figure. He had the misfortune, in this respect, to incur the enmity of the famous contemporary observer Horace Walpole. Apart from putting the worst possible construction on Grenville's political actions, Walpole made this sort of remark: 'Scarce any man ever wore in his face such outward and visible marks of the hollow, cruel and rotten heart within.'[2] Even if such bias is discounted, it is clear that in public life Grenville was tactless, obstinate, and ungenerous. Here is a comment on him by his cousin and friend Thomas Pitt: 'He had nothing seducing in his manners. His countenance had rather the expression of peevishness and austerity. . . . He was to a proverb tedious. . . . He was diffuse and argumentative, and never had done with a subject after he had convinced your judgement till he had wearied your attention. The foreign ministers complained of his prolixity, which they called amongst each

[1] *Historical Manuscripts Commission Reports, Lothian MSS* (1907), p. 259.
[2] Horace Walpole, *Memoirs of the Reign of King George III*, ed. G. F. Russell Barker (4 vols, London, 1894), i, 215.

other, the being *Grenvilisé*.'[3] Yet through all the calumny and candour of contemporary comment there emerges the impression of an upright man, devoted to duty and endowed with an admirable sense of public responsibility.

George Grenville practised law until he became MP for the family pocket borough in 1741. Throughout his life he was dependent on his eldest brother for both his parliamentary seat and his house, held on an annual lease, and much of his quest for family sinecures and his parsimonious attitude to national finance may be explained in terms of this personal insecurity; until he became Prime Minister he saved his annual salary from each office to increase his capital. Grenville entered Parliament as a member of Lord Cobham's band of 'Boy Patriots', seeking office after the fall of Sir Robert Walpole in 1742. For his first twenty years at Westminster he played a subordinate role to William Pitt and brother Richard: and although he held minor posts from 1744 onwards these two self-centred and arrogant men evidently made unscrupulous use of a supporter able enough to win a reputation for himself. Within a decade or so of entering the Commons Grenville was reckoned to be one of the leading members there. He was a professional politician in a sense that few men of his day were: Thomas Pitt recalled that Grenville was 'a man born to public business, which was his luxury and amusement. An Act of Parliament was in itself entertaining to him, as was proved when he stole a turnpike Bill out of somebody's pocket at a concert and read it in a corner in despite of all the efforts of the finest singers to attract his attention.' Grenville came to feel resentment that he was being deprived of a reward proper to his talents. Even in the later 1750s, when Pitt was winning the Seven Years War as Secretary of State and Temple was also in the Cabinet as Lord Privy Seal, they failed to exert their influence on George's behalf, despite many promises and a hint that he would become Chancellor of the Exchequer. Grenville did much of the ministry's parliamentary chores, being reckoned 'the second of Pitt's party' in the House of Commons; and he ran the Navy Office with notable efficiency. But his reaction to his lack of progress was to opt out of the political battle. By 1760 arrangements were in hand for him to become Speaker of the House of Commons, a post that would have well suited a man so concerned with both the procedure

[3] For Thomas Pitt's pen portrait of Grenville see Sir Lewis Namier and John Brooke (eds), *The House of Commons 1754-90. The History of Parliament* (3 vols, London, 1964), ii, 539.

and the prestige of the House. Then Grenville's prospects and career were transformed by the accession that year of George III.

The new King and his favourite Lord Bute had a high opinion of Grenville; and when Pitt resigned as Secretary of State in October 1761 Grenville accepted an invitation to become Leader of the House in his place. His decision to desert his family and political connections must be seen against the long background of disappointment arising out of his political tutelage to Pitt and Temple. Six months later Grenville helped to force the resignation of the Duke of Newcastle from the Treasury by opposing his war finance, and became Secretary of State when Bute succeeded Newcastle. Grenville's career then suffered a setback. Handicapped by Bute's hold on patronage, he had not been a success as Leader of the Commons: and during the summer of 1762 he attacked in Cabinet the peace terms negotiated by Bute. In October he was replaced as Leader of the House by Henry Fox, and demoted from Secretary of State to First Lord of the Admiralty. He had apparently reached his political ceiling. 'Grenville has thrown away the game he had two years ago,' George III commented to Bute when discussing in March 1763 who could succeed his favourite at the Treasury:[4] but the King had to fall back on Grenville as the only man to keep out the opposition leaders Newcastle and Pitt when Fox declined to do so.

Few ministers can have taken office in such humiliating circumstances. Grenville had to accept an administration chosen for him by Bute, even his own Treasury Board; and when he saw George III on 5 April, only the day before the change became public knowledge, the King made it quite clear that he was a poor substitute for Bute and owed his post entirely to the favourite's nomination. News of the ministry was greeted with scepticism about Grenville's ability to stand alone – for although fifty years of age he had hitherto always played a subordinate role – and with derision, the widespread conviction being, as the Duke of Devonshire told Newcastle, that 'Lord Bute undoubtedly means to be the Minister behind the Curtain'.[5] Contemporary opinion was wrong. Bute's intention to retire from the centre of politics, decision-making, was quite genuine: but George III would not let him go. The King insisted on consulting Bute on public business after his resignation. Grenville and his colleagues found themselves with

[4] *Letters from George III to Lord Bute 1756–66*, ed. R. Sedgwick (London, 1939), pp. 200–1.
[5] British Museum Additional MS 32948, folios 86–7.

ministerial responsibility but without the effective power that could only come from complete royal confidence. A Bute problem existed, but not the one depicted by contemporaries and some historians.

Grenville and his two Secretaries of State, his brother-in-law Egremont and the experienced Halifax, formed the inner core of the administration, being known as the 'Triumvirate': they shared responsibility for patronage as well as policy, an arrangement Sir Lewis Namier described as 'the premiership in commission'. After several months of unease they presented the King with an ultimatum. At the beginning of August all three in turn told George III that he had to choose between supporting his existing ministry and forming another one. There followed a political crisis, prolonged by the sudden death of Egremont on 21 August. In negotiations chiefly conducted by Bute, George III found out that any alternative ministry would be even more unacceptable to him than the one he had, and Grenville was able to make the condition that he would continue in office only if the King would 'arm him with such powers as were necessary, and suffer no secret influence whatever to prevail against the advice of those to whom he trusted the management of his affairs'.[6] Bute had created a minister he could neither control nor remove.

The crisis of August 1763 was a triumph of minister over King: but the events also threw the two men closer together. If George III could no longer consult Bute, Grenville had lost Egremont and feared isolation in a Cabinet composed not of his friends but of men chosen to strengthen the King's Government, like the Duke of Bedford and the Earl of Sandwich. On 8 September he told George III that 'these might prove too strong for him; his only reliance was upon his Majesty's truth and honour, and on that he trusted he might depend. The King assured him he might.'[7] When other ministers began to put forward pretensions George III told Grenville that 'he meant to put his government solely into his hands', and refused to consider applications for favours until he had privately consulted Grenville.[8]

Grenville was now Prime Minister in reality, having established his position against both the royal favourite and his Cabinet colleagues.

[6] *The Grenville Papers: Being the Correspondence of Richard Grenville, Earl Temple, KG, and the Right Hon. George Grenville, their Friends and Contemporaries*, ed. W. J. Smith (4 vols, London, 1852–3), iii, 197–201 (Mrs Grenville's diary).
[7] *Grenville Papers*, iii, 205 (Mrs Grenville's diary).
[8] *Grenville Papers*, iii, 207–12 (Mrs Grenville's diary).

His claim to control of patronage was based on his role as Leader of the House of Commons, the unofficial but universally acknowledged position of manager of 'His Majesty's affairs in the House of Commons' which as invariably fell to the First Lord of the Treasury if a commoner as the post of Chancellor of the Exchequer. Grenville's previous failure as Leader caused many to think the task beyond him; but circumstances were now different. Grenville had the power of patronage, the prestige of being the King's first minister – always a great advantage in handling the Commons, and a new self-confidence that was to be reflected in his parliamentary performance. He was to be a notable success even though he at once faced a political crisis that was to blow up into one of the great parliamentary battles of the century. It began with the arrest of MP John Wilkes under a general warrant for a libel in a weekly political paper, *The North Briton*. The decision was made by Secretaries of State Halifax and Egremont, but the whole administration had to face the political consequences.

The ministry at first saw the question as simply being whether or not Wilkes should have been immune from arrest by virtue of parliamentary privilege: and Grenville's strategy was to pass resolutions in the Commons declaring that the offending paper had been a seditious libel and that privilege did not cover such an offence. He proposed to make the subject a vote of confidence and resign if defeated. When the parliamentary session opened in November events showed that there was no danger of that. Grenville won by 300 votes to 111 on the first trial of strength, and carried his resolutions by similar majorities. But after the Christmas recess there came an opposition attack on the procedural issue of the general warrant, an authority to arrest unnamed persons. The use of this had aroused widespread uneasiness, and in February 1764 the administration carried two divisions on the point by narrow margins of ten and fourteen votes. Opposition hopes of overthrowing the ministry were illusory, for many of the hundred or so members who deserted the Government on this subject did not intend to force such a change, and it was not the matter Grenville had deemed a question of confidence; but the parliamentary victory nevertheless represented a personal success for him. Before the crucial debates Grenville briefed meetings of supporters on the line to take, the contention that the matter should be left to the law courts; he made a politic concession over a grievance felt by many MPs, a Cider Tax imposed the previous year; and he himself took the leading part when the parliamentary

battle appeared to swing against him, as even Horace Walpole acknowledged. 'Grenville, not losing courage on this turn of fortune, replied
ably and freely.'[9]

After February 1764 Grenville's hold on the Commons was never
again threatened while he was minister. He had, indeed, already been
well on the way towards winning the confidence of the House. Although no orator, he possessed many qualities that served him well
there, as Thomas Pitt recalled despite the qualification that his

'prolixity rendered him an unpleasant speaker in the House of Commons.
Yet though his eloquence charmed nobody, his argument converted
. . . The abundance of his matter, his experience of the forms and
practice of the House . . . his skill upon all matters of finance, of commerce, of foreign treaties, and above all the purity of his character gave
him weight. . . . He never took notes; he never quitted his seat for
refreshment in the longest debates, and generally spoke the last when
his strength and his memory served him to recollect every argument
that had been used, and to suffer scarce a word of any consequence to
escape his notice.'

Grenville's knowledge of parliamentary lore was invaluable in an age
whose political thinking was typified by his own legalistic cast of mind.
He was reckoned the foremost man in the House for grasp and exposition of national finance, and his economy commended itself to tax-
burdened country gentlemen. He had immediately thrown himself into
the work of the Treasury, and his two Budget Days were personal
triumphs. But his greatest asset was his honest character. Before, during
and after his ministry, on such matters as war and peace, Wilkes and
America, Grenville said and did what he thought was right, without
trimming to the winds of political expediency: and he won respect even
from those who disagreed with him.

Within a year of taking office Grenville enjoyed royal favour to the
exclusion of his ministerial colleagues, and was paramount in the House
of Commons. His is commonly regarded as the strongest ministry of the
troubled first decade of George III's reign. Entrenched in both Court
and Parliament, he bid fair in 1764 to become a Prime Minister in the
mould of Walpole and Pelham. Yet a year later he was dismissed without any prospect of ever returning to office. He had contrived to give

[9] H. Walpole, *Memoirs . . . George III*, i, 291.

such personal offence to the King that George III said afterwards, 'I would rather see the devil in my closet than Mr Grenville.'[10]

Part of the explanation was his verbosity. 'When he has wearied me for two hours,' complained George III, 'he looks at his watch, to see if he may not tire me for an hour more.' This fault was compounded by what Grenville said. Many of these harangues were constitutional lectures, based on the ministerial need for patronage and his suspicion of Bute's interference in that field. Grenville insisted on appointing to every office, and whenever his suggestions met with royal objections he blamed Bute and gave little credence to George III's denials, conveying the impression that he thought his sovereign a dishonest man. This incessant pressure gradually alienated the King. George III later recalled his anger when in October 1764 Grenville 'had the insolence' to tell a Court official 'that if people presumed to speak to me on business without his previous consent he would not serve an hour'.[11] Matters grew worse during the next six months: as Grenville failed to have his way in a series of patronage matters his behaviour became ever more outrageous in the King's eyes. George III had already decided to get rid of him before the Regency Bill crisis of April 1765 which is often said to have precipitated his fall. Grenville, ungracious and uncompromising, survived as minister until July only because the King could not find any alternative administration before then: and George III was so determined to dismiss him that he then called on the young and inexperienced Marquis of Rockingham.

No part of this quarrel concerned policy. George III left that to his Cabinet, and indeed he approved of what the Grenville ministry did with respect to Wilkes, America and Europe. By this time the Cabinet was a small, efficient body, consisting of nine members during the Grenville administration; and decisions were forwarded to the King in the form of minutes embodying recommendations. They were taken after genuine discussion, with particular weight being given to the opinion of the departmental head concerned. Grenville, although Prime Minister, could expect to have his way only over Treasury matters: on other subjects he had to deploy the two weapons of financial costs and his responsibility for government measures in the Commons, arguments

[10] *Memoirs of the Marquis of Rockingham and his Contemporaries*, ed. Earl of Albemarle (2 vols, London, 1852), ii, 50.

[11] *The Correspondence of King George the Third from 1760 to December 1783*, ed. Sir John Fortescue (6 vols, London, 1927–8), i, 168.

not always applicable to the matter under consideration. He often failed to carry his point of view on foreign policy, the province of the two Secretaries of State; for he favoured a firmer line with France over the implementation of the peace terms than that adopted by his colleagues. America fell within the department of the Secretary of State for the South; and on 16 September 1763 Grenville objected in vain to Secretary Halifax's policy of leaving the Mississippi valley without a settled form of government and reserving it for the Indians, which was embodied in the royal Proclamation of the next month. The Prime Minister could thus be overruled in Cabinet on important matters of policy: but Grenville's characteristic application and determination soon enabled him to dominate his colleagues. The Cabinet minutes came to bear the imprint of his dictation; and Horace Walpole later recalled that 'there sprung up out of great weakness a strong and cemented ministry, who all acquiesced in the predominant power of Grenville'.[12]

Contrary to general expectation Grenville had proved big enough for the post of Prime Minister. Here is the comment of one supporter, Lord Buckinghamshire, three months after Grenville's dismissal: 'Reflection but the more convinces me of the calamity England has sustained by his being compelled to quit an office which he is not only the best but the only man in these times duly qualified to fill.'[13] This judgement was implicitly confirmed by men who disliked Grenville. In June William Pitt, when declining to form a ministry himself, had advised George III to continue Grenville at the Treasury: '. . . as things now stood without him he saw nothing in that department either solid or substantial. In opposition too he might give great trouble, his knowlege in revenue matters was considerable and perhaps bitterness and rancour were not the smallest ingredients which went to the composition of his character.'[14] And Horace Walpole made this reflection on Grenville's death: 'Mr Grenville was, confessedly, the ablest man of business in the House of Commons, and, though not popular, of great authority there from his spirit, knowledge, and gravity of character.'[15]

Office had given Grenville stature and a party of his own: and respect

[12] H. Walpole, *Memoirs . . . George III*, i, 234.
[13] *HMC Reports, Lothian MSS*, p. 258.
[14] *The Jenkinson Papers 1760–6*, ed. N. S. Jucker (London, 1949), p. 377. Memorandum by Gilbert Elliot, MP.
[15] H. Walpole, *Memoirs . . . George III*, iv, 125.

for his personal and political qualities enabled him to retain the loyalty of most of his friends even when it became evident that he was doomed by the antipathy of the King to spend the rest of his life in opposition. During his last years Grenville, resigned to the role of elder statesman, was always heard with respect in the Commons, and in 1770 he achieved the remarkable feat of carrying an important Bill against the Government: the so-called Grenville Act established a fairer method of deciding disputed parliamentary election cases. This was a fitting end to the career of a man rooted in the House of Commons, and a more appropriate legacy than the ill-fated Stamp Act of 1765 imposing taxation on the American colonies for which he is best known – a measure no one in office and few in opposition questioned at the time of its passage.

BIBLIOGRAPHY

There is no full biography of Grenville. His career until 1763 has been described in Lewis M. Wiggin, *The Faction of Cousins: A Political Account of the Grenvilles 1733–63* (New Haven, 1958). For an unpublished account of the Grenville ministry see John R. G. Tomlinson, 'The Grenville Papers 1763–5' (University of Manchester MA Thesis, 1956). Grenville's relationship with the King is examined in John Brooke, *King George III* (London, 1972), pp. 102–22; foreign policy in the introduction by Frank Spencer to his *The Fourth Earl of Sandwich: Diplomatic Correspondence 1763–5* (Manchester, 1961); and American policy in my forthcoming book *British Politics and the Stamp Act Crisis*. Papers of especial relevance are Dora M. Clark, 'George Grenville as First Lord of the Treasury and Chancellor of the Exchequer, 1763–5', *Huntingdon Library Quarterly*, xiii (1949–50), 383–97; Ian R. Christie, 'The Cabinet During the Grenville Administration', *English Historical Review*, lxxiii (1958), 86–92; and Sir Lewis Namier's biography of Grenville in Sir Lewis Namier and John Brooke, eds, *The House of Commons 1754–90. The History of Parliament* (3 vols, London, 1964), ii, pp. 537–44.

THE MARQUIS
OF ROCKINGHAM

BY

PAUL LANGFORD

Charles Watson Wentworth, 2nd Marquis of Rockingham, born 13 May 1730, son of the 1st Marquis. Educated at Westminster School and St John's, Cambridge. Styled Viscount Higham 1739–46 and Earl of Malton 1746–50; created Irish peer (Earl Malton) 1750 and succeeded as 2nd Marquis of Rockingham 1750. Married Mary Bright, daughter of Thomas Bright of Badsworth. Took his seat in the Lords May 1751; Lord Lieutenant of North and West Ridings of Yorkshire 1751–62; Lord of the Bedchamber to George II and George III 1751–62; FRS 1751; FSA 1752; Vice-Admiral of Yorkshire 1755–63; KG 1760; PC 1765; First Lord of the Treasury 1765–6 and from 27 March 1782 till his death on 1 July of the same year. Reappointed Lord Lieutenant 1765 and Vice-Admiral 1776; High Steward of Hull 1766.

Charles Watson-Wentworth, 2nd Marquis of Rockingham. Studio of Reynolds

THE MARQUIS OF ROCKINGHAM

It is a minor irony of eighteenth-century history that the Marquis of Rockingham, in many ways one of the least impressive of Georgian prime ministers, should have figured so prominently in the mythology constructed by a succeeding age. To Whiggish Victorians Rockingham's career seemed flawless. As the successor in the Whig leadership to the Duke of Newcastle he apparently cleansed and purified a party soiled by the corruption of the Walpole and Pelham regimes, and by opposing tyranny both at home and in the colonies, he preserved the cause of liberal reform which was to be inherited by the party of Charles James Fox, Lord Grey and Lord John Russell. Moreover as the patron of Edmund Burke he brought into the Whig tradition the man who did more than any other to influence the way in which later generations saw the political history of the late eighteenth century. It is scarcely surprising then that Rockingham came to be seen as such an important figure. He took his place in history as one of those, in Macaulay's words, 'worthy to have charged by the side of Hampden at Chalgrove, or to have exchanged the last embrace with Russell on the scaffold in Lincoln's Inn Fields'.[1]

Yet Rockingham's ministerial career, at least, was extremely insubstantial. He was First Lord of the Treasury for only fifteen months, from July 1765 to July 1766 and again from March 1782 until his death in the following July. Strictly speaking he was Prime Minister for an even shorter period. In the early months of his first administration, it was the King's uncle, the Duke of Cumberland, who was truly Prime Minister. Though he held no official position, Cumberland had been personally commissioned by George III to form a ministry from the opposition Whigs, and took the lead in the direction of policy and patronage. Lord Shelburne's description of the new regime as 'the Duke's Administration, with Lord Rockingham at the Treasury', was extremely apt.[2] In fact Rockingham accepted the Treasury with extreme reluctance and for two reasons only. In the first place he was

---

[1] Lord Macaulay, *Essay on the Earl of Chatham* (London, 1887), p. 151.
[2] Lord E. Fitzmaurice, *Life of William, Earl of Shelburne* (London, 1875–6), i, 335.

very much a personal friend of Cumberland's, and expected to act only as his lieutenant. In the second the obvious alternatives for the office were either unco-operative, like William Pitt, or unacceptable, like the Duke of Newcastle. In any event Rockingham began his tenure of the Treasury without effective power; he became the King's minister quite fortuitously when Cumberland died barely three months after the formation of the new ministry, on 31 October 1765. Even his second period in office after sixteen years in opposition barely entitled him to the status of Prime Minister. He was given the Treasury by George III in March 1782 with extremely bad grace and only because no alternative could be found. To all intents and purposes one of his Secretaries of State, Shelburne, was treated by the King as joint Prime Minister.[3] Such authority as Rockingham retained was shattered by his own illness and the bitter conflict which broke out in his Cabinet between Shelburne and the other Secretary of State, Charles James Fox. In short, only in the winter and spring of 1765–6, in the period between Cumberland's death and his own dismissal, can Rockingham be seen very plausibly as effective premier.

If Rockingham's tenure as Prime Minister was limited, so were his talents. When he was first placed in office in 1765 his political experience was absurdly slight. He had been an independent-minded Court magnate under the Pelhams, and had followed Newcastle and Devonshire into opposition to the Bute and Grenville ministries. He had held no office or position of consequence and outside Yorkshire had played little part in politics. As Horace Walpole remarked he was 'only known to the public by his passion for horse races'.[4] Moreover he was personally ill suited to either ministerial business or political in-fighting. He was ever a valetudinarian, and throughout his life suffered from mysterious and debilitating ailments. In addition his principal characteristic was 'indolence of temper',[5] that is to say, idleness. At the Treasury he depended entirely on his Chancellor of the Exchequer, William Dowdeswell; in the Cabinet he was hopelessly unbusinesslike, on one occasion actually forgetting to attend one of his own Cabinet meetings.[6]

[3] See J. A. Cannon, *The Fox-North Coalition* (London, 1969), p. 5.
[4] Horace Walpole's *Memoirs of the Reign of King George III*, ed. G. F. R. Barker (London, 1894), ii, 140.
[5] British Museum Additional MS 32977, Newcastle Papers, f.39: J. White to Newcastle, 6 Sept. 1766.
[6] Add. MS 32972, f.94: Rockingham to Newcastle, 1 Dec. 1765.

He was also a notoriously poor parliamentary performer. During his first administration he spoke only twice, and on each occasion merely because the taunts and jeers of his opponents compelled him to rise to his feet.[7] In matters of policy he was irresolute, procrastinating and apparently incapable of initiative. George III remarked that Rockingham 'never appeared to him to have a decided opinion about things', and the Duke of Richmond's verdict was similar: 'Lord Rockingham's disposition is always to defer, and by too fine-spun schemes to bring about what he wishes. He loses many opportunities by being always too late and while he is talking and schemeing [sic] perhaps to prevent a thing, it is done.'[8] Though the legislative achievements of his first ministry were not inconsiderable, most of them were either essentially negative, like the repeal of the Stamp Act, the repeal of the cider excise, and the general warrants resolutions, or carried out largely by way of concession to the commercial interests, like the Free Port and American Duties Acts. Grenville's charge in the spring of 1766 that the ministry was little more than the tool of the mercantile pressure groups was not altogether wide of the mark.[9] Finally his political strategy was disastrous. His first administration was short-lived not, as generations of Whig apologists claimed, because the King conspired against it from its inception, but because it proved so inefficient. George III came to see his ministry, as Newcastle remarked, as 'an administration of boys',[10] and certainly Rockingham's political decisions seemed to justify such a description. His ludicrous courtship of the Elder Pitt, his needless alienation of the King and many of his friends at Court, his abysmal complacency and inactivity in the closing stages of the administration, all bore testimony to Rockingham's apparent naivety and incompetence. Junius' comment on the collapse of the first Rockingham administration, that it 'dissolved in its own weakness', was by no means unjustified.[11]

Despite Rockingham's limitations, perhaps because of them, there

---

[7] The two occasions were 20 January 1766 and 28 May 1766.
[8] Fitzmaurice, *Life of Shelburne*, i, 373; 'The Duke of Richmond's Memorandum, 1–7 July 1766', ed. A. G. Olson, *English Historical Review*, lxxv (1960), 479.
[9] Add. MS 32975, f.58: West to Newcastle, 30 April 1766, quoted in L. S. Sutherland, 'Edmund Burke and the First Rockingham Ministry', *Eng. Hist. Rev.*, xlvii (1932), 66.
[10] Add. MS 32976, f.325: Newcastle to C. Yorke, 29 July 1766.
[11] *The Letters of Junius*, ed. C. W. Everitt (London, 1927), p. 105.

were some features of his tenure as Prime Minister that were both unusual and significant. Particularly intriguing was the curious way in
which he treated the King. Since in the eighteenth century prime
ministers were nominees of the Crown above all else, those who
neglected the arts of the courtier did so at their peril. Rockingham's
immediate predecessor at the Treasury, George Grenville, had proved,
despite his mastery of the Commons, an abominably bad courtier and
paid for it with the loss of his ministerial career. It was therefore all the
more incumbent upon Rockingham to secure George III's favour. Yet
he perversely declined to make a point of cultivating the closet and
indeed at times seemed intent on treating the King as a mere cypher.
During the administration of 1765–6 George III was slighted repeatedly.
His views on the Stamp Act crisis were neglected, his recommendations
of an alliance with Lord Bute's friends ignored, his objections to the
appointment of Richmond as Secretary of State in May 1766 overridden,
and his indignation at Rockingham's treatment of the princes of the
blood in the matter of financial provision in June brushed aside. In the
succeeding years attitudes naturally hardened and it was not to be
expected that during Rockingham's brief second administration relations between King and minister would be anything but frosty. However, in 1765–6 Rockingham had every opportunity to establish himself
in the closet; that he failed to do so was very much his own fault. No
doubt his treatment of the Crown looked forward to the views of
Charles James Fox and the practice of the nineteenth century, when the
monarchy's role in politics gradually diminished. But it also did much
to cut short Rockingham's ministerial career and return his party to the
political wilderness.

A further respect in which Rockingham arguably broke new ground
was in his attitude to party. Unlike most politicians of his day, he saw
his party not as a means to power but rather as an end in itself. Indeed
it is scarcely too much to claim that in terms of personal ambition he
valued the leadership of his party far above the premiership. To many
contemporaries this seemed the ultimate proof of his folly, yet it undeniably gave to his political career a peculiar emphasis. Precisely what
kind of party Rockingham led is a matter for dispute. It is possible to
see the Rockingham Whigs either as one of the characteristic aristocratic factions thrown up in the maelstrom of the 1760s, or as a great
country party comparable to the Tories of the previous reigns; the
truth doubtless lies somewhere between these two extremes. What is

certain is that Rockingham's extraordinary worship of his party radically affected his tenure as Prime Minister. 'Lord Rockingham,' Newcastle remarked in May 1766, 'thinks *he* shall keep *the Whig* party together, and I suppose be himself at the head of it.'[12] The results of Rockingham's obsession were seen both in relation to men and to measures.

So far as personnel was concerned it is no coincidence that the Rockingham administrations saw two of the greatest upheavals among office-holders of the century. In 1765 and 1782 old scores were paid off, old enemies ejected from office and a great corps of loyal 'Whigs' restored to place and profit. Still more significant was the firmness with which Rockingham and his friends adopted what amounted to a party programme. 'Then for the first time were men seen attached in office to every principle they had maintained in opposition,' Burke boasted on behalf of Rockingham's first ministry.[13] On all three issues that had principally occupied the opposition to the Bute and Grenville administrations, Rockingham and his colleagues took action when in office. A serious, if largely unsuccessful, attempt to revive the Anglo-Prussian alliance and adopt a tougher line with the Bourbon courts was made, resolutions against general warrants were carried through the House of Commons, and the objectionable elements in Bute's cider excise were repealed.[14] The same concern with consistency dominated Rockingham's thinking during the years of opposition and emerged especially clearly in the discussions that preceded his second administration. The negotiations of 1780, for example, broke down because Rockingham refused to accept the King's stipulation 'that those who come into office must give assurance that they do not mean to be hampered by the tenets

---

[12] *Newcastle's Narrative of the Changes in the Ministry, 1765–7*, ed. M. Bateson (London, 1898), p. 56.

[13] *Burke's Works* (ed. Bohn), i, 330.

[14] Contrary to popular belief, however, the Rockingham Ministry's most important legislative measure, the repeal of the Stamp Act, was not the result of promises made in opposition. Rockingham and his colleagues had done little to oppose Grenville's American measures when they were passed and showed no disposition to repeal them when they entered office. On the contrary the initial response of the Rockingham ministry to the news of the Stamp Act riots in the summer and autumn of 1765 was to threaten enforcement of the Act and repression of resistance by force. Only under the pressure of the business interests in Britain did Rockingham discover a desire to reverse Grenville's colonial policies.

they have held during their opposition'.[15] When George III was eventually compelled to accept Rockingham's terms in 1782 they were carried out to the letter. Not merely the termination of the American war, which was clearly unavoidable anyway, but a detailed programme of 'economical reform' embodied in Burke's Bill, Crewe's Bill and Clerke's Bill, all passed in 1782, bore testimony to the consistency and good faith of the Rockinghams. Contemporaries were struck by the novelty of Rockingham's practice in this respect. As William Knox pointed out in 1789, opposition leaders did not normally adhere in office to the principles that they had espoused out of it: 'When an opposition gets into office and the King trusts them with the exercise of his power, the farce is at an end, and, after a few awkward apologies, and a few ineffectual votes with old connections, by way of consistency, the business of Government is expected to be taken up, and carried on in the usual way. Such however, was not the conduct of the Old Whigs.'[16] Rockingham's behaviour both in 1765–6 and 1782 contrasted markedly, for example, with that of Carteret and Pulteney in 1742 and that of Pitt in 1757.

Rockingham's preoccupation with what today would be described as a party platform was only part of a wider and characteristic concern with public opinion. Again the novelty lay largely in the fact that Rockingham seemed to take seriously principles to which most politicians merely paid lip-service. Whether in office or in opposition his chief consideration was 'the publick in general', 'the general disposition of the publick', 'the general predominant opinion of the nation'.[17] During his first ministry both his greatest blunder and his greatest achievement derived largely from this concern. His failure to establish his ministry on a firm basis was fundamentally a result of his repeated refusals to contemplate an alliance with Bute's friends, a strategy that would have earned him the loathing of the metropolis and the press while making his position at Court and in Parliament unassailable. At the same time his solution to the imperial crisis, the repeal of the Stamp Act, was the

---

[15] *The Correspondence of George III from 1760 to December 1783*, ed. Sir J. Fortescue (London, 1927), v, 3099. See also I. R. Christie, 'The Marquis of Rockingham and Lord North's Offer of Coalition June–July 1782', in *Myth and Reality in Late Eighteenth-Century British Politics and Other Papers* (London, 1970).

[16] W. Knox, *Extra Official State Papers* (London, 1789), pp. 2–3.

[17] *The Correspondence of Edmund Burke*, ed. T. W. Copeland (Cambridge, 1958–), ii, 498; ii, 191; iv, 163.

result not of any great concern for American liberty, but rather of his ready response to the pressure of British merchants and manufacturers. Nothing pleased Rockingham more than to excel even Pitt, the acknowledged master of politics out of doors, in obtaining the applause of the City of London and business communities up and down the country. As the second Earl of Hardwicke told him, in August 1766, 'You are really beating the late Great Commoner at his own weapons and receiving those eulogiums which his *puffs* have hitherto supposed, that nobody was *entitled* to but himself.'[18] Whatever his other faults, Rockingham was not neglectful of opinion outside the restricted world of Whitehall and Westminster.

Together these features of Rockingham's conduct as Prime Minister add up to one straightforward fact: he behaved in power very much as if he were in opposition. His neglect of Court and closet, his preoccupation with his party, his unceasing cultivation of extra-parliamentary support all smacked more of the 'outs' than the 'ins'. George III was puzzled by this – he remarked to Bute on the curious way in which Rockingham and his colleagues were 'still imbibing those strange ideas in government, that they addopted [*sic*] whilst in opposition'.[19] In part this bizarre phenomenon, so much at variance with the attitudes of old corps Whiggism under Walpole and the Pelhams, was the product of the circumstances that had beset the 'Old Whigs' since the death of Henry Pelham in 1754. They had seen the Elder Pitt achieve the heights of power and prestige apparently supported by little but the force of public opinion. They had as they believed been gratuitously humiliated and spurned by the young George III and the upstart Bute. They had had to learn, most of them for the first time in their lives, the arts of systematic opposition, and had witnessed the spectacular embarrassments that John Wilkes had inflicted on the Court. Against this background it need not be altogether surprising that Rockingham and his friends took up rather eccentric positions when they were restored to office themselves. Their animus against the Court and its more loyal adherents, their excessive concern with opinion outside Parliament, their anxiety to establish their new administration on a rigidly partisan

[18] Sheffield City Library, Wentworth Woodhouse Muniments, R1–679: 24 Aug. 1766. I am indebted to the Earl Fitzwilliam and his trustees for permission to consult and quote from these manuscripts.
[19] *Letters from George III to Lord Bute, 1756–65*, ed. R. Sedgwick (London, 1939), p. 242.

basis, all had much to do with their experience of the decade before 1765. But equally important was the mentality that Rockingham personally brought to his party and his administration. Though Rockingham himself had been a courtier in the 1750s he retained in his political make-up an authentic streak of the old country Whiggism which had always been strong in the north. In Yorkshire he was very much at home among the country gentlemen and businessmen to whom the Court mentality was wholly alien.[20] His friends were men like Sir George Savile and David Hartley, themselves thoroughly impractical 'country' politicians steeped in the political traditions of 'independence'. Once Rockingham was released from the Court orbit by the breakdown of relations between George III and the 'Old Whigs' he began to exploit this heritage on the national scene, and with his elevation to the Treasury in 1765 it became a critical factor in the direction he and his party took. Edmund Burke was to weave the party's political experience in the mid-sixties into a sophisticated theory of party and opposition. But at base the traditions and principles that Burke employed to such effect were those of his patron.

In retrospect it is clear that Rockingham's political attitudes did nothing but damage to his own ministerial career. After resigning from the Court of George III in 1762 he spent all but fifteen months of the remainder of his career in opposition. His two brief periods as Prime Minister he owed not in the least to his own tactics or activities. In 1765 it was the accident of Grenville's folly at Court that put him in office and in 1782 it was the accident of military disaster in North America that did so. In each case the failure of the existing regime, not the strength of the Rockingham party, was the decisive factor. Yet the whole story could so easily have been different if in his crucial year of power from 1765 to 1766 Rockingham had adopted a totally different strategy. By resolving to establish himself in the favour of the King, by rebuilding the shattered Court and Treasury party on the basis of an alliance between his own and Bute's friends, by ceasing to seek the patronage of the Elder Pitt, by eschewing mistaken notions of popularity, he could reasonably have remained the King's minister until his death. If he had

[20] On this aspect of Rockingham's career and character see C. Collyer, 'The Rockingham Connection and Country Opinion in the Early Years of George III', *Proceedings of Leeds Philosophical and Literary Society*, vii (1952-5), 251-75; 'The Rockinghams and Yorkshire Politics, 1742-61', *Publications of Thoresby Society*, xli, *Thoresby Miscellany*, xii (1954), 352-82.

any political talents at all they were those of the party leader – shelving awkward questions, averting divisive quarrels, and generally working through compromise. In administration the role of a Lord Liverpool would have suited him temperamentally and it might well have suited the times. Yet Rockingham clung to his 'principles'. In fact so marked was his contempt for the considerations of expediency urged on him by more pragmatic politicians, that some of his friends, perhaps rightly, came to suspect that he valued his public reputation far more than his ministerial career. 'My Lord Rockingham,' Newcastle wrote in June 1766, 'I believe, wishes to go out, and flatters himself that he shall go out with more *éclat* than any man ever did.'[21] Whatever the truth of this, Rockingham's strange conduct, while reducing his term as Prime Minister, contrived to make him the darling of generations of Whigs, a liberal Victorian before his time.

BIBLIOGRAPHY

Unfortunately there is no satisfactory biography of Rockingham. Albemarle's *Memoirs of the Marquis of Rockingham and his Contemporaries* (London, 1852) is useful only for the extracts from Rockingham's correspondence printed, though even these are often inaccurately reproduced and badly edited. G. H. Guttridge, *The Early Career of Lord Rockingham: 1730-65* (University of California Publications in History, xliv, 1952), deals only with Rockingham's younger days. The two Rockingham ministries are covered respectively by P. Langford, *The First Rockingham Administration, 1765-6* (Oxford, 1973), and J. A. Cannon, *The Fox-North Coalition* (Cambridge, 1969). Among the many monographs which touch on aspects of Rockingham's years in opposition, the following are particularly useful: G. H. Guttridge, *English Whiggism and the American Revolution* (Berkeley and Los Angeles, 1963); J. Brooke, *The Chatham Administration, 1766-8* (London, 1956); B. Donoghue, *British Politics and the American Revolution* (London, 1964); I. R. Christie, *The End of North's Ministry, 1780-2* (London, 1958). I. R. Christie's *Myth and Reality in Late Eighteenth-Century British Politics and Other Papers* (London, 1970) has invaluable essays on the Rockingham party in opposition. Finally, though there are very many articles that cast light on various aspects of Rockingham's career, three deserve a special mention. L. S. Sutherland, 'Edmund Burke and the First Rockingham Ministry', *English Historical Review*, xlvii (1932) 46-72, identifies the precise role of Burke and Rockingham in relation to the commercial interests. C. Collyer, 'The Rockingham Connection and Country Opinion in the Early Years of George III', *Proceedings of Leeds Philosophical and Literary Society*, vii (1952-5), 251-75, and 'The Rockinghams and Yorkshire Politics, 1742-61', *Thoresby Miscellany*, xii (1954), 352-82, reveal the importance of Rockingham's Yorkshire background.

[21] Newcastle's *Narrative of the Changes in the Ministry*, p. 75.

WILLIAM PITT, EARL OF CHATHAM

BY

STANLEY AYLING

William Pitt, born 15 November 1708, younger son of Robert Pitt, MP, and Harriet Villiers. Educated at Eton, Oxford and Utrecht. Cornet of Dragoons 1731. MP for Old Sarum 1735–47; Seaford 1747–54; Aldborough 1754–6; Okehampton 1756–7; Bath 1756–66. Dismissed from cornetcy by George II and Walpole 1736; Groom of the Chamber to Frederick, Prince of Wales 1737–45; Commons spokesman for Prince 1737–41. Unsuccessfully demanded action against Walpole on his fall in 1742; inherited £10,000 from the Duchess of Marlborough for opposing Walpole 1744. First acute depressive attack 1744. Excluded from Pelham's government of 1744; Paymaster 1746. Second breakdown 1751–3. Married 1754 Lady Hester Grenville; three sons (including William, second son, later Prime Minister, born 1759), two daughters. Denied Commons leadership 1754. Secretary of State, November 1756 (dismissed April 1757); Pitt–Newcastle coalition 1757–61 (resigned and accepted pension and peerage for wife 1761). Supported repeal of the Stamp Act 1766; formed ministry (Lord Privy Seal) and accepted Earldom of Chatham 1766. Resigned 1768 following third breakdown. On recovery opposed Grafton and North governments. Collapsed while opposing American independence in the Lords, April 1778, and died on 11 May 1778.

William Pitt, 1st Earl of Chatham, by William Hoare

WILLIAM PITT, EARL OF CHATHAM

'The first question I shall ask when I go to town,' wrote Horace Walpole in June 1768, 'will be, how my Lord Chatham does. I shall mind his health more than the stocks. The least symptom of a war will certainly cure him.' Walpole was always amused to wonder 'how much the mountebank had concurred to form the great man', and his uncharitable scepticism that summer, when a desperately ill Chatham lay torpid under his depression, was justified at least to this extent: it was the threats and opportunities of war that had always brought out the best of his ferocious energies. He had first gained prominence in the 1730s, demanding war with Spain: 'When trade is at stake . . . you must defend it or perish.' He had saved his country at a moment of crisis in the subsequent war with France. He had gone on to demand war *à outrance* when the nation, sated by his victories, had had enough of it. And after the peace of 1763, nothing roused his energy and eloquence more than the fear of another war that might bring disaster in America and revenge for France.

From the beginning he had claimed to represent 'the voice of England', and there were times – certainly between 1756 and 1760, and perhaps even as early as 1739 during the clamour against Spain – when the claim was reasonable. The source of Britain's greatness, he always maintained, lay in overseas trade. Her interests were hence global rather than continental; and for many years he preached that her policies ought not to be tied to Hanover's tail – thus by the offence given to George II long precluding himself from major office. Sir Robert Walpole held that commerce would flourish best in peace; Pitt that it required a constant readiness for war. Over Spain, the more vulnerable Bourbon power, his views fluctuated as the years passed; during the fifties he was anxious to secure her neutrality. But towards the formidable power of France he never wavered. Britain's trade, her prosperity and that of her colonies, would not be secure until the French were mastered.

Blackballed by the King and belonging to no parliamentary connection once he had parted company with the 'Patriots' and the Prince of Wales, Pitt until the beginning of the Seven Years War spent his energies either in opposition or in minor office only. During that time the Spanish war ('of Jenkins's Ear') was succeeded by the general European war ('of the Austrian Succession'). Then came a breathing-space with the Peace of Aix-la-Chapelle which, except for Italy, settled nothing. While in Europe preparations continued for a renewal of the war, on the disputed frontier of North America and along the Bengal and Coromandel coasts of India the contest never ceased, as British traders, regardless of the quarrels between Prussia and the Habsburg Empire, or of the necessity of protecting Hanover from the French, fought to secure or enlarge their interests.

This was the struggle that absorbed Pitt's attention. The strategy with which to wage it was developed, in the light of his contacts with merchants trading with the West Indies and America and along the shores of Africa and India, during the long years in which he built up his reputation in the Commons and with the public, ostentatiously waived the customary substantial perquisites of the Pay Office, and manoeuvred fruitlessly for high office. All this time he conducted his fluctuating personal battle with physical illness and mental instability, either (for two prolonged periods) in his private hell of acute depression, or in the public theatre of the Commons, huge-booted and flannelled against his gout, often looking ill enough to convince many he was dying.

During his nine years as Paymaster, Pitt laboured to deserve the promotion that he never doubted ought to be his. Sometimes in the cause of loyalty – and perhaps self-advancement – he sacrificed his better judgement, though he could not resist standing firm against Pelham's naval economies. Several times he earned, and accepted, charges of inconsistency. He had to admit modifying his views on Hanover; he conceded the need for subsidising Britain's European allies; and in 1751 he spoke in favour of a peace with Spain which left Britain miles short of those minimum claims he had earlier laid down as prerequisites for peace. Still George II maintained his ban, and the Pelhams did not labour over-strenuously to break it. Indeed, when Pelham died in 1754, Newcastle, succeeding him, first attempted to manage the Commons through a minor second-rate politician, and then, when this broke down, chose Henry Fox rather than Pitt to lead the House.

Meanwhile events pointed clearly to an early resumption of war, and Newcastle's attempts to avoid it aroused Pitt's scorn only a little less than his subsequent efforts to wage it. For a time a second prolonged mental and physical breakdown held Pitt back. Then the blessing of his marriage, and the access of vigour that coincided with it, helped to make once again a formidable man of him. Released from obligations to Newcastle, appealing now in a torrent of speeches not only to the Commons but over the heads of King and Government to the nation at large, he hammered away from the outset of the 1755 session at the unpreparedness and incompetence which, he claimed, looked like losing command of the seas, sacrificing 'the long injured, long neglected, long forgotten people of America', and frittering away an empire. An electric presence, with his hawk nose and scorching glance, he was mordantly sarcastic at ministers' expense, mournfully eloquent at the nation's plight, arrogantly yet soberly convinced that he and only he could save the country. While 140,000 men were ready to defend Hanover, only 'two miserable battalions of Irish' had been sent to America. We were sending our money abroad 'to buy courage or defence' when we should have been 'like Athens putting ourselves aboard our fleet', reinforcing the American colonies, and building up a militia at home. He prayed to God, he said, the King might not 'have Minorca, like Calais, written on his heart'. When Minorca (the principal Mediterranean base) was indeed lost, followed by the British forts at Oswego on Lake Ontario, and the French finally signed their alliance with the Habsburgs, a Pitt ministry began to look the only alternative to national humiliation. The one possible alternative, which the King would have preferred as the lesser of two evils, a ministry led by Fox, was put out of court by Pitt's refusal to have any truck with it. Pitt held out for his own terms. He must have an inquiry into the late ministry's conduct, have personal access to the King, and be 'in the first concert and concoction of measures'. The 'succour and preservation of America' must have priority, while a home militia must be established. Not specifically demanding the right to name his Cabinet colleagues, he nevertheless tendered his draft list, excluding Newcastle and all his recent chief lieutenants, and suggesting a figure of dignified rank, the Duke of Devonshire, for the Treasury. Pitt himself, in the office of Secretary of State, was of course to be *de facto* Prime Minister.

In one sense it was a false start. 'Great genius,' Lyttelton observed of him, 'is not conducted by the rules of common prudence'; and Pitt, strongly as he enjoyed the support of the merchants and professional classes, and backed though he was by many independent country-gentlemen members, by Tories, and of course by his own family connection of the Grenvilles, had neglected to provide himself with a parliamentary majority. He spurned Fox and the Cumberland connection; he had ousted Newcastle and Hardwicke, who led the main Whig group. Devonshire had accepted the Treasury with mixed feelings and was soon anxious to resign. The King described his ministers as scoundrels. Even the city merchants and public opinion grew cooler in their praise of Pitt when he courageously opposed sacrificing Admiral Byng as a scapegoat for Minorca. Finally Cumberland refused to act as commander-in-chief while Pitt remained chief minister.

Declining to resign, Pitt was dismissed in April 1757, after less than five months in office; but even in that short time the conduct of the war was given a new spirit. The Hessians and Hanoverians whom a scared Newcastle had imported for defence were sent back to Germany, and against the opposition of the Lords a militia was established. New battalions were raised, old regiments expanded, and two new ones formed from recently rebellious Highland clans. (It would 'gain the Scotch', Pitt hoped – and happily they might settle in America at the end of the war.) He husbanded his ships as well as the precarious situation allowed, and immediately laid down an ambitious building programme, with heavy emphasis on a new class of fast frigates. Working with furious energy, and in practice dictator of the Admiralty and War Office as well as both the Secretaries' offices, he set an urgent and novel atmosphere of 'action this day'. He planned general strategy, giving priority to the attack on Canada; but no detail was too small for his attention. He always delegated as little as possible; he himself must attend to the arrangements for convoys, to the preparation of siege trains, even to the condition of a consignment of ammunition flints. His under-secretaries he treated as clerks. Once a dragoon himself, he had studied war, and understood logistics; in contact too over many years with merchants at home and abroad, he was well instructed in the geography and economics of America and the Caribbean. His colleagues found him impressive, but overbearing and more than a little mad. Indeed he never recognised colleagues but only subordinates: as Newcastle was later to complain, 'such treatment cannot be borne . . . he will be Treasurer, Secretary, General, and Admiral'. Towards those inferiors who protested that impossibilities were being asked of them, his scorn could be annihilating. 'Sir,' he said to one, indicating the crutches his gout required, 'I walk upon impossibilities.'

The public support he had accumulated was demonstrated during the eleven weeks when George II looked fruitlessly for a new administration. It 'rained gold boxes', and nineteen of the nation's chief cities offered the discarded minister their freedom. As Johnson remarked, Pitt was 'a minister given by the people to the King' – in itself a phenomenon of significant novelty. Newcastle, seeing that Pitt was indispensable, negotiated an understanding with him; and the King was obliged to reinstate him. Newcastle, appointed First Lord of the Treasury, while twittering querulously that he 'would not be inferior' to Pitt, was realist enough to accept that 'after near forty years' he would leave 'ordinary business' to others and 'desire the King's permission to trouble him only twice a week'. He was quite aware that 'if he whispered in the Closet or gave any disturbance in Parliament . . . he might expect all kinds of hostilitys from Mr P'. In fact, he was to play his part to the general satisfaction and even to Pitt's. Attending to parliamentary management, conferring regularly with Pitt on matters of supply, fretting constantly over the war's expense, chronically alarmed at the rashness of sending so many troops abroad, he privately considered that Pitt's notion 'of being able to extirpate the French from North America' was 'the idlest of all imaginings'. But he soon accommodated himself to the badgering and bullying; and recognising, however ruefully, Pitt's qualities, he was ready to support him even when he was being most outrageous – for example in 1759 when Pitt provoked a crisis by forcing the King to bestow the Garter upon his insufferable brother-in-law Temple. From his side Pitt proceeded on the assumption that his monopoly of policy was absolute. Even in financial matters he was by no means prepared to leave things to Newcastle, especially where the King's German troops were concerned. 'The demand of forage for the Hessians' was 'preposterous'; and how possibly could he persuade the Commons to budget for 'another 38,000 Germans'? 'In the name of God, my Lord, how came such an idea on paper?' In fact the Commons was ready for three years and more to eat out of his hand. 'Mr Pitt declares only what he would have them do,' wrote Chesterfield, 'and they do it *nemine contradicente*'.

Hard as he looked at continental commitments, Pitt had moved a long way from his earlier contempt for Hanover and hostility to the King's 'German business'. He was now ready to contribute a containing force of British or British-hired troops to the continental army led by Ferdinand of Brunswick, and for the rest of his life he was to be a champion of the Prussian alliance, with its wartime obligation of subsidies for Frederick the Great. He was also committed to some much criticised diversionary raids on the French coast. But of the main targets he was never for a moment in doubt – mastery of the seas and, by means of that, the conquest of French overseas trade. Even supporting Prussia was only to 'conquer America in Germany'. Territory in itself, without strategic or commercial advantage, possessed no attraction. It was still arguable in Pitt's day whether the single sugar island of Guadeloupe or the whole of Canada should be reckoned the richer prize – and Pitt himself contended that victory in Canada would be thrown away if it did not carry with it the Newfoundland cod-fishing monopoly, which was worth as much as the rest of Canada's wealth combined. Taking Goree, off the Senegal coast, was a necessary step to damaging the French silk industry (through the trade in gum) and denying France the benefits of the slave trade upon which in turn the sugar trade rested. The capture of Mauritius (contemplated but never actually undertaken) would have undermined the whole French trading position in India. Nothing was more distant from his ambitions than an extensive territorial empire in India; indeed the very successes there of Clive and Eyre Coote were later to cause him problems to which he had no answer. Trade was the goal. The sacrifices involved in its pursuit were an investment for future wealth and greatness.

After two years of setbacks and disappointments but also of wide-ranging and ambitious preparations, in 1758 the tale of victories began to come in. 'God send a miracle to save old England at last,' Thomas ('Diamond') Pitt, then Governor of Madras, had written home to his son – Pitt's father – in 1704, before the news of Blenheim could reach India. By the summer of 1758, and increasingly during 1759, it looked as though his prayer was being posthumously answered, and ironically by one of his own 'cockatrice brood of Pitts', against whom he had railed so constantly. Apart from Clive's extraordinary performance at Plassey, news of which was long delayed, the first successes of this new (so-called Seven Years) war were Prussian – Frederick's defeat of the French at Rossbach and the Austrians at Leuthen. Then in July 1758 Louisbourg, the gateway to the St Lawrence and the strongest fortress in North America, fell to the combined sea and land assault of Boscawen and Amherst. Pitt's reputation as miracle man was established. Thanksgivings in St Paul's, bonfires and illuminations in the City, celebrations throughout Britain and British America greeted the event and its architect. 'Nothing but congratulations to you my dear brother

Louisbourg', wrote Temple, 'I shall never call you by any other name except that of Quebeck in good time.' On the mainland Fort Duquesne on the Ohio was next taken and renamed Fort Pitt; it is the modern Pittsburg. In December Goree was captured. During 1759 the tempo quickened. The French lost Guadeloupe. The continental army defeated them at Minden. Boscawen destroyed part of the Toulon fleet at Lagos Bay – in neutral Portuguese waters; but it would be rather easier, Pitt considered, for Britain to satisfy the Portuguese Court than for the French to replace their battleships. In September the assault on Quebec which Pitt and his advisers had first envisaged a dozen or more years earlier was at last brought to success by Wolfe; and to close a triumphant year came news of Hawke's no less daring victory over the Brest fleet in Quiberon Bay. Naval supremacy, the *sine qua non* of all Pitt's enterprises, was by then secured, and Garrick's company at Drury Lane could celebrate the achievement that New Year's Eve with a popular new number:

> Come cheer up my lads, 'tis to glory we steer. . . .
> > Heart of oak are our ships,
> > Heart of oak are our men. . . .
> We'll fight and we'll conquer again and again.

By September 1760 Montreal had fallen, and with it in effect all Canada. Of major British objectives only Minorca, Martinique and Mauritius remained unattained.

Widely differing circumstances combined at this stage to weaken Pitt's position, public idol though he had become. Two royal deaths contributed. Abroad, Ferdinand VI of Spain, who had pursued neutrality, was succeeded in 1759 by Charles III, who prepared to reactivate the Bourbon Family Compact. At home, George III, succeeding his grandfather in October 1760, was under the influence of Lord Bute, once Pitt's tactical ally but now his most dangerous rival; and Bute stood for peace. George III, wishing to install him as chief minister, looked forward to the day when he could be rid of many of the presiding group of Whig politicians, including both Newcastle, his grandfather's 'knave and counsellor', and 'that mad Pitt', who had treated both Bute and George himself with scant regard and had apparently forgotten that 'a day must come when he must expect to be treated according to his deserts'.

George III did not, however, dismiss Pitt. Pitt dismissed himself.

That this could be accepted without overmuch dismay was partly because, by 1760, he had in large measure performed what the nation had
asked. There was little fear now of invasion. Choiseul's new plans for
yet another attempt inspired no anxiety, except in the breast of Newcastle, where anxiety was endemic. The overseas empire had been
saved, and enough new bargaining counters won to be put into peace
negotiations against the return of Minorca – with ample to spare, both
for glory and the balance-sheets. Most country gentlemen felt it was
time to think of reducing the Land Tax down. Some even of Pitt's
City supporters were nervous about going for a colonial grand slam.
Might not a flood of sugar bring a slump in profits? Influential voices in
the Cabinet and outside spoke of the likelihood of a great European
coalition against Britain if victory was pushed too far. Exploratory
negotiations with France were begun in March 1761, and more than
once Pitt was outvoted in Cabinet on the projected terms. He still
wanted 'the total destruction of the French in the East Indies', and
refused to accept sharing the Newfoundland fisheries with the French.
Now that the French navy had been mastered, he considered that a
Franco-Spanish alliance and an extension of the war could be confidently faced. The Spanish Empire was infinitely more vulnerable in
1761 than the French had been in 1755: 'You are prepared, and she is
not.' In any case, Pitt argued, it was better openly to fight France and
Spain than to be faced by France aided by Spanish money, ships, and port
facilities, which was the likely alternative. When his intelligence sources
told him that Spain's decision to declare war was taken, he argued in the
Cabinet for a pre-emptive strike against her, before her home-coming
treasure fleet could make port. Only Temple supported him – and
resigned with him when the rest of the Cabinet decided to await Spanish
action. He would go on no longer, he declared, since his advice was
spurned. He would be responsible for nothing he did not direct.

The impetus of his direction carried over into the last phase of
hostilities. Belle Isle had been taken a little before Pitt's resignation,
and the great prize of Martinique soon after it; and when the Spaniards
entered the war they were defeated in Cuba and the Philippines. Yet
the peace which Bedford was already negotiating in Paris on behalf of
a government in which Bute was now dominant, restored so much to
France and Spain that the mercantile community was outraged; and
Pitt, pallid and emaciated, gloved and bandaged, was carried into the
Commons to denounce for three and a half hours – much of the time

sitting, and in low spectral tones – our 'treacherous' desertion of Prussia, the abandonment 'of all the Spanish treasure and riches that lay at our feet', and above all the neglect

'of the great fundamental principle that France is chiefly, if not solely, to be dreaded by us in the light of a maritime and commercial power – and therefore by restoring to her all the valuable West Indian Islands, and by our concessions in the Newfoundland fishery, we have given her the means of recovering her prodigious losses. . . .'

For the next three and a half years, while George III struggled with the Whig factions, Pitt stayed in the shadows, invalid but still ambitious and redoubtable; aloof, oracular, unpredictable, and unbending. He could still compel in the Commons the sort of attention given to no one else so intensely, as when he pleaded for the repeal of the Stamp Act and a policy of conciliation towards the Americans. When, however, on repeated occasions negotiations were begun with him upon his conditions for re-entering the King's service and so lending this or that administration the strength and stability his name might bestow, Pitt's responses were devious and ambiguous. He was a master of the opaque rigmarole. He mystified and exasperated. And his ever-shifting relationships with his brothers-in-law, George Grenville and Lord Temple, added fresh dimensions of complication. When all the provisos and qualifications were at last translated into intelligible statements, these usually amounted to a refusal to consider any terms other than those that would make him dictator of policy.

When, after years of ministerial confusion, he finally returned to office in 1766, it was at the head of a government hand-picked to do his bidding; three of his own followers in Grafton, Camden, and Shelburne, and the rest chosen one or two from this group and one or two from that, with the deliberate intention of breaking parties and the spirit of party – 'to root out the present method of banding together', as George III hopefully expressed it. It was to be a government of patriotic renewal. There was certainly no doubt who was to be Prime Minister – few ministers have ever been quite so 'prime' as Pitt in the summer of 1766 – but the post of First Lord of the Treasury (after Temple had bad-temperedly refused it) went to the Duke of Grafton. Pitt knew that his own health was too precarious to be burdened with the weight of Commons business. He had, moreover, never lacked a desire for rank or an esteem for wealth and grandeur. (Since inheriting a large estate in Somerset from an admirer he was during these years overspending wildly and perhaps pathologically upon it.) So now, becoming Lord Privy Seal, he accepted the Earldom of Chatham, and thus at a stroke destroyed one pillar upon which his strength had rested – the magic he could wield as the Great Commoner. As Walpole coolly observed, 'The silence of the House [of Lords], and the decency of the debate there, were not suited to that inflammatory eloquence by which Lord Chatham had been accustomed to raise huzzas from a more numerous auditory.'

Chatham's ministry, declared Burke, the great subsequent champion of party, was 'a tessellated pavement without cement'; and very soon the tesserae began to work loose. The Prussian Ambassador noted how at the King's levee Pitt held his own 'levee' in the ante-room, handing ministers a note as they left him, with their instructions written on it; and Charles Townshend was not the only minister who resented Chatham's style. It proved, moreover, even more difficult to compel policies than men. None of the three major concerns that exercised Chatham at this time, conciliation of the Americans, limitation of the East India Company's powers, and an Anglo-Russo-Prussian alliance against the Bourbons, proved amenable to his efforts. Reasonably fearing French preparations for a counter-stroke, he plunged into the project of the anti-Bourbon alliance as though war were imminent; but neither Frederick nor the Tsarina Catherine showed interest. And the Americans, whom Chatham hoped to be able to treat as patriotic Englishmen happening to live overseas, proceeded to present demands that so dedicated an imperialist could not possibly entertain. The merchants of New York, he was pained to observe, 'disobedient', 'irritable and umbrageous', were 'quite out of their senses'.

Within a few weeks of taking office Chatham had retired to Bath for a month to nurse an attack of gout which had among other things incapacitated his writing hand. During the autumn he was back in London, forcing himself and others along with all his old drive, though the total of his attendances in the Lords during his whole ministry amounted to two only. By Christmas 1766 he had returned to Bath, and only after two abortive attempts managed to get himself back to London by March, when immediately he collapsed again. That he was very sick there is no doubt; but a fair relative appraisal of physical and psychological factors in his complicated and erratic infirmity is not to be determined. Shrewd, but not shrewd enough, Horace Walpole wondered if the 'master dissembler' was being 'extravagant by design'. Many, including the King, for a time suspected some malingering, the more so as he was occasionally reported out horse-riding. But undeniably by the spring of 1767 Chatham was the pitiable victim (it was the third time for him) of what contemporaries sometimes knew as 'gout in the head', their euphemism for madness. He was suffering from fever, digestive disorders, insomnia, giddiness, and palpitations; from irrationality, mental confusions and distortions; and for long stretches from a paralysing stupor that robbed him of the will to move or eat or speak – the extreme depressive stage of his psychosis. His doctor and his devoted wife, who was his secretary, nurse, and guardian angel, hopefully awaited a good strong return of the gout, which it was believed would expel these evil humours.

For the rest of 1767 and throughout 1768 he remained in a generally poor state, sometimes being driven out or even riding, but mostly unable to concentrate, and sometimes almost comatose. Meanwhile his ministers pursued policies and imposed measures – in particular concerning the East India Company and American taxation – which a Chatham in control would not have approved.

In 1766 the East India Company's charter was due for statutory renewal. Chatham had for some years been 'uneasy' over India, as he had told Clive, and even before his collapse the vast recent acquisitions were the subject of Cabinet disagreements. The trade in sugar and slaves by which many of Chatham's City supporters grew rich never roused a whisper from him; but the grandson of 'Diamond' Pitt spoke strongly against those East India merchants who 'lived in riot and luxury' upon 'the ignorant, the innocent, the helpless'. He had never accepted that British conquests in India belonged wholly, by right, to the Company. It would be fanciful to suppose that he ever envisaged any future British *raj* in India; but he did wish to see some of the Company's territorial revenues surrendered to the State. The quarrels, principally with Townshend, had arisen over how, and how much. As Chatham sank into inactivity all he would say was that 'he would make no plan', and that the matter should 'find its way through the House'. It was plain that British-controlled India had become too big to be managed by a body of merchants but, as Rockingham wrote to Burke in 1772, 'In regard to what Lord Chatham's ideas may be on East Indian matters': I am not sure that his Lordship has had *or ever had any* fixed plan or idea on that subject.'

Chatham summoned the strength to resign – or as George III saw it, finally to desert – in October 1768. By then he was on the way to as good a recovery as his battle-scarred constitution was ever likely to manage. By mid-1769 a visitor discovered him 'high in spirits and in fury' at the Government. He was soon in a mood to be 'a scarecrow of violence', to try anything that might topple first Grafton (who had of course originally come in as Chatham's nominee) and then North, who took over as chief minister in 1770 and behind whom stood the King, stubborn as ever but by now experienced too, and determined not to be outmanoeuvred either by Chatham, that 'trumpet of sedition', or by the Whig clans. The combination of the Rockinghams with a Chatham who was now busily repairing his family alliance with Temple and Grenville did indeed sound formidable, but Burke and Rockingham had no mind to accept this cuckoo in their nest.

For two years Chatham attacked on all fronts, echoing the virulence of 'Junius', even on one occasion, like 'Junius' again, unmistakably attacking the King himself. He fulminated against those who had 'laid the axe to the tree of liberty' by expelling Wilkes from the Commons – not that by this time he had any more respect for Wilkes than Wilkes for him ('flint-hearted' Chatham). Upon the newly raised topic of parliamentary reform he would not advocate abolishing rotten boroughs – for several of which he himself had sat – lest, as he said, amputation of dead limbs should kill the tree; but with the Whigs he denounced the 'corrupting' power of royal influence and supported an increase in the representation of what he took to be the uncorrupt counties. He called, too, for triennial rather than septennial general elections. On India, he called vehemently for intervention against 'the lofty Asiatic plunderers of Leadenhall Street'. And on eight occasions he factiously and fierily attacked the North ministry's quiet settlement of the Falkland Islands dispute with Spain. He loved peace, so he protested, but 'if our honour is to be the expense of our tranquillity, let discord reign'.

The American problem remained, and dominated Chatham's last years, while his powers ebbed. Though he unequivocally affirmed Britain's right to regulate imperial trade and impose 'external' taxation, he continued to deny her right to tax 'internally' – a distinction which sounded constructive until an incident such as the Boston Tea Party exposed its limitations. He had once claimed to 'rejoice' at the resistance of the Americans, yet he deeply dreaded the consequences. To safeguard and strengthen the colonies of the western hemisphere had always been at the top of his priorities; and now, partly through the umbrageousness of the Americans but, he considered, vastly more through the blindness of the British, the whole edifice was in danger. Worse, France, rebuilding her navy, was preparing to seize her moment of revenge. In his now rare descents upon Parliament Chatham made repeated pleas for some show of 'affection' to which the English in America might respond. In 1774 he took the Protestant New Englanders' side in their resentment against the Quebec Act, a measure designed to increase the 'affection' of French Americans for British rule. Any concession to the French appeared to him a dangerous mischief.

A Chatham in full control over the years from 1763 could probably have done no more than delay the revolt of the Americans. For all his willingness to 'be to their faults a little kind', and despite his ability to see that even victory must mean defeat ('You cannot *make* them buy your cloth'), his views remained rooted in the old colonial system. The colonies beyond the Atlantic were 'the fountain of our wealth, the nerve of our strength, the nursery and basis of our naval power'. He would never concede that America, in the process of becoming a nation, must sooner or later wish for independence. To accept *that* – he would as soon, he declared, swallow trans-substantiation. When in April 1778 the Duke of Richmond moved that the King withdraw his troops from the revolted provinces, Chatham's concern was 'unspeakable'. Infirm and agitated, he had insisted on travelling to Westminster. He spoke, faltered, and resumed 'with shreds of eloquence' protesting against ignominious surrender, before he suffered his final and fatal collapse. To the last he sustained what Horace Walpole called his one style, the epic; 'the multiplication table' was not for him.

BIBLIOGRAPHY

Brooke, J., *The Chatham Administration of 1766–8* (London, 1956)

Corbett, Sir J. S., *England in the Seven Years War* (2 vols, London, 1907)

Eyck, E., *Pitt versus Fox, Father and Son* (London, 1950)

Hotblack, K., *Chatham's Colonial Policy* (London, 1917)

Kimball, G. S., *Correspondence with Colonial Governors* . . . (2 vols, New York, 1900).

Macaulay, Lord, 'William Pitt' and 'The Earl of Chatham', in *Essays* (London, 1834, 1844)

Namier, Sir L., *England in the Age of the American Revolution* (2nd edn, London, 1961)

Plumb, J. H., *Chatham* (London, 1953)

Robertson, Sir C. G., *Chatham and the British Empire* (London, 1946)

Rosebery, Lord, *Chatham, his Early Life and Connections* (London, 1910)

Sherrard, O. A., *Lord Chatham* (3 vols, London, 1952–8)

Taylor, W. S. and Pringle, J. H. (eds), *Chatham Correspondence* (4 vols, London, 1839)

Tunstall, B., *William Pitt, Earl of Chatham* (London, 1938) (the best one-volume biography)

Williams, B., *William Pitt, Earl of Chatham* (2 vols, London, 1913) (the standard Life)

THE DUKE OF GRAFTON

BY

PETER DURRANT

Augustus Henry Fitzroy, born 28 September 1735, elder son of Lord Augustus Fitzroy (d. 1741) and grandson of the 2nd Duke of Grafton, whom he succeeded in 1757. Educated at Peterhouse, Cambridge, 1751–3. Married (1) 1756 Anne Liddell (Div. 1769); three sons, one daughter. (2) 1769 Elizabeth Wrottesley; five sons, eight daughters. MP for Bury St Edmunds 1756–7; Lord of the Bedchamber to the Prince of Wales 1756–7; Lord Lieutenant of Suffolk 1757–63, 1769–90; Secretary of State for the Northern Department 1765–6; first Lord of the Treasury 1766–70; KG 1769; Lord Privy Seal 1771–1775, 1782–1783. Died 14 March 1811.

Augustus Fitzroy, 3rd Duke of Grafton, by Pompeo Batoni

THE DUKE OF GRAFTON

Grafton's appointment as First Lord of the Treasury in July 1766 was unusual in that he was not thereby appointed Prime Minister. Traditionally the First Lord of the Treasury had assumed the leadership of administration; but in 1766 the King had summoned William Pitt, not Grafton, to form a government. Pitt, however, regarded with distaste the prospect of involvement in the day-to-day business of administration, and he retired to the House of Lords, as Earl of Chatham, to direct affairs from the less demanding post of Lord Privy Seal. Grafton was appointed, in effect, as Chatham's man of business. Not until twelve months later did he assume the leadership of the ministry.

Chatham pressed Grafton to accept office because he realised that in few others was proven ability coupled with such considerable devotion to himself. The Duke had first established himself in politics as a leader of the 'Young Friends' of the Duke of Newcastle in opposition to Bute and Grenville. Such diverse people as George III, Burke and Charles James Fox testified to his ability in debate.[1] He had, moreover, some experience, albeit limited, of office, under Rockingham in 1765–6. Above all he possessed a high personal opinion of Chatham, believing that Chatham's leadership was vital to a successful administration.[2] When Chatham threatened to retire from politics unless Grafton joined him, the Duke had little option but to agree.

It was nevertheless with great reluctance that Grafton accepted the appointment. His early enthusiasm for politics, manifested in 1762–3, had not endured, and he accepted in 1766, as he had done a year earlier under Rockingham, without eagerness and more from a sense of duty than from delight. He much preferred the life of a country gentleman, and he was invariably happier in the country than in London. There he could indulge in pursuits that really interested him: farming, hunting,

[1] George III to Grafton, 15 Feb. 1768, Grafton MSS 120; Burke to Charles O'Hara, 11 Mar. 1766, *The Correspondence of Edmund Burke*, ed. T. W. Copeland (10 vols, Cambridge, 1958–70), i, 244; C. J. Fox to Sir George Macartney, 14 Mar. 1766, BM Add. MSS 47568, f.8.
[2] Grafton had resigned from the Rockingham administration in May 1766 on these grounds.

racing (his fondness for horse-racing, though greatly criticised, was not really exceptional by the standards of the day), and, more unusually, collecting and talking about books. His friends were drawn from men who shared these interests, rarely from the political world.[3] And he greatly preferred to enjoy their company in the relaxed atmosphere of Euston Hall, his Suffolk home, than to immerse himself in the tensions and perplexities of public life.

In unfamiliar society, Grafton seems generally to have been shy and uneasy. His 'dislike of anything of a public nature' had been noted in Italy in 1762;[4] nor had his feelings changed with the passing years. He still disliked the ceremonial aspects of his office, and he was glad to be excused attending Court functions.[5] He could command tact and delicacy in his dealings with people, but he lacked charm and was inclined to seriousness. Under stress he could be short-tempered and irritable, even among friends.[6] Nor was his private life beyond reproach.[7] Casual associates received little encouragement to improve their acquaintance with him, and enemies found him easy material for criticism.[8]

[3] His friends included, for example, Earl Spencer, his neighbour in Northamptonshire; racing men such as Hugo Meynell and the Earl of March; and scholars and intelligent men such as John Symonds, Professor of Modern History at Cambridge; John Hinchcliffe, Bishop of Peterborough and Master of Trinity College, Cambridge; Richard Watson, Bishop of Llandaff and Professor of Chemistry at Cambridge; and Arthur Young, the agriculturalist. The only significant friendships he made through politics were with Camden and Northington.

[4] Sir Horace Mann to Horace Walpole, 12 June 1762, *The Correspondence of Horace Walpole*, ed. W. S. Lewis (24 vols, Yale, 1937–65), xxii, 40.

[5] T. Bradshaw to S. Martin, 4 July 1767, BM Add. MS 41354, f.107; George III to Grafton, 15 Sept. 1768, *The Correspondence of King George III*, ed. Sir J. Fortescue (6 vols, London, 1927), ii, 651.

[6] J. Cradock, *Literary and Miscellaneous Memoirs*, ed. J. B. Nicholls, (4 vols, London, 1828), i, 106.

[7] Grafton's difficulties were considerably increased by domestic unhappiness. Differences with his first wife had led to separation in 1764, when Grafton had taken a mistress. At times of stress, Grafton was prone to be unusually careless of conventional decorum. But it is unjust to call him profligate. He was loyal to his mistress, until his divorce enabled him to remarry. With his second wife he enjoyed more than forty years of contented married life.

[8] He suffered a good deal of adverse criticism, particularly from 'Junius' and Horace Walpole, who between them created a legend of profligacy and indolence which too many historians have been prepared to accept. A man is seldom pictured fairly by his enemies, and much of the criticism they and others levelled against him is merely malicious invention.

Impelled by duty, but hindered by lack of ambition, Grafton never really made a success of his political career. Though he spent most of his life in politics, he was not a career politician. He was a conscientious administrator,[9] attending most of the Treasury Board meetings, and occasionally taking work away with him to Suffolk – where in ten days 'his Grace did more real business than he would have been suffered by solicitors to do for a month in London.[10] He could be resolute and decisive, but his enthusiasm was sporadic, and he very often lacked conviction when dealing with political issues. Partly perhaps because he was pursued by domestic problems, partly because his real interests lay elsewhere, Grafton never really put his heart into politics.

Significantly, he never attached to himself a group of political adherents: when he left the Treasury in 1770 few men followed him. This was partly because his was not an immediately attractive personality: his public aspect did not invite close friendships. But it was also because his own attitude was antipathetic to groups. He was, for example, not interested in building up a following by extending his electoral interests. His only real associates were generally personal friends. During his career he was associated with several political groups, but never as a fully committed member. He was always a little apart. Like his first idol, Chatham, he was something of a solitary figure in politics.

For his first few months in office Grafton relied entirely on Chatham for direction, and would scarcely take even the smallest decision without Chatham's approval. And indeed he was given little encouragement to act independently; for Chatham could be devastatingly critical of anyone who deviated from the path laid down by himself.[11] Yet Chatham's leadership was inadequate from the very beginning. He spent long periods in Bath, too far removed from the centre of affairs to exercise detailed control. By March 1767 he had been overtaken by illness and was completely incapable of political activity. Grafton, who

[9] Except in the matter of electioneering, which he found distasteful and tended to neglect. This admittedly was a considerable failing in a prime minister.
[10] T. Bradshaw to S. Martin, 25 Sept. 1767, BM Add. MS 41354, f. 111. And when in 1782 The King criticised North for being two years behind in completing the quarterly account books of the secret service, he added: 'The Duke of Grafton never let a month elapse after the quarter without getting the book finished and delivering it' (J. Brooke, *King George III* (London, 1972), p. 235).
[11] For example in the case of Charles Townshend over the East India Company business in 1766–7.

had not been appointed to direct affairs, was reluctant to take responsibility, as long as there was a chance of Chatham's recovery. But such a lack of direction was almost disastrous for the ministry. Opposition built up during April and May, and Grafton was faced with the very real prospect of defeat. When the ministry's majority in the House of Lords, normally the stronghold of administration, sank to three (on 26 May 1767), Grafton was very close to resignation. After seeing Chatham – incidentally for the last time in private interview – Grafton resolved to patch up and continue for the rest of the session. But his loyalty to Chatham had almost disappeared. The highhandedness and lack of sympathy that Chatham had shown throughout the preceding year had disgusted Grafton; and by his totally unco-operative response to the King's solicitations during June,[12] Chatham finally forfeited the Duke's regard.[13]

Far from feeling free to retire, however, Grafton felt compelled to carry on by a new loyalty which overpowered his reluctance – a loyalty to King George III. Grafton had always felt a sense of duty towards the Crown; but now this was overlaid and strengthened by a more personal loyalty to the King. And in return he was rewarded with a degree of friendship and support which neither Rockingham nor Grenville had enjoyed. George III and Grafton had been in a similar position *vis-à-vis* Chatham during the preceding twelve months. Both young men who had been in politics for a comparatively short time – and for the King a particularly trying time – they had handed over an unusual degree of authority to Chatham; and he had failed them. Perhaps in this lay the origins of the good relations which indubitably existed between King and minister; relations that were confirmed by Grafton's behaviour at this crisis. For by staying in office he almost certainly averted a political upheaval similar to those of July 1765 and July 1766 – occasions that the King looked back on with dread and that he desperately wished to avoid being repeated. Despite Grafton's faults and even their disagree-

[12] See the letters between George III and Chatham in Fortescue, op. cit., i, 523-4, 530-3, 535-8.
[13] Grafton had no further contact with Chatham except when it was politically unavoidable. He endeavoured to stop Chatham resigning in October 1768, but largely because he feared the effect it would have on Camden, at that time his closest Cabinet colleague. In February 1770, Grafton delivered a blistering attack on Chatham during the debate on the State of the Nation. See Horace Walpole, *Memoirs of the Reign of George III*, ed. G. F. R. Barker (4 vols, London, 1894), iv, 63.

ments, the King's goodwill continued until the Duke resigned in 1770.[14]

Grafton needed considerable resolution to abandon the pleasant prospect of retirement and to face the daunting task of rebuilding the ministry. His situation in July 1767 was altogether unenviable. The pressures of opposition were bad enough; but the situation in the Cabinet was yet worse. Grafton had scarcely one colleague on whom he could absolutely rely.[15] Eventually he turned to Lord President Northington, an old political campaigner who had saved the King during the negotiations of the previous summer. With Northington's agreement, Grafton determined to attempt a showdown with Chatham. Together they insisted to the King that it was essential

'that Lord Chatham should either appear and assist in filling up the vacancies that must immediately happen, or otherwise quit any thoughts of being Minister, as it was impossible to continue longer in this state of suspense, or prevail with men of abilities to undertake a temporary plan, which might be totally reversed whenever Lord Chatham's health permitted him to act.'[16]

The measure of Grafton's courage and resolution at this time – unsurpassed in his career – may be taken from his decision to continue even though Chatham ignored the ultimatum, and remained in office as a permanent embarrassment to the administration. By remaining Grafton had in effect accepted responsibility for the administration. Still only thirty-one, he was *de facto* Prime Minister – the youngest Prime minister, with the single exception of the Younger Pitt, in the 250 years between Sir Robert Walpole and the present day.

The negotiations of July 1767 are important not merely because they

[14] In August 1769 the King, conferring the Garter on Grafton, wrote: 'I can with great truth declare that I never gave a Garter with more pleasure and that it is one of the very few I have given unsolicited' (George III to Grafton, 26 Aug. 1769, Grafton MSS 538).

[15] Indeed, he drew up the King's speech for the end of the session with Marchmont and Dyson, neither members of the Cabinet. See G. F. S. Elliot, *The Border Elliots and the Family of Minto* (Edinburgh, 1897), p. 402n. Of the Cabinet, Conway and Northington were anxious to resign, Camden and Shelburne were devoted Chathamites, Townshend was totally untrustworthy, and Granby and Hawke were service chiefs and political nonentities.

[16] Sir Gilbert Elliot's Memorandum, G. F. S. Elliot, op. cit., pp. 402–3.

mark Grafton's arrival as Prime Minister. Together with those of December 1767 they represent a critical point in the emergence of political stability in the 1760s; and they are crucial for an understanding of the nature of political organisation. Grafton had two fairly straightforward objectives: to increase the support his administration enjoyed in Parliament, and – more important – to bring into his Cabinet some colleagues on whom he could rely. As a disciple of Chatham, Grafton had quoted the master on the subject of forming a ministry composed of the best men from all parties. But experience had not confirmed his belief in this approach. Politicians did to a large extent work in groups. This is not to suggest that parties were fixed and rigid in membership, or that they were the sole units of political organisation. The career of Grafton himself is a denial of this. But parties did exist, and it was necessary in any political calculation to take them into account. Chatham's attempt to build a non-party administration had failed: the Cabinet was in pieces within twelve months of its formation. Grafton had discovered the reality of political grouping in his two unsuccessful attempts to detach individuals from the Bedford coterie. In July 1767 the remains of non-party doctrine were perhaps just evident. Had it been possible, Grafton would have liked to detach support from among the followers of both Bedford and Rockingham – though more to break opposition than to strengthen government. But such a scheme did not preclude the possibility of absorbing a group. Grafton's chief success in July was in dividing the Opposition more firmly into its constituent groups (in itself a useful achievement). That he accepted the fact of party is shown by his willingness in December to take in the Bedfords.

In December 1767 a political party was admitted to administration; but this did not mean that the ministry had become a party ministry. Indeed, one of its chief weaknesses lay in the fact that the Cabinet continued to lack cohesion and unity. In some ways it was as much a collection of individuals as had been Chatham's Cabinet in 1766.[17]

[17] The Cabinet (excluding Chatham) consisted of Grafton himself and nine colleagues. Of these only two, Gower and Weymouth, were from the Bedford group (though the Bedfords had in addition several non-Cabinet posts). North and Hillsborough were primarily king's men. Shelburne remained a Chathamite, and Granby was rapidly becoming one. Camden retained his allegiance to Chatham, but he was wavering, and in October 1768 he declared his support for Grafton, only to return to Chatham in January 1770. Conway was discontented with Grafton, but more inclined to follow his line than any other. Hawke was a nonentity who followed Grafton.

Grafton certainly had colleagues who were thoroughly reliable in their own departments, as Weymouth showed by his handling of the riots in the spring of 1768. But the Cabinet collectively suffered from an inability to make decisions. This weakness was already apparent in February 1768, when the Cabinet failed to give an opinion on the establishment of a legislature in Canada.[18] In part this was undoubtedly due to a genuine divergence of opinion; but to a great extent it was also due to Grafton's failure to give a decisive lead in policy matters.

Within a few weeks of its formation, Grafton's new administration was put to the test by the re-emergence of John Wilkes on to the political stage. Though still outlawed, Wilkes had returned to England in February 1768. The following month he stood as candidate for the City of London in the general election. Defeated but undaunted, he tried again in Middlesex, where, to the accompaniment of much riotous behaviour, he came top of the poll. The ministry was faced with two problems: one was the preservation of public order; the other, a much more delicate political question, was what to do with Wilkes.

On the question of public order, Grafton was quite prepared to back strong measures, as soon as they were seen to be necessary – though he had been reluctant to give the impression of 'finding fault only with the People for their Joy too riotously testified at the late Election'.[19] It was the duty of government to keep order and to preserve society and the Constitution. Though Grafton took little active part in arranging measures – this was Weymouth's department – he gave his approval to a policy of vigour.[20]

In the case of Wilkes himself, Grafton's natural reaction was one of caution. Remembering the trouble that Wilkes had caused Grenville in 1763-4, he had no desire to give gratuitous offence by ill-advised intervention. But those who had pressed for vigorous action against the rioters were anxious to punish Wilkes. The King adopted a similar attitude. Considering his conception of duty to the King and his natural reluctance to assert himself, it is perhaps surprising that Grafton went as far as he did to avoid the application of hard-line measures against Wilkes.

The suggestion that Wilkes be expelled the House of Commons was raised almost as soon as he was elected, and it met with widespread

[18] George III to Grafton, 18 Feb. 1768, Grafton MSS 510.
[19] Grafton to George III, 31 Mar. 1768, Fortescue, *The Correspondence of King George III*, ii, 605.
[20] Grafton to Weymouth, 9 May 1768, Longleat MSS.

approval. The King supported the measure, and 'the ideas of the ministry' also went to expulsion.[21] A meeting of the principal men of the House of Commons independently approved the idea.[22] Nevertheless, Grafton avoided implementing such a course of action. Wilkes had appealed against his outlawry, and Grafton realised that if he was expelled, and then cleared in the courts of law, administration would be very embarrassed; while if his outlawry was upheld, Parliament could most justifiably take action against him. In the event the outlawry was quashed, but a fine and imprisonment substituted for his several offences. Grafton would have been quite happy to leave the matter there; and in spite of the earlier approval for expulsion, he might have succeeded. The matter remained untouched over the summer recess, and the Cabinet was far less sure in October than it had been in April whether to proceed to expulsion.[23] But Wilkes would not accept oblivion. In November, he prepared to present a petition to Parliament. Grafton, hoping to avoid a revival of the problem, endeavoured to dissuade Wilkes by promising that expulsion measures would be dropped if he obliged.[24] But Wilkes refused. The presentation of the petition was the signal for anti-Wilkes speeches in the House of Commons. Barrington, whom Wilkes had particularly libelled, attacked him strongly. Grafton found little support for his attitude.[25] On 3 February 1769 Barrington moved the expulsion of Wilkes. It was carried, and so the farce of the Middlesex elections began.[26]

[21] George III to North, 25 April 1768, Fortescue, op. cit., ii, 613; Rigby to Bedford, 23 April 1768, Bedford MSS, lvii, f.54.
[22] Bradshaw reported to Grafton that the meeting had not been informed that the Government had taken any resolution on the subject of Wilkes (T. Bradshaw to Grafton [25 April 1768], Grafton MSS 309), though those present presumably had some idea of the Government's attitude.
[23] Rigby to Bedford, 31 Oct. 1768, Bedford MSS lvii, f.206.
[24] J. Almon, *The Correspondence of John Wilkes* (5 vols, London, 1805), iii, 293-4.
[25] 'As the times are, I had rather pardon W[ilkes] than punish him. This is a political opinion, independent of the merits of the cause' (Camden to Grafton, 9 Jan. 1769, *Autobiography of the Third Duke of Grafton*, ed. Sir W. Anson (1898), p. 201). But Camden seems not to have supported Grafton in the Cabinet. See H. Walpole, *Memoirs of . . . George III*, iv, 58-9.
[26] Wilkes was expelled on 3 February. He was twice re-elected and twice the elections were annulled by Parliament. After his third re-election in April, the Commons decided that votes cast for Wilkes were invalid, and that Henry Luttrell (defeated by 1,143 votes to 296) had therefore been duly elected. See G. Rude *Wilkes and Liberty* (Oxford, 1962), chapters 3 and 4.

The other major issue that Grafton's administration faced concerned the attitude to be adopted towards the American colonies, which had offered severe provocation during 1768.[27] Grafton was again somewhat awkwardly placed. On this issue the Cabinet was more definitely polarised into authoritarian and conciliatory camps than it had been over Wilkes. Grafton once again favoured moderation, and once again faced a strong force of hard-liners. He certainly cannot be accused of failing to offer a solution to the problem: he had one prepared in November 1768.[28] But it met with little enthusiasm in the Cabinet, and Grafton, though disappointed, did not press it. The crucial decision came in the summer of 1769 when the Cabinet met to decide on the proposals offered by Hillsborough, the Colonial Secretary. They were passed by five votes to four – with Grafton in the minority.[29]

Grafton's failure to provide a commanding leadership in the Cabinet was apparently considerable. The Cabinet clearly had some responsibility for deciding measures. But the extent of the Prime Minister's responsibility for directing policy within the Cabinet was much less clearly defined. Certainly he was not appointed with a 'programme' of measures to put into effect; though it is arguable, with the advantage of hindsight, that the country would have been better served had Grafton pressed his own opinions harder. The Government was the King's Government, carried on with his appointed servants, and Grafton saw his main role as sustaining the King's administration. When it came to negotiation, for example, he was generally prepared to take responsibility; but when it came to deciding policy, he was much less ready to assert himself. Measures had to be favoured by both King and administration before they were possible.[30] The issues facing the administration in 1768–9 were genuinely divisive and Grafton's approach, admittedly not very forcefully presented, failed to find acceptance. But he did not therefore feel it necessary to retire. If the Bedfords gained ascendancy over Grafton – which in itself is doubtful – they did so because they listened more closely to the King.

[27] Hillsborough to George III, 19 and 22 July 1768, Fortescue, op. cit., ii, 637, 638.
[28] Grafton to George III, 29 November 1768, ibid., ii, 673.
[29] Gower, Weymouth, North, Hillsborough and Rochford favoured the measures; Grafton, Camden, Conway and Granby disapproved. Hawke was absent. (Rochford had replaced Shelburne in the Cabinet in October 1768.)
[30] The agreement of both Houses of Parliament was also necessary; but the Court usually had had a potential majority, which only needed cultivating. Grafton was less skilful at this than North.

Grafton left office in January 1770, less because he lost his nerve than because he lost heart. The Rockinghams, who had been involved during the preceding autumn in collecting support outside Parliament, in the form of petititions against the Government's action in the Middlesex election dispute, launched a strong attack on the ministry at the opening of the new session in January 1770. The re-emergence of Chatham on the political stage, now however in opposition, gave courage to the Opposition, and severely discomfited the ministry. The divisions in the Commons showed but a slender majority for the administration. And in the Cabinet Grafton faced desertions: Camden resigned, and then Granby, after wavering, followed suit. The attempt by Grafton and the King to replace Camden with Charles Yorke failed when Yorke died within three days of his appointment. Grafton's half-hearted (and unsuccessful) attempt to persuade the Attorney-General, William de Grey, to accept, strongly suggests that he had had his fill of political responsibility.[31] He knew moreover that he had a potential successor of considerable ability in North. The King considered his resignation a desertion, and it was widely expected that the ministry would fall. But North survived. Grafton had done what he conceived to be his duty. He had served the King in 1767 and for two and a half difficult years since then, and he left his successor a ministry that formed the basis of the most secure administration since the death of Henry Pelham.

Though Grafton resigned office in 1770 he had not done with politics: indeed he was still active thirty years later. He supported North until 1775, when he resigned because he could no longer support a policy of coercion towards America. His support continued to be held valuable, and it was sought by both North (in 1779) and Pitt (in 1784). Grafton took office once more, under Rockingham and Shelburne in 1782–3. But he maintained all the time his old independence of political groups, a detachment that enabled him, towards the end of his life, to achieve something of the reputation and eminence of an 'elder statesman'.

BIBLIOGRAPHY

Though written late in his life and in places coloured by hindsight, *The Autobiography and Political Correspondence of the Third Duke of Grafton*, ed. Sir W. R. Anson

[31] Grafton's *Autobiography*, p. 245–50; Lord Hardwickes 'Memorial of Family Occurrences', BM Add. MS 35428, folios 116–21; George III to Grafton, 15 Jan. 1770, Grafton MSS 543; Jenkinson to [Lowther], 18 [Jan. 1770], BM Add MS 38206, folios 197–8.

(London, 1898), remains the principal and indispensable source for a study of Grafton's career. It includes many letters from the Duke's correspondence: there are, however, several important unpublished letters among the Grafton Manuscripts in the Bury St Edmunds and West Suffolk Record Office. Further letters from Grafton are published in *Correspondence of William Pitt, Earl of Chatham*, ed. W. S. Taylor and J. H. Pringle (4 vols, London, 1838–40), and in *The Correspondence of King George III, 1760–83*, ed. Sir J. Fortescue (6 vols, London, 1927–8); and there are unpublished letters among the Chatham Papers in the Public Record Office. J. Brooke, *The Chatham Administration* (London, 1956), is invaluable for the period 1766–8; there is, however, no adequate survey of the ministry for the period 1768–70. The ministry's attitude to Wilkes is discussed briefly in G. Rude *Wilkes and Liberty* (Oxford, 1962).

LORD NORTH

BY

JOHN CANNON

Frederick North, 2nd Earl of Guilford, but styled Lord North from 1752 to 1790, born 13 April 1732, first son of Francis, 1st Earl of Guilford. Educated at Eton, 1742–8, and Trinity College, Oxford, 1749. Married 1756 Anne, daughter of George Speke; four sons, three daughters. Succeeded as 2nd Earl, 1790. MP for Banbury 1754–90; Lord of the Treasury 1759–65; Joint Paymaster-General 1766–7; Chancellor of the Exchequer 1767–1782; First Lord of the Treasury 1770–82; Home Secretary 1783. PC 1766; KG 1772; Chancellor of the University of Oxford 1773–92; Lord Lieutenant of Somerset 1774–92; Lord Warden of the Cinque Ports 1778–92. Died 5 August 1792.

Frederick, Lord North, by N. Dance

LORD NORTH

Frederick, Lord North, has an unenviable reputation as the worst prime minister of all time. It is an assessment with which, in his more sombre moments, he might have inclined to agree. His continuation as First Lord of the Treasury, he told the King at the crisis of the American war, was 'to be reckoned among the principal causes of the present dangerous position of this country'.[1]

To defend a man from his own strictures may seem unduly zealous. At first sight the case against Lord North is overwhelming. He is the only prime minister to be associated with failure in a major conflict: in 1783, for the first and last time in modern history, Britain tasted the full bitterness of defeat. 'It is a paltry eulogium for the prime minister of a great country,' observed Horace Walpole sourly, 'yet the best that can be allotted to Lord North is that, though his country was ruined under his administration, he preserved his good humour.'[2]

But this is a verdict which is bound to be affected by the lengthening perspective of history. To Lord North's contemporaries the loss of the thirteen American colonies was an unprecedented calamity: it is hardly surprising that most people regarded it as the consequence of gross political blunders. But when independence for the American states was followed in turn by the emancipation of Latin America from Spain and Portugal and by mass de-colonisation in the twentieth century, the broader trends of historical explanation emerged and human culpability diminished: the American revolt then appeared as the first in a series of national colonial risings rather than the unique occurrence it had once seemed. In the same way, it was natural enough for Horace Walpole to assume the ruin of the commonwealth: on this occasion he was in agreement with George III who wrote that the peace settlement completed 'the downfall of the lustre of this empire'.[3] In fact Britain stood on the threshold of those industrial changes that were to give her unimagined political and economic power.

[1] *The Correspondence of George III*, ed. Sir J. Fortescue (London, 1927), iv, no. 2692.
[2] *Memoirs of the Reign of George III*, ed. G. F. R. Barker (London, 1894), iv, 55.
[3] Fortescue, vi, no. 4470.

The shadow of defeat falls so heavily over Lord North's career that it becomes necessary to emphasise how successful were the early years of his administration. After a spell of two years as Chancellor of the Exchequer, North took over the premiership from the Duke of Grafton at a moment of acute crisis. Grafton's ministry had staggered from disaster to disaster since its formation in 1766. First Lord Chatham, the great man on whom all was to depend, went to pieces under the strain of responsibility and for months was totally incapable of conducting business: in October 1768, much to the King's dismay, he insisted on resigning. During 1769 the ministers were plagued by the complications arising out of the Middlesex election and tormented by the dexterous Wilkes and his savage henchman 'Junius'. The Opposition succeeded in drawing together its forces to form a working coalition and, to the amazement of the political world, was joined in January 1770 by Chatham himself, an apparition from the past, miraculously restored and belabouring his former colleagues as enemies of the Constitution. Chatham's first salvo carried away the ministry's Lord Chancellor, Camden, and his successor, Charles Yorke, died after only three days in office. A week later Grafton tendered his resignation and the Opposition seemed on the brink of success. To North the King confessed that there was no peer who could be placed at the head of the Government should he refuse to serve.

Within a few months of Lord North's taking office, the situation was transformed. The Government's majority, down to a mere 40 odd in January, was up to 97 four weeks later. In March the Opposition overplayed its hand with a violent remonstrance from the City of London, which produced another government victory by 271 votes to 108. Before the year was out the Opposition was in complete disarray: there was not 'the least glimmering of hope', Burke warned Lord Rockingham in December 1770.[4]

Circumstances undoubtedly favoured the ministers. The deaths of William Beckford and George Grenville within five months of each other removed two formidable opponents. The opposition alliance had always appeared fragile: it was not easy for the Rockinghams, with their train of pocket boroughs, to collaborate enthusiastically with a group preaching radical reform of Parliament. The excesses of the Wilkite agitation produced a conservative reaction which assisted

---

[4] *Correspondence of Edmund Burke*, ed. L. S. Sutherland (Cambridge, 1960), ii, 176.

government supporters to recapture some of the ground they had lost in city politics.

Nevertheless, North's own contribution was important. Though still a young man, he was portly in build and his flabby cheeks and protruding eyes gave him, according to one witness, 'the air of a blind trumpeter'.[5] But he was a hard-working and capable administrator with ten years' experience in office behind him. He rarely attempted wit, his delivery was portentous and his articulation far from distinct, but his speeches were relevant and seldom tried the patience of the House. Not least among his political assets were his good humour and imperturbability. He was a cultivated and agreeable companion: 'Never was a first minister,' wrote Wraxall who knew him well, 'less intrenched within the forms of his official situation. He seemed, on the contrary, always happy to throw aside his public character.'[6]

His humour was admitted on all sides. He seems to have felt a sense of professional pride in his performance in the House of Commons: the burdens of his private misfortunes were rarely allowed to show through and he possessed a remarkable resilience, bobbing up under pressure like a cork. Two examples must suffice, from the dark days after Saratoga when a joint Franco-Spanish invasion seemed a possibility. He turned on Charles Fox who was eking out an evidently underprepared speech with a good deal of synthetic abuse: it reminded him, said North gently, of those maps by ancient geographers who concealed their lack of knowledge with pictures of elephants and other strange beasts. To Temple Luttrell, a noisy and pertinacious critic of the administration, North was sharper: when Luttrell, in a burst of false candour, hoped that his remarks would not clog the activity of government, North waved him aside with contempt – no more than the fly which, landing on the wheels of a chariot, 'thought she raised the dust with which she was surrounded'.[7]

It was also much to North's advantage that he was a member of the House of Commons. In view of the administrations of Lord Liverpool at the beginning and Lord Salisbury at the end of the nineteenth century it would be idle to claim that a seat in the Commons was an essential condition for successful premiership. Nevertheless it was useful, as Sir

[5] Walpole, op. cit., iv, 52.
[6] N. W. Wraxall, *Historical and Posthumous Memoirs*, ed. H. B. Wheatley (London, 1884), i, 361–2.
[7] *Parliamentary History*, xx, 336; xix, 1387.

Robert Walpole's career had demonstrated, and the point had been re-inforced by the difficulty that subsequent first ministers in the Lords had experienced in obtaining suitable deputies in the Commons. The Duke of Newcastle had found Sir Thomas Robinson useless – the Duke 'may as well send his jackboot to govern us,' Pitt had remarked – while Henry Fox proved demanding. George Grenville, appointed to lead the Commons during the Bute ministry, was not long in discovering his own power and aspiring to first place. The ignorance of Commons management shown by Lords Chatham and Shelburne contributed substantially to their political failures. But North was in a position to keep an eye on those independent members whose support was so necessary to him and his affability ensured that he remained sensitive to changes of opinion in the House.

No less important was the extremely good understanding that North soon reached with the King. The Grenville administration five years earlier, though strong in other respects, had broken down on this very point, the King confessing that he would 'rather see the Devil in his closet than Mr Grenville'. North, by contrast, was on the most cordial terms with the King. In 1771 George wrote offering him the Garter – the first time a commoner had been so honoured since Sir Robert Walpole – and by 1775 could refer to him as 'my sheet anchor'. Two years later he intervened to pay Lord North's personal debts, amounting to some £18,000, putting the proposal in a letter of great kindness and delicacy. 'You know me very ill,' wrote the King, 'if you do not think that of all the letters I have ever wrote to you this one gives me the most pleasure, and I want no other return than your being convinced that I love you as well as a man of worth as I esteem you as a minister.'[8]

The Government's policy during North's early years as first minister was moderate and conciliatory. Though he had taken the lead in the Grafton administration's prosecution of Wilkes, he saw the wisdom of allowing the matter to drop, and when Wilkes took his seat in the House of Commons in 1774 North treated him jocularly: 'He agreed entirely in opinion with the counsellor, whoever he was, that might think one Wilkes sufficient: for indeed he thought that it was one too much in any well-regulated government; though, he said, to do him justice, it was not easy to find many such.' The same cool approach appeared at first to have restored harmony in the American quarrel, which North inherited from previous ministries. By removing all taxes except a small

[8] Fortescue, iii, nos. 1742 and 2059.

one on tea, North hoped to appease the colonists while keeping a token of control to satisfy opinion at home. In April 1771 he could claim that 'the American disputes are settled and there is nothing to interrupt the peace and prosperity of the nation'.[9] His handling of the nation's finances was approved even by his critics and the crisis over the East India Company in 1772 served merely to confirm his resourcefulness and adaptability: though the limitations of his Indian settlement were soon apparent, North's appointment of a Governor-General was an important extension of the principle of public responsibility.

The first few years saw Lord North's administration established almost beyond overthrow. Horace Walpole thought that the session of 1773 had been the most triumphant ever known, with the Opposition itself nearly abandoning the game. 'This is an epoch,' wrote Thomas Dampier in February 1775, 'which will render Lord North's name immortal in our English history.' Though this testimony from the tutor of North's sons in a letter to Lord Guilford may not be wholly disinterested, it is confirmed, if in less ecstatic terms, from other sources. Henry Cruger, newly elected for Bristol and a 'hot Wilkite', admitted in his maiden speech in December 1774 that 'the abilities of the minister it seems are universally acknowledged'.[10]

In presenting his budget of May 1772 to the House of Commons North allowed himself the guess that there was 'the fairest prospect of the continuance of peace' that he had known in his lifetime. The following month a gang of Rhode Island radicals seized the revenue cutter *Gaspée*, wounded the captain and burnt the vessel. The British ministers retorted by authorising the Governor to seek out those responsible and present them for trial. It is not easy to see what else they could have done short of admitting that the British had no authority in the colonies. The Governor failed to discover the culprits. Many Britons concluded that the Americans were incorrigible; many Americans concluded that the British were feeble and despotic. The Boston tea party a year later repeated the affront on the grand scale and the ministry responded with four coercive acts designed to bring the colonies back to obedience. The dispute, North declared, was no longer about taxation: it was whether the British retained any power in America – 'it is very clear

[9] *Parliamentary History*, xviii, 1013; xvii, 165.
[10] *Last Journals*, i, 179; Dampier to Guilford, 6 February 1775, Bodleian MSS North d. 16, f.7; *Parliamentary History*, xviii, 67.

we have none if we suffer the property of our subjects to be destroyed'. North misjudged the situation completely: four or five frigates, he assured members, would be sufficient to do the business without any military force.[11]

The rest of North's ministry was played out in the context of these momentous decisions. Before 1774 was over the first continental congress had been summoned to co-ordinate American resistance. British patriotism rose in reply to American intransigence and left North little room for manoeuvre. 'It was not in the power of the minister to sit still and take no measure,' he admitted, and it is significant that the Opposition did not dare to risk a division on the Boston Port Bill. North and his step-brother Lord Dartmouth battled hard in the Cabinet against the fire-eaters and he took his political life in his hands by pushing the conciliation proposals of February 1775. Indeed, the charge against North might well be the reverse – that his reluctance to abandon plans for retrenchment and economy sent Britain into the struggle less well prepared than she might have been. December 1774 – a month after the King had written that 'blows must decide' – was a strange time for North to move the retention of the Land Tax at three shillings in the pound, together with a naval establishment 4,000 fewer than for the previous year. Two months later the number of seamen had to be increased, but the Land Tax was not raised to four shillings until 1776.[12]

The first two years of fighting in America passed without any decisive encounter. North survived two unpleasant Cabinet crises in late 1775 and 1776 over the conciliation proposals and his parliamentary majority held firm. In 1777 the British devised a plan to end the conflict by splitting New England, the heart of resistance, from the rest of the American colonies: Burgoyne's army, marching south from Canada, was to effect a junction with General Howe, marching northwards from New York up the Hudson river. Throughout the autumn of 1777 North and his colleagues waited anxiously for news. The King's Speech for the parliamentary session, due to open in November, had to be drawn up without their knowing which way the issue had gone. In October came heartening reports that Howe had captured Philadelphia, headquarters of Congress and the largest American city: on 2 December Lord Sandwich wrote to acquaint the King that Burgoyne and his entire army had been

[11] *Parliamentary History*, xvii, 489, 1167, 1172.
[12] ibid., p. 1187.

forced to capitulate at Saratoga. 'The consequences of this most fatal event,' wrote North, 'may be very important and serious, and will certainly require some material change of system.'[13]

Saratoga was Lord North's political death warrant. It was to him what the Norwegian campaign proved to Chamberlain or the Somme to Asquith. Yet circumstances combined to give him a stay of execution that lasted more than four years. The Opposition, of course, professed no doubt that his majorities were sustained by corruption on a massive scale and generations of historians accepted the legend of the King's Friends, oblivious to everything but the service of their master. In fact it is clear that the influence of the Crown was already beginning to shrink.[14] North's survival was in part the work of the Opposition itself which had adopted so extreme a line that it fell into discredit. He was, in addition, the victim of his own remarkable popularity, which gave him a fund of goodwill to draw upon in the moment of crisis. But the essential factor was the King's determination under no circumstances to part with North.

After Saratoga began a tragi-comedy unsurpassed perhaps in British history as the first minister, his nerve gone, begged piteously to be allowed to resign and was refused on literally dozens of occasions. In letter after letter North pleaded his total incapacity to cope with the demands of the situation. 'The anxiety of his mind,' he told the King in January 1778, 'has deprived Lord North of his memory and under-standing.' Capital punishment, he wrote two months later after the King had dropped hints that he might be the first victim of any new political arrangement, 'is preferable to that constant anguish of mind which he feels from the consideration that his continuance in office is ruining His Majesty's affairs'. 'Let me not go to the grave,' he beseeched George, 'with the guilt of having been the ruin of my king and country.'[15]

Each effort the hapless man made to escape was stymied by fate or by the King. In the spring of 1778 he urged George to come to terms with Lord Chatham in the desperate hope that the miracle he had wrought during the Seven Years War might be repeated. If Chatham were not brought in, North wrote on 30 March, the nation was undone.

[13] Fortescue, iii, nos. 2092 and 2095.
[14] I. R. Christie, 'Was there a "New Toryism" in the earlier part of George III's reign?', and 'Economical reform and "the influence of the Crown", 1780', in *Myth and Reality in Late Eighteenth-Century Politics* (London, 1970).
[15] Fortescue, iv, nos. 2179, 2228 and 2329.

A week later Chatham suffered a fatal collapse while speaking in the House of Lords. 'May not the political exit of Lord Chatham,' inquired the King without any elaborate show of grief, 'incline you to continue at the head of my affairs?' After further months of negotiation with the Opposition, North attempted to pass the poisoned chalice to a member of his own Cabinet: 'The person best qualified for that station appears to him to be Lord Suffolk,' he wrote on 16 November. Lord Suffolk, doomed by North's good opinion, keeled over and was dead within three months, at the age of 39.[16]

To all of North's entreaties the King turned a deaf ear. For years he kept him in harness with a subtle mixture of encouragement and reproach. His strongest card was the appeal to North's honour. Was he really prepared to desert his sovereign in the hour of need as the Duke of Grafton had done? Had not the King demonstrated in every possible way not merely his trust, but his affection for his minister? Was the King to be rewarded by being handed over to his political enemies? 'Common honesty and that sense of honour which must reside in the breast of every man born of a noble family' should compel North to stay.

Why was George III so desperately anxious to keep North's services? It would certainly not have been difficult to find people who would have conducted the war with more vigour, and unquestionably more enthusiasm, than North showed. It was not, as was often suggested, that the King had found a first minister pliant and obedient in all things, a willing tool. The fact is that Lord North, for all his limitations which the King knew full well, was an indispensable political asset. It was of critical importance that the chief government spokesman in the House of Commons should be a man of cheerful and amiable disposition, fat and sleepy, demonstrably unwarlike in his conduct and interests, concerned chiefly with retrenchment and fiscal reform – the last man who might be suspected of plunging lightheartedly into conflict. That North, known to stand for compromise and conciliation, should acknowledge the need to carry on the struggle, was in itself a persuasive argument. The Government's case could certainly have been put by tougher and more resolute politicians – Henry Dundas, for instance – but they would have forfeited the reserves of trust that Lord North still commanded. North's character, the source of so many of his misfortunes, was also the source of much of his political strength.

[16] Fortescue, iv, nos. 2257, 2284 and 2452.

North's reasons for continuing were, no doubt, complex. He was by no means indifferent to power and influence and it is noticeable that when the King showed signs of taking the protestations seriously, North was inclined to shuffle. He felt deeply the many favours he had received from the King and particularly the payment of his private debts. But much of the difficulty arose from the ambiguities of the eighteenth-century political system, in which the role of the monarch had never been precisely defined. Where was the line to be drawn between private and public obligations? To what extent was carrying on the government a matter of personal loyalty to the sovereign? In the nineteenth century, Wellington, Peel and Melbourne were all capable of seeing the issue in highly personal terms. 'I am under such obligations to the King,' declared North, 'that I can never leave his service while he desires me to remain in it.'[17] In the context of modern constitutional theory, North's conduct is scarcely defensible: in the eighteenth century, it made some sense.

North's attitude towards the office he held is not easy to ascertain. In public he denied that the Constitution allowed for a prime minister and claimed to be answerable only for his departmental administration of the Treasury: 'He never should be so presumptuous,' he told the House of Commons in May 1778, 'as to think himself capable of directing the departments of others. . . . He did not think our constitution authorised such a character as that animal called a prime minister.'[18] In part this reflected North's reluctance to accept responsibility; in part it was a useful debating ploy and one which the great Sir Robert Walpole, a determined engrosser of power, had not hesitated to use.[19] But in his private letters to the King, North conceded in full the case for a prime minister. 'Whoever may come to the assistance of government,' he observed in the spring of 1778 when overtures were being made to Chatham, 'must be the director and dictator of the leading measures of government. Lord North knows too well his want of ability and decision. . . .' On a subsequent occasion he confessed to the King that he had not that 'authority of character' that the situation demanded: 'In these critical times it is necessary that there should be one directing

[17] Egerton MSS 2232, f.11.
[18] *Parliamentary History*, xix, 1173.
[19] In the censure debate of 1741 he declared that he did 'not pretend to be a great master of foreign affairs: in that post in which I have the honour to serve His Majesty it is not my business to meddle with them.' *Parliamentary History*, xi, 1298.

minister, who should plan the whole of the operations of government.'
North's experience of his own inadequacy seems to have made a lasting
impression on him and convinced him of the need for a prime minister
at all times. When he met Charles Fox in February 1783 to negotiate
the coalition he was reported to have said that there 'should be one
man, or a Cabinet, to govern the whole and direct every measure.
Government by departments was not brought in by me. I found it so,
and had not vigour and resolution to put an end to it.'[20]

So North stayed for four more years, in receipt of a constant parliamentary buffeting from Fox and Burke – augmented after 1780 by
Sheridan and the young Pitt – and threatened continually with impeachment and the block. Politically disastrous, the last years of his ministry
revealed courage of a high order. In between parliamentary sessions
his subordinates Jenkinson and Robinson worked with the King to keep
him going, like seconds trying to get their man into shape to last a few
more rounds. In October 1779 Robinson found his lordship 'much calmer
than usual': a week later North was in 'a state of mind such as it is
melancholy even to reflect on'. Next came a surprising recovery and
a month later he was 'in a good deal of Vigour of Mind and Spirits'.
Alas, it did not last, and before the month was out North was once more
petitioning for release, 'for I must look upon it as a degree of guilt to
continue in office while the public suffers and while nobody approves
my conduct'.[21]

But he struggled on, surviving, with some dexterity, the crisis over
economical reform in the spring of 1780 when the House of Commons,
in a spasm of revolt, carried against him Dunning's motion that the
influence of the Crown had increased, was increasing and ought to be
diminished. The year 1781 even saw a kind of Indian summer with
opposition hushed and administration fortified by delusive gleams of
hope from America. North was released from his treadmill by the news
in November 1781 of the surrender of Lord Cornwallis's army at Yorktown. At last the parliamentary majorities began to melt. Even then it
took a blunt and cogent exposition of constitutional realities before
North could persuade the King to give way: 'The torrent,' North
warned in March 1782, 'is too strong to be resisted. Your Majesty is
well apprized that, in this country, the Prince on the Throne cannot,

[20] Fortescue, iv, nos. 2239 and 2446; *Memoirs and Correspondence of Charles James
Fox*, ed. Lord John Russell, ii, 38.
[21] Fortescue, iv, nos. 2792, 2807, 2828 and 2845.

with prudence, oppose the deliberate resolution of the House of Commons.'[22]

There is much that might still be said on North's behalf but it forms a plea in mitigation rather than a defence. His personal honesty was un-questioned – no small thing in a period that had seen Sir Robert Walpole and Lord Holland make vast fortunes in the service of the State. He was capable of devising schemes of some ingenuity, though usually under pressure of circumstances: his East Indian legislation was forced upon him by the imminent threat of bankruptcy to the Company, while his financial innovations, considered of some importance, were largely a reply to opposition criticisms.[23] He could respond to events but he had neither the foresight, nor perhaps the time, to anticipate them. It is significant that some of his best and most telling speeches were those delivered in support of the *status quo* – against further concessions to the dissenters and against parliamentary reform. His misjudgement of American affairs was one he shared with most of his generation: he was no wiser than they were, which is in part why they found him so com-fortable a leader. He was essentially a man of business above his station – a truth which his superb debating ability concealed from many of his supporters but never from North himself. The troubles facing the country, he told the King in the summer of 1778, might yet be overcome if affairs of state were well conducted: 'They can hardly be well con-ducted unless there is a person in the Cabinet capable of leading, of discerning between opinions, of deciding quickly and confidently, and of connecting all the operations of government, that this nation may act uniformly and with force. Lord North is not such a man. . . .'[24]

His niche in history is as one of the greatest of all parliamentarians. 'That assembly,' wrote Wraxall, 'presented in fact a theatre on which he acted the first personage.'[25] From beginning to end North maintained that the war against America was a war to uphold parliamentary author-ity. In his final speech as prime minister, after he had announced the resignation of the administration, he turned to his supporters and in

[22] Fortescue, v, no. 3566.
[23] His Indian legislation is discussed in L. S. Sutherland, *The East India Company in Eighteenth-Century Politics* (Oxford, 1952), and his financial policy in J. E. D. Binney, *British Public Finance and Administration, 1774–92* (Oxford, 1958).
[24] Fortescue, iv, no. 2334.
[25] *Historical and Posthumous Memoirs*, i, 369.

thanking them showed his awareness of the source of his influence. He wished, he said, to acknowledge

'the very kind, the repeated and essential support he had for so many years received from the Commons of England, during his holding a situation to which he must confess he had at all times been unequal. And it was . . . the more incumbent upon him to return his thanks in that place because it was that House which had made him what he had been.'

BIBLIOGRAPHY

Butterfield, H., *George III, Lord North and the People*, 1779–80 (London, 1949)
Cannon, John, *The Fox–North Coalition* (Cambridge, 1969)
—, *Lord North: The Noble Lord in the Blue Ribbon* (Historical Association pamphlet G 74) (London, 1970)
Christie, I. R., *The End of North's Ministry, 1780–2* (London, 1958)
Lucas, R., *Lord North* (2 vols, London, 1913)
Pemberton, W. B., *Lord North* (London, 1938)
Valentine, A., *Lord North* (2 vols, Oklahoma, 1967)

THE EARL OF SHELBURNE

BY

FRANK O'GORMAN

William Petty Fitzmaurice, born 13 May 1737, the son of the Hon. John Fitzmaurice, 1st Earl of Shelburne. Educated privately and at Christ Church, Oxford and served in the Seven Years War. Succeeded to the earldom 1761 and in 1784 became Marquess of Lansdowne. Married (1) 1765 Lady Sophia Carteret; (2) 1779 Lady Louise Fitzpatrick. MP for Chipping Wycombe 1760–1; First Lord of Trade 1763; Secretary of State for the Southern Department 1766–8; Secretary of State for Home Affairs 1782; First Lord of the Treasury 1782–3. Died 7 May 1805. He was succeeded as Marquess by his son by his first marriage, John Henry Petty; the second marriage was childless. Petty was the name adopted by the first Earl on succeeding to the estates of his uncle.

William, 2nd Earl of Shelburne, from a mezzotint of a group,
by Sir Joshua Reynolds

THE EARL OF SHELBURNE

Shelburne's political career was one of the most remarkable in eighteenth-century history. His tenure of office was not uneventful but it was brief and it ended in failure and humiliation. The measure of his failure is difficult to grasp, tantalisingly elusive to explain. For Shelburne was perhaps the most brilliant intellectual in politics in the second half of the eighteenth century after Burke. He was also the most hated of all politicians. The political career of this curious man spanned the first half of the reign of George III and in a very real sense he was one of its most complete casualties.

Of his intellectual brilliance and personal charm there can be no doubt. Those close to him testified constantly to the generosity of his private manner, his kindness, his wit and his patience. Yet Shelburne was a complex person who may perhaps be described as a compulsive intellectual. He took few ideas for granted and subjected prevailing ideas and institutions to constant analysis. Furthermore, he rather enjoyed making a show of his intellectualism. He must have been one of the very few eighteenth-century statesmen to have enjoyed the services of what the twentieth century would term a 'think tank' in the little coterie of intellectuals which he patronised at Bowood, and to have established a formal secretariat to facilitate his political activities. To his contemporaries, therefore, Shelburne appeared to be something of a 'character'. At the same time, there can be no doubting the sincerity of his involvement in intellectual life. He had a brilliant mind, kept abreast of current developments in a wide variety of subjects and made himself an authority on several. Men of the calibre of Price, Priestley and Jeremy Bentham, while owing much to his patronage, were ready to respect the man himself. The Bowood circle, indeed, pioneered many of the reformist ideas which were to agitate British political life until and after the first Reform Bill. Shelburne strongly supported the notion that the intellectual had an important role to play in politics. The Members he returned in his boroughs – Calne and High Wycombe – were men of a very high calibre. In the whole of the eighteenth century there is no party to compare with his brilliant group of men who sat in

185

the Commons, including Isaac Barre, John Dunning, John Calcraft and Lord Mahon.

Even more remarkable than his intellectual gifts and pursuits, however, is the fact that he was universally detested by his contemporaries. Posterity has not been able to provide satisfactory explanations for it. Historians have usually ascribed it to certain aspects of his personality. Men hated Shelburne because they felt that they could not trust him. They regarded him as utterly without principle and thus completely unreliable. It was not just the fact that he became a 'King's man' in 1782 after he had espoused popular causes for over a decade. Widespread distrust of him antedates the Rockingham-Shelburne ministry of 1782. Essentially, Shelburne lacked the ability to communicate his whole personality to others. He was remote and unreachable, never at ease and never relaxed. His efforts to appear so gave him an air of inconsistency and unpredictability which was exaggerated by his effusive bonhomie. In his desire to present his pleasantest face to the world he indulged in lavish flattery and obsequious ingratiation whose transparent insincerity was manifest. Shelburne, then, was a lonely and isolated individual who did not understand others, and lacking the ability to understand men, their emotions and their motivations, he was perhaps unsuited to politics. But there was more than this to Shelburne's unpopularity. Contemporaries constantly (and completely without foundation) accused him of corruption, immorality, and even subversion. Because he was not trusted, his 'advanced' ideas were treated with fear and scepticism. An aura of secrecy and sinister mystery surrounded Shelburne. It was entirely characteristic of his career that his London residence in Berkeley Square had once belonged to Lord Bute.[1] When the radical reformer of the 1770s became the 'King's man' of 1782–3 contemporaries were shocked but they were not surprised. It was exactly the sort of behaviour they expected from 'the Jesuit of Berkeley Square'.

In 1760 Shelburne launched himself into his political career. His family was Irish and he thus felt no inclination to associate himself with the great Whig aristocracy led by the Duke of Newcastle. Indeed, his earliest political associates were Henry Fox and Lord Bute, and he participated in their endeavours to destroy the political world of the

[1] Bute's abiding influence with the King was constantly assumed by political observers until the end of the 1760s. Shelburne's association with Bute thus provoked comment and raised the issue of his political integrity.

Pelhams. He acted in 1762-3 as a go-between for the King with Fox (whom the King detested) and Bute (whom he loved). He was rewarded with the gratitude of George III but he paid dearly for it. (Already he was beginning to acquire that reputation for intrigue which dogged his whole career.) Shelburne was further rewarded by his appointment as President of the Board of Trade during the ministry of George Grenville. Although he attended assiduously to his departmental duties he revealed qualities of weakness and indecision which, together with his own unpopularity, deprived him of any influence on policy. His resignation in September 1763, less than six months after taking office, created neither surprise nor regret.

It was just at this moment in his life that he came under the influence of William Pitt. For the next five years at least Shelburne was to live under his shadow. Accepting Pitt's principle of 'Measures not Men', he followed his lead over the issue of general warrants in 1763-4 and over his refusal to join the Rockingham ministry of 1765-6. Shelburne's loyalty was rewarded when he received Cabinet office in the Chatham administration of 1766-8. Although he kept something of the spirit of Chatham alive while the ostensible premier nursed his gout at Bath he was unable to persuade his colleagues to follow the policies of the Great Commoner. He was unable, for example, to stop Charles Townshend from pushing through his disastrous scheme to tax the American colonists. Indeed, he became increasingly isolated within the ministry. Differences over policy and patronage led to his resignation in October 1768. Shelburne's future looked bleak. His affection for Chatham was not reciprocated. The early respect of the King had not been maintained. Shelburne had kept aloof from the Rockingham Whigs, the largest opposition party. Fortuitously, the Petitioning Movement of 1769 rescued him from political isolation and gave a new twist to his hitherto wholly unremarkable political career.[2]

Shelburne involved himself in the movement initially because of his desire to follow Chatham's lead[3] but he also wished to preserve the

[2] The Petitioning Movement of 1769 was organised by a temporarily united opposition of Chatham, Grenville and Rockingham protesting against the actions of Grafton's ministry over the Middlesex election, the unseating of Wilkes and the seating of his defeated opponent, Luttrell.

[3] Nevertheless, it was in 1769 that Shelburne began to shake himself free of his subordination to Chatham. Although he remained respectful and even obsequious towards him until his death in 1778 Shelburne emerged as an independent political figure at this time.

following which he had painstakingly built up for himself in commercial circles, particularly inside the East India Company, during the last few years. His support of Wilkes opened up contacts with the radicalism of the metropolis and he threw himself wholeheartedly into the radical movement, playing an essential role in forging a link between the metropolitan radicals and the parliamentary politicians. At this time, too, he came under the influence of the radical ideas of English Dissent. Through the influence of Price and Priestley he came to appreciate the currents of reformist thought which went back to the seventeenth century. After the failure of the Petitioning Movement in 1770 Shelburne remained in opposition, in uneasy alliance with the Rockinghams, dedicated to radical reform of British political institutions.

Conflict with the Rockingham Whig party was to be the dominant theme of the rest of Shelburne's active political career and disputes and disagreements had already begun to manifest themselves in 1769. Fundamentally, Shelburne's reforming principles were different from those of the Rockinghams. They continued to proclaim the traditional complaints of opposition against corruption and secret influence and asserted that these could only be cured by party government. It is doubtful if Shelburne believed, with the Rockinghams, that since the beginning of the reign of George III a deliberate policy of corruption had been undertaken by the Court which had for its object the establishment of an inner Cabinet (whose existence undermined the authority and responsibility of the official Cabinet) and the silencing of Parliament as an organ of protest and opposition. The Rockinghams thought in terms of establishing a different system of government. Shelburne was more radical than the Rockinghams.[4] He was, at the same time, more loyalist than they were. He wished to improve the King's service, not to weaken his ministers. Shelburne objected less to the political role of the Crown than to waste and inefficiency of government. Unlike the Rockinghams, he was concerned with comprehensive administrative reform and bureaucratic efficiency.

Shelburne's economic and imperial thinking was also at odds with that of the Rockinghams and far in advance of it. After he left office in

[4] Although Shelburne's acceptance of parliamentary reform remained largely theoretical it offended the Rockinghams. He advocated an additional Member for each county, but even this very moderate proposal was regarded by them as proof of his readiness to listen to the popular voice. They constantly suspected his 'popular' politics. They found his defence of the Gordon rioters in 1780 distasteful.

1768 he came under the influence of Adam Smith and Dean Tucker and adopted their free trade ideas.[5] He thus came to question the rigid, mercantilist structure of the Empire.[6] He embraced the vision of an abiding imperial partnership and a federal alliance with the Americans based upon voluntary agreement. Consequently, he found the notion of complete American independence unacceptable in the 1770s and was distressed when the Rockinghams began to accept it in 1778. Shelburne perceived that the old imperial system was breaking down and that a new kind of imperial relationship would have to replace it if the Empire were to survive at all. Simply to accept American independence, as the Rockinghams seemed content to do, was to preside over the liquidation of the Empire, and this Shelburne refused to do.[7]

Fundamentally, Shelburne's approach to politics was different from that of the Rockinghams. One of the basic elements in the political thought and practical activities of both Chatham and Shelburne was their detestation of party.[8] Neither of them suffered fools gladly. They were too arrogant ever to have considered themselves to be *members* of a party. They wished to retain their freedom of action and to do so they would endeavour to destroy factions. They would consult the national interest and appeal to the country at large to vindicate their conduct. Shelburne believed that Cabinets ought to include the best men of all parties. The Cabinet would be dominated by a great national leader who would enjoy a unique position of trust and confidence with the King. Members of the Cabinet were to be servants of the Crown and the first minister. It was the function of the Cabinet to approve of

[5] In this area of thought he was far in advance of Chatham. (It confuses the biographies of both men to assume that he was Chatham's pupil in everything.) Chatham remained something of a mercantilist and never grasped the significance of the new free trade theories.

[6] In 1765–6 Shelburne had already opposed the internal taxation of the colonies by the British Parliament. Furthermore, in 1775, when hostilities began, he was prepared to abandon all rights of taxation.

[7] Of American independence Shelburne remarked in a debate in July 1782 that 'he had used every effort in public and in private, in England and out of it, to guard it from so dreadful a disaster'. (William Cobbett, *The Parliamentary History* (London, 1806–20), xxiii, 193.)

[8] 'The fact was, that he was, and had through life stood aloof from parties. He was of no party. It was his pride and principle to be of no faction, but to embrace every measure on its own ground, free from all connection. Such had been his political creed; as such he stood before the people, and as such he coveted to be judged by them.' (Ibid., xxvi, 575.)

policy already decided upon between the departmental head concerned and the King. Individual ministers were responsible for their policy not to Parliament, not to the Cabinet, but to the King. It followed that the King must retain the full exercise of his prerogative of appointing ministers.[9] It is important to understand that the protection of the royal prerogative of appointing ministers was a natural consequence of Shelburne's distaste for party.

It is hardly surprising, then, that after the failure of British arms in America and the resignation of North, the King attempted to persuade Shelburne to lead a new ministry. The King reasoned that, in spite of his radical tendencies, Shelburne had no party to impose upon him. Disagree they might over policy, but at least he had no intention of humiliating the monarchy. But Shelburne was too realistic to have believed that he could have survived for long without the Rockinghams, and he persuaded the King to form a ministry around them but including him. Shelburne may well have been worried by his prospective position in the Cabinet in 1782. He disagreed with the Rockinghams on many matters of policy and principle and saw that their party clannishness could leave him isolated and powerless. His major safeguard against that possibility was the protection of the King. For his part, the King needed a friend in the Cabinet to protect him from the Rockinghams and from the earliest days of the ministry used Shelburne as his agent. The royal riposte to the constitutional revolution of 1782, then, was to use Shelburne to weaken and divide the Rockingham-Shelburne ministry.[10] It mattered little that the Rockinghams obtained the Treasury and the bulk of the offices.[11] Shelburne understood what the King was

[9] Shelburne's ideas, 'which for seventeen years he had imbibed from his master in politics, the late Earl of Chatham', included the conviction that he should 'stand up for the prerogative of the Crown and insist upon the King's right to appoint his own servants'; otherwise 'the monarchical part of the Constitution would be absorbed by the aristocracy, and the famed Constitution of England would be no more'. (Ibid., xxiii, 192–3.)

[10] The King even put into writing a promise of 'full power and full confidence' in Shelburne. (Lord Fitzmaurice, *Life of William, Earl of Shelburne*, (2 vols, London, 1912), ii, 89.)

[11] Even so, of the nine members of the Cabinet, Rockingham could only rely absolutely on three, Fox, Cavendish and Keppel. Shelburne could rely upon Grafton, Ashburton and, in most circumstances, upon Camden, Conway, and possibly Richmond. The ninth member was Thurlow, closer to the King than he was to either Rockingham or Shelburne.

about and prepared to co-operate with him in his scheming. Indeed, he even promised his full co-operation and assistance.[12]

There was bound to be trouble in the Cabinet. Shelburne behaved as though he wished to encourage it. He was enjoying his power and his position. He strutted and boasted, revelling in the King's confidence, delighting in his new-found importance, scorning the Rockinghams and making it very clear to them that although Rockingham might have the Treasury, the King wished the ministry to be one in which 'all ecclesiastical and civil preferments should be jointly recommended'.[13] Furthermore, the King supported Shelburne in his Chathamite conception of the workings of the Cabinet over and against Rockingham's idea of Cabinet solidarity. He would not entertain the Rockingham's 'practice of discussing business and laying advice before the King unasked'.[14] Even in matters where co-operation ought to have been possible between Shelburne and the Rockinghams it was not forthcoming, and Shelburne was at least as much, and possibly more, to blame than Rockingham.[15] For example, when the Rockinghams brought in their economical reform legislation Shelburne did not lift a finger to help them. It is true that his idea of economical reform was somewhat different from theirs but this fact scarcely warranted his ostentatious scepticism towards the Rockinghams' policy. He confessed that there were parts of it which he did not understand and professed it to be too difficult and daunting an undertaking to be carried out at that time.[16]

The most serious area of disagreement between the two wings of the ministry lay in the problem of making peace with America. As we have observed already, the Rockinghams were much readier than Shelburne

---

[12] 'I certainly would not run away from any opportunity of serving his Majesty, or the public.' (Fitzmaurice, op. cit., ii, 88-9.)

[13] The King to Shelburne, 5 April 1782. (*The Correspondence of George III*, ed. Sir J. Fortescue (6 vols, London, 1927), v, 443-4.)

[14] The King to Shelburne, 29 April 1782. (Ibid., 504-5.)

[15] Shelburne's political morality can be assessed from a brief glance at his behaviour over the Irish question. Ireland was Shelburne's responsibility, falling as it did within his department. But when the Rockinghamite Lord Lieutenant of Ireland, the Duke of Portland, recommended that Ireland be granted legislative independence, Shelburne refused to commit himself on the subject. He well knew the King's aversion to legislative independence and saw no reason to share in the royal odium which Portland incurred.

[16] Fitzmaurice, ii, 224-5.

to concede American independence. They believed that such a concession would leave England free to take action against her European enemies. Shelburne and the King wished to move more slowly, to make concessions to the Americans but not to go to the lengths of severing all connections and links with them. Shelburne persisted in his opinion that American westward expansion and, to some extent, even American trade, were matters over which the British Government ought to retain some measure of responsibility. It was not just these differences of opinion that wrecked the ministry. The peculiar administrative structure of the times worsened the existing political and personal discord. Charles James Fox was Foreign Secretary and therefore responsible for peace negotiations with the European powers, but Shelburne, as Home Secretary, had responsibility for the American negotiations. Fox feared that Shelburne was attempting to take over the conduct of the negotiations with France. His position grew increasingly desperate. Shelburne's opinions not only had the support of the King but they obtained the approval of the Cabinet. Further, even the European powers came to regard the negotiations with Shelburne as more official than those with Fox. The matter came to a head when Fox brought the dispute before the Cabinet. At its meetings on 26 and 30 June, however, the decision went Shelburne's way. Independence was not to be conceded initially but was to be part of a general settlement. At this, Fox threatened to resign.

At exactly this point, with the ministry on the verge of disintegration, the Marquis of Rockingham died (on 1 July). Even before his death it was clear that Shelburne would be his successor.[17] His appointment was greeted with the resignations of Fox and Lord John Cavendish, the Chancellor of the Exchequer, from the Cabinet, and some few resignations in the lower offices. Fox protested that Rockingham's successor as leader of his party, the Duke of Portland, and not Shelburne, should have been appointed to the Treasury, on the grounds that Shelburne did not have the confidence of the major part of the Cabinet and the ministry.

It is important to be clear about exactly what was at issue in these disputes, for it was largely because of the principles at stake in them that the ministry of Shelburne has its significance. Most contemporaries, even if they disliked Shelburne, thought that he and not Fox was con-

[17] Especially to Shelburne who, as Rockingham lay dying, was already casting around for support.

stitutionally in the right in July 1782. The King had freely chosen Shelburne to lead the ministry and a ministry had been formed. Until it was proved that the ministry did not enjoy the confidence of Parliament the King's choice must be respected. The behaviour of Fox seemed spiteful and full of pique. His claim that the Cabinet and not the King should choose Rockingham's successor was of very doubtful constitutional propriety indeed. Few people took Fox seriously, for he was attacking openly the royal prerogative of appointing ministers.[18] Although there was not much enthusiasm for Shelburne's administration in July 1782 he did appear to be in a strong position. Fox was discredited and Shelburne was a man of far greater talent than the Duke of Portland. He was, furthermore, the heir of Chatham and of his principles and, in the political conditions of the summer of 1782, the defender of the Constitution and, especially, of the monarchy. He clearly had a *prima facie* right to govern.[19]

Shelburne intended to make full use of the political power which was now his and he entertained far-reaching ideas of reform. His two major preoccupations, however, were to be economical reform and the making of peace. The first was to prove a disappointment, the second a disaster.

Shelburne set himself to eliminate waste, extravagance and inefficiency from the machinery of government with commendable enthusiasm and industry. He saw clearly enough that the persistence of useless and outdated offices owed as much to the lingering concept of office as a freehold as to greed and pluralism. This he could not change overnight. He achieved a substantial number of minor reforms affecting the organisation of the Treasury but he went out of office before he could implement many of his schemes.[20] He attempted with little success to reduce the debt on the Civil List. He improved the supervision of the fees system, removing the worst of the abuses. He did something to

[18] Burke gave Fox some good advice at this point, suggesting that he remain in office until Parliament had had an opportunity to sustain or to defeat Shelburne. Burke's advice would have effectively prevented Fox from seeming factious and, in particular, stirring up the problem of the royal prerogative of appointing ministers. See J. Cannon, *The Fox–North Coalition* (Cambridge, 1969), pp. 21–2.

[19] He was also extremely fortunate in that the parliamentary recess began less than a week after he took office. His ministry was bound to survive, therefore, for at least six months, until Parliament reassembled.

[20] Shelburne himself asserted that he had many economic reform proposals in preparation when he left office. (*The Parliamentary History*, xxiii, 824.)

rationalise the system of estimating the expenditure of various departments.[21] Further than this he did not have time to go. Many of his schemes were taken over by the Younger Pitt and gradually introduced by him but the credit for their initiation really belongs to Shelburne.

The great issue upon which the fate of the ministry hung, however, was that of peace-making. Shelburne hurried to complete the peace preliminaries before Parliament met. This he did when they were signed on 30 November. It should be stressed that for Shelburne to have made a successful and popular peace was quite out of the question. British troops had been humiliatingly defeated in America, and if the war had been lost then the peace could not be won. The British public made a scapegoat of Shelburne and castigated the luckless premier mercilessly, especially over his inability to do anything for the American loyalists. As soon as the preliminaries were made public, Shelburne's ministry began to look very vulnerable indeed. The peace terms were Shelburne's own. He was an autocratic premier[22] and it was his own personal stature that was in question. His political future depended upon his ability or inability to persuade Parliament to approve the preliminaries. On 17 and 21 February his peace was rejected in the Commons by divisions of 224 to 208 and 207 to 190 respectively. Three days later he resigned. What explains his disastrous defeat and his ignominious departure from office?[23]

To a large extent Shelburne's Chathamite principle of refusing to organise a parliamentary following went far towards destroying his ministry. Shelburne had only a small group of followers and he would have to rely for a majority entirely upon the Court and administration group. He really believed that this normally loyal body would be sufficient to obtain a majority for the peace. His advisers promised him a massive majority and he was unwise enough to believe them.[24] Another aspect of his Chathamite principles contributed to his downfall. Shel-

[21] For his economic reform activities, see the authoritative account in J. Norris, *Shelburne and Reform* (London, 1963), chapters 10, 11, 12.

[22] Before the debates on the peace preliminaries Grafton and Keppel had resigned, the former entirely and the latter partly because of Shelburne's high-handedness. Richmond had stopped attending the Cabinet and Camden was extremely unhappy at his own situation.

[23] Ignominious not only because of his apparent cowardice but because during the debates hardly any members, even among those who normally supported him, had a good word to say for him.

[24] Cannon, op. cit., p. 30.

burne believed that the confidence of the Crown was sufficient to keep
a ministry in office. It was not. Unlike Chatham Shelburne did not have
the personal qualities that appealed to uncommitted members. Indeed,
it was Shelburne's unpopularity that made possible the Fox-North
Coalition which turned him out of office. Shelburne might have saved
himself by cultivating North, but his unfounded optimism of the winter
of 1782–3 allowed the Foxites an almost free hand in negotiating with
North.[25] Even when he did approach North the result was disastrous.
He tried to commit him to supporting the peace terms without telling
North what they were. Only Shelburne could have been guilty of such
an indiscretion. Only Shelburne could have been guilty of the fatal error
that precipitated the agreement between Fox and North which was
reached on 14 February, just three days before the first of the two
Commons divisions. Shelburne attempted to frighten North into remaining neutral on the issue of the peace, a blunder which drove that
amiable nobleman straight into the arms of Charles James Fox.

Shelburne's premiership came to an end, then, because of his adherence to Chathamite ideas and his political ineptitude as well as the
peace and his personal unpopularity. But ministries could and did survive occasional defeats in the eighteenth century, even on great issues.
Why did not Shelburne, who after all had only narrowly lost an unpopular peace against a well organised parliamentary opposition, remain in office? The answer is that he had by this time lost the will to
fight. He had no stomach for public, political battles and feared further
defeats at the hands of the Coalition. He no longer believed that he
enjoyed the unlimited confidence of the King. Indeed, he went so far as
to blame his parliamentary defeat upon the King's lack of support. To
the end he believed in his own righteousness.

There was something tragic in his isolation. While there was no
justification for his conviction that the King had been disloyal to him
there can be little doubt that the King's confidence in his minister was
beginning to weaken. His radical ideas had never endeared themselves
to him and Shelburne was of little use to him if he could not even stave
off a defeat in Parliament on a major issue. His Cabinet colleagues provided no support or encouragement. Thurlow had always thought his
economical reform ideas to be nonsensical and had little sympathy for
him. Conway and Grafton, two of the mildest of men, were offended by

25 Even as late as December it was quite obvious that the Northites and the Foxites
were still at odds. Shelburne did nothing to profit from their dissensions.

his high-handedness. Grafton, indeed, resigned because he did not consider himself to be in receipt of 'the fair confidence of the principal minister', and he accused Shelburne of 'attempting to break through that system of *general Cabinet advice*, which has been understood by us all'.[26] In short, his imperiousness had made an enemy of most members of his own Cabinet. Some of them, Richmond and Keppel, for example, yearned for a reconciliation with Fox. By February, then, the remarkable situation obtained where Shelburne had not a single friend in his own Cabinet.[27] Even outside the Cabinet there was no enthusiasm for him. Such political 'friends' as he had, men such as Pitt the Younger and Henry Dundas, were uninterested in saving Shelburne. They had their own careers to look to. It was, perhaps, just as well for Shelburne that he did resign in February 1783. His political isolation would not have allowed him to survive for very long even if he had summoned up the courage to struggle on.

Shelburne left some few constructive achievements to posterity. The peace treaty was renegotiated by the Coalition but they were hardly able to improve on it. He did not stay in power long enough to negotiate the kind of free trade relationship with America of which he had always dreamed. For the same reason his plans for economical reform remained unfulfilled, his other schemes unrealised.

The story of his premiership, however, is strongly suggestive of the state of British politics during the constitutional crisis of 1782–4. For a ministry to survive it was no longer sufficient for the first minister to enjoy the royal confidence and the patronage which possession of the Treasury provided. A ministry had to be led in the Commons and sustained there by a party of supporters. A ministry had to command acceptance among a fairly wide section of opinion and particularly among the Independents. Those statesmen of eighteenth-century Britain like Chatham and Shelburne who did not form parties were naturally more acceptable to monarchs than those who did but they could not survive without organised parliamentary support. This had been the lesson of the Chatham administration of 1766–8 and it was the lesson of

[26] Sir W. Anson (ed.), *Autobiography of the 3rd Duke of Grafton* (London, 1898), p. 362.
[27] However, there appears to be no truth in the old tradition that Shelburne's Cabinet met very infrequently because Shelburne was afraid to assemble it. Between 12 July and 19 December it met at least 26 times. (I. R. Christie, *Myth and Reality in Late Eighteenth-Century British Politics* (London, 1970), p. 69.)

Shelburne's ministry of 1782-3. Lord Shelburne was the last Prime Minister to attempt to govern without the aid of Party.

BIBLIOGRAPHY

The manuscripts of Shelburne have been much neglected by historians. There is a large deposit at Bowood, Wiltshire, and another at the William Clements Library, Ann Arbor, Michigan, USA. The only modern study of Shelburne is that by John Norris, *Shelburne and Reform* (London, 1963), but it is still necessary to consult Lord E. Fitzmaurice, *Life of William, Earl of Shelburne* (3 vols, London, 1875–6), which includes an invaluable autobiographical fragment. There is valuable material on particular aspects of Shelburne's career in: V. T. Harlow, *The Founding of the Second British Empire, 1763–93* (2 vols, London, 1959–64); J. Cannon, *The Fox–North Coalition* (Cambridge, 1969); D. Jarrett, *The Begetters of Revolution, 1759–89* (London, 1973).

THE DUKE OF PORTLAND

BY

E. ANTHONY SMITH

*William Henry Cavendish-Bentinck, born 14 April 1738, son of the
2nd Duke of Portland. Educated at Westminster School and Christ
Church, Oxford. Succeeded as 3rd Duke 1762. Married 1766 Lady
Dorothy Cavendish, daughter of 4th Duke of Devonshire; four sons
and one daughter. Lord Chamberlain of the Household 1765–6;
Lord Lieutenant of Ireland 1782; leader of the Whig party 1782;
First Lord of the Treasury 1783; leader of the Whig Opposition
1783–94; abandoned opposition 1792; joined Pitt 1794; Home
Secretary 1794–1801; Lord President of the Council 1801–5;
First Lord of the Treasury 1807–9. PC 1765; KG 1794; Lord
Lieutenant of Nottinghamshire 1795–1809; Chancellor of the
University of Oxford 1792–1809. Resigned as Prime Minister on
6 September 1809 and died 29 October 1809.*

William Cavendish-Bentinck, 3rd Duke of Portland

THE DUKE OF PORTLAND

If other holders of the office have been nicknamed the 'forgotten' and the 'unknown' prime ministers, William Henry Cavendish-Bentinck, third Duke of Portland, must surely rank as the 'unheard-of' prime minister. Yet he held the post on two separate occasions, no less than twenty-four years apart, and each time he came to 10 Downing Street at the height of a political and constitutional crisis which seemed to threaten the balanced eighteenth-century constitutional relationship between the King and his ministers. In the first instance he came to office as nominal head of the Fox–North Coalition, attempting to assert the supremacy of the Cabinet, backed by a House of Commons majority, over the King's personal will. On the second occasion he volunteered to rescue George III from ministerial domination after the King's quarrel with Grenville's Cabinet on the Catholic question, so repeating the role which Pitt had played against his administration in December 1783. His two periods of office thus offer contrasting views of the constitutional relationship between King and ministers in the late eighteenth and early nineteenth centuries, just at the time when that relationship was passing through a vital transitional period. The decline in the formal 'Influence of the Crown' and the emergence of the new political forces outside Parliament were beginning to change the context of eighteenth-century aristocratic politics, and would eventually transform the Constitution into a parliamentary democracy in which the Crown was to become little more than a figurehead and the prime minister a national as well as a party leader. Portland's career illustrates the limited extent of this development by 1809.

Conscientious and industrious, Portland dedicated himself from the first to the service of the Whig party. 'I consider myself as a servant of the Party,' he wrote to Newcastle in 1766, 'and shall always think it my duty to act in the manner that is most conducive to its support.'[1] Nevertheless, he failed to overcome a natural shyness and dislike of public prominence. He was an affectionate and considerate friend and a devoted family man, but to those who did not know him intimately he

[1] British Museum Additional MS 32977, f.58.

seemed aloof and frigid. Horace Walpole characterised him as 'a proud though bashful man', and a later historian remarked that he was 'an outstanding representative of the aristocratic theories for which he lived'. He was, however, a man of firm principles. Canning called him 'one of the most blameless, and noble-minded of men'.[2] He was one of the few to preserve a spotless reputation in an age when public men were often accused of personal intrigue or underhand dealing, and though he lacked the drive and energy to be a successful party leader in opposition he never lost the respect and, indeed, the devotion of his colleagues. Paradoxically, it was his complete lack of personal ambition that raised him to the premiership. Like Trollope's Duke of Omnium – for whom he might almost have been a model – he became Prime Minister partly because he was a duke, and partly because his appointment to the office enabled other, more vigorous but more abrasive colleagues to serve together under him. In both his administrations the driving force came from others – from Fox and Burke in 1783, from Perceval, Canning and Castlereagh in 1807-9. On both occasions Portland was a 'dummy' rather than a real Prime Minister, but on both occasions the choice met with the general approval of the other ministers. As his grandson Charles Greville later wrote, Portland's election as Whig party leader in July 1782 showed 'how aristocratic that party was, and what weight and influence the aristocracy possessed in those days; they would never have endured to be led by a Peel or a Canning'.[3] Yet Portland's subsequent authority was never questioned by the men of talent in the party.

Despite Portland's election to Rockingham's office as Whig party leader, he did not succeed immediately to the premiership. George III was not yet willing to accept a prime minister at the nomination of a party in the House of Commons, however strong in numbers. The post was offered to Shelburne, who was distrusted by the Foxites. They determined not to serve under him. 'Where there is not confidence, there must be Power,' Fox wrote on 12 July, 'and Power in this country must accompany the Treasury.' He declared to the King that the Whigs would insist on a prime minister of their own choosing.[4] If the King would not accept Portland, he might be forced to do so. In February

[2] A. S. Turberville, *A History of Welbeck Abbey and its Owners* (1939), ii, 319-21.
[3] C. C. F. Greville, *Journal of the Reign of Queen Victoria, 1837-52*, part II (1885), iii, 212-13.
[4] Fox to Portland, 12 July 1782 (*Memorials and Correspondence of C. J. Fox*, iv, 275).

1783 the Government was defeated in the Commons by the Coalition between the two opposition parties of Fox and North. Shelburne resigned, leaving the King to find another combination that could obtain a majority in the Commons. For the second time in the eighteenth century, this requirement dominated the search for a prime minister. Previously, ministers appointed by the Crown had been able to expect support from the Commons almost as a matter of course. In 1782 and 1783 the majority of the Commons was sufficiently intractable and determined to compel the King to submit to their virtual nomination. Fox again declared that the Whigs would not join any government unless Portland were placed at the head of it.[5]

Portland and Fox were not satisfied with a mere commission to form a government. In the first place, remembering the difficulties caused for Rockingham in 1782 by the use of Shelburne as a go-between, they insisted on Portland's receiving the appointment directly from the King. 'If it is his Majesty's pleasure to place me at the head of the Treasury,' Portland wrote, 'it is impossible to suppose that he means to withhold from me any part of his confidence, but it is very necessary that the public should be convinced of that circumstance.'[6] They were also determined that the ministry should institute a new relationship between the King and his servants. At the beginning of the crisis Portland declared: 'If . . . it should be the King's pleasure to place the Government in our hands, the powers of carrying it on must be given to those who are looked upon to be Whigs, and were considered to be such by our late most excellent friend, Lord Rockingham.' In particular, he would not serve unless George abandoned his insistence that Lords Thurlow and Stormont should be in the Cabinet, and when Portland was at last admitted to the royal presence on 23 March he refused to disclose the proposed arrangement of offices except for the Cabinet itself. While giving an assurance that any removals would be made 'as little obnoxious to his Majesty as the case would possibly admit', and in particular that there would be no alterations in the Bedchamber so long as its officers supported the Government, Portland insisted that before he could discuss further arrangements the King must signify his confidence in his ministers by approving the list of the Cabinet and binding himself to accept their recommendations. He therefore submitted only

[5] North to George III, 4 Mar. 1783; George III to Shelburne, 19 Mar. (Fortescue, *Correspondence of George III*, vi, 260-1, 292).
[6] Portland to North, 17 Mar. 1783 (Fortescue, p. 285).

the seven names proposed for the Cabinet. Pitt's refusal to come to the rescue left the King without an alternative and, muttering threats of abdication, George submitted to Portland's demands on 31 March, pleading that only the emptiness of the Treasury prevented him from prolonging the struggle. And if his new minister wished for a free hand in distributing the lesser offices, he should have it. The King insisted on the point that Portland had 'named' rather than 'recommended' the members of the Cabinet, and on 4 April he wrote that he had no desire to interfere with the formation of the Admiralty Board, which Portland could arrange as he liked.[7] On 1 April, the day before the ministry formally took office, the King even wrote to Lord Temple, who had refused to join them, to express the earnest hope that, as William Grenville expressed it, 'those who act with us should hold themselves apart from such a government in order that he may have something else to look to whenever circumstances shall allow it'. In the meantime he declared his resolution to grant no peerages or other honours at the ministers' recommendation, to signal his disfavour to the public at large.[8]

Portland's first ministry set out under conditions unprecedented in the history of British Cabinets, with the sovereign almost publicly avowing his distaste for his ministers, and the events of the next months did not improve the relationship. The settlement of the Prince of Wales's income on his coming of age in August 1783 resulted in a quarrel between Portland and the King when the Duke proposed to allow the Prince – who was associated politically with the Whig party and personally with Fox's circle of friends – an annual sum amounting to double that received by George III when he was heir to the throne, plus a large sum to help pay off his enormous debts. The King refused point-blank so 'to gratify the passions of an ill-advised young man'. 'The reception I met with in the Closet,' wrote Portland to Lord Loughborough, 'was so grievous that I know not how to describe it.' The King threatened to expose the whole affair to the public as a job for the benefit of the

[7] Portland to Temple, 22 Feb. 1783 (*Memoirs of the Court and Cabinets of George III*, ed. Buckingham and Chandos (1853), i, 163); North to George III, 15 Mar., George III to North, 23 Mar., Portland to George III, 23 Mar., George III to Pitt, 23 Mar., to Weymouth, 25 Mar., draft messages of abdication [? 28 Mar.], George III to Portland, 4 April, and his memorandum, 30 Mar. (Fortescue, vi, 280, 298–300, 310, 314–17, 325, 332–3). See also O. Browning (ed.), *Political Memoranda of Francis, Duke of Leeds* (Camden Society, NS xxxv, 1884), pp. 86–7.

[8] George III to Temple, 1 April (Fortescue, vi, 329–30); W. W. Grenville to Temple, 1 April (*Court and Cabinets*, I, 216).

ministers and their friends, and even sent copies of his correspondence with Portland to Lord North in the hope that he and Stormont, both members of the Cabinet, would disavow the Government's policy. Portland had to persuade the Prince to accept his father's offer of half the proposed income plus the Duchy of Cornwall revenues and a capital sum from Parliament to pay his debts. Despite the ministry's parliamentary strength, the King had won a victory, and the Government's life remained precarious.[9]

The fall of the Portland ministry over the India Bill in December 1783 is a story that has often been told.[10] The Bill was a serious attempt to bring the political administration of India under closer public control, but it contained provisions which could be interpreted, like those concerning the Prince of Wales's income, as designed more for the advantage of the ministers than of the Empire. The proposed Commission for the Government of India, to be nominated by Parliament and serving for a fixed term of four years, was to control Indian patronage and administration, and was to consist of close friends and associates of Fox and North. Since the four-year term of office would run beyond the date of the next general election, it was at once assumed that the aim of the Bill was to ensure the ministers' success at the polls in 1786 or 1787 and so to make their tenure of office permanent. It was in response to this threat that Pitt and Temple initiated the well-known plan to secure the defeat of the Bill by the direct use of the King's name with the House of Lords, and to use the defeat as a pretext to dismiss the ministry and appoint a new one under their leadership. On 17 December the Lords rejected the Bill, and on the following day the ministry was dismissed, the King merely sending a messenger to collect the seals of office, 'as audiences on such occasions must be unpleasant'. The ministers considered themselves deceived, as the King had never hinted his disapproval to them; the revelation of the royal displeasure even converted the vote of Lord Stormont, a member of the Cabinet itself, into one against the Bill.[11] The King's action was a foretaste of the tactics which Portland himself was to exploit against Grenville's ministry

[9] George III to Portland, 16 June 1783, and to North, 16 June (Fortescue, vi, 401–3). Portland to Loughborough, 18 June (Portland MSS, PwF 9212).

[10] The most recent account is that of Dr J. A. Cannon in *The Fox–North Coalition* (1969).

[11] George III to North, 18 Dec. 1783 (Fortescue, vi, 476); W. Eden to Morton Eden, 16 Dec. (*Journal and Correspondence of Lord Auckland* (1861), i, 69).

in March 1807 and, as Fox pointed out with some force in the House of Commons, it violated the cardinal constitutional principle of the responsibility of ministers, 'the only pledge and security the people of England possess against the infinite abuses so natural to the exercise of this power. Once remove this great bulwark of the Constitution, and we are, in every respect, the slaves and property of despotism.'[12] If the accession to office of Portland's ministry exposed the limitations of the royal power over the appointment of ministers and determination of policy in face of a strong and determined political party, the manner of its dismissal showed that the King need only find a sufficient degree of support elsewhere in order to recover his position.

Portland remained out of office for over eleven years. In July 1794 the greater part of the aristocratic section of the Whig party joined Pitt, anxious to strengthen the Government's hand in dealing with the twin threats of French aggression abroad and French revolutionary example at home. As Home Secretary, Portland was responsible until 1801 for the maintenance of law and order in the country and the control of popular disturbances. The experience confirmed his strong natural conservatism – he had always been utterly opposed to parliamentary reform and a convinced adherent of the creed of aristocratic Whig paternalism. By 1805, when he went into what he expected to be his political retirement after serving for ten and a half years without a break in the Cabinet, he had come to represent the ultimate in loyalty to King, country and the old Constitution. It was to protect all these that he agreed to assume the burdens of office once more in 1807, nearly a year after Pitt's death.

George III's quarrel with his Ministry of All the Talents over the proposed Catholic Relief Bill came to a head early in March 1807. As in November 1783, the King had given no overt sign of his opinion of the Cabinet's proposal when it was submitted to him for approval, tacitly reserving his freedom of action until the parliamentary situation became clear. On this occasion it was Sidmouth, always a strong anti-Catholic, who became alarmed at the scope of the measure, and his visit to the Palace provided George with evidence that there was a possibility of replacing the ministry with one more agreeable to his own Protestant views. Once again he hinted at the possibility of his using the royal veto against the Bill if it passed both Houses. Such a step, as Lord Mulgrave wrote, would lead to the dismissal or resignation of the

[12] *Parliamentary History*, xxiv, 216–17.

ministry and a dissolution of Parliament, accompanied by 'the greatest agitation . . . both in this country and in Ireland'.[13] To avert the political crisis which would result from the direct involvement of the Crown in a contest with Parliament, the Pittite leaders agreed to offer to form a government, with Portland at its head.

As early as June 1806 the Duke of York had suggested that Portland was the only possible leader of Pitt's former friends, amongst whom there were 'too many persons of the same rank, and nearly the same political consideration', while the King too seemed to regard the Duke as Pitt's natural successor.[14] It was Portland, therefore, who took the initiative when the crisis of March 1807 developed. On the 12th, after consulting Malmesbury, he addressed a long letter to the King, assuring him that 'should . . . the belief I wish to entertain be well founded, and that your Majesty shall not have given your consent to the measure in its present shape, I have little apprehension of disappointing your Majesty when I venture to express my opinion that it may be ultimately defeated . . . in . . . the House of Lords', providing the King's views were made unequivocally plain. He advised George to seek a direct explanation with Grenville, and, in the likely event of the ministry's resignation, declared 'that your Majesty would have an abundant choice of persons capable of managing your Majesty's affairs, and that so circumstanced, those persons would receive the general support of the nation at large'. Finally,' as for myself, incapable as, *I know*, I am from age, infirmity and want of ability to render your Majesty any profitable service, should your Majesty be of opinion that I can be of any use to you, I will do the best I can to serve you to my life's end.'[15]

George III, constitutionally proper as always, sent no formal reply to Portland's letter until after the crisis was over, but there is no doubt that it provided him with the support he needed to act. On the 13th he authorised a message to Malmesbury to declare his unchanged sentiments on the Catholic question. On the same day he saw Grenville, declared his objection to the Bill, and demanded its withdrawal. The Cabinet agreed on 15 March to withdraw, but reserved the right of

[13] Mulgrave to Lowther, 11 Mar. 1807 (Lonsdale MSS, quoted in A. Aspinall (ed.), *Later Correspondence of George III*, iv, 525, n.1).
[14] Malmesbury, *Diary and Correspondence of . . . 1st Earl of Malmesbury* (1845), iv, 359–61.
[15] Portland to George III, 12 Mar. (*Later Correspondence of George III*, pp. 525–8). The King replied on the 22nd (ibid., p. 533).

the ministers as individuals to declare in Parliament their support for the principles behind the Bill. The King demanded in return a pledge that they would propose nothing more to him on the Catholic question, and on their refusal sent for Eldon and Hawkesbury to come to Windsor. They saw him on the 19th, were informed of his wish to change his ministers, and recommended that he should send for Portland, 'as more likely to unite the feelings of persons than any other man'. The King, reported Eldon and Hawkesbury, declared that Portland should have a completely free hand – 'he may dispose of everything'. He was to confer with Chatham and Viscount Lowther, and submit a plan for approval.[16]

Portland accepted the commission on the 20th, though with great reluctance owing to his advanced infirmity. He had been gravely ill for some time, and had only a few months before undergone with great courage the ordeal of 'cutting for the stone'. He realised that the appointment might shorten his life, but, he assured Malmesbury, 'he should by no means regret a few years, or perhaps months, more or less, when he had the inward satisfaction of thinking they were sacrificed in his endeavours to serve his King and his country'. Hawkesbury reported to the King that Portland was 'most ready and willing to lend himself to be the instrument of any arrangement which your Majesty might deem advantageous to your service.'[17] On 25 March Portland and his colleagues were sworn in.

Portland's Cabinet of 1807 was, to appearances, one of the most impressive of the eighteenth and nineteenth centuries. It included three future prime ministers – Perceval, Hawkesbury and Canning – in addition to Eldon and Castlereagh, two of the leading statesmen of the early nineteenth century. Yet it proved to be one of the weakest and least successful of administrations. Portland's continuing and progressively worsening ill health must be held partly responsible for its lack of unity. He had never been an inspiring leader or shown much talent for co-ordinating the efforts of others when he was at the head of the Whig party. Now he was largely ignored by his own colleagues, and on occasions not even summoned to Cabinet meetings. Malmesbury lamented that the Duke 'had so few, or rather *no* person in the Cabinet he could call his personal friend', and noticed that his colleagues 'take a great

[16] Malmesbury, iv, 373–4, 378–81; Camden to Lowther, 19 Mar. (Lonsdale MSS, quoted in *Later Correspondence of George III*, p. 529, n.1).
[17] Malmesbury, iv, 375; Hawkesbury to George III [20 Mar. 1807] (*Later Correspondence of George III*, iv, 530).

deal on themselves, immediately belonging to *him*, and treat him more as a nominal than as a real head of the Ministry'. So, 'if ever he had a point to contend, or ever was disposed to contend one, [he would] be left in a very small minority.' Perceval, as Leader of the Commons, Hawkesbury, Canning and Castlereagh were the major political figures in the ministry, but they were uncomfortable colleagues who failed to work closely together. Unfortunately, too, the remaining members of the Cabinet were less able men who could offer Portland no real support. Portland failed – he did not even try – to weld these discordant elements into a team. The position was summed up by Perceval in August 1809: 'It is not because the Duke of Portland is at our head,' he wrote, 'that the Government is a Government of Departments; but it is because the Government is and must be essentially a Government of Departments that the Duke of Portland is at our head, and is the best head possibly that we could have. I very much doubt us continuing long under any other.'[18] The Cabinet contained a group of self-willed individuals, men of equal importance, so that a 'strong' premier would merely have driven it rapidly to self-destruction. Even Portland's feeble authority could not hold it together when his colleagues began to quarrel amongst themselves. The ministry thus burrowed its way further and further into difficulties, partly of its own making, in the conduct of the war and at home, while the Prime Minister, frequently incapacitated by bouts of agonising pain, was unable to deal effectively with his colleagues. Malmesbury wrote: 'I have often been with him when I thought he would have died in his chair; and his powers of attention were so weakened that he could neither read a paper, nor listen for a while, without becoming drowsy and falling asleep.'[19] He was clearly incapable of handling the dispute between Canning and Castlereagh. Canning's campaign to have Castlereagh removed from the War Office opened in March 1809, and the Duke, instead of stepping in and acting with firmness at the outset, allowed matters to drift on until the end of June, when Perceval found out that Castlereagh was, unknown to himself, virtually under sentence of dismissal. The consequence was a quarrel between Perceval and Canning, and, in September, Castlereagh's resignation and duel with Canning. By then, however, Portland's health had finally given way. In August he had an apoplectic

[18] Malmesbury, iv, 386, 394; Perceval to Huskisson, 21 Aug. 1809 (Perceval MSS, quoted in D. Gray, *Spencer Perceval* (1963), p. 223).
[19] Malmesbury, iv, 413.

seizure on the way to his country house at Bulstrode, and, though he partially recovered his mind and speech, he resigned on 6 September with the Cabinet breaking up around him. He died after a second seizure on 29 October.

If in his first ministry of 1783 Portland represented the Whig claim to the supremacy of Cabinet and party over the Crown, in his second term of office he stood for the preservation of monarchical influence over the rising claims of the politicians. On both occasions he presided over ministries composed of discordant groups and individuals, and he failed to impose a personal authority over them. He allowed Fox to run his first ministry into head-on collision with the King, and Canning to destroy his second. Portland was thus a prime minister in only a limited sense. His role was virtually that of a figurehead for abler men who supplied the real driving power of government, and on both occasions too his tenure of office depended directly upon the King's willingness to allow him to hold it. Portland's career shows that even by 1809 the authority of a prime minister still depended on the personal attitudes of the sovereign and of the individual members of the Cabinet.

BIBLIOGRAPHY

Aspinall, A., (ed.), *Later Correspondence of George III* (Cambridge, 1962–70), vol. iv
Fortescue, Sir J. (ed.), *Correspondence of George III* (London, 1927–8), vol. vi
Diaries and Correspondence of James Harris, First Earl of Malmesbury, edited by his grandson, the 3rd Earl (1845), vol. iv
Welbeck MSS (Nottingham University Library)
Cannon, J., *The Fox–North Coalition* (Cambridge, 1969)
Gray, D., *Spencer Perceval, the Evangelical Prime Minister* (Manchester, 1963)
Turberville, A. S., *A History of Welbeck Abbey and its Owners* (London, 1939), vol. ii

WILLIAM PITT 'THE YOUNGER'

BY

PETER DOUGLAS BROWN

William Pitt, born 28 May 1759, son of William Pitt, MP (cr. Earl of Chatham 1766) and Lady Hester Grenville, daughter of Richard Grenville, MP. Educated at Pembroke College, Cambridge; Lincoln's Inn 1778; called 1780; MP Appleby 1781–1784; Cambridge University 1784–1806; PC 1782; Chancellor of the Exchequer 1782–1783; First Lord of the Treasury and Chancellor of the Exchequer 1783–1801, 1804–1806; Lord Warden of the Cinque Ports 1792. Unmarried. Died 23 January 1806.

William Pitt, 'the Younger', by John Hoppner

WILLIAM PITT 'THE YOUNGER'

William Pitt became Prime Minister at the age of twenty-four and proceeded to manage the affairs of a great empire for seventeen years without interruption, an achievement unique in the parliamentary annals of any country. Born during the Annus Mirabilis of 1759 and conditioned by the universal adulation for his father, politics were for him the only concern. Chatham, discerning a true senator, himself trained the boy in oratory. A Cambridge undergraduate at fourteen, William had as tutor the Reverend George Pretyman-Tomline, whom he would one day appoint Bishop of Lincoln. Though he was far from being head of a coterie, a good many of his university acquaintance were destined to serve under him. Granby (soon to be fourth Duke of Rutland), John Pratt, son of Chatham's Lord Chancellor Camden, and the tenth Earl of Westmorland all became Viceroys of Ireland; Althorp as second Earl Spencer would be First Lord of the Admiralty when Nelson fought at Aboukir. Pitt watched House of Commons debates and met Charles James Fox, already prominent in Parliament, but whose unstable ways were a source of alarm to his friends.

With Pitt ebullience took the form of a happy ambition, tempered by a serenity reminiscent of those classical sages whom men of the eighteenth century sought to emulate. In respect of the appetites, his temper had no difficulty in meeting the moderation demanded by his circumstances. Chatham's financial embarrassments precluded provision for a younger son and Pitt would be the first future Prime Minister ever to undertake a profession: Cambridge was followed by practice at the Bar. When in 1780 the King sprang a general election Pitt, just come of age, manifested that optimistic courage which would always be one of the most appealing sides to his greatness. He offered himself for the representation of his university but ended bottom of the count, though not ignominiously. Rutland introduced him to Sir James Lowther, the greatest parliamentary patron in England, and Pitt, after some misgivings about representing a private borough, accepted his nomination for Appleby. What practical advantages membership of Parliament might bring were however far from evident, for North, as the King intended, had held on to a majority in the House of Commons, and for Chatham's son the apostasy of seeking his board from that ministry was unthinkable.

That Pitt should have become Prime Minister scarcely less than three years after entering Parliament was not, and never could have been, due solely to the concurrence of precocious abilities with the public memory of Chatham. So meteoric a transformation could take place only in consequence of a cataclysm so great as to throw party alignments into utter confusion. The American war, whether decided in terms of unity or division between the English-speaking peoples, must dominate allegiances at Westminster. But when Pitt embarked on politics the coming disaster was not in evidence, for the war situation, though unpromising, was not hopeless.

Pitt's sympathies naturally lay with the opponents of the war which his father had deplored. He had a young man's enthusiasm for the re-form of the House of Commons, which his father had advocated and the cause of America had made hugely topical. He was also an admirer of Adam Smith and his free trade principles, which belonged to the generation after Chatham. For Pitt there was an obvious leader in Shel-burne, his father's disciple, the most intellectually pioneering man in the politics of the day. Pitt was welcomed into that eclectic circle of the man who might well be a prime minister for the future. It would not however be correct to call him Shelburne's follower: already his insularity matched his gifts. Pitt owed his introduction to the moderate parliamentary reformer Wyvill not to Shelburne, but to his cousin Lord Mahon. In the House of Commons, with the ease of a total unself-consciousness, Pitt established a reputation as a first-class debater. News of Yorktown made certain the opening of a new chapter but the prospects of Shelburne, let alone Pitt, were hard to discern. Shelburne had the asset of Chatham's reputation but also the disadvantage of his very small parliamentary following. Yet while North's ministry was crumbling, Pitt declared before the House of Commons his unwilling-ness ever to condescend to junior office – a most ill-judged essay in conceit from anyone but himself.

True to his word Pitt refused a minor place in the Rockingham ministry. The piecemeal harassment of the Civil List, after the prin-ciples conceived by Burke for limiting the 'influence' of the Crown, could not spark off his enthusiasm. Shelburne became the Secretary of State with the main responsibility for negotiating peace with America, in a most unenviable situation, hated by Fox and Burke. Pitt, acting in concert with Wyvill, called for a select committee of the House of Commons on parliamentary reform. He was beaten 161–141, a respectable defeat which would be the best the reformers would manage in Pitt's lifetime. On Rockingham's death Shelburne was appointed Prime Minister and Fox hastened back to the game of opposition. But Fox was considered even by some of his friends to be resigning on grounds purely personal.

The King would have liked Pitt at the Home Office but for the jealousies so rapid a promotion must arouse. Pitt was happy to be Chancellor of the Exchequer with a seat in the Cabinet. Shelburne had a most ambitious programme to cover the deficiencies laid bare by the war. All depended upon the ministry building a majority and Pitt indicated that, though he would not be a party to a coalition with North, an arrangement with Fox might be palatable. But Fox made clear to Pitt that he would not serve with Shelburne. So Fox and North got together and Shelburne, his plans for peace with America and France thrown out by the House of Commons, resigned. To some extent Pitt, by his obduracy towards North, had been responsible for his chief's downfall, but his subsequent consistency of conduct would redeem him. From Shelburne Pitt had learnt much, above all the ideal of sound administration as an end in itself, and not merely as a means to the diminution of 'influence'. He also recognised that Shelburne had come to grief in part because his plans were far too comprehensive for any House of Commons to swallow at once. Reform would have to be gradual, step by step, and as little alarming as possible to interested parties.

In George III's eyes Shelburne was a broken reed, and as he had no intention of treating with Fox and North, to invite Pitt to become Prime Minister was not so very surprising. But despite the pleas of Shelburne and Dundas, Pitt declined the opportunity, offered twice within a month, because his majority would have to depend upon North's goodwill. He thereby preserved his freedom of action and proved to the world that, unlike Fox, he would not compromise his principles for power. The way was open for the Infamous Coalition of Fox and North with Portland Prime Minister. Pitt stood forth as the champion of parliamentary reform and during May and June put forward a series of resolutions which won moderate support. But the stance of the Government was most impressive and Pitt made plans to resume his Bar career. Then Fox threw the game away by his India Bill, a most unpopular measure which vested Indian patronage in a committee to be nominated by the Coalition's majority in the Commons. Pitt considered Fox's Bill barely constitutional, doubted its passage through the Commons and was certain the Lords would block it. He spoke loud and clear against, and here opened his great parliamentary duel with Fox, 'Cicero in Catilinam', that would last their days. On this occasion Pitt misjudged the Commons, who passed the India Bill by a handsome majority in one of the most important divisions of the century. The King's next line of defence was the House of Lords but the consequences of challenging the Commons had first to be considered. The chances of a new minister establishing a majority were exactly counted, and also the probable outcome of a general election: both calculations were found to leave 'no manly ground for apprehension'. Pitt agreed to take the risk, the alternative being to leave the King shackled with Fox and North for ever and so destroy every chance for himself. A message entrusted to Pitt's first cousin, the second Earl Temple, informed the peers that anyone who voted for Fox's India Bill would be considered a personal enemy of the King, and this secured its rejection. On 19 December 1783 George III dismissed the Coalition and Pitt was appointed Prime Minister.

Forming a ministry was not easy; with what Henry Dundas censured as great cowardice, Temple retracted his acceptance of a Secretaryship of State. The Government which emerged was not impressive. Thurlow, so long the King's man, was bound to come back as Lord Chancellor. Lord Sydney, conscientious but rather dull, returned to the Home Office. For Foreign Secretary Pitt took the Duke of Leeds's heir, Carmarthen, indolent and ineffective. The second Earl Gower as Lord President and Rutland temporarily Lord Privy Seal brought borough influence and historic connections. All the Cabinet were peers and, Thurlow excepted, not one a statesman of even second-class rating. Shelburne was not invited into the Government but had to console himself with the marquisate of Lansdowne: Pitt had no wish for a rival. His real trust lay in a circle of close friends, especially his first cousin William Wyndham Grenville, Dundas and George Rose, but at first they could be given only junior places.

Pitt saw that, rather than ask for a dissolution, he would be wiser to face the House of Commons, let members see him in action and for the man he was, pilot through the budget and leave Fox to do his worst. Fox hoped to turn Pitt out by the votes of the existing House of Commons who, he held, had the right to dictate the choice of prime minister. Pitt admitted that a minority government was 'unusual' but upheld the prerogative of the King. In truth his situation was more unknown than 'unusual', and the penalty for losing what was really a fight to the death between George III and Fox could be impeachment. The King, who had soon lived down what unpopularity he had acquired owing to the American war, happily dilated on the rights of the executive in a 'mixed Constitution'. Fox did himself the greatest harm by his dissolute manner of life, his open and constantly reiterated abuse of the King and his association with the open whore-mongering of the Prince of Wales, gleefully reported in the newspapers. The King showed his confidence by the creation of some peers; Lowther became Earl of Lonsdale. The Freedom of London which Pitt received on 28 February was a very distinct mark of popularity. The King and Pitt as champions of the Constitution were far more convincing than 'Carlo Khan', the libertine, who had tried to filch the riches of the East. Fox's Whig friends stayed firm. But North's followers had for years been happy to look to the approval of George III and man by man they deserted to Pitt. Fox dared not lay himself open to the charge of disrupting government by refusing supply. The Mutiny Bill through, the King dissolved Parliament on 24 March.

No eighteenth-century government ever lost a general election but the extent of Pitt's victory was astounding. He had a personal triumph in this time being elected for his university. Fox was again returned for Westminster, but through the country 160 of the men who had voted for his India Bill were thrown out. In the debate on the Address when Parliament met, Pitt's majority was 282–114. It was the coincidence between the King's judgement and that of the electorate that made the decision so complete. The ultimate future lay not with prerogative, but in Fox's concept of the functions of the House of Commons: this however was for the next generation.

In the hour of triumph Pitt made a mistake. Motivated by spite he attempted on a technicality to prevent Fox from taking his seat: the good sense of members prevailed and Pitt met his first defeat. But this was none the less essentially Pitt's House of Commons. The landed gentry would readily support him as representing a stable government and the type of Member desirous of office would rally to his banner. Eden did not heed the charge of tergiversation he was bound to attract on joining Pitt in 1785, and Jenkinson crowned a lifetime of service by his presidency of the Board of Trade, which won him the earldom of Liverpool. Pitt did not attempt to become a party leader in the sense ascribable to Walpole, Pelham and in some respects to North. For the first ten years he was the only member of the Cabinet not to be a peer. His personal following in the House of Commons never exceeded fifty and he depended upon the typical man of goodwill customarily ready to vote for administration. Apart from his natural aloofness Pitt was of the tradition of Chatham, who had thought the idea of party as defined by Burke positively harmful. His interest lay in seeing that the King's Government was carried on, and well; for that he had all the necessary support. By way of paradox Fox, though leader of a permanent minority, played the party game. He held his men together and of those who had survived the general election few deserted. He never forgave Pitt the way of his coming to power and castigated him as the reimbodiment of North's system. Pitt was not completely dependent upon the King, for both knew the alternative might be Fox. But just as the prerogative had been essential for his survival, so the understanding that he had the King's confidence was necessary for keeping his majority together. The King found that generally he and Pitt saw eye to eye over policy, left him to carry on business, and over patronage they compromised.

Pitt's India Act went through comfortably though at the cost of condoning some past abuses. The system of dual control thereby established lasted until 1858. Political power was exercised by the Board of Control in London, whilst on paper patronage stayed with the Company. Cornwallis embarked upon his great career as proconsul by becoming Governor-General, and from home Dundas at the Board of Control gradually established his all-pervasive influence. Though the Company lobby remained important, India ceased to be in the forefront of interest and Fox was completely dished over his pet topic. So far as the affairs of Warren Hastings were concerned neither Pitt nor Fox intervened initially. But Fox, anxious to get his own back, joined the attack as a political manoeuvre. Pitt's vote for a prosecution on the Benares charge, which made impeachment certain, astounded his friends and the King, but he seems simply to have changed his mind in the light of the evidence. At first the trial superficially compensated the Opposition for their ineffectiveness in Parliament, but as time drew on people became disgusted at the perversion of a legal process for party interest and the Whigs lost reputation.

With India out of the way Pitt could turn to the problems bequeathed by the American war. The loss of the American markets and shipyards was expected to be catastrophic. In the opinion of the Emperor Joseph II Britain was a second-class power. With this the views of Pitt and the King coincided in the sense that an adventurous foreign policy was economically out of the question. But Pitt had before him Shelburne's ideal of free trade as the means to recovery. The Americans would have welcomed a trade treaty but Pitt knew the House of Commons would never allow a return to the reciprocities of the old Empire now the political link had gone. Soon the disadvantages of the commercial breach with America would be more than offset by an immense upsurge in British production and trade which continued unbroken even during the French revolutionary wars. In the case of Ireland, constitutionally autonomous since 1782, closer links were imperative. Here Pitt's vision passed beyond the bounds of economics: if reciprocity in trade could be accompanied by an Irish contribution to imperial interests, and some parliamentary reform in Dublin, Britain and Ireland would enjoy a common polity, with domestic concerns left to the local legislatures. The Dublin Parliament substantially cut the proposed contribution to the Navy, and trouble there was not unexpected, but Pitt had not bargained for the storm of protest from merchants and manufacturers in Britain. The concessions to Ireland had to be curtailed so drastically that there was no hope of acceptance in Dublin. The Crown was left the only point of union between the two countries. The peace treaties had required a trade agreement with France, which during 1786 Eden negotiated on highly favourable terms. To Fox's objection that France was the natural enemy of Britain Pitt retorted that 'to suppose that any nation could be unalterably the enemy of another is weak and childish'. The treaty was approved by a large majority.

Pitt, after the manner of Walpole, Pelham, and of North as minister in time of peace, built his reputation upon his mastery of the national finances. At the opening of his ministry the interest on the National Debt, the Civil List and military and naval expenses exceeded the appropriated revenues by £2 million. There was the burden of an unfunded debt of £14 million carrying a discount of 14–15 per cent. Pitt's genius as an administrator was ideally suited to the mood of business optimism. He reduced the duties on those articles most extensively smuggled, cut drastically the duty on tea and substituted a Window Tax graduated to hit large houses. In the year 1787 alone Pitt carried nearly 3,000 resolutions through the House of Commons to remodel the port and excise duties. Already he had built a revenue surplus of nearly £1 million and set up a Sinking Fund for the reduction of the National Debt. Pitt depended very greatly upon his Treasury staff, especially Rose, for his own arithmetical calculations were frequently inaccurate and his immaculately presented budgets were the fruit of much correction. Financial prosperity gave power at the international level and in 1787 Pitt had no difficulty in checking the designs of France upon Holland, and an alliance followed with Prussia, the other interested power. Britain was back in the comity of Europe.

In respect of economical reform Pitt avoided offending interested parties by a sweeping clearance of dead wood. Sinecure offices and pensions were quietly abolished on the death of the holders and the diminution in the 'influence' of the Crown that resulted was an incidental result rather than a publicly declared objective. But in the long term Pitt's reductions were far more extensive and above all administratively efficient than anything Burke had envisaged. So penetrating was Pitt's decomposition of the ancient tissues of reward that he had to resort to peerage creations and baronetcies. He has been held responsible for an alleged decline in the intellectual standards of the House of Lords and for honouring wealth rather than merit, criticisms without foundation. Until 1784 the Hanoverians had been so parsimonious that new creations had barely exceeded extinctions. Pitt's policy, although prompted by the erosion of patronage, also reflected the great expansion of the moneyed class. A House of Lords which comprised Liverpool, Barham, Auckland (Eden), Wellesley and a promotion for Cornwallis cannot be called undistinguished.

The scheme for parliamentary reform which Pitt put forward in the House of Commons on 18 April 1785 turned out to be no more than an episode in his ministry. It was planned to re-allot seventy-two rotten boroughs among the counties and London, by buying the rights of the owners, subject to their consent. Pitt may have been sincere but by this time parliamentary reform stood no chance. The King did not trouble to manifest his opposition; his views were well known and he appreciated that even Dundas, Rose and Grenville were against. There was, as North was quick to point out, little popular demand for change and the measure was defeated 248–174. The men who had voted against reform had no wish for Pitt's resignation. Pitt probably realised that his successes in other fields had assuaged the discontents of the North era. To put forward changes not desired by the King or the House of Commons was a pointless exercise and his was to be a ministry not of reform but of sound government. The nonconformists, closely identified with the movement for parliamentary reform, had with considerable reason expected Pitt to prove himself the Prime Minister who would secure the repeal of their disabilities. Pitt in 1787 and again in 1789 opposed the repeal of the Test and Corporation Acts; there was already liberty of worship and a free Constitution did not call for the abolition of the Anglican monopoly of political power.

Amidst the stubborn conservatism of Pitt's Britain the movement for the abolition of the slave trade was a brilliant beacon of praiseworthy endeavour. Only in this country was the cause taken seriously, in the sense that the Government was committed, which as the trade was a bulwark of the mercantilist economy was all the more remarkable. It was on Pitt's advice that Wilberforce decided to raise the issue in Parliament, though party was not involved for Fox and Burke were equally enthusiastic. In Wilberforce's absence through illness, Pitt on 9 April 1788 introduced and carried a Commons resolution for an investigation as early as possible. Abolition was made a Cabinet matter and over the next two years Pitt and Grenville did all they could. Two great obstacles were that the refusal of the French Government to show interest made any infringement of British mercantilism appear one-sided: also, though the great men were for abolition, the dwarfs were obscurantist. Unfortunately time slipped by until the French Revolution cast its shadow.

Suddenly, in November 1788, Pitt's Government – indeed it seemed possible his whole career – was put to hazard when the King fell dangerously ill. Modern medicine has diagnosed porphyria, but then his delirium was thought to betoken insanity. Evidently a Regency might prove essential, a prospect delightful to the Prince of Wales who would make Fox Prime Minister and then demolish Pitt's power by exactly the same methods his father had used to destroy the Whigs. Acting on impulse, Fox produced the distinctly un-Whiggish doctrine that the Prince had an inherent right to the Regency with full monarchical authority, the function of Parliament being restricted to naming the inauguration date. This turned out to be giving the game to Pitt, who admitted that only the Prince could be Regent but also maintained that Parliament must first nominate him, subject to such restrictions as the precedents might indicate. Superficially it might seem that Pitt and Fox had swapped creeds, with the Prime Minister as the man of 'the people' and Fox the advocate of prerogative. In fact Fox's motives were so obviously selfish and the Prince's deportment so very unseemly that the public preferred Pitt's insistence upon constitutional propriety. But then Fox was convinced that the illness was chronic and a Regency unavoidable. Pitt, who knew the King intimately, was not so sure but some decision could not long be delayed. Already Thurlow was showing himself only too ready to ease Fox's way, provided he remained Lord Chancellor. The conditions embodied in the House of Commons resolutions of 16 December were very restrictive, which would seem to guarantee Pitt's dismissal. Disturbing news came from Dublin, where the Irish House of Commons had offered to acknowledge the Prince as Regent without limitations, irrespective of what might happen at Westminster. Then the King recovered and the air cleared, almost as though nothing had happened.

Pitt's ministry, essentially a one-man government, enjoying a general rather than a party support, emerged unscathed, whilst Fox had lost ground badly. Pitt's character had become set; distant as ever, he reserved his gay side for his small circle and there was no sign of his wishing to marry. The incompleteness of his domestic side perhaps went together with his Philistine blindness in respect of contemporary art and literature. With the King his relations were always formal, but politically as one they embarked upon their glorious autumn and neither perceived the significance of the taking of the Bastille that summer. If Fox thought that event heralded a new era in human relations, Pitt was happy to see France bankrupt and ruined by dissension. In truth the Revolution placed the Whigs in dire peril. Burke's *Reflexions upon the Revolution in France*, though leading directly to a breach between him and Fox, did not at first affect the Whig party. But time would prove that the French Revolution was very different from the Glorious Revolution and the Whigs were in no position to face an event bound to force upon all men a reappraisal of political values. Pitt was happy to fish in troubled waters and already he saw that their divisions would work to his own advantage. At the general election of 1790 Pitt's majority was increased and the opportunity was taken to give a peerage to Grenville, who had never fared outstandingly in the House of Commons and might counteract the sinister machinations of Thurlow. Two years later Thurlow had to be got rid of for attempting to tamper with Pitt's Sinking Fund Bill. He had no parliamentary group to fall back on so with the King's agreement he was succeeded by Loughborough. The old independence of the eighteenth-century Lord

Chancellor was ended and in future he would have to submit to the principle of Cabinet solidarity. The King would always fear a return of his illness and saw the need to take things steadily. Increasingly he settled at Windsor, a willing absentee from London, though he never neglected his dispatch boxes. But he could sometimes be tiresome about appointments, promotions and vacant Garters. One day he would very properly refuse Pitt's request to have the rather secular and, by episcopal standards, unscholarly Tomline translated to Canterbury. Though the King could not save his favourite Lord Chancellor he knew what to look for in his archbishops.

That the embarrassment of the French Court was to Britain's advantage seemed proved when in 1790 a crisis arose with Spain because a British trading station on Nootka Sound in Vancouver Island had been destroyed. Spain regarded the Pacific as her monopoly, a claim Pitt would not tolerate, and in May he obtained a vote of credit for the Navy. The quarrel was similar to that over the Falkland Islands in 1770–1 and France once more was in no condition to back her ally by force. In the event of war Pitt was ready to co-operate with potential rebels in the Spanish Empire by an expedition to Mexico. On 28 October Spain agreed to a Convention by which the Vancouver settlement was allowed and the freedom of British navigation in the Pacific and trade north of California was recognised. Though Pitt's direct interest was only commercial the future existence of the colony of British Columbia was in fact assured.

The Constitution of Canada set up by North's Quebec Act required attention. The influx of American Loyalists had greatly increased the English-speaking population. Though there was an unofficial majority, French and English, on the nominated legislative council, Loyalists who had settled in New Brunswick enjoyed a representative Assembly and Crown Colony government had never been popular with the merchant community. The French might by now be deemed suitable for representation but Pitt was firmly against the hazard of combining the two communities under one Assembly. Grenville, who had succeeded Sydney at the Home Office, had no doubt that the British Parliament was exportable and he drafted the required legislation. There were to be two Canadas, Upper and Lower, each with two legislative houses, one elected, the other nominated. This solution reflected much thought upon the theory of colonial government, for the terrible American example was held to have resulted from too little control, yet regard must be paid to the natural rights of British subjects. Though not entirely satisfactory in practice, the Canada Act of 1791 remained the Constitution until the Durham Report and the changes of 1840.

The continental powers were not deeply concerned about the French Revolution until Louis XVI, by attempting to flee the country, turned his people against him and endangered the dynasty. Tension lay in the east, where Russia, Prussia and Austria were bent upon dividing Poland. There British interests were not affected but Pitt was concerned at the designs of Austria and Russia upon Turkey. In 1790 the Emperor Leopold II agreed to an armistice returning to the *status quo*. But Catherine the Great snubbed Britain and went ahead with the establishment of a naval base at Otchakoff (Odessa) on the Black Sea. On 22 March Pitt obtained the consent of the House of Commons to a naval armament, but finding the prospect of war generally unpopular he decided to back down. The Duke of Leeds, as Carmarthen had become, resigned – no great loss – and Pitt's position was strengthened by the appointment of Grenville, one of the greatest Foreign Secretaries of all time.

At the opening of 1792 Pitt cut taxation and reduced the Navy by 2,000 men. He forecast that in fifteen years a further £25 million of the National Debt would have been paid off, possibly only in ten: 'There was never a time when, from the situation of Europe, we might more reasonably expect fifteen years of peace than we may at the present moment.' But in August France declared war on Austria and Prussia, Louis XVI was deposed and the British Ambassador withdrawn. The French army overran Belgium and the Scheldt was declared an open river. The threat to Holland revived the tensions which had nearly brought about war in 1787. But for the present the Government in Paris was flirting with the idea of an accommodation with Britain as between the free nations of Europe. French agents were in London and Edinburgh spreading revolutionary propaganda, and on Pitt's advice the militia was called out and an Aliens Bill passed, as a precaution against the thousands of émigrés, refugees and agitators entering the country. When in January Louis XVI was executed Grenville ordered the French agent Chauvelin out of the country and a French declaration of war soon followed.

Under the impact of an ideological war Britain became a less free society. Obviously the correspondence between liberal-minded circles in Britain and France as of late had to be suppressed. But also freedom of political association and comment for purposes exclusively British, parliamentary reform included, were severely circumscribed. Fox's Libel Act of 1792, which Pitt had supported, gave some protection to publications of a nature once deemed innocent but now liable to penalties. Pitt's war policy lay in the formation of a grand coalition against France and between March and October 1793 Russia, Sardinia, Spain, Naples and Portugal, moved by fear of the French Revolution, joined Austria and Prussia as England's allies. Pitt thought French finances extremely precarious and expected only a short war. Already he was showing that sanguine over-confidence that marked one of his failings as a war leader. Grenville from the start had few illusions about what the country was up against. To him and also to the King the war was always ideological, a contest between forms of government as well as a clash between the essential interests of nations. Pitt had to keep the House of Commons happy and he always made clear that the war aim was self-preservation and not, as Fox alleged, to foist the Bourbons back onto the French people. But arguments theoretical or material did not serve to keep Prussia or Russia in the field, with the partition of Poland still uncompleted. By the end of 1795 Austria was the only great power actively engaged against France.

To support the war must entail some parliamentary co-operation with the Government, and on this issue the Whig party split. Canning, the great catch among the young generation, whose early friendships had been with Fox and Sheridan, chose to enter Parliament under Pitt's auspices. In July 1794 Portland, with great reluctance, decided to join Pitt's Government, and with him went Spencer, Fitzwilliam and Windham. They had to make a farewell to all the Foxite lore about Pitt acting as the King's tool in undermining the principles of parliamentary government established by the Glorious Revolution. Portland at the Home Office and Spencer at the Admiralty were assets from the administrative point of view. Windham, forceful and versatile, became the first Secretary at War to sit in the Cabinet. Fox was left with a party of only about fifty. British politics would never again be the same, for here was the foundation of the Tory party of the future, leaving Fox and Grey to liberalise the Whigs.

Pitt was the first British statesman whose career would be broken by Ireland. It was the example of the American Revolution, together with economic disadvantages, that had caused the constitutional revolution in Dublin of 1782. Since then the Protestant aristocracy had been in control and for them as well as for the English Whigs the French

Revolution possessed a magnetism. Of British rule only the Crown and the Privy Council's veto remained, but British mercantilism still had a sore edge. The Catholic peasantry in their turn had grievances against Protestant landlordism. Pitt believed the Catholics to be basically conservative and in 1793 Irish Catholics with the property qualifications were given the vote in parliamentary elections, which enfranchised many smallholders. The remaining Catholic disabilities were exclusion from the major offices and from the right to sit in the Dublin Parliament. In 1794–5 Pitt acceded to the request of Fitzwilliam, one of the greatest landowners in Ireland, for the Viceroyalty, though on the understanding that no sweeping changes were to be attempted. Fitzwilliam's instructions were not exact but he exceeded their spirit by dismissing Tory officials and promising full Catholic political rights at once. The King intervened to make clear his opinion that Catholic emancipation would divide rather than unite the two countries, and was in any event a constitutional question beyond the competence of 'any council of ministers'. After only two months Pitt recalled Fitzwilliam, who got a cold reception from Portland. Catholic opinion was deeply exasperated and a train of events set alight which would lead Ireland into a terrible rebellion.

Napoleon's conquest of Italy in 1796 closed any possibility of forcing the French back to their original frontiers. By the end of 1797 the position of Britain seemed desperate. The Navy had mutinied and when in October the Emperor was forced to make peace before Napoleon's army marched on Vienna the fighting on the Continent was ended. But despite disaster Pitt maintained a surface calm, though inward anxiety was undermining his health. The business of managing a war was not his *métier*, for far from being spontaneously exact and prompt he was a terrible correspondent and lacked altogether the natural dispatch required. Fortunately he had no political difficulties, for the 1796 general election confirmed his leadership and Fox unwisely seceded from House of Commons proceedings. The vast sums needed for the war were cheerfully voted, not that Pitt's efforts to meet the bills were uniformly successful. His famous Income Tax, a frightening innovation, yielded only six millions instead of the ten he had expected. His continuation of the Sinking Fund while borrowing at inflated rates has been justly condemned. Where Walpole, Newcastle and North had come to grief over war, Pitt survived the most costly disasters Britain had known that century, and it was universally agreed that provided he and the King stayed together, his administration was as solid as a rock. The country knew that in revolutionary France Britain was confronted by a novel enemy and Pitt was the only man.

The Irish rebellion of 1798 presented Britain with the most mortal threat since the Battle of the Boyne. Pitt thought the British Empire in danger of disruption, and in June reached the conclusion that a union between Britain and Ireland was essential and must be of the closest description, a joining of Parliaments. Often he had speculated in general terms on the possibility of union being produced by the natural course of events and now he made it his policy. The danger that the French might invade Ireland was frustrated by the Navy and instead Napoleon sailed to Egypt. It was a happy moment, for Nelson's victory on the Nile put new heart into Britain and enabled Pitt to build a second coalition with Austria and Russia. When at the close of the year Napoleon as First Consul had the impertinence to write a personal letter to George III suggesting peace, Pitt and Grenville brushed him aside.

The Union with Ireland was Pitt's most controversial achievement. India and Warren Hastings, parliamentary reform, nonconformist relief, even the harsh regulation of the press, pale beside the intensity of the passions aroused then and since by Pitt's failure to secure the right of Catholics to sit at Westminster as a condition of suppressing the Dublin Parliament. To Pitt it was out of the question to allow a Catholic majority to dominate a legislature already practically independent of imperial control. On the other hand to combine a union of Parliaments with Catholic emancipation would present no hazard, because the Protestants must always be in a majority at Westminster. The objections of the Protestant landowners, who since 1782 had had the run of things, at the loss of their legislative independence would have to be overcome. The consideration uppermost in Pitt's mind was imperial solidarity, and he saw a union as incorporating the Irish people in the metropolitan leadership of a great empire, with all the concomitant advantages. He did not consider religion the only issue at stake, or placating the Irish Catholics by full equality the sole advantage. He looked forward to the participation of the Irish nation in a project which he hoped would prove as outstandingly successful as the Union with Scotland. The dimensions of Pitt's thought were not mean or sectarian but conceived in a design of grandeur, to the advantage of the British Isles considered as one.

When Pitt took his decision the Irish rebellion was at its height and the Protestant landowners thoroughly frightened. The first step was to meet Camden's request to be replaced. Cornwallis, whose term in India had been most successful, was appointed Viceroy. The King understood well that union was the objective and made the shrewd suggestion that the panic gave an easy opportunity to overcome any objections in Dublin. At the same time, recalling the Fitzwilliam episode, he made absolutely clear in a letter to Pitt that further concessions to the Catholics were not open to consideration. Pitt knew very well that on a subject of that nature the King would never change his mind, and therefore if Catholic emancipation was presented to the Westminster Parliament as part of the union deal, he would face a crisis. The King's hint to rush matters was not taken. The rebellion was going from bad to worse but Cornwallis pursued a clement policy while, in accordance with Pitt's custom, the practical problems of union were investigated. At the end of December 1798 Pitt and the Cabinet drew up a plan based upon the Scots precedent. By this time the rebellion had subsided and fear of French invasion was no more. When therefore in January that able young man Castlereagh, just become Irish Secretary, presented his proposals to the Dublin Parliament, he was faced with an outburst of nationalist opposition. In the last week of the month Pitt carried his union resolutions through the House of Commons, with practically no opposition. There was not, and never had been, any question of Catholic emancipation being part of the proposed Act but Pitt, while expressly discounting any commitment in point of time, pointed out that the admission of Catholics to full privileges might be agitated with greater safety in a united Parliament. During the autumn of 1799 Pitt authorised Cornwallis and Castlereagh to approach the Catholics in terms suggestive of an early review of their disabilities, once union was secured. Cornwallis also went to work with the Irish Parliament, with promises of peerages and favours. The Irish borough owners were richly compensated. Inevitably the magnates came begging to London and Pitt met their expectations. But only the scale of corruption merits criticism, for the methods were of a kind always required to secure major legislation. During the spring of 1800 Union was agreed in both Parliaments by majorities of 158–118 in Dublin and 236–50 in Westminster.

Soon Cornwallis and Castlereagh were reminding Pitt of his promises. He knew that he would have to confront the King with a united Cabinet. When at a meeting of 28 September he explained his plan to relax the oaths of allegiance in a sense acceptable to the Catholics,

Loughborough alone dissented. The first Parliament of the United Kingdom met on 22 January 1801 and Pitt carried the Address by 245–63; but already the King was contemplating a change of ministry. At the levee six days later he declared to Dundas of emancipation: 'I shall reckon any man my personal enemy who proposes any such measure. The most Jacobinical thing I ever heard of.' Next day the King sent Addington to Pitt with the request that Catholic emancipation be abandoned. Pitt wrote to the King arguing that emancipation would present no dangers, offering his resignation as the alternative and finally deprecating his sovereign's direct employment of his authority. To this the King replied with his favourite argument, that his Coronation Oath precluded his consent to emancipation, but asking Pitt to stay on for the remainder of the reign. Pitt none the less resigned on 3 February and two days later Addington agreed to form a government.

Grenville, Dundas, Spencer and Windham went out with Pitt and in Dublin Cornwallis and Castlereagh followed. Canning too resigned, contrary to Pitt's advice, and constituted of himself a sort of unofficial opposition, more Pittite than Pitt. Of the younger generation Pitt much preferred Perceval and is said to have seen in him the future Prime Minister, although he was an opponent of emancipation. Portland, Westmorland and Chatham were ready to serve under Addington. Hawkesbury succeeded Grenville as Foreign Secretary and embarked upon the course that, as second Earl of Liverpool, would make him Prime Minister. The great Pitt ministry was ended, his parliamentary majority broken up, and he was left with his personal following of around fifty. Pitt's situation was painfully isolated, for Dundas particularly was deeply indignant at his abdication in favour of Addington, whom he thought incapable of maintaining sound government.

The question was what Pitt would do next. Before the end of the month the return of the King's malady promised still greater confusion. The Prince of Wales suggested that this time the attack might be prolonged, which drew Pitt's comment: 'Thy wish, Harry, was father to that thought.' Pitt promised Cornwallis and Castlereagh that he and the outgoing ministers would do their utmost for the Catholics. But only four days afterwards, deeply stung at a spiteful remark by the King that he was to blame for his illness, Pitt gave his famous pledge never again to raise Catholic emancipation during the reign. The King's attack lasted only three weeks but Pitt had fallen into a manifestly contradictory position. Having completed the budget Pitt handed over to Addington on 14 March, ignoring the suggestion of his friends that he might, in view of his pledge to the King, carry on.

Pitt's conduct of the Irish crisis cannot be explained with complete satisfaction. If political circumstances, especially the King's objections, made impossible the achievement of Union with full rights for Catholics, then Pitt's allowing Cornwallis and Castlereagh to promise emancipation was, on the face of it, perfidy. Probably, as during 1784 and 1788, he had meant to feel his way to safety, but he showed none of the buoyancy of his early years. His actions after his resignation, meekly supporting Addington and especially his double pledges to the Catholics and to the King, have no satisfactory explanation in terms of justice to Ireland. But Pitt never looked upon Union in an exclusively domestic context. Imperial interests in time of war were the paramount consideration and to that end the exclusion of the Prince of Wales from power by protecting the King's health was essential. The undertakings to the Irish Catholics were always general and though any reading of Pitt's character excludes trickery, he knew that the political balance at Westminster must condition their fulfilment. The King's distaste for Catholic emancipation and national opinion could well have been at one: Britain was still a Protestant country. Addington's victory at the general election of 1802 and the ease with which, after Pitt's death, the King dismissed his next Prime Minister, Grenville, for demanding Catholic emancipation, would indicate that an attempt to form an opposition party on that issue would have added to political confusion without bringing nearer the ideal of religious equality.

The peace preliminaries agreed by Addington and Hawkesbury towards the end of the year widened the breach between Pitt and his friends. The limitation of France to her 1792 boundaries, let alone a Bourbon restoration, were simply out of the question. Pitt, consulted towards the end of the negotiations, thought the terms 'highly creditable and on the whole very advantageous'. Grenville could not forgive a treaty which abandoned every colonial and maritime conquest except Trinidad and Ceylon. Peace depended upon Napoleon's moderation, and the weakness of the Peace of Amiens concluded in March 1802 was that the independence of the Dutch and Italian republics guaranteed under the Treaty of Lunéville with Austria was not reaffirmed. Soon Napoleon would show all too clearly that these were but client states of France. Pitt, who never attended properly to his household bills or kept an eye on his servants, was racked with anxiety over debt. His health was very poor and had not been helped by heavy drinking sessions with Dundas over the years. Strongly though Pitt disapproved of Addington's budget of 1803, he resisted the entreaties of Canning and Rose to come out into the open against the Government, for he felt his ground far from certain. Dundas, who had vowed never to bow to Addington, had accepted a peerage as Lord Melville. Then in March Addington sent Melville to Pitt as emissary to negotiate a coalition. Pitt had no intention of being less than the head and the comment reported of him was: 'Really, I had not the curiosity to ask what I was to be.' Pitt's terms were that the King, Addington and the Cabinet should give him the undisputed leadership, and that Grenville, Melville, Spencer and Windham be included. But the resurrection of the great Pitt ministry was impossible, partly because he himself would not force Addington's hand. The failure to provide Britain with a strong government was one reason for Napoleon's willingness to reopen the war.

When early in 1804 Grenville reached an understanding with Fox to work for a broad-based ministry, a new party alignment was formed which could not work to Pitt's advantage. That April Pitt decided to form a ministry and would readily have employed Fox, but the King would not listen, which therefore prevented Grenville from serving. So Pitt had to head a ministry which included Addington himself and six ministers who had served under him. A crisis with Spain, whose Bourbon King was ready to be the ally of Napoleon, brought out Pitt's old fire. He retaliated in the way his father had desired in 1761 and had the Spanish treasure ships destroyed on the high seas. The expected Spanish declaration of war placed the entire west European coastline in Napoleon's hands, and the sharp criticisms of Grenville completed the breach of an old friendship. The ministry was under constant strain and though Addington, with some demur, took a peerage as Lord Sidmouth, some of his friends were promoted, to the intense irritation of Rose and Canning. Then in April came the blow of Melville's impeachment for malversation. Two months later Sidmouth and some of his friends resigned because, owing to their attitude to Melville, Pitt refused them advancement.

Pitt had been engaged in negotiations with Austria and Russia which he hoped might lead to a third coalition. He laid down two principles, which were to be the foundation of the peace settlements negotiated by Castlereagh in 1814: France should be surrounded by strong buffer states and the whole guaranteed by international agreement. The talks with Russia nearly broke down owing to Tsar Alexander I's demand for Malta. But then Napoleon, by having himself crowned King of Italy, so provoked Austria and Russia that the coalition came into being. Much depended upon the willingness of Prussia to join but Frederick William III's greedy designs upon Hanover frustrated this. News of the battle of Ulm was soon followed by Trafalgar: Britain could not be destroyed by France but Austerlitz ended the war of the third coalition. Pitt died on 23 January 1806, twenty-five years after he first entered Parliament.

Pitt had been the greatest Prime Minister since Walpole and until Peel no man comparable would appear. In the magnitude and variety of his commission, shouldered over so long a period, he stands alone. Pitt was not the founder of a political party. His government was one of business, based upon a leadership personal rather than of principle. The Tory party which came after him was not of his intention but was forged by war and fear of revolution. It was in the achievements of peace that Pitt's creative powers excelled. Fundamental changes of policy in home finance, overseas trade, colonial government and foreign policy, and finally the Union between Britain and Ireland, all fell within Pitt's compass. During the years of peace fate was on his side. The work of reconstruction following the American war was guaranteed success by the spontaneous and fortunate eruption of industrial enterprise on an unprecedented scale. In terms of constitutional as distinct from administrative reform, directly considered, Pitt in truth achieved nothing at home. The innate conservatism of the eighteenth century and, it might perhaps be suggested, of the British genius, was against Pitt the young reformer. A Prime Minister unable to secure the abolition of the slave trade could not have reformed Parliament. Pitt's great achievement is to be found not in the formal but in the conventional and more important aspect of the Constitution. He established decisively that Britain has a Prime Minister, a description which from being one of doubtful repute came by his example to personify the government of this country.

For the Empire Pitt accomplished much. The East India Company was given a new respectability and the government of India that centralised force which enabled Wellesley to render British supremacy unchallengeable. The government of Canada was established so that the British and French could expand peaceably. The foundation of the settlement of Botany Bay for transported criminals was also an achievement of the great Pitt ministry, though he did not visualise the future Australia. Britain without the American colonies emerged with a new identity, and the optimism which inspired survival from Napoleon and finally glorious victory.

The French Revolution involved the greatest cleavage in European civilisation since the Reformation. The division between revolutionary France and the old Europe was by no means entirely founded upon ideology. French patriotism, hitherto so affronted by the deceits and inefficiency of the royal government, blazed forth with a new confidence and exerted a corresponding attraction over other nations. The Belgians, Dutch, Italians and Germans had in many respects suffered as much as the French by the failure of the ancient governments to meet the aspirations of the peoples. How far Pitt appreciated the importance of nationalism may be doubted. Britain was not seriously affected by a malaise of regime and her citizens for the most part considered King George and the House of Commons to represent their interests. As a war leader Pitt in no way compared with Chatham in strategical concepts or in that determined efficiency essential in mounting military operations. He represented the national will to resist tyranny: 'England has saved herself by her exertions, and will, I trust, save Europe by her example.'

BIBLIOGRAPHY

Aspinall, A., (ed.), *The Later Correspondence of George III, December 1783–December 1810* (Cambridge, 1962–70)

Bolton, G. C., *The Passing of the Act of Union* (Oxford, 1966)

Brooke, John, *King George III* (Constable, 1972)

Coupland, Sir Reginald, *Wilberforce* (Collins, 1945)

Ehrman, John, *The Younger Pitt* (Constable, 1969)

Magnus, Sir Philip, *Edmund Burke* (Murray, 1939)

Marshall, Dorothy, *The Rise of George Canning* (Longmans, 1938)

Mitchell, Leslie, *Charles James Fox and the Disintegration of the Whig Party 1782–94* (Oxford, 1971)

Rose, J. Holland, *William Pitt and National Revival* (G. Bell, 1911)

Rose, J. Holland, *William Pitt and the Great War* (G. Bell, 1911)

Watson, J. Steven, *The Reign of George III* (Oxford, 1960)

White, R. J., *The Age of George III* (Heinemann, 1968)

HENRY ADDINGTON, VISCOUNT SIDMOUTH

BY

PHILIP ZIEGLER

Henry Addington, born 30 May 1757, eldest son of Dr Anthony Addington and Mary Hiley. Educated at Cheam School, Winchester and Brasenose College, Oxford. Married (1) 1791 Ursula Mary Hammond; two sons, four daughters. (2) 1823, Mary Anne Townsend; no issue. Admitted to Lincoln's Inn and read for Bar; MP for Devizes 1784; seconded the address 1786; Speaker of the House of Commons 1789–1801; Prime Minister 1801–4; created Viscount Sidmouth 1805; Lord Privy Seal in Ministry of All the Talents 1806–1807; President of the Council 1812; Home Secretary 1812–1821; Member of Cabinet without Portfolio 1821–24. Died 15 February 1844.

Henry Addington, 1st Viscount Sidmouth, by George Richmond

HENRY ADDINGTON,
FIRST VISCOUNT SIDMOUTH

—————

When Addington became Prime Minister in March 1801 he took the place of William Pitt; when he resigned in April 1804 William Pitt replaced him. When he took office the Napoleonic wars were spluttering on, when he left it the brief truce was over and we were at war again. All that had changed significantly in the intervening years was Addington's own reputation. When his ministry began he was generally esteemed if not revered, a man of honour and proven ability whose new appointment seemed surprising but not absurd. When it ended he was derided where he was not detested, his government dismissed as a catastrophic failure. Whether either or both these judgements were correct is the most important question that the student of Addington must answer.

The most remarkable feature of Addington's life is that a man whom not even the most benevolent critic could credit with transcendent talents should have risen from bourgeois origins to supreme office in an intensely aristocratic society and under a king who felt few things to be more detestable than the middle classes. The Addingtons were yeomen farmers who, over the previous century, had edged nervously into the minor gentry. Henry's father, Anthony, chose medicine as his road to fortune and mental illness as his particular field of expertise. The choice was a shrewd one. Few ailments were more fashionable than insanity and it was not long before he was established in London and a regular visitor at many of its greatest houses. By the time Henry was born on 30 May 1757, his father had become a Fellow of the College of Physicians and had built up a most lucrative practice.

Addington's education – Cheam, Winchester, and Brasenose, Oxford – was conventional and notable, principally, for the energy with which he built up the circle of loyal friends who were to remain closely linked with him throughout his political life. Four members of his first administration were at the same preparatory school as himself, two more were added at Winchester. None of them was of outstanding quality yet none of them was less than competent. Divided they would have been of trivial importance, united they formed the Addingtonian Interest in Parliament and were a force to be reckoned with. It is a curious paradox that a man whom all agreed to be devoid of personal magnetism or outstanding charms should nevertheless have commanded and retained the loyalties of this far from inconsiderable band.

But Dr Addington gave his son more than a sound education and a useful if unspectacular circle of acquaintances; he gained him also the patronage of Lord Chatham and the comradeship of Henry's contemporary, William Pitt. Dr Addington had graduated from the role of medical adviser to that of Chatham's confidant and counsellor. The two families saw much of each other. At first Henry, the successful schoolboy home on holiday, tended to patronise his shy and sheltered friend, and for the first year or two in which they were reading for the Bar in London and were much in each other's company, he seemed still the more mature and independent of the two. It was not to last. Pitt flourished, moved into a more brilliant and sophisticated circle and, finally, 'went into the House of Commons as an heir enters his home'. Addington dwindled into a dowdy country cousin, dependable and decent enough, but to be tolerated rather than courted. Still, they remained close to each other, and when at the election of March 1784 Pitt shattered the Foxites and Addington entered Parliament for the first time as Member for Devizes, no one doubted that the ranks of the Pittites had received a staunch and potentially valuable recruit.

It cannot be said that Addington's early years in Parliament were crowned with glamorous success. It was nearly two years before he spoke at all, and then only because Pitt forced his hand by choosing him to second the Address. 'He was *very* little embarrassed,' wrote his brother Hiley approvingly; 'Not destitute of grace and dignity,' noted Wraxall; but he was not encouraged to repeat the effort. It was more than a year before he spoke again and then only briefly on a technical point connected with the Horse Tax. But he did not waste his time. He was sensible and industrious on committees; indefatigable in widening his acquaintance, even among the Opposition; and renowned as an expert on the rules and precedents of Parliament. It was his reputation as a good House of Commons man that emboldened Pitt to give him dramatic promotion in 1789.

The Speakership had fallen into sad disrepute over the last decade, culminating in Charles Cornwall who had kept a supply of porter underneath his chair and sipped it noisily during debates. When Grenville was elected early in 1789 it was felt that things were looking up, but, arrogant and ambitious as all his clan, he stayed in the post only long enough to savour the quality of the perquisites and was then on the way to replace Lord Sydney as Home Secretary. Was the Chair, demanded Burke, to become 'a succession house, a hot bed for statesmen'? He spoke for many members, and the general indignation convinced Pitt that he must find a safe man for the post – a man who would be free from higher ambitions and prove himself a devoted servant of the House. Addington's eligibility seemed obvious. Not everyone agreed. The Whig candidate for the Speakership wrote with disgust: 'Pitt could not have made a more obnoxious choice. . . . He is the son of Lord Chatham's physician and is in fact a sort of dependant to the family. The Chair has hitherto been filled by persons of quite a different description.' But Elliot was exceptional in his judgement. Most people thought Pitt had chosen well and though the Whigs dutifully divided against him it was done with little animosity. 'We were all very sorry to vote against you,' Sheridan told him affably.

Whatever strictures may be passed on other stages of his career, no one can deny that Addington proved an uncommonly good Speaker. He was patient, diligent, invariably courteous, well versed in the rules of the House and yet aware that sometimes they must be ignored, a thoughtful negotiator when disputes threatened the smooth running of affairs. Above all he was impartial, a quality today taken for granted in the Speaker but in 1789 an agreeable rarity. Only in one way were his future prospects damaged by his incumbency of the Chair. Any chance there ever was that he might become a competent parliamentary debater now disappeared. His latent vices of pomposity and prolixity flourished horrifyingly in this sympathetic atmosphere; free from heckling he never learnt to think on his feet or to deal with interruptions. Most dangerous of all, he lost all capacity to see when he might make himself absurd: the notes he prepared for a debate in 1800 on the corn shortage, in which he extolled the virtues of bran as opposed to grain and dwelt lovingly on 'the rarefying warmth, the solvent moisture and the grinding action of the stomach', show either that he did not know his nickname was 'The Doctor' or that he was disastrously unaware of the damage that could be done by ridicule. Such indifference was endearing, admirable even, but it boded ill for his future if he ever stepped outside the parliamentary asylum offered by his present office.

In every other way his stature grew during his twelve years in the Chair. His friendship with Pitt grew close again and his influence increased, so that he formed with Granville, Dundas and Loughborough an informal inner council which the Prime Minister found convenient to consult on many issues. Such conduct may not seem wholly Speaker-like but he justified it by the paramount needs of the war. Indeed, by 1794 all but a tiny rump of Whig irreconcilables under Fox had rallied to the Government. Often these latter did not attend debates at all; when they did their very weakness made it easy for Addington to defend their interests without damage to the cause he had espoused. Without shame he vowed allegiance to his glorious friend. Pitt and he dined together, talked together, drank far into the night together. On one occasion they were almost mobbed together. After a banquet at Canterbury a hostile crowd booed them heartily. 'A pretty story will this make in the papers,' said Pitt. 'The Minister and the Speaker dined with the corporation, got very drunk and were hissed out of town!'

Towards the end of 1793 Pitt offered Addington Dundas's seat in the Cabinet. Addington refused; he was quite happy where he was. Then in 1797 Pitt contemplated resignation on the grounds that a new prime minister could more easily reach a settlement with the French. In such a case his successor, it was secretly agreed, would be the Speaker. This too came to nothing but it is of importance as showing that, to the King and Pitt at least, the idea that Addington might one day head the Government was not a sudden whim but a long-meditated project. In 1799 another link in the chain was forged. The Bill for the Union of Ireland and England was debated in the House of Commons. Pitt believed that a Union would be disastrous unless swiftly followed by Catholic emancipation; Addington would not wholly commit himself but argued that emancipation would be unthinkable in present circumstances and hinted strongly that he could not imagine what might occur to make him ever change his mind. At Windsor the words made pleasant hearing; one follower of Pitt's at least would oppose a step which George III considered would be not merely dangerous folly but in violation of his Coronation Oath.

In October 1801 Pitt decided to force the issue. If the King would not accept emancipation for the Catholic Irish then he would have to find a new prime minister. 'Is such an enterprise necessary?' asked Auckland in dismay. 'Is it expedient a *Cui bono*? With what view? To what end?' Many of Pitt's followers were asking the same questions and the King now called on Addington to 'open Mr Pitt's eyes on the danger arising from the agitating of this improper question'. Dutifully Addington laboured to avert the crisis but Pitt proved implacable. The King's riposte was to send for the Speaker and ask him to form an administration. Addington, with patent sincerity, pleaded that Pitt must be prevailed upon to stay and that, even if he did not, someone more worthy should be found to fill his shoes. 'Lay your hand upon your heart,' said the King grandiloquently, 'and ask yourself where I am to turn for support if *you* do not stand by me.' Pitt now added to the pressure. Addington *must* take his place, no one else would be generally acceptable. He would urge his supporters to serve in the new administration and, for himself, pledged 'the most uniform and diligent support'.

Whatever Pitt might urge, however, not many of his former ministers were prepared to take jobs under Addington. Men like Dundas, Spencer and Windham felt themselves committed to the principle of emancipation while the smaller fry such as Canning could not bring themselves to desert their beloved chief. Addington quickly found that he would have to make do with the rump of the old Government – including Pitt's elder brother Chatham as a testimony of continuing goodwill; a handful of new recruits of stature like St Vincent and Hawkesbury, later to be Lord Liverpool; and a topping up of friends and relations from the 'Addingtonian Interest'. 'The Goose Administration', Canning called it. 'Wretched, pusillanimous, toad-eating . . .' Yet in fact it promised to be business-like enough. In Portland, Perceval and Hawkesbury it contained three future prime ministers and its law officers were of impressive quality. The average Member thought well of it: 'Thank God for a government without one of those damned men of genius in it,' as a Tory squire is said to have exclaimed. At any rate, it promised well enough for Addington to report optimistically to George III. 'The King cannot find words sufficiently expressive of His Majesty's cordial approbation of the whole arrangements,' wrote the delighted monarch. 'Addington', he told his new Prime Minister face to face, 'you have saved the country!'

Not everyone was satisfied with the official account of Pitt's resignation. 'Pitt went out,' judged Malmesbury, 'because he felt himself incapable either of carrying on the war, or of making peace.' This is not the whole truth, but there is still something in it. Military disasters and the defection of his allies had left his European policies wholly barren. Near starvation, mutinies and discontent at home completed the pattern of a war which it seemed could never be won and yet might well be lost. Pitt's earlier efforts to make peace had failed dismally and several of his ministers would have opposed any new negotiation. Part of the heritage he passed on to Addington was the need to bring about an honourable peace and the assurance that, from him at least, the Prime Minister could count on every help to make it possible.

In his first speech in the Commons the new minister pledged himself to take all possible steps to secure a peace. It can be argued that he was in too great a hurry, that he allowed his perception of his own problems to blind him to the still greater difficulties of the French, but it is hard to see that further delay would have done more than prolong the agony. Addington's belief was that Britain needed a truce more than France so as to rebuild the economy and allow its continental allies a breathing-space in which to recover their strength and their will to fight. The argument was a reasonable one and, if it be accepted, then the case for urgent negotiations needs no further defence.

Once begun, the discussions with the French were carried through with commendable secrecy and speed. By the beginning of October the preliminary terms had been worked out. It was clear that we were to give away a lot in the way of wartime conquests but Addington was not alone in attaching little importance to colonial kickshaws which could anyway be quickly retaken when and if war broke out again. More important was the proposal to abandon Malta. 'I have no idea how the effect of this measure is ever to be recovered,' wrote Windham. 'Chance may do much, but according to any conception I can form, the country has received its death blow.' Nelson supported the Government's decision but Addington himself had doubts and it is noteworthy that it was the British failure to evacuate Malta, in defiance of our treaty obligations, that eventually gave Napoleon his most justifiable complaint against us. All criticism of the peace was, anyway, of trivial importance. Pitt himself was satisfied and the people were delighted. The carriages of the French emissaries were towed in triumph from St James's Square to Downing Street and all the cows, calves and asses of Falmouth were bedecked with ribbons. Addington's stock was high.

Behind the euphoria, however, certain built-in weaknesses persisted. Addington as prime minister suffered from three handicaps which were to cripple and, in the end, destroy him. He was not an aristocrat, he was not an orator and he was not William Pitt. It was surprisingly common for an industrious young man from the middle or lower-middle classes, with luck and an influential patron, to break through into the ruling elite, but to be prime minister was another matter. On top of this there was the freakish fact that for a prime minister to be a doctor's son was not only socially unpardonable but irrepressibly comical as well. 'The Doctor', with flowing coat-tails and clyster pipe sticking from his pocket, became the cartoonist's butt, and the sniggers of smart society rippled out throughout the country until the idea that the Prime Minister was at least faintly ridiculous became common currency in every home.

Addington's second handicap, his lack of oratory, at first seemed almost an asset. The House of Commons was sated with fine speaking. 'At the close of every brilliant display,' wrote Sydney Smith of Pitt, 'an expedition failed or a kingdom fell. God send us a stammerer!' Now the stammerer had come. But the charm of Addington's stumbling sentences soon passed and when the House cried out for inspiration and leadership nothing was offered them. The contrast with his great predecessor was nowhere more striking.

And in the continued and conspicuous existence of this predecessor lay Addington's most considerable handicap – not the Pitt of reality but a larger-than-life, an infallible, a dream Pitt. The redeeming feature about John Brown was that, though his soul might go marching on, his body at least was safely mouldering in the grave. The unfortunate Addington had to compete with a rival who enjoyed all the privileges of a sanctified spot in the obituary column and yet was evidently and embarrasingly alive. For the moment he might be benevolently disposed towards the new administration, but not all his benevolence could curb the malicious mischief-making of his young acolyte Canning. In the end it was the benevolence that was to be eroded.

For the moment, however, all seemed set fair. The King treated Addington with singular affection, installed him in a handsome house in Richmond Park and sent him seven cows from the royal herd as a special mark of his esteem. The Prime Minister was conscious, however, of the weakness of his ministers in debate. He made tentative overtures toward the Whigs: 'Sheep that he is,' wrote Canning fretfully, 'he is calling in the wolves to his assistance.' But the wolves would not answer the call and on the whole Addington was more relieved than sorry. A union with the Whigs would not have pleased either Pitt or the King and in them lay his sure support. As George III had put it: 'If we three do but keep together all will be well.'

The period from the announcement of the Preliminaries of Peace to the signature of the formal treaty was Addington's golden age. His first budget, in which the ending of the war allowed him to abolish the 'monstrous', 'inquisitional', 'boldly tyrannical' Income Tax, was a triumphant popular success. The election that followed also went well; Pitt's massive majority was retained even though the master himself was absent from the field. 'It was the fashion at first to say *that it would not do*,' observed Wilberforce. 'I always maintained the contrary, and the event has justified my expectations.' Yet in Addington's very success lay danger. It is one thing to protect and patronise a failing government, another oneself to be patronised by one's prosperous successor. After eighteen months in retirement Pitt seemed further than ever from a return to office, and Addington took less trouble to cajole and propitiate his former master. Pitt was too big and honest a man to turn against Addington simply because he felt an itch for office, but it became more and more certain that he would look with suspicion and disfavour on any action of the present Government. His friends fostered the conviction that, if war broke out again, his leadership would be indispensable. Canning hailed him as 'the Pilot that weathered the storm', to whom the nation would turn as soon as the winds began to blow again. The analogy was perhaps flattering to Pitt who had committed the offence, surely reprehensible in a pilot, of abandoning his vessel in mid-tempest, but it reflected the feeling of many who were still numbered among the Government's vociferous supporters.

In the autumn of 1802 the storm began. Napoleon complained about the activities of the royalist emigrés in Britain and the excesses of the London press; then, in October, marched his troops into Switzerland. With the resumption of war appearing ever more inevitable Addington introduced a sensible but conservative budget and looked hopefully to his friend for support. He looked in vain. Pitt sulked in Bath while his minions in London fed him with slanted reports of the Government's ineptitude and hostility to their predecessors. Addington's followers behaved little better, his brother Hiley, in particular, excelling himself in the venom of his attacks on the Pittites. By January 1803, when the two men met again, Pitt had almost been persuaded that it was his duty to strike down his unworthy surrogate and take back the reins of power.

For a man who was well pleased with his own performance Addington proved astonishingly ready to adopt the same point of view. He knew as well as anyone how much of his parliamentary support depended on Pitt's goodwill and was quite prepared to sacrifice his own position in the interests of a settlement. First he proposed that both men should serve under a third party – perhaps Pitt's elder brother Chatham. Pitt dismissed the idea out of hand. 'Really,' he commented disdainfully, 'I had not the curiosity to ask what I was to be.' Then Addington went still further. He and his most intimate cronies would resign to make way for Pitt – his only condition was that some of the other ministers should survive and a few of his most embittered enemies be, temporarily at least, excluded from office. This too Pitt rejected: he must have absolute freedom to reshape the ministry as he chose. Negotiations broke down. 'It was a foolish business from one end to the other,' grumbled the King. 'It was begun ill, conducted ill and terminated ill.'

So the resumption of war in May 1803 found Addington still in office. His conduct of the war has been much criticised, both at the time and by posterity. Such criticism rests for the most part on the assumption that he was trying to wage the same sort of war as Pitt before him by launching – usually futile – forays in every direction and welding France's continental enemies into new coalitions against Napoleon. But this was not Addington's policy. He believed that the conditions which had made stalemate inevitable in 1801 still obtained. Whoever took the initiative would court disaster; victory would go to the side that remained inactive longest. Napoleon's Army, staring in frustration across the Channel, would either take to the sea and be dealt with by the British Navy or remain ashore and suffer in health and discipline. The strategy was hardly a noble one, nor free from risks, but it was still reasonable and consistent with the view of affairs which had led Addington to conclude the Peace of Amiens. The history of the next few years was to suggest that it was at least as successful as any alternative Pitt had to offer.

On the economic side, certainly, the Prime Minister coped with striking competence. In his budget of 1803 he introduced a new-styled Income Tax based upon fundamentally new principles, introducing a daring innovation which was to survive to the present day and to be known as 'Taxation at the Source'. The results were electrifying. Pitt's Income Tax, at 2 shillings in the pound, had yielded some £5.3 million in 1800; in its first year Addington's new tax, at only 1 shilling in the pound, produced £4.7 million. Though Pitt deplored the innovation in the debate in the House of Commons he made no important changes in his own budget the following year. Addington had laid the economic foundations of the system that was to carry Britain to victory.

Nevertheless, from the moment war was declared, the only question was how long Addington's administration would survive. It is easy to chart the course of the illness, the gradual ebbing away of strength, the phases of fitful recovery, the inevitable relapses and the sudden, catastrophic deterioration which heralded the end. But diagnosis is another matter, for though it was clear that the Government was dying it was harder to understand exactly why.

One problem was that, though its strengths and successes were inconspicuous and slow-maturing, its blunders and weaknesses were embarrassingly obvious. The pattern was set by Addington's pitifully inept performance when he broke the news to the House of Commons that war had been resumed. At such moments a parliament demands inspiration; it got a trickle of stumbling platitudes. Instead Pitt seized the occasion to make one of his greatest speeches – so much so that even Fox had to declare: 'If Demosthenes had been present he must have admired, and might have envied.' Worse followed when the time came to enlist the armies needed for Britain's defence. The Government recruited far more men than it could arm or train and was forced into a humiliating reversal of policy. No other single misfortune could so immediately have diminished its reputation in the eyes of the people at large.

In the last resort, however, it was a question of confidence. All government rests fundamentally on an act of faith: the belief of ministers that they have a right to command and of the people that they have a duty to obey. From Addington's administration the faith had seeped away. 'They are, upon my soul, the feeblest – lowest almost – of men, still more so of Ministers,' wrote the choleric Creevey. It was an absurd misjudgement, but increasingly ministers behaved as if they believed it to be correct. Though the King was still loyal to his favourite prime minister not even he could protect the Government from a combination of Whigs and Pittites, and though Pitt still hesitated to commit himself to all-out assault, Fox's offer to join him in 'solemn union against the Doctor' was a temptation which could not long be resisted.

It was the desertion of Addington's Lord Chancellor, Eldon, that precipitated the end. Acting as self-appointed representative of certain disaffected ministers he opened private negotiations with Pitt and offered to act as intermediary between him and the King. When the keeper of the royal conscience cast himself in such a role, Pitt could hardly be blamed for assuming that the Government was doomed. With every vote Addington's majority in the Commons crumbled further. On 29 April 1803 he told his Cabinet that he could no longer carry on. 'Why are we to part?' asked the King in anguish. 'Can I do nothing to reconcile you and Mr Pitt?' The answer was too obvious to need spelling out; Addington's Government was at an end.

Addington himself claimed to believe that, if he had dissolved Parliament, he could have won an election by a large majority. He did not do so only because he feared to throw the country into confusion while invasion still threatened. His prediction was the less convincing for the care he took not to put it to the test, but it was not wholly ridiculous. There was still much goodwill in the country towards the Doctor and his ministry. Addington had proved himself an honest and usually competent administrator; his conduct of the nation's finances had been always capable and sometimes masterly; his foreign policy and direction of the war had been uninspired but far from disastrous.

Yet few governments can have been more generally denounced or have lost the confidence of so many of their closest supporters. It is this contrast between performance and reputation that provides the most intriguing feature of Addington's administration. His failure, one can only conclude, was primarily a failure of communication, a failure to put himself across so that his authentic talents could be as readily remarked as his equally real but, on the whole, less significant defects. In all he did he seemed to exude an aura of pettiness – 'the indefinable air of a village apothecary inspecting the tongue of the State' was Rosebery's vivid phrase. It was the conviction that he was too small for his job that drove his peers into irrational opposition. His failure was not so much one of achievement as of personality and of will. He was not a bad prime minister but he was bad at behaving like a prime minister and at convincing others that he was an effective prime minister. In the end he could not even convince himself.

In 1803 Addington was forty-six years old. As Lord Sidmouth he had more than thirty years of active political life ahead of him. The supine and fatuous Doctor, butt of the political cartoonists, the 'pitiful, squirting politician . . . not fit for anything but a shop' was to be mysteriously transformed into a harsh and fanatical reactionary who honeycombed Britain with a network of spies and whose policy of repression and persecution drove his country to the verge of revolution. Sidmouth of the Six Acts, of Oliver the *agent provocateur*, of Peterloo, was rivalled only by Castlereagh in the rogues' gallery of the Radicals:

> . . . two vultures sick for battle,
> Two scorpions under one white stone,
> Two bloodless wolves whose dry throats rattle,
> Two crows perched on the murrained cattle,
> Two vipers tangled into one.

It would be out of place to examine here Sidmouth's record as Home Secretary or in the other posts which he filled before his final retirement. A man of deeply conservative disposition with an exaggerated reverence for law and order, it was inevitable that he would gain – and indeed largely earn – the label of diehard reactionary. With no conception that the hideous poverty and misery of the working classes could be in any way the responsibility of government, it would have been futile to look for even a glimmering of reforming zeal. And yet within the moral code of his time he was a humane man, benevolent whenever benevolence seemed in order, fair and, on the whole, moderate where he felt repression was essential. His caricature as a cruel and evil tyrant was still less convincing than the earlier version of a flabby puppet who sprang into political motion only when the strings were pulled by William Pitt.

Indeed, it is his consistency that impresses. At every point in his career his deficiencies were obvious. He lacked imagination and a broad grasp of policy; he lacked flexibility; he lacked enterprise; above all he lacked grandeur and the art of kindling enthusiasm in the public. But he had qualities too. He was determined; he was courageous; he was thorough; he could command the devoted loyalty of his closest friends and allies. And among his qualities were several which are not invariably associated with the trade of politics. Integrity can be a dangerous asset and Addington's inability to conceal or compromise his often wrong-headed principles won him many enemies and little respect. Courtesy is frequently taken as the defence of the feeble and he was often dismissed as a flatterer and a hypocrite. Consideration for others is a grave handicap for the ambitious and he found himself ruthlessly thrust from the path of those with a clearer eye for the main chance. 'I am not aware', he wrote in old age, 'of having ever wilfully injured or given pain to any human being.' It is hardly the boast of a successful politician but it is not a bad epitaph for all that.

BIBLIOGRAPHY

The only recent biography of Addington is Philip Ziegler's own: *A Life of Henry Addington, First Viscount Sidmouth* (London, 1965). George Pellew's three-volume *Life and Correspondence* (London, 1847) is the only other full-scale biography. It is neither stimulating nor reliable. F. O. Darvall's *Popular Disturbances and Public Order in Regency England* (Oxford, 1934), Professor Feiling's *Second Tory Party* (London, 1938) and Steven Watson's *The Reign of George III* (Oxford, 1960) provide useful background to Addington's career. *The Diary and Correspondence of Lord Colchester* (London, 1861) is probably the most relevant of the innumerable biographies and autobiographies which relate to the period.

LORD GRENVILLE

BY

PETER JUPP

William Wyndham Grenville, born 24 October 1759, third son of George Grenville (q.v.) and Elizabeth, daughter of Sir William Wyndham. Educated at Eton and Christ Church, Oxford. Married 1792 the Hon. Anne Pitt, elder daughter of Thomas, 1st Baron Camelford. PC 1783; created Baron Grenville 1790. MP for Buckingham 1782–4 and Co. Buckingham 1784–1790. Chief Secretary 1782–3; Paymaster-General 1783; Joint Paymaster-General 1784–9; Board of Control 1784–90 (President 1790–1793); Vice-President of the Board of Trade 1786–9. Speaker of the House of Commons 1789; Home Secretary 1789–91; Foreign Secretary 1791–1801; Auditor of the Exchequer 1794 until death in 1834; First Lord of the Treasury 1806–7. Chancellor of the University of Oxford 1810 until death on 12 January 1834.

William Grenville, 1st Baron Grenville, by John Hoppner

LORD GRENVILLE

The news of Pitt's death, as it sped through London on 23 January 1806, cast gloom upon a dim and uncertain future. The Government, as it confronted the opening of Parliament on the 26th, was weak and in need of reinforcement; the continental situation, in the wake of Ulm, Austerlitz and the capitulation of Prussia, was perilous. Lord Grenville, Pitt's cousin, heard the news at Camelford House on the corner of Oxford Street and Park Lane. Deeply saddened, he scribbled a note to his brother, the Marquis of Buckingham, that he was retiring immediately to Dropmore, his country residence in Buckinghamshire, where he hoped to 'restore my mind tolerably to its level'; he added that he would return to London in two or three days 'at latest'.[1]

Grenville's concern to return to London reflected the general view that he would be involved in any negotiations leading to the formation of a new government. Together with the 'Grenvilles' (the thirty or so relations, friends and supporters who looked to him for political guidance), he was associated with the Foxite whigs in a loose opposition coalition formed in March 1804 to urge more effective measures of domestic policy. With more than a hundred supporters, the coalition was, after the Pittites, the largest single party in the Commons. Furthermore, his long service under Pitt until 1801 and the sincere respect between the two men since then, encouraged some Pittites to regard him as only temporarily estranged from their cause and as a likely future ally. Finally, few could match his administrative experience, particularly in the field of foreign affairs. In terms of his political pedigree and the strength of his party associations he had strong claims to office and perhaps, to the premiership. As an individual, however, he possessed qualities of character and ability, which at both the private and public levels made these claims less formidable.

In public Grenville appeared (as in his portrait) to be of singularly strong, self-willed and independent character: cold and distant and deserving of the nickname 'boguey' or bugbear.[2] This exterior, however,

[1] Huntington Library, Stowe MSS, STG Box 41 (4).
[2] Applied as early as 1787. See Countess of Minto, *Life and Letters of Sir Gilbert Elliot* (London, 1874), i, 140.

concealed tensions between his personal instincts and proclivities and the normal demands of public life. The main feature of his private life was his dependence upon a narrow family circle in which he neither assumed nor aspired to a dominant role. The youngest of three sons, his parents died when he was a young boy and he soon fell under the influence of Buckingham, to whom he was to accord constant gratitude and deference. In the world beyond his relation's homes and estates he was ill at ease and insecure. His marriage to a distant cousin in 1792, and their move to a small estate in Buckinghamshire, has therefore a special significance. Dropmore became an increasingly welcome retreat from public life – a sanctuary where he could develop his strong inclination for the private study of classical literature and religion. Within a year or two of leaving office in 1801, domestic habits had taken a firm root. In October 1803 he wrote: 'I can hardly keep wondering at my own folly in thinking it worthwhile to leave my books and garden, even for one day's attendance in the House of Lords.'[3]

The main feature of his public life was his relatively modest ambitions. His decision to enter politics was the inevitable choice of a younger son of no estate and with a very small income.[4] Later, as he scaled the political ladder, he was continually torn between settling for financial security in a modest political backwater and the more glittering prospects that went with the key offices of state. By 1794 political independence had come with a peerage while financial security had been achieved with the sinecure office of auditor of the Exchequer. His course thereafter was beset with fears of the effects of office upon his health and his domestic life. These fears persisted after his resignation in 1801 and were a reason for his unwillingness to adopt the role of a party *leader* with any vigour. As he put the matter to his banker in April 1805: 'I deprecate any event which would again impose on me the burthen of fatigue and disquietude inseparable from a public situation.'[5]

Grenville's political thinking was strongly conservative. With regard to the Constitution he believed that measures of economical reform had, by the beginning of 1783, produced a reasonable balance between the powers of the Crown, executive and Parliament. Government, he thought, was best conducted by a strong Cabinet system and he dis-

[3] The Duke of Buckingham, *The Court and Cabinets of George III* (London, 1855), iii, 331.
[4] Approximately £1,500 in 1782.
[5] Coutts MSS 1090: Grenville to Thomas Coutts, 28 April 1805.

approved strongly of 'the wretched system of a Cabinet of cyphers, and a government of one man alone',[6] which he deduced was a feature of Pitt's last ministry. As for MPs and their attitude to political issues, he believed that actions should be guided by informed considerations of policy and took the view that 'systematic' opposition was foolish and dishonest. After 1801 he eschewed such a course and insisted upon purely 'prospective' opposition.

Abroad he looked to a stable Europe and an expanding Empire. He thought that the first objective was best achieved by the subduing of Republican France by continental armies subsidised by Britain, a policy he had pursued as Foreign Secretary and which was hotly opposed by Fox. As for the Empire, he believed that its future depended upon the success of his European policy but that in the interim, policies should be governed by the requirements of security. Thus in the case of Ireland he supported the Union and Catholic emancipation as ways of quietening a troublesome dependency.

As for his authority in the political world, it rested almost entirely upon his prodigious capacity for hard work, his experience in nearly every department of state, and hardly at all upon a personal magnetism. After 1801 his prominence derived from his trenchant attacks upon government policies and his view that Britain's future depended upon an ordered policy in which the priorities were: first, a union of political parties headed preferably by Pitt – a ministry of all the talents; second, the stabilisation of Ireland by Catholic emancipation and the strengthening of Britain by a reorganisation of her armed forces and a reform of her national finance. These were the qualities which enabled his friends and relations and the Foxite Whigs to look to him for their future. For the arts of leadership and the managing of policy he had little aptitude. His preference, as he said himself, was to 'rather follow than lead',[7] and when confronted with the problem of finding the means to suit the ends of policy he had often displayed an inflexibility of mind and a weakness of spirit.

As Grenville mourned, the King consulted his ministers in the hope that they could reshuffle their pack and continue in office. They refused, arguing their weakness in the Commons; instead they advised the King to consult Grenville. He was their obvious choice for of the other party

[6] *Court and Cabinets*, iii, 422.
[7] Fitzpatrick, W. (ed.), *The Dropmore Papers* (HMSO, 1892), i, 194.

leaders Fox, as Pitt's bitterest enemy, and Sidmouth, who had recently resigned from the Government, were out of the question. In addition, many Pittites recognised that Grenville's views upon foreign policy were similar to their own, and some predicted that if this were to break the loose coalition between the Grenvilles and the Foxites then he would have to look to them for support.[8] Grenville simply appeared the best insurance for the survival of Pittite policies and, perhaps, their return to office. The King reluctantly accepted their advice and on 27 January asked Grenville to prepare a plan of government 'without exclusion', thereby recognising that the serious situation demanded that he accept Fox into Cabinet rank.[9]

In the construction of the Government during the following three weeks Grenville's initial steps were hesitant. The King asked him to plan, not to form, a government and he initially expressed his reluctance to take the position of First Lord and urged the claims of Lord Spencer.[10] His reasons were an unwillingness to take the lead and a concern that by so doing he would be obliged to resign his auditorship of the Exchequer, leaving him in the situation in which 'I should in fact receive no addition to my present income and must incur a very great additional expense'.[11] When pressed by his brothers and by Fox, who agreed to introduce a Bill enabling the auditorship to be conveyed to a trustee, thus guaranteeing Grenville's financial security, his reluctance to take the lead was assuaged. From that moment (30 January) his course was more determined and he set about trying to form a government which in terms of both policy and personnel would have some flexibility in the future. The King's objections to the Government's plan to reorganise the administration of the Army and do away with the power and patronage of the commander-in-chief, his son the Duke of York, were firmly resisted. On 3 February, having agreed to the first list of recommended appointments, the King expressed himself as satisfied with Grenville's insistence that he and his colleagues required time to prepare measures

[8] See e.g. Rev. L. V. Harcourt, *Diaries and Correspondence of George Rose* (London, 1860), ii, 313; Scottish RO, Melville MSS: Robert Dundas to Melville, 11 Feb. 1806.
[9] It is interesting that on the morning of 22 Jan. the King held a long conversation with Buckingham's close friend, W. H. Fremantle, about the Grenvilles and their likely course in office. (Huntington Library, Stowe MSS, STG Box 33 (17): Fremantle to Buckingham, 24 Jan. 1806.)
[10] *Court and Cabinets*, iv, 15-16; *Dropmore Papers*, vii, 346-7: Auckland to Grenville, 28 Jan. 1806.
[11] Stowe MSS, STG Box 41 (5): Grenville to Buckingham, 30 Jan. 1806.

in detail and that they recognised his right to veto any they submitted to him.[12]

As to the political character of the Government Grenville believed that in view of the 'evils and dangers' that faced the country, it should rest ideally 'upon the most extended basis' and include all four political parties.[13] The obstacles in the way of achieving such a policy immediately were certainly forbidding. The opposition of the Foxites to a Commons vote of funeral honours to Pitt on 27 January had indicated their hostility to such a course and determined some Pittites that they could not take a part. In addition, it was doubtful whether the number of offices available could accommodate the pretensions of more than three of the parties. Nevertheless if Grenville had been in a vigorous frame of mind he could have set himself above the claims of his immediate colleagues and made the attempt. He did not. Instead he adopted the more modest course of trying to persuade some junior members of the old Government to stay in office and to keep the door open for future admissions by insisting upon 'no proscription' against Pittites in matters of patronage and a benevolent attitude to their past conduct in government.[14] Even this proved too modest a policy to succeed and when Grenville made firm offers, to Lord Bathurst to remain at the Mint and to Charles Long to stay in Ireland and become Chancellor of the Irish Exchequer, they were refused as not being sufficient to attach the Pittites as a body to the Government.[15] Only a pale reflection of the policy remained. Fox intimated that it might be a good idea to admit Pittites in the future and a few of their number, including Canning, Castlereagh and Perceval, felt that enough had been done to determine them not to refuse to take a hand when the right opportunity arose.[16]

The Government was therefore constructed from three of the four parties. Lord Sidmouth and his thirty or so Commons votes were taken in because this step was warmly recommended by the Prince of Wales (who regarded himself as guardian to the new administration), and

[12] *Dropmore Papers*, viii, 8–9: the King to Grenville, 3 Feb. 1806; Northants RO, Fitzwilliam MSS: Grenville to Fitzwilliam, 3 Feb. 1806.
[13] *Dropmore Papers*, vii, 332: Grenville to Wellesley, 23 Jan. 1806; British Museum Additional MS 41852, folios 213–16: Grenville to T. Grenville, 24 Jan. 1806.
[14] Public Record Office, Granville MSS: Morpeth to Leveson Gower, 7 Feb. 1806; *Dropmore Papers*, viii, 44–5.
[15] BM Fortescue MSS: Bathurst and Long to Grenville, 7 Feb. 1806.
[16] *Diaries and Correspondence of George Rose*, ii, 246–51; Countess Granville, *Private Correspondence of Lord Granville Leveson Gower* (London, 1916), ii, 178.

because it suited Grenville's desire for a comprehensive government.[17] Sidmouth became Lord Privy Seal, and his acolyte Lord Ellenborough Lord Chief Justice with a seat in the Cabinet, an appointment which, as it united judicial and excutive functions in one person, caused a minor storm in the Commons. The remaining Cabinet posts and the bulk of the junior appointments were dealt out amongst the Foxites and the Grenvilles in a proportion to their voting strength in the Commons which favoured the Grenvilles. Five Cabinet posts went to the Foxites, Fox at last becoming Foreign Secretary, and three, including Spencer at the Home Office and William Windham as Secretary at War, to the Grenvilles. A number of critics concluded that this was 'a Fox or a Sidmouth Government with a little of Lord Grenville', but this was far from the truth.[18] Admittedly the omission of Grenville's brothers appeared a sign of weakness but then Buckingham made it clear that he did not want to load 'a cart already too heavily charged', while Tom Grenville had no wish to attend Parliament with any frequency.[19] However, the notion rested upon little more than a casual glance at the list of appointments. Close study would have revealed that while Fox and his friends were strong in the Commons and clearly dominated foreign affairs, the Grenvilles controlled the efficient offices connected with domestic policy. As First Lord of the British and Irish Treasuries, with a (Foxite) Chancellor of the Exchequer in Lord Henry Petty who at twenty-six was too young and inexperienced to stray far from his orbit, and with friends taking two of the three junior lordships of the Treasury, the senior and vice-presidencies of the Board of Trade and the Irish Exchequer, Grenville took a firm control of financial policy. With Spencer at the Home Office he had the last word in Irish and, as it transpired, Scottish affairs, including the all-important question of the distribution of patronage. And finally there was Windham who, as an old colleague under Pitt and an early associate in opposition to Addington, was at least within Grenville's sphere of influence if not a slavish Grenvillite. In terms of numbers and debating strength the Government was largely Foxite; in terms of decision-making Grenville's influence was certainly as strong as that of Fox. Further, Grenville was regarded by his colleagues from the outset as the effective head of the Government.

Of more accuracy were the gibes that this was far from being a

[17] Devon RO, Sidmouth MSS: Sheridan to Sidmouth, n.d. (30 Jan. 1806).
[18] Carlisle R.O., Lonsdale MSS: Robert Ward to Lonsdale, 1 Feb. 1806.
[19] Bucks R.O., Cottesloe MSS: Buckingham to Fremantle, 27 Jan. 1806.

ministry of all the talents. The absence of the leading Pittites made that inevitable but Grenville had at least kept the door open for them. The omission from high office of those peacocks in the Whig camp – Sheridan, Tierney and Whitbread – was certainly striking, and can be accounted for by Grenville's distaste for them and their pretensions and Fox's instinctive preference for men of more considerable social standing. However, in filling up the sixty or so vacancies and dealing with the flood of applications for favours, Grenville looked to talent and efficiency rather than to ornamental qualities. He deliberately kept his Cabinet as slim as possible, did his best to avoid the appointment of nonentities to junior posts, and took little interest in creating peers, baronets and privy councillors. He even eschewed an earldom for himself.[20] Nevertheless it was not a ministry of *all* the talents as Grenville had initially hoped and what talent it precisely possessed was yet to be discovered.

The main lines of policy were established by the end of March at a series of Cabinet meetings which exhibited 'the most perfect and cordial harmony'.[21] One reason for this unexpected feature was the division of responsibilities between Fox and Grenville. The other was that in the field of foreign affairs the differences between the two men had dissolved under the hammer blows that Bonaparte had inflicted upon the third coalition. By the end of December 1805 France had occupied large portions of the Austrian Empire, given Russia her marching orders from Moravia, Hungary and Galicia and had forced Prussia to a treaty. The differences between Fox and Grenville over the virtue of fighting the war with continental allies became merely 'speculative'.[22] In addition, the previous Government left little behind it in the way of contingency planning and Grenville was thus able to lend himself in mid-February to Fox's attempt to negotiate peace. His view was that any terms agreed by the French would prove unacceptable to Britain, but that sufficient time would be bought to consolidate the country's strength for the inevitable struggle ahead. Fox, for his part, proved to be more than the submissive negotiator that Grenville had feared. He agreed that the basis of any terms should be '*uti possidetis*', and that

[20] BM Add. MS 41852, folios 225–6, 251: Grenville to T. Grenville, 30 Jan., 26 Mar. 1806.
[21] *Dropmore Papers*, viii, 107–8: Grenville to Fox, 19 April 1806.
[22] *Court and Cabinets*, iv, 12–13: Grenville to Buckingham, 14 (not as printed 13) Jan. 1806.

Britain should insist upon a joint negotiation with her ally Russia, as a means of laying the basis for future continental co-operation against France. Further, he entered fully into the measures taken against Prussia as a result of her annexation of Hanover in February 1806. Thus until Fox's health deteriorated in late June there were few differences in the Cabinet upon foreign affairs,[23] leaving Grenville able to concentrate upon the cultivation of what he was later to refer to as a 'defensive and husbanding system' on the domestic front.[24]

Grenville's strong preference for a 'system' that emphasised the need for domestic security flowed from a number of considerations. It derived from his view that Britain was in a perilous position; it built upon the basis of the co-operation established between the Foxites and the Grenvilles; it demonstrated his anxiety to obtain a political consensus and it reflected his instinct for 'systematic' government. Its central features were as follows. First, a reorganisation of the armed services which Grenville, in the company of others, had been urging since the renewal of the war with France. Second, a reform of national finances so as to deal with the recurring problem of raising enough money to pay for the war. Third, a policy of 'conciliation' towards Ireland in terms of both political management and measures, combined with a strengthening of the Union. Grenville's reasoning as to management was that the traditional distribution of Irish offices upon political grounds strengthened divisions within the Protestant ascendancy, alienated Catholics from the administrative system and made the task of managing the Irish MPs in the interest of government more difficult. Fourth, the adoption of the similar principle of 'moderation' with regard to Scottish patronage in order to unite the Scottish MPs in support of government and as a means of ensuring that 'the administration of Scotland should no longer be considered as separate from the rest of the Empire'. And, finally, the avoidance of measures that would force the Pittites into active opposition. In short, Grenville had in mind a United Kingdom prepared for the vicissitudes of war if Fox failed to secure an honourable peace.[25]

[23] See e.g. BM Add. MS 47569, folios 275-8: Fox to Bedford, 26 April 1806.
[24] BM Fortescue MSS: Grenville to Fitzwilliam, 9 Jan. 1809 (copy).
[25] This view of Grenville's policy depends upon a quantity of documents too numerous to mention here. For Ireland, however, see in particular BM Add. MS 47569, f. 284: Fox to Bedford, 13 May 1806; for Scotland, Scottish RO, Melville MSS: Robert Dundas to Melville, 26 Feb. 1806; BM Add. MS 41852, f. 241: Grenville to T. Grenville, 6 Mar. 1806; BM Fortescue MSS: Grenville to the Marquis of Douglas, 27 June 1806.

When the parliamentary session ended on 23 July, Grenville had failed to impress this cautious programme upon the minds of his colleagues as a blueprint for positive action. This was one reason for its general lack of success. He simply had no experience of firm leadership. In earlier days Pitt had solved the problem by restricting his Cabinet confidants to less than a handful and, in order to concentrate upon essentials, had often dropped whole areas of policy. Grenville, on the other hand, in conformity with his expressed hostility to government 'by one man alone',[26] took everyone into his confidence, and while allowing departmental heads a fair degree of independence, attempted constant supervision of all their activities. Moreover, rather than adopting a policy of supervision by a few brisk directives, Grenville preferred to cosset and coddle. He even moved from Oxford Street to 10 Downing Street in order to be close at hand, a move which he regarded as 'irksome' and which annoyed the Chancellor of the Exchequer who argued that the house was annexed to his office and not that of the First Lord.[27] The result was that instead of impressing the overall strategy of government upon his colleagues, he found himself attending to the details of its individual components. This diffusion of energy was carried further by his taking up matters that were extraneous to his real purpose, such as the reform of the Scottish court of session, the giving of statutory permanence to a proclamation prohibiting the importation of African negroes into colonies acquired during the war, and, throughout June, the investigation into the conduct of the Princess of Wales, the report of which he largely wrote himself. He therefore indulged his capacity for business and neglected its management with the result that few, if any, of his colleagues were given a clear idea of the direction in which they were travelling.

The other reasons why government measures failed to impress the parliamentary public lie more with lack of time to prepare them properly and the weaknesses and inexperience of individual ministers.[28] The reorganisation of the armed services amounted to no more than an

[26] See p. 255.
[27] *Dropmore Papers*, viii, 20-1; BM Fortescue MSS: Grenville to the Bishop of Lincoln, 15 April 1806. He moved to 10 Downing St, in April. There he found Hoppner's portrait of Pitt and hung it in a place where it would escape dust.
[28] A detailed study of the Government's measures can be found in A. D. Harvey, 'The Talents Ministry', *Historical Journal*, xv (4), 619-49. I have therefore only provided references for details or interpretations not found there.

increase in Navy pay and Windham's army plan which was novel only in that it dealt at a stroke with all three forces – the militia, volunteers and regular. Its central features were a pruning of the militia and the volunteers and the application of the long-discussed principle of limited service to the Regular Army in order to improve recruitment. Lack of time to prepare the measures properly and Windham's inability to think a problem through produced measures which reduced the volunteers but failed to increase recruitment into the regulars. Further, Windham's slackness in presenting his plan in the Commons, combined with his caustic criticism of the much loved volunteers – 'painted cherries', he once called them – alienated the country gentlemen and the Pittites.

In the financial sphere, where Grenville's authority was strongest, the Government proved to be unprepared for an immediate comprehensive measure. The budget had to be presented quickly and as a result Grenville and Petty fell back upon measures largely foreshadowed by their predecessor. Two acts improved methods of public accounting: the treasurership of the ordnance was regulated and a watchful eye kept upon the matter of reversionary offices. As to the budget, the property tax was raised, as had been widely expected, and in order to meet the remaining deficit the assessed taxes were raided after an attempt to produce the money from two alternative sources had been beaten off in Parliament. This package, which tended to underline the need for comprehensive reform, again led to severe Pittite criticisms.

As to Ireland, Grenville's policy prevailed, although only after a Foxite shot across its unionist bows. Immediately prior to the Government's taking office, Fox had inferred in the Commons that he would like to repeal the Union. Passions in Ireland waxed warm[29] until Fox, when in office, retracted. This conversion symbolised Grenville's control over Irish affairs. When the new Viceroy, the Duke of Bedford, left for Ireland in March, he had agreed to pursue the 'system of conciliation' in matters of patronage[30] and although Fox later lamented his acquiescence, it was largely upheld.

In the case of Scotland, the prospect of a Whig manager of patronage was killed and Pitt's friends were assured that in that sphere Grenville

[29] Dublin SPO, 531/225/3: Charles Long to Marsden, 17 Feb. 1806; BM Fortescue MSS: Lord Glandore to Grenville, 27 Feb. 1806.
[30] Durham University, Grey MSS, Box 6, file 17 (8, 9): Bedford to Howick, 5 Jan. 1807 and reply on 15 Jan.

and Spencer would have the last word.[31] Scottish party politics, however, proved more difficult to manage than the Irish, and by July the
policy was beginning to creak and groan under the weight of the
mutual suspicions of both the Whigs and the Pittites.

In several respects, therefore, Grenville's plan had come to very
little. This, together with the fact that the conduct of government
business was admitted by even a junior minister to be 'loose and
desultory'[32] led the Pittites to abandon their policy of 'forbearance' and,
in June and July, to enter into spirited opposition.[33] Throughout this
campaign the Government maintained sufficient majorities but it was
generally admitted that it could not take on another session without
some addition to its debating strength. It was reported that Lord
Lowther told Grenville to his face that 'the weight of debate (Fox of
course excepted, but Fox only) was wholly on the side of the Opposition', that 'the Government was thought and felt to be exceedingly
inadequate; that upon this point country gentlemen and others not
politicians, felt sore and ashamed; and were obliged to confess, that the
Opposition made the Government appear weak and ridiculous.'[34]

Thus by the end of the session Grenville was confronted with severe
problems. His 'system' had made little impression upon his ministers,
and they in turn had hardly made a favourable impression upon Parliament. He was no doubt aware of his difficulties. As early as May he had
confessed to Buckingham that he did not believe his continuance in
office could do much good and might well 'destroy my own happiness'.[35]
His confidence might well have declined further had it not been for the
steady deterioration in Fox's health during July and the fact that the
full control of the Government fell into his hands. By force of circumstance, Grenville's attention was diverted from domestic security
and the difficulties he had encountered, to strengthening the Government in the House of Commons and the direction of foreign policy.

On 16 July he adopted the comforting but hardly imaginative policy
of introducing his brother Tom into the Cabinet as President of the
Board of Control. During August he negotiated with George Canning of the Opposition, but finding him unwilling to act separately

[31] See p. 258.
[32] *Dropmore Papers*, viii, 285: Auckland to Grenville, 16 Aug. 1806.
[33] Welbeck MSS: Canning to Titchfield, 26 April 1806.
[34] Harewood MSS: Canning to his wife, 16 June 1806, reporting Lowther's remarks.
[35] *Court and Cabinets*, iv, 29–31.

263

from his colleagues decided (after some wavering) that he could not introduce the Pittites as a party into the Government. When Fox died on 13 September Grenville was therefore forced to reshuffle his Cabinet from the three parties in the Government.[36] His real hope was to put Windham out of harm's way by elevating him to the Lords and thus allow Tom Grenville to take one of the two remaining secretary-ships of state that could be held in the Commons, thereby strengthening his own influence. Windham refused, however, and Grenville did not insist. Instead he fell back upon putting Lord Howick into Fox's place and Tom Grenville into that of Howick at the Admiralty. As his brother was not regarded as a first-class debater, the accession of strength was minimal.

On the continental front Grenville began to broaden the range of policy to the point where a basis for comprehensive allied action was its main aim. On 4 September, having heard that the Tsar had rejected any possibility of a separate treaty with France, he put Britain's negotia-tions in Paris upon a footing in which the accommodation of Russia was a priority. In the instructions sent to Paris, emphasis was placed upon the need to recognise Russia's special interests in the Adriatic and the Mediterranean; in particular, a firm resolution was taken that as Russia requested, Britain would insist that Sicily be retained by the King of Naples. Further, the terms of 'uti possidetis' were added to by the inclusion of Buenos Aires, the news of whose capture by a free-booting British force arrived on 12 September. When it became known that Prussia was showing a determination to resist Bonaparte's encircling movements, Grenville requested that the Foreign Office consider the formation of a Northern League to which Britain would be a party. On 20 September the Cabinet decided to open negotiations with Prussia for the restitution of Hanover and the establishment of a general con-

---

[36] A warm feeling had existed between Grenville and Fox since their political association in 1804. However, Grenville never found it easy to deal with friends outside his family circle and he was never upon intimate terms with him. The nature of the relationship is captured by a few words he said to Lord Lauderdale on 31 July just as that close friend of Fox was leaving an interview he had had with the Prime Minister. He said that 'he had many times abstained from going to Stable Yard (where Fox lived), from an apprehension that if Mr Fox should know he was there, he might suppose he was come upon business and make an effort to see him, which might do him harm; but that if he followed the dictates of his own inclination, he should be there every day.' (The Earl of Ilchester, *The Journal of Lady Holland* (London, 1908), ii, 171.)

cert. On 3 October, two days after Prussia presented France with an ultimatum, he was willing to consider a Prussian subsidy, a matter which he concluded would certainly require endorsement by Parliament before Christmas. And finally, a fresh look was given to the feasibility of putting a British force upon the Continent.[37]

As Grenville took these tentative steps forward, news arrived in London on 8 October that the Paris negotiations had broken down over the question of Sicily. In view of this and the outbreak of the Franco–Prussian war, he concluded that 'vigorous resolutions' might be called for, which, if taken, would require the sanction of Parliament. The question was therefore raised of the Government's security in the existing House of Commons. Despite the fact that it had enjoyed sufficient majorities in June and July, Grenville concluded that it was less than gilt-edged. His reconstructed Cabinet desperately needed a boost to its strength and authority. Further, there were persistent rumours that members of the Opposition were to be seen at Windsor and were undermining the King's confidence in his ministers. Grenville therefore decided to seek a general election. As governments did not lose general elections at this time, it would increase the Government's strength and, as the power of dissolving Parliament rested with the King, would, if granted, demonstrate clearly his support of the Government. In short, Grenville sought absolute security at home before venturing abroad. On 12 October he requested, and the next day received, the King's agreement to a dissolution of Parliament.

In principle his policy was safe and sound. In practice, however, while it increased the Government's strength by about forty votes, it diverted Grenville's attention still further from the overall direction of policy. He took upon himself the management of the election campaign in which, in conformity with his earlier policy of 'moderation', he attempted to see that government favour was given to those who were generally in support of the Government rather than simply to thick and thin party men.[38] This ensured that the campaign was particularly complicated and onerous. As Bonaparte followed up his decisive victory

---

[37] *Dropmore Papers*, viii, 312 (Cabinet minute), 324–6, 352–5; A. Aspinall (ed.), *The Later Correspondence of George III* (Cambridge, 1962–70), iv, 471–5; Durham University, Grey MSS, Box 21, file 2: Grenville to Howick, 27 Sept., 3, 11 Oct. 1806, which indicate Grenville's superintendence of foreign affairs.

[38] For the 1806 general election consult M. G. Hinton, 'The General Elections of 1806 and 1807', an unpublished University of Reading PhD thesis.

over the Prussians at Jena on 14 October, the British Prime Minister threw himself into decisions about the merits of this or that electoral interest in a hundred and one far-flung places.

Thus when the new Parliament assembled on 15 December, Grenville was mentally tired and in no mood to spirit his Cabinet into the 'vigorous resolutions' that the allies were now demanding in the wake of the French occupation of Berlin on 25 October. Prussia requested a subsidy; Russia, extended credit; and Sweden some money to strengthen her forces at Stralsund, a port that gave British commerce access to northern Europe and could be used as a springboard for a military adventure in Bonaparte's rear. Throughout the period during which the Cabinet considered these matters (until 18 March), it was strongly affected by Grenville's gloom and despondency at the failure of Prussia and his view that without more independent resolution on her part 'a complete submission of the Continent under the name of peace' was likely before the spring.[39] Thus instead of making a warm response to outstretched hands, he allowed arguments against positive action to prevail and showed more enthusiasm for what were essentially diversions, such as the recapture of Buenos Aires, which had been lost almost as soon as it was won, various schemes that the Board of Trade put forward for enriching colonial trade, and, to some extent, a naval attack upon Turkey, then at war with Russia. A mere pittance was offered to Prussia; suspicions that Russia would be unable to meet the interest upon British credit, and fears that Parliament might not sanction what might amount to a loan resulted in an offer that proved offensive to Russian dignity. As for the Baltic, consideration of the fact that British action at sea or upon land would require warm weather and either Denmark's co-operation or defeat led to indecision. And finally, the question of military action at any point on the Continent was complicated in the minds of ministers by fears of the cost and the likely drain upon defensive forces which they still regarded as inadequate. It is true that some of Grenville's colleagues were opposed almost as a matter of principle to both continental alliances and the prospect of military action in Europe, and that if he had decided upon vigorous measures, he would have had to battle hard in the Cabinet. However, the firm conclusion to be drawn from the evidence of the Cabinet's deliberations is that numbed by Prussia's defeat, Grenville failed to bring his colleagues to clear-cut decisions. Once again he chose to concentrate upon domestic

[39] *Court and Cabinets*, iv, 127.

security. Here the burden upon Grenville proved considerable and under its impact his thinking narrowed to the point at which he became convinced that security depended upon the success of his policies in two of the three remaining areas that he had regarded as government priorities on coming into office: national finance and Ireland.

Since his resignation in 1801 Grenville had become increasingly interested in the question of political economy, and upon taking office in 1806 had looked for a comprehensive answer to the question of raising money for an extended war. During December and January he produced with the advice of Petty and others 'our great plan', which sought to peg war taxes at an acceptable minimum through the creation of an extra Sinking Fund.[40] Although a lively debate upon its merits took place over the next six years, it seems likely that if it had been put into full operation it would not have succeeded.[41] However in the first two months of 1807 the important fact is that it was not received with any enthusiasm in Parliament and in fact was virulently attacked by Canning and Castlereagh in the middle of February. One of the bases upon which Grenville hoped to make Britain capable of extended offensive or defensive action was thereby undermined. This seems to have stiffened his resolve, at a critical time in the life of the Government, that in Ireland his policies had to succeed.

In the case of Ireland it was characteristic of Grenville's thinking that he was to regard the policy he eventually decided upon as the solution to a range of problems that the Government confronted in its quest for security. In the autumn of 1806 serious disturbances occurred in the midland and western counties and there was some evidence that they were connected with republican feeling and French agitators. At approximately the same time the Catholic leaders in Dublin intimated that they would seek to petition the new Parliament for Catholic emancipation. For a long time Grenville had believed that stability in Ireland was essential to Britain's security; he also knew that the King would not countenance Catholic emancipation and that a Catholic petition would be likely to divide and destroy his Cabinet. For the

---

[40] BM Fortescue MSS: Grenville to Wellesley, 26 Jan. 1813; the collection also contains a file of papers relating to the plan, in which it seems likely that David Ricardo had a hand.

[41] Its main defect was to fix war expenditure at an annual sum of £32 million, which was soon exceeded. For a lengthy discussion of the plan see A. Alison, *History of Europe* (London, 1848), x, 198–208.

future he therefore looked to a comprehensive (but diversionary) policy comprising tithe reform, an increase in the parliamentary grant to the Roman Catholic College at Maynooth, state provision for the Catholic clergy and a reform of the Established Church.[42] For the present he decided upon extending to the United Kingdom the Irish Act of 1793 which allowed Catholics to hold commissions in the Army up to the rank of general. To Grenville's mind this measure would kill three birds with one stone. It would pass as a limited concession to Catholics and perhaps forestall the presentation of a petition. It would, by enabling Catholic officers to serve in Britain, solve some of the problems created by the failure of Windham's Army plans.[43] Finally, as Catholic regiments were to be raised in the west of Ireland, it would curb the disaffection there without recourse to the proclaiming of whole areas under the terms of the dreaded Insurrection Act.

If Grenville had decided upon the extension of the precise terms of the Irish Act (a measure which it could be argued was complementary to his general policy of completing the Union), then the Government would have survived longer into history. He did not. Instead he decided in the first week of February, as a result of sustained pressure from the Catholic leaders in Ireland for a substantial concession, that the terms of the Act had to be added to so as to enable Catholics to be generals on the staff.[44] As a result of that decision he was confronted over the next five weeks with two main problems. The first was that when the matter was brought to the King's attention, he was to be persuaded to agree to an extension of the terms of the Act to Britain but not to any addition to them. The second was that Lord Sidmouth threatened his resignation if the terms were added to, while Lord Howick appeared destined to leave the already fragile Treasury bench for the House of Lords in view of the imminent death of his father.

Grenville did not choose to meet any of these problems head on. He

[42] *Dropmore Papers*, viii, 486–8: Grenville to Bedford, 29 Dec. 1806, which should be compared with Lord Holland's memorandum of ministerial discussions on the Irish question of 17 Dec. 1806 in the Holland House MSS.

[43] As early as August Grenville had calculated the likely deficit in the regular forces and had concluded that extra Catholic troops would be required for overseas duties. (Huntington Library, Stowe MSS, STG Box 170 (12), 7 Aug. 1806.)

[44] Detailed narratives of the crisis over the Irish question can be found in M. Roberts, *The Whig Party 1807–12*, pp. 7–34; M. G. Hinton, 'The General Elections of 1806 and 1807', and A. Aspinall (ed.), *The Later Correspondence of George III*, iv, xxxviii–xli.

did not clarify to the King the situation with regard to the Catholic question, partly as a result of a genuine misunderstanding as to the King's views, and partly because of his fears of the King's likely reaction. As to the problems of the Cabinet, he once again threw out a lifeline to Canning, although on this occasion he considered broadening the base of the Government to include both Pittites and radical members of the Whig party.[45]

Neither parry succeeded. The King was forced to clarify the Catholic question to the Cabinet by making it clear on 13 March that he would not accept a measure that did not conform exactly with the terms of the Irish Act of 1793. The following day Canning threw back the lifeline and urged upon Grenville the general view of the Opposition that he should drop the Catholic measure (now in the form of a Bill) and stay in office.[46] Thus when the Cabinet met on 15 March neither the King nor the Opposition was pressing for the Government's removal. In order to stay in office Grenville had to choose between two alternatives, neither of which was particularly attractive. He could either modify the Bill until it conformed exactly with the terms of the Irish Act or drop it altogether. In either case he would have to confront the wrath of those in the Cabinet who were now determined to stand by the enlarged measure and that of the Catholic leaders in Dublin. On the other hand, neither course would be opposed by the King and most of the Pittites. However, Grenville was in no mood to take on a struggle with his friends. Constant participation in the problems of every government department, and the piloting through the Lords of new measures to reform the Scottish court of session and to abolish the slave trade had borne him down. To be confronted now with the problem of managing a policy he regarded as essential to his whole 'defensive and husbanding system' proved too much. On 7 March he had informed Buckingham that he longed 'daily and hourly' . . . 'for the moment when my friends will allow me to think that I have fully discharged (by a life of hitherto incessant labour) every claim that they, or the country can have upon me'. He continued with a thought prompted by problems elsewhere but which well applies to those he confronted with his Cabinet: 'I want one great and essential quality for my station, and every hour increases the difficulty . . . I am not competent to the

[45] Harewood MSS: Canning to his wife, 4, 7, 11–14 Feb. 1807, are particularly valuable sources.
[46] ibid., Canning to his wife, 17, 18, 20 Mar. 1807.

management of men. I never was so naturally and toil and anxiety more and more unfit me for it'.[47] In this mood Grenville sought for himself and his friends an honourable release. On 17 March the Cabinet agreed to drop the Bill but reserved the right to express their views as individuals on the Catholic question, a move that given the King's sensibilities was tantamount to asking him to look for another government. On 18 March, having asked and been refused the Cabinet's agreement not to raise the Catholic question to him again, this is exactly what the King set about doing. In his resolution to retire from office, Grenville had sought to secure a politically face-saving dismissal.[48]

Having therefore failed to achieve the security he believed necessary to his country, Grenville returned quickly to Dropmore. On 20 March Lord Howick requested him to attend a meeting to discuss measures of opposition. He replied: 'I feel very repugnant to any course of active opposition having been most unaffectedly disinclined to take upon myself the task in which I have been engaged and feeling no small pleasure in an honourable release, I could not bring myself to struggle much to get my chains on again.'[49] Nor did he, although for the next ten years he lingered on in public life as an ill-fitting and ever-drooping figurehead to the Whig party.

Five days after he had replied to Howick's letter, he surrendered his seals of office. On the same day the royal assent was given to the measure that would stand to the lasting credit of the ministry of 'all the talents' – the abolition of the slave trade. Ironically it had never been sponsored by Grenvilles's Cabinet.

BIBLIOGRAPHY

Alison, A., *History of Europe, 1789–1815* (London, 1848), x, 168–249

Aspinall, A. (ed.), *The Later Correspondence of George III* (Cambridge, 1968), pp. 26–41

Fitzpatrick, W. (ed.), *The Dropmore Papers* (HMSO, 1912) viii, 7–49; (HMSO, 1915), ix, 7–26

Harvey, A. D., 'The Ministry of All the Talents', *The Historical Journal*, xv, no. 4 (1972), 619–49

Roberts, M., *The Whig Party 1807–12* (London, 1939), *passim*

---

[47] *Court and Cabinets*, iv, 132–3.
[48] In a letter to Lord Derby on 24 March Grenville made it clear that the Cabinet had not resigned but had been 'turned out'. (BM Fortescue MSS.)
[49] Durham University, Grey MSS, Box 21, file 2.

SPENCER PERCEVAL

BY

JOYCE MARLOW

Spencer Perceval, born 1 November 1762, second son of the 2nd Earl of Egmont and Catherine, daughter of Charles Compton. Educated at Woolwich, Harrow, Trinity College, Cambridge and Lincoln's Inn. Married 1790 Jane Spencer-Wilson; six sons, six daughters. Joined Midland Circuit 1786; Deputy Recorder Northants 1787; Junior Counsel Crown prosecution of Tom Paine 1792 and of Horne Tooke 1794; KC 1796. MP for Northampton 1796; Solicitor-General 1801–1802; Attorney-General 1802–1804; again Attorney-General 1804–1806; PC 1807; Chancellor of the Exchequer 1807; Prime Minister 4 October 1809 till 11 May 1812, when murdered in the lobby of the House of Commons.

Spencer Perceval, by G. F. Joseph

SPENCER PERCEVAL

When the Duke of Portland's administration staggered to its close in the early autumn of 1809, there was one seeming front runner for his job, the brilliant, wayward Canning. But Canning had intrigued too many times, he had alienated too many people, he had wanted the highest office too obviously and too passionately, and the unsavoury scent of the duel with Castlereagh hung too closely over him, for sufficient support to be forthcoming. The man for whom adequate factional support was eventually fashioned was Spencer Perceval. It was the combination of professionalism (although it is doubtful whether his contemporaries would have recognised it as such) and the sound reactionary views that led to sufficient backing for his candidacy. And to George III, Perceval was eminently acceptable because of his proven championship of the Crown and Constitution and his opposition to Catholic emancipation.

Spencer Perceval ranks high among Britain's unremembered prime ministers, but he has two distinct claims to fame that posterity might recall. He remains the only man to have held the offices of Solicitor-General, Attorney-General and Prime Minister; and the sole man holding the last office to have been assassinated. His ability to survive politically is also worthy of more attention than it has generally been accorded.

Perceval was born in London in 1762. He was the second son of the second marriage of the second Earl of Egmont, which meant his inherited financial prospects were never good and he always needed to earn a living. As a young man he showed no outstanding qualities. Samuel Romilly, who liked him, described him as a person 'with very little reading, of a conversation barren of instruction, and with strong and invincible prejudices on many subjects'. But if he was not an intellectual Perceval had a mind capable of absorbing and utilising facts, he had application and he had an equable temperament. After leaving Cambridge in 1781 he entered Lincoln's Inn and then joined the Midland Circuit as a barrister. By the early 1790s he had begun to establish himself, and he attracted Pitt's interest. The attention was not gained by any brilliant performances at the Bar but by steady, plodding industry and by the soundness of his invincible prejudices.

From childhood Perceval had been deeply religious, and he matured with a fervour that was evangelical in its attachment to the Church of England, both as a religious creed and as the lynch-pin of the Constitution. His fervent Anglicanism meant that he was opposed to Catholic emancipation, and he therefore appealed to an influential sector of the ruling elite. On the question of the war with France he proved himself equally sound. Perceval believed as absolutely as he disbelieved in Catholic emancipation that the war must be fought to a conclusion. Unless Napoleon could be brought to his knees, the British way of life was doomed. All reasonable men of whatever class must grasp this obvious fact. They must accept that the prosecution of the war to final, decisive victory was the first priority of the age. As this was the view held by a majority of those possessing power and influence, Perceval's appeal grew wider.

In 1796 he was invited to stand for Parliament as a Tory candidate, and was duly returned without difficulty. Initially Perceval attended the House of Commons infrequently, concentrating on his legal career to obtain the necessary money to support a large family. When he did attend he was not at first a success. In court he could deliver his thoroughly prepared briefs to a captive audience whereas in Parliament he was shouted down and forced to extemporise. Such experiences left him stuttering and stammering. But Perceval was a worker by temperament and circumstance, and he had acquired a leech-like tenacity, probably more through the circumstance of having to earn a living than from inherent character. During Addington's brief reign as Prime Minister, it was chiefly he who defended the shaky administration with a mounting skill and confidence. It was during Addington's tenure of office that he was offered, and accepted, first the post of Solicitor-General, then of Attorney-General. He continued to hold the latter post in Pitt's last administration.

When Pitt died in 1806, Perceval had built up a solid reputation, as both lawyer and politician. (In the former capacity he was extraordinarily successful, earning 5,000 guineas a year at his peak.) Generally his reputation was solid. His private life was exemplary. He was a devoted father and husband, and unlike many of his parliamentary and legal colleagues he neither gambled nor drank. He had demonstrated his soundness on the entwined subject of the Constitution and the

Church of England and on the subject of the French war. But he had also shown that he could fight for an unpopular view if he believed in it, and that he was nobody's puppet. As Attorney-General he had refused to equate the Government with the masters in the growing volume of trades union disputes. He had sponsored a Bill to alleviate the horrors of the convict passage to New South Wales, and he had been a consistent supporter of Wilberforce in his anti-slavery campaign.

The quality that was increasingly impressing his contemporaries was his integrity. When bribery and corruption were such integral parts of the power structure, a man who was relatively indifferent to the lure of money and position in return for vote or support was exceptional, but useful. With Perceval's relative disinterest in patronage went a positive distaste for intrigue which again was useful for those manipulating the eternally shifting sands of parliamentary alliance. Once Perceval committed himself to a man and his policies, it was a safe assumption that his allegiance would be retained, as it had been by his first patron and hero, Pitt.

Perceval's unusual qualities of industry, integrity, loyalty and commitment were based on the fact that he was of an emergent species. He was a professional in the last full tide of the amateur, a man who got on with the job in dedicated, earnest fashion when to be seen to be earnest or dedicated was regarded as un-English and un-gentlemanly. Perceval can be viewed as an early Victorian, a herald of a new approach to the business of governing the country. However, this was only in respect of his approach to earning a living and concentrating on the job. In other ways he remained solidly eighteenth-century. He had no sympathy with or understanding of the ideas that had already germinated and were increasingly to preoccupy his descendants. He did not believe in corporate responsibility for the less fortunate members of society or that the Government should interfere in trade, industry, education or any facet of the average citizen's life. For him, as for many others, there was an ordained hierarchy. Some were born rich, more were born poor, a few intelligent, the majority stupid. He believed that one should be personally kind and considerate, and accept responsibility for one's immediate inferiors; but to contemplate interfering by legislation in the way a man conducted his estate or factory, to consider upsetting the preordained natural structure of life, was both dangerous and sacriligious.

Despite the King's approval and the promises of parliamentary support, it was with extreme difficulty that Perceval formed a government. MPs might in theory be prepared to accept him as the least objectionable candidate of ability but in practice few of any calibre were willing to serve under him. Canning refused, certain Perceval could not function without him; the small band of Canningites therefore also refused; Castlereagh held aloof; Addington, now Lord Sidmouth, refused; and he failed to enlist the Whig support of Grey or Grenville. But eventually Perceval succeeded in filling his vacancies, his strongest ministers being Lord Wellesley at the Foreign Office, Lord Liverpool at the War Office and Lord Eldon as Lord Chancellor. However, in the first week of its life Perceval's administration was defeated four times, and Canning was not alone in considering him the most compromise of candidates and his ministry the most stop-gap of measures.

The problems facing Perceval as he became Prime Minister and First Lord of the Treasury were daunting. Britain had already been at war with France, apart from the brief respite of the Treaty of Amiens, for seventeen years. The economy was consequently stretched to its limits. In fact he assumed office at a moment when trade was enjoying a boom because of the opening of the South American markets, but this boom proved as temporary as the Peace of Amiens. Behind him, and mountingly ahead of him, stretched the adverse effects of Napoleon's Berlin and Milan decrees which had closed continental markets to British goods; the equally adverse effects of the retaliatory British Orders in Council which had imposed a blockade on Napoleon's Europe; and the closing of the United States markets by the Americans, who had become entangled in the European embargoes and sanctions.

As a result of the trade war, large sections of the population had already suffered greatly, no sections more disastrously than the new manufacturing districts in the North and Midlands. It was these areas that were also, obviously, bearing the brunt of the Industrial Revolution. But that there had been any sort of revolution was scarcely recognised. The effects of a changing life-style, a booming birthrate, the new concentrations of population, the inevitably new relationships between masters and men, the shifts of wealth and emphasis, were being largely ignored. The country was still being ruled by its old system or lack of system; a totally unrepresentative Parliament, an anomalous jumble of local government, a creed of vague paternalism based on a policy of *laissez-faire* and non-interference by the State.

The problems of the year 1809 would have daunted a better man than Spencer Perceval. On the one hand there was an apparently endless, economy-draining war that had to be fought to a conclusion; on the other hand there was a divided, restless, distressed country. Moreover, as Perceval assumed office, the consequences of unplanned industrialisation allied to the economic stresses of the French war were patently building to a head that could burst at any moment. It was not expected that he would long survive such a combination of problems and pressures.

But Perceval astonished everybody, initially by remaining in office longer than the predicted few months, then by surmounting a succession of difficult or potentially disastrous situations that should in theory, without doubt, have toppled him. He survived George III's ultimate descent into madness and the passing of the Regency Act, the latter of which events should definitely in theory have removed him from office. The newly empowered Prince Regent was supposed to be a friend both of Canning and the Whigs, and furthermore Perceval had earlier alienated the Regent by defending his wife, Caroline, in the 'Delicate Affair' of her supposed pregnancy. But Perceval's tenacity won the day, and the Prince Regent did not dismiss him. He went on to survive the disastrous economic effects of the collapse of the briefly opened South American markets, followed by the United States Non-Intercourse Act which finally closed their markets to British goods and thereby plunged the manufacturing districts into even greater distress. He survived the Luddite Riots, those potentially so dangerous eruptions of the long-simmering discontent which first surfaced early in 1811 and were still flaring at the time of his death. He survived a monetary crisis involving the mounting National Debt, the absence of a gold standard and the value of paper money. And he survived the resignation of Lord Wellesley, the elder brother of the Duke of Wellington, from the Cabinet.

Part of the reason why Perceval not only survived, but was beginning to show signs of prospering when the assassin's bullet cut short his life, lay in the qualities that had led him unspectacularly but doggedly upwards: the determination, the dedication, the professionalism, the will and ability to fight that so many had underestimated. Grattan said, 'He is not a ship of the line, but he carries many guns, is tight-built, and is out in all weathers.' He also survived and started to prosper for the very reason that he was *not* 'a ship of the line', because he was a mediocrity when placed alongside the foremost politicians or statesmen.

Ideally, the times needed a man of genius – and on the military front they got one in Arthur Wellesley, soon to be created Duke of Wellington. But torn by internal dissensions and jealousies, with the shadow of the French Revolution looming over them, fearful that a similar event might happen in England, the ruling classes did not really want a man of genius on the home front. They wanted somebody who would not rock the boat. Perceval might be castigated as 'a little man with a little mind' by a few, but for the majority of those wielding power in and out of Parliament he fought for what was desired – victory over Napoleon; and delivered what was required – a preservation of the *status quo*. Certainly Perceval endured because of his own tenacity and determination, but the strength of his reactionary beliefs, reflecting the mood of the ruling classes, played its part in his survival.

The strength of Perceval's beliefs has since led him to be listed among the most repressive and reactionary of nineteenth-century prime ministers. It is true that he sat on the keg of gunpowder known as the Luddite Riots and did nothing other than have them put down by the use of troops, transportation to New South Wales and executions. Retrospectively, the eruption of Luddism is the most crucial event of Perceval's tenure of office. At the time, despite the French revolutionary fears, it was remarkable how little governmental interest was shown in the riots. The surprising indifference arose basically because of the lack of centralised government in England. The Home Office obtained information and received cries for help from the local magistrates in the disturbed areas; but these same magistrates were empowered to call for military aid without sanction from Westminster; there was no central body collating the extent of the disturbances. The fact that 12,000 troops were used in suppressing the Luddite Riots – more than the future Duke of Wellington had at his disposal in Spain – was never commented upon, if indeed realised. Further, although it was appreciated that distress caused discontent, it was felt there was nothing the Government could do to ameliorate conditions. Time, the recovery of trade, sensible arrangements by the masters, would eventually effect improvements. In the meantime the only course of action for the good of the country was to suppress the discontent as evinced in the machine-breaking and general rioting, in piecemeal fashion when and where it occurred.

The causes of Luddism – why the riots were occurring – never impinged upon Perceval. He never began to appreciate that the severe distress was linked to the growing dependence of an industrial economy on the reaction of world markets. Nor did he realise that Luddism had much deeper roots, that the breakdown of the old quasi-paternalist system and the onset of industrialisation demanded a new approach to the country's government, political and social as well as economic. But then the causes of Luddism did not penetrate the minds of other members of the Cabinet or of Parliament or of the ruling classes as a whole. Again Perceval reflected the prevalent atmosphere. Some governmental action was taken against the riots – frame-breaking became an offence punishable by death early in 1812. But on the whole, ironically if disastrously for the starving stockingers of Nottinghamshire, the hosiers of Leicestershire, the hand-loom weavers of Lancashire, and the croppers of Yorkshire, Perceval and the country bobbed up from the shock-waves of Luddism because nobody in power took them too seriously. The outbreaks had to be put down, and if some men had to be hanged that was a necessary measure 'called for by the circumstances of the time' (as Perceval had earlier said of Pitt's Gagging Acts). If 12,000 troops were required in the process that was a surprising but again unfortunate necessity. It was ostensibly on the grounds that Perceval was starving his brother of sufficient troops and supplies to conduct the Peninsular campaign that Lord Wellesley resigned. But in the resignation there was no hint that one of the reasons Wellington was being starved of troops and supplies was because they were tied up on home duty, suppressing the Luddite Riots.

Had a man of greater vision, comprehension or social conscience been Prime Minister at the period, the sufferings of the new working classes might have been less prolonged, the future social struggle less traumatic, but such men are not thick upon the ground in any era and they were not conspicuous in the early 1800s. Any man who had grasped the implications of industrialisation, and had been able to read the storm warnings of Luddism clearly, would also have needed to have been a master politician and tactician to have carried extensive remedial legislation through a Parliament consisting of country gentlemen and the scions and protégés of the great landed families. Perceval obviously did not possess such attributes. Given the existing circumstances and political and social climate, his basic achievement was to have survived. Perhaps his second achievement was to have pumped sufficient troops and supplies into Spain to have allowed Wellington to consolidate his position. Whatever Lord Wellesley claimed when he resigned, between 1809 and 1812 the Peninsular campaign more than got off the ground. Napoleon's troops were for the first time defeated on land by a British-led force, and the seeds of victory were planted. After two decades of war there was little likelihood of serious attention being given to the distress at home until Napoleon had been finally defeated. Of its own volition the war had become the first priority, and Perceval was probably right to pursue it as such. Up-ending the priorities at this stage could have created even greater problems.

Allowing that the war had to be fought to the bitter end, Perceval could and should have taken some remedial measures at home. His record as Prime Minister was essentially negative. But if he had a little mind it was not a mean one, and he did much to encourage young politicians – Palmerston and the young Peel were among his notable protégés.

Had Perceval not hung on, would the situation have been any better for the distressed masses? If Perceval had fallen within the predicted few months would a man with a broader, more comprehending mind have been likely to assume office? The answer is almost certainly, no; and Perceval's successor, Lord Liverpool, did not noticeably change tactics or alter policies. But when Lord Liverpool became Prime Minister there was greater political stability than there had been three years previously. This surprising stability, however unsurprisingly repressive it was, can be attributed to Perceval's capacity for survival. If his Government had collapsed within the predicted few months, the consequences would undoubtedly have been a succession of squabbling ministries. Confidence abroad would have been undermined, trade would have slumped deeper into the mire, the task of rallying the anti-Napoleonic forces in Europe would have been more difficult than it was, and the war would have dragged on longer than it did. The alternative was home-brewed revolution, a doubtfully beneficial occurrence when successful. As the forces of radicalism and discontent lacked a great leader in the same measure as did the ruling classes, anarchy or greater repression would have been the more likely outcome. It can be said that Perceval's negative, repressive three-year tenure of office provided a framework for stability.

Despite the repression, it was not a starving weaver or a revolutionary idealist who cut short the life of the Prime Minister who had survived against the odds. It was a man called John Bellingham. He had been arrested and imprisoned while trading in Russia and when eventually released became convinced that the British Government owed him financial redress for his sufferings. Failing to obtain satisfaction from various ministers, he transferred his obsessional sense of grievance to the Prime Minister. On 11 May 1812, Bellingham stationed himself in the lobby of the House of Commons, a revolver hidden in the specially tailored pocket of his coat. The only connection with the economic distress that had surrounded Perceval's administration was tangential and unrelated to the assassin. When Bellingham shot him, Perceval was on his way to attend a session of the committee that had finally been appointed to inquire into the adverse trade effects of the Orders in Council. Bellingham shot at point-blank range, and Perceval died almost immediately.

Bellingham was brought to trial on 15 May. His counsel's plea of insanity was rejected and on 18 May he was hanged. His counsel's was one of the very few voices to protest at the unprecedented speed of the proceedings. Perceval was eulogised as 'the model of a high-minded, high-principled, truthful, generous gentleman, *sans peur et sans reproche*', and Parliament voted large sums of money to support his widow and family. There were some murmurings about a revolutionary plot, and some vague attempts to tie up the assassination with the Luddite Riots. On the whole life in the country continued as before, singularly unaffected by the first – and hopefully the last – assassination of a British prime minister. That life did continue without interruption, that neither the Radicals nor the distressed masses utilised the melodramatic event, can be viewed as proof of the stabilising effect of Perceval's capacity to survive, or evidence of the law-abiding nature British discontent had already acquired.

BIBLIOGRAPHY

A Full Report of the Trial of John Bellingham (London, 1812)

Darvall, F. O., *Popular Disturbance and Public Order in Regency England* (Oxford University Press, 1934)

Gray, Denis, *Spencer Perceval* (Manchester University Press, 1963)

Treherne, Philip, *The Rt Hon. Spencer Perceval* (London, 1909)

Walpole, Sir Spencer, *The Life of the Rt Hon. Spencer Perceval* (London, 1874)

Williams, C. V., *The Life and Administration of the Rt Hon. Spencer Perceval* (London, 1872)

THE EARL OF LIVERPOOL

BY

NORMAN GASH

Robert Banks Jenkinson, born 7 June 1770, son of Charles Jenkinson (created Baron Hawkesbury 1786 and Earl of Liverpool 1796). Educated at Charterhouse and Christ Church, Oxford. Married (1) 1794 Lady Louisa Hervey and (2) 1822 Mary Chester. MP for Appleby 1790–96, Rye 1796–1803; India Board 1793; Master of Mint 1796; Foreign Secretary 1801–3; called to the Lords as Baron Hawkesbury 1803; Home Secretary 1804–6, 1807–9; succeeded as 2nd Earl of Liverpool 1808; Secretary for War and Colonies 1809–12; Prime Minister 1812–27. Died 4 December 1828.

Robert Jenkinson, Lord Liverpool, by Sir Thomas Lawrence

LORD LIVERPOOL

Who was prime minister at the time of the Battle of Waterloo? The question is rarely asked. Robert Banks Jenkinson, second Earl of Liverpool, is one of the least known and most underrated prime ministers in British history. When his name is recalled, it is more often in the depersonalised phrase 'the Liverpool administration', a label of a government rather than the evocation of a personality. Even contemporaries felt this anonymity. The savage caricatures of the period seized on Castlereagh, Sidmouth and Eldon, hardly ever on Liverpool. When his premiership ended abruptly in 1827, the dominant feeling was not a sense of personal loss but a realisation that an era in British politics had come to an end. Liverpool had been Prime Minister for fifteen years, longer than all his successors and all but one of his predecessors. He had gathered round him an unsurpassed array of talent. Castlereagh and Canning were his Foreign Secretaries; Wellington was a member of his Cabinet; Peel was his Home Secretary; Huskisson his President of the Board of Trade; Robinson – 'Prosperity Robinson' – his Chancellor of the Exchequer. Of the next ten prime ministers, six had served his administration.

His early career seemed almost a curriculum for the premiership. His father had held office under Grafton, North and Pitt, made a position for himself as one of George III's most trusted political servants, and was rewarded with an earldom before the end of the century. The education of his eldest son – Charterhouse, Oxford, and the Grand Tour – was conventional, though the additional grounding in French, history, mathematics and political economy prescribed by his father opened up to young Jenkinson a wider intellectual horizon. The man who told the House of Lords in 1815 that he 'had been bred up in a school where he had been taught highly to value the commercial interest', and the King in 1824 that the steam engine was 'the greatest and most useful invention of modern times', possessed from the start a more open mind than most of the squirarchy from which his family came. Elected for a pocket borough in 1790 before he came of age, he was appointed by Pitt to the India Board three years later. After that

he was never out of office, except for the thirteen months of the Grenville administration in 1806–7. By 1809 he had held all three secretary-
ships – Foreign, Home and War – and was the anchor man of any
ministry formed on Pittite–Tory principles. Only accident and his own
native caution had kept him from even greater eminence. George III
had wanted him to be chief minister in 1806 and again in 1807. If in
1809 Perceval and Canning could have agreed to serve together under
a peer, Liverpool would have been their choice. Few prime ministers
have made such a measured ascent to supreme office or been prepared
for it by such comprehensive experience. Nothing could have been
more natural after Perceval's assassination in 1812 than the view of
the Cabinet that if they were to continue, it must be under his leadership.

Long before that date age and office had enabled Liverpool to master
his highly-strung temperament. The awkward, bookish undergraduate,
alternating between shyness and pomposity, had turned into a modest,
conciliatory politician. The irresolution and procrastination that marked
his early career had been replaced by calmness and resolution. The
lanky, shambling, melancholy figure depicted in Hickel's picture of the
House of Commons in 1793 was becoming the stout, serious, ungrace-
ful and reflective man of the Lawrence painting in the National Portrait
Gallery. The public did not realise, as his colleagues did, that the
imperturbability and courtesy of his outward manner concealed a tense
personality. He had, wrote his biographer C. D. Yonge, 'an anxious
temperament'. His patronage secretary Charles Arbuthnot, who knew
him more intimately than possibly any man, spoke of 'a most nervous
mind'. Consciousness of impending difficulties tended to throw him into
what Huskisson called his 'grand fidgetts'. His agitation over the Cabinet
changes in 1822 at some stages, reported Canning, 'amounted almost
to illness'. He was profoundly distressed by personal conflict and un-
kindness. He had few relaxations; he lacked sociability. He had, wrote
Henry Hobhouse, Under-secretary of State at the Home Office, 'fewer
personal friends and less quality for conciliating men's affections than
perhaps any Minister that ever lived'. Politically he was always a
solitary person. 'I feel,' he wrote in 1820 in a moment of depression, 'I
have few, very few publick friends in the world.' To his wife, who died
in 1821 after twenty-seven years of married life, he was devotedly
attached; but it was perhaps indicative of his need for domestic comfort
that he married again almost immediately. Hardly any of his corres-

pondence with his wives exists because he was hardly ever separated from them.

To his public life, however, he brought qualities which in aggregate few prime ministers have equalled. In grasp of principles, mastery of detail, discernment of means, and judgement of individuals he was almost faultless. Cautious and unhurried in weighing a situation, he was prompt and decisive when the time came for action. In debate he was not only informed, lucid, and objective, but conspicuously honest. It was said that you could make a speech against him and leave the Chamber, knowing that in his reply he would state your arguments as fairly as yourself and probably more clearly. Though his colleagues might occasionally disagree with him, he never lost their respect or their trust. He repaid them in full. He never dismissed a minister; he was never ungrateful or disloyal. Kind by temperament, he had an instinctive tact in dealing with others. His conciliatory manner smoothed away innumerable personal difficulties. He was a man whom it was almost impossible to dislike; and he himself could find something to like in almost everyone. Few, for example, who had to work with Wellington's vain and pompous brother, Lord Wellesley, had much good to say of him. But, Liverpool wrote characteristically to Arbuthnot in 1823, 'the truth is, he is a great *compound*, and if one is to have the use of him, it must be by making as little as possible of some of his absurdities. . . . A man may be wise in some things & most foolish in others.'

Yet intellectually he could be as hard as rock. 'We wish,' he wrote to Castlereagh, when discussing plans for the disposal of Napoleon after Waterloo, 'that the King of France would hang or shoot Buonaparte as the best termination of the business.' He refused to interfere with Ney's execution since he thought that Louis would never be safe on his throne 'till he has dared to spill traitors' blood'. In the less sanguinary field of British domestic politics he did not hesitate to make an example when clemency would have been taken as weakness. The Earl Fitzwilliam was removed from his lord lieutenancy for identifying himself with radical protests after Peterloo; and the riotous scenes which turned the Queen's funeral in 1821 into a political demonstration were answered by the dismissals of an Army officer and a metropolitan magistrate. On patronage, which he administered with puritanical integrity, he could be immovable even against the highest suitors. He rejected Wellington's solicitations for a bishopric for his brother, a married clergyman living apart from his wife. He refused to allow Lord Conyngham, husband of the King's favourite, to be made Lord Chamberlain, or to sanction a canonry at Windsor for Sumner, a curate who tutored the Conyngham children. When in 1823 Arbuthnot warned him of the royal displeasure and urged him to conciliate the Court by making Knighton, the King's private secretary, a Privy Councillor, Liverpool's reply was brusque and uncompromising: 'The K. will find himself very much mistaken if he supposes that if he dismissed me . . . Canning, Peel or anyone of my colleagues would remain behind. . . . Let the K. take care that he does not make the close of a reign which has been hitherto most glorious, & on the whole most prosperous, stormy and miserable.'

As Prime Minister he maintained the integrity both of his own office and of the parliamentary Constitution over which he presided. When Castlereagh, despite his description of the Holy Alliance as a piece of sublime mysticism and nonsense, suggested that the Prince Regent might sign the document as an 'autographic avowal of sentiment between him and the sovereigns, his allies', Liverpool was adamant. For the Prince to sign the Act of Accession, he wrote back, would be 'inconsistent with all the forms and principles of our Government'. Within the Cabinet he permitted no cabals or divisions. When Wellesley complained in 1812 of not having the weight he expected in the Government, Liverpool told his brother that Wellesley on his side had failed in his obligations as a colleague: 'Government through a Cabinet is necessarily a Government *inter pares* in which every man must expect to have his opinions and despatches canvassed.' Eleven years later when the alliance with the Grenvillites had been cemented, Liverpool flatly refused to allow Buckingham to enter the Cabinet as their representative: 'I cannot bear the idea of the Cabinet being a connection of little knots of parties.' On the other hand he maintained stubbornly the right of the prime minister to choose the men he thought fittest for any particular post. When the King in 1821 seemed to be putting an absolute ban on Canning's return to the Cabinet, Liverpool was prepared to use the ultimate sanction at his disposal. 'Upon such a principle, so applied,' he wrote to Arbuthnot, 'I cannot agree to remain at the head of the Government.'

The traditional interpretation of Liverpool's administration divided it into two contrasting phases: 'reactionary Toryism', dominated by Castlereagh, Sidmouth, Eldon, and Vansittart; and 'liberal Toryism', dominated by Canning, Peel, Huskisson and Robinson. The ministerial reconstruction of 1821–2 marked the division and provided the explanation. On this analysis Liverpool's role was that of a neutral chairman, taking his colour from his colleagues. Such a view will hardly survive even a cursory examination. Liverpool was never a mere chairman presiding over a Cabinet of superior talents. Disraeli's disparaging epithet of the 'Arch-mediocrity' was as shallow as most of his historical judgements. The precise influence of a prime minister over his colleagues is always difficult to assess. But it is clear that the guiding lines of policy were always firmly in Liverpool's hands, in consultation with an inner ring of ministers: Castlereagh and later Canning, the successive leaders in the House of Commons; Bathurst, the influential elder statesman of the Cabinet; and Wellington, whose unique standing in politics transcended any particular office. Liverpool himself kept a close supervision of all the main departments, including the Foreign Office; and in matters of trade and finance was always the dominating figure. Commenting on the new Chancellor of the Exchequer in 1823 Wynn observed casually that 'Robinson will be a decided improvement on poor Van, both in manner and popularity with the House, but as to measures, Liverpool must of course give the orders, and he obey'. To make the Cabinet reconstruction of 1821–2 the dividing-line in the history of the Liverpool administration is to distort it in another way. It leaves in the background the first four years of his premiership, which were occupied in winning the war against Napoleon. Lord Liverpool is unique among British prime ministers in that he not only led his country to victory in the greatest and most expensive war it had ever fought, but grappled with post-war economic and social difficulties of a kind that were not to recur for another century, and finally won through to years of prosperity and social stability.

The achievement is more remarkable since Liverpool had to face a Parliament which had lost most of the apparatus of eighteenth-century administrative influence without gaining the discipline of nineteenth-century party organisation. The regular Government supporters in the Commons were hardly more numerous than the permanent Opposition, and the balance was held by a heterogeneous mass of Independents whose support fluctuated with the measures proposed and the mood of the country. For most of his premiership Liverpool had to reckon with an unstable, critical and occasionally hostile House of Commons. The ministry itself had a sickly birth. It could only exist at all by agreeing

289

to shelve the major issue of domestic policy, Catholic emancipation; and for a while it seemed a caretaker government, holding office while the grandees in opposition considered on what terms they might consent to take power. Only the necessities of war enabled Liverpool to survive his first testing years. It was an additional misfortune that the administration was particularly weak in the Commons. In the absence of able and experienced politicians, Liverpool had (as he modestly wrote) 'no recourse but to bring forward the most promising of the young men . . . I should be most happy to see another Pitt amongst them. I would willingly resign the government into his hands for I am fully aware of the importance of the minister being if possible in the House of Commons.'

Fortunately for the ministry, Liverpool's four years as war leader saw the military success that had defied his predecessors. The Spanish revolt in 1808 for the first time enabled British sea power to be translated into effective operations on the continental mainland. But everything depended on the ability of the Government to discern and their will to exploit the opportunity. As soon as he became Secretary for War in 1809 Liverpool concentrated on success in the Peninsula. 'I laid it down as a principle,' he wrote, 'that if the war was to be continued in Portugal and Spain, we ought not to suffer any part of our efforts to be directed to other objects.' As prime minister three years later he maintained the Peninsular strategy unflinchingly against the defeatist criticisms of the Whig Opposition. From the start he realised that in Spain, unlike the states of central Europe, Napoleon was faced with the opposition of an entire people. He was equally quick to appreciate the strategic effect of Napoleon's disastrous expedition to Russia. 'The Spanish War,' he wrote to the British Ambassador in Moscow in 1812, 'is the only national war in which Buonaparte has been engaged before the present. The Russians have therefore the example of Spain and the success of Spain before their eyes.' To his own commander in the field he gave unwavering political support, unprecedented financial backing, and the widest latitude of action. The alliance of Wellington, Liverpool, and Bathurst, his successor at the War Department, was in fact the most efficient combination the country produced in twenty years of conflict.

But the financial cost had been enormous. After Waterloo the Government faced a House of Commons clamouring for instant tax reduction and a public that complained of the inflation of the war while resenting the economic adjustments to the peace. 'The country at the moment is peace mad,' the Prime Minister wrote to Castlereagh early in 1815, 'Many of our best friends think of nothing but the reduction of taxes and low establishments.' The refusal of Parliament in 1816 to renew the Income Tax left the ministers to meet an expenditure of £30 million with a revenue of £12 million and made inevitable the ruinous policy of borrowing and raids on the Sinking Fund from which they did not extricate themselves for another five years. It was not a defeat for the Government; only for its policy. The independent MPs did not wish to displace Liverpool and his colleagues. But they were determined to set limits to government expenditure and insist on administrative economies beyond anything that the ministers themselves thought reasonable or even practicable. In 1817 and 1818 the Cabinet found itself fighting desperately not merely to preserve a minimum revenue for its ordinary needs but to safeguard the basic administrative structure of the State. Savage reductions in military and naval establishments, a drastic over-haul of civil offices, a cut in the Civil List, and a 10 per cent deduction from official salaries in 1817 merely fed the appetite for economy in the country without curing the Government's weakness in Parliament.

What paradoxically helped to maintain the ministers in office was the widespread disorder and violence, and the semi-seditious activities, which marked the economic depression of the post-war period. Liver-pool himself was convinced that what confronted the Government was a dangerous combination of economic distress and revolutionary doc-trine which would not have emerged but for the example of the French Revolution. In one who had witnessed the storming of the Bastille in 1789 it was not a surprising attitude; and it was shared by most of his class. It is easy in retrospect to criticise the Government for reacting too strongly to casual disorder and for believing too easily in the exist-ence of a genuine revolutionary spirit in the country. But the emblems and vocabulary, and occasionally the actions, of many extreme Radicals after Waterloo gave colour to that belief. The Government had no organised police at their disposal; they found it difficult to get exact information; and they were dependent on the support of an unpaid, amateur magistracy. Nevertheless, unlike his more alarmist advisers, Liverpool always tried to distinguish between distress and agitation. The repressive legislation passed in 1817 and 1819 was only that which he thought any responsible government ought to undertake; and it was based in good faith on such evidence as the Government could collect.

If he erred, he did so in good company; and the House of Commons supported him with sweeping majorities. His prime object was to isolate the agitators, support the magistracy, and protect law-abiding subjects from intimidation. He was defending, not bending, the Constitution. 'Fear of the mob,' he told the House of Lords, 'invariably led to arbitrary government.' It was this fear he wished to dissipate; arbitrary government he wished to avoid. Moderate firmness at the start would, in his view, prevent more brutal measures later. Like most Englishmen of his generation, he had learnt from France how easily timidity of authority in the face of disorder can lead to anarchy.

For a prime minister who sought to separate economic grievance from political agitation, there was a further handicap. The accepted doctrines of political economy – and Liverpool was above all a political economist – taught that government could do little to remove the causes or alleviate the effects of economic distress. 'There was a doctrine that could not be too often or too strongly impressed on the people of this country,' he observed bravely in 1819. 'They ought to be taught that evils inseparable from the state of things should not be charged on any government.' Even if government sought to intervene, he believed that the effects would at best be short-lived; at worst positively harmful. 'I am afraid,' he wrote, 'that government or Parliament never meddle with these matters at all but they do harm more or less.' Nevertheless, though imbued like most educated men of his generation with *laissez-faire* philosophy, he was not a doctrinaire and was prepared to break with theory if circumstances made it necessary. The piecemeal measures passed by the Government in 1817, including a Poor Employment Act sanctioning state loans for promoting useful works, at least indicated the Government's awareness of the social problem and their readiness to consider short-term palliatives. To the working classes Liverpool's attitude was paternalistic. His million-pound Church Building Act in 1818 was the first time for a century that the central government had acknowledged direct responsibility for the spiritual needs of the growing urban population. He supported efforts to improve educational facilities for the poor. He favoured a reform of the Game Laws and welcomed the elder Peel's Factory Bill to protect children in the cotton industry.

Liverpool in fact was a conservative statesman in the fundamental sense. He wished to avoid organic change by pursuing administrative reform. But he was neither a bigot nor a reactionary. He was opposed to Catholic emancipation because, as he put it with unusual bluntness in 1825, 'the Protestant gave an entire allegiance to his sovereign; the Catholic gave a divided one'. But the issue for him was political, not religious: the future of the Irish Union. The previous year, when Lansdowne had introduced Bills to enfranchise English Roman Catholics and admit them to the magistracy, he had both spoken and voted in favour. In the same spirit, though he refused to repeal the Test and Corporation Acts, he had passed a Relief Bill for dissenters in 1812 which was hailed by many of them as a second Toleration Act. 'An enlarged and liberal toleration,' he told the Lords, 'was the best security to the Established Church.' He disliked any general scheme of parliamentary reform but was prepared to support the disfranchisement of individual corrupt constituencies. In such cases he preferred to transfer the seats not to the populous towns, whose representatives were 'least likely to be steadily attached to the good order of society', but to the counties. The county MPs, he observed to his Cabinet, 'if not generally the ablest members in the House, are certainly those who have the greatest stake in the country and may be trusted for the most part in periods of difficulty and danger.'

Yet all this, as he realised, was only scratching the face of the main problem. The real solution lay in a return to general prosperity which would benefit poor as well as rich. By 1819, dissatisfied at the slow recovery of the national economy, Liverpool was ready to give a lead to the country. The 1819 Currency Commission and the return to the gold standard provided the necessary financial stability and Vansittart's budget of that year marked a real attempt to end the chronic post-war insolvency and initiate a constructive financial policy. More would have been done in 1820 had not the Government been paralysed by the Queen's divorce. After that the work was resumed and gained momentum with the ministerial changes of 1821-2. The importance of those changes has, however, been both exaggerated and misinterpreted. They were in fact part of a regular process of renewal which had been both checked and made more urgent by the depressing effects on the Government of the Queen's trial. The considerations that weighed with Liverpool were personal rather than political. He wished to improve the parliamentary efficiency of the ministry, strengthen the House of Commons front bench, and deny the King the nucleus of an alternative administration. But the shift of policy had already started. The substitution of Canning merely meant the continuation of the new line in foreign affairs which had been emerging before Castlereagh's death. The first of Peel's legal reforms had been prepared under Sidmouth. Before Robinson became Chancellor of the Exchequer, Liverpool and Vansittart were already laying the foundation of the new financial policy and Wallace, the able Vice-president of the Board of Trade, was initiating the changes in the commercial code later identified with Huskisson.

What was cardinal to the changed direction of government in the 1820s was the great commercial policy which had been signalled in 1819 and received its first authoritative exposition in Liverpool's speech on free trade in 1820. His purpose was threefold: to move from a high tariff to a low one; to modify the rigidity of the Navigation Acts in favour of a more flexible mercantile system; and to substitute for the monopolistic Corn Law of 1815 a protection that would recognise agriculture as one, but only one, of the great interests of the country. The essence of the new approach was that it took into account not only the needs of the producer but the interests of the consumer. What the farmers needed, Liverpool told the House of Lords in 1822, was not high protection but a market. The low prices of which they complained, he added pointedly, did in fact benefit the great majority of the people. Before the end of his ministry he was planning the significant modification of the Corn Laws which issued in the Act of 1828. Even in 1825, with the confidence of success, he was able to enunciate with authority 'the general principle of free trade as the great foundation of national prosperity'.

For the 'unprecedented, unparallelled prosperity', as he described it, in which the country was basking in 1825, Liverpool could legitimately take much personal credit. The new commercial policy of the 1820s owed everything to government initiative, nothing to external pressure or parliamentary tactics. Had he been given time and opportunity, he would have gone further. By 1824 he was convinced that tax reduction had gone too far and what was needed was a substantial surplus to make possible further tariff reforms. If ministers did what they ought to do, he told Canning ('Do not be alarmed, I am not going to propose it') they would increase direct taxation by £2 million and reduce tariffs by double that amount. He had always regretted the abolition of the Income Tax; nothing that could be substituted for it, in his view, was 'so equal and just'. But it was not until after his death that ministers could even talk of reviving it; and not until 1842 that Peel was able to accomplish it. At this, as at almost every other point, Liverpool was faced with unsurmountable limitations on his freedom of action.

Within the Government his difficulties were ironically greater than before. The Queen's divorce case in 1820 had been forced on the Cabinet by the intransigence of both parties. Once the peaceable compromise for which he had worked proved unattainable, Liverpool's conduct of the Bill in the House of Lords was exemplary in its fairness and dignity. But the collapse of the proceedings created a resentment in the King which threatened the actual existence of the Government. Only the lack of a congenial alternative deterred George IV from inaugurating his reign with a change of ministry. Much of his anger was directed against Liverpool personally and the friction continued in later years. Within the Cabinet the old harmony broke down after 1820 and was never restored. 'Ours is not, nor never has been a *controversial* Cabinet,' said Wellington in 1821; but everything seemed to change with the return of Canning. There were conflicts over his flamboyant diplomacy and irritation at Liverpool's apparent subservience to his old college friend. Many of his colleagues thought Canning was a disloyal intriguer; and though their suspicions were usually baseless, the distrust which Canning engendered was a political reality. It was only Liverpool who kept the discordant elements together.

Liverpool's partiality derived, however, as much from intellectual conviction as personal friendship. On foreign policy there was a clear identity of minds. Though Liverpool had admired and trusted Castlereagh – 'the right arm of the administration', as he called him – he himself was always insular rather than European. His constant argument from 1815 onwards was that Britain could not enter into further engagements with her wartime allies and that the nature of British parliamentary government put it in a class apart from the autocracies of Europe. One of the difficulties with Wellington was that he was heir to the Castlereagh tradition. 'He is rather *more continental*,' Liverpool wrote in 1822, 'than we either are or ought to be *permanently*.' His support for Canning's South American policy was based on an appreciation of the commercial advantages for Britain; and his forceful reaction to the threatened Spanish attack on Portugal in 1826 showed how far he was from being a reluctant follower of his Foreign Secretary. Nevertheless, Canning, by his restlessness, his badgering of the Prime Minister, and his advocacy of Catholic claims, was a continual drain on Liverpool's emotional strength. Canning's move in 1825 to make the Catholic question no longer an open one almost broke up the Cabinet; and only the reluctance of his 'Catholic' colleagues to support him saved the day.

As it was the Prime Minister felt that the end of his ministry was approaching. Early in 1827 he told Arbuthnot that he had made up his mind to retire and leave to others the inevitable settlement of Catholic claims. By that date he was a tired and prematurely aged man. The strains of the 1820–2 period had brought him to a pitch of nervous frustration from which he never fully recovered. The irritability, pessimism, and unusual bursts of temper noted by observers in those years were probably the marks of physical deterioration. Increasingly he began to speak of his declining health and inability to continue in office. 'It is not affectation in me to say that I am ill in body, as well as in mind,' he wrote to Arbuthnot in June 1821. It is possible that it was at this time that he suffered the organic heart damage indicated by his later symptoms. Lassitude and a disquietingly low pulse rate caused him to take a cure at Bath in 1824. At the end of 1826 renewed illness again turned his thoughts to resignation. His doctors sent him off for a month to Bath but the effects were brief. The stroke which in February 1827 ended his career was, as far as can be diagnosed, the result of a chronic hypertensive condition. He lingered on, a mental and physical wreck, until December 1828.

By that date he was already a figure of the past; and in a few more years a gulf seemed to have opened up between the Age of Reform and the Age of Peterloo. Yet the more the nineteenth century is put into perspective, the more significant does Liverpool's role appear. It was not merely that his political skill had kept an administration together so long or that his sheer professionalism as an administrator had enabled him to master all the diverse needs of government between 1812 and 1827. Even more important is that in the face of enormous practical difficulties he opened up the road along which early Victorian Britain was to travel with increasing certainty and profit in the next generation. The work of Peel's great ministry of 1841–6, for example, can only be appreciated when it is seen as a conscious resumption of the principles and policies initiated in 1819–27. Liverpool was the pioneer who prepared the ground and provided the training for his greatest pupil. In his emphasis on the need to promote general prosperity, in his insistence that agriculture and industry were not conflicting but interdependent interests, in his determination that executive government should follow a national and not a class policy, he laid down the maxims that Peel was to follow fifteen years later.

BIBLIOGRAPHY

Aspinall, A., *Correspondence of Charles Arbuthnot* (Camden series, lxv, 1941)
—, (ed.), *Letters of George IV* (3 vols, Cambridge, 1938)
Brock, W. R., *Lord Liverpool and Liberal Toryism, 1820–7* (Cambridge, 1941)
Buckingham, Duke of, *Court and Cabinets of the Regency* (2 vols, London, 1856)
—, *Court and Cabinets of George IV* (2 vols, London, 1859)
Petrie, C., *Lord Liverpool* (London, 1956)
Yonge, C. D., *Life of Lord Liverpool* (3 vols, London, 1868)

GEORGE CANNING

BY

ELIZABETH LONGFORD

George Canning, born 11 April 1770, only son of George Canning and Mary Anne, daughter of Jordan Costello. Educated at Eton and Christ Church, Oxford. Called to the Bar 1791. MP for Newport, Isle of Wight, 1794. Married Joan Scott (a wealthy heiress) 1800; four children of whom the third became Earl Canning, Governor-General of India. Foreign Secretary 1807. Fights duel with Castlereagh 1809. Rejected Foreign Office 1812; Ambassador to Lisbon 1814; Foreign Secretary 1822; Prime Minister and First Lord of the Treasury 1827. Died 8 August 1827.

George Canning, by Sir Thomas Lawrence

than Irish reunification, the negotiations were payment on account, as far as he was concerned, whilst Chamberlain regarded them as a final settlement. Hitler would not be limited to expansion in German populated areas as Chamberlain hoped. Perhaps Chamberlain's political security at home made him underestimate the forces of political unrest in Germany which provided both the impetus and the Achilles' heel of Hitler's regime. There can be little doubt that Chamberlain (and others) overestimated the armed strength of Germany and, in particular, that country's unity.

As far as Colvin and other critics of Chamberlain are concerned, he stands condemned at the bar of history for three main reasons. Firstly, for failing to rearm in time; secondly, for surrending in Czechoslovakia in 1938 when he need not have done; and, thirdly, for failing to achieve an alliance with Russia. None of these charges stands too deep an investigation. There can be few historians left who still regard Chamberlain as a simple opponent of rearmament. Chamberlain's role in the mid-1930s was that of Chancellor of the Exchequer, faced with an uphill economic recovery from the slump, whose job it was to fight large demands for the armed services from scarce economic resources. Naturally, the Chancellor protected his own field, but there was more to it than that. Chamberlain and the Treasury regarded a strong national financial position as being an indispensable weapon in a long war. Thus, when Prime Minister, Chamberlain aimed at limiting defence expenditure over the next four years to £1,500 million, to maintain balanced budgets, and to concentrate on defensive arms expenditure, rather than offensive. Under the last heading, Chamberlain switched resources from the building of bomber aeroplanes to that of fighters and attained agreement in the Cabinet to concentrate on imperial defence rather than on maintaining a sizable army available for immediate use on the Continent. Chamberlain's rearmament policy fitted in logically with other plans he had; by limiting arms expenditure he hoped that social reforms could be continued; by restricting offensive arms expenditure he hoped that Hitler would feel less threatened and therefore be more amenable.

Chamberlain's policy of 'business as usual' only ended after Hitler had incorporated Austria in the Reich in March 1938. Chamberlain then cancelled the policy adopted in 1934, that rearmament should only be undertaken on the understanding that it did not interfere with normal foreign trade or alter the industrial capacity of the nation in any marked way.

The policy adopted at Munich and Chamberlain's rearmament policy stand or fall together, as they formed part of the same plan. It is a fact that Chamberlain's personal diplomacy failed, but it is not at all clear that any alternative policy would have fared better (unless one accepts the very dubious argument that war in 1938 would have been better than war a year later). Chamberlain followed the lessons of Canning's diplomacy, that to threaten without the means or the will to execute your threats is a fatal form of diplomacy. He tried to come to terms with what he regarded as legitimate German grievances, whilst at the same time trying to limit further German aggression and, incidentally, placing British reasonableness in the face of American opinion. The policy was a failure, but it was neither indefensible nor irresponsible.

Although Chamberlain was probably prejudiced against Russia, he cannot be blamed for failing to secure a Russian alliance in 1939. A Russian alliance would have defeated the whole purpose of his diplomacy, which was to convince Hitler that there was no attempt to encircle him, and to maintain the utmost diplomatic flexibility. As it happened, Russia put forward terms that were unacceptable to the British. It is important not to exaggerate Chamberlain's control of events; an expert on Britain's inter-war foreign policy, Professor Medlicott, concludes that it cannot be shown 'that he took the conduct of foreign affairs into his own hands or peregrinated abroad to anything like the same extent as Lloyd George, or Churchill, or even Disraeli, or MacDonald or Macmillan did on occasion'.[11] In fact, Chamberlain revived the Cabinet foreign policy committee and presided over at least fifty of its meetings between 1937 and 1939.

The real basis of criticism of Chamberlain's premiership does not lie in his broad strategy but rather in his faults of manner and tactics. Chamberlain lacked the ability to 'sell himself'; he could not inspire others. He was a very poor war premier, probably worse than Asquith. Chamberlain's paternalism, his firm belief in free enterprise, and his acerbic debating tongue, did not win him the support of Labour leaders, who were eventually responsible for his overthrow in May 1940. His policy of 'business as usual' could never have been less apposite – his Government completely failed to exploit the national mood.

Significantly, Chamberlain stayed on as party leader after he had resigned the premiership. He had been Chairman of the Conservative

[11] W. H. Medlicott, *Contemporary England 1914–64* (London, 1967), pp. 357–8.

party at the turn of the decade and as Premier had done much to inject party solidarity into the nominally National Government of the 1930s. However, the historian of the Conservative party, Lord Blake, has argued that Chamberlain's attitude and policies hardened the divisions within the Conservative party and made them much worse than they had been under Baldwin: 'They left a lasting mark on the party, not wholly obliterated even as late as 1957.'[12] Twenty Conservative MPs abstained in the vote after Eden's resignation and between twenty-five and thirty abstained over Munich later in the year. Chamberlain was finally ousted on a vote of censure in which his majority dropped from 200 to 80. He made the mistake of identifying his party with appeasement; he would have been much wiser to spread the responsibility for unpopular but necessary decisions by widening his Government during 1939 to include the Labour party.

Neville Chamberlain died only months after leaving office. There can have been few more luckless politicians. Perhaps his worst misfortune was being born too late! One feels he would have made an eminently successful Prime Minister in the age of *Pax Britannica*, whereas he appears lost in the world of *Blitzkrieg*.

[12] Robert Blake, *The Conservative Party from Peel to Churchill*, paperback edn (London, 1972), pp. 238, 240.

SIR WINSTON CHURCHILL

BY

M. R. D. FOOT

*Sir Winston Leonard Spencer Churchill, born at Blenheim on 30
November 1874, elder son of Lord Randolph Churchill, third son
of the 7th Duke of Marlborough, and Jennie, second daughter of
Leonard Jerome of New York. Educated at Harrow and Sandhurst.
Served in the 4th Hussars in Cuba, Malakand, Tirah and Soudan
1895–98. War correspondent in South Africa 1899–1900;
captured and escaped. MP (Cons) for Oldham 1900–05; (Lib)
N.W. Manchester 1906–08; (Lib and Co-Lib) Dundee 1908–22;
(Cons) Epping 1924–45; Woodford 1945–65. Married 1908
Clementine, daughter of Colonel Sir H. M. Hozier and Lady
Blanche Ogilvy; one son, three daughters. Under-Secretary of State
for Colonies 1906–08; President of the Board of Trade 1908–10;
Home Secretary 1910–11; First Lord of the Admiralty 1911–15;
Chancellor of the Duchy of Lancaster 1915; commanded 6th Royal
Scots Fusiliers 1916; Minister of Munitions 1917; Secretary of
State for War 1919–21; Secretary of State for Colonies 1921–22;
Chancellor of the Exchequer 1924–29; First Lord of the Admiralty
1939–40; Prime Minister and Minister of Defence 1940–45;
Leader of the Opposition 1945–51; Prime Minister 1951–55,
and Minister of Defence 1951–52. PC 1907, CH 1922, OM
1946, KG 1953. Hon. DCL (Oxford; Rochester, USA); Hon.
LLD (Belfast, Bristol, Harvard, McGill, Brussels, Louvain,
Miami, Columbia, Aberdeen, St Andrews, Liverpool); D. Litt.
(London); etc. Died 24 January 1965. Author of* The River War,
1899; The World Crisis *(5 vols), 1923–31;* Marlborough *(4
vols), 1933–38;* The Second World War *(6 vols), 1948–54;* A
History of the English-Speaking Peoples *(4 vols), 1956–58;
etc, etc. Nobel Prize for Literature 1953.*

Sir Winston Churchill. Photo by Vivienne

SIR WINSTON CHURCHILL

Churchill's ancestry and character provide the keys to understanding his achievement; before we can consider what he did, we must remember who he was. He never forgot that on his father's side his roots lay in the western English countryside, that his people had long been of tremendous social standing, and that his forbears included one of the greatest captains of all known time. His father, a political comet that for a moment outshone even Gladstone in the bright sky of the mid-eighties, rose to great but not to the greatest heights in Conservative politics; fell correspondingly fast and far; and died, mad, when his elder son was barely twenty. His mother, still bewitchingly lovely, re-married five years later. By the social conventions of the day, he and she could not see a great deal of each other, even when he was an infant. But the practical, inventive Jerome strain in him was strong – stronger, some close friends thought, than the somewhat etiolated strain of the Churchills.

From his ducal descent he derived the hauteur of his manner. Though never as insolent as his father had been, he was often grumpy or downright rude; his scowl was notorious, and he was not an easy man to work for at close quarters. On the other hand, he was a good diner-out if he got a chance to talk, and liked to scintillate among cronies. Beneath the abrasive social manner, common in the upper class into which he was born, lay a much more formidable strength: a tough tenacity, a refusal to be overwhelmed by adversities, for which his half-American birth bears some responsibility.

His tenacity and resilience, almost as well known as his super-abundant energy, hardly need recall to a readership whose fathers at least knew him. He inherited another quality, that was reinforced by his upbringing, and is rare enough in politics to deserve remark: generosity. Gentlemen, he learnt in boyhood, ought never to be mean; and in later life he seldom was. It is almost impossible for a prime minister to avoid occasional touches of the appearance, at least, of meanness; public life is notoriously a hard taskmaster. But Churchill carried over into his principles of grand strategy the line of generous conduct he was taught

677

to approve in the nursery. This may not always have been wise; at least it was not mean.

Again, he shared with the polo-playing and fox-hunting companions of his youth the quality of courage; gentlemen no more flinch than they are mean. As a subaltern, he rode without a tremor in the lancers' charge at Omdurman; saying afterwards that his time was so taken up with sheathing his sword and drawing his pistol at the gallop, that he had no time for alarm. A couple of years later, he spent over an hour under fire, trying to shift a derailed armoured train in South Africa; to the warm admiration of those who saw him. His months in the trenches in France in 1916 left him equally unperturbed. And as an old man, during the bombardment of London, he said simply to Pile, the anti-aircraft commander, 'I love the bangs!'

This brings out an unexpected quality in any prime minister, particularly in one who did not attain the post till he was sixty-five: boyishness. A strong streak of the schoolboy remained near the surface of his character, long after it had been suppressed in his staider contemporaries and in many younger people with whom he had to work. This was not naughty-boyishness, but impishness without malice; what his age called cheek. With it went a delight in gadgets, codes, covers, minor and major mysteries, and a robust sense of humour. This made him original, rather than reliable, as a leader in difficult times.

From an early age he had had dinned into him that deadly text round which the nineteenth-century public schools revolved: 'Unto whomsoever much is given, of him shall be much required.'[1] His parents were not wealthy, his mother had sore financial troubles after his father's early death, and one of his own main reasons for writing was to make money; but he always believed that he was one on whom fortune had smiled, and that his birth had given him a flying start in life. He was aware that he had powers, and determined in due course to exercise them; he had ambition to match his energy, which was well beyond the common run. Where did it lead him?

He did badly at Harrow, and only scraped into Sandhurst; he understood that his father thought him a fool, and had to make clear to himself at least that Lord Randolph had been wrong. He was indeed a late and slow developer intellectually. 'I knew nothing of science,' he once said, nor was he a linguist. But he absorbed a lot of history, and formed himself a distinct and characteristic style, both for writing and for speak-

[1] Luke xii: 48.

ing. He conflated Gibbon, Macaulay, and the necessary brevities of campaign life to produce English that was always vigorous, sometimes racy, and usually clear.

As he was his father's son, and as he became a newspaper correspondent in the intervals of regimental duty, he attracted publicity; but he was not merely a newspaperman's hero. He was not too proud to write for a paper that would pay him a decent fee, but he did not envisage a career in Fleet Street; any more than he fancied one in Grub Street. He was too disdainful of journalists and of the public they served.

His personal life was of course hedged round, as closely as his professional life in the Army or in politics, by rules about how one should behave. At the fourth attempt, he was accepted in marriage – in August 1908 – by the beautiful Clementine Hozier, whom he married the following month. This gave him a perfectly firm personal base for the rest of his long life; she still survives him. As his future mother-in-law remarked at the time, 'He is gentle and tender, affectionate to those he loves, much hated by those who have not come under his personal charm.'[2] His great gifts for making enemies, as well as friends, need to be remembered: they were among the brakes on his action, when he reached the summit and before.

Two important enemies were obstacles to him in the Army. Neither Roberts nor Kitchener had wished to forward his military career, and each felt himself offended when Churchill outflanked him, got to a scene of action, and started writing to the newspapers about it. He resigned his commission early in 1899; the South African war provided him with the opportunity he eagerly sought, to enter Parliament. He won Oldham, which had rejected him at a by-election in July 1899, at the khaki election of 1900; having meanwhile been out to the Front, been captured, and escaped. Thereafter he rose like a cork. He was just under twenty-five when he went to Westminster; elected as a Conservative, he went as a Free Trader to sit on the Liberal benches in May 1904. He had just turned 31 when he entered Campbell-Bannerman's ministry, as Under-secretary for the Colonies, at the end of 1905. Asquith brought him into the Cabinet at 33, as President of the Board of Trade, and moved him before he was 35 to the Home Office, traditionally one of the three or four topmost posts in the government. But it was over thirty years more before he reached the summit.

[2] Lady Blanche Hozier to W. S. Blunt, in R. S. Churchill, *Winston S. Churchill* (London, 1969), ii, 268–9.

What happened in those thirty years could not help affecting the way he behaved then, and deserves a moment's attention from us now.

At the Colonial Office he learnt how the Civil Service works, and how to speak for a department in the Commons; but had no time to make any mark on colonial policy. At the Board of Trade, under the guidance of his predecessor Lloyd George – with whom he began a close friendship at this time – he carried on with the origins of the mid-century Welfare State: labour exchanges and unemployment insurance. At the Home Office, he was able to do something to soften the harsh regime in prisons; though a single episode from his spell there is more generally remembered. When a small murder gang barricaded themselves in Sidney Street, Stepney, and fired on the police, his adventurous and boyish streak surfaced: he went down to the East End to watch the shooting. Oddly enough, this scuffle is better known than all the rest of his eighteen months' work at the Home Office put together; save for the legend that he sent troops to put down a riot at Tonypandy, which is pure fiction.

In October 1911 Asquith sent him to the Admiralty, where for the first time he made an impact of first-class importance on the nation's life. He turned out an admirable continuator of the work of the recently retired Admiral Fisher. Fisher and Churchill had been on opposite sides in the controversy over the naval estimates for 1909;[3] but Churchill as usual came fast under the influence of his technical advisers, formed a warm friendship with Fisher, and carried Fisher's reforms further. He made the Dreadnoughts of 1906 obsolete with the Queen Elizabeth class of fast super-Dreadnoughts; he began the naval air service; still more important, he began the conversion of the whole fleet from coal to oil fuel, a conversion that made a mark on British foreign policy that lasts to this day. In short, he maintained continuous pressure for reform on a traditionally conservative and slow-moving service. As a result, the outbreak of war in 1914 found much the world's strongest fleet fully mobilised at its war stations, and able to exercise an international impact which, over four and a quarter years, proved decisive. This impact was as much Fisher's achievement as Churchill's, but neither could have done as much as he did without the other.

During the Great War, Churchill at first played a, but not *the*, leading part in forming British strategy. As Liddell Hart has observed, his activities outside the German far right had a perceptible influence on

[3] cp. p. 550 above.

the battle of the Marne;[4] and he was one of the three people who influenced the development of the tank, the weapon that broke the deadlock on the Western Front that derived from the Marne. The other two, Swinton and Hankey, were probably more important; but Churchill's help here was critical.

His other principal contribution to the conduct of the war was his sponsorship of the Dardanelles expedition. There is no point in stirring the still glowing embers of that controversy here. Instead, let us look at his retrospect:

'. . . power in a national crisis, when a man believes he knows what orders should be given, is a blessing. In any sphere of action there can be no comparison between the positions of number one and numbers two, three, or four. The duties and the problems of all persons other than number one are quite different and in many ways more difficult. It is always a misfortune when number two or three has to initiate a dominant plan or policy. He has to consider not only the merits of the policy, but the mind of his chief; not only what to advise, but what it is proper for him in his station to advise; not only what to do, but how to get it agreed, and how to get it done. Moreover, number two or three will have to reckon with numbers four, five, and six, or maybe some bright outsider, number twenty. . . . I was ruined for the time being in 1915 over the Dardanelles, and a supreme enterprise was cast away, through my trying to carry out a major and cardinal operation of war from a subordinate position.'[5]

The strategy was sound, the execution was weak: he could not get the best men to help him carry it out. In his own Admiralty headquarters, he had brought Fisher back as First Sea Lord when an absurd press campaign drove out Prince Louis of Battenberg; the strain was too much for the termagant old man. 'Fisher went mad', as Churchill put it succinctly, and flounced out in May 1915. The Conservatives heard of this, and moved in to evict Churchill, whom they detested.

They did not only hate him as a renegade; the black core in the party had never forgiven him for ordering a battle squadron to Lamlash, in the Isle of Arran, during the Ulster crisis in March 1914.[6] (Lady

[4] In A. J. P. Taylor et al., Churchill: Four Faces and the Man (London, 1969), pp. 165–8.
[5] Winston Churchill, The Second World War (London, 1959), ii, 14–15.
[6] See A. T. Q. Stewart, The Ulster Crisis (London, 1967), pp. 148 ff., 163.

Milner held forth to the present writer at length about the unforgivable enormity of this order, thirty-five years after the event. The fact that no ship in the squadron then got nearer to Lamlash than the Scillies made her no less angry.) Mean revengers made sure that he left the Admiralty; as Chancellor of the Duchy of Lancaster he found that he had no real hand in running the war.

So he went to France, to command an infantry battalion at the Front. This places him in a special category of prime ministers, in which Wellington is his only predecessor. Several others had heard shots fired in anger: Liverpool at the taking of the Bastille, Russell as a tourist in the Peninsula, Asquith and Lloyd George as visitors to quiet corners of the Western Front; Aberdeen had ridden over the battlefield of Leipzig, and could still hear the cries of the wounded forty years later; Canning had fought a duel. But only Wellington, till Churchill, had been resident in danger; had been personally a target for enemy fire, for a living, for months on end. This brings a real grasp of what war is like, though it does not always bring steady judgement. Attlee, Eden, Heath, and Macmillan have gone through the same mill; Wilson and Home have been bombarded from the air, which is not exactly the same.

Soon after Lloyd George replaced Asquith, he recalled Churchill from France, to take over the Ministry of Munitions; where Churchill made no particular mark. In the winter of 1918–19 he moved on to a pair of secretaryships of state, for war and air, where he had more influence. On the air side, he accepted Treasury advice and was sorely cramped in the peacetime RAF; on the military, he handled demobilisation sensibly, but then got entangled in the Russian revolutionary civil war.

'The foul baboonery of Bolshevism', one of his more memorable phrases, revolted him, and all through 1919 and 1920 he urged his colleagues to adopt a resolute policy of intervention against it: in vain.[7] Intervention had begun in 1918 as an anti-German measure – originally, at the Bolsheviks' own request. Churchill tried to turn it into a successful anti-Bolshevik war, and failed; made no secret of his efforts; and was widely mistrusted on their account by those of the British working classes who felt instinctive sympathy with their Russian opposite numbers.

This mistrust helped to lose him his seat at Dundee in 1922, and was

[7] See R. H. Ullman, *Britain and the Russian Civil War* (Princeton, 1968), especially pp. 298–304.

strengthened during the General Strike of 1926. Unexpectedly made Chancellor of the Exchequer by Baldwin, he played a prominent part in the counter measures mounted against the strike as editor of the *British Gazette*, which strikers found provocative. As Chancellor, he put Great Britain back on the Gold Standard, at the pre-war parity of £1 = $5, a measure that boded little good to British industry; and, prisoner as before of departmental views, he severely pruned the service estimates. Much of the Grand Fleet he had built up in 1911–14 was broken up, as a result of his financial stringency, in 1924–9: with bitter consequences arising from British impotence later.

Soon after the end of the Great War, he had begun to assemble material for a history of it; as a friend said, 'Winston has written an enormous book about himself and called it *The World Crisis*.' He wrote most of it when out of Parliament in 1922–4, and had much more leisure to write in his ten years out of office, from 1929 to 1939. Delving deep, with professional help, in the papers at Blenheim, he wrote a detailed life of his direct ancestor, the great Duke of Marlborough; the task gave him leisure to reflect on the problems of coalition warfare, and so had an importance for history as well as for literature. Much of his time in Parliament was taken up with a struggle against the extension of Indian powers of self-government; he still saw India through the eyes of a cavalry subaltern of the nineties.

This shows how far he was out on the margin of politics. Shades of Lamlash for the few, of Gallipoli and Murmansk for the many, overlay his reputation; he was thought restless, excitable, bellicose, unreliable. In the second half of the thirties, he gathered round him a group of well-informed backbenchers, who preached danger from Hitler to deaf ears. Churchill knew a tyrant when he saw one, and was not afraid to say so; saying so did not make him more popular with an electorate and a ruling class that disliked excitement and suspected 'cleverness'. He tried to form a 'King's party' during the Abdication crisis of 1936, but Edward VIII's established enemies were too nimble for him: again, he seemed a rogue elephant.

When his preachings turned out true and war began again, in September 1939, he returned to the Admiralty. In his eight months there, he galvanised the entire naval service with inquiries, investigations, ideas; few of the ideas came to much in the short run. One of them, the Naval Wire Barrage (known afloat as the Pig Trough), an anti-aircraft rocket device adopted at the behest of Churchill's scientific adviser F. A. Lindemann, may have destroyed *Hood* in the spring of 1941.[8] But he woke everybody up, and stretched everybody to his limit: an enormous achievement in wartime.

He did the same for the whole nation when he became Prime Minister, at one of the darkest moments in England's history, on 10 May 1940. He was more nearly lost at once than is generally recalled. On 12 June, on his way back from an attempt to stiffen the faltering French Government at Briare, the crew of his unarmed and unescorted airliner had 'seen two German aircraft below us firing at fishing-boats. We were lucky that their pilots did not look upward.'[9] So were we all. He has already been quoted on the advantages of being in command. The passage goes on:

'At the top there are great simplifications. An accepted leader has only to be sure of what it is best to do, or at least to have made up his mind about it. The loyalties which centre upon number one are enormous. If he trips he must be sustained. If he makes mistakes they must be covered. If he sleeps he must not be wantonly disturbed. If he is no good he must be pole-axed.'[10]

There was talk of pole-axing him in the spring of 1941, when the war was going poorly, and again in the summer of 1942, when things seemed worse still; but there was no one, absolutely no one, to match him in powers of leadership, at home or abroad. It is certainly true that he sustained, it is hardly too much to claim that he saved the country in the summer crisis of 1940. His gifts of oratory may in the end have bored sophisticated MPs,[11] but the age of broadcasting had now begun, and he continued to delight a listening public, both sides of the Channel. Had those two German pilots looked up and seen his Flamingo – but speculation is supposed to be unhistorical. He survived; the country survived. Our least passionate historian ends a biographical thumbnail sketch of him with the words 'the saviour of his country'.[12]

The heart of his war policy was to act. He knew that indecision, Asquith's bane, is the one catastrophic vice in a war leader. He often

[8] A. J. Marder in *English Historical Review*, supplement 5 (1972), pp. 9–10.
[9] *The Second World War*, ii, 141.
[10] ibid., p. 15.
[11] R. R. James (ed.), *Chips* (Penguin edn, 1970), pp. 375, 378, 388–9.
[12] A. J. P. Taylor, *English History 1914–1945* (Penguin edn, 1970), p. 29n.

acted wrongly; but even acting wrongly was as a rule better than not acting at all. Most military, like most political, choices are between two evils, and in wartime people hardly ever had enough data before them to be quite sure that they were always quite right. Churchill was ready to undertake the responsibility of being wrong; he preferred doing that to doing nothing.

To uphold Great Britain against Germany was no mean achievement. To uphold her against Germany, Italy, and Japan combined turned out to be possible, but fatal to her greatness. Many detailed, technical criticisms are made of Churchill as a war leader. As research on the recently opened war archives gets under way, there will be more pieces of tactic or branches of strategy to deplore; some of these attacks will be sound. The grand fact remains as Taylor states it. Yet in saving England he ruined her: because he could not bear to be mean.

When Japan entered the war, in December 1941, British resources in men and women, in machines, in foreign reserves, were already nearing exhaustion. The prudent course would have been to retire from the war as far as possible, or even altogether; leaving it to Germany and Japan to wear themselves out eventually against the superior wealth of the United States and the superior manpower of the Soviet Union. Churchill would have none of this: the only decent, honourable course was to fight on, however ruinous that course might prove. 'We shall go on to the end . . . we shall never surrender', he had said in one of his most famous and most electrifying speeches;[13] was he the prisoner of his own rhetoric? No: he meant what he said. If he was a prisoner, it was of his own upbringing.

That upbringing led him never to say 'I told you so' to those who had derided him in the days before the war when he had spoken of a German danger and opposed 'appeasement'. The attitude, again, is creditable to him, and was appreciated by public and private figures alike. He has been reproached for not perceiving, or rather for not preventing, the rise to world power status of Soviet Russia; a task beyond any Englishman's capacities. To have upheld the free world was a feat: wherever the free world may have gone since. The current (summer 1973) scandals on both sides of the Atlantic are nasty enough; but they are not nasty in the way that Himmler's camps were nasty. To resist Himmler, Hitler, and their friends with all one's force was wise and

[13] House of Commons, 4 June 1940; reprinted in *Blood, Sweat and Tears* (New York, 1941), p. 297.

humane; even if it meant making friends, when they changed sides, with Stalin and Beria, whose camps were not much more fragrant. Nor is it clear how Stalin's rise to world power could have been checked, unless by making friends with people who were even fiercer and more treacherous than he.

In occupied Europe, Churchill's name carried weight; more in some countries even than Stalin's or Roosevelt's. Millions of people looked to him, for he saw – even foresaw – resistance as the means by which they would recover their own moral balance after the shock of defeat, and throw the Nazis out; and he at least was a man who had never succumbed to any of Hitler's blandishments. Through Churchill, and SOE which Churchill created and supported, and through the RAF, a vast reserve of pro-British goodwill was built up in the western half of Europe; most of it squandered, it is true, by subsequent British policies, some of them Churchill's.

In home affairs his touch was much less sure than in foreign. They interested him little, and he left them to his able coalition assistants, Anderson, Bevin and Morrison. The achievement of a coalition, at a moment of intense crisis, appeared a personal triumph for him; he was in fact sustained, much as Lloyd George had been in 1916, by the anxiety of politicians to forget old scores and get on with the war. He has himself testified to the sloth of the Conservative party in welcoming him as its leader: indeed he did not formally take up that position till October 1940, shortly before Chamberlain's death.[14] The Labour party, which supported him against Chamberlain, did not support him against itself; as the war went on, and Labour ministers – Bevin particularly – proved their worth in office, the Labour politicians drew somewhat away from him. They held off from his offer of a renewed coalition after the defeat of Germany.

His 'caretaker' Government, purely Conservative, only made one decision of importance: 'unanimous, automatic, unquestioned agreement' to the use of atomic weapons on Japan.[15]

In the general election campaign of June and July 1945, he made a tour of the industrial Midlands. Wherever he went, crowds turned out to see him. He was not often punctual, nor always visibly sober, on this trip; and the map of election results showed a swathe of labour gains across the country, following roughly in his track. It was not that the

[14] *The Second World War*, ii, 8–9, 211, 438–9.
[15] ibid., vi, 553.

electors were ungrateful to him for rescuing them; but they felt that his tremendous gifts as a war leader fitted him less well for the tasks of reconstruction and social reform than did those of his wartime deputy, the meticulous Attlee.

He had a quiet six years in opposition. We need only note his speech in 1946 at Fulton, Missouri, on the Russian danger, which gave currency to the phrase 'iron curtain'. He was of course a cold warrior *par excellence*, as he had been a hot one, and a strong supporter of NATO. Now that the cold war appears to be over, we need not be too hasty in assuming it was a mistake to wage it.

He came back to power in October 1951, having only missed it by half a dozen seats eighteen months earlier, but his parliamentary majority was only seventeen, and the total of votes cast in the country showed a majority for Labour of some 200,000. So, the steel industry apart, his Government left most of their predecessors' socialising reforms alone; and he kept up his own interests in strategy and foreign affairs. He continued the production of British atomic weapons, and did his best to foster the European Defence Community. It was approved in 1952, but two years later the French Assembly refused to ratify it, and it never came into actual being. He did approve, in 1954, the withdrawal of British troops from Egypt, a decision his successor tried with unfortunate results to reverse soon afterwards. For he was very old; by 1955 even his walk was tottery, and he was persuaded it was time to go. He settled down to publish a history of the English-speaking peoples and to die with dignity; a process drawn out for nearly ten years more, till the seventieth anniversary of Lord Randolph's death.

When he died, his body lay in state in Westminster Hall, as Gladstone's alone among commoners had done before him. Many scores of thousands of people, most of them too young to recall him at his zenith, queued for long hours – a wait in the snow from two to six a.m. was common – to file past. At his funeral, which began in St Paul's, grown men were weeping in the streets; and every crane driver in the Pool of London dipped his crane in salute when the coffin appeared at the water's edge on its last journey, carrying him back to the graveyard in north Oxfordshire where his father's body lies.

Whatever else he did, he left a mark on his day; he was much hated, but he was also much loved. Of him it can be said by every Englishman now alive – and of no one else in this book is this true – 'Had it not been for him, I should not now be here.'

BIBLIOGRAPHY

Churchill wrote several volumes of autobiography. A monumental life of him, begun by his son Randolph, who died in 1968, is being completed by Martin Gilbert. Three volumes, accompanied by five volumes of supporting texts, have so far appeared (1966–72); they advance the life to 1916. Two other posthumous books and a short monograph deserve note: Lady Violet Bonham Carter's *Winston Churchill as I Knew Him* (London, 1965), A. J. P. Taylor and others, *Churchill: Four Faces and the Man* (London, 1969), and A. J. Marder, 'Winston is Back: Churchill at the Admiralty 1939–40', *English Historical Review*, supplement 5 (1972).

CLEMENT ATTLEE

BY

RICHARD ROSE

Clement Richard Attlee, created 1st Earl Attlee 1955. KG (1966), PC (1935), OM (1951) CH (1945) FRS (1947). Born at Putney 3 January 1883 and educated at Haileybury College and University College, Oxford (MA, Hon. Fellow 1942). Called to the Bar 1906. Secretary Toynbee Hall 1910; Lecturer Ruskin College 1911; Tutor and Lecturer, London School of Economics 1913-23; served in Gallipoli, Mesopotamia and France 1914-19; Major 1917; Mayor of Stepney 1919, 1920; MP (Lab.) Limehouse 1922-50, W. Walthamstow 1950-55; Under-Secretary of State for War 1924; Chancellor of the Duchy of Lancaster 1930-31; Postmaster-General 1931; Deputy Leader of the Labour Party in the Commons 1931-35; Leader of the Opposition 1935-40; Lord Privy Seal 1940-42; Secretary of State for Dominions Affairs 1942-43; Lord President of the Council 1943-45; Deputy Prime Minister 1942-45; Prime Minister and First Lord of the Treasury 1945-51; Minister of Defence 1945-46; Leader of the Opposition 1951-55. Attended San Francisco and Potsdam Conferences 1945; Leader of UK Delegation to the General Assembly of the UN 1946; led the UK Delegation to the Paris Peace Conference 1946. Hon. DCL (Oxford), Hon. LLD (Cambridge, London, Wales, Glasgow, Nottingham, Aberdeen, etc.), Hon. DLitt (Reading), Hon. FRIBA. Hon. Fellow Queen Mary College (London), London School of Economics. Married 1922 Violet Helen, daughter of H. E. Millar; one son, three daughters. Died 8 October 1967. Author of The Social Worker, The Town Councillor, The Will and the Way to Socialism, The Labour Party in Perspective, As It Happened, *etc.*

Clement Richard, 1st Earl Attlee, by G. Harcourt

CLEMENT ATTLEE

The political career of Clement Attlee challenges many preconceptions about political leadership. Attlee did not stand out among his contemporaries as a forceful orator or as a man of magnetic personality. Nor did he stand out as an original thinker, or a proponent of a particular brand of Socialism. He did not dominate the organisational life of the Labour party, nor was he the head of a powerful trade union. Yet among twentieth-century party leaders, Clement Attlee ranks first, if the test of political leadership is survival; his twenty-year tenure of the leadership of the Labour party is unrivalled in any party. Moreover, his experience as deputy Prime Minister in the wartime coalition of 1940-5, followed by six years as Prime Minister, put him at the centre of power longer than any other prime minister of this century, with the exception of Stanley Baldwin.

The question arises: why? Unlike other little men, physically and politically (Harry Truman is a good example), Clement Attlee did not compensate for his stature by a pugnacious manner, or self-assertiveness. Instead, his political style matched his physical demeanour: short, unprepossessing statements, delivered in a clipped manner without much argument. These are the mannerisms one might expect of a City solicitor advising a client, rather than the mannerisms of the leader of the Labour party in its most challenging and successful decades.

The distinctive feature of Clement Attlee's style of leadership is carefulness. He was cautious when confronted with political problems; yet cautiousness did not make him timorous. Once sure of political support, he could act swiftly, even ruthlessly. He was solicitous of the feelings and opinions of political colleagues; he never claimed to have discovered the one true path to socialism. Attlee was fond of quoting the remark of a Labour MP of the inter-war years, Tom Shaw: 'When I was young I was always talking about my conscience. When I grew older, I discovered it was just my blooming conceit.' Care also showed in the economical use of words; one was employed where other politicians would use a dozen. The words chosen were sometimes opaque and often vague, or harmless. When doctrinaire colleagues waged battle about the meaning of Socialism, Clement Attlee was careful to avoid inflaming others, or entangling himself in their controversies.

Not least, Clement Attlee was full of care for the conditions of ordinary Englishmen, most of whom had been born and raised in conditions far less comfortable than his own. He did not enter politics to seek fame, power or money. The impulse that led him into politics was moral and philosophical; it was a decision, based on first-hand experience of social work in the East End of London, that 'the economic and ethical basis of society was wrong'.

In the course of a political career that almost exactly spanned the first half-century of the Labour party, Clement Attlee developed personally as the party itself grew. The party reached national prominence before the man. The man grew into authority as a servant of the party rather than as a creator of the party, as did Ramsay MacDonald. The career of the man cannot be understood apart from the life of the party. Nor did the man himself see the situation otherwise. His long innings as leader resulted from an ability to assess carefully the state of opinion and the balance of power within the party, never acting outside these constraints, while promptly acting when the exigencies or evolution of events gave an opening to take a major decision.

The upbringing of Clement Attlee was, in his own words, that of 'a typical family of the professional class brought up in the atmosphere of Victorian England'. His father was a successful City of London solicitor: uncles and great-uncles were millers, brewers, farmers, doctors and an occasional clergyman. The Attlees were established in Surrey centuries before the county became part of commuters' London. The family home at Putney was still surrounded with fields, farms and country pubs when Clement Attlee was growing up in the final decades of Victoria's reign. A half-century after the event he could write of the news of Queen Victoria's death as 'a tremendous shock'.

There was nothing in this upbringing to make Clement Attlee particularly conscious of the conditions in which millions of people were then living 'In Darkest England'. His family and residence left him remote from industrial life. Nor was there anything in this upbringing to make a career in Parliament seem either likely or desirable. The family were predominantly Conservative, strictly sabbatarian supporters of the Church of England. They were not politically active.

The education of Clement Attlee was for service, not leadership. By coincidence, his sisters' governess had also been governess to Winston Churchill. The young Churchill, grandson of a Duke, could be imperious even when young; once he rang a bell and, when a maidservant appeared, announced that the governess should be taken away, as she was very cross. This could not have happened in the more modest Attlee household.

At public school, Haileybury, the dominant ethos was service in the Army or in India. The school's imperialist tradition emphasised service in the officer class, but not aspiration to a field-marshal's rank or the eminence of a viceroy. As a Commoner at University College, Oxford, Attlee did not seek the limelight. He read history and poetry for pleasure, and was too shy to attempt speaking in the Oxford Union. In politics, he held to the family's Conservatism, affecting a worldliness above concern with great religious or social questions. In 1904, Attlee went down to London to begin studying for the Bar, a career chosen less from a desire to shine as a barrister, than from its obvious appropriateness to family circumstances.

Neither calculation nor ambition started Clement Attlee on the trail that led to Downing Street. Instead, it was the strong tradition of social service, inspired by church, school and family. In October 1905, Attlee began going one night a week to Haileybury House, a boys' club in Stepney, one of the poorest parts of the East End of London. In 1907 he became the club's manager, and moved from Putney to begin a fourteen-year residence in the East End. In the same year he became a Socialist, joining the Independent Labour Party; he preferred its religious and ethical approach to social problems to the dogmatic Marxism of the Social Democratic Federation, or the pragmatic gradualism of the Fabian Society. Until the outbreak of the First World War, Attlee was a Socialist propagandist and held a variety of positions in the East End concerned with social betterment. This gave him great first-hand knowledge of the conditions and attitudes of ordinary working-class people. In later years Attlee was careful not to deduce their attitudes from theories of class conflict, but to argue them from this inductive knowledge.

The outbreak of the First World War united the country politically, except for the Labour movement. Unlike some members of the ILP (and some well-born, well-educated Radicals in the Liberal party), Clement Attlee responded to the call of patriotism. Just as boys from the East End joined the ranks and became NCOs, Attlee entered as an officer in the South Lancashire Regiment, and ended a Major; he served at Gallipoli and in the trenches in France, and was wounded in action. Service as a soldier appears to have confirmed Attlee's early patriotism. It also gave him a keen interest in military affairs. As he later recalled, 'Many Labour people in fact seemed to be of the opinion that an inefficient army was less wicked than an efficient one. Having served in the First World War, I did not share that view'.

The first political office that Clement Attlee ever held was Mayor of Stepney. He was co-opted to the borough council after Labour gained power there for the first time with a spate of inexperienced candidates in the local elections of 1919. He held the post for two years, and served as a Stepney alderman for eight. These offices brought him first-hand experience of local government possessed by very few twentieth-century prime ministers, except Neville Chamberlain. In 1922 marriage to Violet Millar, daughter of an old family friend, led Attlee to leave his East End residence for suburban Essex, and then move to Middlesex. But his political connections there were lifelong, for he sat in Parliament from 1922 to 1950 for Limehouse, and from 1950 to his retirement in 1955 for West Walthamstow.

There was no glamour and little publicity in the offices Attlee held during the 1920s. But the man was not a seeker of the spotlight, nor did his personality invest his every activity with the aura of importance, or attract press publicity. The platform speaking of pre-war days, useful in overcoming shyness and as preparation for the rough-and-tumble of parliamentary debate, was not his natural role. Nor did his lecturing post at the London School of Economics imply academic brilliance; he held a post in social administration because of his practical knowledge of social conditions.

In the period up to the 1931 Labour collapse, Clement Attlee established himself as a respected member of the Parliamentary Labour Party. By virtue of his class and educational background, he was more at home with the printed word and the intricacies of legislation and administration than many Labour MPs who had come from the work-benches or the pits to Parliament. By the same token, the emotionally charged (but administratively hollow) rhetoric that marked the leading working-class orators was alien to him. Nor did he seek to compensate for his background by becoming, like Sir Oswald Mosley or John Strachey, a spokesman for extremist views.

Service as parliamentary private secretary to Ramsay MacDonald when MacDonald was leader of Labour in opposition, 1922–3, was followed by an Under-secretaryship in the War Office in the first Labour Government. In the late 1920s Attlee gained experience of overseas affairs as a member of Sir John Simon's Indian Statutory Commission. When Labour returned to office in June 1929, Attlee was not offered a ministerial post. When the post of Chancellor of the Duchy of Lancaster became vacant in May 1930, he moved there from the back benches. When H. B. Lees-Smith was moved up to a Cabinet post in March 1931, Attlee became Postmaster-General. None of these appointments brought Cabinet rank. Retrospectively, these varied tasks can be seen as useful background for a person required to assume general oversight of policy as Prime Minister. At the time, they were no more than way stations along a path that was not meant to lead to any eminence.

Events, not personality, catapulted Clement Attlee forward as a Labour leader. The general election of October 1931, held after Ramsay MacDonald left the party to become Prime Minister in a National Coalition, removed nearly all senior Labour politicians from the House of Commons, as well as creating a vacancy for the post of leader. Attlee was fortunate in scraping back at Limehouse with a majority of 551 votes. The Parliamentary Labour Party of less than fifty was short of men of experience. George Lansbury was elected leader of the Parliamentary Labour Party and Attlee was elected deputy leader without opposition. Together with a new recruit to Labour's cause, Sir Stafford Cripps, they shared the burden of leading the party through hopeless years of opposition.

With the great fall in Labour's numbers, the work load of individual Labour MPs rose. Attlee suddenly found himself pushed into the position of responsible spokesman for the party in many fields. From 1931 to 1935 his routine was to leave home at 9 a.m. and not return until near midnight on days when the House of Commons was sitting. In his second year as deputy leader, he filled more columns of Hansard than any other MP, not because of garrulousness but because of the party's need for a man who could speak and speak reliably on many subjects. By contrast, Sir Stafford Cripps was suspect for lack of judgement, and George Lansbury was ageing and unsuited to debating the details of legislation. In 1934 Lansbury was in hospital for months, thus placing Attlee in the post of acting leader of the Labour party.

Events again favoured Attlee when the leadership of the Labour party unexpectedly fell vacant before the 1935 general election. He was the only candidate for the post at that time, but the choice was seen as temporary. The 1935 election trebled the size of the Parliamentary Labour Party. The new MPs, including men who had been senior to Attlee in the party prior to the 1931 débâcle, were offered three candidates for the leadership: Attlee, Arthur Greenwood and Herbert Morrison. On the first ballot, Attlee received 58 out of 135 votes. He gained the leadership because Greenwood's supporters swung almost *en bloc* to his side. The narrowness of Attlee's victory rankled for years with Herbert Morrison, who periodically sought to displace him. It seemed to have little effect on Attlee's self-confidence. He had gained his eminence by acting as the spokesman for the majority of opinion in the party. He saw his new role as remaining the careful articulator of the views of the party. This role was in keeping not only with his temperament and aptitudes, but also with the temper of the times: Ramsay MacDonald and Sir Oswald Mosley had frightened Labour by first swaying opinion within the party and then deserting it.

The first four years of Attlee's leadership were the most difficult for the party, but less so for the man on top. While debates raged within the party between proponents and opponents of rearmament, Attlee carefully stayed on middle ground. When the issue of collaboration with Communists or Liberals came forward, Attlee avoided encouraging such alliances; he also remained aloof from the intense controversy required to defend the party's *status quo*. When left-wing Socialists thundered about the extremist measures that might be required to build Socialism in Britain, Attlee sympathised with many of their aspirations, but refused to endorse methods alien to parliamentary traditions. In one respect he did take the initiative: he used his position and European Socialist contacts to travel widely on the Continent, meeting a variety of political leaders and becoming familiar with the threat of totalitarianism at first hand.

In 1937 Clement Attlee published *The Labour Party in Perspective*, an exposition of his political ideas. At a time of great ideological strife between and within parties, the author characteristically concentrated upon a few things of general importance and general agreement. The book was self-consciously ethical and undoctrinaire. Notwithstanding support of the League of Nations, it was also patriotic, presenting the Labour party as 'typically British' and Socialism as 'a characteristic example of British methods, and as the outcome of British political instincts'. It was gradualist in temper and recommendations. Yet there was no attempt to be all things to all men. In the 1930s there was not enough common ground among the electorate (let alone among MPs) to permit a party leader to avoid commitment to distinctive party principles. Attlee's characteristic mixture of ethical and Socialist concerns is epitomised in the objectives he defined for the party: freedom, economic security, equality, democracy, common ownership of the land and major industries, beauty and internationalism.

The realisation of many of the ideals expressed in Attlee's pre-war writings and speeches was made possible in the aftermath of the Second World War. It was not made inevitable. If Attlee's wartime colleagues deserve some of the credit for anticipating actions undertaken by the post-war Cabinet he headed, so it might be claimed that Attlee himself deserved credit for actions undertaken by the War Cabinet in which he was important.

When the downfall of Neville Chamberlain as Prime Minister was imminent, Attlee was not prominent in the negotiations that dislodged Chamberlain and brought in Churchill in his stead. Attlee concentrated upon two points: the need to create a coalition government with the will and means to pursue the nation's defence; and, by acting carefully and correctly according to the party constitution, to ensure that the Labour party was united behind those invited to sit in Cabinet with such old enemies as Churchill and Lord Halifax. Fortuitously, the occurrence of the party's annual conference during delicate negotiations concerning the Coalition enabled Attlee to enter government with the expressed support of the whole party.

Initially, the Labour leader was appointed Lord Privy Seal, and awarded residence at 11 Downing Street. Attlee was effectively deputy Prime Minister, a title granted formally in 1942. He was vice-chairman of the Defence Committee of Cabinet and latterly became head of the Cabinet's Committee on the Home Front. In the Commons as well as in Cabinet, he acted as Prime Minister when Churchill was abroad.

The contribution of Clement Attlee to Britain's war effort was general, rather than specific. He neither directed grand strategy like Churchill, nor did he carry diplomatic responsibilities, like the Prime Minister and his Foreign Secretary, Sir Anthony Eden. On the domestic front, Herbert Morrison as Home Secretary and Ernest Bevin as Minister of Labour respectively organised civil defence and the massive mobilisation of labour. Sir Stafford Cripps re-emerged as a responsible political figure within the Labour movement as Ambassador to the Soviet Union and then Minister of Aircraft Production.

Attlee's role was to hold the party together; by doing this, he enabled the Coalition Government itself to hold together. The intrigues and political disruption of the First World War provided cautionary tales of what could happen if party leaders quarrelled about the spoils of office in the midst of the havoc of war. In demeanour as in political objectives, Attlee was an exemplary foil for Churchill. He was careful not to insist upon party claims at a time when wartime mobilisation was leading the country's diplomatic, economic and social policy along lines he had long urged: an international alliance to secure collective security; full employment and state direction of the economy; and 'fair shares' rationing of food and other resources, based upon need rather than wealth.

When the war in Europe ended in May 1945, Attlee once again carefully consulted colleagues before departing from the Coalition. If Labour was to suffer defeat, the leader wished to assure that all were equally implicated. The Conservative terms for continuing the Coalition were unacceptable to the party's National Executive Committee; a general election was held forthwith. The result was victory for the Labour party by a landslide margin that surprised Attlee by its extent. At the age of sixty-two, Clement Attlee became Prime Minister, notwithstanding last-minute efforts by a small clique to substitute Herbert Morrison in his place.

Clement Attlee entered 10 Downing Street with great political advantages. He was careful to maintain them, as far as possible, during his six years in office. He knew how to manage the House of Commons, a skill acquired in the early 1930s; and how to conduct Cabinet business, learned on the job as Deputy Prime Minister. Experience had given first-hand familiarity with political problems at every level from local government to international diplomacy. In addition, he could call upon the talents of experienced and able Labour politicians from all wings of the party. Men of the calibre of Ernest Bevin, Herbert Morrison, Hugh Dalton and Sir Stafford Cripps greatly strengthened the effectiveness of the 1945-51 Labour Government. Its aims could not be achieved by the efforts of a single man. For every major task, Attlee had a man with the ability and experience to do the job. As long as the Cabinet held together, Attlee was proof against rebellion in the House of Commons. The Cabinet held together not only out of regard for their chairman, but also because they disagreed bitterly about who should inherit his position, if and when he left. Ernest Bevin's consistent support of Attlee and refusal to allow his own name to go forward as a replacement gave the Labour Prime Minister great security against the intrigues that inevitably arise when a government goes through an unpopular period.

The achievements of the 1945–51 Labour Government were far greater than the accomplishments of any single individual. The Government introduced the National Health Service and a national insurance scheme that abolished the old means test; it also sustained full employment in peacetime. Coal, gas, electricity, the railways and the steel industry were nationalised. Food subsidies and rationing were continued to prevent inflation and allocate basic goods by reference to need, not income. A new Representation of the People Act established the principle 'one man, one vote'; the delaying powers of the House of Lords were also reduced. The post-war demobilisation of the wartime fighting services was carried out satisfactorily. All of these measures were measures that the Prime Minister, as well as many rank-and-file members of the Labour party, had long advocated. They were thus a collective achievement; as leader of a team, Attlee deserved the credit due to a successful captain.

In international affairs, Clement Attlee could claim personal credit for effecting the transition from Empire to Commonwealth. This change was forced forward by the granting of independence to India and Pakistan in 1947. Difficult decisions were required before this could be achieved. In the transition from war to peace, Attlee was also personally concerned with the decision to build British atomic weapons, following the breakdown of Anglo-American wartime co-operation. Most foreign affairs achievements of the 1945–51 Labour Government reflected the efforts of his Foreign Secretary for almost six years, Ernest Bevin. In Attlee's own words: '"If you have a good dog, don't bark yourself" is a good proverb, and in Ernest Bevin I had an exceptionally good dog.' These two Englishmen, one a trade unionist raised in rural poverty and the other a social worker with a private income, had a common view of the realities of the post-war world. Collaborating closely with the American Government of President Truman, the Labour Government transferred its responsibilities for the defence of Greece and Turkey to the United States in 1946, participated in the establishment of the

Marshall Plan for the post-war economic recovery of Europe, the air-lift to counteract the Berlin blockade, the establishment of the North Atlantic Treaty Organisation for the defence of Europe, and, after the outbreak of the Korean War in 1950, commenced rearmament against a potential Russian threat.

The acts of omission are fewer and more controversial. The Government turned down continental requests to join a nascent European Coal and Steel Community, withdrew troops from Palestine rather than mediate indefinitely between Jews and Arabs, and withdrew from the oilfields of Iran, rather than intervene with troops following the nationalisation of British oil interests there in 1951.

The great personal contribution of Clement Attlee was to ensure that the disparate talents and interests of the members of his Government were concentrated upon common goals. Success was gained by carefully calculating the tolerances of different individuals and groups within the Labour movement. By meeting party expectations in domestic policy, credit was gained within the party, useful to offset frustrations arising from the inability to meet expectations in the rapidly changing currents of foreign affairs.

That success was due to the skilful management of political forces, rather than to a compelling personality, was clearly demonstrated by the record of Attlee's last five years as Labour leader. Prior to the election of 1950, divisions were beginning to show within the party between those who wished to carry out more Socialist policies, and those who wished to consolidate legislation realising the promises of a generation. The election result left Labour with a precarious overall majority of five. The failing health of Bevin and Sir Stafford Cripps deprived Attlee of two great stalwarts in Cabinet. The claims of rearmament upon domestic resources triggered off a battle in Cabinet, climaxing in the resignation of Aneurin Bevan and Harold Wilson in April 1951. Herbert Morrison proved unable to carry the full responsibilities of the Foreign Office at a time when foreign affairs and defence were of great urgency. The Prime Minister's health suffered, requiring hospital treatment for a duodenal ulcer and eczema. Uncertain of support, uncertain of direction and uncertain of the men needed to share the burdens, Attlee called a general election in October 1951. A small Labour majority was turned into a slightly larger Conservative majority.

Out of office, Clement Attlee showed once again the care with which he led the Labour party. In a very different political situation –

personally as well as in party terms – he avoided fully committing himself on divisive issues. For three years a great debate raged within the party about the propriety of rearming Germany. With it were linked disputes about the furtherance or consolidation of nationalisation. Aneurin Bevan and the *Tribune* group of MPs used rank-and-file antipathy towards Germany to advance a broad left-wing attack on the party's programme. Herbert Morrison and Hugh Gaitskell defended the position of the second Labour Government. As in the late 1930s, Attlee saw his role as reflecting the balance of power in the party, rather than as an active determinant. When the crucial vote on German rearmament was taken in the House of Commons, he recommended that Labour MPs abstain.

Unlike most prime ministers, Attlee retired from politics in good health, and with the praise of the nation. The controversies within the Labour party made it inopportune for MPs to choose a new Labour leader before the May 1955 general election could be held. In December 1955 the 72-year-old Attlee announced his retirement. The Queen conferred an earldom. The ex-Prime Minister retired to the Lords, appearing from time to time in print, television, or on the lecture circuit with his reminiscences, but rarely entering party controversy. Uncharacteristically, he did allow his name to be used as Honorary Chairman of the moderate Campaign for Democratic Socialism when it was founded in 1961 to defend Hugh Gaitskell from the left-wing critics who had also harassed Attlee. Advancing years gradually restricted his movements, prior to his death on 8 October 1967.

If not one of the very greatest prime ministers, Clement Attlee was, at the least, a very good prime minister. He was less the cause of events than the means by which great events came to pass. He spoke little, but when he spoke it was to the point. He usually did not speak until and unless he was sure he could speak with good effect. In foreign affairs he played a weak hand, but he played it well. In domestic affairs, the actions of his Government, rather than the phrases of its leader, are memorable. The statute books from 1945 to 1951 are a memorial of his work, and more than that. The achievements of that Government were also the achievements of tens of thousands in the Labour movement who committed themselves to Socialism in times and places as inauspicious as that chosen by the youthful Attlee. If fortune or events had taken a different turn at any number of points in his political career, Attlee's name would be little more familiar than the names of his Stepney comrades, or of his comrades in the pathetic battles in opposition in the early 1930s. There is no doubt that he, like them, would have been satisfied enough by collective success, without personal fame.

While Clement Attlee was a dedicated Socialist during his half-century in politics, he was throughout his life an Englishman, dedicated to maintaining and advancing all that he thought best in a land that has a Radical as well as a Tory tradition, and respect for social service as well as deference in its culture. In the final paragraph of his autobiographical memoir, Clement Attlee succinctly sums up what he saw as the chief features of his life: 'I have been a very happy and fortunate man in having lived so long in the greatest country in the world, in having a happy family life, and in having been given the opportunity of serving in a state of life to which I had never expected to be called.'

BIBLIOGRAPHY

Writings by Clement Attlee
As It Happened (London, 1954)
Empire into Commonwealth (London, 1961)
The Labour Party in Perspective (London, 1937)
A Prime Minister Remembers (by Francis Williams, based on the private papers and a series of recorded conversations) (London, 1961)
Purpose and Policy: Selected Speeches (London, 1947)
The Social Worker (London, 1920)
The Town Councillor (co-author W. A. Robson) (London, 1925)
War Comes to Britain (speeches) (London, 1940)
The Will and the Way to Socialism (London, 1935)

Books about Clement Attlee
Jenkins, Roy H., *Mr Attlee: An Interim Biography* (London, 1948)
Murphy, John T., *Labour's Big Three* (London, 1948)

SIR ANTHONY EDEN

BY

ANTHONY NUTTING

*Anthony Eden, created Earl of Avon 1961. Hon. DCL (Oxford and
Durham); Hon. LLD (Birmingham, Bristol, Cambridge, Leeds,
Sheffield, Belfast, etc). Born 12 June 1897, son of Sir William
Eden, Bart. Educated at Eton and Christ Church, Oxford (BA
1922). Served in the European War 1915–19; Bde Major (MC).
Contested (Con.) Spennymoor 1922; MP for Warwick and
Leamington 1923–57. Parliamentary Private Secretary to Sir
Austen Chamberlain (Foreign Office) 1926–29; Parliamentary
Under-secretary for Foreign Affairs 1931–34; Lord Privy Seal
and Minister for League of Nations Affairs 1934–35; Foreign
Secretary 1935–38; Dominions Secretary 1939–40; Secretary of
State for War 1940; Foreign Secretary 1940–45; Leader of the
House of Commons 1942–45; Deputy Leader of the Opposition
1945–51; Foreign Secretary and Deputy Prime Minister 1951–55;
Prime Minister and First Lord of the Treasury 1955–57. Chairman
of the OEEC 1952–54; Trustee of the National Gallery 1935–49;
Chancellor of the University of Birmingham 1945; President of the
Royal Shakespeare Theatre 1958–66. Married (1) 1923 Beatrice
Helen Beckett, one surviving son (one son killed on active service);
(2) Clarissa Anne Churchill. Author of* Places in the Sun,
Freedom and Order, Days for Decision, The Eden Memoirs, *etc.*

Robert Anthony Eden, 1st Earl Avon. Photo by Vivienne.

SIR ANTHONY EDEN

After the 1955 general election a friend of mine in the Labour party told me that what clinched the victory for the Tories was a poster which appeared on almost every hoarding in Britain depicting Anthony Eden's face with the brief and simple slogan underneath, 'Working for Peace'. If there had ever been any chance of Labour regaining power, 'that poster', said my friend, 'finally disposed of it'.

As one of Eden's ministers especially deputed to speak on foreign affairs during that election campaign, I know just how true this was. For one thing the poster reminded the electors of the Prime Minister's reputation as a master practitioner of international negotiation. More important still, it emphasised how, largely due to his personal and prodigious efforts as Churchill's Foreign Secretary over the previous three and a half years, most of the conflicts across the world which the Tories had inherited from the Labour Government in 1951 had been peaceably resolved; and at that moment in time there was no actual war in progress anywhere on the surface of the earth.

Consequently the 1955 election not only gave Eden, as Churchill's successor, a renewed mandate to carry on the Conservative Government and to continue 'working for peace'; it also gave him a majority in the new Parliament more than three times that which his illustrious predecessor had gained at the previous contest in 1951. Those middle-of-the-road voters who had earlier felt a certain anxiety at the thought of Sir Winston with his bulldog image leading the nation at a time when world peace seemed to hang in the balance, had no such qualms about Anthony Eden. To them the new Prime Minister epitomised their idea of the perfect peace-maker – a man who had been instrumental in halting the war in Korea and bringing about a ceasefire in Indo-China, who had resolved Britain's disputes with Persia and Egypt and who had initiated the first tentative steps towards ending the Cold War between the West and the Communist bloc. And with the first post-war Summit Conference between the leaders of America, Russia, Britain and France about to take place, it seemed inconceivable that the search for peace should be entrusted to anyone but the man who had brought about this remarkable sequence of settlements.

Indeed seldom has any Prime Minister of Britain taken office under more auspicious circumstances or with a greater fund of goodwill at home and abroad, in Parliament and in the councils of the world outside. Yet within less than two years, Eden was to throw that goodwill away and to bring about his own downfall by plunging into a conflict that was as unnecessary as its outcome was mortifying for him and for the nation he aspired to lead. By one of the most tragic paradoxes of modern times, after the 'belligerent bulldog' Churchill had retired, leaving behind him a long line of peaceful arrangements, the deft diplomatist who had been the principal architect of these settlements was to bequeath to his successor a legacy of war, humiliation and confusion. In so doing, he lost not only his reputation as a peace-maker *par excellence* but also the premiership for which he had worked and waited for so long. And whereas his record as Foreign Secretary was studded with one brilliant success after another, his brief reign as Prime Minister will be remembered only for the titanic disaster of Suez.

To understand how so experienced and pre-eminent a statesman as Eden came to break all the rules that had hitherto governed his political career it is necessary to turn the pages of history back to the time when he first took over the office of Foreign Secretary at the end of 1935 at the tender age of thirty-eight. In a brilliant personal portrait Lord Vansittart, then the permanent head of the Foreign Office, described how his political chief rose to such dizzy heights at so early an age:

'Young Eden, straight from charm school, omitted nothing to deserve his promotion. . . . His appearance went far to ensure that he would get what he wanted, and that was a lot. . . . Zealous, affable, intelligent . . . he possessed early the makings of a good House of Commons manner. Desirous and deserving of praise, he avoided suspicions of brilliance or originality [and] he said the right thing so often that he seemed incapable of saying anything else. . . . In three years he was Lord Privy Seal, in four Foreign Secretary. It all seemed probable.'

During these formative years it was for the most part plain sailing for 'young Eden'. Always a glutton for work, he revelled in the activity of international conferences and parliamentary debates. Both in the

House of Commons, where he served his apprenticeship as Under-secretary of State for Foreign Affairs, and then as Britain's spokesman in the League of Nations, he quickly established himself as a most skilful parliamentarian and negotiator. True, when Mussolini set the pattern of Fascist aggression in the thirties by attacking Abyssinia, Eden failed to mobilise sufficient international support for effective sanctions against the aggressor. Yet it was generally recognised that this was not for want of trying on his part. Hence he personally bore no share of blame for the failure of the sanctions policy. Even the scandal of the Hoare-Laval plan for buying off Mussolini, by awarding him a substantial portion of Abyssinian territory, had no adverse effects on Eden who, together with the Prime Minister, Stanley Baldwin, and the rest of the Cabinet, contrived to dissociate himself from what the Foreign Secretary had agreed with his French opposite number. And when Hoare, finding himself disowned by his colleagues and pilloried by the press, resigned from the Foreign Secretaryship, Eden was, despite his youth, the natural and inevitable successor.

However, within three months of his succession, his days of plain sailing were brought to an abrupt stop and the first major crisis of his political life burst upon him, which no amount of 'charm school' training could help him to surmount and which was to scar him for all the rest of his political life. In March 1936 Hitler tore up the Versailles peace settlement and the Locarno treaty by sending German troops to reoccupy the Rhineland, which Germany had agreed under both of these treaties should remain demilitarised.

Up to this point Eden's aim had been to do all in his power to avert a second war with Germany, to which end he was, as he told his Cabinet colleagues, fully prepared to make 'concessions of value to her as part of a final settlement. . . .' Although the Germans had announced in March 1935 that, contrary to the Versailles terms, they already possessed an air force and would shortly have a conscript army of thirty-six divisions, Eden continued to regard Mussolini rather than Hitler as the principal villain of Europe and to contend that a settlement with Germany would be possible if only she would play her part in the League of Nations and sign a disarmament treaty.

Hitler's reoccupation of the Rhineland should therefore have come as a serious setback to such hopes. Yet, far from abandoning his appeasement policy, Eden's reaction was to persist in his search for an accommodation with Nazi Germany. Brazen though it was, he told his colleagues, Hitler's move had been most skilfully contrived. And while it might now be clear that the German leader would repudiate any treaty if convenient, the Government could not ignore the fact that 'not one in a thousand Englishmen' was prepared to resist the reoccupation of the Rhineland by force of arms. British public opinion, along with most of the Cabinet, felt that Germany had a right to send troops into a piece of her own territory. And a lot of people thought that there was something to be said for Hitler's argument that France had been the first to break at least the spirit of the Locarno treaty by her recent alliance with Russia, which had effectively encircled Germany. Moreover, the Government had also to take into account that, even as his army marched into the Rhineland, Hitler had offered a new European settlement which included the creation of a demilitarised zone on both sides of Germany's frontiers with France and Belgium.

It was all very well, Eden contended, for the French to call for a military showdown with Germany on this issue. But Laval's recent attempt to inveigle Britain into betraying Abyssinia and the League scarcely suggested that French counter action would in practice be more than a bluff which Hitler would be certain to call. Therefore he suggested, to the infinite relief of the Cabinet, that in view of 'Germany's growing strength and power of mischief', Britain should continue to seek 'as enduring a settlement as possible while Hitler is in the mood to do so'. And since there was no alternative but to submit to the reoccupation of the Rhineland, it would be preferable for Britain to persuade France to accept the *fait accompli* 'while surrender still has a bargaining value'. All that Eden asked of Hitler was that, to show good faith, the Germans should withdraw all but a token force from the former demilitarised zone while the proposed new treaty was being negotiated. And when the answer came that Germany could only guarantee not to increase the existing occupation army, his sole practical riposte was to announce that France had been invited to join in staff talks in London.

As a result the Germans got what they wanted over the Rhineland without being obliged even to spell out their proposals for a new Locarno, let alone to enter into any fresh engagements. Yet, as late as the end of 1937, only a few weeks before he resigned from Neville Chamberlain's Government, Eden was still talking of the need for a settlement with Hitler. Harold Nicolson records that, at a meeting of Tory MPs, Eden asserted that there was no imminent likelihood of war.

Despite Hitler's repudiation of the peace settlement, he told them that there was now a better than ever prospect for a policy of appeasement and that Britain should seize the opportunity to reach a general settlement with Germany. Moreover, in order to clear the decks for the appeasement approach, Eden had shunted the resolutely anti-Nazi Vansittart from the post of Permanent Under-Secretary at the Foreign Office into a sinecure assignment whence he could exercise no effective influence on policy. And even although his attitude towards Hitler hardened somewhat after his resignation and more especially after Munich, he steadfastly refused to join in any backbench campaign to stiffen the Government's resistance to the Nazi menace.

It would, of course, be grossly unfair to say, with the advantage of hindsight, that Eden ought to have acceded to French demands for joint military action in March 1936 and that, when his colleagues rejected such counsels, he should have resigned. Although the French persisted in saying so, nobody could then have been certain – as we are now from the German documents which have since come to light – that Hitler would have backed down, if he had been confronted by an Anglo-French show of force. But it was because Eden knew, on reflection, that he had been responsible for what Sir Alexander Cadogan afterwards called this 'great and tragic appeasement', that he himself was to state in his own memoirs that Britain and France 'should have attempted the impossible' and braved the public outcry against forcing Germany to withdraw her armies from the Rhineland. And to a former private secretary, Sir Pierson Dixon, he confided some twenty years later that if Britain had resisted Hitler in 1936, the Second World War might have been avoided, in which case 'millions of lives would have been saved'.

Thus it is clear that, for all the rest of his most distinguished political career, Eden was scarred by a feeling of guilt for his inaction over the Rhineland. Yet far from suffering any censure for his tame surrender, his reputation as Foreign Secretary went from strength to strength. And when he finally resigned early in 1938, having found that he could no longer work with his Prime Minister, Neville Chamberlain, he was revered by all those who opposed appeasement as a man of conscience and courage who wanted to stand up to the European dictators, Hitler as well as Mussolini.

In fact Eden's resignation, when it came, had nothing to do with Hitler and, so far as it concerned the Government's attitude towards Mussolini, it turned on an issue more of procedure and timing than of principle. Whereas Baldwin had been largely uninterested in international affairs and so had left his Foreign Secretary a very free hand, Chamberlain, deeming it his duty to pacify the situation in Europe, intervened constantly in the conduct of foreign policy after he succeeded to the premiership in 1937. Being essentially more vain than most politicians, Eden soon came to resent such interference after the relative freedom of action he had enjoyed under Baldwin. And although, to begin with, Eden told a close friend that Chamberlain had the makings of a great Prime Minister, within a very few months his opinion of his chief underwent a drastic change. In January 1938, President Roosevelt proposed to Britain a conference of the major European powers and the United States to discuss and, if possible, settle outstanding international problems. The Foreign Secretary was abroad at the time on a brief spell of leave and, as if deliberately taking advantage of his absence, Chamberlain dashed off a damping reply saying that he was hoping to reach a settlement with Hitler and Mussolini and that he did not want any crossing of wires at this delicate juncture.

Eden exploded with rage when he learnt of this, and on his return to London promptly sent Roosevelt a message designed to mitigate the Prime Minister's negative response. After a week of arguing he prevailed on Chamberlain to cable the President that he warmly welcomed his initiative and would support it whenever he decided to launch it. But although Roosevelt replied that he was deeply gratified by the Prime Minister's second message, the damage had been done and nothing more was heard of the President's project.

Convinced that Chamberlain had torpedoed the best, if not the only, hope of the Americans throwing their weight behind the European democracies' search for peace, Eden now began to realise that he would never be able to work harmoniously with his Prime Minister. And when Chamberlain insisted on holding formal discussions for a settlement with Mussolini, based on Britain's *de jure* recognition of the Italian conquest of Abyssinia, he argued strongly that only informal talks should take place unless and until the Italian dictator made some gesture of good faith, such as withdrawing the troops he had sent to fight for General Franco in the current Spanish Civil War. Various attempts were made by Eden's friends in the Cabinet to draw up a compromise formula on which both the Prime Minister and the Foreign Secretary could agree. But to no avail. Chamberlain was no less delighted to get rid of Eden than Eden was determined to stick to his guns. And in February 1938 the two men formally parted company.

However, after an interval of less than two years during which, to the dismay of his supporters in Parliament and the press, he preserved an uncritical silence on foreign policy issues, Eden returned to Chamberlain's Government as Dominions Secretary following the outbreak of World War II. In this capacity he chafed at the relative inactivity and it was with the greatest enthusiasm that he took over the War Office when Churchill was precipitated into the premiership in the spring of 1940. Churchill had long been an admirer of Eden, who he thought was by far the best member of those governments of the 1930s from which he himself had been excluded. And when Eden had resigned, he described how for once sleep deserted him: 'From midnight till dawn I lay in my bed consumed by emotions of sorrow and fear. There seemed one strong young figure standing up against long, dismal, drawling tides of drift and surrender. . . . Now he was gone. I watched the daylight slowly creep in through the windows and saw before me in mental gaze the vision of death.'

Not surprisingly therefore, when Lord Halifax, who had succeeded to the Foreign Office in 1938, was appointed as Ambassador to Washington three years later, it was Eden whom Churchill chose as Foreign Secretary. With his customary love of hard work, Eden once more plunged into the direction of British foreign policy and soon became, along with Lord Beaverbrook and Field-Marshal Smuts, a member of the most intimate circle of Churchill's friends. And although Churchill interfered constantly in foreign policy matters, any differences between the two men were mostly of method only and, more often than not, Churchill would be able to charm his lieutenant into agreement. Indeed one of Churchill's private secretaries has stated that only on one occasion did he ever witness an open disagreement between Eden and his Prime Minister in all the five years in which they worked together during the war.

So great was the harmony of this partnership that Churchill very soon nominated Eden as his successor over the heads of several senior ministerial colleagues and in 1942 asked him to take on the task of leading the House of Commons in addition to his Foreign Office responsibilities. Realising that the intention was to groom him for the eventual succession to the premiership, Eden accepted these additional burdens with alacrity. And although his Foreign Office advisers complained that he henceforth became more than ever what Cadogan called 'a cat on hot bricks', and never had enough time to discuss foreign policy, his three years' spell as Leader of the House was a brilliant success, from which he emerged as a parliamentarian of the very highest order.

However the burden of combining these two jobs, with the Commons then sitting morning and afternoon, eventually undermined his health, and just before the 1945 general election he was stricken with a virulent jaundice which effectively prevented him from any participation in the campaign. This was the first warning that physically he was no superman, however much he might rely on his abundant store of nervous energy to get him through his work. But Eden refused to admit the fact, and after he became Foreign Secretary for the third time when the Tories were returned to office in 1951, he would take elaborate steps to demonstrate his physical fitness to the world and to conceal from all but his closest advisers that he could be laid low by so much as a head-cold. Working from before breakfast to the early hours of the next morning his day was a non-stop series of Cabinet meetings, conferences and interviews, with questions or debates in Parliament to answer at least once a week. Never able to be alone for more than a few minutes at a time, he loved to preside over large gatherings of ministers and Foreign Office officials. And on these occasions he would more often than not put on the kind of performance that prompted Anthony Quayle, who met him during the war, to remark that he seemed like some actor playing the part of Eden. To save time, meetings with his closest advisers would frequently take place with him in bed, sun-bathing on a terrace or dressing for dinner – and occasionally even in the bath-tub. Indeed, except for his few hours of sleep, there was never one moment in the day or night when he ever seemed to want to relax.

Inevitably the strain of such working hours was to take its toll and early in 1953 he was wheeled off to hospital to have his gall-bladder removed. Then, as ill luck would have it, he suffered a serious relapse due to trouble with the bile-duct, the exhaust-pipe of the human system, from which he was never to recover fully and which kept him away from the conduct of foreign affairs for the next months.

Nevertheless, despite this setback, there can be no doubt that the third spell as Foreign Secretary marked the high point of Eden's political career. Taking over at the height of the Cold War between the West and the Soviet bloc, he set about trying to reduce international tensions and to substitute discussion for diatribe as the means of diplomatic communication. When he took office, in addition to the overriding problems of the Cold War with Russia, the armistice talks in Korea were deadlocked, the Communists were threatening to take over all Indo-China, British oilmen had been thrown out of Persia, relations with Egypt were in a state of undeclared war over the presence of the British bases on the Suez Canal and, for good measure, Italy and Yugoslavia were at odds over the future of Trieste. Yet when he succeeded to the premiership three and a half years afterwards, all these critical issues had been settled, largely, and in some cases entirely, due to his persistent diplomacy; and relations with Russia had improved to the point where the first post-war Summit Meeting was about to be held in Geneva. Seldom in history has Britain and a British Foreign Secretary been so highly revered in the councils of the world.

Well might two of his senior Foreign Office advisers, Cadogan and Lord Strang, say of Eden in their memoirs that no other Foreign Secretary whom they served could excel him in finesse as a negotiator or in a sense of international relationships. Nobody appreciated this better than Churchill who, even as he formed his last Government at the age of seventy-six, was thinking of retiring in the near future. But after Eden's grave illness in 1953, Churchill began to wonder if his chosen successor was physically and mentally strong enough to take over as Prime Minister. At the same time, he was determined that no one else should succeed him and so, although he himself suffered a serious stroke in 1953, he held on to the premiership hoping that the interval would give Eden the necessary time to recoup his strength. Nevertheless Churchill's puckish sense of humour could not resist the occasional opportunity to tease his successor, as happened when he announced, during a visit from Dean Acheson, the American Secretary of State, that he intended to cut down the trees in the Downing Street garden. Eden protested that he had no right to do so. Living at No. 10 did not mean that he owned the place. 'I see what you mean,' Churchill replied with a mischievous twinkle, 'I'm only the life tenant, you're the remainder-man.'

But Eden could not understand why Churchill continually postponed his retirement and he persisted, with more petulance than discretion, in telling his friends and colleagues that the 'old man' was playing cat and mouse with him. For, sad to say, he never really reciprocated Churchill's feelings of real affection for him. Indeed he was sometimes extremely jealous of his chief. Dixon cited an instance in his diary when, after the Yalta Conference in 1945, Eden became furious with Churchill for insisting on accompanying him on a visit to newly liberated Athens where he had hoped to have all the limelight. The Prime Minister's decision, Dixon recorded, 'reduced Eden to such a state of exasperation that he sulked all the afternoon, refused to look at any work and then complained . . . when he did read some telegrams that matters of importance had been kept from him'

What is more Churchill was not the only object of Eden's jealousy. During the war he resented the independent status Harold Macmillan enjoyed as Minister Resident in North Africa and Italy, and wanted him to be subordinate to his orders as Foreign Secretary. Then, when he himself became Prime Minister, he very soon realised that Macmillan, whom he first appointed to the Foreign Office, was too strong a character to work as a subordinate in the sphere of foreign affairs, where he intended as Prime Minister to exercise no less paramount an influence than before. Not only had the new Foreign Secretary gained the credit and distinction of signing the long delayed Austrian peace treaty, but he had also shown a far greater understanding of the Greek Government's attitude in the Cyprus dispute than Eden was prepared to concede. Consequently, at the first available opportunity in the late autumn of 1955, Macmillan was transferred to the home front as Chancellor of the Exchequer in place of Rab Butler who was in need of a change after four anxious years at the Treasury.

Not surprisingly such jealousy towards his political contemporaries made it extremely difficult for Eden to give his friendship wholeheartedly to any of his senior colleagues. Consequently he was a very lonely man, and although he made sure that he was seldom without company, his choice of companions generally fell on men much younger than himself who could not possibly represent any threat to his supremacy and who, as Dixon once described them to me, were more like 'buddies' than real and enduring friends.

Nor were these egocentric susceptibilities confined to personal relationships. As Butler wrote in his autobiography, Eden was extremely sensitive to criticism, especially in the press. Many is the time that he called me at home before breakfast to complain bitterly about some editorial which was not to his liking. Occasionally he would hit back justifiably, as happened when the *Sunday Express* once launched a most unjust attack on a senior Foreign Office official who had no right to reply for himself. But, less wisely, he would all too often allow himself to be goaded by some personal criticism into an outburst of rage reminiscent no doubt of his father, an irascible baronet who, when a downpour of rain ruined a day's partridge shooting, is alleged to have beaten with his fists on the drawing-room window shouting, 'Oh! God, how like You!'

As Eden climbed to the top of the political ladder, these quirks of his character seemed to grow rather than to diminish. In part this could be attributed to the debilitating after-effects of his illness in 1953. But aside from that, he found himself altogether too isolated as Prime Minister. Unlike the Foreign Office where he was constantly surrounded by hordes of experts and officials, No. 10 was a very lonely pinnacle. And Eden compensated for this loneliness by continually intervening in the work of his ministers, especially those at the Foreign Office, even to the point of sometimes countermanding decisions which, although they conformed to established policy, had not been specifically referred to him for approval. As Butler put it, the Prime Minister was driven to making 'innumerable telephone calls on every day of the week and every hour of the day which characterised his conscientious but highly strung supervision of our affairs'. And as one who was frequently at the receiving end of those calls, I can honestly say that Eden in his days as Foreign Secretary could never have suffered more interference from his various chiefs than Selwyn Lloyd and I endured during his brief premiership.

As this interference increased so a sense of frustration and distrust began to pervade the atmosphere of Whitehall which did not take long to communicate itself to Fleet Street. And before Eden had been in office for six months, the press began to attack him for lack of effective leadership. Inevitably comparisons were made between him and his predecessor from which he emerged dwarfed by the mantle of Churchill. And as if this were not hurtful enough to his vanity, a scathing attack appeared in an editorial in that archetypal Tory newspaper, the *Daily Telegraph*. Describing how, when making a speech, Eden would often stress a point by putting the clenched fist of one hand into the palm of the other, the editor commented, 'But the smack is seldom heard', and he went on to say that it was high time that the smack of firm government was heard from No. 10.

Eden had never been exactly the darling of the Conservative right who had consistently opposed him and supported Chamberlain's policies in the late thirties. Also, during his last spell as Foreign Secretary, they had bitterly criticised him for tamely giving way to nationalist pressures from Nasser's Egypt and agreeing to remove the British bases from the Suez Canal Zone. Being as always highly sensitive to criticism from the press and now nagged by deteriorating health, he responded to the *Daily Telegraph* editorial like a kicking mule. Instead of following his own natural bent as a deft diplomat and negotiator *par excellence*, he decided totally out of character to show his critics that he was the strong man who could wear Churchill's mantle without being bowed down by it. Talleyrand was to play the part of Napoleon. Eden was to silence his critics of the right by joining them.

Thus when, two months later, King Hussein of Jordan dismissed his British Commander-in-Chief, General Glubb, at twenty-four hours' notice, Eden reacted violently. Instead of taking care to discover what motives lay behind this sudden action, he immediately concluded that it was Nasser's doing. Gone was the desire to get on terms with the new Egypt which, as Foreign Secretary, he had expressed to me when Nasser and I signed the agreement about the British bases less than two years before. Arab nationalism, which had earlier been a legitimate aspiration in his sight, had become what he termed a 'bacillus' which had to be exterminated. As he now told me, Nasser must be destroyed and it was only a matter of waiting for a suitable pretext to do so.

From that moment onwards, therefore, Eden declared a personal war on Egypt's ruler. Nasser, he asserted, was the sworn enemy of Britain throughout the Middle East. Not satisfied with getting the British to remove their troops from Egyptian territory, he was engaged in a conspiracy with Arab nationalist forces everywhere to destroy all British influence and interests in the Arab world. And as he pondered how best to kill this mad dog before every other Arab was bitten and infected by its rabid poison, the memory of 1936 came back to haunt him. World War II might not have happened, he told himself, if Britain and France had stopped Hitler when he marched into the Rhineland; and he felt that he bore a major share of the responsibility for their failure to do so. Now, twenty years later, he felt he had the chance to expiate his inaction at that fatal turning-point in history. Come what might, he would not be found wanting a second time.

To compare Nasser with Hitler, or even Mussolini, was of course grossly to misread his motives and even to exaggerate his power to challenge Britain's position in the Middle East. For Egypt had neither the strength nor the intention to remove more than Britain's military presence from Arab soil. Yet when Nasser nationalised the Suez Canal

Company in the following July, Eden contended that his action was proof of his implacable hostility to every British interest in the area and of the need to crush him without delay.

In the event, such was Nasser's skill in avoiding any open collision with British interests, following the nationalisation of the Canal Company, that Eden was obliged to wait until he could concoct with the French and the Israelis the necessary pretext to destroy his enemy by force of arms. And when, as was inevitable, the pressures of world opinion, led by America and Russia, brought about the withdrawal of the Anglo-French force that had been sent to seize the Suez Canal, the Prime Minister's strong-arm policy lay in ruins. Britain and France, together with Israel, had been branded throughout the world as aggressors for their gunboat diplomacy and were obliged to withdraw without achieving any of their objectives. Not surprisingly in a sick man, a total breakdown of Eden's health now followed, as the fevers induced by the damaged bile-duct became more frequent and violent with the nervous strain of those last terrible weeks. And when the doctors told him that he could not carry on, he had no alternative but to tender his resignation to the Queen.

In one way, perhaps, the fates were kinder than they seemed when they decreed that Eden should retire for reasons of health. For it is hard to see how he could have carried on as Prime Minister after the sordid fiasco he had brought about. Indeed, from his performance throughout his twenty-one nervous months at No. 10, it is more than likely that, even if Nasser and Suez had never happened, he would not have been able to hold down the premiership for very long. Brilliant diplomatist and parliamentarian that he was, when put to the test he did not have the right temperament for the tasks involved.

If the premiership were merely a prize for diligence and hard work, no one ever earned it more than Eden. But, as it turned out, he had neither the confidence in himself nor the trust in others to fulfil the expectations of his admirers. When things went wrong he answered his critics from an injured vanity rather than a sense of purpose. In part, this was because he had for too long been the Golden Boy of the Tory party, the glamorous Crown Prince awaiting the summons to mount the throne in place of the ageing Emperor. This inevitably made it that much harder for him to rise above the criticisms that descended upon his head once he had reached the summit. In part also his failure was due to his inability to think and plan strategically. Consummate tactician that he was, both in diplomacy and politics, he lacked the strategist's sense of direction and, when blown off course, his helmsmanship degenerated into a series of reckless manoeuvres designed to court an ephemeral popularity and so undermined still further that sense of confidence among his colleagues which is quintessential to a successful premiership.

Would that Eden had heeded the lines of the poet Longfellow:

> 'Not in the clamour of the crowded street,
> Not in the shouts and plaudits of the throng,
> But in ourselves are triumph and defeat.'

For if only he could have accepted ultimately to be judged on his own real merits and achievements, he would not have needed to seek 'the shouts and plaudits' of a fickle public.

But it was not to be so. Unable to be true to his own nature, on the morrow of his greatest diplomatic triumphs, he plunged into a suicidal and ignominious defeat. That Eden should have failed so miserably in the office for which he had waited for so long was tragic indeed. Yet more tragic still was the fact that in those last few disastrous months of his career, he destroyed so much of the respect and esteem which he had earlier won for himself and for Britain among the nations of the world.

BIBLIOGRAPHY

Acheson, Dean, *Present at the Creation* (London, 1970)

Avon, Lord, Eden Memoirs: *Facing the Dictators* (London, 1962); *Full Circle* (London, 1960)

Butler, Lord, *The Art of the Possible* (London, 1971)

Cadogan, Sir Alexander, *Diaries 1938–45* (London, 1971)

Churchill, Sir Winston, *The Second World War*, vol. i, 'The Gathering Storm' (London, 1959)

Cook, Don, *Floodtide in Europe* (New York, 1965)

Cooper, Duff, *Old Men Forget* (London, 1953)

Dixon, Pierson, *Double Diploma* (London, 1968)

Harvey, Lord, *Diplomatic Diaries of Oliver Harvey 1937–40* (London, 1970)

Johnson, Alan Campbell, *Viscount Halifax* (London, 1941)

Macmillan, Harold, *Riding the Storm* (London, 1971)

Murphy, Robert, *Diplomat among Warriors* (London, 1964)

Nicolson, Harold, *Diaries and Letters 1930–9* (London, 1956)

Normanbrook, Lord, and Colville, John, *Action This Day* (London, 1968)

Nutting, Anthony, *No End of a Lesson* (London, 1967)

Strang, Lord, *Home and Abroad* (London, 1956)

Taylor, A. J. P., *English History 1914–45* (Oxford, 1965)

Trevelyan, Lord, *Worlds Apart* (London, 1971)

Sherwood, Robert, *White House Papers of Harry L. Hopkins*, vol. ii (London, 1949)

Vansittart, Lord, *The Mist Procession* (London, 1958)

HAROLD MACMILLAN

BY

DUNCAN CROW

*Maurice Harold Macmillan, PC (1942), FRS (1962). Born 10
February 1894. Educated at Eton and Balliol College, Oxford.
Served in the Grenadier Guards 1914–18. Married Lady Dorothy
Evelyn Cavendish, one son, two daughters. ADC to the Governor-
General of Canada 1919–20. MP for Stockton 1924–29 and 1931–
45, for Bromley 1945–64. Parliamentary Secretary to the Ministry
of Supply 1940–42; Parliamentary Under-Secretary of State for
the Colonies 1942; Minister Resident at Allied HQ in North-
West Africa 1942–45; Secretary for Air 1945; Minister of Hous-
ing and Local Government 1951–54; Minister of Defence 1954–
55; Secretary of State for Foreign Affairs 1955; Chancellor of the
Exchequer 1955–57; Prime Minister and First Lord of the Treasury
1957–63. Chancellor of the University of Oxford from 1960;
President, Macmillan (Holdings). Hon. DCL (Oxford) 1958,
LLD (Cambridge) 1961, (Sussex) 1963. Author of (Memoirs):*
Winds of Change, *1966;* The Blast of War, *1967;* Tides of
Fortune, *1969;* Riding the Storm, *1971;* Pointing the Way,
1972; At the End of the Day, *1973. Also* Reconstruction; A
Plea for a National Policy, *1933;* Planning for Employment,
1935; The Middle Way, *1938; etc.*

Maurice Harold Macmillan. Photo by Vivienne

HAROLD MACMILLAN

EARLY POLITICAL CAREER

Maurice Harold Macmillan was born in London on 10 February 1894, the youngest of the three sons of Maurice Crawford Macmillan and Helen *née* Belles, the daughter of Dr Joshua Tarleton Belles of Spencer, Indiana, USA. His paternal grandfather, Daniel Macmillan, and Daniel's brother Alexander, who were brought up in extreme poverty in the west of Scotland, founded the family's publishing house of Macmillan. In 1855 they published their first best-seller, Charles Kingsley's *Westward Ho*! One of Daniel Macmillan's greatest friends was another Christian Socialist, the Reverend Frederick Denison Maurice. The admiration he felt for Maurice was perpetuated in the name of one of his sons, Harold's father, who carried on the link, as indeed did Harold himself in his turn.

Harold Macmillan was educated at Summerfields (a preparatory school in Oxford), Eton (where he was a Scholar and which he had to leave prematurely because of ill health), and Oxford (Balliol as an Exhibitioner), 1912–14 (a First in Classic Moderations). During the period between Eton and Oxford he had a series of tutors including Ronald Knox who, he wrote later, 'had a profound influence upon me, both then and afterwards'.

He was commissioned in the King's Royal Rifle Corps in 1914, then transferred to the Grenadier Guards in which he subsequently became a captain. He was wounded at the battle of Loos in 1915, and on the Somme in September 1916. This latter wound shattered his pelvis, keeping him out of action and mostly in hospital for the rest of the war. Not until 1920 did the wound finally heal.

In 1919 he went to Canada as ADC to the Governor-General, the ninth Duke of Devonshire. He became engaged to the Duke's daughter, Lady Dorothy Cavendish, returned to England with her in January 1920, and was married at St Margaret's, Westminster, three months later. Soon afterwards he joined the family publishing firm.

His political career began at the general election in December 1923 when he stood as Conservative candidate for the north of England industrial constituency of Stockton-on-Tees. In a three-cornered fight he lost to the Liberal by 73 votes with the Labour candidate 1,042 behind in third place. At the next general election, in October 1924, he won Stockton by 3,215 votes from the Labour candidate with the Liberal third. He made his maiden speech in the Budget debate on 30 April 1925.

Macmillan was MP for Stockton from 1924 to May 1929 when he lost the seat to Labour by 2,389 votes with the Liberal again third. In the October 1931 election he beat the Labour candidate by 11,031 votes in a straight fight. He retained the seat in the November 1935 election with a 4,068 majority over Labour, the Liberal losing his deposit, and continued as Conservative Member for Stockton-on-Tees until he was defeated in the July 1945 election.

Macmillan, who had great ability and was deeply interested in politics, was nevertheless much neglected during his years in Parliament before the outbreak of World War II. He earned for himself the reputation of a rebel. When he entered the House of Commons in 1924 he gravitated towards the left wing of his party and was one of a group who were nicknamed 'The YMCA' – as opposed to another section of the Conservative party called by their opponents 'The Forty Thieves'. The young enthusiasts of 'The YMCA' were keen advocates of social reform and of a planned economy. In 1927, with Robert Boothby, John Loder and Oliver Stanley, Macmillan published *Industry and the State*, which was regarded as a manifesto of the progressive Conservatives. From then until the outbreak of war he continued to write books and pamphlets (*The State and Industry* 1932, *The Next Step* 1932, *Reconstruction* 1933, *Planning for Employment* 1935 (joint author), *The Next Five Years* 1935 (joint author), *The Middle Way* 1938, *The Price of Peace* 1938, *Economic Aspects of Defence* 1939), which propounded his unorthodox Conservative views.

For Macmillan the stimulus for planning and reform was the constituency he represented, acting on an awakened social conscience that had been stirred by his experiences in the trenches. Stockton-on-Tees was one of many depressed areas where widespread unemployment that went on year after year made a mockery of 'the land fit for heroes' that had been promised to the returning soldiers of the 1914–18 war. This dreadful evidence of human waste that surrounded him in his constituency affected Macmillan throughout his political career – as indeed it lingered with anyone who saw the hopeless street-corner groups of unwanted men that haunted Britain in the years between the two world wars.

Although Macmillan still maintained a close interest in social and economic questions, after 1935 he began to turn his attention more and more to foreign affairs and to defence. The *Zeitgeist* was changing. Abyssinia, Hitler, and the Spanish Civil War were beginning to overshadow Jarrow and the hunger marchers. When sanctions against Italy were abandoned in 1936 he was one of only two Conservatives to vote with the Labour Opposition against the Government on a three-line Whip, supporting the motion 'That His Majesty's Government by their lack of a resolute and straightforward foreign policy, have lowered the prestige of the country, weakened the League of Nations, imperilled peace and thereby forfeited the confidence of this House'. Immediately after this act of open mutiny he resigned the party Whip, on 29 June, and remained as an Independent Conservative until 27 July 1937, when he wrote to Chamberlain, who had succeeded Baldwin as Prime Minister, asking for re-admission to the Whip. His return to the ranks of Conservative respectability was hardly wholehearted. In October 1938 he supported the Independent Socialist candidate, Dr A. D. Lindsay (later Lord Lindsay of Birker), against the official Conservative candidate, Quintin Hogg (later Lord Hailsham), in the Oxford City by-election. Macmillan, like Lindsay, was opposed to Chamberlain's Munich policy. There was now no chance of his getting office under Chamberlain. Not until the premiership passed to Churchill, whose firm supporter he was, did Macmillan at last get office. He was forty-six.

On 15 May 1940 Churchill gave him his first ministerial appointment as Parliamentary Secretary to the Ministry of Supply. Up till then his sole job connected with the war had been as a member of a committee set up to organise aid for the Finns in their Winter War against the Russians, and as a representative of that committee he had visited Finland in February. He remained at the Ministry of Supply under three successive ministers (Herbert Morrison, Sir Andrew Duncan, and Lord Beaverbrook) until 4 February 1942, when he became Parliamentary Under-secretary at the Colonial Office under Lord Cranborne (later Lord Salisbury). Neither of these positions was of any great consequence in the hierarchy of political power and they brought him to the brink of resignation. Then all at once he came to the top. At the end of December 1942 Churchill appointed him Minister Resident at Allied Force Headquarters in North-west Africa and he became a member of the Cabinet (though not of the War Cabinet) with direct access to the Prime Minister.

Macmillan held this office for thirty months, during which its title changed slightly as AFHQ moved to Italy and General Maitland Wilson succeeded General Eisenhower as Supreme Commander for the Mediterranean. It was a position of immense importance and immense power. It demanded a quite remarkable ability for its success. As the course of the war brought the Allies to North-west Africa and then to Italy the political problems that emerged, and which had a profound effect on the military campaign, had to be solved in concert by the Americans and the British in relation to those factions of the French and Italian schisms that could wield significant power. And after French North Africa and the new government in Italy came the attempted Communist takeover of Greece and the Yugoslavian Communist irredentism under Tito. In all these affairs of nations Macmillan played a dominant role in his three-cornered hat as British Resident Minister in the Mediterranean, Political Adviser to the Supreme Allied Commander, and Acting President of the Allied Commission for Italy.

Macmillan's Mediterranean duties came to an end on 26 May 1945 and he returned to the United Kingdom. From his heights of power as virtual Viceroy of the Mediterranean he, like others in his party, went into the wilderness of political frustration. After two months as Secretary for Air in the Caretaker Government he lost his seat at Stockton in the general election of July 1945 by 8,664 votes to the Labour candidate, with the Liberal nowhere.

His absence from Parliament was, however, brief. In August 1945 he was adopted as Conservative candidate for Bromley, and at a by-election on 16 November 1945 he won a three-cornered fight with a majority of 5,557. He retained the seat at the general elections of February 1950 and October 1951 with majorities of 10,688 and 12,125 respectively. Macmillan was not enthralled by opposition work and the return to power of a Conservative Government under Churchill in October 1951 seemed to augur well for his own return to a Cabinet post of significant power. But Churchill offered him the Ministry of Housing.

After the years in the Mediterranean and the discreet wielding of great power in the councils of nations it was hardly an appointment to enthuse him. Even in the years of opposition he had, at Churchill's request, taken a considerable part in the European movement and had been a delegate to the Council of Europe. From this to building houses, even for the former Member for Stockton-on-Tees, was surely a political backwater of dreadful stagnancy. It would, said Churchill, make or mar his political career, and he pressed him with tears and Victorian mottoes ('Every humble home will bless your name'). Macmillan took time to decide. Then he accepted – and succeeded in building the number of houses promised. He established a reputation as a man 'who could get things done' and was consequently the darling of the 1952 Conservative Party Conference.

After three years at Housing ('three of the happiest years of my life') Macmillan succeeded his friend and wartime Mediterranean colleague Earl Alexander of Tunis as Minister of Defence in a Cabinet reshuffle on 18 October 1954. He held that office for six months. On 6 April 1955 Eden succeeded Churchill as Prime Minister and the following day Macmillan became Foreign Secretary. Once again it was a short tenure. Reluctantly he left the Foreign Office on 20 December 1955 (where he was succeeded by Selwyn Lloyd) and went to the Treasury as Chancellor of the Exchequer in succession to R. A. Butler. His time at the Foreign Office included the Austrian peace treaty in May, the first Summit Meeting at Geneva in July (and the subsequent Foreign Ministers' Conference there in October–November), and the defection of Burgess and Maclean in November. At the Treasury he introduced one Budget only, which included the starting of Premium Bonds. By the time the next year's Budget was due he was no longer at the Treasury but found himself, almost unbelievably it might seem to those who had studied his earlier political life, in No. 10 Downing Street as Prime Minister.

PRIME MINISTER

Harold Macmillan's appointment was only the second occasion this century on which the Crown exercised its prerogative in choosing the Prime Minister. The first was in 1923 when Baldwin was preferred to Curzon on the resignation of Bonar Law through ill health. With the resignation of Eden, also through ill health, on 9 January 1957, there were again two contenders: Macmillan and R. A. (later Lord) Butler.

Eden held his last Cabinet at five o'clock on the day of his resignation. After it was over Macmillan and Butler left separately, while the remaining ministers were asked to see Lord Salisbury (the Lord President), who was the senior Cabinet minister, and Lord Kilmuir (the Lord

Chancellor), one by one in the Lord President's room in the Privy Council offices, which could be reached without leaving the building. As each came in he was asked by Salisbury, 'Well, which is it, Wab or Hawold?' Kilmuir and Salisbury also consulted the Chief Whip, Edward Heath, and the Chairman of the Conservative party, Oliver (later Lord) Poole. The Chairman of the Conservative backbenchers' 1922 Committee gave his opinion. 'An overwhelming majority of Cabinet Ministers were in favour of Macmillan as Eden's successor, and back-bench opinion, as reported to us,' wrote Lord Kilmuir in his memoirs, 'strongly endorsed this view'.

Usually the choice of the next Prime Minister is so clear that there is no need for the Crown to take advice. In this case, because of the doubt, the Queen, on the following morning, consulted some of the 'old Tory hands'. These were: Lord Salisbury (who simply conveyed the general view in the party as gleaned from his canvass with Lord Kilmuir); Lord Waverley (better known in public life as Sir John Anderson); Lord Chandos (Oliver Lyttelton); and Sir Winston Churchill. The answer of all four was 'Macmillan'. Eden was not asked for his advice, nor did he volunteer it.

At 2 p.m. on that same day, 10 January, the Queen received Harold Macmillan and asked him to form a government. However long she may have expected it to last, neither Macmillan himself nor the generality of politicians expected it to be more than a stopgap. They could hardly have been more wrong – just as the generality of political journalists could hardly have been more wrong in prognosticating that the Queen would choose Butler. Only Randolph Churchill in the *Evening Standard* got the right answer.

When Lord Melbourne was offered the premiership in 1834 it is said that he was at first reluctant to accept it on the grounds that it was a 'damned bore'. But a friend pointed out that such a position was never held by any Greek or Roman and that even if it only lasted three months it would be 'worth while to have been Prime Minister of England'. Although Harold Macmillan showed no reluctance and required no friendly persuasion, his own estimate of how long his new Government would last was only half that 'worth while' period. He told the Queen that he doubted if it would last six weeks. Six years later, when he was still Prime Minister, she reminded him of his pessimism. Indeed, despite the rickety foundations on which it was built his premiership lasted for six years nine months, the longest unbroken term since Asquith's.

The reason for his initial pessimism was not that he had any doubts about his ability to discharge the duties of Prime Minister – indeed his American mother had always spurred his ambition to that end and he himself had always been confident of his ability. His feelings of imminent mortality for his Government were caused by the political circumstances in which he found himself. To his old friend and colleague Lord Salisbury, when Salisbury resigned from his Cabinet on 29 March 1957 over the decision to release Archbishop Makarios from his sequestration in the Seychelles, Macmillan wrote that he deeply regretted the resignation because he had 'taken on a very difficult job in circumstances almost unparalleled in political history', and he wished that Salisbury could have stayed with him to see it through.

Before examining those circumstances it is worth commenting on Macmillan's generalisation that they were almost unparalleled. His great relaxation was reading and one of his foremost traits was his knowledge of history. His conversation, wrote Sir Robert Menzies, was 'garnished with analogies from the European past', and 'had he not chosen the more arduous paths of political service, [he] would have made a professor of Modern History whose classes would have been thronged with delighted students'. Another friend and Cabinet colleague told me: 'If you got him on the day something happened – and this was before he flowered with the responsibility of the premiership – his opinion was one of the best I know. Leave him for half a dozen days and it was one of the worst. This was because he saw everything very much against a historical background.'

That Macmillan was faced with a task of great difficulty, even if not unparalleled, is without question. He took office in the bitter aftermath of Suez when his party was in disarray and the country was still in a fury of frustration and recrimination. For Britain the Suez operation had the same shatteringly divisive effect as the Dreyfus case had had on France at the turn of the century. This deep division in the instincts of the nation was caused because on the one hand there were many who felt that Britain should never have embarked on the operation at all, and on the other there were perhaps just as many who felt that having done so it should have been carried through to a successful conclusion and should not have ended in the bitter demonstration that Britain was no longer a Colossus that bestrode the world but was only a small island on the shoulder of Europe. It was the unwelcome proof that an era had ended.

Surveying the range of his immediate problems on taking office Macmillan listed six main ones.[1] 'The first need was to restore the confidence of the people in their Government and in themselves. . . . The fact that France and Britain, even acting together, could no longer impose their will was alarming. Never before in history had Western Europe proved so weak.' Secondly there were the practical problems of reopening the Suez Canal, ensuring the flow of oil, and getting compensation for losses to British subjects as a result of Nasser's actions – all of which would no doubt involve the imposition of indignities 'which we must struggle to resist'. Thirdly there was the United States. Suez had destroyed the alliance that had begun in World War II. How could that alliance 'which I knew to be essential in the modern world', be reestablished? Fourthly there was the economic situation. Having just spent a year as Chancellor of the Exchequer Macmillan was well aware of the great difficulties involved in maintaining the British economy at the correct level between inflation and deflation. The fifth problem was defence, including the true value of Cyprus as a base in Britain's defence pattern. Finally there was the future of the Commonwealth: was Macmillan 'destined to be the remodeller or the liquidator of Empire'?

If we add two further problems to the above list we have a broad appreciation of the main themes in Macmillan's premiership. These two additional problems were the East-West split across the Iron Curtain, and the relations between Britain and Europe.

The solution of the first problem was not achieved overnight; but it was achieved. At the parliamentary level the fact that the Government had a majority of forty-nine after the final debate on the aftermath of Suez on 15 and 16 May 1957 was generally regarded as proof of this. As to the restoration of confidence in the country at large Macmillan had certainly achieved this in sufficient measure by October 1959 to give his Government a substantially increased majority at the general election, an election in which Suez played no significant part. By that time indeed even the financial negotiations with Egypt had been concluded, the oil was flowing, and the Canal had been reopened – only to be closed again for a much longer period after the Arab-Israeli Six Day War of 1967. In 1967, however, the fleet of giant tankers that was gradually taking over so much of oil transportation, and the dominance of the aeroplane over the ship, were both turning the Suez Canal into a stretch of industrial archaeology.

[1] Harold Macmillan, *Riding the Storm 1956-9* (London, 1971), pp. 198-200.

While the aftermath of Suez was taking its course Macmillan was already in the thick of the other immediate problems. His most urgent task, as he saw it, was to repair the breach with Washington. Closely linked to this was Britain's defence situation. Was Britain to rely on the nuclear deterrent, as a White Paper published when Macmillan was Minister of Defence had suggested? If so, the Americans must be persuaded to repeal the McMahon Act which prevented the sharing of American nuclear information.

At President Eisenhower's suggestion Macmillan went to Bermuda in March 1957, taking with him Selwyn Lloyd, the Foreign Secretary. There they met the President and the Secretary of State, John Foster Dulles. Although, as Macmillan wrote in his autobiography, neither he nor his colleagues were prepared 'to appear in a white sheet' because they felt that they had been 'let down, if not betrayed, by the vacillating and delaying tactics which Dulles had pursued in the earlier stages of the Suez crisis and by the viciousness with which he and his subordinates had attacked us after the launching of the Anglo-French operation', and although for their part, Eisenhower and Dulles, as the President recorded, found it difficult at first 'to talk constructively with our British colleagues about Suez because of the blinding bitterness they felt towards Nasser', the Bermuda Conference nevertheless succeeded in its object: the alliance was re-established and Macmillan and Eisenhower, already old friends from the days of AFHQ, instituted a system of constant and frank communication that lasted throughout Eisenhower's presidency and was continued throughout Kennedy's. The renewal of close relations was such that when menacing issues arose, as for example they did in 1958 over Jordan and the Lebanon and over the off-shore islands and Formosa, and in 1962 over Cuba, there was no question of Britain's view being ignored. 'Our relations with America were so good,' wrote Macmillan, 'that our influence could during my term of office be exerted to the full.'[2] This did not mean, however, as has sometimes been suggested, that Macmillan put Britain in America's pocket. A clear example was over Indo-China. Macmillan was determined that Britain should not get involved in any military commitment in that area. When Kennedy asked for British help there, Macmillan refused.

There were three specific agreements reached at Bermuda. The first was that the United States would join in the work of the Baghdad Pact's

[2] *Winds of Change 1914–39* (London, 1966), p. 28.

731

Military Committee; the second, that the United States would supply Britain with guided missiles; and the third, that both countries would continue with nuclear tests. Also arising out of the Conference was the release of Makarios from the Seychelles. This was something that Eisenhower wanted, that Macmillan agreed to, and that Lord Salisbury resigned over. His resignation without any shattering effect on the Government was the first sign of Macmillan's growing political strength. Two years later, in February 1959, the Cyprus agreement was signed, and on 16 August 1960 Cyprus became an independent republic under the presidency of Makarios.

Consequent on the agreements reached at Bermuda the final revision was made to a British Defence White Paper. It was a drastic document. It announced the end of conscription. It announced the reduction of the armed forces from 690,000 to 375,000 in five years. And it announced the reliance on nuclear forces as Britain's main means of defence. The following month, on 15 May, the first British H-bomb was exploded.

Looking back on this 1957 Defence White Paper in the fifth volume of his autobiography, Macmillan wrote that 'for good or ill' it marked a new era.

'Our decision to develop and maintain an effective nuclear deterrent had important consequences both internationally and nationally. It involved the British Government in the problem of convincing our NATO allies both of its wisdom and its consistence with the theme of interdependence which I had agreed with President Eisenhower and preached in and out of season as a sound basis for the effective defence of the non-Communist world. Equally it engaged Britain, as one of three nuclear powers, in the long arguments on tests and negotiations for their restriction or abolition. It may indeed be claimed that our determination, in spite of heavy expense and many technical difficulties, to remain in the nuclear club at least allowed us to play an important and perhaps decisive part in the negotiations which finally led to the abandonment by the Three Powers of all atmospheric tests.'[3]

The Test Ban Treaty was eventually ratified on 8 October 1963, at the very end of Macmillan's premiership. It was one of his greatest triumphs.

The visit to Bermuda was the first of many journeys that Macmillan made and visits that he received from other national leaders during his

[3] *Pointing the Way 1959–61* (London, 1972), p. 249.

years as Prime Minister. Outstanding among these journeys was his visit to Russia in February 1959, a year after Krushchev had become Premier of the Soviet Union. The visit arose out of an invitation that had been given to Eden as Prime Minister when Krushchev and Bulganin visited Britain in April 1956. This was not Macmillan's first visit to Russia. He had previously been there in 1932. This new 'Voyage of Discovery', as he called it in his memoirs, was not an unqualified success at the time; snubs punctuated the cordiality. But it achieved Macmillan's object, which was to lessen the tension in East-West relations that had reached danger point as a result of Krushchev's ultimatum over Berlin the previous November, and to make some progress, however slight, towards a nuclear test ban treaty. The visit also helped to make possible the ill-fated Summit Meeting in Paris in May 1960. That this took place at all was the result of Macmillan's perseverance, and when it was broken off because of the shooting down of an American U2 aircraft over Russia his disappointment amounted 'almost to despair – so much attempted, so little achieved'. The unresolved problem of Berlin 'hung over the whole world, like a dark cloud' throughout the rest of his premiership and beyond.

As well as his frequent meetings with the American Presidents, Eisenhower and Kennedy, and his repeated exchange of visits with the French and German leaders, Macmillan kept his personal links with the Commonwealth as close as possible. During his premiership there were Commonwealth Prime Ministers' Conferences in 1957, 1960, 1961, and 1962, and he himself made two Commonwealth tours – the first in January-February 1958 to India, Pakistan, Ceylon, Australia and New Zealand; the second, exactly two years later, to Africa, where he visited Ghana, Nigeria, Rhodesia, and South Africa. It was on this second tour that on two occasions, once in Accra on 9 January 1960 and the second time in Cape Town on 3 February, he used the phrase 'the wind of change'. On the first occasion it passed unnoticed in the world press; the second time it echoed round the world:

'The most striking of all the impressions I have formed since I left London a month ago is of the strength of this African national consciousness. In different places it may take different forms, but it is happening everywhere. The wind of change is blowing through the continent. Whether we like it or not, this growth of national consciousness is a political fact. We must all accept it as a fact.'

The wind of change blew the British Colonial Empire out of existence, and especially out of Africa. It did this mainly during Macmillan's premiership, so that whether or not time will show that he did any remodelling of the Empire it is already clear that he liquidated it. Nor was this liquidation carried out without grave difficulties. In particular, 'the complications, confusions and conflicts of Central Africa seemed never to be absent from our minds' throughout the whole of his time as Prime Minister. And in place of a Colonial Empire overseas the British got the Empire in their back garden through immigration. This was not to the taste of the whole community and in August 1958 there were race riots in Nottingham and Notting Hill.

These journeys and meetings of Macmillan's were part of a new pattern of international practice, especially between the major powers, which he largely created. To some extent, it is true, he inherited the 'summit idea' from Churchill, but more than that his experiences as 'Viceroy of the Mediterranean' had shown him what the personal touch could achieve in international affairs. Only a few months after he became Prime Minister the first sputnik went into orbit. His whole approach to the overriding problem of East-West relations was a complete acceptance of the technology the sputnik and the H-bomb represented. This in a way was curious because his intellectual background, his distaste for any aspect of the 'permissive society', and his manner of an 'unflappable' Edwardian gentleman to whom politics was simply 'fun' would suggest that he would have been unwilling, or at least would have found it difficult, to accept the realities of the space age. Not a bit of it. He adapted the technique of the Field of the Cloth of Gold to the era of the jet aircraft, and he did this as far as the public was concerned with a panache and insouciance which, at any rate in the first years of his premiership, made Bevan's jibe and Vicky's cartoon character into complimentary realities. Macwonder and Supermac were just what he was, not only because of his skill in international negotiations but because of the boom that came to Britain in the early years of his premiership.

Economically the Britain of 1957 was very different from the Britain of twenty and thirty years earlier. To a politician like Macmillan who had represented Stockton-on-Tees throughout its years of misery, the face of Britain when he became Prime Minister was so changed that it seemed as if only a miracle could have wrought the transformation. It was with this in mind that he told an audience at Bedford on 20 July

1957, 'Let's be frank about it; most of our people have never had it so good. Go around the country, go to the industrial towns, go to the farms, and you will see a state of prosperity such as we have never had in my lifetime – nor indeed ever in the history of this country.' But, he went on,

'What is beginning to worry some of us is "Is it too good to be true?", or perhaps I should say, "Is it too good to last?" For, amidst all this prosperity, there is one problem that has troubled us – in one way or another – ever since the war. Its the problem of rising prices. Our constant concern today is – can prices be steadied while at the same time we maintain full employment in an expanding economy? Can we control inflation? This is the problem of our time.'

The problem was still there long after Macmillan's departure from office. Many attempts were made by his and subsequent Governments to solve it. None appeared to succeed. The first of these attempts was debated in the House of Commons five days after Macmillan's Bedford speech. This was the Government's decision to set up an independent Council on Prices, Productivity and Incomes – 'The Three Wise Men'. The Prime Minister repeated his 'Never had it so good' phrase; but he repeated it in its context, as an achievement and again as a preface to a warning, not as a boast. A third time he used it, on another occasion, and the phrase began to assume an individual existence as the slogan for Macmillan's administration and of the boom that was taking television sets and washing-machines into millions of homes and was changing the stream of bicycles that emerged from factory gates at the end of the day's work into a stream of cars bought on hire-purchase.

Not that the boom was without its setbacks. There was a cut-back in government spending and a 2 per cent rise in Bank Rate to 7 per cent in September 1957. Macmillan was not prepared to accept a continuing policy of deflation, however. In January 1958 the Chancellor, Thorneycroft, and his political lieutenants at the Treasury resigned rather than approve estimates for increased government expenditure in the following year. Macmillan was on the eve of departing on his first Commonwealth tour. He referred to the resignations in press and television interviews as 'little local difficulties' compared to the wider vision of the Commonwealth. The phrase became part of his image. He was the man who 'played it cool'. This in itself contributed importantly to the restoration of national confidence.

Macmillan's calm was something new in his political career. Lack of power had made him extremely restless, and even when he held a senior position in the Cabinet the restlessness was still there. This stemmed from his feeling that a full use was not being made of his unusually complete personality. He seemed to at least one of his friends to be 'much in touch with the press and apt to inspire rumours that stirred things up a bit'. He had considered resigning from the Colonial Office in November 1942 because his career seemed to be reaching a dead end; he was even closer to resignation from the Chancellorship of the Exchequer in February 1956 over his determination to remove subsidies from bread and milk. Unlike Thorneycroft's disagreement with his colleagues, Macmillan's was eventually resolved by compromise. Both could have brought down the Government.

When he became Prime Minister all this changed almost literally overnight. The restlessness disappeared. So too did the intriguing. It was no good intriguing for anything more. You were Prime Minister and, for better or for worse, that was it! Greater even than Viceroy of the Mediterranean, you were now Prime Minister of the United Kingdom – 'worth while', as Melbourne acknowledged, if only for a few months. And so the restlessness disappeared and in its place – and it was a curious transformation to those who watched it – there emerged a great calmness which was characterised in the press as 'unflappability'. Harold Macmillan, whose mother had insisted on his becoming a French linguist, believed with the French that *on ne règne sur les âmes que par le calme*. Indeed, though it may have been his instinctive formula for exercising power, it was also a conscious attitude. On No. 10 Downing Street notepaper, in his own hand, he wrote out a text from *The Gondoliers* for his aides in his private office and the Cabinet room: 'Quiet, calm deliberation disentangles every knot. H.M.' Sometimes, it is true, the calmness was only skin-deep. At the time of the landings by British and American troops in Jordan and Lebanon in July 1958 he wrote in his diary of 'trying to . . . hide his sickening anxiety'. Outwardly, however, the resignations of three ministers from the Treasury in January 1958 were 'little local difficulties'.

Thorneycroft was replaced as Chancellor of the Exchequer by Heathcoat Amory. When signs of a slump appeared later in 1958 measures were taken to reflate the economy. The 1959 Budget was expansionist. This cannot have been without its effect on the result of the general election in October that year. It had been a glorious summer, the economy was booming, the Conservatives increased their majority over all other parties to 100. Macmillan himself, whose majority in the 1955 election had been up by 1,014, was now returned with an even larger majority.

It was held against Macmillan by many, including Archbishop Fisher of Canterbury, that his Bedford phrase, 'Never had it so good', was a reprehensible slogan of out-and-out materialism. Lord Salisbury, too, took him to task for its sentiment. Later, in a speech in November 1961, Macmillan tried to put across the fact that the phrase, now become notorious, had continually been used out of context and had in the process totally lost the import he had intended. He reminded his audience that the phrase had been embedded in a paragraph that was far from hubristic. But the attempt to repaint the phrase in its true colours was totally unsuccessful. Like Asquith's 'Wait and see' (the parallel with which Macmillan drew in his autobiography), 'Never had it so good' was given a lasting life in a sense that was never intended. None the less, as a straight statement of fact it was incontrovertible. The outstanding domestic phenomena of Macmillan's years as Prime Minister were the multiple signs of what was being called the Affluent Society. The British people had only recently been totally rid of the austerities of rationing. It was hardly surprising that the demand for consumer goods welled up and that the drab macintosh days of post-war Britain gave place to the cheerful fashions of a new age.

Admittedly there were grim black clouds mounting above the economic horizon. Their message read, 'Is it too good to last?' Selwyn Lloyd, who replaced Heathcoat Amory as Chancellor in July 1960 and whose Budget in April 1961 continued the expansionist theme, was forced to introduce a 'Little Budget' on 25 July 1961 because of a full-scale sterling crisis. It included a 'pay pause' to stop spiralling wages. 'Though clumsily enforced, and very badly presented', wrote one of Macmillan's biographers, 'it represented the first serious attempt towards an incomes policy, which five years later was to be far more widely accepted.'[4]

In an endeavour to run the economy in a manner that would allow expansion without an unacceptable level of inflation, Macmillan made planning a respectable part of Conservative orthodoxy: 'Neddy' (National Economic Development Council) was set up in 1961, 'Nicky'

[4] Anthony Sampson, *Macmillan: A Study in Antiquity* (Harmondsworth, 1967), p. 198.

(National Incomes Commission) in 1962. But neither the pay pause nor the credit squeeze did anything to endear the Prime Minister or his party to the electorate. Nor did mounting unemployment. The days of Supermac were over. The by-elections of March 1962, especially the one at Orpington, proved the point.

Throughout Macmillan's premiership the economic position of Britain steadily declined. Partially this was because her competitive power in world markets deteriorated; partially because she could not face the challenge of the European Economic Community. Macmillan, with the experience of two wars behind him, had always been in favour of a closer unity in Europe. He had helped in the formation of the European movement. But he had not gone against the tide when the Treasury, the Foreign Office, the Board of Trade, and many of his Cabinet colleagues in the post-war Conservative governments, had been opposed to Britain's taking any part in the budding Common Market. Later he recognised his mistake, for which, he wrote in the Prologue to his autobiography, published in 1966, 'I shall never cease to blame myself'.

Scrambling along behind the increasingly powerful EEC Britain in November 1959, having failed to inveigle the Common Market countries into a wider free trade area, signed the European Free Trade Agreement with the other countries of the 'Outer Seven'. This too proved insufficient to solve the market problems of British industry. At last, on 10 August 1961, Britain applied to join the EEC. The negotiations were begun under the leadership of Edward Heath. They continued throughout 1962. But de Gaulle was not disposed to accept this British 'Johnny-come-lately' with its schizophrenic ambivalence between Europe and the Commonwealth. On 14 January 1963 he gave a press conference. France would impose her veto. Britain was to be shut out of Europe.

As Macmillan wisely foresaw in the Prologue to his autobiography de Gaulle's veto proved to be only the end of a chapter, not the end of the story. The successful outcome of that story was to belong to the man who had led the negotiations in 1961–3 and who had staked his career on Britain's joining the Common Market. But the veto in January 1963 emphasised the change that had taken place in Macmillan's image with the public and in Parliament. Little was going right. In July 1962, in response to growing unrest in the party that resulted from continuing evidence of the Conservatives' unpopularity in the country, he had dramatically reconstructed the Cabinet, replacing Selwyn Lloyd by

Maudling at the Treasury, making Butler Deputy Prime Minister and First Secretary of State, Brooke Home Secretary, Manningham-Buller Lord Chancellor in place of Kilmuir, Thorneycroft Minister of Defence, and introducing seven new men into the Cabinet (including Thorneycroft). At the end of the year the Radcliffe Tribunal on the Vassall case resulted in journalists being sent to prison for refusing to disclose the sources of their allegations. This caused bitter resentment in the press, which was to stand Macmillan in no good stead when the Profumo scandal broke about his head the following summer. The British public was in one of its periodical fits of morality, egged on by a Fleet Street that was thirsting for revenge over the Radcliffe Tribunal. His enemies saw the perfect chance to get rid of him. He himself was undecided. He survived the Profumo debate on 17 June – the fourth time in eighty years that British political life had been rocked to its foundations because of a woman – but he wondered whether he should resign. The decision was taken out of his hands. On 8 October he went into hospital for an operation on his prostate gland. The following day he announced his intention to resign. His intention was read out to the Conservative Party Conference at Blackpool by Lord Home, who eventually proved to be his successor. On 19 October Macmillan sent his resignation to the Queen.

Macmillan has often been characterised as 'The Old Entertainer' or criticised as an 'actor-manager'. In the present-day world this is more a compliment than a criticism as far as a prime minister is concerned. Macmillan's flamboyance, which so irritated his political opponent Hugh Gaitskell, was only his public face; privately, and especially in Cabinet and in committee, the casual, colourful approach disappeared and he was master of the table, brilliantly in command.

When he resigned he accepted none of the honours traditionally bestowed on departing prime ministers; neither an earldom, nor the Garter, nor even one of the life peerages that had been introduced under his aegis in 1958. He resigned as Prime Minister of the United Kingdom, but remained Chancellor of Oxford University, which he had been since 1960, another 'worth-while' office for an old Balliol Exhibitioner.

BIBLIOGRAPHY

Macmillan's Memoirs, 6 volumes, 1966–73
Winds of Change (London, 1966); *The Blast of War* (London, 1967); *Tides of Fortune*

(London, 1969); *Riding the Storm* (London, 1971); *Pointing the Way* (London, 1972); *At the End of the Day* (London, 1973)

Egremont, Lord, *Wyndham and Children First* (London, 1968)
Hughes, Emrys, *Macmillan: Portrait of a Politician* (London, 1962)
Sampson, Anthony, *Macmillan: A Study in Ambiguity* (London, 1962)

SIR ALEC DOUGLAS-HOME

BY

IAIN SPROAT

Sir Alec Douglas-Home, Born 2 July 1903, eldest son of the 13th Earl of Home. Succeeded his father in 1951 but disclaimed his peerage for life 23 October 1963. Educated at Eton and Christ Church, Oxford. Married 1936 Elizabeth Hester Alington; one son, three daughters. MP (South Lanark) 1931–45, Lanark division of Lanarkshire (1950–51), Kinross & W. Perth (1963–   ). Parliamentary Private Secretary to the Prime Minister 1937–40; Joint Parliamentary Under-Secretary, Foreign Office, 1945; Minister of State, Scottish Office, 1951–55; Secretary of State for Commonwealth Relations, 1955–60; Deputy Leader of the House of Lords 1956–57; Leader of the House of Lords and Lord President of the Council 1957–60; Foreign Secretary 1960–63; Prime Minister and First Lord of the Treasury 1963–64; Leader of the Opposition, 1964–65. Hon. DCL (Oxford); Hon. LLD (Harvard, Edinburgh, Aberdeen, Liverpool, St Andrews); Hon. Master of the Bench, Inner Temple. Foreign Secretary 1970–74.

Sir Alec Douglas-Home. Photo by Vivienne

SIR ALEC DOUGLAS-HOME

The Earl of Home became Prime Minister on 19 October 1963 when
the fortunes of the Conservative Government were at a very low ebb,
and, as Sir Alec Douglas-Home, left that office on 16 October 1964.
Within that short period he came within a hair's breadth of achieving
what no British prime minister has ever achieved for his party: the
winning of a fourth general election in a row.

This feat was the more remarkable in that Sir Alec had to overcome
a series of obstacles dauntingly numerous and varied. In October 1963
the Conservative Government was still tainted by scandal from the
Profumo and Vassall affairs. After twelve years the Cabinet was in
grave danger of becoming stale, of losing intellectual and political
dynamic. Sir Alec himself had been absent from the rough-and-tumble
of Commons debate – so different from the more courteous and leisurely
attitude of the Lords – since he became the Earl of Home in 1951, and
the troops on the Conservative benches behind wanted, as always, a
leader who could raise their morale by patently and decisively crushing
Labour spokesmen. Harold Wilson was a formidable opposition leader,
with a ready debating wit and a command of economic fact and jargon,
which was far from being Sir Alec's strength.

The Tory ranks in the Commons were in disarray, with memories of
Harold Macmillan's wholesale Cabinet sackings of July 1962 still
smouldering. Even more importantly, two able and respected ministers
of long experience, Iain Macleod and Enoch Powell, refused to serve
in Sir Alec's Cabinet. This disarray in the House of Commons was
reflected, if not so strongly, in the Tory ranks in the country. And in
addition to all this, there were growing economic difficulties; there was
a yawning gap in policy left by the failure of the Common Market talks
the year before; there had been morale-sapping by-election defeats;
there was the charge, difficult to counter, that after twelve years it was
'time for a change'. Above all, there was an acute shortage of time, and
the concomitant factor that Sir Alec must fight with a Cabinet largely
not of his own choosing.

All these factors Sir Alec had to overcome before a general election in November 1964 at the latest.

There were, of course, advantages also to hand. Although the team was mainly Macmillan's, it contained men of outstanding calibre and experience like Edward Heath, R. A. Butler and Reginald Maudling. Sir Alec could rely confidently on these ministers to pursue government policies with sense and vigour without interference from No. 10. This left the new Prime Minister able to concentrate on what was virtually twelve months of non-stop electioneering.

Furthermore, Sir Alec could call on what Lord Kilmuir, Macmillan's last Lord Chancellor but one, described as the Tories' secret weapon: loyalty. In spite of many media prophecies to the contrary, the passing over of the vastly experienced Butler, and the resignation of Macleod and Powell, caused no major splits within the party in the country. A strain on loyalty, some disgruntlement, and even the odd resignation in constituency associations, there certainly were; but there was never the slightest question, when it came to the crunch, that the Tories would develop and nourish a Butlerite faction, as the Labour party so disastrously had earlier a Bevanite; and the personality of the new Prime Minister, and the natural inclinations of his supporters, effected an almost solid closing of the party ranks long before the election came. The only initiative of the Home Government to operate against Conservative unity, in any major way, was that on the abolition of Resale Price Maintenance, which considerably angered small Tory shopkeepers. For this reason Sir Alec was much less keen to push the measure through than Heath, who as the minister involved, was convinced of its importance.

But in addition to the ability of his colleagues and the traditional loyalty of the Conservative party to its leader, there was another factor which accounted greatly for the astonishing proximity to electoral success that Sir Alec achieved – astonishing, that is, to most of the media, who consistently underrated him – and that was the particular, if elusive, indeed deceptive, personality of the man.

The deceptive aspect of Sir Alec's character was that, unusual in anyone who has climbed to the top of the political ladder, it was strong without many of the normal outer signs of strength, decisive without the usual trappings of decisiveness. Sir Alec was not arrogant, bullying, abrupt, ruthless, cold, egocentric or determinedly charismatic; he did not parade himself as a great orator. On the contrary, he was amiable –

a virtue which, perhaps significantly, Jane Austen once wrote of as especially British – approachable, and unfailingly courteous, whether to opponents or to the least important of his party's supporters. Tory audiences loved him; they loved his straightforwardness, his manner that was both gentle and crisp; they warmed to him – as they never warmed to one of his chief rivals for the premiership, R. A. Butler, although Butler had given unparalleled service to the Tory party for a generation. Among Tory audiences there was an affection for Sir Alec, which his rivals, Butler, Hailsham, Macleod or Maudling, could not command, however much respect, admiration or even fervour they could evoke. In 1964 the British public still loved, if less a lord, then certainly a 'gentleman', and whatever precise definition of gentleman you preferred, Sir Alec looked like, acted like, and indubitably was a 'gentleman'. Sir Alec's own party, and indeed the country at large, could recognise in him a disinterestedness in personal ends. When, for example, Iain Macleod, that politician of brilliance, tragically never destined to fulfil his great potential, dazzled a conference by his oratory, there was always a thought that he was delighting in the personal impression he was making; that he was tacitly asking the audience to mark what an exceptional fellow he was. That was never so with Sir Alec: he made a speech because he quite simply wanted to communicate what he considered an important message, divorced from personalities. He was obviously not ambitious for himself. He was born with social position; he was born rich; he had already achieved high office: it was clear to even his bitterest opponent that he accepted the office of prime minister because – rightly or wrongly – he believed it to be his duty to his country. All this gave Sir Alec a moral stature which no other politician of the day could match.

Much of the strength of Sir Alec's character sprang from an ultimate confidence in his own beliefs. Behind his agreeable manner, he hid a number of steely convictions, much tougher, in fact, than those held by many of his apparently more abrasive colleagues. It was the confidence of someone born well socially at a time when such birth still meant much; the confidence of someone of great inherited wealth; the confidence of someone whose natural abilities and apparently languid charm had shielded him from most of those vicissitudes, at school and at university, to which his money and station might still have left him vulnerable. Sir Alec could have possessed all these attributes, and still done little with them; but in fact they did give him a solid bed-rock of confidence, which an agreeable diffidence of manner might sometimes conceal, but never erode.

Sir Alec also possessed a moral certainty that sprang from the strength of his religious convictions. During his time as Prime Minister, he was perhaps the only important figure in political life who regularly worked into his speeches references to Christianity in a manner acceptable to his audience. Not, of course, that he was the only man in politics to hold such convictions. But where others were content to omit references to them, or, as in the case of Quintin Hogg, to speak of them in a manner much more high-flown, and occasionally at the risk of making some of his audience uneasy, Sir Alec did so in a matter-of-fact way that heartened those who shared, or at least inclined towards, his religious beliefs, and to many agnostics or atheists, lent him a comforting reassurance whose source they might not accept, but whose results they did.

A third factor that deepened and strengthened Sir Alec's political convictions arose from what at the time must have seemed to him the cruellest misfortune. In 1940 he aggravated an old injury, and for the next two years he was compelled to lie on his back. At that time he was thirty-seven, an age when most men in his position have reached certain conclusions about life – however inadequate those conclusions may be – and from then on they continue down their chosen paths, thinking freshly less and less and merely reacting to outside events more and more. Enforced inactivity gave Sir Alec a chance to look at himself, to examine and sift what he had learnt from life, and to remedy by study any gaps in his knowledge which such an examination might reveal. This chance he took. He read widely and deeply, and in particular he studied everything on which he could lay his hands about the theory and practice of Soviet Communism. When, later, he became Foreign Secretary, Prime Minister, and then Foreign Secretary again, he viewed the moves and counter moves of the Kremlin in a long perspective, and, it must be said, in a far more suspicious and hostile light than did many of his colleagues. During the years in hospital he reached certain sombre conclusions about the nature of Soviet ambitions, which the optimism or the wishful thinking of others in British public life never dispelled. What had largely been, during his pre-war years as an MP, the natural political instincts of someone from his particular background, now became hardened during this period into conscious, thought-out political convictions.

Nevertheless, it was not until Macmillan had made what seemed to many at the time the astonishing choice of Home as Foreign Secretary that the toughness and the independence of his mind made much public impact. But thereafter he soon developed an individual manner of speech which endeared him at first to Tory audiences, and, as it turned out, later to a wider section of the public. He spoke more directly, more clearly, and more forcefully than was usual in Foreign Secretaries. He had no constituents to worry about; he was not made cautious by amibition. For example, in April 1963 he was speaking of the H-bomb in these terms: 'The great advantage of the nuclear bomb is that at last ordinary decent men have been given a weapon which can stop the wicked from achieving their ends by war.' There was a *simpliste* note about that, combining the words of politics with those of morality, that many found appealing. Again, there was his famous, or infamous, speech at Berwick-on-Tweed in December 1961, in which, although he came down in favour of retaining the United Nations, he refused to indulge in the fashionable hypocrisy about its virtues and attacked it for irresponsibility; and publicly said that the barbaric chaos in the Congo had been the result of that country's getting its independence too soon. That was strong meat from a British Foreign Secretary.

This political confidence and outspokenness in Sir Alec were a late flowering, and a long way from the politician of whom Winston Churchill remarked, when he was recommended by the then Chief Whip, James Stuart, as Minister of State at the Scottish Office in 1951: 'Never heard of him.'

Naturally, there were those to whom Sir Alec's views and outspokenness as Foreign Secretary were abhorrent. When he became Prime Minister, however, the main matters upon which the Opposition sought to blacken him in the eyes of public opinion were different.

The first of these was the charge that Sir Alec knew nothing of domestic matters, and, in particular, was spectacularly ignorant of even the rudiments of economics. This was at a time when it was a maxim of accepted wisdom that 'Politics is Economics'. Sir Alec had added fuel to the these flames by saying in an interview that when he opened a newspaper he turned to the sporting pages first, and that he liked to use a box of matchsticks to help him in his economic calculations. Harold Wilson thereafter made much of scathing references to 'matchsticks'. It was at this time that Wilson was successfully developing his theme of harnessing science to Socialism, and he would contrast the future possibilities for Britain in the 'white heat of the technological revolution' with the supposed economic and technological illiteracy of Sir Alec. In fact, this campaign by Wilson may have slightly back-fired with the wider public, as there was in Sir Alec's approach something that appealed to the traditional British love of the amateur.

Labour's second main charge against Sir Alec was connected with the first; it was, quite simply, that he was an aristocrat, a fourteenth Earl, and thus out of touch with the ordinary man, with the modern world, and was indeed a living symbol of the reactionary, old-fashioned order that Labour was pledged to sweep away in every field. It was a charge that found a responsive echo in the minds and hearts of those to whom the theme of harnessing science to Socialism most appealed. There was no doubt that Sir Alec was vulnerable to both charges, but the second, the charge of being 'the fourteenth Earl', he neutralised to a considerable extent by pointing out good-naturedly that 'if you came to think about it', Mr Wilson was presumably 'the fourteenth Mr Wilson'. None the less, behind the specific charge lay a general feeling in the country – rightly or wrongly – that it was time for thrusting new measures, and Sir Alec had difficulty in projecting himself to the dynamic young executive – a much quoted and appealed-to figure at the time – as the man best suited to bring such measures about. Of course, he could point to abrasive and dynamic figures under his command in the Government, like Heath. If anyone said he himself was far removed from the world of young executives, he could point out the fallacy, which Dr Johnson's ridicule first demolished in the famous remark, 'Who drives fat oxen must himself be fat'. He could try to convince the public that unless the defence of the country was guaranteed, nothing else mattered, and that Labour, with their pacifist and extreme left-wing factions, were tragically ill suited to dealing with defence and foreign policy matters. He could project himself as an honest, reliable man above political ambition.

All of this Sir Alec did in the year of his premiership; but it was an uphill struggle. Except on defence matters, it was nearly always Wilson on the attack – although, of course, the electorate often found Sir Alec's defences more convincing than Wilson's attacks. Ridiculous as it seems in .the light of subsequent events, Wilson sought to attach to himself some of the glamorous dynamic which at that time adhered to President Kennedy, and was not unsuccessful in the attempt. Kennedy-

Wilson's supposed youthful drive was contrasted with Sir Alec's supposed reactionary irrelevancy to the twentieth century.

During his brief twelve months as Prime Minister, Sir Alec was acting against a background of difficulty simply in presiding over the tail of twelve years of Conservative government. This meant not only that there was a genuine danger of the Cabinet's running out of steam; not only that there was little, if any, time for fresh political initiative to capture the support of the electorate; but also, so long was it since Labour were last in power, that there was almost no problem facing the country for which Harold Wilson could not attempt to pin blame on the Tories. Slum housing, poor schools, the plight of old age pensioners, low wages, industrial unrest, poor road and rail communications, inadequate hospitals, scandal in high places, low investment, falling production – everything was grist to Labour's mill.

But there was a deeper background of difficulty than this against which Sir Alec must act. In 1963, Britain was still on the path of retreat from world possession and power. Empire had been largely turned into Commonwealth. Macmillan's concept of being the 'honest broker' between the United States and the Soviet Union, diminished a role as that was, was now the maximum to which Britain could aspire: very useful, but ultimately not crucial. World markets had long since ceased to be the easy targets they had once been for British manufacturers. The people of the United Kingdom were uneasily aware that they were being steadily overhauled by their erstwhile enemies, Germany and Japan, whom less than twenty years before they had seen crushed in ruin. In national terms, it seemed a time of running downhill, of contraction all round. Actually, the wonder was that the retreat from Empire, and all that meant, caused as few socio-political traumas as it did, that the British remained as sane and tolerant as they did in the face of their vastly altered world position.

Sir Alec, therefore, knew that he was facing a holding position not only with regard to winning a new term of office for the Conservative party, but on a more important level waiting for the opportune moment to start negotiations again for the entry of the United Kingdom into Europe, which alone, he believed, would halt and reverse the retreat and contraction.

In Sir Alec's mind the priority was clear from the moment he succeeded Macmillan. As he put it to a Conservative audience in November 1963: 'From this moment on, the fact that there is a general election

ahead of us must never be out of our minds.' And during the by-election
at Kinross to get him into the House of Commons, after he had renounced his peerage, he already appeared to be electioneering for the
national campaign that was to come, rather than the one he was then
fighting. He promised 400,000 houses a year, £350 million a year for
higher education, £800 million a year for hospital building, £100
million a year for roads by 1969, and £400 million a year for schools
by 1968. At the end of 1963, he accepted the recommendations of the
Robbins Report for vast increases in university education: the doubling
of higher education places by 1973, and concomitant capital expenditure.

During what, therefore, amounted to a year of almost continuous
election campaigning, Sir Alec personally concentrated on getting himself more widely known to the public. He initiated no unexpected new
major policy decisions, but restored drive and gloss to what was already
under way. He envisaged fighting on a variant of Macmillan's successful domestic maxim of 1959, 'You've never had it so good', combined
with his own personal stature as Foreign Secretary, and such government foreign affairs successes as the Test Ban Treaty, signed in Moscow
in the summer of 1963. Even when the Conservatives were trailing to
the Socialists in the polls in every other aspect of policy – the balance
of payments, which became a serious issue from February 1964, house
prices and mortgages, technological advance – the Government were
always ahead in questions of foreign policy.

Sir Alec's major tactical decision was when to call the election. At
the time, there were Tory voices calling for a June poll. This was mainly
because, in spite of some serious by-election swings against the Government in May 1964, it was believed that the economic situation was
deteriorating fast, and that it would certainly be worse in the autumn
than it was in the summer. The first major shock had been in February,
when the very day after Sir Alec had claimed in a television interview
that the economy was extremely healthy – as indeed in a long-term
prospect it was – trade figures were released showing an alarming
deficit in the balance of payments. Furthermore, no government likes
to be pushed right up against the final time limit for holding an election,
with no room for manoeuvre. Nevertheless, Sir Alec took the decision
to go to October; and almost certainly, on balance, he was right, for
although the economic situation did indeed deteriorate as Maudling,
the Chancellor of the Exchequer, had predicted, the extra months were

needed for the consolidation of Sir Alec as leader, for allowing the public time to forget the distasteful Profumo scandal of the previous year, and for the party to recover from the strain of Macmillan's resignation and the consequent jockeying for position between Home, Butler, Macleod and Powell. Indeed, there were many in October 1964 who believed that had Krushchev fallen a day or two before the election, instead of just after, the Conservatives might have won because of the greater public confidence in the Tories to deal with an uncertain foreign situation.

Conducting what, therefore, was essentially a holding operation, Sir Alec was obliged to make the difficult choice between, on the one hand, taking few major policy initiatives, and thus opening his Government to a charge of inertia from a vociferous Opposition already in full cry against thirteen 'stagnant' years, and on the other hand, risking upsetting his own ranks or the uncommitted electorate by introducing controversial measures. Such latter considerations affected his postponement of plans to make labour contracts legally binding, but did not prevent the courageous decision to abolish Resale Price Maintenance, a policy relentlessly pushed through by Heath although deeply resented at the time by small shopkeepers.

During the election campaign itself, Sir Alec pressed strongly on the issue of nuclear defence in almost every major speech he made: his theme was the necessity for the United Kingdom to retain her own independent deterrent. This policy was very much a part of Sir Alec's personal political thinking, as opposed to those other Tory policies with which, to be sure, he did not disagree, but which lay in fields, such as economics, where he had little expertise. And because of the strength of his own feeling on this matter, he commanded a fluency, a comprehensiveness, and a conviction that he was not always able to display elsewhere. On this and on foreign policy, he was most himself and most successful. Particularly on these issues, Sir Alec possessed an air of statesmanship to which Wilson, whatever his other considerable skills, could not aspire. Furthermore, not only was Sir Alec at his best, but Labour were at their weakest: they could not disguise entirely from the British electorate that they had a considerable, pacifist and far left wing, which had always been antipathetic to the mainstream of political tradition in this country. It must be said, however, that apart from the staunchest Tory newspapers, Sir Alec did not receive much support in the media: fashionable thinking was largely opposed to his nuclear concepts, even derisive. Nevertheless, probably in strategic terms, certainly in political terms, Sir Alec's personal judgement was right in that these concepts undoubtedly found an echo not only in nearly all Tory hearts, but also in Labour ones – not among Labour's articulate intellectuals but among its many traditional supporters, who, for example, had taken no little semi-jingoistic satisfaction in the Suez operation. And in the event, Wilson in office was to adopt a nuclear policy not much different in practice.

Sir Alec Douglas-Home was not Prime Minister for long enough to fashion fresh Conservative policies after his own philosophy. What he was required to do was to restore the assurance of integrity in high places, to unite a battered party both at Westminster and in the country, and to win the fourth general election running for his party. He succeeded wholly in the first; he succeeded largely in the second – with the exceptions of Macleod and Powell at Westminster, and none of significance in the country outside; and came within a hair's breadth of the third. It was an astonishing achievement. It was Sir Alec's fortune that the diffident, if crisp, manner by which he did this caused others to underestimate the magnitude of his achievement. It was his happier fortune that circumstances contrived to return him to office as Foreign Secretary in the Heath administration of 1970, where he exerted a profoundly formative and significant influence at a watershed in British history, in taking the United Kingdom into the European Economic Community.

No prime minister in modern times achieved his office with so little seeking of it. No leader of the Conservative party so gracefully relinquished that post, as did Sir Alec in 1965. In the regions of high office, Sir Alec's was a unique character.

BIBLIOGRAPHY

Brittan, Samuel, *The Treasury under the Tories, 1951–64* (London, 1965)
Butler, D. E. and King, A., *The British General Election of 1964* (London, 1965)
Churchill, Randolph, *The Fight for the Tory Leadership*, 2nd edn (London, 1964)
Dickie, J., *The Uncommon Commoner: Sir Alec Douglas-Home* (London, 1964)
Eden, Sir Anthony, *Memoirs: Full Circle* (London, 1960)
Macmillan, Harold, *Tides of Fortune* (London, 1969); *Riding the Storm* (London, 1971); *Pointing the Way* (London, 1972)
Taylor, A. J. P., *Oxford English History, 1914–45* (Oxford, 1965)
Thomas, Hugh, *The Suez Affair* (London, 1967)
Young, Kenneth, *Sir Alec Douglas-Home* (London, 1970)

HAROLD WILSON

BY

GERARD NOEL

James Harold Wilson, PC, CBE, FRS, born 11 March 1916 and educated at Wirral Grammar School and Jesus College, Oxford. Lecturer in Economics, New College, Oxford, 1937; Fellow of University College, Oxford, 1938; Praelector in Economics 1945; Director of Economics and Statistics, Ministry of Fuel and Power 1943–44; MP for Ormskirk 1945–50; Parliamentary Secretary, Ministry of Works, 1945–47; Secretary for Overseas Trade 1947; President of the Board of Trade 1947–51; MP for Huyton 1950–   ; Chairman, Labour Party Executive Committee, 1961– 62; Chairman, Public Accounts Committee, 1959–63; Prime Minister 1964–70; Leader of the Opposition 1970–74; Prime Minister 1974–   ; President of the Royal Statistical Society 1972–   ; Hon. Fellow of Jesus and University Colleges, Oxford; Hon. LLD (Lancaster, Liverpool, Nottingham, Sussex); Hon. DCL (Oxford); Hon. DTech. (Bradford and Essex). Married; two sons. Author of New Deal for Coal, *1947;* In Place of Dollars, *1952;* The War on World Poverty, *1953;* The Relevance of British Socialism, *1964;* Purpose in Politics, *1964;* The Labour Government, 1964–70, *1971; etc.*

James Harold Wilson. Photo by Vivienne

HAROLD WILSON

It is impossible to assess the distinctive contribution of Harold Wilson as Prime Minister to British political history without a fairly intimate familiarity with the history of British Socialism. And the soul of such Socialism is unknowable to anyone mystified by such names and phrases as Robert Owen, Cold Bath Fields, Chartism, Tolpuddle, Taff Vale, Hyndman, Conrad Noel and the Bridlington Rules. The examples spring readily to the pen and are written down almost at random; but one of them is particularly important: Bridlington Rules. Did these – do they yet – mean much to those who felt (and still feel) that the Government's 1969 'showdown' with the trade unions was actually a surrender? It is the sort of question that must be borne in mind when considering that particular, and very revealing, example of Wilsonism in action at 10 Downing Street.

It is equally impossible to have a full understanding of Harold Wilson without an authentic insight into the world where Socialism is anathematised with as much fervour as elsewhere it is professed. And one is speaking of nothing as nebulous as the 'middle' and professional strata of society in general but of that rarefied upper-class enclave, that inaccessible holy of holies which is fully comprehensible only from within. This resilient citadel still exercises immense if almost wholly unsuspected influence, and its often invisible power operates at every level of British life. The infinitely complex socio-industrial network through which it works – greatly helped by the struggle in each generation to climb the social scale – had, *until Wilson's day*, made Conservative government the natural kind for Britain, and Socialist government the exception.

Wilson's whole career, however, has been inordinately overshadowed by this circumstance of power-from-the-top. He has always been acutely sensitive to its subtle but formidable strength, and has often over-reacted against it. Though far too intelligent to suffer from the inferiority complex of lesser Socialists, he has detonated so many depth-charges in the wells of power as to bring to the surface a bitter personal animosity against him experienced by very few of his Downing Street predecessors. Wilson has thus paid a high price in personal terms for a political achievement that has outstripped that of former Labour Prime Ministers. For if Ramsay MacDonald made Labour government possible, and Clement Attlee made it respectable, it is Harold Wilson who has made it successful; and the assumption that this success had been permanently curtailed by the setback of 1970 was rudely displaced by the shock defeat of an over-confident Conservative Party in February 1974. But his very success, considerable if unfinished, and his relentless pursuit thereof at every stage, have provoked an implacable hostility that has had the twofold effect of damaging his image and, at the same time, spurring him on to greater efforts, by similar means, in pursuit of yet further successes. In this sense Wilson, so far anyway, has been imprisoned in a sort of vicious circle; his future fortunes may well depend on the extent to which he has now escaped.

Well known by now is the saga of progress from staunchly Congregationalist lower-middle-class Yorkshire surroundings, via great brilliance at pre-war Oxford; vital and formative, if underestimated, wartime civil service; and post-war political high-flying, to ultimate tenure of 10 Downing Street. It represented not only a remarkable personal triumph but also a long-delayed one for the Dissenting Radicalism that had inspired even the High Church Gladstone in the eighteen-seventies and Lloyd George in the Edwardian era; only now did it find its natural home in the Labour Party.[1] But Wilson has not always seen Socialism as necessarily the only vehicle capable of forwarding the great Radical dream; he is not only extremely cautious by nature, but, with the razor-sharp instincts of the thoroughbred political animal, he has never ignored the vital role of balance in the affairs of the body politic.

He flirted with Liberalism at Oxford, when Gladstone was still his principal hero. But the decision to become a practising Socialist was a case of unambiguous commitment. To Wilson Socialism is unquestionably 'a moral crusade'. 'But his socialism is fundamental; it is the dropped clue in the common interpretation of him and his work that causes

---

[1] Wilson's religious convictions – very strong and notably different from those of either Ramsay MacDonald or Clement Attlee – made him the first Nonconformist Labour Prime Minister. See *The Churches and the Labour Movement*, by Stephen Mayor (Independent Press, 1967), which remarks (p. 382) on the 'extraordinary feature of English life that the Socialist movement, to which Marxian – and Owenite – sceptics and Secularists had contributed so much, produced as its first three premiers a sincere if obscure Theist, a solid Anglican, and a representative Noncomformist'.

criticism to miss its mark. It is, as he has said, not "a revealed dogma, but a spirit and a tendency": *it is a principle at once of efficiency and of service*.[2] These words were originally written of Ramsay MacDonald.[3] They are of interest because of the uncanny degree to which they apply also to Harold Wilson, for whom 'British Socialism is essentially democratic and evolutionary'.[4] One phrase is italicised as being particularly applicable to the present Labour leader for whom ideological advance (in education, social security, welfare, etc.) is inseparable from economic expansion, greater dynamism in industry and, in fact, a fundamental scientific revolution. His view of Socialism, in other words, is an 'essentially pragmatic conception, related to the age in which we live'.[5]

If efficiency and service are thus quintessential in this context, Wilson has always possessed in addition the prowess to will the means as well as the end. This has involved a principle at all times central to his political thinking, namely party unity. He has long realised that if this is lacking all is lost, not least because of his ever-present awareness of the strength of opposition – social, psychological, personal and political – to his aims and methods. Wilson's approach to party unity involves assessment of where the ideologically true centre of gravity is – *or should be* – at any given moment; and this often involves support for minority as opposed to majority views, so as not to upset that overall 'balance' previously referred to. It is thus a mistake to suppose that Wilson has made a point of favouring popular causes; the opposite has more often been the case, particularly between 1951 and 1962.

After his legendary rise to Cabinet rank in the late nineteen-forties – when he himself was just over thirty – Wilson suddenly resigned, in 1951, from the Presidency of the Board of Trade. For reasons vital to an understanding of his political make-up this resignation did not, *in the long run*, damage either party unity or his own future career. The issue concerned Hugh Gaitskell's proposed £4,700 million arms programme which would have involved an expenditure cut in the social services. Aneurin Bevan resigned on principle because 'his' Health Service would be the prime sufferer. Wilson, helped by his experiences at the Ministry

[2] Italics added.
[3] By Mary Agnes Hamilton in *The Book of the Labour Party*, ed. Herbert Tracy (Caxton, 1926), iii, 141.
[4] cf. Harold Wilson, *The Relevance of British Socialism* (Weidenfeld & Nicolson, 1964), p. 2.
[5] cf. Harold Wilson, *Purpose in Politics* (Weidenfeld & Nicolson, 1964), p. 270.

of Supply in 1940, resigned because he was convinced that the proposed programme could not be fulfilled in the time stated and that it was unnecessary and wrong to attempt to finance an unrealistic arms programme by the measures proposed. Bevans's resignation was entirely dogmatic. Wilson's was guided by greater sensitivity to reality and the future as well as to the fundamentals of Socialism; by a principle, that is, 'at once of efficiency and service'. Wilson turned out to be right, though the subsequent arms cut-back was, ironically, made by a Conservative government. It is important to recall, meanwhile, that Wilson was never a 'Bevanite', and even remarked that there was never really any such thing as 'Bevanism'. Wilson, in other words, has never looked on Socialism as a theory to be molly-coddled in a vacuum; still less has he ever expected it to flourish in a Labour movement damaged by its age-old proneness to internal division. It was thus that Wilson took his stand on the twin pillars of party unity, as against Bevan in 1954, and fundamental Socialist ideology, as against Gaitskell in 1960.[6]

On the former occasion Bevan resigned from the Shadow Cabinet, and Wilson, being next in line, was automatically deemed the man to replace him. As he wrote, however, to the Secretary of the Parliamentary Labour Party: 'I am in entire agreement, as the Party know, with Aneurin Bevan on the policy issues involved – on the dangers not only of Mr Dulles's policies in South-east Asia but also of German rearmament. Obviously, therefore, it is extremely difficult to accept co-option to a vacancy caused by his resignation. Nevertheless what matters in the last resort is the unity and strength of the Party.'

The latter situation came about through the new line taken (in 1960) by party leader Hugh Gaitskell who regarded Clause Four, the main plank of Labour policy since 1918, as ripe for immediate scrapping. But within the context of evolutionary Socialism, the very vagueness of this Clause – the product of Sidney Webb's fertile brain – with its demand for the common ownership of the means of production, distribution and exchange, was its strength, for it permitted flexibility in any Labour programme. To Wilson it seemed a grave error to delete, by a stroke of the pen, so basic an article of Socialist faith when the question of nationalisation had, in any event, to be decided on the individual merits of each particular case. In fact Gaitskell's defeat over Clause Four at the next conference was not as serious for him as the defeat of the Executive (at the same conference) on the question of defence, when a

[6] cf. Gerard Noel, *Harold Wilson* (Victor Gollancz, 1964), p. 119.

resolution for unilateral disarmament was carried by a small majority.

It was this (not the Clause Four battle) that originated Gaitskell's famous phrase that he would 'Fight, fight and fight again' to ensure that the decision was reversed. Wilson was no unilateralist but he did differ from Gaitskell as to the means of achieving a similar aim. He wished, in fact (and in a manner typical of him) to retain the basis of the official defence statement without condemning the wishes of the party conference.

With Hugh Gaitskell's untimely death (early in 1963) Wilson inherited the leadership of a party whose new-found unity owed more to himself than any other individual. During his first administration (1964–6) such unity was not likely to be seriously threatened because of the razor-thin majority secured by Labour in the 1964 general election.[7]

The scene was wholly different in the late sixties when the mammoth battle to restore the balance of payments was finally won but only at the cost of much extremely unpopular legislation. Party unity moreover – inevitably vulnerable during the false security of a substantial parliamentary majority – faced a crucial test at this time on the question of industrial relations. It was a question of party unity, not alone but in conjunction, as invariably with Wilsonian political philosophy, (and the pattern in this regard is remarkably consistent) with national efficiency and basic ideologies. In April 1969 legislation on prices and incomes was being phased out in favour of a voluntary incomes policy; at the same time the Chancellor of the Exchequer, Roy Jenkins, was to announce in his Budget speech the decision to introduce an interim Industrial Relations Bill. One of the main purposes of this Bill was to curb unconstitutional and unofficial strikes. Its passage was considered by the Prime Minister[8] to be essential to the Government's continuance in office *unless* the TUC came forward – as they had been invited to do – with equally effective alternative proposals. With the threat of legislation in the background it was, in the event, such very alternative proposals that were finally adopted. They took the form of a 'binding agreement', that is a 'rule of Congress' similar to the Bridlington Rules of 1939; and the latter, which governed inter-union relations, were the most binding Congress had ever imposed. Without some knowledge of what this implies in trade union parlance, one may well be as sceptical

---

[7] In this election, held on 15 October 1964, the final figures were: Labour 317; Conservative 303; Liberal 9; the Retiring Speaker 1.

[8] In a speech outlining the proposals to the weekly party meeting on 17 April 1969.

as to the obligations involved as foreigners have often been about the Englishman's interpretation of a 'gentleman's agreement'.

It is difficult, in summing up the net result of the whole incident, to improve on the candour of Wilson's own description:

'The issues posed in Barbara Castle's White Paper *In Place of Strife* had therefore been settled by a decision to introduce legislation to enact the positive provisions of the Donovan Report, and by our decision of 18th June to follow Donovan in not proceeding with punitive legislation. For good or ill, we had accepted the views of the TUC, but only because under the catalytic action of our legislative proposals, they had "moved forward forty years in a month". . . . The advance we had won was the unanimous decision of the TUC to use its powers both in inter-union and in unofficial disputes. Although there would be cases that neither it nor any other agency could hope to settle, there would also be a large number of cases where none but the TUC would have the authority or power to settle.'[9]

Whether Wilson was wise to overemphasise, as he seemed (intentionally?) to be doing, the dependence of the Government's continuance on the 'passage of this Bill' is a very different matter. Knowing as he did the strength of the opposition press – and all that this implies in terms of power-from-above – he took what one can only call an uncalculated (or perhaps miscalculated) risk. He was and is entirely satisfied himself that the operative words were fully qualified by others used in the same speech, and that the overall context of his message was quite clear – as indeed it appears when the whole speech is read with care in the cold light of day. But he might well have anticipated that his opponents would champion a different interpretation. The net upshot of the whole affair was that Wilson got what he wanted in the national interest by methods favourable to both party unity and Socialist philosophy; but he paid a heavy price for his victory, for at that moment a new anti-Wilson legend was born and subsequently nurtured with dedication and skill.

Perhaps the most important of the test cases whereby Wilson, as a political thinker-cum-practical politician may be judged, is his stance on the European Economic Community. Its consideration, however,

[9] Harold Wilson, *The Labour Government 1964–70. A Personal Record* (Weidenfeld & Nicolson and Michael Joseph, 1971), p. 662.

should come at the end of the essay, both chronologically and logically, in view of its on-going relevance to Britain's present and future political scene. The title of this book moreover implies that final judgement on the men in question must be attempted primarily on the basis of their actual performance while holding the highest office in the land.

No Prime Minister in history had, so soon after going back into opposition, more painstakingly provided as much and as revealing information about himself while in power as did Harold Wilson in 1971. Nothing, least of all so brief a summary as the present one, can replace the massive 'Apologia' contained in his *Personal Record*. Its close study is indispensable for any clear understanding of Wilson as British Premier. It is better than any of the many books written *about* him, particularly those written with supposedly intimate knowledge but providing only the most superficial of analyses. Indeed it reveals even more of the subject than probably the author himself intended.

It portrays a man almost obsessively preoccupied with the minutiae as well as the memorabilia of prime ministerial responsibility; with the paraphernalia as much as with the potentialities of power: but aware throughout of the humbling no less than the exhilarating effects of high office. It remains true, more than ten years after his becoming party leader, that Wilson is, as he was then, 'indefinably but distinctly modest, though in no way self-effacing or retiring', while Sir Alec Douglas-Home is 'retiring and self-effacing but not particularly modest'.[10] But one might bring the generalisation up to date by saying that Sir Alec was fairly sure of himself even when he was wrong (and never felt the need for elaborate self-justification); while Wilson is not always completely sure of himself even when he is right. This, at least, is the impression that emerges strongly from his own devastatingly detailed account of his first six years of power – the sort of book, incidentally, that Sir Alec would never think of writing.

The very preoccupation with minutiae enhances rather than deprecates the overall picture of Wilson as Prime Minister: his life at Downing Street and Chequers exhibits none of the hauteur of incumbents affecting concern only with the great moments of history.[11] Apart from

[10] Gerard Noel, *Harold Wilson*, p. 35.

[11] As he wrote in 1964: 'What one learns in British politics, and in my case, this realisation has inevitably been more forcefully expressed since I was elected Leader of my Party, is the essential unity of the problems we are facing, the need for

anything else, Wilson enjoys his work at Downing Street far too much not to be a glutton for even some of its most extreme demands. He is conscientious to a fault in matters of protocol, procedure and preparation. During the sometimes feverish activity between 1964 and 1970 he managed almost always to remain, at least outwardly, calm. The actual volume of mental and physical exertion he expended was phenomenal, almost incredible; and there are constant reminders – with little relaxation allowed during plane, train and even car journeys – of a maxim he had devised himself when collaborating with Beveridge before and during the war, namely that there is no substitute for self-executed work. Thus, behind the hazy impression most people have of Wilson the Prime Minister – headline-hunter, hustler, traveller, debater, memory man, reparteeist, negotiator, media master, 'starring' here, 'flopping' there – there is the hidden reality of Wilson the footnote-fiend, drafting for himself his own most important speeches and statements, revelling in rather than retreating from tight corners and hostile crowds, and never – but never – neglecting his endless 'homework'.

One naturally reads and re-reads his remarkable personal narrative with constant 'interlinear' reference to the other written records of the period. By doing this and by letting Harold Wilson speak for himself, as I have done, in private question-and-answer session, one feels that one has got as close to Britain's present Prime Minister as is practical for the purposes of writing a realistic short essay about him. Anyone with more intimate knowledge would probably be 'too near' for this purpose; but neither is anyone who has not pored over the hundreds of thousands of words written by and about him likely to be very close to the mark in summing him up.

Personal diplomacy was, above all, what gave flesh to the basic bone structure of Wilson's tenure of prime ministerial office between 1964 and 1970; a distinctive style was strikingly evidenced by the encounters and relationships with world figures no less than in direct interventions (fewer than often imagined) in industrial disputes.

During his five and a half years as Premier, Wilson intervened directly in only five disputes. The first intervention was just before the 1966

harmony and integration between domestic and overseas affairs. This is why I have more than once described the task of a party leader, be he Leader of the Opposition or Prime Minister, as essentially that of conducting a mighty orchestra. One false note, one badly scored part, can destroy the unity of the whole.' *Purpose in Politics*, p. viii.

general election and ended the railway dispute; but the net effect of this on electioneering was negligible. If domestic affairs dominated this election, the most prominent of other issues during the campaign was that of the Common Market. Wilson, during a speech at Bristol shortly before polling day, said: '. . . given a fair wind, we will negotiate our way into the Common Market, head held high, not crawl in. And we shall go in if the conditions are right. . . . Negotiations? Yes. Unconditional acceptance of whatever terms we are offered? No. We believe that given the right conditions it would be possible and right to join the EEC.'[12]

With supreme irony, as it turned out, Wilson's fifth prime ministerial intervention into an industrial dispute came just before the 1970 election and broke the deadlock that had caused all national newspapers to suspend publication. Wilson thus, in the cause of free and full comment on the issues before voters, enabled two newspapers in particular to unleash attacks of unprecedented ferocity against him. His intervention, in fact, virtually lost him the election, though one Conservative paper paid handsome tribute to him for enabling the papers to resume publication. The article containing the tribute, however, did not appear until after polling day.

Personal diplomacy with regard to world figures, however, was probably the most fascinating single aspect of the Wilson years from 1964 to 1970. It deserves a whole book to itself. The passages in the *Personal Record* that touch on it stand apart, to a great extent, from the rest of the narrative; they have a more intimate and informal, but at the same time even more urgent, tone, exhibiting both spontaneous personality interaction and a sense of achievement that was extra-dimensional to orthodox politics. And this indeed was what actually happened, to the extent, for example, that peace in Vietnam (on terms better than those settled for in 1973) came within a hair's breadth of resulting from the cliff-hanging Wilson-Kosygin London talks in early 1967. The killing of the plan in Washington was a historic if tragic turning-point; but the whole episode makes gripping 'personality-politics' reading.

If this particular diplomatic exercise was the most dramatic of those engaged in by Wilson, the saving of the critical 1969 Commonwealth Conference, and the attempts on *Tiger* and *Fearless* to negotiate

---

[12] The state of the parties after this general election (held on 31 March 1966) was: Labour 363; Conservatives 253; Liberals 12; Republican Labour (N. Ireland) 1; the Speaker 1; Labour majority over Conservatives 110, overall 97.

meaningfully with Rhodesia's mercurial Ian Smith, do not rank far behind. But the same note of urgency and total immersion – and almost always of remarkable *rapport* even in the most unpropitious circumstances – emerges in varying degrees from all such Wilsonian encounters: with Lyndon Johnson, de Gaulle, Terence O'Neill, Kenyatta, Kaunda, Nkrumah, Pompidou, Moro, Gowon and many others.

Few reminders are needed that, on the home front, Wilson's first administration inherited an unprecedented adverse balance of some £800 million. It was not generally anticipated in the 'money' world that – in his second administration – this would be put right; but it was. And Wilson thus came within an ace of being the first man in history to be elected Prime Minister three times running. But his departure from Downing Street in 1970 turned out to be only a temporary separation.

Harold Wilson's initial overall achievement as Prime Minister went, of course, far beyond the mere balancing of Britain's books. The pace he set himself and sustained to the bitter end (future historians may judge this to have been a mistake) was flat out from the word go. An almost immediate decision was made to proceed as if there were a majority not of five but of a hundred. This was to establish the paramountcy of long-term aims in contrast to the atmosphere of electioneering that had been going on for the previous year and a half. The international financial position was the first priority. The principal weapon adopted with a minimum of delay was a 15 per cent surcharge on all imports except food, tobacco and raw materials. And the pattern for the early days of Britain's first Labour Government for thirteen years was then outlined in the Queen's Speech: in overseas affairs emphasis was laid on interdependence, on nuclear questions and on the United Nations and its agencies; at home, principal stress was on economic strength and social progress, with special provision for regional planning and the development areas.

The deficit inherited in 1964 has been played up and played down for purposes of party propaganda. (And when the Labour leader returned to Downing Street in March 1974, the balance of payments position was no less than five times worse than it had been ten years earlier.) Some have felt that Wilson allowed himself to become disproportionately influenced by this problem in the late sixties and almost obsessively preoccupied by its solution. The decision to impose surcharges had been preceded by a fateful decision by the new Prime Minister, during the first weekend, not to devalue sterling. To do so, within twenty-four hours of taking office, would have been politically tempting; but the temptation was resisted. When, three years later, devaluation was forced on the Government, it was at least recognised (and internationally backed) as an economic necessity rather than a political expedient.

Wilson will long be remembered for his immense energy, unremitting attention to detail and almost incredible resilience in times of adversity. All three qualities were much in evidence during his celebrated 'first hundred days' of office. The quality of resilience was particularly needed after a shock defeat in a by-election at Leyton in January 1965, when Patrick Gordon Walker narrowly lost to the Conservatives.[13] This reduced the Government's majority from five to three. Lord Longford (Lord Privy Seal) could hardly believe how outwardly unconcerned Wilson seemed when discussing routine business with him within hours of so unnerving a development. But Wilson is very good (perhaps too good) at hiding his acute sensitivity; though inwardly shaken he not only refused to bow to the inevitable feeling around him that the end was nigh, but became more determined than ever to govern according to mandate. His approach to this task was characteristic; for the extent to which Wilson (and even his rivals are quick to confirm it) stays near to people is remarkable. Even at the busiest moments he has never neglected close personal contact with constituents and other voters. At the beginning of 1965 it seemed clear to the Prime Minister that his ministers were operating, however conscientiously, at one step's remove from the party in the country as a whole. A back-to-the-grass-roots process was set in motion by the Premier himself; very possibly it was this, more than anything else, that enabled him to survive for another year before having to call a general election.

Before 1965 was out the worst financial implications of the balance of payments deficit had been blunted, and the distinctive hand of Wilson had been imprinted on the foreign field as well: what he referred to as the 'pretence' of nuclear independence had been ended, as had the controversial 'Multilateral Force'. Wilson's Scarborough philosophy on technology[14] was beginning to bear fruit in terms of acceptance by

[13] Patrick Gordon Walker had been Wilson's first choice as Foreign Secretary but he had been defeated at Smethwick at the general election. The by-election at Leyton, made possible by the elevation of Frank Bowles to the Lords, was won by the Conservatives by a majority of 205.
[14] As set out in his speech to the Labour Party Conference of 1963.

British industry, and the new corporation and capital gains taxes had inaugurated a virtual fiscal revolution. The size and scope, in fact, of the new Government's legislative programme up to that time exceeded any two legislative sessions between 1951 and 1963. With hardly a pause for breath the programme for the next session seemed even more ambitious, foreshadowing, as it did, the Prices and Incomes Bill among its most important provisions.

What stands out sharply, however, from the mass of detailed history for this period, is the driving force of the Prime Minister himself. It was almost entirely due to this that, in the country at large, confidence in the Government was increasing. This meant that an election was not vital; but for the sake of a more clear-cut mandate it seemed eminently desirable, being held, and triumphantly won, on the last day of March, 1966. The victory had important personal effects for Wilson. He became freer to spend more time in different parts of the country, something he was always very anxious to do. He had the welcome opportunity of looking for himself at housing progress and other social problems, and for visiting industrial organisations, research stations and trade union conferences. And as 1966 went on it became clear that the trade deficit had been forced back to a point almost of balance. From now on the Prime Minister could address himself to his favourite themes of social reform, and a more human future for ordinary people, from a position of economic strength. Had it not been for a prolonged and somewhat shattering seamen's strike during the summer of that year, a sort of economic-social miracle might have been in embryo. As it was the strike proved an acid test of government determination to preserve the criteria laid down for an incomes policy. The test was passed, but at heavy cost. The earlier advances – the first fruits of Wilson's personal dynamism – began to be counterbalanced. The Prime Minister, in a doughty, dogged style now becoming familiar to viewers and voters, hit out not only at the employers, but also, on the union side, at 'pressures which are anything but democratic'. This was an obvious reference to the notorious fact of Communist or near-Communist terrorising tactics against moderate members of the seamen's Executive. Wilson did not hesitate to name names when challenged to produce evidence for his charges.

All of this helped to highlight the difficulty of retaining as Minister of Technology (an entirely new creation under Wilson) a man, namely Frank Cousins, who was at the same time General Secretary of the

Transport and General Workers' Union. The appointment – a typical example of Wilsonian *penchant* for balance and consensus thinking – had worked well to begin with. But a tougher incomes policy – as foreshadowed by the Queen's Speech following the 1966 election – had practical implications which Cousins could not conscientiously accept. He was replaced at this (by now greatly enlarged) Ministry by Tony Benn, hitherto a highly successful technological Postmaster General and, though often misunderstood, already looked on by many as a possible future prime minister.

Wilson's astonishing resilience was never more needed than in the grim period between the summer of 1966 and the end of the following year. The damaging seamen's strike turned out to be the first in a series of fortuitous economic setbacks. Stringent economic measures and a prolonged wage freeze postponed but could not prevent the need to devalue the pound in November 1967. There was evidence, however, that Wilson's personal magic *vis-à-vis* ordinary people was still working behind an economic screen now in need of more armour plating. The wage freeze, though total, was honoured without exception. The only major dispute during its six-month duration (October 1966–April 1967) was a strike against redundancies in BMC's radiator factory at Oxford.

Devaluation when it came occasioned one of Harold Wilson's major mistakes while in office. The actual decision to devalue was made imperative not by any failure of the policies which had in fact already turned the famous deficit into a surplus. The decisive factors were the consequences of the crisis in the Near East – notably the closure of the Suez Canal – combined, at home, with dock strikes in Liverpool and London, followed by financial manoeuvring within the Common Market (then generally referred to as 'the Six'). Wilson's mistake was in not presenting devaluation to the nation as a reverse of fortune, although this had been his original intention. He was persuaded by others, notably Richard Crossman, to describe it in more euphoric terms. This marked a psychological turning-point in Wilson's premiership. Having played down defeat in 1967, he was unable, in 1970, to extract full electoral mileage from what was in fact an immense personal triumph: his holding together of a notoriously divisible party through the six most momentous and difficult years of its history, while simultaneously winning the battles for solvency and his concept of a Socialist New Britain.

His tactical error did not, of course, prevent his exploiting, with the plentitude of his political and economic expertise, the full potentialities of devaluation. By the end of 1969 he could make a 'look around' speech at the party conference at Brighton which, with justification, painted a rosy picture. A man with less steel-like political nerves might well have been got down by the Opposition's supreme confidence that neither he nor any other Socialist leader could get the economic situation right. But he had done so, and by early 1970 opinion polls were showing a marked trend toward Labour. The gap in Wilson's favour appeared to widen into a chasm, and there was talk of a possible Labour landslide. But there is often talk of landslides, which seldom happen; and anyone over-confident of a Labour victory was reckoning without the expensive and formidable machinery of Conservative organisation, especially in such moments of supreme emergency. To the computerised strength of Central Office moreover were allied strong, silent armies of Conservative ladies in town and hamlet: an example of power-from-above at its most intangible and most intense. Wilson was defeated by it in June 1970.

Though, in his *Personal Record*, he disclaims having been certain of winning this election, he clearly expected to do so. The aftermath of defeat was traumatic for such a personality as Harold Wilson as he looked back in anguish during the months that followed. Then came the pouring out onto paper of the chronicle of his years of office; and the very method, apart from the content, of this chronicle greatly helps to fix Wilson's 'place' among the prime ministers. For he worked on the book not only at home with all records of events readily available, but with equal speed during odd hours and in all sorts of different places while travelling around, relying for the most part on his remarkable facility for total recall. This precious inheritance from a very gifted father enabled him to put a personal stamp on his premiership in a manner equalled by few if any other prime ministers. But it was a weakness as well as a strength. For it was linked to something first acquired during a key wartime job involving familiarity with the Civil Service and then, after the war, as Parliamentary Secretary at the Ministry of Works: intimate practical acquaintance – the salient facts never being forgotten – with every single ministerial department. As a consequent perfectionist and demon for detail, this led Wilson, the possessor of a prodigious memory, to enunciate a highly individualistic view of a premier's function:

'Every Prime Minister's style of government must be different, but I find it hard to resist the view that a modern head of government must be the managing director as well as chairman of his team, and this means that he must be completely *au fait* not only with the developments in the work of all main departments, including the particular responsibility of No. 10, but also with every short-run occurrence of political importance. And all he does, and says, must be part of a coherent political strategy.'[15]

This has been a source of immense strength at most times, particularly when things were going really well. It has enabled him to take a broad and long-term view, to be a step ahead of others, and – because of his memory, grasp of detail and late-flowering dialectic skill – to sparkle in debates and interviews. (Not the least considerable of Wilson's personal triumphs was to graduate from being considered, in the late forties, one of the dullest and flattest orators in the House, to dominating its proceedings, both in Opposition and as Prime Minister, through most of the sixties.) But the very breadth of his strategic concept can be a cause of weakness in times of adversity; for it necessarily involves, at all stages, the provision of alternative policies ('leaving the options open'). And although these are invariably adverted to in advance by Wilson, they usually come under the heading of 'small print' as far as the general public (to say nothing of the Opposition) are concerned. And when options left open have finally had to be exercised, Wilson has come to be looked on by many as a short-term tactician rather than a long-term strategist. To make matters worse for his 'image' he has, despite his basic cautiousness, an inclination to live dangerously in certain directions, generally reserving, for example, his criticisms of trade unionists for trade union conferences and those of speculative excesses and unpatriotic attacks on sterling for City audiences. Those who have, year after year, worked very closely with Wilson laugh at the description of his being wily and devious. They know him to be neither. But it may be that the outward appearance of one or the other has, at times, been an unconscious cover for acute sensitivity to criticism.

He was naturally apprehensive of an overdose of this on the morrow of his 1970 electoral defeat. Little consolation, at that moment, were certain undisputed facts: the beginnings of his 'New Britain' with sweeping reforms in the realms of education, social security, welfare,

[15] *Personal Record*, p. 45.

transport, taxation, and the mining and the other industries. And this had been achieved not at the cost of bankrupting Britain, but simultaneously with turning the unprecedented deficit into a large surplus. The cost was of a different kind. It was a cost as personal to Wilson as was the degree of his own responsibility for the achievement involved. And this was considerable. But of the many mistakes inevitably made in the course of its pursuance, perhaps the greatest was allowing an aura of infallibility to grow up around Downing Street, thus obscuring the true Wilson: a genuine man of the people who, idealistic and supremely talented, had got to the top in a pitilessly competitive world.

At the moment of electoral defeat in June 1970, Wilson remarked, in answer to a journalist's question:

'No incoming Prime Minister, if Mr Heath takes over, in living memory has taken over a stronger economic situation. I wanted to use that as we have never been able to, in the past five or six years, to use the economic situation for building on what we have done, for example in the social services, health and education and social security and housing – to accelerate what we have been doing, to intensify and develop it. Now we hand over the means to do that, to somebody else.'

The strong economic position inherited by the incoming Prime Minister would be of particular significance in the attempt to enter the EEC 'from a position of strength'. The Labour Government's application for EEC membership came at a time when sterling was strong and Britain's economic position improving; it was endorsed in Parliament by a vote of 488 to 62.

In 1972, on the other hand, legislation to enable Britain to join the EEC at the end of the year was subject to certain crucial divisions in the House of Commons. That the Government's majority was on occasion down to a single figure was due not to the fact that Wilson, now in opposition, had changed his mind on the whole issue, but to the fact that he hadn't. His most succinct statement on the matter had been made as far back as 1962, when he said, 'Our position is that if we can get the terms, then we go in.'[16] Despite the millions of words and thou-

16 House of Commons debate, 8 November 1962. The sentence quoted above was immediately preceded by the following passage: 'The third thing I must say – and

sands of negotiating man-hours that have been devoted to this subject in the interim, there has never been any change in this basic Wilsonian stance as regards the EEC; but there is of course a considerable difference between the circumstances wherein entry was being sought in 1967 and those wherein it was actually achieved in 1972. The 1972–3 terms were not 'the terms the Labour Government told Europe in 1967 would be necessary for British entry'.[17] And in addressing the Socialist International Congress in Vienna in June 1972, Wilson reminded his audience: 'The decision, of Conference and of the Parliamentary Party, has not changed. The policy of the British Labour Party is one of opposition to the terms negotiated by the Conservative Government, not to the principle of entry on the right terms'.[18]

In other words, the lapse of six years, during which so many changes had occurred, had convinced Wilson – rightly or wrongly – that the terms felt acceptable by the Government in 1972 for EEC entry would, mainly through the heavy demands of the Common Agricultural Policy, produce disadvantages – particularly in terms of rising prices at home – insufficiently counterbalanced by the advantages envisaged. Soon after Wilson had become Prime Minister again in 1974, the first steps were taken by the new Foreign Secretary, James Callaghan, towards renegotiating the terms of British EEC membership.

Light is above all shed on Wilson's political approach to such major problems by his personal-cum-parliamentary diplomacy during the early seventies. It was in a sense the supreme test for his leadership, certain to have similar but ever-further-reaching effects on his own future and that of his party than his actions in the early fifties. In 1971–2, with the two main parties divided on the Common Market issue, the task of both party leaders was delicate. Fortunately for Mr Heath, Conservative anti-Marketeers were unwilling to push their opposition

---

it is perhaps a pity that I need to say it, but our position has been misrepresented so much – is that our attitude is not based on national sovereignty. We are not clinging like woad-painted aboriginal Britons to outmoded concepts of national sovereignty. In our first debate in August 1961, I said: "The question is not whether sovereignty remains absolute or not, but in what way one is prepared to sacrifice sovereignty, to whom and for what purpose. That is the real issue before us. . . ." That has been our attitude right through.'

[17] Wilson's speech to the Labour Party Conference, Blackpool, 1972. The speech is important as containing detailed examples of respects in which conditions for EEC entry as insisted on in 1967 differed from those accepted in 1972.

[18] Labour Party Information Department, *News Release* S. 153/72.

to European entry to the point of bringing down the Government. Wilson's problem, meanwhile, was to pilot the official Labour policy of 'entry on the right terms' as between the Jenkins line of accepting the terms then offered and views of those (a much smaller group) opposing entry altogether.

The climax came at the 1972 Labour Party Conference where the spirit of tolerance overcame any tendency toward a major split. Veteran politicians could recall the contrast with 1939 when Cripps, Bevan and Strauss were expelled from the party for opposing official Labour policy with their demand for a popular front against the appeasement of the Chamberlain Government. Though unity was restored under Clement Attlee, it was lost again in the days of Gaitskell, who, with all his virtues, seemed powerless to prevent deep bitterness between himself and other leading party members. Such bitterness came to an end with Wilson. Preservation of party unity has been his special achievement and was a key factor in winning the general elections of February and October 1974.

Historical parallels, if seldom wholly exact, are invariably helpful, for example Asquith with Burleigh, Macmillan with Walpole, Churchill with the Elder Pitt, Heath with Peel. But particularly useful is the comparison between Wilson and George Savile, Marquis of Halifax, provided one makes full allowance for the changed interpretation, during three centuries, of the word 'Trimmer'. For Halifax, a key political figure in the reign of Charles II, the word signified 'no more than this, that if men are together in a boat, and one part of the company would weigh it down on one side, another would make it lean as much to the contrary'.[19] Macaulay says of him:

'He was the chief of those politicians whom the two great parties contemptuously called Trimmers. Instead of quarrelling with this nickname, he assumed it as a title of honour, and vindicated with great vivacity the dignity of the appellation. Every good thing, he said, trims between extremes. The temperate zone trims between the climate in which men are roasted and the climate in which they are frozen. . . .

Thus Halifax was a Trimmer on principle. He was also a Trimmer by the constitution both of his head and of his heart.'[20]

[19] H. C. Foxcroft, *Character of the Trimmer* (Cambridge, 1946).
[20] Macaulay's *History of England*, i, chap. 2.

The application of such principles, duly brought up to date, has obvious relevance to the Labour Party of today, never more so than during the run-up to the general election of February 1974; and the state of the parties after all the votes had been counted[21] made another election inevitable in the near future. But it was with characteristic determination and confidence that Harold Wilson, in March 1974, kissed hands for the third time as Prime Minister, to become head of the first minority government of recent years. It was a dramatic and historic moment with nothing but imponderables and uncertainties lying ahead. Wilson, however, applied himself to the land's highest office with his customary energy and dynamism, now tempered by a concern to delegate more authority to others and to mastermind affairs from what he called a 'half-back' position. His interesting choice for the key post of Secretary of State for Employment was the colourful veteran parliamentarian Michael Foot; and his concept of a new 'social compact' to govern industrial relations found favour with voters in the General Election of 10 October 1974. Harold Wilson was on this date returned to prime ministerial office for the fourth time in a victory which was more impressive than at first appeared from the final state of the parties.[22] For the same forces – unknown to any computer – that had defeated Labour in June 1970 were strongly at work in marginal constituencies in October 1974;[23] and the same prior presumption of overwhelming Labour success had sprung from yet another opinion poll miscalculation. Wilson nevertheless achieved a majority over all the other parties of an unprecedently fragmented 'opposition', and the Conservatives received the lowest percentage of popular votes recorded this century. Short of extreme partisanship there was no belittling this triumph for a Labour leadership whose mantle now appeared more likely than ever to fall eventually on Anthony Wedgwood Benn, a politician with the advantageous distinction once enjoyed by Wilson of being exaggeratedly attacked and complacently underestimated by his opponents.

To none, perhaps, more than to observers belonging, like myself, to no political party, did October 1974 seem to portend a major turning point in British political history. For the Labour Party now began to

[21] Labour: 301; Conservative: 296; Liberal: 14; Others: 23.
[22] Labour: 319; Conservative: 276; Liberal: 13; Scottish Nationalist: 11; United Ulster Unionist: 10; Plaid Cymru: 3; Others: 3.
[23] See page 768.

look unmistakably like becoming – in fulfilment of Wilson's great ambition – the normal governing party of the future. And the man who had kept this party united as well as inspired had simultaneously set his seal on the most successful peacetime premiership of modern times. Described, on the day after the election, by so leading a conservative as Edward du Cann as 'the most accomplished politician of our generation', Harold Wilson had already staked a claim to ultimate recognition as one of the greatest of all the Prime Ministers.

BIBLIOGRAPHY

Books by Harold Wilson
New Deal for Coal (London, 1945)
War on World Poverty (London, 1953)
Purpose in Politics (London, 1964)
The Relevance of British Socialism (London, 1964)
The Labour Government 1964–70. A Personal Record (London, 1971)

Foot, Michael, *Harold Wilson. A Pictorial Biography* (London, 1964)
Noel, Gerard, *Harold Wilson. A Political Biography* (London, 1964); *The New Britain and Harold Wilson* (London, 1966)
Smith, Leslie, *Harold Wilson* (London, 1964)

EDWARD HEATH

BY

ANDREW ROTH

Edward Richard George Heath, PC, MBE, born 9 July 1916 and educated at Chatham House School, Ramsgate, and Balliol College, Oxford. Served in France, Belgium, Holland and Germany 1940–46; Major, 1945; Lieut-Col. commanding 2nd Reg HAC (TA) 1947–51. MP (Cons) for Bexley 1950–74, Sidcup 1974– ; Assistant Whip, February 1951; Lord Commissioner of the Treasury, November 1951; Joint Deputy Chief Whip 1953–55; Parliamentary Secretary to the Treasury and Chief Whip 1955–59; Minister of Labour 1959–60; Lord Privy Seal 1960–63; Prime Minister, 1970–74; Chairman, Commonwealth Parliamentary Association, 1970– ; Member of the Council of the Royal College of Music 1961; Chairman, London Symphony Orchestra Trust 1963–70; Vice-Pres., Bach Choir 1970– ; Fellow of Nuffield College, Oxford, 1962–70; Hon. Fellow 1970. Co-author of One Nation, a Tory Approach to Social Problems, *1950; author* Old World, New Horizons, *1970.*

Edward Richard George Heath. Photo by Vivienne

EDWARD HEATH

'None goes so far as he who knows not
whither he is going.' Oliver Cromwell

Edward Heath's narrow defeat in the February 1974 general election
only began the process of a bipartisan assessment of his three and a half
years in office. Initially, his defeat partly freed the voices of Tory backbenchers. Their criticisms of his style of leadership while in government
had been muted previously, out of both loyalty and self-interest. But
they soon began to make known their dissatisfaction when he changed
tactics without consulting backbenchers soon after Harold Wilson
had replaced him. But the narrowness of the Conservative defeat, and
uncertainty of when the next election would be held, did not free the
tongues of front bench Conservatives who had observed him more
closely from within his Cabinet. Since he might soon again be Prime
Minister, with the power to distribute Cabinet posts, this reticence was
understandable. It did, however, inhibit the judgement of political
historians anxious to fill out an assessment of where Mr Heath stands in
the parade of British prime ministers.

Partly because of his spasmodic interest in the 'One Nation' Group,
Edward Heath has been attracted by the figure of Disraeli, who started
as an 'outsider' but came to dominate Toryism. If comparisons are to
be made, however, Heath has a greater resemblance to the man Disraeli
destroyed: Robert Peel.

Robert Peel, the son of a Lancashire calico-printer, was also an
'outsider' in a party dominated by the landed gentry. He, too, had been
a 'gentlemanly commoner' at Oxford. Pushed by his party because they
thought him an efficient servant, he turned out to be a tough-minded
master. With a shy and secretive manner, he refused to take the Conservative rank and file into his confidence. His smile, said Daniel
O'Connell, 'was like a silver plate on a coffin'. Peel, too, despised the
'narrow representation' of interests on the benches behind him. Returned
by the squires to protect the Corn Laws which ensured high prices for
their produce, he became a convert to free trade in corn even before the

Irish potato blight and a poor English harvest gave power to his aboli-
tionist elbow. Mr Heath has applauded Mr Peel's decision to put 'the
national interest' before 'the landowning interest'.

It is difficult to assess whether Mr Heath will split the Tories as badly
as Peel while he is still in mid-stride. Nor is it easy to assess in which
direction he now faces (summer 1974). Prime ministers are often 'blown
off course', but few have put about as dramatically, or as secretively,
as Mr Heath. The inside story of the dramatic change from an almost
pre-war right-wing Conservatism to a very left-wing Keynsian pump-
priming was long one of the best-kept secrets of any post-war regime.
The proposal for naval co-operation with the South Africans with
which the Heath Government was launched was soon sunk without
trace. Detested offspring of the Wilson Government – boards to control
prices and incomes and government investment in industry – were
first buried with relish only to be dug up with life blown into them under
different names.

This Heathian ability to change his mind did not disturb the inner
core of his Cabinet – Whitelaw, Carrington, Barber, Carr. They saw
him not as a fancy-talking philosopher, but as a resolute man of decision. They saw him as capable of keeping his eye on the target and
persevering in that direction when all but him have lost heart and courage. His lieutenants have fought willingly by his side because they
have found in him a command quality and daring rarely seen among
post-war politicians. They felt that nobody else would have kept believing he could win the 1970 election. Nobody else, they feel, would have
pushed through the Industrial Relations Act, despite the opposition of
Labour and the trade unions and the thinly concealed scepticism of
industrialists. Only Heath, they feel, could have secured Britain's entry
into the EEC by January 1973, in the face of Labour opposition, a
divided Tory party and the drag of traditionalism and chauvinism. Who
but Heath, they insisted, could have jettisoned his long-standing opposition to a prices and incomes policy to claim as a revelation and a revolution a version of President Nixon's three-phase fight against inflation?

It was difficult to arouse similar enthusiasm among backbenchers
and activists in the country. Darting raids in different directions are
suitable for a small, mobile commando. But it is difficult for a large and
traditional army of politicians organised for set-piece confrontations.
It was difficult for an ordinary Tory MP, elected on a 1970 platform
favouring slashed government spending, to defend overnight the July

778

1971 decision to spend £4,000 million on 'pump-priming' to escape 'stagflation'.

Mr Heath's Cabinet lieutenants and activists in the country have largely kept their safety belts fastened and their mouths shut because of the evident risks of going 'hell for broke', as Anthony Barber described it. But by the end of 1972 the desired 5 per cent growth target had been reached, although the 1971 favourable balance of £1,000 million had been completely erased. The pound sterling continued to float, although this proposal had been rejected when Enoch Powell had proposed it and it was continued long after January 1973, when Britain had committed itself to anchor its currency. His lieutenants continued to have faith that the economy would be riding high in the autumn of 1974, the target date for a general election.

This inflationary 'gamble on growth' was overtaken in the autumn of 1973 by the worldwide inflation in raw material costs, spearheaded by skyrocketing oil prices. On top of this came the strike of the coalminers at the end of 1973. Mr Heath had never forgotten his humiliating defeat by the miners two years before. It was largely to avoid another similar capitulation he had erected his elaborate three-phase prices and incomes policy. He was willing to make the miners the most generous offers possible within his policy of dictating the limits of prices and incomes increases. But he was not willing to buy the miners off with the extra two or three pounds beyond Phase Three which would have avoided the miners' strike. Once the strike was on, his Government broadened the confrontation by imposing a three-day week. Mr Heath initially resisted the argument from Conservative Central Office and the bulk of his Cabinet colleagues that he should go for an early election. This was based on the assumption that the bulk of the middle class would vote Conservative rather than give the victory to the miners. Another assumption was that the economy would get much worse later in the year. Mr Heath delayed for three weeks before agreeing to hold a general election. In the event enough of the middle class voted Liberal to allow Labour to gain a five-seat plurality of seats. For a few days Mr Heath tried to hold on to Number Ten by offering the Liberals a coalition before handing over to Labour.

Mr Heath's willingness to take chances almost of a swashbuckling quality owes little to a background more suitable for a suburban architect or insurance executive. He was born in the middle-class seaside town of Broadstairs, Kent, on 9 July 1916, into the family of Will Heath, then a carpenter and later a small builder, and the former Edith Annie Pantony, the daughter of a poor and illiterate farmworker who had been a domestic. If, as psychologists suggest, being the indisputable favourite of your mother gives you the feeling of a conqueror, then young Ted had early reason for his obsessional drive. 'She worshipped him,' recalled a family friend. His mother gave him not only every opportunity the family could afford, but also the upward-looking aspirations and puritanical inhibitions that one would expect of an ambitious, respectable, churchgoing Victorian mother.

The mother-encouraged hard work of a bright young boy enabled him to get his foot on the crucial rungs of the musical and educational ladders. First was the best local grammar school, Chatham House School in Ramsgate down the coast. He spent nine years there, with his eye on a scholarship to Balliol College, Oxford. He failed his scholarship examination in French. But a loan from Kent County Council and his mother's willingness to pledge another £120 a year secured him entry; it was only after entry that he won the needed organ scholarship.

'Balliol opened all the doors for me,' Heath has said. Under A. D. (later Lord) Lindsay, Balliol had been broadening its intake to produce a more encompassing 'democratic aristocracy'. With a pleasant but inexorable drive, which a contemporary *Isis* compared to that of a tank, Heath made his mark across the whole range of Oxford activity. He formed the Balliol Choir, joined the Oxford Union and the Oxford University Conservative Association. Although his political ambitions were strongly evident during his four years at Oxford, so was his loathing for the dominant Chamberlain appeasers. After a trip to Spain, he was the leading anti-Franco young Tory at Oxford. He won the presidency of the OUCA against a pro-Franco Tory. He campaigned alongside Harold Macmillan against Quintin Hogg, the pro-Chamberlain Tory in the Oxford by-election. He won the presidency of the Union as an anti-Fascist candidate. His Union activity enabled him to join in a debating tour of the United States, where he warmed to 'the social freedom, the classlessness . . .'.

Heath spent six formative years, 1940–6, in the Royal Artillery, largely as Adjutant of the 107th Heavy Anti-Aircraft Regiment. As a person he was a 'loner', avoiding drinking with brother officers and regarding women as plague-bearers. As an officer he was enormously hard-working and efficient, even if given to over-documentation. His unit was the second into liberated Antwerp in September 1944. His band played at a 'liberation dance', but Captain Heath spent most of the night doing paperwork in his makeshift office. A Major in command of his own battery in January 1945, he was transferred to the 86th HAA Regiment of the Honourable Artillery Company only after the war was over. His rank of Lieutenant-Colonel was acquired in 1947 when he reformed a Territorial HAA regiment for the HAC. This led to his becoming Master Gunner within the Tower, 1951–4.

THE NEW MEMBER

By this time Heath was already a new Conservative MP for Bexley, in south-east London's Kentish suburbs. Like many another politically ambitious Tory returned officer, he had had difficulties in finding both employment and a winnable seat in the Labour-governed Britain to which he returned. After passing out joint top for his age in the Civil Service examination, he was assigned to the Ministry of Civil Aviation's Directorate of Long-Term Planning under Peter Masefield. But he did not find this congenial and was not sorry to resign on being adopted for Bexley in October 1947.

Even that marginal seat was hard to find. He had been beaten at Ashford by William Deedes, a descendant of local squires. He was beaten for East Fulham. He was beaten again for Sevenoaks. He struck it lucky at Bexley, partly because his witty friend, Ian Harvey, had been placed the week before at Harrow East. This made it easier for local activists who wanted a local boy from an ordinary family. But he had to disarm local women with 'I have no prejudice against matrimony. I just think it is not a matter that should be rushed.'

Over the next two years Heath worked very hard, attacking the 'specious promises' and 'lack of leadership' of the Attlee Government. Meanwhile, he supported himself first, unhappily, as well-paid news editor of the *Church Times*. Then, more happily but at a third of the pay, he became a trainee in the City merchant bank, Brown, Shipley. Finally, in February 1950, his gamble paid off: he was elected by a majority of 133 votes in a four-way contest in which a Communist took almost four times that margin from the Labour candidate.

Heath, already greying and plump, was one of a hundred new Tory MPs in the famous 'Class of '50', which included other ex-officer newcomers like Powell, Maudling and Macleod. They demonstrated that the domination of Old Etonians, squires and business magnates was being assaulted by professionals. Despite this, Heath had a social identity problem in what remained a class-conscious political community. He saw no point in identifying with fellow ESBs (elementary school boys), preferring to emphasise that he was a Balliol man, the Lieutenant-Colonel of an HAC regiment and a 'City banker' (at £200 a year).

Heath made a number of shrewd initial decisions. He joined the 'One Nation' Group with Angus Maude, Robert Carr, Iain Macleod and Enoch Powell. He made an impressive maiden speech in June 1950 urging European unity. He accepted in 1951 an invitation from Patrick Buchan-Hepburn to join the Whips' Office. It was as an extremely efficient, flexible and rapidly promoted member of that Praetorian Guard to successive Tory prime ministers that Heath made his mark, particularly after succeeding Buchan-Hepburn as Chief Whip in December 1955. His great achievement was in holding the Tories together in the wrenching days after the collapse of Sir Anthony Eden's Suez intervention in 1956. But Heath only came to public attention in January 1957 when the press discovered him celebrating Harold Macmillan's victory over R. A. Butler with oysters, game pie and champagne. A fellow Balliol man who had campaigned with Macmillan against Quintin Hogg in the 1938 Oxford by-election, Heath was very much a 'Macmillan man' from the outset and was trusted and consulted as such.

Heath's first chance as a minister was in Labour, beginning in 1960. His brief, nine-month role there was played very much in the pacifying Monckton tradition, very different from the part he sought to play a half-dozen years later. He was plucked out of this obscurity to make his reputation as Mr Macmillan's 'Mr Europe' and No. 2 to Lord Home at the Foreign Office, beginning in 1961. Over the next eighteen months Heath flew 100,000 miles in pursuit of terms for EEC entry that would satisfy both a divided Cabinet and a President de Gaulle mordantly suspicious of Britain as America's 'Trojan Horse'. When de Gaulle slammed the door on Britain in January 1963, he made Heath the beneficiary of popular sympathy and his own prediction: 'The Labour Party will come to power for a short and disastrous period, to be followed by the Conservatives, with Heath at their head. It is he who will enable Britain to enter Europe.'

Initially, de Gaulle's prediction seemed a nonsense. When Macmillan's prostate enabled him to throw in the towel at the Conservatives' turbulent October 1963 Blackpool conference, Butler and Hailsham were the leading contenders for the succession. Only Maudling among Heath's contemporaries had a chance. After Hailsham threw away his chance to lead the 'stop Butler' movement, on Macmillan's advice Heath threw in his lot with Lord Home to enable him to buy time to overtake Maudling.

Heath's reward was the Board of Trade, with his title upgraded at his request to 'Secretary of State for Industry, Trade and Regional Development and President of the Board of Trade'. With typical dynamism, he chose to make his mark in the year left before the general election with an attack on Resale Price Maintenance. This aroused Cabinet dissension because it was seen as divisive and a provocation to the Tory shopkeepers. But he got his legislation – and the subsequent credit for it.

Heath was deeply shocked by Labour's narrow victory in October 1964 because he could not hide his contempt for Labour as a ruling party. Sir Alec Douglas-Home named Maudling his deputy, but gave Heath the pace-setting job of policy planner and economic spokesman. While Maudling devoted much of his time to his City directorships, Heath (with only a Brown, Shipley directorship) was in command of the assault on Callaghan's mammoth 1965 Budget, with the aid of lieutenants like Anthony Barber and Peter Walker. When it became clear he was running neck-and-neck with Maudling, Heath discreetly supported the 'Alec Must Go!' campaign launched by PEST.

When Sir Alec unexpectedly decided to step down in July 1965, an over-confident Maudling confided his campaign to a diffident aristocrat, Lord Lambton, while Heath put his in the hands of efficient, thrusting Peter Walker. *The Economist* thought him more 'abrasive' and a 'riskier choice,' but he had the better record on EEC entry and the encouragement of competition. He was 'the cannon' who would 'batter down the walls'. Heath had the majority of the press, Maudling most of the Tories outside. In the Conservatives' first democratic election for leader, Heath secured 150, Maudling 133 and Powell 15.

From the outset the Heath-Wilson battle more resembled a Sicilian vendetta than Britain's normal gentlemanly politicians' rivalry. Wilson, who preferred Maudling, tried to destroy Heath by splitting the Tories three ways over Rhodesia. Heath regarded Wilson as a tricky opportunist, willing to sacrifice the national interest for party advantage. Heath surprised even enthusiasts like *The Economist* by how far right he went as Opposition leader. He ridiculed Wilson's prices and incomes policy as threatening a 'totalitarian society'. When he lost the March 1966 general election by a hundred-seat majority, Heath survived because he had performed creditably as a campaigner and because the Tories had no heart for another leadership struggle.

Heath tried to keep party unity behind him by setting a fast attacking pace led by younger men. He shelved veterans Selwyn Lloyd, Duncan Sandys and John Boyd-Carpenter and promoted younger 'Heathmen' from modest backgrounds like Geoffrey Rippon and Peter Walker. He urged party Chairman Edward du Cann to purge elderly squires from the candidates' list.

Heath made his comeback through Wilson's economic difficulties after July 1966. He attacked Wilson for devaluing in November 1967. He profited from Wilson's unpopularity as a result of post-devaluation economy measures like prescription charges. He began to win safe Labour seats in by-election swings of over 20 per cent.

Heath kept burnished his links with de Gaulle. He spoke vaguely of Anglo-French nuclear collaboration. He demanded Wilson disavow his Defence Secretary, Denis Healey, for attacking de Gaulle as a 'bad ally'. 'A Europe without France in the long run makes as little sense as a Europe without Britain,' he told a Hague meeting.

Unlike de Gaulle, Heath remained a strong defender of the United States role in Vietnam after his 1965 visit. He attacked Wilson for dissociating the Labour Government from the US bombing near Hanoi and Haiphong. In private he argued strongly with his Defence spokesman, Enoch Powell, also a critic of the Americans in Vietnam.

Although Powell made a lot of guerrilla raids on fellow Tory frontbenchers' ideological positions, he decided to commit himself most heavily on race. After some weeks of heightening attacks, Heath sacked Powell after his explosive April 1968 Birmingham speech, which he thought 'racialist' in tone. This dismissal produced widespread pro-Powell demonstration, including a march on Parliament by Fascist-led Smithfield porters and dockers. Heath had the support of the establishment, Powell of the back-street Tories. When Powell turned against EEC entry in March 1969 it was clear he was trying to destroy Heath as the young Disraeli had destroyed Peel.

Heath was furious at these stabs in the back just when the Tories were poised on the brink of victory on a rather right-wing platform, as unveiled at the Selsdon Park Hotel in January–February 1970. A strengthened police force and a stronger law on trespass was promised to block unruly pickets and anti-Apartheid demonstrators. Direct taxation would be cut. Agreements with trade unions would be made legally binding. Immigration controls would be tightened. Heath also swung rightwards on education by dropping his liberal friend Sir Edward Boyle and replacing him with a grocer's more right-wing daughter, Mrs Margaret Thatcher.

Suddenly Tory confidence plummeted at the end of April 1970 when the Harris Poll and Marplan both showed Labour in the lead for the first time since 1967. Wilson called for a general election. Leading Tories, who had hoped that Heath's attractiveness had been enhanced by his winning the Australian ocean yacht races, resumed their conviction that he was the party's albatross, to be jettisoned as soon as the election was over. Only Anthony Barber and Lord Aldington shared Heath's unbending self-confidence. In fact, the tide shifted in the last week. Tory market researchers had discovered that their best hope was to persuade working-class housewives that they could curb price rises. Heath resisted, but on 15 June a monthly trade deficit of £31 million was announced. Next day reporters were given a statement signed by him that tax cuts and curbs on nationalised industries' prices 'would, at a stroke, reduce the rise in prices', while Labour might bring in another devaluation.

When Edward Heath became Britain's unexpected Prime Minister in June 1970, he had 'made it on his own', owing little to anyone else. Most of his Cabinet appointments – Maudling (Home Office), Macleod (Treasury), Sir Alec (Foreign Office), Carrington (Defence) – were predictable. Some – Prior (Agriculture) and Peter Thomas (Wales *and* party Chairman) – owed more to loyalty than to proven ability. His exclusions – particularly of Powell and du Cann – showed how strong could be his pique.

His initial policies were right wing enough to be almost pre-war in quality. He told the October 1970 Blackpool conference he was trying to persuade 'our fellow citizens to recognise that they must be responsible for the consequences of their own actions'. His Minister of Technology, John Davies, predicted that 'lame ducks' would be plucked. The October 1970 'mini-Budget' cut expenditures on school milk and subsidies on council houses and increased prescription charges. The interventionist Industrial Reconstruction Corporation and the Prices and Incomes Board were both wound up. Thomas Cook was tagged for denationalisation. As if to make clear that a new man was in charge who would not accept dictation from the black Commonwealth leaders, an unnecessarily exaggerated campaign was launched to announce the sale of arms to South Africa. It was 'sold' as necessary to protect the vast Indian Ocean against a massive Soviet naval influx. But in the end all that was involved was the sale of a few helicopters and frigates. It seemed hardly worthwhile souring the Singapore Commonwealth Prime Ministers' Conference in January 1971 over this.

This policy of unnecessary confrontation carried on longest with the trade unions, partly because Heath believed both in curbing trade union power and giving more incentives to entrepreneurs. He made this most evident on a *Panorama* programme on BBC-TV on 9 November 1971 when he denounced as 'blatantly nonsensical' the arguments used in the Scamp pay award of a 14 per cent increase for dustmen while applauding as 'incentives' the tax cuts promised the middle class in Anthony Barber's mini-Budget the month before. This policy of confrontation began to crumble. The Cabinet stood up to the electricity workers, but the award of the Wilberforce tribunal turned out to be an 18 per cent increase. In January 1972 Heath decided to fight it out with the miners, with the assurance that there was eight weeks' supply of coal above ground. In February, just before the country ground to a complete halt, the Government gave the miners almost exactly what they had demanded. The patent failure of confrontation made the Industrial Relations Act almost a dangerous irrelevance, which neither the Government nor industry wanted to invoke.

More fundamental was the search for a new formula for keeping the mixed industrial economy working at full stretch while making its living in an increasingly competitive world. The need to rescue Rolls-Royce airplane engines by nationalisation in February 1971 knocked off one leg of a doctrinaire approach. The need to prevent the death of shipbuilding on the Clyde severely damaged the other. But the very seat of Tory belt-tightening was blocked by the discovery that the policies of the outgoing Labour Chancellor, Roy Jenkins, had been much more powerful than anticipated in cutting imports while expanding money in circulation. When Heath suggested cutting the money supply to Bank of England chief Sir Leslie O'Brien, on top of his budget-cutting activities, he was warned that it would mean widespread bankruptcies and unemployment would expand far beyond the 600,000 inherited. By the late spring of 1971 this figure had expanded to 750,000, with the assurance that it would top one million by the next winter. The Cabinet faced the danger of continuing 'stagflation' and the consequent loss of by-elections at a time when the contested European Communities Bill would be wending its protracted way through a Commons, where the thirty-man Tory majority could be eroded by a score of hardline anti-Marketeers.

In July 1971 Mr Heath put the helm smartly to port, with no fanfare. His Cabinet decided to pump £1,900 million into the economy during the first year, and more in the second year, in order to go 'hell for broke' (Barber) for an annual increase in production of 5 per cent. This hope became a reality in the first quarter of 1973. By that time, unemployment, declining at 30,000 a month, had ceased to be a political problem.

The serious problem then was inflation, both international and internal. By the autumn of 1972 this threatened to become a runaway inflation. Heath tried to secure a voluntary anti-inflation agreement by negotiations with the CBI and TUC in the summer of 1972. When this failed, he took a leaf out of President Nixon's book and proclaimed a three-phase statutory control of prices and incomes, beginning in November 1972 with a standstill. Heath proclaimed this as a historic turning-point, completely ignoring the vitriol he had poured on Wilson's efforts in 1965 and 1966.

It did indeed represent a turning-point in his own attitude because he increasingly attempted to become a Peel-like Tory spokesman of the 'national interest' rather than the sectional interest. The CBI complained that the draft of the Price and Pay Code lowered the ceiling so low on possible price increases as to discourage industrial investment. The final form, which came into effect in April 1973, was slightly more flexible. But Mr Heath was still able to claim that it imposed the tightest price control since World War II, albeit without the price-reducing subsidies that had made British food prices relatively cheap before EEC entry.

As Heath entered the home stretch of his foreshortened term of office, he was much nearer the centre of the political spectrum than anyone could have anticipated at its beginning. Tories suspected him for having stirred sleeping dogs by searching for a socially just society. And trade union leaders were beginning to think that he was a man with whom they might possibly negotiate. But all that went sour with the miners' strike on which he lost the February 1974 general election.

Mr Heath's Labour opponents won a lead of only five seats over the Tories on that occasion, without an overall majority over all parties. For a weekend he remained in 10 Downing Street in the hope that his policies favouring the European Community and government-determined prices and incomes could be retained with Liberal support. But Liberal leader, Jeremy Thorpe, found it impossible to be identified with the 'architect of confrontation' unless Mr Heath could concede the proportional representation which would further enhance the Liberals but ensure that the Tories would never again win a majority on their own.

After his replacement at 10 Downing Street by Labour leader Harold Wilson, Mr Heath's bruised ego was salved by the renewal of a Chinese invitation to visit the People's Republic. When he flew to China in May, in every city he visited thousands of schoolchildren danced their welcome and tens of thousands were mobilized along the streets to demonstrate the intensity of China's official welcome. It was Chairman Mao Tse-tung's public demonstration that he preferred the pro-EEC, anti-Russian posture of the Tory leader to the anti-EEC, relatively pro-Russian attitudes of his successor, Harold Wilson. In his private conversation with Edward Heath, Chairman Mao made it clear that he hoped the Tory leader would again lead Britain and perhaps the Community into an anti-Russian position which would serve China's interest equally with that of Britain.

On his return to Britain in the summer of 1974, it became increasingly clear that Mr Heath could not escape from his winter reputation, among working people in particular, that he was the architect of confrontation and the main begetter of the winter's three-day weeks. This was not, of course, his own view. He had prided himself as being the Prime Minister who had spent more time talking to, if not listening to, trade union leaders than any of his predecessors.

When the October 1974 general election approached, he and his colleagues desperately attempted to shed the 'confrontation' image. In their manifesto they pledged themselves not to restore the union-hated Industrial Relations Act. If the Tories were returned with a majority, he promised, they would organize a government of national unity, including others besides Tory politicians – all unspecified. But the man who could not reflect in his Cabinet the broad coalition of attitudes represented in the Conservative Party found it difficult to persuade voters that he could reflect more disparate political and non-political elements. His party lost almost another score of seats, enabling Labour to emerge with a wafer-thin majority of three overall.

His loss of the third of the four general elections into which he had led the Tories opened up a new barrage of attacks on his leadership.

Even among his pro-European, pro-consensus friends there was an argument over whether they could better maintain his policies by jettisoning him. His anti-European Tory opponents wondered how they could best get rid of his policies as well as Edward Heath himself. Even among those Tory MPs who most admired his prime ministerial and parliamentary qualities, there were hardly any who thought he would be anything but a continued disadvantage at the next general election. The only questions posed when Parliament reassembled after the general election was not whether he would be deposed, but when and how.

BIBLIOGRAPHY

Roth, Andrew, *Heath and the Heathmen* (London, 1972)

NOTES ON THE AUTHORS

AYLING, Stanley. Born 1909 and educated at Strand School, London, and Emmanuel College, Cambridge (Goldsmiths' Company exhibitioner). Married; two sons. Worked for many years as a schoolmaster. Author of *Portraits of Power*, *Nineteenth Century Gallery*, *George the Third*. Currently working on a biography of the elder Pitt.

BLAKE, Robert Norman William, MA FBA, DLitt, FRHistS, created Lord Blake 1971. Born 1916. Lecturer at Christ Church, Oxford, 1946–47; Student of Christ Church, 1947–68; Ford Lecturer, 1967–68; member of the Oxford City Council, 1957–64; JP Oxford City, 1964. Governor of Trent College, Bradfield College, King Edward VI School (Norwich), Malvern College and St Edward's (Oxford). Provost of Queen's College, Oxford, since 1968. Married; three daughters. Publications: *The Private Papers of Douglas Haig* (ed.), 1952; *The Unknown Prime Minister, the Life and Times of Andrew Bonar Law*, 1955; *Disraeli*, 1966; *The Conservative Party from Peel to Churchill*, 1970.

BREWER, John. Born 1947 and educated at Liverpool College and Sidney Sussex College, Cambridge, BA (History, Class I with distinction) 1965–68, MA (1972), PhD (1973). Henry Fellow, Harvard University; Fulbright Travelling Fellow (1968–69); Research Fellow, Sidney Sussex College, Cambridge (1969–73); Visiting Professor, Washington University, St Louis (1972–73); Visiting Fellow, Huntington Library, San Marino, California (1973); Fellow, Corpus Christi College, Cambridge (1973–); Assistant Lecturer in History, Cambridge University (1973). Author of *Perspectives in American History* (1972); *Political Argument and propaganda in England 1760–1770* (forthcoming), and contributor to *The Historical Journal*.

BRIGGS, Asa. Born 1921. Married; two sons, two daughters. Fellow of Worcester College, Oxford, 1944–55; Reader in Recent Social and Economic History, Oxford, 1950–55; Professor of Modern History, Leeds University, 1955–61; Professor of History, Sussex University, since 1961 and Vice-Chancellor since 1967; Visiting Professor, Australian National University, 1960; University of Chicago, 1966 and 1972; D.Litt (Hon) East Anglia 1966 and Strathclyde 1972; LLD (Hon) York (Canada) 1968; Hon. Fellow of Sidney Sussex College, Cambridge, 1968 and of Worcester College, Oxford, 1969. Author of *Victorian People*, 1954; *Friends of the People*, 1956; *The Age of Improvement*, 1959; 3 volumes of the *History of Broadcasting in the United Kingdom*, 1961–70; *William Cobbett*, 1967; *How They Lived, 1700–1815*, 1969; etc.

BROWN, Peter Douglas, MA. Born 1925 and educated at Harrow and Balliol College, Oxford. Author of *The Chathamites*, 1967; and presently working on a life of *William Pitt, Earl of Chatham*.

CANNON, John. Educated at Peterhouse, Cambridge, and did research at the University of Bristol into eighteenth century electoral history. Served in the History of Parliament Trust with Sir Lewis Namier. Presently Reader in History, University of Bristol. Author of *The Fox-North Coalition*, and *Parliamentary Reform, 1640–1832*.

CLARKE, John. Born in Oxford 1947 and educated at Magdalen School, Brackley (Northants), and Wadham College, Oxford. Fellow of All Souls College, Oxford, 1967. Contributor to various journals. At present working on the Russia Company in the eighteenth century.

COOK, Christopher. Educated St Catharine's College, Cambridge (first class honours in history). Research at Nuffield College, Oxford, under supervision of A. J. P. Taylor. Lecturer in politics at Magdalen College, Oxford; subsequently appointed Senior Research Officer at the London School of Economics. Co-editor of *Sources in British Political History, 1900–51; British Historical Facts, 1830–1900; The Decade of Disillusion; European Political Facts, 1918–73; By-Elections in British Politics*. Joint editor of Pears Encyclopedia.

CROW, Duncan. Born Aberdeen and educated in Edinburgh and London, Grenoble and the Army. Served throughout World War Two in the Royal Armoured Corps and the 'Phantom' Regiment. Author of fourteen books including *The Victorian Woman*. Television broadcaster and editor of *Armoured Fighting Vehicles of the World*.

DERRY, J. W. Born 1933 and educated at Gateshead Grammar School and Emmanuel College, Cambridge. Lecturer, London School of Economics, 1961–65; Fellow and Director of Studies in History at Downing College, Cambridge, 1965–70; Lecturer in History, University of Newcastle-on-Tyne, 1970–73, and Senior Lecturer since 1973. Author of *William Pitt*, 1962; *The Regency Crisis and the Whigs*, 1963; *Reaction and Reform*, 1963; *The Radical Tradition*, 1967; *Charles James Fox*, 1972.

DICKINSON, Harry Thomas. Born 1939 and educated at Durham University (BA 1960, DipEd 1961, MA 1963). PhD (Newcastle) 1968. Earl Grey Fellow, Newcastle University, 1964–66. Lecturer in History, University of Edinburgh, 1966–73. Promoted to Reader in History, 1973. Married; one son, one daughter. Author of *Bolingbroke*, 1970; *Walpole and the Whig Supremacy*, 1973; editor of *The Correspondence of Sir James Clavering, 1708-40*, 1967; *Politics and Literature in the Eighteenth Century*, 1974; contributor to historical journals.

DURRANT, Peter. Born 1948 and educated at The Grammar School, Haywards Heath, Sussex, and Manchester University. At present working on a full-length political biography of the Third Duke of Grafton.

FEUCHTWANGER, Edgar Joseph, Reader in History and Deputy Director, Department of Extra-Mural Studies, University of Southampton. MA, PhD., FRHistS. Born 1924. Married; one son, two daughters. Author of *Disraeli, Democracy and the Tory Party*, 1968; *Prussia, Myth and Reality*, 1970; *Gladstone, a Political Biography*, 1975; and contributor to various historical journals.

FOOT, Michael Richard Daniell, Professor of Modern History, University of Manchester 1967–73. MA, BLitt, FRHistS. Born 1919. Married; one son, one daughter. Formerly lecturer at Keble College, Oxford (1952–59) and Trinity College, Oxford (1956–59). Author of *Gladstone and Liberalism* (with J. L. Hammond), 1952; *British Foreign Policy since 1898*, 1956; *Men in Uniform*, 1961; *SOE in France*, 1966; editor of *The Gladstone Diaries*, 2 vols, 1968; *War and Society*, 1973.

FORREST, D. M., born Worcestershire, educated at King's School, Worcester, and King's College, London. Worked as journalist in Oxford and Birmingham. Later Assistant Editor of *The Countryman*. Freelance correspondent in Paris. Joined Tea Bureau after World War II to edit technical and historical publications and became head of the organisation; retired 1965. Author of *A Hundred Years of Ceylon Tea*, 1965; *The Oriental*, 1968; *Tiger of Mysore*, 1970–73.

GASH, Norman. Born 1912 and educated at Oxford University (BA 1933, MA 1938, BLitt 1934). FRHistS, FBA, FRSL. Temporary Lecturer, Edinburgh University, 1935–36; Assistant Lecturer, University College, London, 1936–40; Lecturer, St Salvator's College, St Andrews, 1946–53; Professor of Modern History, Leeds University, 1953–55; Visiting Professor, John Hopkins University, Baltimore, 1962; Ford Lecturer, Oxford, 1964; Vice-Principal, St Andrew's University, 1967–71; Professor of History, St Salvator's College, St Andrews, since 1955; President of St Andrews British Historical Association 1955–70; Member of the Council of the Royal Historical Society, 1961–64. Married: two daughters. Author of *Politics in the Age of*

Peel, 1953; *Mr Secretary Peel*, 1961; *Reaction and Reconstruction in English Politics, 1832–52*, 1965; *The Age of Peel*, 1968; *Sir Robert Peel*, 1972. Contributor to historical journals.

GRIMOND, Joseph, PC, TD, LLD, DCL, MP. Born St Andrews 29 July 1913. Educated Eton and Balliol College, Oxford. First class honours in politics, philosophy and economics. Practised as a barrister until 1939–45 war. Served in the 2nd Fife and Forfar Yeomanry and as major on the staff of 53rd Division. MP (Liberal) for Orkney and Shetland since 1950. Liberal Whip, 1950–56. Party leader 1956–67. PC 1961. Director of the 'Manchester Guardian' and 'Evening News' since 1967. Rector of Edinburgh University 1960–63, and of Aberdeen University 1970–73, Chancellor of Kent University 1970. Broadcaster and newspaper contributor. Married; three children.

HOLMES, Geoffrey, born in Sheffield 1928 and educated at Woodhouse Grammar School, Sheffield, 1938–45, and Pembroke College, Oxford, 1945–8, 1950–51. On the staff of the Military Adviser to the UK High Commissioner in India, 1949–50; Assistant Lecturer, Lecturer and Senior Lecturer in History, University of Glasgow, 1952–69; Reader in History, University of Lancaster, 1969–72; Professor of History at Lancaster (Personal Chair) since January 1973. FRHistS. Married; two children. Author of *British Politics in the Age of Anne*, 1967; (with W. A. Speck) *The Divided Society*, 1967; (editor and contributor) *Britain after the Glorious Revolution*, 1969; *The Trial of Doctor Sacheverell*, 1973, and contributor to historical journals.

HOWAT, Gerald M. D., BLitt, MA, FRHistS, DipEd. Born 1928. Educated at Trinity College, Glenalmond; Exeter College, Oxford, Edinburgh and London Universities. Head of the Department of History, Culham College, Nuneham Park, Oxford, until 1973. Presently Head of the History Department, Radley College, Oxford. Author of *From Chatham to Churchill* (1966); (with Anne Howat) *The Story of Health* (1967); *Documents in European History, 1789–1970* (1973); *Stuart and Cromwellian Foreign Policy* (1974); *Learie Constantine* (in preparation). Editor of *Dictionary of World History* (1973); Consultant Editor, *Who did What* (1974). Author of an Historical Association pamphlet on Commonwealth History, and of articles on history, the teaching of history, and education.

JAMES, Robert Rhodes, MA, FRSL, FRHistS. Born 10 April 1933 and educated privately in India and England, Sedbergh School and Worcester College, Oxford. Assistant Clerk of the House of Commons, 1955–1961; Senior Clerk, 1961–1964; Fellow of All Souls, Oxford, 1964–1968; Kratter Visiting Professor, Stanford University, California, 1968; Director of the Institute for the Study of International Organisation, 1968–1973; Principal Officer, Executive Office of the UN Secretary-General, 1973; UN Consultant on the Human Environment, 1971–1972; UK member, UN Human Rights Sub-Commission, 1972. Author of *Lord Randolph Churchill*, 1959; *An Introduction to the House of Commons*, 1961; *Rosebery*, 1963;

Gallipoli, 1965; (ed.) *Chips: The Diaries of Sir Henry Channon*, 1967; *Memoirs of a Conservative* (Lord Davidson), 1968; (ed.) *The Czechoslovak Crisis, 1968*, 1969; *Britain's Role in the United Nations*, 1970; *Churchill – a Study in Failure, 1900–39*, 1970; *Staffing the United Nations Secretariat*, 1971; *Ambitions and Realities*, 1972; etc. Awarded the John Llewellyn Rhys Memorial Prize 1961; Heinemann Literary Award, 1964; FRSL, 1964; FRHistS, 1973. Married, four daughters.

JONES, George William. Born 1938 and educated at Jesus College, Oxford (BA 1960, MA 1965); doctorate for research at Nuffield College, Oxford, 1965. Assistant Lecturer in Government, Leeds University, 1963–65 and Lecturer 1965–66; Lecturer in Political Science, London School of Economics, 1966–71, and Senior Lecturer since 1971. Married; one son, one daughter. Author of *Borough Politics*, 1969; co-author of *Herbert Morrison: Portrait of a Politician*, 1973. Contributor to journals on Central and Local government.

JUPP, Peter. Educated at Owens School, Islington, and the University of Reading. Lecturer in Modern History, Queen's University, Belfast since 1964; Visiting Fellow, Huntington Library, San Marino, California, 1972; Visiting Fellow, Wolfson College, Cambridge, 1973–74. Author of a thesis on *Irish Parliamentary Representation, 1801–20*, a contribution to the official History of Parliament, 1790–1820; also a number of articles on aspects of British and Irish politics in the late eighteenth and early nineteenth centuries and *British and Irish Elections 1784–1831*, 1973.

LANGFORD, Paul. Born at Bridgend (Glamorgan) 1945 and educated at Monmouth School and Hertford College, Oxford. Elected to a Junior Research Fellowship at Lincoln College, Oxford in 1969, and to a Tutorial Fellowship in 1970. MA, DPhil. Has specialised in British domestic and imperial politics in the eighteenth century. Author of a book on Rockingham and articles on the Elder Pitt and the American Revolution.

LONGFORD, Countess of, Elizabeth Pakenham, born 30 August 1906, daughter of N. B. Harman, FRCS. Married 1931 the Hon. F. A. Pakenham, now 7th Earl of Longford; four sons, three daughters. Educated Headington School and Lady Margaret Hall, Oxford. WEA and University Extension lecturer 1929–35; contested (Lab.) Cheltenham 1935, Oxford 1950; Trustee, National Portrait Gallery since 1968; Member of the Advisory Council of the V & A Museum since 1969. Hon.DLitt (Sussex) 1970. FRSL. Author of *Victoria R.I.*, 1964; *Wellington, Years of the Sword*, 1969; *Wellington, Pillar of State*, 1972.

LOWE, Peter Carlton, BA, PhD, FRHistS. Born 1941. Assistant Lecturer, Manchester University, 1965–68; Lecturer in History, Manchester University since 1968. Author of *Great Britain and Japan 1911–15*, 1969; 'The Rise to the Premiership, 1914–16' in *Lloyd George: Twelve Essays*, (ed.) A. J. P. Taylor, 1971; contributor to historical journals.

MARLOW, Joyce. Born in Manchester 1929 and educated at local State schools, which she left at the age of seventeen to train for the theatre. Worked for seventeen years as a professional actress in repertory, West End, films and television. Married; two sons. While acting she had her first book, a children's adventure story, published in 1964, followed by two more children's books and a novel (*Time to Die*). Author also of *The Peterloo Massacre*, 1969; *The Tolpuddle Martyrs*, 1971; *Captain Boycott and the Irish*, 1973; *The Life and Times of George I*, 1973.

MARSHALL, Dorothy. Born 26 March 1900 at Morecambe, Lancashire and educated at Park School, Preston, and Girton College, Cambridge, BA 1921, PhD 1925. Temporary Instructor, Vassar College, USA 1924–5; Senior History Mistress, Reigate County School, 1925–7; Temporary Lecturer, University of the Witwatersrand, 1927–8; Assistant Lecturer, Bedford College, London, 1930–34; Senior Tutor, St Mary's College, and Lecturer, Durham University 1934–6; Lecturer, Senior Lecturer and in 1965 Reader in History in the University of Wales at University College of Cardiff and Monmouthshire 1936–67; Visiting Lecturer at Wellesley College, USA, 1960–61. Author of *The English Poor in the 18th Century*, 1926; *The Rise of George Canning*, 1939; *English People in the 18th Century*, 1956; *Eighteenth Century England*, 1962; *John Wesley*, 1965; *Dr Johnson's London*, 1968; *Life and Times of Queen Victoria*, 1972; *Industrial England 1776–1850*, 1973.

McCORD, Norman. Born 1930. Educated at Tynemouth High School, King's College, Newcastle and Trinity College, Cambridge. BA, PhD, FRHistS. Assistant Lecturer in History, Cardiff, 1958–60; Lecturer in History, Newcastle, 1960–69; Reader in Modern History, Newcastle, 1969–70; Reader in Economic and Social History, Newcastle since 1970. Author of *The Anti-Corn Law League*, 1958; *Free Trade*, 1970; *Industry in the Nineteenth Century*, 1971; etc., and contributor to various historical journals.

MIDDLEMAS, Robert Keith. MA (Cambridge), DPhil (Sussex). Born 1935 and educated at Stowe and Pembroke College, Cambridge (first-class Honours in history). Served for eight years as Clerk in the House of Commons. Since 1965 lecturer in modern history at the University of Sussex. Married; four children. Author of *The Clydesiders*, 1965; *Baldwin* (with A. J. L. Barnes), 1969; *Diplomacy of Illusion*, 1972; (ed.) Thomas Jones *Whitehall Diary*, published 1969–71.

NEWMAN, Aubrey Norris. Born 1927 and educated at Glasgow (MA 1949) and Oxford University (BA 1953, MA 1957, DPhil 1957). FRHistS 1964. Research Fellow, Bedford College (London), 1954–55, 1957–58; part-time temporary lecturer Nottingham University, 1958–59; Assistant Lecturer, Leicester University, 1959–

61; Lecturer 1961–69, Senior Lecturer 1969–72, Reader in History since 1972; Research Assistant, History of Parliament, 1955–59. Married: one son, three daughters. Author of *The Stanhopes of Chevening*, 1969; *Leicester House Politics, 1750–60*, 1969; (with H. Miller) *A Bibliography of British History, 1485–1760,* 1970; etc.

NOEL, Hon. Gerard Eyre Wriothesley, son of the 4th Earl of Gainsborough. Educated at Georgetown, USA and Exeter College, Oxford. MA (Modern History). Called to the Bar, 1952. Publisher, author and journalist. Literary editor, *Catholic Times*, 1958–61; Assistant editor, *Catholic Herald*, 1968, Editor since 1971. Director, Herder Book Co., 1959–66; Chairman, Sands and Co (Publishers) Ltd, since 1967. Married; two sons and one daughter. Author of *Paul IV*, 1963; *Harold Wilson*, 1964; *Goldwater*, 1964; *The New Britain*, 1966; *The Path from Rome*, 1968; *Princess Alice*, 1974; etc.

NUTTING, Rt Hon. Sir (Harold) Anthony, Bt, PC. Born 11 January 1920, third son of Sir Harold Stansmore Nutting, 2nd Bart. Educated at Eton and Trinity College, Cambridge. Served in the Leics. Yeomanry 1939, invalided. Foreign Service 1940–45. MP (Cons) Melton, 1945–56, resigned. Chairman, Young Conservatives, 1946; National Union of Conservatives and Unionist Association, 1950; Conservative National Executive Committee, 1951; Parliamentary Under-Secretary of State for Foreign Affairs, 1951–54; Minister of State for Foreign Affairs, 1954–56, resigned; leader of UK delegation to the UN General Assembly and to UN Disarmament Commission 1954–56. Married; two sons and one daughter. Author of *Europe Will Not Wait*, 1960; *Lawrence of Arabia*, 1961; *The Arabs*, 1964; *Gordon, Martyr and Misfit*, 1966; *No End of a Lesson*, 1967; *Scramble for Africa*, 1970; *Nasser*, 1972.

O'GORMAN, Frank. Born 1940 and educated at the University of Leeds. BA (Leeds) 1962; PhD (Cambridge) 1965. Lecturer in Modern History at the University of Manchester since 1965. Author of *The Whig Party and the French Revolution*, 1967; *Edmund Burke: His Political Philosophy*, 1973; *The Rise of Party in Britain* (in preparation); and contributions to historical journals.

PALMER, Alan Warwick, MA, BLitt. Born 1926 and educated at Bancroft's School and Oriel College, Oxford. Author of *A Dictionary of Modern History*, 1962; *Yugoslavia*, 1964; *The Garden of Salonika*, 1965; *Napoleon in Russia*, 1967; *The Laws Between*, 1970; *Metternich*, 1972; *Alexander I*, 2974.

PREST, John Michael. Born 1928 and educated at Bradfield College and King's College, Cambridge. MA Cambridge, MA Oxford. Fellow and Tutor in Modern History, Balliol College, Oxford, since 1954. Vice-Master 1971–74. Married; two sons and one daughter. Author of *Lord John Russell,* 1972; *The Industrial Revolution in Coventry,* 1959.

RAMSDEN, John. Born 1947 and educated in Sheffield and at Corpus Christi College, Oxford. Student at Nuffield College, Oxford, 1969–72; lecturer in modern history at Queen Mary College, London, since 1972. Author and co-editor of *By-elections in British Politics,* 1973. Currently engaged in research for a book on the history of the Conservative Party from 1902 till 1940.

RIDLEY, Jasper, FRSL. Born 25 May 1920 and educated at Felcourt School, the Sorbonne, and Magdalen College, Oxford. Called to the bar 1945. Member St Pancras Borough Council 1945–49. President of the Hardwicke Society, 1954–55. Contested (Labour) Winchester 1955, Westbury 1959. Married; two sons and one daughter. Author of *Thomas Cranmer,* 1962; *John Knox,* 1968; *Lord Palmerston,* 1970; etc.

ROBBINS, Keith Gilbert, MA, FRHistS. Born 1940, educated Bristol Grammar School and Magdalen College, Oxford; Gladstone Memorial Prize, 1960; first class honours modern history; Senior Scholar, St Antony's College, Oxford, 1961–63; DPhil 1964. Lecturer in History, University of York, 1963–71. Professor of History, University College of North Wales, Bangor, since 1971. Married; three sons, one daughter. Author of *Munich 1938,* 1968; *Sir Edward Grey,* 1971; contributor to historical journals. Currently engaged on a study of pacifists in the First World War and on a biography of John Bright.

ROSE, Richard, Professor of Politics, University of Strathclyde since 1966. BA DPhil. Born 1933. Married; two sons, one daughter. Formerly lecturer, Manchester University, 1961–66. President of the Scottish Political Studies Association 1967–68 and 1972–73; Secretary of the Committee on Political Sociology of the International Sociological Association; Member of the US-UK Fulbright Commission. Author of *The British General Election of 1959* (with D. E. Butler); *Must Labour Lose?* (with Mark Abrams), 1960; *Governing Without Consensus,* 1971; *Politics in England, Today,* 1974; editor of *Studies in British Politics,* 1966, and contributor to *The Times, New Society,* etc.

ROTH, Andrew. Born in New York in 1919, attended City University (BSS), Columbia University (MA), Michigan and Harvard. He was working on his PhD in Far Eastern history and teaching history in a New York secondary school when he joined the US Navy as an Intelligence officer in 1941, to be trained in Japan. Author of *Dilemma in Japan*; *Enoch Powell*; *Heath and the Heathmen*, 1972. He settled in Britain in 1950 and became a British citizen in 1965, and is the editor of *Westminster Newsletter*.

SMITH, Ernest Anthony. Born 1924 and educated at Cambridge University (BA 1949, MA 1955); DipEd (Reading) 1950; FRHistS 1957. Assistant Lecturer in History, Reading University, 1951–54; Lecturer 1954–64; Senior Lecturer since 1964. Married; one son, one daughter. Author of *History of the Press*, 1968; Editor of *The Letters of Princess Lieven to Lady Holland, 1847–57*, 1955; (ed. with A. Aspinall) *English Historical Documents*, (Vol. XI, 1783–1832), 1959. Contributor to historical journals.

SPROAT, Iain MacDonald. Born 3 November 1938 and educated at Melrose, Winchester and Magdalen College, Oxford. MP (Cons) for Aberdeen (South) since 1970. Parliamentary Private Secretary to the Secretary of State for Scotland, 1973–74. Serving officer in the 4th (Vol.) Battalion, Royal Green Jackets, and has lectured at the Royal College of Defence Studies on guerrilla warfare. Chairman, Sproat Group of Companies.

THOMAS, Peter David Garner. Born 1930 and educated at the University College of North Wales (BA 1951, MA 1953), and University College, London (PhD 1958); FRHistS; Assistant Lecturer, Glasgow University, 1956–59; Lecturer 1959–65; Lecturer, University College of Wales, 1965–68; Senior Lecturer 1968–71; Reader in History since 1971. Married, two sons, one daughter. Author of *The House of Commons in the Eighteenth Century*, 1971. Contributor to historical journals.

VAN THAL, Herbert. Born 1904 in Hampstead and educated at St Paul's School, London. Entered the book trade by way of bookselling and later migrated to publishing. Author of *Ernest Augustus, Duke of Cumberland*; *The Tops of the Mulberry Trees*, and a biography of Mrs Lynn Linton (in preparation); editor of biographical anthologies of Belloc and Landor, Thomas Adolphus Trollope's autobiography; etc.

VINCENT, John Russell, Professor of Modern History, University of Bristol. Born 1937. MA, PhD. Author of *The Formation of the Liberal Party, 1857–68*, 1966; *Pollbooks: How the Victorians Voted*, 1967; *Lord Caringford's Journal, Reflections of a Cabinet Minister*, 1971 (with A. B. Cooke); *The Governing Passion: British Cabinet Government and Party Politics 1885–86*, 1974 (with A. B. Cooke).

WILSON, The Hon John, CMG. Born 1924. Educated at Eton and King's College,

Cambridge. Served in the Royal Navy in the 1939–45 war, in the Foreign Office 1944–5; as Third Secretary at Ankara, 1948, and Tel Aviv, 1950; Second Secretary at Rio de Janeiro, 1953; First Secretary at FO, 1956; Washington 1959; and at FO, 1961. Counsellor at the British Embassy in South Africa, 1965, and head of the West African Department, Foreign and Commonwealth Office, 1968. Concurrently Ambassador to Chad from 1970. Now Ambassador to Turkey. Married; two sons and one daughter. Author of *C.B., a Life of Sir Henry Campbell-Bannerman* (1973).

WOODBRIDGE, George. Professor Emeritus, Barnard College, Columbia University. Born 1908 and educated at Columbia University (AB 1927 and MA 1934) and the University of Wisconsin (PhD 1937). Taught at Columbia University, 1937–42, and Barnard College, 1960–73. Visiting Professor at Queen Mary College, University of London 1968–69. Author of *UNRRA : The History of the United Nations Relief and Rehabilitation Administration*, New York, 1949; *The Reform Bill of 1832*, New York, 1971.

YOUNG, (Charles) Kenneth, FRSL. Born 27 November 1916 and educated at Queen Elizabeth's (Wakefield), Coatham School (Redcar) and Leeds University (first-class hons, English). Served 1939–45 in the Royal Corps of Signals and the Intelligence Corps, and the Foreign Office. Joined BBC European Service 1948, *Daily Mirror* 1949, *Daily Mail* 1950, *Daily Telegraph* 1952–60, and was editor of the *Yorkshire Post* 1960–64. Political and literary adviser to Beaverbrook Newspapers since 1965. Married; three sons and two daughters. Author of *John Dryden*, 1954; *A. J. Balfour*, 1963; *Churchill and Beaverbrook*, 1966; *Rhodesia and Independence*, 1967; *The Greek Passion*, 1969; *Sir Alec Douglas-Home*, 1970; (ed.) *Diaries of Sir Robert Bruce Lockhart*, Vol. I, 1973, Vol. II, 1975.

ZIEGLER, Philip Sanderman. Born 1929 and educated at Eton and New College, Oxford (1st Class Honours Jurisprudence; Chancellor's Essay Prize). HM Diplomatic Service 1952–65, serving in Vientiane, Paris, Pretoria and Bogotá. Editor, William Collins and Sons, 1966–73. FRSL 1972. Married (1) Sarah Collins (deceased), one son, one daughter; (2) Clare Charrington, one son. Author of *The Duchess of Dino*, 1962; *Addington*, 1965; *The Black Death*, 1968; *William IV*, 1972; *Omdurman*, 1973. Currently at work on a biography of Melbourne.

GEORGE CANNING

Canning, like Anthony Eden, is a Prime Minister chiefly remembered for having been Foreign Secretary. To this paradox is added an enigma. Was he – would he have become – a great all-round statesman? For he succumbed to the illness which afflicted him throughout his brief premiership, and died at the politically youthful age of fifty-six.

A special dazzle still hangs about Canning, recognisable to this day. There is the Canning Club, to which Tories are proud to belong. He is seen, rightly or wrongly, as an innovator. He is looked to as the prophet of British nationalism. Because he was held to be 'of the people', and knew how to win popularity while never idolising the people, he is popular still.

George Canning was born in London on 11 April 1770, the same year as his future Cabinet colleagues, Henry Huskisson and Lord Liverpool; a year after Wellington, Castlereagh and Napoleon. His early childhood was passed in harsh circumstances. His father, who came from Northern Ireland, having quarrelled with his family, died in penury on 11 April 1771. His mother, also Irish, went on the stage to keep herself and married a villainous actor who set young George 'on the highroad to the gallows'. Rescued by his uncle, Stratford Canning, a City banker, George found himself enjoying an elitist education: preparatory school near Winchester, followed by Eton. He shone as a scholar, debater and model pupil. From the experiences of a childhood so nearly wrecked he must have gained his determination to succeed, and to succeed through the most single-minded dedication to hard work and what passed in those days for abstinence.

His uncle, being a prominent Whig, introduced him to Whig politicians like Burke and Fox, whose cause he ardently espoused. At Oxford he made friends with young Tories until, with the coming of the French Revolution, he was converted by William Pitt, the Prime Minister, to Toryism. As a frequenter of the London debating clubs, Canning was noted for his elegant figure, expressive face and air of perfect breeding. But his enemies would never accept him as a gentleman. The murk of his childhood stuck, down to the unprepossessing name of his second stepfather, a silk mercer called Hunn; for the rest, the man was just too sharp. He revelled in vituperation, invective and satire. In ridiculing the Philosophic Radicals of the 1790s, he threw off many verses which, though now rendered innocuous in the anthologies, were then the cause of much pain and anger:

> But of all plagues, good Heaven, thy wrath can send,
> Save, save, oh! save me from the *Candid Friend!*
> (New Morality)

Yet these 'candid friends' were the very Whigs whose principles Canning had once so volubly defended. Now he was excoriating them, together with the philosophy of the French Revolution, in a fortnightly publication, the *Anti-Jacobin*. Canning had done what Winston Churchill was to do: changed sides, not gravely like Mr Gladstone, but impudently, with wicked laughter. Young George, like young Winston, could be represented by critics as something of a bounder.

Canning entered Parliament for a Tory pocket borough in January 1794 and for two years supported Pitt and the war against France from the back benches. This entailed supporting the Aliens Act and the suspension of Habeas Corpus. It was observed that the youthful orator put on an 'air of surprise' when defending the indefensible. He was rewarded in 1796 with a government post: Under-Secretary at the Foreign Office. So successful was he that a leading Whig, the future Earl Grey, took to quitting the Chamber ostentatiously when Canning was up.

By 1800 Canning had also established his material and emotional life. He married Joan Scott, an heiress. The marriage was idyllic; indeed, but for this unruffled zone of happiness, he might not have lived as long as he did.

The delicate role he had to play as liaison officer between Pitt and Grenville (Foreign Secretary) aroused some suspicion. His refusal after Pitt retired to serve under Grenville and Charles James Fox in the coalition ministry of 'All the Talents' (1806) changed suspicion into pronounced distrust. His game seemed to be too clever by half. In justifying Pitt's war policy, Canning inevitably slashed at Fox's attempts to make peace. His vehemence may have helped to drive Fox to his death, much as Grey's hostility was to hound Canning to death some twenty years later. Poetic justice destined Canning to die in the same house as Fox. When George III brought down the 'Talents' ministry by his refusal to consider the Catholics' claim to equality of civic status, Canning celebrated the ministers' demise with his usual joky rhymes:

> Though they sleep with the devil, yet theirs is the hope,
> On the downfall of Britain to rise with the Pope.

The real joke was that Canning himself was eventually to 'rise with the Pope', for he was later to lead those Tories who advocated Catholic emancipation.

The aged Duke of Portland now formed a purely Tory government (1807) with Catholic emancipation forgotten and only the war against Napoleon pursued. It assembled many of the great Tory names of the next twenty years: Canning as Foreign Secretary, Castlereagh at the War Office, Liverpool at the Home Office, Wellington as Irish Secretary. Just before taking office again, Canning had been described by a diplomat as 'very clever and very essential to government; but . . . *hardly yet a statesman*' because of 'his dangerous habit of *quizzing*'. Canning's reputation for quizzing (destructive criticism), in addition to Portland's somnolent senility and the exigencies of the war, soon dragged the ministry into fierce trouble. Castlereagh's handling of his department, culminating in the disastrous Walcheren expedition, had convinced Canning that the War Minister ought to be moved to a different post. Instead of acting at once, Portland let the plan leak out and haughty Castlereagh, hearing of it, regarded it as a typically low intrigue prompted by Canning's plebeian ambition. Tempers flared, and in one of his rare waking moments Portland joined Canning and Castlereagh in resigning. The latter two fought a duel in which War slightly wounded Foreign Affairs; Portland expired. Yet still the blight seemed to hang over politics and the war. Portland was succeeded as Prime Minister by unexciting Mr Spencer Perceval, who ended his tenure after two and a half years with a burst of uncharacteristic melodrama: he was assassinated in the House of Commons.

There followed a prolonged spasm of manoeuvring by the Prince Regent (later George IV) and elbowing by the politicians, in which Canning's staunch ally, the Marquis Wellesley, tried and failed to form a government. Possibly because he thought the Government which Lord Liverpool then constructed would not last, Canning declined to serve the new Prime Minister as Foreign Secretary, a refusal he soon came to regret. This fresh eclipse was the worst, and from 1814 to 1816 he was an expatriate. When he returned to the Cabinet it was only to the Board of Control, the Government's liaison office for Indian affairs. Even from this peripheral position he once more had to resign in 1820. King George IV had forced the Cabinet to bring Queen Caroline to trial, and she had been friendly with Canning and his wife. The new hiatus, it was proposed, should be filled by appointing him Governor-General of India. Suddenly this came to nothing by the most unexpected turn of the political wheel. Lord Castlereagh, Foreign Secretary since 1812, committed suicide in August 1822. And despite Canning's past mistakes and consequent effacement, it seemed to those in the inner circles of power that he must be his former enemy's successor.

His record so far was marked by many signs of potential and not a few of actual distinction. In 1807 his bold initiative had pre-empted Napoleon's secret plot to seize the Danish fleet – a drama not altogether unlike the Norwegian campaign of 1940, but with very much more skill and luck on the British side. Moreover Canning understood economic and currency questions far better than any ministers before Peel and Huskisson, and was able to make riveting speeches even about bullion. The work he put into his speeches and dispatches was immense. 'Nothing can be done without a great deal of pains,' he once said. 'I prepare very much on many subjects; a great part of this is lost and never comes into play, but sometimes an opportunity arises when I can bring in something I have ready, and I always perceive the much greater effect of those passages upon the House.' His constituency from 1812 to 1822 was the great and growing city of Liverpool. It taught him to appreciate the commercial middle classes. In their interest he spouted eloquently and frequently at democratic meetings, a quirk not shared or approved by most of his colleagues. His reconciliation with Castlereagh after their duel showed that he had charm and no vindictiveness. His loyalty to strange characters like the Marquis Wellesley and Queen Caroline went deep, as did his faithfulness to the principles of his political preceptor, the younger Pitt: only after George III's mind and health went completely in 1811–12 did Canning feel himself absolved from Pitt's promise not to raise Catholic emancipation during the old King's lifetime. His sympathy for the country's industrial classes brought him into alliance with a like-minded statesman and economist, Henry Huskisson. Together they recommended greater freedom in trade and a modification of the Corn Laws for the sake of cheaper bread. Along with these signs of liberalism went contempt for what Canning called the 'proud combinations' of aristocrats. He abused Britain's most powerful vested interest as 'our agricultural grandees'.

He was none the less a Tory. When the 'discontented and restless spirit of the age' (to quote his words) expressed itself in the march of the Blanketeers, followed by the 'Peterloo massacre' and finally by the Cato Street conspiracy, Canning was in full agreement with the repressive severities of his fellow Tory ministers. Though he had indeed supported Catholic emancipation since 1812, he was never willing to liberate Protestant dissenters by repealing the Test Acts. As for a parliamentary Reform Bill, he regarded this like any regular die-hard as a recipe for revolution.

So now the complex problems arising in 1822 after Castlereagh's suicide had to be solved. Was it to be the viceroyalty of India for Canning, or the European influence of the foreign secretaryship boosted by leadership of the House of Commons into the foremost power in the State? On the King's side, was not HM in honour bound to turn down the man who had been his detested wife's friend? 'You hear, Arthur,' he huffed and puffed to his closest adviser, 'on my honour as a gentleman?' But Arthur Duke of Wellington would have none of the royal posturing. Firmly he insisted that Canning must be Foreign Secretary. When Canning kissed hands in September 1822 his final struggle with King and countrymen had begun. He likened his appointment by the reluctant sovereign to receiving an entry card to Almack's most gentlemanly club and finding written on the back, 'Admit the rogue'.

There were political as well as personal reasons why George IV should not welcome his new Foreign Secretary. Canning had no use for Europe's congresses. Starting with the Congress of Vienna in 1814 and reaching the last in the series at Verona in 1822, to which he must unwillingly send a British delegate, Canning had no use for the methods which monarchical Europe had chosen to organise peace since the late war. What came to be known as the 'Congress system' was initially intended to supply 'the sovereign remedy' for all the ills thrown up by revolution and Napoleonic empire. From it arose a number of alliances, among which the Quadruple Alliance between Britain, Austria, Russia and Prussia was the most effective. England was not a member of the Holy Alliance, rightly described as a piece of 'sublime nonsense' by Lord Castlereagh. The Quadruple Alliance of 1815, by way of contrast, had his and Wellington's full support, including as it did in its aims the saving of Europe from revolution. Canning also wanted to be saved from revolution, but not to be saved by Congress. In his eyes Britain, having saved Europe by her exertions and example (to telescope Pitt's famous words), stood in mortal danger of losing her proud independence from the Continent, now represented by absolutist emperors and kings. An outpost of liberty, she was forced to watch the autocratic dynasts suppress the constitutional urges of their peoples, wherever a Habsburg or Bourbon, a Romanov or Hohenzollern bore sceptre and crown.

As disciples of Pitt, Castlereagh and Canning were agreed on restoring the European balance of power. This, in economic terms, was always the least costly foreign policy as long as Britain's maritime rights remained intact. But whereas Castlereagh hoped to safeguard that balance through alliances, Canning was resolved to disengage his country from all European entanglements, and then re-enter the arena to mastermind a balance on his own terms.

He therefore had no intention whatever of attending the Congress of Verona in person, as Castlereagh had planned to do, albeit with misgivings. He sent Wellington instead. His final instructions to the great European commander were such as only a soldier trained in implicit obedience to the civil power above him could carry out. Wellington had to inform Congress that British policy in Europe was – non-intervention. This, to a Congress waiting hopefully to sanction, with British backing, a French invasion of anti-Bourbon, extremist Spain, was a bombshell. The invasion did indeed take place in 1823 and was swiftly successful; but with Britain opposed to it, it could no longer be promoted as a European crusade to rescue the King of Spain from his subjects. Canning, speaking ironically enough through the mouth of Wellington, had torn the old system to shreds. 'So things are getting back to a wholesome state again,' he wrote, well pleased. 'Every nation for itself and God for us all.' God and Canning had cast England in the role of 'spectatress'. Exit the Concert of Europe: 'For *Europe* I shall be desirous *now and then* to read *England*'; 'For "Alliance" read "England"', and you have the clue to my policy.' Canning's was not to be a Little England, however, but an England-on-top.

His nationalism belonged to a brand of patriotic thinking always acceptable to the offshore islanders, and it was at once hugely popular. Significantly, Castlereagh had believed 'unpopularity to be the more gentlemanly fate for a politician'. If Canning was a populist, Castlereagh was an 'unpopulist'.

Meanwhile the pro-Europeans, ranging from Wellington and the foreign ambassadors at the Court of St James to Metternich on the Continent, battled against Canning for possession of the King's soul. What was known as the 'Cottage Coterie' was formed among the diplomats who visited George IV in his luxurious *cottage orné* at Windsor. Their object was to jockey the King into making Lord Liverpool dismiss Canning. Wellington for one did not rate their chances of success high. As a prematurely aged man who was said to need a whiff of ether before making a speech, Liverpool was bound to depend more and more on the glamour and vigour which Canning's oratory had brought to his wilting Government in place of Castlereagh's 'gentlemanly' coldness. Once or twice the Duke was heard to say that Liverpool was behaving towards Canning like a 'spaniel' or a 'common prostitute'.

In minor ways, moreover, Canning had made progress with the King himself. That bored old voluptuary was kept awake and amused by Canning's tangy wit. He also appreciated Canning's tactful use of Foreign Office patronage on behalf of the royal circle. Lord Francis Conyngham, son of Lady Conyngham the royal favourite, was given a post there; in return, Lord Francis kept Canning informed of the Cottage Coterie's machinations. Later on, one of Lady Conyngham's ex-lovers, Lord Ponsonby, was posted to South America, a removal for which the suspicious King was duly grateful.

South America, in Canning's political vision, was no mere oubliette for the King's supposed rivals. It was the positive reverse of his European negative. Spain's South American colonies had broken away from the mother country. In doing so they offered rich markets to any country in either hemisphere which would recognise their independence. Castlereagh had desired a slow approach towards *collective* recognition by the European alliance. Not so Canning. His aim was immediate and unilateral recognition by England, so that England's commercial classes could snatch the lion's share of trade. His dynamic policy was more than welcome to the country, where he put it across in public meetings fully reported by the press. This 'speechifying', as his detractors called it, temporarily lowered his stock once more with the King, who asked Liverpool to call the Foreign Minister to heel. (Half a century later Queen Victoria was to make similarly fruitless efforts to curb Gladstone's whistle-stop oratory.) At the same time the diplomats' Cottage Coterie, the ultra-Tories in Parliament, the Duke of York's cronies and other reactionary groups were trying out new ways of poisoning the King's mind against Canning's South American policy. If successful, they hoped to resuscitate the moribund Congress system at the eleventh hour.

The battle over South America, however, could ultimately be won or lost only in the Cabinet. Here, Canning had a secret weapon: he threatened to expose in Parliament the attempts of foreign diplomats to interfere. And stage by stage, with verbal blows given and taken in an orgy of mutual colleague-bashing, Canning pushed his policy through. By July 1824 the sending of commercial attachés to the South American republics was agreed upon. By December there was a Cabinet majority for full diplomatic recognition. Canning was exhausted and exalted. 'I am really quite knocked up by it', he wrote. 'The fight has been hard, but it is won. The deed is done. The nail is driven. Spanish America is free; and if we do not mismanage our affairs, she is English.' Two years later, when the forcibly restored King of Spain was threatening constitutional Portugal, England's ancient ally, Canning brought off a triumphant parliamentary double. In words that link him with Palmerston, he thrillingly announced military aid for the potential victim: 'At this very hour . . . British troops are on their way to Portugal!' The House burst into a roar of astonishment and applause. As for Spain, continued Canning in response to a heckler, even if she did commit aggression (in fact she withdrew) Spain was no longer the awesome imperial power which had loomed so large in our island story. If the invasion of 1823 had won back Spain for despotism, at least it was not 'Spain with the Indies'. To a House electrified by his eloquence Canning declared: 'I called the New World into existence to redeem the balance of the old.'

During this same glorious year, 1826, Canning made his leap back into Europe. He sent Wellington to Russia with an offer of British mediation between the Tsar and the Sultan of Turkey, on behalf of the Turks' oppressed Greek subjects. (Up to now, Canning had merely recognised Greek belligerency, while aiming to 'stay the plague both ways'.) A protocol was signed in St Petersburg which set on foot the liberation of Greece.

But what if there still remained certain benighted Europeans who ignored the lead Britain was giving in freer trade as well as free institutions? When the Dutch minister, M. Falck, persistently rejected a reciprocal lowering of shipping duties, the irrepressible Canning

cyphered a dispatch to his Ambassador at the Hague, ordering reprisals – in verse:

> In matters of commerce the fault of the Dutch
> Is giving too little and asking too much;
> With equal advantage the French are content,
> So we'll clap on Dutch bottoms a twenty per cent.

> *Chorus of Douaniers:* Twenty per cent,
> Twenty per cent,
> Nous frapperons Falck with twenty per cent.

Canning's last year, 1827, opened with a royal death which, on
paper, removed yet another obstacle from his victorious path. The Duke
of York had recently proved himself the most effective and bigoted
opponent of Catholic emancipation. He died in January. His state
funeral took place at Windsor in dark and deadly cold. Canning was
among the many who caught severe chills. While still convalescing at
Brighton in February, he heard that the Prime Minister had suffered a
totally incapacitating stroke. There seemed only one possible successor
to Lord Liverpool. But this time Wellington did not tell the King that it
must be Canning. On the contrary, Canning's commitment to Catholic
emancipation ruled him out in the view of Wellington and Peel, as
well as of all the 'right wing'. It was the 'right wing' nevertheless that
finally, though unwittingly, fixed the King's choice upon Canning. A
group of ultra-Tory peers made their way into the King's presence and
urged him to choose Wellington. As soon as Canning heard of this
little expedition he astutely appealed to the King's pride: 'Sir, your
father broke the domination of the Whigs; I hope your Majesty will
not endure that of the Tories.' The King replied promptly, 'No, I'll
be damned if I do.' On 10 April he commissioned Canning to form a
plan for reconstructing the Government, and on the 12th Canning
received loud cheers as Prime Minister.

At once a new crisis broke. The King might be damned if he'd submit
to ultra-Tory pressure; the ultra-Tories, who for this purpose included
Wellington, Peel and half the previous Government, were damned if
they'd serve under Canning. All the old mistrust of the abrasive *parvenu*,
heightened by the recent split over foreign policy and topped up with
the conviction that Canning would sooner or later introduce Catholic

emancipation – these things combined to produce massive resignations. Still racked by rheumatic pains, Canning turned perforce to the highways and hedges and filled up the gaps in his Government with Whigs. Even here the spectre of past animosities arose to damage him. Lord Grey, the ill-tempered leader of the Whig Opposition who long ago had walked out of the House rather than listen to Canning's barbs, now attacked the Prime Minister with every species of virulence, personal and political. Deeply wounded, the victim considered taking a peerage in order to refute Grey face to face.

Furthermore, what Canning called his two 'buggaboos', Catholic emancipation and Corn, were holding up progress on the domestic front. Emancipation had already been defeated in the Commons by four votes on 7 March, and was consequently 'out' for that session. Through a misunderstanding between Wellington and Huskisson exploited by Grey, the Government's attempt in May to liberalise the Corn Laws was thwarted. Only one major undertaking was Canning able to fulfil. In July he drove through a treaty between Britain, France and Russia by which the Sultan of Turkey, unless he accepted an armistice with the hard-pressed Greeks, would be forcibly prevented from destroying them. Three months later, though Canning was not there to hear it, news reached England that the Turkish fleet was at the bottom of Navarino Bay and Greece saved.

Parliament had been prorogued on 2 July. That same month the King, who had come greatly to enjoy the prestige with which Canning's foreign policy invested His Britannic Majesty, wrote sincerely hoping that the Prime Minister was 'rapidly recovering from the odious lumbago'. Far from it, alas; at the beginning of August Canning was lent the Duke of Devonshire's villa in Chiswick where Fox had died. Huskisson visited him and was shocked to see his yellowing complexion. Though Canning assured his friend that it was only a reflection from the bedroom curtains, he died soon after 4 a.m. on 8 August 1827.

From 12 April to 8 August was exactly one hundred days. When measured by the magnitude of Canning's power and glory throughout Britain and Europe, they were days of consummate greatness. But they were only days. If he had lived for a normal span of years, could he have converted the King and the Tory party to Catholic emancipation, and himself to Reform? We shall never know. Nor is it possible to judge how far his hitherto somewhat narrow patriotism, with its passing jingoist undertones, could have developed into a broader states-manship. He had always derided any politician who was internationally-minded:

> A steady patriot of the world alone,
> The friend of every country but his own

– which was a long way from Dr Johnson's 'Patriotism is the last refuge of the scoundrel'. Canning certainly did much for his own country; much also for Greece and Portugal. If he tangled needlessly with the United States over 'calling the New World into existence', this was partly due to his distrust of their republican influence. Perhaps his place among British prime ministers is best symbolised by an incident after his death. He was buried in Westminster Abbey at the feet of his master Pitt; Canning's disciple Gladstone came as a boy to pray and meditate beside the grave.

There was a febrile streak of irritability in the man Canning which ultimately consumed him. It separated him from the giants. Beyond this temperamental defect lay a further weakness. Style, corrosive wit and vivid imagery are no substitutes for the passion that profoundly moves. Canning could play the kettle-drum but not the deep music of humanity. He supported popular movements but not the 'sovereign people'. He used the media of press and publicity but saw nothing whatever wrong beneath the surface of English life. Yet if Peel, Palmerston, Gladstone and Disraeli all looked up to him for inspiration, as they did, he surely belonged to the great liberal–conservative tradition.

BIBLIOGRAPHY

Arbuthnot, *The Journal of Mrs Arbuthnot*, ed. Francis Bamford and the Duke of Wellington (2 vols, London, 1950)

Aspinall, A., *The Formation of Canning's Ministry*, Camden 3rd Series (London, 1937)

—, *The Letters of George IV* (3 vols, Cambridge University Press, 1938)

Bagot, J. F., *George Canning and his Friends* (2 vols, London, 1909)

Briggs, Asa, *The Age of Improvement* (London, 1965)

Gash, Norman, *Mr Secretary Peel: The Life of Sir Robert Peel to 1830* (London, 1961)

Hinde, Wendy, *George Canning* (London, 1973)

Longford, Elizabeth, *Wellington: The Years of the Sword* (London, 1969)

—, *Wellington: Pillar of State* (London, 1972)

Marshall, Dorothy, *The Rise of George Canning* (London, 1938)

Petrie, Sir Charles, *George Canning* (London, 1930)
Rolo, P. J. V., *George Canning* (London, 1965)
Stapleton, A. G., *George Canning 1822–7* (3 vols, London, 1831)
Temperley, H. V., *Life of Canning* (London, 1905)

New Cambridge Modern History, ix, 1793–1830 (Cambridge, 1965)

VISCOUNT GODERICH

JOHN DERRY

Frederick John Robinson, born 30 October 1782. Educated at Harrow and St John's College, Cambridge. Married 1814 Lady Sarah Hobart, daughter of the 4th Earl of Buckinghamshire; one surviving son, George Frederick Samuel, later 1st Marquess of Ripon; one son and one daughter died in childhood. MP for Carlow 1806 and for Ripon 1807; Vice-President of the Board of Trade 1812; President of the Board of Trade 1818; Chancellor of the Exchequer 1827; Colonial Secretary and Leader of the House of Lords 1827; Prime Minister and First Lord of the Treasury 1827–8; Colonial Secretary 1830–4; President of the Board of Trade 1841; President of the Board of Control 1843–6. Created 1st Viscount Goderich 1827 and 1st Earl of Ripon 1833. Died 28 Jan. 1859.

Frederick Robinson, 1st Viscount Goderich, Earl of Ripon, by Sir Thomas Lawrence

VISCOUNT GODERICH

The brief premiership of Frederick John Robinson, Lord Goderich, which lasted for a mere five months, has become notorious as a futile episode in the confusion that followed the retirement of Liverpool and the death of Canning. For most of his administration Goderich was preoccupied with trying to keep it together, and his failure is often cited as evidence of his own ineptitude. While Goderich fell below the standards of management set by Liverpool it is erroneous to suppose that only his limitations prevented the formation of a stable ministry. The behaviour of the King, dissensions within the Tory party, disagreements over Catholic emancipation and foreign policy, and the unreliability of several members of the administration, all contributed to Goderich's discomfiture. Goderich contributed little to the development of the premiership, but his abortive ministry throws light on the state of party politics in the late 1820s and reveals the ambivalent nature of the premiership at that period.

Goderich owed his appointment to the favourable reputation he had built up throughout his political career. He was respected as a man of considerable administrative experience, whose integrity, common sense and fair-mindedness were never in question. He was a good, if not a brilliant, debater, and he was a popular parliamentarian. He was acceptable to most of the factions within the Tory party, while being identified with none. For this reason it was hoped that he would be able to emulate Liverpool in holding disparate elements together. High Tories remembered Goderich's links with Castlereagh; Canningites recalled his sympathies with those commercial policies which were coming to be described as liberal. At the Board of Trade Goderich had played a significant part in the move towards freer trade, though he was never a doctrinaire free trader. His contribution to the nation's growing prosperity had earned him the nickname 'Prosperity Robinson', but the recession of 1825 tarnished his reputation, somewhat unfairly, and what had originally been meant as a tribute came to be regarded simply as proof of his good-natured optimism. His cautious advocacy of Catholic emancipation was cited as further evidence of his ability to see both sides of most political questions. He was never afraid to change his opinions, and although his reasons for doing so were not always clear to his contemporaries he usually succeeded in convincing them of his sincerity without giving offence. It was, therefore, wholly reasonable that there should be widespread agreement that he was as well qualified as anyone to hold together a party which had been shocked by Liverpool's stroke and Canning's death, and which was divided over the Catholic question and uncertain about British policy in the Near East. Goderich's acceptability to the Tory party is a reminder of the mediating role of the premier, who was expected to reconcile conflicts within a government rather than impose policies of his own upon a ministry. Prime ministers habitually conceded a wide discretionary freedom to their colleagues, and ministers regarded themselves as colleagues of the prime minister rather than subordinates. Though Goderich failed to fulfil the expectations which his previous record inspired this does not alter the character of the role he was expected to play. There were some reservations about his capacity to head an administration, and these were notably expressed, with characteristic firmness, by Wellington, but nevertheless no one in the Government expected him to be a dominant prime minister.

Goderich's appointment was also an indication of the continued importance of the King in politics. When George IV chose Goderich to succeed Canning everyone respected the King's right to choose his first minister. Though George IV was in a weaker constitutional position than his father had been forty years earlier he was expected to take the initiative in forming a new government. The King was also able to lay down conditions which he considered binding upon his new minister. No members of Lord Grey's group of Whigs were to be admitted to the ministry, and although George failed to impose stricter limitations on the question of Catholic relief than those that had operated under Canning, he was able to ensure that the issue would remain an open question in the new government just as it had done in the old, and this favoured the anti-Catholic party. The King made suggestions to Goderich affecting several of the most important appointments. Goderich's freedom in choosing his colleagues was therefore severely limited, and in his attempts to broaden the base of his administration he was constrained by the King's prejudices. The appointment of Herries as Chancellor of the Exchequer posed special problems, and it was only with difficulty that Lansdowne, who distrusted Herries as an anti-

Catholic Tory, was prevailed upon to serve as Home Secretary. Goderich was dependent on the King's confidence, and when this was withdrawn his ministry collapsed. Yet the price of the King's support was the exclusion of several moderate Whigs who would have been preferred by Goderich if he had been in a position to press for their appointment. Lord Holland, a Whig favourable to Catholic relief, was kept out of the Government, and from the beginning the Catholic question ominously heightened suspicions which various members of the administration entertained towards each other. The King and the High Tories were determined to prevent any accession of strength to the emancipationists in the Cabinet. There was general respect for Goderich, but little enthusiasm, and he could not rely on the committed personal loyalty of his colleagues.

It was soon evident that without a strong personality at its head the ministry was vulnerable to all the rivalries and confusions within the Tory party. Goderich presided over a ministry which lacked party discipline, essential agreement on fundamental issues, and a sufficient measure of internal harmony to enable it to withstand unforeseen embarrassments. Co-operation was possible only by agreeing to differ, but should any issue provoke major disagreement or any resignation disturb the balance of the ministry it would be difficult for the premier to maintain his position or for the Government to continue. Anti-Catholic Tories regarded Goderich's open-mindedness as a liability. He was thought to be too sensitive to changing circumstances, too willing to accede to reformist policies, too unsound in his commitment to Toryism of the more traditional type, and too generous in his attitude to moderate Whigs. Goderich was a victim of circumstances outside his control. If the King wavered he would be in an impossible position, since he would then be unable to withstand internal criticism. Goderich's ministry was virtually a prolongation of the Canning administration, but the fundamental tensions within the Tory party remained unsolved, and those qualities which had made Goderich acceptable as a prime minister eventually made it impossible for him to reconstruct his ministry on a sounder basis.

He soon found that his ministry was under strain because of dissensions over foreign and domestic policy. When Herries threatened to resign as Chancellor of the Exchequer the King's confidence in Goderich collapsed. But initially improving trade suggested that Goderich might be able to carry out further fiscal and commercial reforms, while a conciliatory policy in Ireland was contemplated. Unhappily the critical situation in the Near East, reaching as it did a climax at the Battle of Navarino in October 1827, heightened the stresses within the ministry. Huskisson was sympathetic to Russia but uneasy about Codrington's destruction of the Turkish fleet. Herries was opposed to any action that might damage Turkey still further. Goderich was proud of Codrington's victory but uncertain about the direction of British policy over Greece. Mistrust between ministers over foreign affairs spilled over into other matters. Herries and Huskisson became involved in a dispute about the appointment of Althorp as chairman of a financial committee. Goderich failed to restore discipline and his reputation with both sides slumped. Goderich sought desperately to strengthen his ministry, but the Huskissonites and Canningites feared any extension of High Tory influence while the more conservative Tories remained bitterly suspicious of the more liberal wing of the Government. When Goderich suggested bringing in both Lord Wellesley and Lord Holland the King rejected the proposal.

By the middle of December 1827 Goderich was exhausted and depressed. In addition to his public worries he was tormented by anxieties about his wife's health. When Goderich wrote to the King, seeking to explain his own feelings of inadequacy, George IV's confidence in his minister was sapped still further. Later the King chose to regard this letter as an offer to resign. Nevertheless Goderich still sought a way out of the impasse. With the support of Huskisson he pressed for Holland's inclusion in the ministry, putting forward Wellington's name in addition to that of Wellesley in the hope that this would make Holland's admission less objectionable to the King. The King consulted Huskisson about the possibility of his taking over as prime minister, but when Huskisson refused it seemed that Goderich might, after all, be able to continue. Though the Prime Minister's morale fluctuated he began to think of preparing for the meeting of Parliament that was due early in the new year, but the King was intransigent in his opposition to Lord Holland's appointment.

Rumours about the disagreements within the ministry were rife, and Huskisson's nerve collapsed. No sooner had he asked leave to resign than the unfortunate Prime Minister was faced with a deliberate challenge to his authority. On 21 December Herries revived the dispute about Althorp's chairmanship of the financial committee and threatened to resign if Althorp were appointed. Huskisson reiterated that he would resign if Althorp were not appointed. Other members of the Government became uneasy and there was talk of other resignations. Goderich was blamed for the breakdown of the Government's will to survive. But when he made another attempt to reconcile the discordant factions within his Cabinet he found Herries obstinate and unyielding. Goderich visited the King on 8 January 1828, intending to inform him of the deadlock within the Government, but he found that George IV already regarded the ministry as dissolved, referring to Goderich's earlier letter as tantamount to resignation. There was nothing for Goderich to do but accept the inevitable.

Though Goderich lacked the strength of personality to pull through the governmental crisis he had been unfortunate in facing a foe as malevolent as his Chancellor of the Exchequer. He was unlucky in that so many of his colleagues were deficient both in loyalty and firmness of purpose. Even Huskisson had been less than consistently reliable. Called to the premiership by the King Goderich had also been deprived of assured royal support. Prepared to broaden his ministry by admitting Whigs he had not only found the King hostile to Holland's admission, he had found Grey hostile and aloof. Goderich had inherited a difficult situation; it soon became an impossible one. The Catholic issue exercised a baleful influence upon the conduct of both pro-Catholic and anti-Catholic Tories.

Goderich's experience demonstrated that the premiership did not, of itself, confer pre-eminent leadership or control in the circumstances of the 1820s. The difficulties encountered by Wellington echoed many of the problems that had forced Goderich out of office. Only a stronger sense of collective responsibility within the Cabinet and a growing appreciation of party loyalty in the Commons eventually made it easier for premiers to avoid Goderich's humiliating experience. Yet, though Goderich did not create the divisions that had brought about his downfall, he was reluctant to place party priorities above more traditional ideas of public service. Goderich later served under both Grey and Peel, his career illustrating how loosely he regarded party ties and how deferentially he placed the service of the Crown first in his concept of political duty. The frustrations of his premiership were themselves evidence of the way in which his outlook was becoming inadequate. Sadly, Goderich's premiership showed that integrity, open-mindedness and loyalty to the service of the Crown were incapable of resolving the tensions that were destroying the Tory party, and that finally brought Grey into office in 1830.

BIBLIOGRAPHY

The definitive modern work on Goderich's political career is Wilbur Devereux Jones's *Prosperity Robinson: The Life of Viscount Goderich 1782–1859* (London, 1967), which is based on thorough primary research. But for those interested in the background to the formation of Goderich's ministry G. I. T. Machin, *The Catholic Question in English Politics 1820–30* (Oxford, 1964) is essential reading.

THE
DUKE OF WELLINGTON

BY

JOHN CLARKE

Arthur Wellesley, born c. 29 April 1769, fourth son of the 1st Earl of Mornington and Anne Hill, daughter of the 1st Viscount Dungannon. Educated at Eton and at Angers. Married 1807 Catherine Pakenham, daughter of 2nd Earl of Longford. MP for Trim 1790. Aide-de-camp to the Lord Lieutenant of Ireland 1790; major and then lieutenant-colonel of the 33rd Foot, 1793; Flanders campaign 1794; major-general 1799; KB after the Battle of Assaye 1804. MP for Rye 1806. Chief Secretary for Ireland 1807. Copenhagen expedition 1807. Spanish Peninsula 1808. Created Viscount Wellington 1809. Entered Madrid 1812. Field-Marshal and KG 1813. Victorious in Peninsular War 1814. Created Duke and Ambassador to Paris 1814. Waterloo 1815. Joined Liverpool's administration as Master General of Ordnance 1817. Congress of Vienna 1820; Congress of Verona 1822. Resigned from government 1827. Resumed command of the Army 1827. Prime Minister 1828–30, Lord Warden of the Cinque Ports 1829. Failed to form a government 1832. Took over government 1834 pending Peel's return; Foreign Secretary 1834; Leader of the House of Lords 1841; reappointed to the command of the Army 1842. Died 14 September 1852.

Arthur Wellesley, 1st Duke of Wellington, by J. Jackson

THE DUKE OF WELLINGTON

WELLINGTON THE SOLDIER

Arthur Wellesley, first Duke of Wellington, was born in Dublin on 29 April 1769. As fourth son of the Earl of Mornington, Wellesley became a part of the 'Protestant Ascendency' or small minority which had monopolised all power and influence in Ireland since the end of the seventeenth century. After a short, unhappy and impoverished stay at Eton, it was decided that 'ugly boy Arthur is fit food for powder'. Wellesley was sent to Pignerol's military academy at Angers; he was just in time to experience life in France before the Revolution. After joining the British Army in March 1787, Wellesley was made aide-de-camp to the Lord Lieutenant of Ireland and in 1790 he was elected to the Dublin Parliament as member for Trim, County Meath.

In 1794 Wellesley joined the Duke of York's ill-fated expedition to the Low Countries, but most of his military experience was acquired in India where his elder brother, Richard, was Governor-General. Wellesley was soon given the command of the Army of Mysore and later directed the campaign against the Mahrattas. He returned to England in 1804 to defend his brother's expansionist policy, but in 1807 he was appointed Chief Secretary of Ireland. Wellesley combined this job with an active military career. In July 1807 he was sent to Spain with a force of 8,000 men and given instructions to collaborate with those Spaniards who were opposed to the regime of Joseph Bonaparte. In the early years of the Peninsular War, Wellesley was hampered by inadequate numbers of troops, a great deal of ill-informed criticism in England and the incessant quarrels of his Spanish allies. Gradually things improved and Wellesley's objective of driving the French out of Spain was achieved by the victories of Salamanca and Vitoria.

After the abdication of Napoleon, Wellesley, already a marquis, was made Duke of Wellington; hosts of foreign honours were poured on him. In the short period before Napoleon's return he was British Ambassador in Paris and attended the closing stages of the Congress of Vienna. The Battle of Waterloo, Wellington's most famous victory, ended Napoleon's bid to regain power. Wellington was now given command of the Army of Occupation and for three years was the effective ruler of France. At the end of 1817 Wellington joined Lord Liverpool's Cabinet as Master-General of Ordnance; many thought him the most reactionary member of a very conservative government. He despised politicians who tried to obtain 'vulgar popularity', he thought that newspapers abused their relative freedom of comment, he frequently declared that the admission of Roman Catholics to Parliament would mean the end of British greatness and was a strong supporter of Sidmouth's Six Acts. The Duke represented the British Government at the Congress of Verona in September 1822, and in 1826 he was sent to St Petersburg in an attempt to avert war between Russia and Turkey. Wellington's sympathies were with the Holy Alliance powers and he frequently found himself at odds with the liberalising policies of Canning. Disagreements over Spain, South America and Greece brought Wellington close to resignation.

When Canning became Prime Minister in April 1827, Wellington did resign – because he believed that Canning was motivated by hatred of the landed aristocracy and was certain to upset Liverpool's careful balance between those who were in favour of Catholic emancipation and those who opposed it. Wellington also resigned as Commander-in-Chief, a move which was bitterly resented by George IV. After Canning's death, Wellington agreed to resume the command of the Army but made it clear that he did not support Lord Goderich's coalition Government of progressive Tories and Whigs. It was clear that the ineffective and often tearful Goderich could not last long. He resigned on 8 January 1828 and the King invited Wellington to form a government.

WELLINGTON THE PRIME MINISTER

The Duke of Wellington had some important advantages as premier. Above all he was the national hero who had beaten the French. In political terms this meant that he enjoyed the respect of the ordinary people he so much despised. The House of Lords deferred to his every word and was unlikely to make the sort of difficulties that often wrecked the governments of lesser men. The King, whose influence in politics was still enormous, treated him as an equal. Wellington was universally admitted to be a man of high principles and great energy. He was a hard worker and would not spare himself in his determination to master all the details of government. For a man who had little contact with commerce, he was surprisingly expert in financial matters.

These advantages were balanced by serious weaknesses. Now that Tories like Peel, who had once seemed even more conservative than Wellington, were beginning to pay lip service to the ideas of progress, the Duke appeared to be hopelessly out of touch with the mood of the age. Napoleon's doubts whether a man who had enjoyed so much power could ever be content to relinquish it were shared by many Englishmen. Some Whigs like Brougham claimed that soldiers were naturally contemptuous of constitutional government and inclined to tyranny. In fact, no one could have had a more exaggerated respect for the British Constitution than Wellington, but unscrupulous opponents realised that 'liberty in danger' was always a powerful slogan. Wellington's manner sometimes gave colour to these allegations; he seemed to behave with an aloofness more appropriate to a monarch than a subject. Even the King resented this aspect of Wellington. George IV was not a man whose friendship and support could be relied upon; joking references to 'King Arthur' contained a strong element of jealousy.

Wellington's real trouble was that he had come to politics late in life. He was still fundamentally ill at ease in political circles and his apparent aloofness was really more due to shyness than hauteur. It is absurd to say that Wellington was not a politician. No man can become prime minister without being a politician but no other British prime minister has owed his position more to what he did outside politics. Wellington was still a beginner; he had not even learnt the art of deception properly and so was to be caught out more often than his highly professional colleagues. Unlike most premiers, he had only limited experience of the House of Commons, he took no joy in the rough and tumble of debate and had no 'feel' for the mood of Parliament. He was a poor speaker; when nervous he was liable to keep up his own courage by making more and more extreme statements – without the usual qualifications and escape routes. In short, his whole outlook was very different from that of the men with whom he would have to work.

Wellington disliked coalition governments as 'unprincipled' and disapproved of members of the previous administration who had sacrificed traditional loyalties to their desire for office. Even if the Whigs had been prepared to go on, Wellington was right in thinking that a coalition would have been an unstable affair; Lansdowne and Holland were already under strong pressure from Lord Grey to go over to active opposition. But equally Wellington had no desire to form an extreme conservative, or 'Ultra' government. He wanted to restore the position of Lord Liverpool's time when the progressive and conservative wings of the Tory party had been equally balanced.

At the cost of disappointing some close friends, like Harriet and Charles Arbuthnot, who were expecting a more decidedly conservative Cabinet, Wellington succeeded in his objectives – although it was dangerous to upset the King by refusing to recall the Ultra, Lord Eldon, to the Woolsack. Despite the *Manchester Guardian*'s complaints of 'an utter ignorance of the principles of philosophical legislation', it was a strong Cabinet. With Peel as Home Secretary, Huskisson at the Colonial Office and Palmerston Secretary at War, no one could pretend that the administration lacked talent. Whether it possessed unity was another matter. Wellington had complained about Canning's lack of principle but there was scarcely anything important that his own ministers could agree upon. The best thing that could be said was that there was a precarious agreement to disagree on a number of fundamental questions, notably Catholic emancipation and the redistribution of seats. Wellington could only lead a secure government so long as these issues were kept under the carpet. Both the Ultra and Canningite sections of the Cabinet were led by men who were much concerned with their own dignity and very sensitive to imagined insult. A word or even a gesture implying too much support for one side or the other could produce wholesale resignations. Army life was not the best training for such a delicate situation.

Although Wellington was naturally inclined to the Ultras, he was politician enough to appreciate that some progressive measures were essential. Apart from a sop to the Ultras in the King's speech regretting the Battle of Navarino – which effectively secured Greek independence – the record of the first few months was astonishingly liberal. When the House of Commons approved Lord John Russell's motion to repeal the Dissenters Disabilities Acts – against government opposition – Wellington changed his mind and announced that he would now support repeal. These Acts were the last pieces of serious discrimination against Protestant dissenters. Nonconformists in public office had to endure the humiliation of an annual Act of Indemnity to protect them from the penalties of holding an official position without being practising Anglicans. Few now imagined that the dissenters presented any threat to the Constitution, but once Nonconformists were admitted to full equality with Anglicans it would be much harder to defend the continued exclusion of Roman Catholics from Parliament. To Ultras like the King's forceful brother the Duke of Cumberland, this concession was an obvious thin end of the wedge tactic. It is possible that Wellington was already beginning to contemplate Catholic emancipation, but at least for the moment, he could argue that satisfaction of Nonconformist grievances would make influential dissenters less eager to support the Catholic cause. At the same time, the Prime Minister bowed to Canningite pressure in the Cabinet and agreed to a modification of the 1815 Corn Laws in an attempt to lower the price of bread in years of bad harvest. Despite his reputation for bigotry, Wellington had achieved two important reforms; a sensible observer would have said 'so far so good'.

A number of influential government supporters had voted against the repeal of Dissenters Disabilities; if Wellington's balancing act was to continue, it was quite sensible to follow the reforms with a period of caution. Wellington was not sympathetic to the demand that the seats of Penrhyn and East Retford, two notoriously corrupt boroughs, should be transferred to Birmingham and Manchester, which were still without parliamentary representation. With some logic, the Prime Minister argued that it would be wrong to penalise all the voters in a constituency because some had taken bribes, and that an enlargement of the number of voters by incorporating surrounding villages was the best way to defeat corruption. Huskisson spoke against this reasoning in Parliament and after an undignified squabble as to whether he had or had not asked to resign, the three leading Canningites, Huskisson, Charles Grant and Palmerston, left the Government. Experienced politicians would have realised that a little loss of face was necessary to preserve the balance of the administration. Wellington was either too vain or too unsophisticated to appreciate this. Endless wrangling in the Cabinet had weakened his fragile temper. Wellington took the easy way out, but by letting the Canningites go, he drastically curtailed his own freedom of action.

CATHOLIC EMANCIPATION

The usual picture of Wellington as military genius but peacetime Blimp is unfair. The Duke may have wanted to be a reactionary but he recognised that he could not be. Despite his general hostility to change, his approach to the problem of Catholic emancipation was empirical. Unlike George IV and Cumberland, he did not look at 'The Protestant

Constitution' through a reverential mist of pious observanticism. His ideal solution would have been one of gradual concession; complete equality had to be contemplated but with good management the evil, if inevitable, day might be postponed.

For some time Wellington had been toying with the idea of a Concordat with the Papacy which would admit Catholics to Parliament but give the British Government a veto over the choice of Irish Catholic bishops. If the bishops were safe men who could be relied upon to use their great influence to prevent the election of those who would destroy the Union and threaten property itself, then emancipation might not be a complete disaster. On 10 June 1828 Wellington appealed for tranquillity in Ireland and hinted that if this condition was fulfilled, then something might be done. Events were overtaking the Prime Minister.

Most of the places left by the departure of the Canningites were filled by 'non-political' soldiers. The one progressive appointment was the choice of Vesey Fitzgerald, an untypically good Irish landlord and a supporter of emancipation, to succeed Grant at the Board of Trade. Fitzgerald sat for County Clare and on accepting office would have to fight a by-election. As Wellington was generally believed to be absolutely opposed to the admission of Catholic MPs, his Government was extremely unpopular in Ireland. On 24 June the Catholic leader Daniel O'Connell decided to contest the Clare seat himself. Although a Roman Catholic could not sit in Parliament, there was nothing to prevent him from standing. If O'Connell was elected and then refused admission to Westminster, the always difficult Irish situation was certain to become explosive.

Even if O'Connell could be excluded, the long-term prospects were grim. The franchise in Ireland was surprisingly wide. Roman Catholics could vote and the 40 shilling freehold qualification meant that many voters were practically paupers. This group had little to lose. Even in the 1826 election the Catholic voters had rebelled against the nominees of the Beresford family – probably the most influential in Ireland. At the next general election it was likely that a large number of men like O'Connell would be elected and unable to take their seats because of their religion. There was a danger that this group would form an unofficial Parliament, destroy the Union and encourage popular revolution against the landlords. The best way of meeting this danger would be to take the vote away from those who had no real interest in the preservation of property. This is what Wellington decided to do. He saw that he might be able to trade Catholic emancipation in return for a reduction of the electorate. Like the Concordat scheme this would have the advantage of keeping out extremists. Wellington was not a cynic but a cynic might add that the scheme also had the advantage of opening up a difference of interest between the Catholic peasantry and the Catholic middle classes. As far as Wellington was concerned, although Catholic emancipation was unfortunate, the damage it would cause to the Constitution was minimal compared to that which would result from its continued refusal.

It was an act of statesmanship to decide on emancipation but it was a question of politics to persuade many important people that Wellington was not planning an abject surrender but merely a calculated strategic retreat. O'Connell had been elected but the obstacles facing Wellington were formidable. The Cabinet presented less of a problem than might have been expected. After much agonising, the leading anti-Catholic, Robert Peel, accepted Wellington's arguments. Cabinet ministers are by nature sympathetic to arguments of necessity and expediency. Others can afford to be more inflexible. For the moment Wellington was able to allay Ultra fears by dismissing the pro-Catholic Lord Anglesley from his post as Lord Lieutenant of Ireland.

The main obstacle to emancipation was expected to be the King; it seemed likely that the issue would expand into a trial of strength between royal influence and that of the Prime Minister. In most previous contests the King had won. Despite his general indifference to religion, George IV had frequently declared that if he accepted Catholic emancipation he would be breaking his Coronation Oath, and because of this appalling blasphemy would cease to be King in the sight of God. To Wellington's great surprise, George seemed to agree to his plans. The King was naturally lazy and wanted a quiet life; by the autumn of 1828 he was also a sick man who had to take heavy doses of laudanum to relieve the pain of prostate trouble. It is likely that when George seemed to agree to emancipation, he had not fully appreciated the significance of his actions. The problem for Wellington was whether the Duke of Cumberland would return to England from Berlin in order to open the King's eyes. Cumberland had great influence with his brother so it was vital to keep him out of the country. Wellington was guilty of obvious deception when he wrote to Cumberland that emancipation was not even contemplated when, in fact, plans were well advanced.

Emancipation, combined with proposals to increase the property qualification for Irish voters from 40 shillings to 10 pounds, was announced in the King's speech of 5 February 1829. The King's apparent acquiescence in alliance with the Duke's enormous influence meant that a surprisingly large number of bishops, peers and MPs persuaded themselves that a measure of emancipation from Wellington and Peel was less dangerous than one from genuine pro-Catholics. Drastic changes are more likely to gain acceptance when introduced by conservatives than by those notoriously committed to change. With royal support, Catholic emancipation would have been easy, but it was still not quite clear whether the King's influence would be behind Wellington or Cumberland.

Cumberland returned to England, explained to the King that Wellington had deceived him and obtained an opinion from Lord Eldon that it would be constitutionally proper for George to veto emancipation even if a Relief Bill was passed by both Houses of Parliament. Wellington could only respond with an ultimatum that he would resign unless he received royal support. On 4 March 1829 the King was forced to give way. Despite a rather unnecessary duel between Wellington and Lord Winchelsea the issue was no longer in doubt. For a very short time the Prime Minister became the hero of progressives.

Wellington had exploited his position with the King very cleverly. The Ultra party was essentially one of backwoodsmen. The only member of the Cabinet who supported them was the Attorney-General, Sir Charles Wetherell. They simply did not possess sufficient talent or experience to form a government; their leader, the Duke of Cumberland, would never have been acceptable as Prime Minister – not only because he was a Royal Duke but also because there had been some highly questionable episodes in his past.

Cumberland had probably been the greatest single danger, but his opinion was by no means untypical. There were a number of influential peers, led by Lord Winchelsea, who felt that emancipation must be resisted at all costs. Peers were influential in their own right and often controlled the votes of a number of MPs. When the Catholic Relief Bill eventually passed through the Commons, no fewer than 112 members voted against. Even this represented only a shadow of the anti-Catholic feeling in the country. Emancipation was not a popular cause; hosts of ordinary people believed that a single Catholic in Parliament would mean the end of British freedom. It was only fifty years since the Gordon Riots and if the matter had been decided by referendum, it is certain that there would have been an enormous majority against. Catholic emancipation was one of the many reforms carried through by a fairly enlightened elite against public opinion; with a wider franchise, the measure might have been delayed for some years.

Although emancipation was well received in Ireland, much of the political capital Wellington had made was forfeited by the unnecessary insult of refusing O'Connell admission to Parliament unless he stood for re-election. Obviously the measure prevented the realisation of Wellington's nightmare of a separate Parliament. It was certainly an enormous step forward for religious liberty but, whatever else it did, it did not solve the problem of Ireland. In many areas violence remained almost a way of life. An enormous number of practical grievances remained. Emancipation was really 'too little, too late'.

REFORM

It is a matter of some debate amongst historians whether Wellington's downfall in 1830 is best explained in terms of the Prime Minister's failure to reunite his party, or in terms of the profound social changes which were taking place in a country in the throes of industrialisation. Both were important but the first explanation seems to fit the facts better than the second.

Wellington had now succeeded in alienating both left and right wings of the Tory party. The Whigs were still the largest opposition group in Parliament, but they seemed unlikely to achieve much unless they could make a common cause with the Ultras and Canningites. The Prime Minister's task was to prevent the emergence of such a common cause but, as the two-party system had disintegrated in 1827, any grouping was now possible. The Whigs and Canningites had supported the Government over emancipation; the Prime Minister believed that neither group really wanted to replace him. Wellington strongly disliked Huskisson and hoped that the Canningites would remain quiet even if their leaders were not invited to rejoin the Cabinet. Any formal alliance with the Whigs was ruled out because the King had made it clear that he would never accept Lord Grey as a Cabinet minister. Wellington had been hurt by Ultra allegations of 'betrayal' in 1829 but his natural sympathies were still with this group. At the beginning of 1830 the Prime Minister thought that, by demonstrating his hostility to further change, he could bring the Ultras back to their party allegiance.

The Prime Minister had made two mistakes. He had underestimated the Canningites' desire for office; they were essentially career politicians who felt that their superior talents and experience gave them a natural right to ministerial rank. Unless Wellington was prepared to offer clear-cut terms, he was certain to find the Canningites voting with Grey who would be forced to give them important positions if he ever came to power. Similarly Wellington did not understand the Ultras; he sympathised with them but his thought processes were not the same as theirs. A group of about forty hard-line Ultras were now the Government's most violent adversaries in Parliament. Unlike the Canningites, few of them were professional politicians; they were not interested in being bought off with offices. Wellington's overtures were rejected; regardless of any other considerations, the Ultras wanted revenge for emancipation.

Some of the Ultras can be safely dismissed as 'blockheads' (Peel's contemptuous description) but there were intelligent men amongst them. In fact, there was more in common between the Ultras and groups to the left of the Government than might seem possible. The Ultras were essentially rural landowners but landowners who were very dissatisfied with the depressed state of agriculture. The gentry felt that Wellington had betrayed them, not only by emancipation, but also by his relaxation of the Corn Laws, his deflationary tax policy and his refusal to consider giving up the gold standard as a means of raising agricultural prices. In this sense, the gentry were almost a Radical group; even more important, their belief in inflation as a means of curing distress was shared by many manufacturers and provincial bankers – of whom Thomas Attwood of Birmingham is the best example. Thus the links between rural and urban discontent were surprisingly close.

Wellington was wrong in thinking that he could regain the Ultras by resolute hostility to a reform of Parliament. It was already clear that a wider electorate might have delayed emancipation; men like Sir Richard Vyvyan and Sir Edward Knatchbull seriously believed that Reform might retard rather than accelerate the dreaded 'march of progress'. Many country gentlemen came to the conclusion that their economic ills could not be cured without a drastic reduction in taxes, and that the best way to achieve this was to make MPs more directly responsible to the taxpayers. The demand for Reform had been fairly dormant since the early 1820s; it is important to appreciate that its rather unexpected revival in 1830 was essentially a by-product of a demand for economy. Advocacy of economy and denunciation of 'government waste' are splendid weapons in politics; more than any other issue they have the advantage of appealing to a wide range of opposition factions who can agree on little else. This is what Wellington was now up against.

Seen in this light, many of the traditional explanations of the demand for Reform look unconvincing. The campaign was already well under way before there was news of a revolution in France. Reform was certainly not a contest between town and country, middle class and landowners. In fact all sectors were divided on the issue. It is probably far better to see Reform as yet another round in the endless battle between 'Court and Country'. The sort of redistribution of seats and extension of the franchise contemplated by most people was much less drastic than the proposals introduced by the Whigs in 1831; a very moderate Reform Bill would have satisfied the country and probably destroyed the Whig party for ever. Perhaps Wellington showed that he was fundamentally Irish, not English, by his correct appreciation of the issues of emancipation and his failure to understand the forces at work over Reform. Why was he so wrong?

Towards the end of 1829 it seemed that the economic difficulties that produced discontent were disappearing. Government revenue is a good indication of the level of economic activity; arrears of taxes were being reduced and there was a general building boom. Unfortunately, these signs of recovery were destroyed by an appalling winter, the worst for nearly a century. With so large a proportion of people working out of doors and so much of industry dependent on canal transport, a prolonged period of ice and snow was bound to result in massive unemployment. In January 1830 it was certainly true that 'what was happening at Westminster or in the City was of small account compared to what was happening in the heavens'. Instead of decreasing, discontent was spreading. To make matters worse, it was clear that George IV could not live much longer, and opposition politicians were beginning to step up their attacks on the Government in readiness for the general election which would follow the accession of the new King. It was clear that ambitious men like Henry Brougham would be prepared to inflame opinion out of doors and inject an artificial element of class hatred which grass roots discontent had hitherto lacked.

In the eighteenth century, governments did not lose elections; administrations whose record was far worse than Wellington's could expect a handsome majority. By and large prime ministers only fell when they lost the King's confidence, and William IV quickly indicated that he was satisfied with the ministers he inherited from his brother who died in June 1830. Wellington may have been in favour of old-fashioned policies but his views on political morality were modern. He did not believe that prime ministers should use public money to ensure the election of government candidates and was opposed to the use of sinecure offices to buy the votes of MPs and peers.

Much government patronage had been reformed away in the 1820s; in 1828 Wellington himself complained that he could offer potential supporters nothing more tangible than 'smiles and a dinner'. The Duke did not appreciate, however, that a certain amount of corruption was necessary for political stability, and that the fragmentation of the Tory party was, in part, attributable to the decline in 'places'. Wellington was too idealistic; despite the urgent appeals of the Chief Whip, William Holmes, he did not even utilise the patronage that remained. The Duke fought the election following the death of George IV with one hand tied behind his back.

This election of July 1830 was a muddled affair; it is even an oversimplification to say that the Government was defeated. In the absence of party discipline many 'neutrals' were returned; William Holmes thought that most of the neutrals could be turned into government supporters and calculated that, with good management and sensible policies, the Duke would increase his majority by seventeen seats. It was still not too late – although the fact the new King had no personal animus against Grey meant that Wellington no longer enjoyed a virtual monopoly of the premiership. The election had increased the members who believed that economic distress could be cured by Reform; discontent which had been largely rural was now echoed by a revival of agitation in the towns. For the first time since 1820, Radical demagogues like Cobbett, Carpenter and Hunt, with their talk of Revolution commanded a sizable following.

The Government was in for a difficult time but it is nonsense to suggest that Wellington should have resigned before Parliament met. The Duke could certainly have 'hooked' the Canningites. Huskisson's tragic death at the opening of the Liverpool to Manchester Railway in September 1830 meant that the group was leaderless and seemed ready to return to the Tory fold. Wellington did approach Palmerston who said he would join the Government if another two Canningites were approached as well. Wellington's rejection of these reasonable terms was his fatal mistake – the last chance to restore a 'balanced' Tory party. Again his motives were too honourable; the appointment of three Canningites would mean the dismissal of three loyal supporters – Murray, Beresford and Calcraft. Orthodox politicians would not have been troubled by such scruples but it is not surprising that the Canningites lost patience and finally cast their lot in with the Whigs. There remained only the Ultras.

At the end of August 1830, rural discontent exploded into the Swing Riots. Landowners who attempted to fight falling profit margins by cutting back their wage bill and replacing men with threshing machines saw their machines destroyed by the rioters. Wellington and Peel received hundreds of panic letters from squires declaring that England was on the brink of anarchy and revolution. The Swing Riots do not receive much mention in most histories of Reform. It is true that the farm labourers' cause had little in common with that of the urban middle class, but Swing was crucial to what happened later. The Prime Minister took his cue from the countryside, not the towns. Wellington did not understand the new manufacturing areas; indeed, in 1830 there were not that many factory towns in existence. Wellington saw Swing as conclusive proof of the fragility of civilisation; the smallest concession to popular pressure would lead to anarchy. Conviction was strengthened by political considerations. Swing would have the beneficial effect of bringing the rural Ultras to their senses and make them realise the folly of their flirtation with Reform.

With these two reinforcing considerations in mind, Wellington faced Parliament on 2 November 1830. His speech was a sensation; he went so far in his denunciation of Reform that he declared that even if he were asked to design a Constitution from scratch, he would still incorporate in it all the apparent anomalies of the existing British system of representation. The message was clear: Reform was the same as Revolution. At the end of his speech even Wellington realised that he had probably gone too far. The last bid to gain Ultra support failed. Wellington was wrong; conviction and interest were not the same. The Whigs, now sure of the Canningites, were bidding hard for the vital Ultra vote. Lord Grey announced that the first priority on taking office would be the relief of distress: he opposed the Government's moves towards free trade and had an 'open mind' on the gold standard question. This was insincere pandering to obscuranticism of a kind Wellington would never have stooped to; it was none the less effective. The decision of much of the Tory right to support Grey was strengthened by the conviction that Swing demonstrated not the danger but the necessity of Reform.

Wellington's speech had a bad effect 'out of doors'. The Funds fell, there was sporadic rioting in London and a royal visit to the Guildhall had to be cancelled for fear of an attempt to kidnap the King. The fury had arisen very suddenly. When the Civil List was discussed on 15 November the Government was defeated by 233 votes to 204 – 34 Ultras voted with the Opposition. The Duke was glad to take the opportunity to resign.

Wellington was never again Prime Minister; in May 1832 he made an unsuccessful attempt to form a government and in November 1834, when William IV dismissed Melbourne, he was acting Prime Minister for three weeks before Peel returned from Italy. Between 1830 and 1834 Wellington was something of a bogeyman who was seen as the embodiment of all reactionary prejudice. Analysis of the Duke's premiership shows that this picture is wrong. His failures can usually be attributed to excessive high-mindedness. Catholic emancipation made the idea of changing the Constitution really respectable for the first time; to some extent it made Reform possible. Whether willingly or not, the Duke of Wellington speeded up these two most important changes. When he died, on 14 September 1852, he was again a national hero.

BIBLIOGRAPHY

Best, G., 'The Protestant Constitution and its Supporters 1800–29' (*Transactions of the Royal Historical Society*, 1958)
Bird, A., *The Damnable Duke of Cumberland* (London, 1966)
Davis, R. W., 'The Strategy of Dissent in the Repeal Campaign 1820-8' (*Journal of Modern History*, 1966)
Flick, C., 'The Fall of Wellington's Government' (*JMH*, 1965)
Foord, A. S., 'The Waning Influence of the Crown' (*English Historical Review*, 1947)
Longford, E., *Wellington: Pillar of State* (London, 1972)
Machin, G. I., 'The Duke of Wellington and Catholic Emancipation' (*Journal of Ecclesiastical History*, 1963)
Moore, D. C., 'The Other Face of Reform' (*Victorian Studies*, 1962)
Palmer, A., *George IV* (London, 1972)

EARL GREY

BY

GEORGE WOODBRIDGE

Charles Grey, born 13 March 1764, eldest surviving son of General Sir Charles Grey, afterwards 1st Earl Grey. Educated at Eton and Trinity College, Cambridge. Married Mary Elizabeth Ponsonby 1794; fifteen children. MP for Northumberland 1786–1807; Appleby 1807; Tavistock 1807. Succeeded as 2nd Earl Grey 1807. First Lord of the Admiralty 1806; Foreign Secretary 1806–7. Succeeded Fox as leader of Foxite Whigs 1806 and became Whig leader 1821. Prime Minister 1830–4. Died 17 July 1845.

Charles, 2nd Earl Grey, by Sir Thomas Lawrence

EARL GREY

Charles, second Earl Grey, was born 13 March 1764 into a long-established Northumberland family. His uncle (whose property he ultimately inherited) was a baronet; his father became an earl. At the age of six he was sent to a boarding preparatory school in Marylebone, entering Eton at the age of nine. After eight years there (1773–81) he went on (aged 17) to Trinity College, Cambridge. Apparently a competent but not an outstanding student, he did not take a degree. He went on a Grand Tour in 1784 to 1786, mostly to southern France, Switzerland, and especially Italy. His education at least gave him a real knowledge of Greek, Latin, French, and Italian; the latter two he could speak as well as read.

At a by-election in July 1786, while he was still on the Continent, he was elected (aged 22) a county Member of Parliament for Northumberland. He first took his seat in the House of Commons in January 1787, and continued to sit for that county until defeated in 1807. He then successively represented two boroughs: Appleby, May to July 1807, and Tavistock, July to November 1807. After his father's death on 14 November 1807, he took (aged 43) his seat as the second Earl Grey in the House of Lords, and, of course, remained in that House until his own death (aged 81) on 17 July 1845.

He married Mary Elizabeth, daughter of William Brabazon (Ponsonby), first Baron Ponsonby, on 18 November 1794. He was thirty; she was twenty; they had fifteen children. His wife and almost all of his children survived him. His married and family life seems to have been unusually happy. He may, on occasion, have been stiff in his social and political relations, but never with his family. It is noteworthy that, despite the evidence of Jane Austen and others regarding contemporary practices, his wife did not address him as Mr Grey or Earl Grey; rather she referred to him by the affectionate nickname of 'Car' both in letters to him and to their children. There is no doubt that he thoroughly enjoyed family life and life at Howick in Northumberland (perhaps three or four days' journey from London). This was not always a help to his political career.

When he took his seat in the House of Commons in 1787 his family political connections, if any, were probably moderately Tory. However, he was attracted by the views of Charles James Fox, and their relationship ripened into friendship. Grey became and remained a Foxite Whig. He was throughout his political career a competent speaker and on occasion a very good one.

In 1788 he became associated with Burke, Fox, and Sheridan in the management of the impeachment of Warren Hastings. On 12 April 1791 he moved, 'That it is at all times, and particularly under present circumstances, the interest of the country to preserve peace.' The avoidance of war, if at all possible – in the age of the French Revolution and Napoleon it was not easy – remained a consistent political view.

In 1792 Grey and other young associates founded the Society of the Friends of the People with, among others, the avowed purpose of forestalling radical reform by introducing moderate reform. In this area it achieved no success. Nevertheless, its relatively brief existence had some important permanent results.

It was the last straw that led to the secession of the Portland Whigs. They were opposed to any reform and objected to the Society and its aims. Fox, who was not a member of the Society but was the acknowledged Whig leader, supported the Society, so Portland and his followers left the party to join Pitt and the Tories. The Society collected and published a report on the manner by which members were 'elected' to the House of Commons (more details on this below). This report became a mine of factual information for reformers then and for historians since. Finally, the Society established the Whigs as the party of moderate reform and Grey as the leader of the moderate reform movement. As such, several times in the 1790s he introduced what may be called embryo Reform Bills; all were rejected on first reading.

After 1800, however, Grey seemed to lose his active interest in reform. He did not support various radical proposals, generally involving a wide extension of the franchise. He became (aged 42) in 1806 a member of the Ministry of All the Talents as First Lord of the Admiralty and in September, after the death of Fox, he succeeded him as Secretary of State for Foreign Affairs. He carried to a successful conclusion Fox's Bill for abolishing the slave trade. When the Government fell, he left office and did not again hold a position in the Government until 1830.

Having succeeded Fox as leader of the Foxite Whigs in 1807, Grey became the Whig leader in 1821 when Grenville and his followers left the party, some (but not Grenville himself) joining the Liverpool Government. During the whole period from 1807 to 1830 Grey was only occasionally an effective leader of the Opposition. From time to time, he offered to withdraw, and often seemed reluctant to visit London. He was firm in his opposition to the restrictive legislation of 1819; he did maintain a 'pure' Whig image by refusing to consider entry into the Canning Government, though he raised no serious objections when some of his followers did.

During this period various Reform Bills were proposed to Parliament, by Burdett, Lambton (later Baron then Earl of Durham), and, especially in the 1820s, by Lord John Russell. Grey made it clear, as did the Whigs as a group, that he would not support proposals for universal manhood suffrage. Since none of the Bills ever got beyond first reading in the Commons, none ever reached the Lords, so Grey had no occasion to support them and did not. Interest in reform, both in the country and in the Commons, waxed and waned in the 1820s, but waxed again at the end of the decade. The Marquis of Blandford introduced Reform Bills in June 1829 and February 1830, as did O'Connell and, once again, Russell, in May 1830.

George IV died in June 1830. Wellington, at odds with the Ultra Tories ever since his Government had passed a Catholic Emancipation Bill in 1829, was only uncertainly supported in the Commons. Accordingly, though he could have waited up to six months, he called for elections in July. Then, and even now, there was no agreement as to the results: had Wellington gained or lost? It seems clear that after the election, as before, he needed additional support to maintain a firm Government.

The new Parliament was formally opened on 26 October 1830. The King's Speech was delivered, and the Address Debate began on 2 November. Many, including Peel (who was to oppose vigorously the Reform Bills), assumed that reform would be a principal topic of debate during the session, but no mention was made of it in the King's Speech. In the debate on that speech, Viscount Althorp in the Commons, and Grey in the Lords, both raised the question. They referred to the disturbed conditions of the country and stressed the urgency of some measure of reform to preserve the Constitution. Wellington made his famous reply, insisting that the existing Parliament answered all good purposes, that he was not prepared to bring forward a reform measure, and that he would resist any such measure proposed by another. This statement almost certainly ensured the defeat of his Government.

On 15 November it was beaten, 233 to 209, in the Commons on a motion to refer the Civil List estimates to a committee. The majority was made up of a motley group of Whigs, Canningites, Ultra Tories, and Members who simply did not like Wellington. He seized the opportunity to resign and wrote that he did so to prevent consideration of a motion for reform submitted by Brougham.

The King sent for Grey. He became Prime Minister (aged 66) on 16 November, remaining in that office until his resignation (aged 70) on 8 July 1834, a period of just under four years. During this period his Government passed a number of very important legislative acts. Of these, however, by far the most important, and the one that most involved Grey, was the Reform Act of 1832. Grey's reputation as a Prime Minister rests largely on his handling of the various Bills leading to this Act. While this is not the place to discuss in detail the long efforts to secure passage, attention must be focused on the part played by Grey. It was his finest hour. It may be said that the frequent nervous illnesses that had plagued him during London visits in the 1820s never troubled him in this period. He was healthy, buoyant, and energetic, and he seemed to enjoy the exercise of power, at least until the Bill that was his personal concern became an Act.

His first task was to put together a Cabinet. This he did in a few days. He included Whigs of his generation – Lansdowne and Holland; younger Whigs – Althorp, Stanley, Graham, and Russell (the last not at first in the Cabinet); Canningites – Melbourne, Palmerston, Goderich, and Grant; Radicals – his son-in-law Durham (Hobhouse, also a Radical, later became Secretary at War but was not in the Cabinet); and even an Ultra Tory – Richmond. His most difficult problem was Brougham, fresh from a great election triumph in Yorkshire. Althorp was to be Chancellor of the Exchequer and Leader of the House of Commons. He was very effective in the latter capacity. Brougham, a more brilliant speaker, wayward, and independent, would certainly have been a difficult colleague. After one false start, Grey solved the problem tactfully by persuading Brougham to become Lord Chancellor.

This Cabinet was very mixed, as indeed was essential if a majority was to be obtained in the Commons. (There was certainly no clear Whig majority.) Goderich had already been Prime Minister; Melbourne, Russell, Stanley, and Palmerston were to be. Stanley and Graham were to become Tories and were to serve under Peel. Grey is said to have boasted that his Cabinet owned more acres of English land than any preceding Cabinet. It was emphatically 'aristocratic'. There were different views, stresses, and strains, but tactful and firm leadership held the members together, in spite of recurrent threats of resignation, until much important legislation had been accomplished.

When Grey took office the southern counties were troubled by the Captain Swing Riots, handled firmly, even severely, by Melbourne. In the winter of 1831-2 there was a cholera epidemic. The autumn of 1831 saw riots in Nottingham, Bristol, and elsewhere, and trade and agriculture were depressed in the winter of 1831-2. Not until the summer of 1832 could the country be said to enjoy peace, order, and some measure of prosperity. Abroad, the Government inherited a Belgian crisis, well handled through the winter of 1830-1. Thereafter the international scene was comparatively peaceful.

Grey made his first speech as Prime Minister on 22 November 1830. He said he had been allowed to indicate that he had the King's approval to introduce a Reform Bill. During the next few months his Cabinet survived rather than governed. Budget changes were forced upon it; minor measures were lost. But the Opposition, indeed the whole country, waited for the Reform Bill and tolerated, if they did not endorse, the Government. In the matter of reform Grey moved ahead early and steadily, but not unduly rapidly. He had many problems with which to contend, problems of which he was always keenly aware but which were often overlooked by partisans for or against reform and even sometimes by subsequent commentators.

The resultant Act, by modern democratic standards, was, of course, a moderate, indeed a very moderate, measure. It must, however, be considered in the historical context. The existing parliamentary system had been crystallised about the middle of the seventeenth century. Thereafter there had only been very few and very minor changes. On the whole, certainly until the advent of the Industrial Revolution, it had worked well. The great challenges of France, for example those of Louis XIV, the French Revolution and Napoleon, had been contained and beaten. For all the poverty and misery that existed in it, England had nevertheless become the richest and most powerful nation in the world. The existing system – and Grey certainly planned to make changes within the existing system and not by revolutionary measures outside it – gave much influence to those who controlled it. Any changes, except the most minor, were bound to excite firm resistance.

Among the problems that faced Grey were, first and foremost, what should be the nature of the Reform Bill? Second, Cabinet solidarity; third, the King; fourth, at least at the outset, the Commons; fifth, the Lords; and sixth, the public or at least that portion of the public (skilled workers, masters, the middle classes) that had the greatest interest in the subject. The Bill had to be acceptable to all, or at least to a majority. Some of the Cabinet, the King, and the Lords wanted little; some of the public wanted much – both sides had to be satisfied and convinced. Though now discounted by some historians, the threat of disorders and even revolution could not be ignored by a responsible government.

Before considering the nature of the Bill that Grey wanted, it is necessary to sum up briefly the existing parliamentary framework. There were rotten boroughs, in which the population had dwindled to little or nothing, and pocket (or nomination) boroughs, where one or very few men controlled elections, in effect appointing Members of Parliament. The report of the Society of the Friends of the People indicated that 154 individuals sent 307 (out of 658) Members to the Commons. In the late 1820s, Croker, a Tory opposed to reform, concluded that at least 276 (out of 489) English Members were returned by patrons. There was a very uneven distribution of Members in relation to population. For example, more Members were elected in the two counties of Cornwall and Wiltshire than in the five counties of Middlesex, Somerset, Warwickshire, Worcester, and Yorkshire, though the latter had a combined population of more than ten times that of the former. The franchise, with few exceptions, was very limited. Even in Westminster, generally considered a very democratic constituency, less than one quarter of adult males could vote. Though county constituencies enjoyed a uniform franchise, there was no uniformity in the borough constituencies in which about 82 per cent of the English Members were elected. These were the main features that the Government set out to alter.

Shortly after taking office Grey appointed a committee, consisting of Durham, Russell, Graham, and Duncannon, to prepare a Bill. He instructed them that their proposals should be based on property, existing territorial divisions, and fundamental forms, but should be inclusive enough to forestall further demands for reform. He wanted, it may be said, a Bill with the minimum that would satisfy the reform-demanding public and the maximum that would be acceptable to both Houses of

Parliament and the King. The committee completed its work by the end of 1830 and its proposals were discussed by the full Cabinet in January 1831. There some slight changes were made, generally in a conservative direction. When there were disagreements, decisions were apparently taken by Grey.

Next, he personally took the proposed Bill to the King; it was essential for its passage that the King should agree with it or, at least, not strongly oppose it. Through the whole course run on three Bills, it was Grey who always handled the King. He kept William IV fully informed; he was careful to record their conversations and agreements in letters to the King, written immediately after every meeting; he always replied immediately to any letters or comments of the King. In his first interview on the Bill Grey used a technique he was to use on other occasions. He discussed with the King not only the proposed provisions but also those more radical proposals that he and the Cabinet had rejected, thus suggesting that if the King did not go along with the proposals, he might have to put up with something more extreme. While the King, with one possible exception, behaved loyally to his ministers, his personal entourage was always opposed to reform and continually worked on him to oppose it. This was just one of Grey's many problems.

The long-awaited Bill was at last presented to the Commons on 1 March 1831 by Russell. The Bill proposed the complete elimination of about sixty boroughs. This was the famous Schedule A that caught most attention, winning the approval and support of the Radicals and exciting the greatest opposition from opponents. It also proposed the elimination of one Member from a number of boroughs (Schedule B); the redistribution of seats taken from these boroughs, some to go to counties, some to hitherto unrepresented boroughs, both more or less in proportion to population; a slight extension of the county franchise by including some leaseholders; and the establishment of a uniform borough franchise for residents (the famous 10 pound householder vote). Though the number of voters might be reduced (for example by the exclusion of non-resident voters) in a few boroughs, it was increased in most. (All, however, who had the right to vote but did not qualify under the new dispensation, retained the right for life, if residents.)

After an unprecedentedly long debate lasting several sittings the first reading was carried without a division. After further debate, in an all-night sitting, 22–3 March, the second reading was carried in an unusually large house by 302 to 301. Thus the first hurdle – perhaps the most important – was surmounted by one vote.

Shortly thereafter in committee stage a crippling amendment, designed to destroy the Bill, was carried. Grey immediately asked the King for a dissolution and persuaded him to grant one.

In the subsequent election the reformers achieved a substantial victory. The new Parliament was opened on 21 June. Six days later, with no waste of time, a new Reform Bill was introduced. The second reading was carried 6 July by 367 to 231, a majority of 136. Thereafter Grey had no problems with the Commons. He had timed the election well.

The committee stage lasted the whole summer. The third reading was not carried until 21 September. In the Lords the first reading was not opposed. Debate on the second started on 3 October and lasted for five sittings. It was concluded on the night of the 7–8th, in another all-night session. Grey opened and closed the debate for the Government and made at least one significant statement: he indicated that he would accept minor changes but warned the Lords that if they rejected the current Bill, they would sooner or later have to accept a Bill at least as 'efficient'. In spite of accusations made then and later that he was will-ing and even anxious to weaken the Bill, in fact he never departed from his demand for a Bill as 'efficient' as the one he was proposing. In the early hours of the 8th, the Lords rejected the Bill, 199 (including 49 proxies) to 158 (30 proxies), a majority of 41.

The next day the King asked Grey not to resign. He also indicated, however, that he was not surprised by the rejection (suggesting, no doubt, that he thought the Bill had gone too far), and affirmed that it could not be passed by the creation of new peers. Grey undertook to remain, provided he was allowed to proceed with another Reform Bill basically similar to that rejected. After the Commons had expressed approval of the Government's reform policy by a majority of 131, Grey and Althorp announced in their respective Houses that they would remain in office only if there were reasonable hope of passing an effec-tive Reform Bill. Parliament was then prorogued.

For the next eight months Grey personally assumed most of the responsibility and work in connection with the progress of another Bill. Immediately he was confronted with two problems: a divided Cabinet and unrest in the country.

The Cabinet was divided and remained divided, first on the reform issue and later on other issues, but knowledge of this was fairly well kept from the country. There were those, in the autumn of 1831, who recommended a weakened Bill that would be acceptable to the Lords. On the other hand, there were those who demanded an immediate and firm request for more peers. Somehow Grey kept them all together.

The unrest in the country was potentially dangerous. There were riots in Derby, Nottingham and elsewhere, and a three-day destructive riot in Bristol. Although largely resulting from local issues, they were not entirely divorced from the popular demand for reform. At the same time the existing political associations (the Birmingham Political Union was the most influential of them) renewed their activities and new ones were formed (in London the National Political Union under the leadership of Francis Place). If the unrest got out of hand, it was likely to destroy support for an effective Reform Bill. Alternatively, if repression were too severe, it would forfeit support for the Government. Grey resolved the problem by issuing a royal proclamation declaring illegal those associations with a military character. This satisfied the King, who disliked all political unions and hoped they would be suppressed. Through intermediaries the Birmingham Political Union was asked to refrain from some contemplated activities that might have brought it under the ban. It and others complied. The unrest died down; the unions were not prosecuted and continued their work.

While no problem was expected with the Commons, difficulties with the Lords were certain if another Bill as 'efficient' as that rejected in October were to be passed. Four possibilities were open to Grey:

(1) He could weaken the Bill sufficiently to satisfy the Opposition. This he never considered.

(2) He, and others, could talk to individual peers, including bishops, with the object of converting them. This was actually done with some success. (In October there were only two bishops for and twenty-one against; in April there were to be eleven for and twelve against.)

(3) Discussions could be held with groups of peers. Perhaps not enthusiastically but with the clear intention of satisfying the King that he was trying all possible approaches, Grey negotiated, in two separate periods, with Wharncliffe and Harrowby and their small following, known as the Waverers. (They got no encouragement from the opposition leaders; Peel wrote a strong letter to Harrowby urging him not to compromise and firmly to resist a new Bill.) The first discussion, held late in 1831, produced no agreement. The Waverers really had little to

offer for the concessions they wanted. Grey was adamant on Schedule A, on the proposed new London metropolitan boroughs, and on the 10 pound householder franchise; but he was willing to discuss alterations in Schedule B and some in the proposals for redistribution of seats. Although no agreements were reached in the second discussions in 1832, the Waverers indicated that they would support the second reading, while preserving the right to try to amend the Bill in the committee stage and to vote against it on the third reading if suitable changes were not made.

(4) Grey's fourth option was to push for the creation of more peers. Some of his Cabinet were very eager for this approach, but there were serious difficulties. At that time, the accepted interpretation of the Constitution held that the final decision in this matter rested not with the ministers but with the King, who had already indicated his lack of enthusiasm. There was the question of how many would be required. The second Bill had been beaten by forty-one votes. In March 1832 Grey was to estimate that if slightly more than that number were created (certainly an unprecedentedly large creation – Anne's famous new creations, the one precedent, had involved only twelve), some who had voted for the Bill would turn against it, while others who had not voted would also vote against it. He concluded, therefore, that many more than forty would be required and that the King's consent would be unlikely. But in January 1832 he approached the King in somewhat vague terms since he himself was uncertain as to how many new creations he would need. At one time about twenty-one were suggested; later a number not greatly exceeding that amount. By the end of January the King agreed, in principle, to an unspecified but clearly not to an unlimited number of new creations provided that they were, for the most part, limited to eldest sons and other heirs of existing peers.

Somewhat unexpectedly Grey reconvened Parliament on 6 December 1831. A third Reform Bill was introduced on the 12th and the second reading was passed on the 17th. The committee stage occupied some weeks after the Christmas recess and the third reading was passed, by a majority of 116, on 22 March 1832. There had never been any doubt of the result. But the resistance of the Lords remained.

Early in March Althorp decided that immediate creation of peers was required and threatened to resign if Grey did not present a firm request to the King. Grey wrote him a masterly letter, arguing against such a precipitous step. This letter has sometimes been interpreted as revealing Grey's basic conservatism and a willingness to compromise. In fact it was intended to soothe the King, who had indicated that he might retreat from his promise of some new creations. To him a copy of the letter was sent. The letter accomplished exactly what Grey wanted: the Cabinet was held together and the King was persuaded that Grey was a right-minded man who would not request extreme measures unless their use was proved absolutely necessary. But Grey staked his political fortune on the prediction that the Bill would pass the second reading in the Lords without new peers.

In the House of Lords the first reading passed unopposed on 26 March. The debate on the second reading began on 9 April and occupied four sittings, being concluded on the night of 13–14 April. Grey again opened and closed the case for the Government. He concluded with a highly political and very clever speech, suggesting that all that was at stake was the acceptance of the principle that there should be some reform, leaving the exact details and the degree of reform to be settled in the committee stage. Still another all-night sitting resulted in a victory by a majority of nine (184, including 56 proxies, for; 175, 49 proxies, against). Grey's work and judgement were justified.

On 7 May a crippling amendment was carried in the committee. The next day Grey offered the King two choices: immediate creation of new peers or his resignation. The King chose the latter but asked Grey to remain in office until a new government had been formed. Grey, of course, consented. A week later Wellington informed the King that he could not form a Government. The King, then, had no choice; he had to retain Grey.

On 18 May the reluctant King at last agreed to the creation of the necessary number of new peers. That evening Grey and Althorp announced to their respective Houses that they were staying in office because they had been assured of the necessary means to pass the Bill. The Opposition concluded that further resistance was futile and all but a few die-hards withdrew from further sittings concerned with the Bill. It passed rapidly through the committee stage in the Lords and on 4 June the third reading was carried 106 to 22. The next day the Commons accepted some minor amendments. On 7 June the Royal Assent was given by Commission and the Bill became the Reform Act of 1832.

Thanks to Grey's steadiness, good judgement, and firm but tactful handling of the King, his Cabinet, and the political unions, the country had, if not exactly the first Bill, which had been subject in the second and third versions to many minor revisions, nevertheless, in terms of 'efficiency' and impact, what may justly be termed the Bill, the whole Bill, and nothing but the Bill. Scottish and Irish reform Bills were passed during the summer.

It may be suggested that the next two years, so far as Grey personally was concerned, were anti-climactic. His great work was done. Rifts in the Cabinet became greater and harder to heal; his London ill health again began to plague him.

The only serious foreign affairs problem that confronted the Grey Government had in fact started before he came to office: the Belgian revolution. It was, on the whole, favourably received in England. Grey's Government and the public were not prepared to have the Russians, Prussians, Austrians, or even the Dutch re-establish Dutch rule, but neither were they prepared to allow France, either directly or indirectly, to establish its control over Belgium or any part of it. The British negotiations were conducted primarily by Palmerston, the Foreign Secretary, but with the help and the constant personal interest and assistance of Grey. With the co-operation of Talleyrand, whom Grey frequently saw, a successful and peaceful solution was reached.

The first election held under the terms of the Reform Act took place in December 1832 and resulted, on the surface, in a victory for the Government or at least a defeat for the conservative Opposition. The Government's nominal supporters were, however, divided between those who wanted a vigorous programme of reforms and change and those who wanted only a moderate programme. Satisfying both groups was to prove impossible.

In spite of constant difficulties with the Irish question, which in the end led to Grey's resignation, the accomplishments of his Government in 1833 were considerable. The evidence indicates that they were not, as the Reform Act certainly was, Grey's own measures in which he took a strong personal interest and for which he exercised vigorous leadership. Nevertheless, it was his Government that was responsible.

Among the more important accomplishments was, first, the abolition of slavery throughout the British Empire. Grey had played an important role in the ending of the slave trade, and his son, Howick, did the same in the ending of slavery. Also in 1833 a Factory Act was passed; it was associated with Ashley, though in its final phase it was piloted through the Commons by Althorp. It was important because it established inspectors. In the same year the Government of India Act eliminated the last vestiges of the East India Company's trade monopoly, and established the great principle that government offices in India were to be open to qualified persons without regard to race, creed, or colour. An Irish Church Bill, which did not, due primarily to opposition in the Lords, go as far as the Government had hoped, at least relieved the Irish people from the necessity of paying 'vestry cess' to support the established Protestant Church. A Bank Charter Act helped modernise the banking system. Two law reform acts, especially that establishing a permanent judicial committee of the Privy Council, likewise modernised and improved the handling of justice. A grant for education, though small, marked the beginning of a development that would lead to a national system of free primary education for all. The following year the Commons passed a significant Poor Law Reform Act that was not completed in the Lords until after Grey's resignation.

Throughout its life, the Grey Government struggled with Irish problems. It hoped to mitigate them by reform of the (Protestant) Church of Ireland. Some members of the Cabinet were anxious to move far and vigorously on this path; others hardly at all. Grey hoped to keep them together. Shortly after Russell took a public and strong position on the issue, Stanley, Graham, Richmond, and Ripon (Goderich) resigned. Soon thereafter Althorp and others were unable to persuade Grey and the Cabinet to support modifications, which had been leaked to O'Connell, of a proposed Bill. Althorp resigned and Grey also, on 9 July 1834. Grey in fact had already resigned in January when the Cabinet would not support his Portuguese policy, but had been persuaded by the King and the Cabinet to continue. However, the divisions on Ireland and the Church were too great.

Grey was, perhaps, not a great Prime Minister. Others held the office for longer periods. Others played a more active role in developing parties, programmes, and legislation. He was, however, responsible for what one of its chief opponents, Sir Robert Peel, called the most important Act passed by Parliament in more than a hundred years. Because of Grey's leadership in connection with that Act, it has been said of him that he justly deserves to be 'renowned through all English history'.

BIBLIOGRAPHY

The standard life of Grey is still G. M. Trevelyan, *Lord Grey of the Reform Bill* (London, 1920). The standard account of the Reform Act has for a long time been J. R. M. Butler, *The Passing of the Great Reform Bill* (London, 1914). It has now been superseded by Michael Brock, *The Great Reform Act* (London, 1973). There is a short account by George Woodbridge, *The Reform Bill of 1832* (New York, 1970). For a different interpretation, see the articles of D. C. Moore, especially 'The Other Face of Reform', *Victorian Studies*, ii (1961), 7–34. Professor Moore's other articles are listed in the bibliography of Woodbridge, op. cit. Probably the two most important printed sources are the appropriate volumes of *Hansard's Parliamentary Debates* (3rd series, 1830 onwards), and *The Correspondence of the late Earl Grey with his Majesty King William IV and with Sir Herbert Taylor*, edited by Henry, Earl Grey (2 vols, London, 1867). The works of Butler, Brock, and Woodbridge listed above all have bibliographies.

VISCOUNT MELBOURNE

BY

DOROTHY MARSHALL

William Lamb, 2nd Viscount Melbourne, born 15 March 1779, second son of Peniston Lamb, 1st Viscount. Educated at Eton and Trinity College, Cambridge. Called to the Bar 1804. Married 1805 Lady Caroline Ponsonby, only daughter of the 3rd Earl of Bessborough; separated 1825; MP for Leominster 1806–1812; Northampton 1816; Hertford 1819–25; Secretary for Ireland 1827–8; entered Lords 1828; Home Secretary 1830; Prime Minister 1834 (dismissed same year); Prime Minister 1835–9 and 1839–41; stroke ended political career and died 24 November 1848. No surviving children.

William Lamb, 2nd Viscount Melbourne, by J. Partridge

VISCOUNT MELBOURNE

The life span of William Lamb, second Viscount Melbourne, who was born in 1779 and died in 1848, covered some of the most formative years in English history, when a hierarchical, pre-industrial society was moving irrevocably towards one dominated by urban and industrial pressures. During this period Lord Melbourne was Prime Minister for seven years, from 1834 to 1841 except for the break of a few months. How important was his ministry? This depends on the angle from which it is viewed. Melbourne's direct influence on national policy and constitutional developments was curiously negative. Yet his name is more widely known than is that of some prime ministers whose tenure of office yielded more positive and visible results because to Melbourne fell the task of smoothing the path of monarchy for the young Victoria when she became Queen in 1837. Any assessment of his premiership therefore falls into two parts, the first from 1834 to 1837, the second from 1837 to 1841.

The negative quality of the earlier period was inherent in William Lamb's personality and background. As a second son he had not been intended for a political career, and after Eton and Cambridge had been called to the Bar in 1804. A year later his elder brother died leaving young William heir to the viscounty and, as was customary for the eldest sons of peers, he gave up the Bar in favour of politics, being returned for the Whig interest as MP for Leominster in 1806. His brother's death had equally important consequences for his private life; it made him an eligible match for that wayward, passionate character Lady Caroline Ponsonby, better known under her married name as Lady Caroline Lamb. June 1805 saw the beginning of their storm-tossed marriage. In contrast his years in the House of Commons were calm. Though he could speak well on occasion he never had the 'feel' of the House that Lord North had possessed, and though he was a Member from 1806 to 1812 and again from 1816 to 1829, when on his father's death he went to the Lords, so far his political career had been undistinguished. It was not until 1827, at the age of forty-six, that he first held office as Secretary for Ireland in Canning's short-lived administration. This was in part due to the political set-up of the inter-vening years. A Whig by tradition he could not have held office under the Ultra Tories led by the Duke of Wellington. His opportunity came when, on the death of Lord Liverpool, the Tories split into two oppos-ing camps, the Ultras under the Duke and the moderates under Can-ning, whose middle-of-the-road politics in domestic affairs seemed to Lamb to hold out the best hope for stable government, always his prime and possibly his only political objective. Accordingly when Canning asked both him and Lord Palmerston to join the Government William, though without undue eagerness, did so.

His first taste of office was short. On Canning's death in 1828, after the brief and inglorious premiership of the tearful Goderich, the Ultra Tories came back under Wellington. Nevertheless it had been an en-couraging and revealing experience. As far as anyone in the perpetually troubled state of Ireland could be successful William Lamb could be so counted. For this his personality was largely responsible. His methods of doing business were informal, as indeed they were to be throughout his official career. He would on occasion even interview his callers while shaving, or in his bedchamber, arguing that they would probably prefer to be seen thus than not at all. This lack of ceremony, a willing-ness to welcome all shades of opinions to his house and his apparently unflappable easy manner commended him to the Irish. Melbourne was a man of few positive political views but an inborn scepticism inclined him to the virtues of tolerance. He had little use for bigoted Protestants and was sympathetic towards Roman Catholic emancipation. This in itself was a useful attribute in an Irish Secretary and one likely to make him popular in Dublin. Nevertheless he left Ireland in 1828 with few illusions. When later faced with the problem of Irish unrest, both as Home Secretary and as Prime Minister, he had little faith in the remedies pressed upon him by either O'Connell or his own colleagues. Roman Catholic emancipation, granted in 1829, had merely led to further demands and Melbourne's growing conviction was that 'it was the natural disposition of the people' and not specific grievances and mis-government that lay at the root of the Irish problem.

After a brief period out of office, during which Wellington and his right hand man, Peel, tried to stem the rising demand for parliamentary reform, the Whigs came back under the leadership of the ageing Lord Grey. In the new ministry Lord Melbourne was Home Secretary. On the surface it was a surprising choice for a ministry pledged to reform.

In no sense was Melbourne a reformer. His first instinct was to leave everything alone in the belief that to right a minor wrong, or to remove a minor injustice, was more than likely to create worse problems than it solved, and that to tinker with either the existing state of society or with existing constitutional arrangements might bring everything crashing down. In these views he was far from unique. Though the eighteenth-century Whigs had campaigned for parliamentary reform their aim had been to curb the power of the Crown in favour of the aristocracy, not to usher in popular democracy. Only the Radicals cherished any such aspirations. But by 1830 the demand of the middle classes, who felt that their wealth and material and intellectual contributions to society entitled them to a greater share in the running of the country and in the shaping of policy, combined with the resentful mass of the working population, who had come to see in parliamentary reform the best solution for their economic ills, had produced a restlessness that threatened to slip into revolution. To Melbourne and his contemporaries this was something to be avoided at all costs. This fear, combined with the memory of the excesses of the French Revolution, provides the clue to much of the politics of the post-war decades and explains why the aristocratic Whigs placed themselves at the head of the demand for reform on the well-known principle, 'If you can't beat them join them'. Melbourne therefore joined Lord Grey's ministry partly because during his period as Irish Secretary he had discovered an unexpected scope for his very genuine abilities and partly because, though he disliked reform, he realised that in some shape it had become politically necessary, and that it was better to ride the tiger than be eaten by him, a principle to which he adhered throughout his career.

In the fight for the Reform Bill Melbourne himself played very little part. His responsibility was not so much to steer it through the Lords as to back up the forces of law and order at a time when these seemed to be threatened by a new militancy on the part of the masses. Though their misery could be, and to some extent was, exploited by radical reformers and hotheads, the economic lot of the average landless countryman in overpopulated rural areas was stark enough to explain the waves of agrarian unrest that marked 1830, when the sky was lit by burning ricks and unpopular farmers and landowners were harassed by mobs demanding better wages. The immediate repression of such riots was the business of the local magistrates and the courts but clemency lay with the Home Secretary. It would be unfair to say that this was not exercised. In accordance with common practice, of those condemned to death only the ringleaders were actually hanged, though many of the rioters were transported, but Lord Melbourne put the full weight of his authority behind the work of suppression. He was to do the same in 1834 when the labourers of Tolpuddle strove to emulate the widespread formation of trade unions by the new type of industrial workers. In spite of a petition reputed to have been signed by some quarter of a million persons the Dorset labourers, convicted under an anti-revolutionary law of 1799 against illegal oaths, were transported. Lord Melbourne's view of society remained hierarchical; he was willing to do his duty by his inferiors who accepted their traditional place within it, but he had neither liking for nor understanding of the new middle classes and the desperate workers who swarmed beneath them. Within his own circle he was tolerant, kindly, even sentimentally emotional and sensitive, but the plight of people in the mass, whose lives lay outside his own experience, left him unmoved. His duty as he saw it was to stamp out and extinguish revolutionary fires even by blood if necessary, a duty made easier for a man of his temperament by the fact that it was his role to issue impersonal orders in London without having to come face to face with the personal anguish that resulted. Thus, in spite of his position as Home Secretary in a ministry that not only brought in the great Reform Bill but also passed the first effective Factory Act in 1833 and the Poor Law Amendment Act of 1834, his contribution was largely negative. He stamped out disorder: he suggested no innovations with which to deal with its causes.

By the spring of 1834 Lord Grey's ministry was in difficulties. Once again Irish affairs were producing divergent views within the Cabinet over the form that a renewed Coercion Bill should take, and as a result of intrigues and counter-intrigues Lord Althrop, the indispensable leader of the Commons, resigned. Lord Grey, whose enthusiasm for office after the strain of the last four years was low, declared it impossible to carry on without him and also resigned. It was not easy for William IV to find a replacement. The Whigs still had a majority in the Commons and therefore, though the King would have preferred Wellington and Peel, the new prime minister must be a Whig. The choice was not great. Both Lord John Russell and Lord Brougham would have been unacceptable to important elements in the party, if any group of men so weak and so divided can be dignified by that name. Melbourne seemed the best choice. William IV disliked him rather less than he did his other possible choices and his appointment seemed unlikely to upset the rest of the Cabinet. Melbourne himself is reported to have described the prospect as 'a damn bore' and hesitated as to whether to accept. This is not the stuff out of which great prime ministers are made! Melbourne lacked both the driving force of ambition and that of any deeply held convictions. Not for him was Chatham's 'I know that I can save this country and that no one else can'. Throughout his career Melbourne preferred to temporise and postpone. Nevertheless in the political circumstances of the day William IV's choice was not a bad one. It was true that Melbourne was the last man to deal constructively with the needs of a society in flux, when growing towns were posing ever greater problems of sanitation and power-driven factories were absorbing more and more of the labour force, while in rural areas the harshness of the new Poor Law was biting deep into agrarian society. Like Galileo Melbourne 'cared for none of these things'. It was only the disorder that they brought in their train that caused him concern. Nevertheless, because he was the kind of person he was, placed in the situation in which he found himself, he was able to do what a man of more drive and ambition could not have done, namely hold the Government together. This was no easy task. Parties were only beginning to develop much more than a rudimentary organisation; as a cohesive factor men were still more important than programmes in holding an administration together. It is still less misleading for modern readers to speak of Whigs and Tories than of a Whig or a Tory party, though there was probably more cohesion among the latter than the former.

This lack of common ground among the Whigs, many of whom called themselves Whigs not from any belief in a common policy or shared outlook but merely because they belonged to families tradition-ally Whig, was at once the great cause of Melbourne's troubles as Prime Minister and the reason why he was able to retain that office for so long. The Cabinet, which he inherited from Grey, contained too many divergent personalities, each with his own political programme, for his task to be an easy one. Lord John Russell was a man of doctrin-aire outlook wedded to a limited conception of personal liberty. Lord Durham was wealthy, difficult to handle and Radical in his views. Lord Brougham, the Lord Chancellor, was wildly ambitious, a man of ideas and energy, a brilliant exhibitionist with considerable capacity for intrigue. Lord Palmerston, the Foreign Secretary, saw himself as the champion of constitutional liberty and was prepared to hector and bully autocratic rulers in a way that certainly did not make for smooth diplomatic relations. In contrast Lord Stanley, the future Lord Derby, leant to the extreme right and had more in common with Wellington than with Palmerston. To add to Melbourne's troubles this diverse bunch of Whigs did not by themselves command a majority in the Commons but were forced into an uneasy co-operation with the Radicals and the Irish under Daniel O'Connell. The Radicals can be described as a 'ginger group' ever pressing for further instalments of reform. They were critical of the Church, anxious to remodel the municipal corporations, anxious to cut out the dead wood of tradition from every part of the national administration and to reform it along the lines associated with the Benthamites. To please them was to antagonise the bulk of the true Whigs; to ignore their demands totally was to risk losing their support. The Irish were another headache. In spite of Roman Catholic emancipation Ireland had not settled down and O'Connell was now campaigning for a repeal of the Union. There was also the difficult question of the Protestant Church in Ireland. Should the Irish Catholic majority be forced to pay tithes for its upkeep? Should some of its revenues be diverted to secular ends, such as education? Whatever was decided was bound to displease one section of the uneasy triangle that between them supported the Government.

In circumstances where little could be done without everything collapsing Lord Melbourne's capacity to do absolutely nothing unless driven and then to do as little as possible was a definite asset. So too were his good looks, persuasive charm and his flair for personal relations. It was very difficult to pin him down and equally difficult to resent a failure that was masked by such good-humoured tact. Moreover behind his aversion to change for change's sake, and his conviction that to meddle with established practices would be productive of more harm than good, was a hard-headed realisation that he could not, any more than King Canute, hold back the tide, and that by conceding a little here and a little there, now conciliating the Radicals, now the Irish, and by keeping his colleagues from each other's throats, the Government could be carried on, even though its weakness was patent and it limped from crisis to crisis. This was possible, at least in part, because neither the Radicals nor the Irish genuinely wanted to pull the Government down if Melbourne were to be replaced by Wellington, from whom they expected even less than they were getting from the unsatisfactory, temporising Melbourne. Nor was Peel, now the effective leader of the

Tories, anxious to move prematurely; he was prepared to wait his time until his prey grew still weaker. The person who precipitated the crisis was William IV himself. Though Melbourne handled him with skill and the King had no personal animosity towards him, the royal preference was for Wellington and Peel, and when an opportunity occurred to get rid of the Whigs William IV seized it.

Lord Althrop, whose resignation over the Irish Coercion Bill had given Grey his excuse to resign also, had been persuaded to withdraw his resignation and serve in Melbourne's administration in his old capacity as Leader of the House. Unfortunately for the stability of the ministry his father, Lord Spencer, died, which meant that Althrop went to the Lords. This created a vacancy which Melbourne found difficult to fill. The King disliked the suggestion that Lord John might lead the House and, exercising for the last time the royal prerogative of dismissing a prime minister who still had the confidence of the Commons, asked for Lord Melbourne's resignation. William IV then sent for Wellington to hold the Government together until Peel, who was on a visit to Italy, could return and take over. In the few months that followed Melbourne played a passive part. He had found being Prime Minister a troublesome business and he hated trouble. It is interesting to speculate whether, in addition, he was influenced by the older tradition that the ministers were the King's servants and as such ought to be supported unless to do so were obviously against the national interest. On the score of national interest he would have had no qualms, having in many ways much more sympathy with the Tory outlook than with that of his own troublesome team. His period of release proved short. In January 1835 Peel went to the country and though in the general election the Tories increased their majority they remained a minority government, the Irish, despite their threats, having decided to support the Whigs as the lesser of two evils. Even so Melbourne did not force the issue and it was not not until Peel was defeated on the contentious question of the revenues of the Irish Church that the King was forced to ask Melbourne to form a new government. This he was reluctant to do; never possibly was there a more reluctant premier than he. Unfortunately for his peace of mind there seemed no alternative. Grey refused to come back and the moderate Tories, when approached, refused to form a coalition government. Because of his conviction that the King's government must be carried on Melbourne came back, though he was able to secure a slightly less troublesome Cabinet by refusing to include the difficult Lord Brougham in the new administration. Melbourne was to remain in office until 1841.

The results of his premiership were meagre if measured in the concrete terms of legislation. After difficulties and opposition in the Lords the Radicals succeeded in carrying the Municipal Government Act which effectively put the middle classes in control of urban local government in the boroughs. Something was also done to relieve the dissenters from the worst of their disabilities with regard to tithe. The registration of births, marriages and deaths was made official, so that for the first time reliable vital statistics were available. But the Irish problem continued to bedevil politics, and tinkering with it by introducing a new Poor Law, not well adapted to Irish conditions, did little to improve the situation. Melbourne was however lucky in his Undersecretary, Thomas Drummond, who was able, until he died of overwork, to blunt the edge of Irish discontent by providing that country with a competent administration. But for the most part, like the Abbé Sieyès who, when asked what he had done during the French Revolution replied that he had survived, Melbourne could only claim the same feat for his Government. This, until the accession of Victoria, was his major contribution to English political life. To Melbourne and his contemporaries this record would not seem as meagre as it may to his twentieth-century critics. In their eyes the responsibilities of government were confined to keeping order, raising taxes, dealing with foreign policy and, if war should break out, directing it. Men of the eighteenth century who dominated government circles saw no need for social change or for legislation to ease the process. Holding such views in an age in which both the economy and the society based on it were changing with a hitherto unknown rapidity Melbourne's contribution could not fail to be negative. His role was that of a caretaker until men of the stamp of Peel, heirs to the new industrial Britain, were able to take over the controls and leave the eighteenth century behind.

With the accession of Queen Victoria in 1837 a new chapter in both the history of the monarchy and in Melbourne's premiership opened. It was one in which all his talents and abilities, all the rich warmth of his charm and the depth of his maturity could be called into play. As a mentor to the young Queen he was able to assume a responsibility for which he was wonderfully fitted. Tiresome colleagues still remained; his parliamentary majority was small; Palmerston was still troublesome, forcing on Melbourne a foreign policy in the Middle East far too adventurous for his taste, but the burden that had seemed so heavy became bearable because Victoria depended on him. This was not surprising. The Duchess of Kent's strained relations with William IV and the ambitions of Conroy had isolated Victoria from the political world so that, with the exception of Baroness Lehzen, there was no one in her past on whom she could rely. She promptly therefore fell a willing victim to Melbourne's good looks, urbane charm and sympathetic manner. Almost immediately she was writing in her diary that she had had 'a comfortable talk' with him, while he found in her company something that had been lacking all his life. Melbourne was a man who needed female company; his mother, with whom his ties had been extremely close, died in 1818; his marriage had been disastrous; his long association with Mrs Norton had led to the scandal of the divorce court, even though his name had been cleared of adultery; Emily Eden and Lady Holland were not women who could fill his emotional needs. Now, at last, Fate had thrown him into the closest relationship with a girl of eighteen, full of vitality and a zest for life, yet in many ways naive and surprisingly innocent, whom it was his official duty to serve and his pleasure to train to fit herself for her role as Queen. His success in so doing must be the measure of his right to be considered among the more important of Britain's prime ministers.

To assess Melbourne's influence over Victoria is more difficult than at first sight might appear in view of the amount of time they spent together and her obvious admiration and affection for him. Contemporaries commented on the way in which her eyes would follow him, while she in turn could easily move him to tears of tender affection. To him fell the task of initiating her into the inner mysteries of political life, which the role of the monarchy in a changing world made it essential for her to develop if co-operation between the Crown and the Cabinet were to be smooth. Melbourne's own difficulties with William IV had made him all too conscious of this need. In 1837 the Crown was still far from being the mouthpiece of its ministers, though the balance of power was rapidly tilting in favour of the latter. Every morning Victoria and Melbourne discussed political business. As he informed Peel later, the Queen insisted on being kept in the picture but disliked having to listen to long involved expositions of a theoretical nature for which her mind was too concrete. His method was to explain in simple terms the basic problems and practical issues on which action had been taken from day to day as the need arose. It was an *ad hoc* way of educating the Queen in her political duty which was both painless and effective. It had however its dangers and its limitations. With a prime minister of Melbourne's tact and charm it worked well, but it left her ill prepared to deal with men like Gladstone or Palmerston who refused to play the game under the rules which Melbourne's initiation had conditioned her to expect. Moreover in order to lighten the burden of her official duties he told her that it was unnecessary for her to study in detail the mass of routine papers submitted to her. Baron Stockmar was later of the opinion that her failure to discuss political business with Albert in the early days of their marriage arose not so much from her reluctance to do so as from her inability because her mastery of detail was inadequate. In the years to come this pre-digestion of her official correspondence was a task that the Prince took over himself. Meanwhile it was natural that the young Queen should rely so heavily on her ever-helpful Prime Minister. But this reliance had its disadvantages in that it bred, or perhaps it would be more accurate to say confirmed, in Victoria a spirit of partisanship that was increasingly to come into conflict with the growing political convention that the Crown must be neutral and stand above party conflict, though it is true that neither of her royal predecessors had done so. This partisan quality, which Victoria was never to lose, set the pattern of her relationships with her prime ministers throughout her reign; the nearer they conformed to that which existed between her and Melbourne the more successful they were.

Even in the early years of her reign Melbourne had less influence over his royal mistress than might at first sight be supposed; nor was he always capable of applying the brake to her impulsive actions. This was demonstrated first in the unfortunate affair of Lady Flora Hastings and secondly in the so-called 'Bedchamber Crisis'. In her early years as Queen the deeply buried resentment that she had felt against the domination of her mother, the Duchess of Kent, and the Comptroller of her household, Sir John Conroy, showed itself in a cold dislike of anybody associated with them. When therefore Victoria and Baroness Lehren observed a change in the figure of Lady Flora Hastings, her mother's Lady-in-Waiting, after she returned from Scotland in company with Sir John, they immediately assumed that she was with child by him. The rumours grew and the Court buzzed with gossip, a gossip that should have been stilled but was not when an examination carried out by two doctors pronounced Lady Flora to be a virgin. As the

Hastings were an important Tory family the affair got considerable publicity, and when later it was proved that Lady Flora had died of a malignant tumour Victoria's own popularity was much damaged. How much blame for the mishandling of this affair accrued to Melbourne it is difficult to establish. In its early stages he had followed a policy of drift and almost seems to have shared Victoria's suspicions, though whether this was due to his desire not to cross her or to the laxer moral code of his youth can only be surmised. He was not likely to be shocked if Lady Flora was indeed pregnant. Though his mother was a woman who managed her domestic life with the utmost discretion Melbourne himself was quite well aware that gossip had it that the first Viscount had not been in fact his father. What is surprising is not that he believed the rumours about Lady Flora but that, used as he was to irregularities in the best families, he handled this particular scandal with so little discretion and with so little finesse. He was certainly aware of the dangers of publicity yet he failed to impress on Victoria the need to behave in such a way as to scotch them, which argues that it was never he but always she who was in command of the situation.

This is true also of the Bedchamber Crisis, though here Lord Melbourne's conduct was constitutionally correct. In spite of Victoria's unflinching support his control of the Commons was slipping. His majority had been still further reduced in the general election of 1837, obligatory on the accession of a new monarch, the Cabinet was neither strong nor united while the difficulties of being forced to rely on the co-operation of the Radicals and the Irish remained. In addition there was unrest in Canada and in Jamaica. The former, too complicated to be dealt with here, had arisen from the antagonism between Upper and Lower Canada and between the French and British settlers. It was not an issue about which Melbourne cared deeply, and it did appear to present him with an opportunity to get rid of that difficult colleague the Earl of Durham by sending him to deal with the aftermath of rebellion. This he did effectively but in so high-handed a manner as to provoke criticism in Parliament which, because of Melbourne's lukewarm defence, led to the Earl's resignation and further criticism of the Government. The trouble in Jamaica, which had arisen out of the difficulties inherent in the freeing of the slaves, had more immediate repercussions. Melbourne's majority on a motion to suspend the Constitution of the island sank to four, so that he felt it necessary to resign. In spite of his personal grief – both he and Victoria were near to tears –

Melbourne did everything he could to make the change easy for the Queen, perhaps too easy, because in the hope of softening the blow he had left her with the belief that her Ladies, all of them Whigs, would not be changed. Apart from that he did everything in his power to reconcile the Queen to accepting Peel as her new minister with a good grace, and while negotiations for a new government were in progress he refrained from dining with her. What followed provides an interesting barometer of the extent of his influence over her political conduct when this went against the grain. Victoria did not like Tories and she did not like Peel; when therefore a misunderstanding arose as to whether Peel had insisted on replacing some or all of her Whig Ladies by Tories the indignant young woman manoeuvred Peel into declining to form a ministry and the whole Cabinet into supporting her, though Melbourne was somewhat disconcerted to discover that in fact Peel had only asked for some replacements. As a consequence Victoria gained her point and retained Melbourne as her prop and stay until his defeat in the Commons by one vote on a motion of no confidence in June 1841. Though by this time she was becoming more and more dependent on Albert, the Queen made a last effort to save Melbourne, insisting against his better judgement in appealing to the country. The verdict went against him and he resigned. By then her apprenticeship was over.

Melbourne's influence over Victoria was not confined to training her to become a constitutional monarch. Her education had been limited and her knowledge of the world around her bounded by her mother's rigid determination to keep her daughter from all doubtful contacts. Nowhere could she have found a better mentor to broaden her interests beyond those of the schoolroom and to mature her outlook than Lord Melbourne. The mornings were devoted to public business but he usually dined with the Queen three or four times a week; he was a frequent visitor at Windsor when the Queen was there and often they rode together. In these early years her diary is full of his conversations on these occasions, which Victoria found highly entertaining and amusing, and which ranged widely over personalities past and present, over literature and painting and the world as he had known it, so that inevitably she began to see through his eyes. Contemporaries were agreed as to the stimulating flood of paradox, irony and observation that poured forth with a richness that even Victoria found too abundant to record in her journal. Yet even here it is difficult to estimate the

permanence of Melbourne's influence because later it was to be overlaid by that of her 'dear Angel' Albert. Melbourne's own sense of values
was that of an eighteenth-century nobleman, tempered in his conversations with her by the moral and religious restraints that he felt necessary
when communicating with a young woman of impeccable moral
standards. To his credit he strove to imbue his pupil with some of his
own tolerance towards human frailties and some realisation that as
Queen she must learn to show at least some measure of social com-
plaisance towards persons whom she neither liked nor respected, trying
to tone down with a little grey the black and white of her moral palette.
But though he endeavoured to soften her judgement of people he did
little to waken in her any understanding of the social problems that confronted the new industrial urban Britain. In so far as Victoria ever
developed a social conscience, it was due to Albert. Nor did Melbourne
contribute anything towards her later emotional response to the idea of
empire.

Victoria was sad when Melbourne took his final leave of her as Prime
Minister and for some months continued to keep up a regular correspondence with him, in itself an act of some constitutional impropriety
which Baron Stockmar was terrified might reach the ears of her new
Prime Minister, Sir Robert Peel. In this, as in the Bedchamber Crisis,
the Queen went her own way; in both cases Melbourne allowed his
heart to rule his head. Nevertheless any significant part that he had
played both in the life of Britain and in that of her Queen was over by
1841. Life can be dull for prime ministers who have outlived their use-
fulness: this was to be Lord Melbourne's fate. When he died in 1848 his
death brought to Victoria only the gentle grief of nostalgia: the era of
her hero worship was long past. Even today it is as a man, as the husband
of Lady Caroline Lamb and as the guide, philosopher and friend of the
young Queen Victoria, and not as a prime minister *per se*, that Lord
Melbourne is best remembered. How then is one to sum up his place
in the gallery of Britain's prime ministers? He was responsible for no
innovations in constitutional practice, no important legislation. He
remained either unaware or disapproving of the changes that were taking place at home and in the colonies. His views on the role of government remained those of the eighteenth century. Even the extent of his
long-term influence over Victoria is easy to overestimate. Though
between her accession and her marriage he was the best-loved figure
in her life, 'dear Lord M.', later she adopted Albert's values rather than

his. Nevertheless during his term of office Lord Melbourne performed two valuable services for Britain. He held government together and maintained law and order until the country was ready to move forward under Peel. Above all he gave Victoria a breathing-space in which to prepare herself under his understanding and loving guidance for the tasks that lay ahead. She was the niece of George IV and William IV and a passionate, self-willed young woman when she came to the throne. Without the apprenticeship to constitutional monarchy that she served under Melbourne she might well have been a less successful queen.

BIOGRAPHICAL NOTES ON PERSONS MENTIONED IN THE TEXT, OTHER THAN PAST OR FUTURE PRIME MINISTERS, WHO WILL BE FOUND UNDER THE APPROPRIATE ESSAYS IN THE VOLUME

Lord Althrop, John Charles Spencer (1782–1845), later Earl Spencer. Leader of the House of Commons under Lord Grey. He was not a brilliant speaker, and preferred the life of a country landowner to that of a politician, but was completely trusted by friends and opponents alike because of his truthfulness and integrity.

The Benthamites. Followers of Jeremy Bentham (1748–1832), writer on ethics, jurisprudence, logic and political economy. Preached Utilitarianism based on the greatest good of the greatest number.

Lord Brougham, Henry Peter (1778–1868). Prominent lawyer. Defended Queen Caroline at her trial (1820). Active in promoting popular education, was instrumental in the founding of London University, the Society for the Diffusion of Useful Knowledge, etc. Became Lord Chancellor in 1830 and was created Baron Brougham and Vaux.

Conroy, Sir John, 1st baronet (1786–1854). Equerry to the Duke of Kent and after his death Comptroller of the Duchess's household. Intrigued to have the Duchess made Regent for Victoria if she succeeded to the throne before reaching the age of 21 in the hope of being the power behind the Duchess. Victoria detested him.

Lord Durham, John George Lambton (1791–1840). Created baron in 1830 and earl in 1832. Played an active part in the fight for the Reform Bill and headed the radical wing of the Whigs. Was sent as ambassador extraordinary to St Petersburg 1835–7 and sent to Canada to deal with the aftermath of the rebellion there in 1839. His subsequent report on British North America had considerable influence on subsequent British policy there.

Eden, Emily (1797–1869) daughter of William Eden 1st Baron Auckland. Traveller and novelist. Her 'The Semi-Attached Couple' and 'The Semi-Detached House' give very authentic pictures of the society in which she moved.

Fox, Elizabeth Vassall, Lady Holland (1770–1845). Born in Jamaica, married Sir Geofrey Webster, eloped with Lord Holland and married him 1797. A great Whig hostess who made Holland House a centre for politicians and men of letters.

O'Connell, Daniel (1775–1847). Called 'The Liberator'. A prominent Irish political leader. He led the successful fight for Catholic Emancipation (1829) and subsequently led the fight in the House of Commons for the repeal of the Union.

Baron von Stockmar, Christian Fredrich (1787–1863). Entered the service of Prince Leopold of Saxe-Coburg, afterwards King Leopold of the Belgians, as private physician in 1816 and remained the close friend and confidential advisor to the Coburgs.

SIR ROBERT PEEL

BY

ASA BRIGGS

Robert Peel, 2nd Bart., born 5 February 1788, son of Robert Peel, wealthy manufacturer. Educated at Harrow and Christ Church, Oxford. In 1809, aged 21, MP for Cashel, Tipperary; afterwards for Chippenham; University of Oxford 1817–29; Tamworth 1830–50; Under-secretary for War and the Colonies 1810; Chief Secretary for Ireland 1812–8; Home Secretary 1822–1827 and 1828–1830; Prime Minister, First Lord of the Treasury and Chancellor of the Exchequer 1834–5; Prime Minister 1841–5 (resigned) and 1845–6 (resigned). Died 2 July 1850. Married 1820 Julia Floyd; five sons and two daughters.

Sir Robert Peel, by John Linnell

SIR ROBERT PEEL

When an obscure journalist, W. T. Haly 'of the Parliamentary Galleries', published a book in 1843 called *The Opinions of Sir Robert Peel*, he told his readers in the preface that the book was designed to be 'a sort of dictionary of general political knowledge'.

Peel was then fifty-five years old and had been Prime Minister for two years, a strong Prime Minister, concerned personally and directly with the management of all the affairs of the country, economic and political, domestic and foreign. During the course of his long political life, which had begun in 1809 when his father bought him a seat in the House of Commons, he had expressed opinions on all aspects of national policy in a changing society. Just before he became Prime Minister in 1841 he had made a speech in Parliament attacking the Whig ministers in which he very characteristically posed two rhetorical questions which Haly could take as the motto of his book and print on his title page. 'Where is the man who has more explicitly declared than I have, his opinions upon all the great constitutional questions that have of late years been raised? . . . Have I not, when any question has been brought forward of important public interest, invariably expressed my opinions in plain and explicit terms?'

Yet the 'political knowledge' which Peel acquired and expressed and which Haly accumulated was essentially practical rather than theoretical. It could be and even recently has been set out in the form of maxims, almost as succinct as those of Mao Tse-tung. 'There seem to me very few facts, at least ascertainable facts, in politics.' 'The great art of government is to work by such instruments as the world supplies.' 'No government can exist which does not control and restrain the popular sentiments.' 'I am not sure that those who clamour most suffer most.' 'There are many things which I know to be morally wrong, with which neither I nor you can interfere in the way of legislation.' 'The longer I live, the more clearly do I see the folly of yielding a rash and precipitate assent to any political measure.'

Peel had great intellectual power – he had been outstandingly successful in his examinations at Oxford in 1808 only one year before he entered Parliament – but it was the kind of intellectual power that drove him with unremitting industry from logical analysis first to determined advocacy and second to executive action. Harriet Martineau, who admired the way in which he brought about the repeal of the Corn Laws in 1846, his greatest and most controversial act, called him 'a great doer of the impossible'. Necessarily this meant that he frequently changed his mind on major issues, as he did in the case of the Corn Laws, whilst maintaining great consistency in the way in which he confronted every issue when it arose. In describing how he had selected extracts from Peel's writings and speeches Haly observed that scrupulous care had been taken 'never to injure a context' and that the extracts had been assembled irrespective of their specific content. Peel would have strongly approved of this approach. Knowledge for him was always related to context: the content of what he said at particular times, he argued, had to be interpreted and re-interpreted in the light of his unceasing endeavour to discover the necessary operational truth for the particular occasion. His contemporary and admirer, Guizot, who as Premier of France in 1847 and 1848 had to cope with revolutionary 'political knowledge' of a very different variety, wrote a book about Peel in 1856 in which he called him 'a man of essentially practical mind, consulting facts at every step, just as the mariner consults the face of heaven'. His close political colleague and equally fervent admirer, the Duke of Wellington, testified in the House of Lords after Peel's death that his oustanding quality was veracity: 'I never had in the whole course of my life, the slightest reason for suspecting that he stated any thing which he did not firmly believe to be the fact.'

Yet not everyone was unduly impressed by these qualities. Walter Bagehot wrote an essay on 'the character of Sir Robert Peel' in the same year as Guizot published his book. He acknowledged the veracity and the fact that Peel did not get 'into scrapes', like Lord John Russell, and he admitted that he got nearer than anyone else to 'our definition of a constitutional statesman'. Bagehot's half cynical definition of such a statesman, however, was that he combined 'the powers of a first-rate man and the creed of a second-rate man'. And so the brilliant essayist went on, comparing Peel unfavourably with his Harrow schoolfellow, Byron, whilst recognising that Byron could never have been a statesman. Byron's mind was volcanic: the lava flowed. 'The mind of Peel was the exact opposite of this. His opinions far more resembled the daily accumulating, insensible deposits of a rich alluvial soil. The great stream of time flows on with all things on its surface; and slowly, grain by grain, a mould of wise experience is unconsciously left on the still, extended intellect. You scarcely think of such a mind as acting; it always seems acted upon.'

From his mid-Victorian vantage point Bagehot looked back to Peel's early career as a member of Lord Liverpool's Government – Chief Secretary for Ireland from 1812 to 1818 and Home Secretary from 1822 to 1827 – commenting *en passant* that he had once defended the attitude of the authorities at Peterloo in 1819, the passing of the Six Acts, the Imposition of Tests and the rule of Orangemen. He had been once known, indeed, as 'Orange Peel'. He had started office as Under-secretary for War and the Colonies from 1810 to 1812, 'the chosen representative of a gentry untrained to great affairs, absorbed in a great war, only just recovering from the horror of a great revolution.' That was the original substratum.

'From a certain peculiarity of intellect and fortune, he was never in advance of his time. Of almost all the great measures with which his name is associated, he attained great eminence as an opponent before he attained even greater eminence as their advocate. On the Corn Laws, on the currency, on the amelioration of the criminal code, on Catholic emancipation . . . he was not one of the earliest labourers, or quickest converts. He did not bear the burden and heat of the day; other men laboured, and he entered into their labours. As long as these questions remained the property of first-class intellects, as long as they were confined to philanthropists or speculators, as long as they were only advocated by austere intangible Whigs, Sir Robert Peel was against them. So soon as these same measures, by the progress of time, the striving of understanding, the conversion of receptive minds, be-came the property of second-class intellects, Sir Robert Peel became possessed of them also. He was converted at the conversion of the average man.'

This alternative verdict is interesting but inadequate. It leaves out Peel's courage and it underestimates the power of prejudice not only inside Peel's own party – the wartime party of Pitt, which Peel more than any other man transformed into a viable Conservative party – but inside 'the average man'. Nor does it place in European perspective, as Guizot was able to do, Peel's character and achievements as a

Conservative statesman. The time perspective was wrong also, for we can now see clearly, far more clearly than in 1856, that without Peel's reforms there would have been no golden age of Victorian Britain. Bagehot was right, however, to add to his verdict that Peel was 'a great administrator':

'Civilisation requires this. In a simple age work may be difficult but it is scarce. There are fewer people and everybody wants fewer things. . . . Anybody can understand a rough despotic community – a small buying class of nobles, a small selling class of traders, a large producing class of serfs, are much the same in all quarters of the globe; but a free intellectual community is a complicated network of ramified relations interlacing and passing hither and thither, old and new – some of fine city weaving, some of gross agricultural construction. You are never sure what effect any force or any change may produce on a framework so exquisite and so involved. Govern as you may, it will be a work of great difficulty, labour and responsibility.'

Whatever our twentieth-century verdict on Peel, we must continue to take account of the relevant components to which Bagehot directed attention – not just intellect, fortune and character, but 'the progress of time' and the increasing complexity of society. We must note that Peel was not only able but rich, that the country in which he lived was only partially industrialised but that it was becoming more and more industrialised each year, that between the world of the Six Acts and the year of Peel's death in 1850 Luddites had given way to Chartists, broadsheets to newspapers and stage-coaches to railways. Given the flux, government depended not only on making wise choices but on making them at the right time. Moreover, because government was increasingly difficult, it had both a political and a moral dimension. The former was altered but not transformed after the passing of the Great Reform Bill of 1832, which gave the vote to large numbers of middle-class people: the latter was to be transformed mainly after Peel's death under the influence of Gladstone who started life as a High Tory – higher than Peel had ever been – and after the splits of 1846 became a 'Peelite'.

As for the added sense of responsibility, there was no one in the country who was more clear about this than Peel. Dedicated to an ideal of public service and as willing as Wellington to respond to the call, he felt many of the strains. As Prime Minister, he was general manager rather than co-ordinator, and there is no more systematic evidence of the strains of difficult management in any age than we can find in the voluminous private papers of Peel. Others could play with issues: he had to settle them. And he knew the cost. One of the most revealing letters he wrote was in 1845, when his party was already bitterly divided, particularly on the Corn Laws, and he himself was being subjected to unparalleled pressures:

'The fact is that the state of public business while Parliament sits is becoming in many ways a matter of most serious concern. I defy the [Prime] Minister of this country to perform properly the duties of his office – to read all he ought to read, including the whole of the foreign correspondence; to keep up the constant communication with the Queen *and the Prince*; to see all whom he ought to see; to superintend the grant of honours and the disposal of civil and ecclesiastical patronage; to write with his own hand to every person of note who chooses to write to him; to be prepared for every debate, including the most trumpery concerns; to do all these indispensable things, and also sit in the House of Commons eight hours a day for 118 days. It is impossible for me not to feel that the duties are incompatible, and above all human strength – at least above mine.'

Peel had great human strength. He needed every ounce of it. But he had to work unbelievably hard. In an age when exploited working men were pressing for a Ten Hours Bill to shorten the length of the working day, Peel never applied the limitations of a Ten Hours Bill to himself.

Peel was profoundly interested in the fortunes of working men in the changing society. 'What struck me above all in conversation with him,' wrote Guizot, 'was his constant and passionate preoccupation with the state of the working classes in England.' He described them as 'a disgrace as well as a danger to our civilisation'. His own fortune and background were directly relevant both in this connection and in the broader context of the development of his opinions. He was born in Lancashire, the son of one of England's greatest and richest industrialists, who had made a fortune out of the cotton industry, and the grandson of a man who had started life as a small Lancashire yeoman farmer. He never tried to hide this background, and he was often taunted for it by members of his own party who were willing to nickname him 'the Spinning Jenny'.

When during his great ministry of 1841 to 1846 he was forced to grapple with economic issues which fundamentally affected the interests of landlords, farmers, industrialists, traders and working men alike, he was fully aware of what was at stake in each case. He was an enlightened landlord, an improving farmer who was proud of his model farm at Drayton, and leader of a party which was still dominated by the agricultural interest. Yet his own origins lay in industry, and his father had risen by self-help not by privilege to a position of influence, whereby he could buy his son a seat in the House of Commons where he already sat himself. If any man was fitted by social upbringing to reconcile conflicting interests in an industrialising society, it was Peel. Significantly Richard Cobden, leader of the Anti-Corn Law League (whose love-hate relationship with Peel is one of the fascinating themes of the 1840s), said in a speech long before Peel decided to repeal the Corn Laws, 'I do not altogether like to give up Peel. You see he is a Lancashire man'. Likewise, Ebenezer Elliott, the Anti-Corn Law rhymer, commented in 1842, 'Peel, I have long thought, understands our position, and will do his best to prevent the coming catastrophe'.

Neither Elliott nor Cobden completely understood Peel's own position. After he had repealed the Corn Laws Cobden wrote to him privately urging him to dissolve Parliament and go to the country on the cry of 'Peel and Free Trade'. 'You represent the *idea* of the age,' he said, 'and it has no other representative among statesmen.' Peel could never have contemplated himself playing such a role. He did not want repeal of the Corn Laws to ruin agriculture or to destroy the power of the landlords; he disliked the thought of 'a dull succession of enormous manufacturing towns, connected by railways, intersecting abandoned tracks which it was no longer profitable to cultivate'; he tried to give guarantees to agriculture, maintaining that 'the land is subject to particular burdens' and that compensation was necessary in some form or other to replace the unconditional loss of duty; and he refused to consider seriously anything like a new middle-class system of government which would have meant revision of the tax system and further assaults, of the kind the Anti-Corn Law League had specialised in, on the social position of the landlord. Repeal, in his view, had become necessary by 1845 in the national interest – and because of what was happening in Ireland – and not in the interests of one class: its object was 'to terminate a conflict which . . . would soon place in hostile collision great and powerful classes in this country'. His reply to Cobden, therefore was reserved and dignified, tempered, perhaps, with mild contempt.

'If you say that I individually at this moment embody or personify an idea be it so. Then I must be very careful that, being the organ and representative of a prevailing conception of the public mind, I do not sully that which I represent by warranting the suspicion even, that I am using the power it confers for any personal object. . . . I must also ask you to consider this. After the passing of the Corn and Customs Bill, considering how much trade has suffered of late from delays, debates and uncertainty as to the final result, does not this country stand in need of *repose*? Would not a desperate political conflict throughout the length and breadth of the land impair or defer the beneficial effect of the passing of those measures?'

It was because Peel had an instinctive feeling for 'repose' and a deep-rooted fear of disorder (strongly influenced by his early experiences in Ireland) that he was Conservative. He did not wish to see ancient institutions lose their hold or crucial decisions about national policy be determined by 'agitation'. 'This country has been governed better than any other country on earth,' he argued in 1831 in the middle of the debates on the Great Reform Bill to which he was opposed. A few months later, when it was clear that the Reform Bill would be passed, he told a colleague that it was the task of their party

'to teach young inexperienced men . . . charged with the trust of the Government that, though they may be backed by popular clamour, they shall not override on the first spring tide of excitement every barrier and breakwater raised against popular impulses. . . . [and] that the carrying of extensive changes in the Constitution without previous deliberation shall not be a holiday task.'

Two years after that, when the Reform Act was a *fait accompli*, the Tamworth Manifesto, an address to his own constituents, urged the necessity of preserving limited constitutional monarchy and the rights of each branch of the legislature, of maintaining the establishment, property and privileges of the Church, and of resisting a series of specious reforms which would together convert Britain into a democratic republic. In 1848, when revolution was sweeping Europe and he had been out of office for more than two years, Peel reaffirmed the same convictions. 'I hope the people of this country has sense enough to comprehend the lesson which is written for their instruction and will cling the more strongly to their own institutions. Democracy on the continent is teaching us what it can do for the security of Life, Liberty and Property, as compared with Monarchy.'

Peel's intellectual and administrative ability as Prime Minister between 1841 and 1846 was one of the factors that saved Britain from revolution. He made necessary economic adjustments to the fiscal and banking system which ensured long-term economic prosperity just as he had made necessary religious adjustments in 1829 when he and Wellington (against their previous opinions and inclinations) carried Catholic emancipation. He was never reactionary. In his very first speech to the House of Commons after the general election which followed the passing of the Great Reform Bill he had looked to the future, not to the past, and had accepted what had happened without approving of it: he had added for good measure that 'he was for reforming every institution that really required reform; but he was for doing it gradually, dispassionately, and deliberately in order that reform might be lasting'. Thereafter he deliberately set out to win the support of middle-class manufacturers, traders and shopkeepers as well as aristocrats and country gentlemen. 'We deny that we are separated by any line of interest or any other line of demarcation, from the middling classes', he exclaimed in 1834 when for a hundred days he was Prime Minister for the first time with a majority of Members of the House of Commons against him. His predecessor, the languid Whig Lord Melbourne, who had been dismissed by William IV, belonged to the aristocracy: did not he, Peel, by contrast proclaim the possibilities of something more than continuingly exclusive aristocratic government?

'What was the grand charge against myself – that the King had sent for the son of a cotton-spinner . . . in order to make him Prime Minister of England. Did I feel that by any means a reflection on me? . . . No; but does it not make me, and ought it not make you, gentlemen, do all you can to reserve to other sons of other cotton-spinners the same opportunities, by the same system of laws under which this country has so long flourished, of arriving by the same honourable means at the like destination?'

When during the ministry of 1841 to 1846 he prepared the great budgets which involved drastic reductions in protective duties and in the range of articles subject to tariff protection, the re-imposition as a fiscal imperative of the Income Tax, and the balancing of the Government's accounts not by expedients but by deliberately planned policies, he was not making concessions either to vested interests or to ideological groups, but acting in conformity with his own convictions. And when he was converted to belief in free trade in corn, the biggest fiscal reform he could make, he was willing to provoke the interests without accepting any free trade ideology. He was influenced by industrial depression in England before he was forced, along with his colleagues, to make up his mind about the emergency situation in Ireland. 'Can we vote public money for the sustenance of any considerable portion of the people, on account of actual or apprehended scarcity,' he asked his colleagues in November 1845, 'and maintain in full operation the existing restrictions on the free import of grain?'

Once he had been converted, Peel felt that he could win working-class support on social grounds as well as middle-class support on economic grounds. It was not theory that had made him change his mind but experience: 'You may talk of improving the habits of the working classes, introducing education amongst them, purifying their dwellings, improving their cottages; but, believe me, the first step towards improvement of their social condition is an abundance of food.'

The change could be defended, he argued, on Conservative rather than on Radical grounds. 'I have thought it consistent with true Conservative policy, to promote so much of happiness and contentment among the people that the voice of disaffection should no longer be heard, and thoughts of the dissolution of our institutions should be forgotten in the midst of physical enjoyment.'

When the Corn Laws were in the last stages of being repealed, Peel dealt with what was basically the same point in his peroration to his last speech in the Commons on the subject, a speech which is too impregnated with self-praise to appeal without qualification to posterity:

'I shall leave a name execrated by every monopolist who . . . clamours for protection because it accrues to his individual benefit; but it may be that I shall leave a name sometimes remembered with expressions of goodwill in the abodes of those whose lot it is to labour, and to earn their daily bread by the sweat of their brow, when they shall recruit their exhausted strength with abundant and untaxed food, the sweeter because it is no longer leavened by a sense of injustice.'

In dwelling on this theme Peel was to win short-term dividends. He was cheered in the streets as he left the House of Commons, he was praised in the provincial newspapers and in *Punch*, and when he died in 1850 after a riding accident in the heart of London, popular funds were raised throughout the country to perpetuate his memory in statues and parks. The pennies of the poor were collected without difficulty. 'I thought he had a great hold on the country,' wrote Sir James Graham, who had been his Home Secretary and *alter ego* in the ministry of 1841 to 1846, 'but had no idea it was so deep and strong and general as now appears.'

The short-term dividends acquired long-term value as the country moved into quieter and more comfortable times during the middle years of the nineteenth century, what W. L. Burn called 'the age of equipoise'. We can see in retrospect how important Peel's conception of politics was in a political system where the majority still did not have the vote. 'I have a strong belief,' he had declared during the debates on repeal, 'that the greatest object which we or any other government can contemplate should be to elevate the social condition of that class of the people with whom we are brought into no direct relationship by their elective franchise.' Peel recognised that if these people were to remain disaffected and opposed to government, there would be such tensions and upheavals that demands for large-scale parliamentary and social reform might prove impossible to resist.

None the less, through the act of repealing the Corn Laws Peel broke up the party which he had laboriously built and faced an angry Opposition in Parliamen which not only pushed him from power but made the process painful and at times humiliating for him. The fact that he had been such a powerful parliamentarian, in many respects the most powerful of his times, made the fall more dramatic. In 1836, when he was in opposition, a parliamentary commentator, John Grant, described in detail how Peel was especially effective 'in the serious mode of address'.

'No man in the House can appeal with a tittle of the effect with which he can to the fears of his audience. . . . The deepest stillness pervades the House while he is speaking. Even in the gallery, where there is generally a great deal of noise from the exits and entrances of strangers, the falling of a pin might be heard. All eyes are fixed on Sir Robert.'

Grant went on to note how Peel, who loved applause in Parliament, would often turn his face round to his own party and his back on the Speaker when he was

'urging any argument which appears to him particularly forcible, and which he thinks likely to be received by them with particular applause . . . which is scarcely ever refused him. . . . Never had the leader of a party a more complete ascendancy over that party than has this Tory Coryphaeus over the Conservatives in the House of Commons.'

All the same, Grant recognised that Peel had his 'sore points'. He could be too 'suspicious' and hold things back from his own followers. He was vulnerable in debate when anyone contrasted his professions and performance. Above all he was sensitive to one particular line of attack.

'There is not a man in the House more sensitive on the subject of honour than Sir Robert. You may apply to him epithets which are synonymous with fool, blockhead, &c, if you please, and he utters not a word of complaint; you may brand him with the name of bigot, either in politics or religion if you are so inclined, and he murmurs not a word of resentment; but charge him with anything, either in his private or public capacity, inconsistent with the character of a man of honour, and that moment he demands an explanation.'

There had always been some Conservatives who disliked Peel both on private and public grounds. Lord Ashley, for example, the Evangelical sponsor of the Ten Hours Bill, said that Peel reminded him of 'an iceberg with a slight thaw on the surface': all Peel's 'affinities', he maintained, were 'towards wealth and capital'. There was also a loosely organised cluster of Tory country gentlemen, each priding himself on his independence and distrusting everything that Peel had ever done – from his currency measures of 1819 ('the return to gold'), down through his creation of the Metropolitan Police and his emancipation of the Roman Catholics ten years later, his support of the New Poor Law of 1834 and the Municipal Reform Act of 1835, down to his fiscal policies of the 1840s. These Tories not only thought differently from Peel: they felt differently too. At heart they were critical of industry, cities, international trade and most foreigners. Their protectionism in 1846 was only one facet of their philosophy, and their philosophy was grounded in a way of life.

Peel was only half right when he wrote to a friend in 1845 that 'people like a certain degree of obstinacy and presumption in a Minister. They abuse him for dictation and arrogance, but they all like being governed'. There may have been reason behind such a claim so long as 'the country party' could not find alternative sources of leadership, but by 1845 Tory critics of Peel were listening intently to the gibes of the young Disraeli, whose background and personality were even more different from theirs than Peel's, and by early 1846 to the savage onslaughts of Sir George Bentinck, who possessed impeccable social qualifications, including membership of the Jockey Club. When the break finally came, Peel remarked that he was more surprised that the union had lasted so long inside his party than that it had been 'ultimately severed'. Graham had remarked earlier that 'the country gentlemen cannot be more ready to give us the death-blow than we are prepared to receive it'.

Disraeli, in particular, revelled in the opportunity of exploiting old memories of treachery and charges of misappropriation. He accused Peel of lacking any ideas of his own and of betraying every interest that had looked to him; and he well deserved Ponsonby's handsome tribute: 'I doubt if any classic orator of Rome or England ever did anything so well as you crucified Peel. Had I been him, I would have rushed at and murdered you, or run home and hanged myself.' Yet Disraeli was not content with a crucifixion scene. He profited from the divisions of 1845 and 1846 to enunciate far-reaching ideas of party which went much further than Peel himself or current usage accepted. While Peel looked to posterity to justify him, Disraeli pointed out that posterity was a limited assembly, 'not much more numerous than the planets', and that in the last resort free politics were more dangerous than free trade. He had a word of constitutional advice which could be set alongside Peel's maxims: 'Maintain the line of demarcation between parties, for it is only by maintaining the independence of parties that you maintain the integrity of public-men, and the power and influence of public men.' Disraeli in later life was to hold to this doctrine no more than he was to hold to the doctrine of free trade. Yet the fact that it was advanced so brilliantly at the time was an important by-product of the fiscal debate.

Peel himself stuck to his own doctrines of public service when pressed, very similar to the doctrines of Wellington. 'I am as proud of the confidence as any man can be, which a great party has placed in me; still I never can admit that he owes any personal obligation to those Members who have placed him in a certain position.' He made this statement not in relation to the Corn Laws but to the Maynooth grant, a grant to a Catholic college in Ireland which angered many members of his party and produced some strange temporary alliances. 'I claim for myself the right to give to my sovereign at any time,' he concluded, 'that advice which I believe the interests of the country require.' Taking the evidence of his career as a whole, it seems likely that he would have been willing to repeat this claim with equal force on the last day of judgement.

BIBLIOGRAPHY

Norman Gash, *Mr Secretary Peel* (Longmans, 1961); *Sir Robert Peel*, (Longmans, 1971); C. S. Parker, *Sir Robert Peel from his Private Papers* (3 vols, 1891–9); G. Kitson Clark, *Peel and the Conservative Party* (1929)

PART TWO

THE PRIME MINISTERS

LORD JOHN RUSSELL TO EDWARD HEATH

INTRODUCTION BY ROBERT BLAKE

THE PRIME MINISTER 1835–1974

THE PRIME MINISTER 1835-1974

In the period with which we are concerned the premiership became, more even than before, the goal on which politicians set their sights, the final object of their ambition. Melbourne was perhaps an exception. When sent for by the King he told his private secretary that 'he thought it a damned bore and was in many minds what he should do – be Minister or no'. His secretary ('a vulgar familiar impudent fellow', according to Greville, from whom the story comes) replied 'Why damn it, such a position never was occupied by any Greek or Roman, and, if it only lasts two months, it is well worth while to have been Prime Minister of England'. Melbourne decided to accept. A hundred and twenty-one years later Clement Attlee quoted the same expression in ironically congratulating Anthony Eden on his accession to office at a time when an election was generally regarded as imminent. Few people after Melbourne would have regarded the premiership as 'a damned bore'. Nearly all of them would have privately echoed the sentiments of his secretary.

Melbourne's own career symbolised and emphasised the most important single change which affected the post of prime minister since the days of Walpole – the change from the concept of government as the King's government to government as party government. Lord Liverpool, the Duke of Wellington, Grey, Melbourne himself, insofar as they reflected on the matter, would have thought of themselves primarily as servants of the Crown – and of course there is a sense in which prime ministers still rightly think of themselves in that light today. The difference is that until 1832 the Crown could within certain limits choose a prime minister who would be sure to win an ensuing general election. This was because of the 'influence' which automatically went to him by virtue of his position as First Lord of the Treasury. It is significant that from 1715 to 1835 no government actually lost a general election. Even in 1830 Wellington was not defeated at the polls. In such a situation, although the Prime Minister had to be able to manage Parliament and was liable to be pushed out if he was palpably incompetent to do so, it was even more vital for him to manage the monarch.

All this was changed – though not immediately – with the events of 1834-5. In November 1834 the death of Earl Spencer and the succession of his son Lord Althorp to the peerage created a vacancy in the leadership of the House of Commons. Rather than accept the nomination of Lord John Russell, William IV in effect dismissed Melbourne, making the same interpretation of his own constitutional role that his father had made when dismissing the Fox-North coalition half a century earlier. He assumed that Peel, after a few weeks in which to collect his forces together, would dissolve, and win the next general election even as the younger Pitt had done in 1784. But events did not work out that way, nor did either Wellington, or Peel who took office with reluctance, expect them to do so. The world of 1834 was very different from that of 1784, and not only because of the Reform Act. For many years past 'royal government' had been running down. By the 1820s there were signs that the supply of patronage – the oil that greased the moving parts of the old machine – was beginning to be insufficient. Successive Tory governments in 1818, 1820, 1826 and 1830 managed to win, but with increasing difficulty. The general election of January 1835, however, saw the first clear decision against a prime minister who had the avowed support of the King. Peel tried to carry on, but the Whigs were determined to force him out. After numerous defeats he resigned in April. The King was obliged to send for Melbourne and to accept Lord John Russell as Leader of the House. It was by the old standards a humiliating rebuff.

Never again was a monarch to dismiss a prime minister, although some monarchs continued to talk as if they could, and in the Ulster crisis of 1912-14 such a course was urged by the hotter headed Unionists. When once it was clear that the Crown could no longer ensure electoral success for its own nominee there was really no choice between the risk of open political partisanship which the Crown could not in the end survive, or withdrawal to the position of neutrality which prevails today.

Yet the logic of the situation was not at once apparent. The Bedchamber Crisis of May 1839 is one example. Neither Peel nor Melbourne would have behaved quite as they did if the Crown had been regarded as a neutral factor in politics, and the situation was made no easier by Melbourne's dual role as Prime Minister and Queen's Private Secretary – a combination which was ended soon after her marriage to Prince Albert who took on that task himself. But as late as 1841 the Prince was horrified to find that money from the Privy Purse had been used towards Whig expenses in the general election of that year. The Queen was, moreover, still sufficiently imbued with the notion that the government were 'her' servants to declare privately that she would not have agreed to a dissolution if she had expected Melbourne to lose.

Although the 1830s were marked by this important change from Crown government to party government, it would be a mistake to think that it was the sort of party government which we know today. The Prime Minister did, it is true, have to keep his party behind him if he was to survive, as Peel found to his cost in 1846. But parties were not the cohesive all embracing organisations familiar to us. They were ill disciplined groups, each with a fringe of those independent members whom Disraeli described as members who could not be depended upon. If power had passed from the Crown it had not yet moved to the electorate. In fact the period from 1835 to 1868 saw the heyday of the supremacy of the House of Commons – the situation so brilliantly described by Bagehot, at the very moment that it was on the verge of being transformed into something quite different. The Cabinet was a committee of the legislature. The House of Commons rather than the electorate made and unmade governments. Six parliaments were elected between 1841 and 1868. In the case of five of them the House of Commons had brought down at least one administration, sometimes two, before its dissolution. The only exception was the parliament of 1859 to 1865 which Palmerston controlled virtually from start to finish.

This period of governmental instability, more reminiscent of the French 3rd and 4th Republics than the British system of today, began to change in the 1870s. Whether or not it was a matter of cause and effect, the Reform Act of 1867 was followed by a series of general elections which gave far more decisive results in the House than anything since 1841 and this trend continued after further extensions of the franchise. It was symbolic of the new pattern of politics that in 1868 Disraeli resigned on the morrow of the general election without waiting to test the opinion of the House, so clear had been the verdict of the polls. Some people grumbled and said his conduct was unconstitutional, but Gladstone reluctantly followed the same course in 1874, and Disraeli repeated his action in 1880. Since then it has only been in highly exceptional circumstances (e.g. 1924 or 1974 when the election result was ambiguous), that a Prime Minister has failed to accept at once what appears to be the decision of the electorate. Even in 1964, despite one or two suggestions to the contrary, Sir Alec Douglas-Home resigned as soon as the results were in, though Labour's victory was by the narrowest margin ever known.

A corollary of this development has been the rareness since the 1880s of any government falling to an adverse vote in the House. Gladstone was defeated on a major bill (Irish Home Rule) in 1886. He promptly dissolved Parliament and lost the ensuing election. Rosebery resigned on an adverse vote in 1894, but he need not have done so, for the issue was a minor one. Ramsay MacDonald was defeated in 1924, and followed the same course with the same result as Gladstone thirty-eight years earlier. The last occasion on which the House can be said to have forced the Prime Minister to resign was the fall of Neville Chamberlain in 1940, but he was not actually defeated. It was a massive slump in his normally overwhelming parliamentary majority which decided him to go.

From the 1870s onwards party government in the modern sense has prevailed. It is during this period that the mass party organisations in the country established themselves – a recognition that power has shifted to the electorate. Gladstone appreciated the change when he wrote to Rosebery in the 1880s: 'What is outside Parliament seems to me to be fast mounting, nay to have already mounted to an importance much exceeding what is inside'. The Birmingham 'Caucus', the National Union of Conservative Associations – these were the typical institutions of the new era. Prime Ministers had become heads of one or other of two great political parties with electoral committees or associations in almost every constituency. Of course Peel and Melbourne, Russell and Derby had also been leaders of parties. The difference after 1867 was that Gladstone and Disraeli led parties which not only operated in Parliament but had spread their roots throughout the country.

By a natural process of development the leaders of these parties came to symbolise the cause or causes for which they stood. It is often alleged that this personification of politics is a new phenomenon, caused in part by the exposure to the mass media. It is no doubt true that every elector nowadays knows what Mr Heath and Mr Wilson look like. They would not be as lucky as Peel, who escaped assassination because the lunatic who intended to kill him shot his private secretary instead. But by the time of Gladstone and Disraeli most electors must from cartoons and other representations have had a fair idea of the appearance of the great rivals, and there can be no question that their personalities dominated the whole political scene, not merely, as for example in the case of Pitt and Fox, the House of Commons. Writing of the passions provoked by the Eastern crisis in 1878 Henry Loch, Governor of the Isle of Man commented.

'. . . when the questions are discussed, which they are morning, noon and night by all classes and by both sexes there is an intensity of excitement that frequently breaks out in the most violent language – and it is all *purely personal*, the divergence of opinion being not so much upon the merits of the questions which seem seldom understood, but upon the feelings that are entertained either towards Lord Beaconsfield or Mr Gladstone.'

There is nothing new during the last hundred years in this polarisation of personalities. It depends upon the personalities. There have been many times since the days of Disraeli and Gladstone when it did not apply – for example after Disraeli's death when Northcote and Salisbury opposed Gladstone. Again between 1902 and 1911 when on the one side Balfour and on the other Campbell-Bannerman and Asquith led their respective parties, one may well doubt whether personality was particularly relevant. Forty-five years later with Churchill and Attlee it was relevant, and also during the period when first Mr Macmillan confronted Hugh Gaitskell and later Sir Alec Douglas-Home and then Mr Heath confronted Mr Wilson. But there is no clear trend. We can go back to a time before the great duel between Disraeli and Gladstone and find Lord Shaftesbury writing after the election of 1857. 'There seems to be no measure, no principle, no cry, to influence men's minds and determine elections; it is simply, "Were you or were you not? Are you, or are you not, for Palmerston?"'

The question of personality leads to the question of power – one of the most keenly debated subjects in the historiography of the post of Prime Minister. Are Prime Ministers more powerful now than ever before? Has 'Prime Ministerial' Government replaced Cabinet Government? If so when has the change taken place? What are the reasons for it? Is it a good thing? How is it related to Presidential Government in the American mode? No one can deny that a great change has taken place since the era described by Bagehot. It is perhaps doubtful whether even in his day one could correctly describe the Cabinet as 'a board of control chosen by the legislature' or the Prime Minister as 'elected by the representatives of the people'. Certainly such descriptions would be inadequate in the 1970s. Indeed it could be argued that they have been inadequate for the last hundred years, although it was not until L. S. Amery's *Thoughts on the Constitution* (the Chichele Lectures delivered in Oxford soon after the end of the second World War), that the all-pervasive Bagehot myth was finally blown away.

Bagehot's picture of the working of the constitution does not correspond to modern reality. Nor did it correspond to reality as long ago as the era of Disraeli and Gladstone; the important question is what changes have taken place since then. The most interesting and controversial discussion of this matter is the late Mr R. H. S. Crossman's introduction to the new edition of Bagehot's *The English Constitution* published in 1963 just before Mr Crossman himself became a member of the Labour Cabinet. His theme is that the power of the Prime Minister has enormously increased during and since the second World War. Bagehot had described the Cabinet as 'the hyphen which joins, the buckle which fastens, the legislative part of the state to the executive'. According to Mr Crossman that role is now fulfilled by a single man. 'The post war epoch has seen the final transformation of Cabinet Government into Prime Ministerial Government.'

Mr Crossman discerns three causes for the change. There has been the growth of the power of party which has reduced that of the individual MP, diminished his chances of defying party orthodoxy and removed the real debate on political issues 'from the floor of the Commons to the secrecy of the Committee rooms upstairs'. This enhances the power of the Prime Minister in his capacity as the party leader. 'Politics is inevitably personified and simplified in the public mind into a battle between two super-leaders – appointed for life or until they are removed by an intra party *coup d'état*.' Secondly there was the ending of Cabinet informality by the creation of a secretariat to keep the minutes and circulate papers. This occurred soon after Lloyd George became Prime Minister, and inevitably enhanced the Prime Minister's powers by giving him what was tantamount to a department of his own.

Lloyd George was also involved in the third of Mr Crossman's suggested causes of change – the unification of the civil service, with the Permanent Under Secretary of the Treasury at its head. This occurred in September 1919 when Sir Warren Fisher persuaded the Prime Minister that the talents of civil servants would be better recognised and used if people could move from department to department, instead of staying for the whole career in the same one – the prevailing practice hitherto. A further regulation 'laid down that the consent of the Premier (which in practice meant the head of the civil service) would be required in all departments to the appointment of permanent heads and their deputies.' The upshot, so Mr Crossman argues, was the creation of a 'group of super-bureaucrats each confident that he can take charge at a few weeks' notice of a Ministry of which he has had no previous experience'. This has replaced the old system of a cluster of departments with their own traditions, styles and methods of recruitment.

Here Mr Crossman perhaps proves too much. The power of the Prime Minister over his Cabinet colleagues may well have been increased by the unification of the civil service, for Ministers no longer appoint to the permanent headships of their departments, but Mr Crossman agrees that it is not really the Prime Minister who takes over that role. In practice it is the head of the Civil Service. So, if the Prime Minister has gained power as regards Ministers, can it not be argued also that he has in some measure lost it to the 'super-bureaucrats'? This raises a wider question. Is it clear that Peel who was his own Secretary to the Cabinet and the Treasury and who supervised every department of state, had a less powerful position than Sir Alec Douglas-Home who was operating when the changes described by Mr Crossman should have had ample time to become fully effective? Prime Ministerial power is not a simple or straightforward concept. There is obviously one sense in which any modern prime minister has more power than Peel, Gladstone, Lloyd George or Neville Chamberlain, because government itself controls a far wider part of national life than it ever has before. The real question is the balance of power within the governmental system at this or that moment of time. It is doubtful whether the change has been as definite as Mr Crossman implies. In an illuminating study of the British constitution – *The Body Politic* (1969) – Mr Ian Gilmour who like Mr Crossman has come into office subsequently (though on the opposite political side) puts the point clearly.

'The writers of the Prime Ministerial school make the same mistake as the Whig historians made about George III and the monarchy: they overrate his power today and underrate the power he had in the past.

The development of the office has not been all one way. The progress towards Caesarism has been uneven and its starting point uncertain.'

Lord Morley in his *Walpole* (1889) said: 'The flexibility of the Cabinet system allows the Prime Minister to take upon himself a power not inferior to that of a dictator, provided always that the House of Commons will stand by him'. Morley was writing about the first prime minister, but he certainly had in mind the office as he knew it. He had been a member of Gladstone's Cabinet in 1886. He perceived the great power which lay in the hands of someone determined to use it, and also the limitations; the House of Commons did not stand by Gladstone in 1886 and he was defeated on the second reading of the Irish Home Rule Bill.

The truth is that the powers of the Prime Minister have varied with the personality of the Prime Minister or with the particular political circumstances of his tenure. No one has come nearer to Presidential government on the American model than Lloyd George. Yet none of the factors which Mr Crossman sees as causing this development in the second half of the twentieth century applied then. The cabinet secretariat and the unification of the civil service were indeed the results of decisions by Lloyd George but they cannot have had much effect before 1922. As for the position of the Prime Minister as leader of his party, Lloyd George was especially ill placed. He led no party, only a Liberal splinter group. In the end this weakness was fatal, but it did not handicap him at the height of his prestige when, after virtually abolishing the old Cabinet system, he said, perhaps half in jest, that he thought of doing without the Cabinet altogether, when he conducted foreign policy through a private office of his own, 'the garden suburb', by-passing the indignant Lord Curzon, and when he effortlessly dominated the House of Commons, carrying his way on almost every issue.

Lloyd George was not the first Prime Minister to treat his Cabinet in this cavalier way. Campbell-Bannerman never revealed to the full Cabinet the staff conversations with the French initiated in December 1905 by Sir Edward Grey. His latest biographer, Mr John Wilson, considers that this was a deliberate decision taken in order to avoid a row with the radical wing of the ministry. In 1877, during the Russo-Turkish war, an even more striking instance of Prime Ministerial secrecy occurred. Disraeli had tried to persuade the Cabinet to issue an ultimatum to Russia, threatening war in the event of a second campaign against Turkey in the spring of the following year. The Cabinet, as so often at that time, would neither agree nor disagree. Disraeli, accordingly, sent a secret emissary to St Petersburg to inform the Tsar that the

Cabinet was entirely united in its determination to go to war, if there was a second campaign. The other ministers, including the Foreign Secretary, were kept in ignorance of this démarche by their chief, and some of them would undoubtedly have raised the strongest objections had they known.

Modern Prime Ministers have been much more 'correct'. Oddly enough the two instances of Prime Ministerial indifference to Cabinet responsibility quoted by Mr Crossman do not really support his case. He makes much of Attlee's alleged by-passing of the Cabinet over the construction of the atomic bomb, but the facts do not substantiate the charge. The decision, it is true, was taken by the Defence sub-committee of the Cabinet, but the minutes were circulated to all members of the Cabinet. Moreover it was communicated to Parliament in answer to a question on 12 May 1948. He is possibly on better ground over the Suez crisis. The facts here are more obscure, but it seems on balance that, although some ministers may have felt that they had been 'bounced', the correct constitutional procedure was formally followed. No doubt much more was known by some than others, and the detailed planning was done by a group in close sympathy with Anthony Eden's aims. This, however, is common form. Neville Chamberlain constituted with himself, Lord Halifax, Sir John Simon and Sir Samuel Hoare just such a group at the time of Munich in 1938. In every Cabinet some ministers are more equal than others.

Of course Mr Crossman is quite right to point out some of the changes which have altered the constitutional framework within which the Prime Minister operated. The positions of the civil service, the political parties, the Crown, the legislature, are not the same as they were a hundred years ago, and they were not the same then as they had been fifty, let alone a hundred years before that. The enormous extension of the powers of government, in Britain as in all countries, in itself changes the role of the Prime Minister, just as it has changed that of the President of France or the President of the United States.

Nevertheless, the position of the Prime Minister in terms of an internal balance of power has not changed as fundamentally as all that. The differences are still largely between personalities – the way in which this or that occupant of 10 Downing Street in the light of his own circumstances feels that he should or can behave. Lord Liverpool was described some forty years after his death as the last prime minister to have governed Britain. He was succeeded by Goderich, 'a transient and embarrassed phantom' who lasted a few months and resigned before he met Parliament – one of the very few Prime Ministers in history to have escaped this not unimportant duty.

The study of Prime Ministers' lives is one of perpetual fascination. It is rash to lay down any hard and fast rules about the nature of the position. Perhaps in this respect one can echo the words Disraeli put into the mouth of one of the characters in a novel, 'Read no history, only biography, for that is life without theory.'

LORD JOHN RUSSELL

BY

JOHN PREST

Lord John Russell, created Earl Russell and Viscount Amberley 1861. KG 1862. Born 18 August 1792, the third son of the Sixth Duke of Bedford. Educated at Westminster School and Edinburgh University. MP (Whig) for Tavistock 1813, 1818, 1830; Huntingdonshire 1820, Bandon 1826, S. Devon 1831, Stroud 1835–41, City of London 1841–61. Married (1) 1835 Lady Ribblesdale (who died in 1838), four step-children, two daughters; (2) 1841 Lady Fanny Elliot, three sons and one daughter. Paymaster of the Forces 1830–34; drafted the Reform Bill 1830; entered the Cabinet 1831. Following his choice as Leader of the Commons in 1834, William IV dismissed his ministers. Home Secretary 1835–39, Colonial Secretary 1839–41; Prime Minister 1846–52; joined Aberdeen's ministry of 1852 as Leader of the Commons until 1855; Foreign Secretary 1859–65; Prime Minister 1865–66. Died 28 May 1878. Author of Memoirs of Affairs of Europe, *1824;* History of the English Government and Constitution, *1821; etc.*

Lord John Russell, by F. Grant

LORD JOHN RUSSELL

Lord John Russell regarded Peel's fall as marking the end of an experiment. Politicians on all sides – and not least Lord John, who had drafted the Bill – expected the Reform Act of 1832 to diminish the influence of ministers, and to increase the pressures which public opinion and a majority in the House of Commons could exercise upon the government of the day. Melbourne accepted this, and in 1835 he allowed his administration to be committed to the appropriation of the surplus revenues of the Church of Ireland at the instance of Lord John and the coalition of advanced Whigs, Radicals and Irish by whom he was supported.

Peel, on the other hand, regarded 'weak' government as a great evil, and when he took office in 1841 he deliberately attempted to impose a 'strong' executive upon the reformed Parliament. Indeed, he aimed, Lord John thought, 'at a much greater agreement of opinion, and at a much greater identity of conduct on the part of the members of his Administration, and of his party generally' than had been achieved even by the most distinguished of his predecessors of pre-Reform Bill days, Pitt and Liverpool. Simultaneously he set his face against the Manchester manufacturers' campaign for the repeal of the Corn Laws, and brushed aside the Whigs' plea for a concession in season. 'For a time,' Lord John continued, 'from his great talents' and 'great power in conducting a ministry', Peel was successful. But the very unanimity of his Cabinet alarmed his supporters, who resented being whipped into line by threats of resignation and anticipated a *volte face* upon free trade, and in 1845 Disraeli spoke of having a commission issued 'to inquire into the tenure by which Downing Street is held'. When the disease of the potato made the demand for the repeal of the Corn Laws irresistible, Peel's failure was complete. 'Stout resistance' to extra-parliamentary agitation was followed by 'unqualified concession', and that in turn by the disintegration of the Conservative party. Peel had ridden on too tight a rein, and the crash of 1846 was proportioned to the over-confidence of the rider. As Lord John understated it, Peel's approach was not likely to be successful again, or to be advantageous to the country. His ministry had served, as many ministries do, not to solve the problem, but to eliminate one of the possible routes to its solution, and when Lord John took office it was apparent that there must be a new departure. 'Any government to be formed at present or in the future', and especially a Liberal one, must be conducted in a more responsive manner. Lord John would not attempt to stamp his own personality upon the affairs of every department, and he would tolerate wider divergences of opinion within his Cabinet than his predecessor had done.

Melbourne's administration had taken its policy from its majority in the House of Commons, Peel's from the aims of its chief. Lord John Russell's problem was that the attempt to rule Parliament through a strong executive having failed, it was impossible simply to fall back upon a party majority, because there was none. Lord John took office with about 250 supporters in a House of 658, and for a whole year, while he hoped that the general election in 1847 would do something to get the House back into two parties and give the Whigs a reliable majority, he was sustained in office by the mutual antipathies of the Protectionists and the Peelites. But the Peelites fought the election as a separate party, and the result was to weaken and fragment the Opposition still further. The Whigs, Liberals and Radicals came back about 330 strong, but parties take their cohesion from each other, and with disarray to the right of him, while the Irish famine of 1846 led on to the financial panic of 1847, the revival of Chartism in 1848, and a contest over all Europe between Jacobin and Absolutist principles, Lord John inevitably found himself cast as the defender of order. This meant that his ministry was bound, even more than Melbourne's after 1837, to fall out with its own left wing – the new generation of Radicals and 'Economists', about eighty strong, thrown up by the general election, and fanatically committed to the reduction of government expenditure. Far from having got the House back into two parties, it soon appeared that the election had further divided it into four. The consequence was that throughout his ministry from 1846 to 1852 Lord John was obliged to take account of the fact that any one of several possible combinations of opponents might lead to a defeat, and to calculate, occasion after occasion, much more carefully than any of his predecessors, where his majority was to come from. An open Cabinet faced an independent House of Commons, and the change from the Peel era was epitomised in 1849, when Lord John invited the Irish MPs to choose for themselves whether to support the insolvent Poor Law Unions by an income tax or a rate in aid.

Circumstances had not, however, reduced Lord John to the mere chairman of an open meeting of Parliament. The great issue of the day was free trade, and here conviction and opportunity coincided. Lord John had contested the general election of 1841 upon a free trade platform. He had since spent much of his time in opposition reading the works of the classical economists, and by the time he published his Edinburgh letter in November 1845 he was knowledgeably filled with the beneficent truths of the doctrines of *laissez-faire* and *laissez-passer*. In February 1846 he 'lent' Peel his supporters in order to carry the Bill to repeal the Corn Laws through the House of Commons, and in May he crushed a revolt among the Whig peers in favour of a Whig–Protectionist alignment. By the time he became Prime Minister free trade was a matter upon which he could not compromise if he was to retain credibility as a public figure.

Between 1846 and 1852 the immediate object of the free traders was to stand firm upon the repeal of the Corn Laws, and the prospective object was to carry the policy to its logical conclusion and to abolish the remaining protective duties. Two parties shared these objects, the Whigs and the Peelites, and between them they could command a majority – the one secure majority (apart from the Protestant one) in the entire period 1846 to 1868. Accordingly from the very first day of his ministry to the last Lord John used his authority to confirm his party in its free trade policy, and sought to attach the Peelites to him. Upon taking office he offered places to three of Peel's former ministers, and renewed his approaches upon no fewer than five occasions in 1847, 1849, 1851 (twice) and 1852, arguing each time that 'Whigs and Peelites ought to govern the country and not to quarrel about trifles'. But the Peelites did not recognise numbers as an argument for merging their identity in that of the Whigs; they did not accept that Lord John's title to the premiership lay in his having taken up the cause before Peel, who was a late convert; and they had not given up all hope of returning to the head of affairs themselves. They preferred their independence. Discouraged, but not deterred, Lord John continued to keep the Peelites apprised of his intentions while receiving no confidence in return, and strove to re-draw the lines of party politics with Free Traders on one side and Protectionists on the other. He bravely staked the existence of his ministry upon the passage of the Bill to repeal the Navigation Laws through the House of Lords, and upon that occasion, pocketing the Whig principles of his upbringing, he made such free use of the Queen's name and influence to ensure a favourable outcome that the Protectionists themselves, of all people, began to question the extent of royal power. If one is looking for consistency of purpose, and for 'strong' government in Lord John's career as Prime Minister, then this is the field in which to find it.

Lord John correctly identified the first objective of sound policy for the United Kingdom as being the maintenance of free trade, but the most urgent problem he was called upon to deal with was the famine in Ireland, where among a population of 10 millions, two persons in five were accustomed to living at subsistence level and were without their food.

Here Lord John had no regular majority in the House to guide him, but in 1846–7, at any rate, the gravity of the crisis was universally recognised, and there was a disposition among all parties not to embarrass the ministry and even to help it out. It was open to Lord John, therefore, to frame the measures he thought best, and in many ways he was well fitted for his task, for he was one of the handful of English statesmen who believed that Irishmen had a right to equal treatment under the Act of Union, and in the 1830s he had communicated his own crusading zeal to the regime in Dublin Castle. But a decade later, in her hour of need, Ireland cried out not for civil rights but for exceptional consideration. To some extent it was granted. Gigantic schemes of public works were put in hand under the Labour Rate Act of 1846, and throughout the spring and summer of 1847 the Government provided soup kitchens to keep the people alive. These measures cost £10 million, which was about one hundred times as much as any government had ever spent upon such an occasion before, and the worst that can be said of them is that they followed one step behind the course of the crisis (as one supposes any government's measures would have done).

But even at this early stage of the famine, which lasted until 1849, Lord John revealed an inflexible attachment to his newly assimilated rules of political economy, which his historical studies somehow failed to tell him were not as applicable to backward Ireland as they were to Britain. His refusal to allow the Government to purchase corn upon world markets can be defended on the ground that intervention would not have increased the amount of corn available and would have raised the price. But there seems to have been no satisfactory reason why the ministry should not have diverted corn from Britain to Ireland, and why it should not have stored and distributed more grain in the west of Ireland, where there was no retail trade, and death and disease struck hardest. Irish MPs coming to Lord John to represent the state of famine existing in their districts were referred (all too relevantly if the dogma alone is to be considered) to the fifth chapter of the fourth book of Adam Smith's *Wealth of Nations*.

Worse was to follow. The amount already being spent upon relief was bound to necessitate an increase in taxes, and the old Parliament itself would not, in any case, have been so lavish again. Then, at the general election in July 1847, the English and Scots constituencies revealed that they, like the Treasury, were determined to shift the burden of Irish paupers onto Irish landlords, who still enjoyed the privilege of paying no income tax. The country was passing through a financial panic, and the new Parliament was certain to parade a stony heart. Anticipating what was to follow, Lord John promptly terminated his programme of aid to Ireland in August and September. The decision was harsh, and it did not satisfy: when he came before the House of Commons in February 1848 to ask for an increase in the income tax, in order to pay for the expenditure incurred the year before, there was an outcry in the press, and a revolt among the economical Radicals who left the party and formed an organisation of their own. Lord John, fearing that a defeat would lead to a Protectionist administration and the revival of the Anti-Corn-Law League, gave way, and after that there was no possibility of the Government's being able to obtain any more money for the relief of Irish distress from the Parliament of 1847–52.

When we turn from the immediate problem of famine relief to survey the Government's long-term measures for the reconstruction of Irish society, we find a similar pattern. In many ways the ministry rose to the occasion: it was determined to turn the disaster to good use, and its proposals were startling in their magnitude. Through the agency of an Encumbered Estates Act, insolvent Protestant landlords were to be sold up and their estates transferred to Catholic merchants from the towns. Landlords being of the same religion as their tenants, land wars would then cease. Capital being made available for investment in agriculture, the process already begun by the Labour Rate Act of substituting wage labour for peasant farming would continue apace, productivity would rise, employment would be made more secure, and solvent landlords and tenants would be able to support their remaining poor, who would be given a right to relief, through the rates. Finally the priests would be attached to the new order by the provision of state stipends, and all would then be in harmony.

The ministry was not able to carry out this programme in its entirety, because the proposal to endow the priests excited the jealousy of the Irish hierarchy and must in any case have foundered in that most Protestant of nineteenth-century parliaments. But the main charge against it is not that it was guilty of taking up a proposal which it could not carry – rather that in its long-term plans as in its temporary relief measures, it was insensitive and dogmatic. And this time the dogma was the superiority of British society and institutions. Everything was to be rearranged after the British model, and Lord John completely misconceived the speed with which it would be possible, in his words, to change the habits of a whole people, and brushed aside the need for the Government to provide generous and even massive financial assistance in the transition period. He allowed himself to be overawed by the economical Radicals, took it for granted that it would be as difficult to obtain money for reconstruction as it was for relief, and when Peel spoke out in favour of appointing a commission to manage the distressed areas in the west, replied that that was the sort of proposal that could only have come from an opposition bench.

Irish affairs did not cause much friction between the executive and the House of Commons. The Irish MPs did not know what they wanted, and the Government willingly adjusted its course to the wishes of the English and Scottish MPs who did. But here, indeed, as we can now see, was a failure of the new system of open government. Prime Minister and Cabinet took their tone from the majority when it was wrong to do so, and were laxly doctrinaire when they ought to have been resolutely humane. It is difficult to resist the conclusion that Malthusian fears led both them and the Parliament of 1847–52 virtually to welcome the opportunity of clearing the surplus population of Ireland off the land and Anglicising the remainder. As the years passed and the survivors of the famine became aware of the extent of the disaster, which counted anything up to 1 million dead and 2 million emigrants, the conviction grew that more could have been done by the richest nation on earth to save the inhabitants of the most poverty-stricken province in Europe and to respect the native way of life. The legacy of bitterness, whose fruits included the rebellion of Young Ireland during Lord John's ministry, and the Fenian movement, founded and financed by the exiles in America, in his lifetime, was incalculable.

Lord John held staunchly to the free trade policy, and more timidly did what he could for Ireland within the Parliament of the day. It remains to be seen how his new course of 'low profile' government worked out in other fields of domestic policy. In his first few months he could afford, like any prime minister, to be bravely opportunistic. In 1846 he lowered the duties on sugar, and a majority voted for him rather than turn him out after one month. The next year he overhauled the English Poor Law to the indignation of the anti-centralisers, extended the scope of the State's provision for education in the face of virulent abuse from the Whigs' old allies the Dissenters, and went into the same lobby with the Protectionists in support of Fielden's Ten Hour Bill. 1847 was not a bad year for legislation, and it is doubtful whether any minority government before or since has ever left so deep a mark upon the statute book.

Lord John had taken his chance to do some good along a broad front while circumstances were favourable. But he must have wondered how long he could go on leaning first one way and then the other, and after the general election of 1847 it became clear that the honeymoon period was over. Thenceforth, the success of his measures would depend, as Disraeli put it, 'on a variety of small parties, who, in the aggregate, exceed in number and influence the party of the ministers'. In these circumstances ministers might have been forgiven if they had been content just to defend the free trade policy and to keep afloat. Instead they attempted more, and the first Health of Towns Act, passed in 1848, and the Act of 1850 establishing what was virtually a self-governing dominion in Australia, were both substantial reforms of a liberal character. But in order to achieve anything in that Parliament ministers were bound to expose themselves to the risk of being labelled bad work-men. Both the Health of Towns Bill and the Bill to repeal the Naviga-tion Laws were abandoned one year and reintroduced the next. The Encumbered Estates Act of 1848 was ineffective and had to be replaced (at Peel's suggestion) by a better one the following year. Time and again apparently settled questions like the sugar duties and the ten-hour day were reopened in response to outside pressures, the ministry en-countered unprecedented difficulties in continuing established policies like the maintenance of a naval squadron to suppress the slave trade, and even Bills which were eventually passed by large majorities en-countered an unusual degree of obstructive opposition on the way. The result was that when the Government's measures did receive the royal assent the impression left upon the public was, as Disraeli expressed it with mocking exaggeration, that they were 'so altered, remoulded, remodelled, patched, cobbled, painted, veneered, and varnished' that at last no trace was left of the original scope and scheme.

Within three years of taking office it appeared that Lord John's legislation could be amended at will by almost any and every little faction which chose to oppose it, and the Radicals then advanced beyond obstruction and began to take initiatives of their own, by proposing a reduction in official salaries, and limiting the income tax to one year. Graham thought the middle ground could have been more firmly held – Dunfermline, an ex-Speaker, blamed the forms of the House, and regarded Parliament as unworkable. The latter was nearer the mark, and it is scarcely to be wondered at that, as his Government wallowed in a sea of troubles caused by Peel's destruction of the party system, Lord John became ill, that he reminded himself ominously that Fox and Canning had both broken down at his age, that he contemplated reducing his labours by taking a peerage, that he became cross with his colleagues, and above all that he resented the contrast so often made between Peel's 'strong' Government and his 'weak' one.

The strain and the worry began to affect his judgement, so that when, in 1850, the Pope divided England into sees, Lord John reacted with a public letter to the Bishop of Durham in which he accused both the Roman Catholics and their fellow travellers within the Church of England, the Puseyites, of casuistry bordering upon a conspiracy to hand England over to Rome. His letter was the most popular thing he ever wrote, and the subsequent Ecclesiastical Titles Bill passed by an enormous majority. But the fact remained that Lord John had mistaken a piece of cheek in usurping the Queen's authority to confer territorial titles for an invasion by a hostile power, and that it was undignified for a nineteenth-century prime minister to put himself at the head of a Protestant hue and cry. Worst of all, however, from Lord John's point of view, was the fact that the Durham letter offended both the Irish MPs and the Peelites. There was no future for Lord John in the combination of Whig and Protectionist votes by which the Ecclesiastical Titles Bill passed the House of Commons (nor did he wish it), and he had by his own action forfeited an important part of his regular support, and made it certain that the union of Whigs and Peelites, which was his dearest political object, would not take place under his leadership.

From that moment Lord John was powerless and adrift, and the result was that the public generally began to agree with Brougham, who had argued as early as 1847 that 'a strong Government, which was not to be much liked . . . was, on the whole, to be preferred to a weak one. . . . Any Ministry was better than a Ministry without power.' So that Lord John's ministry in its turn seemed to have eliminated another possible approach to the problem of the relations between the executive and the legislature, and served to recreate a preference for a stronger form of government, without, however, pointing out any very obvious way in which one was to be obtained, though men looked increasingly to Peel, and after the Don Pacifico debate and Peel's death in 1850, to the claims of Palmerston. Simultaneously, the Government's majorities in the House of Commons fell away dramatically as it became increasingly difficult to persuade supporters to attend debates. No ministry with such a large paper strength ever went out upon such a small vote. In 1851 Lord John was defeated by 100 votes to 54, and although he was restored to office, his ministry was finished off the next year by a vote of 136 to 125. Rightly or wrongly open government now appeared futile, and *l'Angleterre s'ennuya*.

Lord John himself shared the public's increasing disillusionment with the work of the Parliament of 1847. But the problem, as he saw it, did not lie in any failing of his, and the answer was not simply to substitute a more powerful person at the head of the executive, but to obtain a solid party majority, either frankly Liberal or frankly Conservative, which would itself uphold a more effective government. Taking his inspiration from his own experience, his mind went back to the 1830s, which now appeared, in retrospect, as a golden age. Following the Reform Act of 1832 the executive had been conspicuous neither for its homogeneity (under Grey) nor for its capacity (under Melbourne), but the House of Commons had contained a Liberal majority, and for four years, from 1832 to 1836, Parliament had been visibly on the move, legislating in accordance with the spirit of the age. Not surprisingly Lord John Russell now began to wonder whether like causes might not produce like effects. For the first time since he took his stand upon 'Finality' in 1837, he began to consider reopening the whole question of parliamentary reform, and he at last acknowledged what eleven years of Chartist agitation, from 1838 to 1848, had never yet brought him to admit, that the Act of 1832 had shut out the working classes. It does not seem to have occurred to him that in the mid-century there might not be anything that could actually be identified as the spirit of the age at all, and that a Liberal majority, if one could be obtained, might not agree upon the objectives it wished to pursue. Nor did he ponder whether a working-class franchise was at that time more likely to add to or to diminish the forces of the economical Radicals, opposed to all legislation involving the action of government, who were the bane of the 1847 Parliament. He just took it for granted, until there was proof to the contrary, that the will to legislate was there, and that it was some fault in the existing arrangements that prevented him, as Prime Minister, from giving it expression.

Extending the franchise to the working classes might be expected to lead to a consolidation of party allegiances in the House of Commons and to a more firmly based Liberal administration with a clear line of policy. But this would be worse than useless, and might even be dangerous, if it subsequently led to a renewal of the deadlock between the two Houses which had taken place in 1836, when every measure of improvement for Ireland was blocked by the Orange peers. Admittedly the House of Lords had kept to the background since Lord John took office in 1846, but that was mainly because a landlord Cabinet and a minority government was apprised of and to some extent anticipated their wishes. The fact that the peers were still an obstructive force to be reckoned with was revealed by their opposition to the new Poor Law of 1847 in Ireland, by their coming within ten votes of throwing out the Bill to repeal the Navigation Laws in 1849, and by their vote of censure upon the Government's handling of foreign affairs the year after. Lord John decided, therefore, to try to reform the House of Lords at the same time that he extended the franchise, and in order to do this he returned to his favourite proposal, which Melbourne had snubbed in 1837, for the creation of life peers.

The facts are quickly told. Lord John began with his notion for life peers, and tried it out upon the Cabinet in 1849, in 1850, and again in 1851. The Queen and the Prince expressed cautious approval, and it was agreed that, if the experiment were to be made, it ought to be confined to eminent lawyers, and to Liberal Scots and Irish peers effectively excluded under the existing representative system. But when, early in 1851, Lord John invited Dr Lushington to become the first life peer, he declined to become a guinea pig, and the Cabinet, which had never been enthusiastic, thereupon slid backwards and concluded that life peers would lower the composition of the Upper House. So there was a divergence of opinion in his own Cabinet which Lord John could not overcome, and he had still not succeeded in creating a life peer by the time he left office.

Lord John would have preferred to have opened up the House of Lords before extending the franchise. But he did not make it an absolute condition, and in any case a second Reform Bill might turn out to be a prerequisite for the reform of the Upper House, so that each time he was thwarted in his wish to create life peers he turned instead to his argument in favour of a second Reform Bill. The Act of 1832 was interpreted by the working classes as an Act to enfranchise their employers, and in Lord John's view it would be better to make a reasonable and voluntary concession in time rather than to wait (like Peel) until he was obliged to yield more to agitation. This was the pure and even noble Whig doctrine with which he sought to persuade his Cabinet in 1849 and 1850. But his Cabinet, alas, knew less about Whig doctrine than he, and as long as the country was quiet, simply could not see the need. Their attitude left Lord John despondent and frustrated, and early in 1851, without consulting his colleagues, who then recalled that they had not been consulted about the Durham letter either, he committed the Government to bringing in a Bill the next year. In the autumn he drove his reluctant Cabinet into appointing a committee to draft Bills for England, Scotland and Ireland. The details were finalised in December, whereupon Palmerston, who had always been the most proudly wayward and mutinous member of the Cabinet, brought the ministry down in his own way, by acts of insubordination and revenge, which none of Lord John's colleagues approved of, and none regretted.

Thirteen years elapsed before Lord John became Prime Minister again. In the meantime the junction of Whigs and Peelites took place under Aberdeen, and the leadership of the Liberal party passed to Palmerston. Free trade budgets apart, the legislative record of those years of 'equipoise' was poor. But there was no popular cry for Reform; Lord John's Reform Bill of 1854 was abandoned upon the outbreak of war with Russia, and that of 1860 perished for want of interest in the House of Commons. While Palmerston lived Reform was dead, and in 1861 Lord John accepted a peerage and became Earl Russell.

Palmerston lived just long enough to hold a general election, so that when Russell succeeded him and became Prime Minister for the second time in October 1865, he was handicapped by a 'cave' of Palmerstonians, forty strong, in a House of Commons where the Liberals nominally enjoyed a majority of seventy. Russell did not hesitate: he was seventy-three, it was sixteen years since he had begun to advocate an extension to the franchise, and ten since Palmerston had brought politics back to 'the do-nothing days of Castlereagh'. But Gladstone had been converted to the cause in 1864, and now became the leader of the Liberal party in the House of Commons. Gladstone was at times dismayed by Russell's 'rapidity', but he scarcely attempted to check it, and at the very first Cabinet meeting after Palmerston's death it was agreed that there was to be a Reform Bill. The measure, lowering the county franchise from £50 to £14 and the borough franchise from £10 to £7, brought squawks from the more timid members of the Cabinet, the Cave duly rebelled, and in eight months all was over and Russell ceased to be Prime Minister and never held office again. But this time he had raised a question that must be answered – Bright saw to that, and a year later Disraeli's Reform Bill passed both Houses of Parliament.

And then was seen the foresight and sagacity of Lord John Russell. The second Reform Act, like the first, got Parliament on the move again. The general election of 1868 produced a revival of interest in party organisation, a clarification of party lines, and a Liberal majority large enough, for the time being, to overawe the House of Lords. Gladstone did not find the Liberal party subservient, and had Peel been alive to contemplate it he would not have classified Gladstone's first ministry as a 'strong' government. But Gladstone was at least able to carry on from the point at which the reforming impetus of the 1830s had come to a halt, to disestablish and disendow the Church of Ireland, and to take up great social questions like the relations of landlord and tenant, which had proved too much for the governments of the 1840s and 1850s. There had been no period of legislation to equal that of 1868–74 since the House of Lords put a stranglehold upon the reformers in 1836–7, and the fact that Lord John Russell's analysis turned out in the event to be correct means that our final view of him must be an appreciative one. As Prime Minister he held to his creed that governments have a responsibility to be active in the promotion of the public welfare, and when Parliament ceased to be up to its share of the work, he recognised the evil, and pointed to a remedy. He did not advocate democracy, but he did turn to the unenfranchised masses, who knew what the problems were, and looked to an infusion of popular votes and a better balance among the classes to reactivate the failing machinery of the State.

BIBLIOGRAPHY

Gooch, G. P. (ed.), *The Later Correspondence of Lord John Russell 1840–78* (2 vols London, 1925)

MacCarthy, D. and Russell, A. (eds), *Lady John Russell: A Memoir with Selections from her Diaries and Correspondence* (London, 1910)

Prest, John, *Lord John Russell* (London, 1972)

Reid, S. J., *Lord John Russell* (London, 1895)

Russell, Lord John, *Recollections and Suggestions 1813–73* (London, 1875)

Russell, Rollo (ed.), *Early Correspondence of Lord John Russell 1815–40* (2 vols, London, 1913)

Tilby, A. W., *Lord John Russell* (London, 1930)

Walpole, Spencer, *Life of Lord John Russell* (2 vols, London, 1889)

THE EARL OF DERBY

BY

DENYS FORREST

Edward George Geoffrey Smith Stanley, 14th Earl of Derby, born 29 March 1799, eldest son of the 13th Earl. Educated at Eton and Christ Church, Oxford. MP (Whig) for Stockbridge 1820, Preston 1826, Windsor 1830, North Lancashire 1832. Entered the House of Lords as Lord Stanley of Bickerstaffe 1844; succeeded as 14th Earl in 1851. Married 1825 the second daughter of Edward Bootle-Wilbraham; two sons and one daughter. Junior Lord of the Treasury under Canning 1827; Under-Secretary for War and Colonies under Canning and Goderich 1827–28; Chief Secretary for Ireland under Grey 1830–33; Secretary of State for War and the Colonies 1833. Resigned 1834 and joined the Conservative Party 1837. Reappointed under Peel 1841, but resigned over Corn Laws 1845 and became leader of the Protectionists. Prime Minister 1852, 1858–59, 1866–68; resigned through ill health. Died 23 October 1869.

Edward Stanley, 14th Earl of Derby, by F. R. Say

THE EARL OF DERBY

In the little group of British statesmen who have had more than two
separate terms as Prime Minister – Gladstone (four), Derby, Salisbury
and Baldwin (three each) – Derby came first. But he remains the most
difficult to know. The fact that each of his periods of office, though they
became progressively longer, lasted less than two years, that each time
he was in a minority, that there was a repetitive pattern of general
elections which he just failed to win and that he never reached power
except after a maze of negotiations with much the same people – all this
creates a blur, even for the moderately assiduous political student. The
common reader of Victorian history and biography is in worse case.
Derby the statesman simply eludes him, and he makes do with Derby
the collection of catch phrases – 'The Rupert of debate', 'Scorpion
Stanley', 'The Derby Dilly', 'Dishing the Whigs', 'A leap in the dark'.[1]
All are valid in their way, but they are inadequate signposts to a career
which, although so little of it was spent in the supreme post, stretched
over nearly half a century.

Edward Stanley was born and bred a Whig, *pur sang*. He wore the
'old Whig uniform of blue and buff' when at the age of twenty-one he
entered Parliament for Stockbridge, a Rotten Borough bought for him
from a Tory peer, who in turn had acquired it from a hard-up West
Indian planter (politics unspecified). And when in 1826 he transferred
to the family borough of Preston, he warned his constituents flatly that
he was no Radical reformer, but 'an old constitutional Whig'. His
acceptance of minor office under Canning and Goderich was an early
hint of his future. In due course the old constitutional Whigs turned reformers themselves, but the dashing young Stanley did not exactly leap
into the front line. His reaction to the first Reform Bill was in fact
incredulous laughter. He recovered himself, and delivered one of those
speeches which sent a whisper along the benches, 'This is the man who
should be our leader.' Yet the picture is of the trusty in-fighter who has
received his instructions, rather than of the go-go reformer pawing the
ground. What the talent-spotters divined in the heir of the Stanleys

[1] See Note pp. 427–8., for the origin and bearing of these phrases.

(then by no means one of the great political families) was a brilliant mind and a blossoming genius for debate.

Both qualities were tested when he became Grey's Chief Secretary for Ireland. Though he genuinely attempted to balance coercion with cautious reform, he was always, for his great antagonist O'Connell, the 'snappish, impertinent, High Church Stanley', graduating to 'Scorpion Stanley' in due course. It was probably wisdom in Grey to move him to the Colonial Secretaryship (then combined with War). Here he found waiting for him a great measure, the freeing of slaves throughout the British dominions, which chimed completely with his own religious convictions. Unfortunately, it was these convictions that forced him into the first of the two 'walk-outs' which were critical to his career. When in May 1834 he realised that the Cabinet was not behind him in his defence of that highly vulnerable body the Irish Church Establishment, he and a handful of colleagues resigned. Thus was formed the briefly famous 'Derby Dilly' or third party, the vehicle whereby Stanley passed over to the Conservative camp. Its life would have been even shorter had Stanley felt able to accept office during Peel's '100 days', but by early 1837 he had come to realise the futility of trying to wield the balance of power from somewhere near the middle of the road.[2] He had long been in the inner councils of Conservatism when he took his place as War and Colonial Secretary in Peel's Cabinet of 1841.

Colonial affairs, notably the winding up of the 'Opium Wars' with China and the dispute over Maori lands in New Zealand, gave scope for the pacific element always present in Stanley's make-up. Yet he felt he was being sidetracked as a front bench speaker, and at his own request he was called to the Upper House as Lord Stanley of Bickerstaffe. At least that is what the published correspondence between him and the Prime Minister implies, however Peel may not have been sorry to place a little more distance between himself and this rather careless, outspoken grandee, with his 'chaffing' ways.

The move turned out to be crucial. It meant that when the great Conservative schism came over the repeal of the Corn Laws, and Stanley emerged as the head of the Protectionist faction, the leadership of that faction in the Commons was thrown into the lap of Benjamin Disraeli.

The relationship between these two men is a fascinating study. The

[2] As W. D. Jones points out in his valuable study, *Lord Derby and Victorian Conservatism* (Oxford, 1956), p. 56, the middle of the road was then somewhat overcrowded with moderate Reformers.

truth about it lies in neither of the two opposing myths – of Stanley as Disraeli's aristocratic puppet or front man, and of Disraeli as Stanley's low-born hireling, who eventually took control. Fortuitous in its origins, their partnership was genuine and lasting. What they actually thought of each other is not so easy to say. Now and then Dizzy would work off his frustrations by petulant outbursts to his lady correspondents about what he regarded as the dilettantism of his chief, who nevertheless kept a highly professional eye on any Disraelian plotting in unsuitable quarters. Very rarely (at any rate in his published correspondence) Stanley would also advert to Disraeli's insecure personal and political standing. On the one notable occasion[3] when he described him as 'unpopular' and not seeing enough of the party in private, he seems to have been retorting complaints against himself for not entertaining the rank-and-file.

Stanley refused to join in the Disraeli–Bentinck witch-hunt against Peel, and no amount of rebuffs ever cured him of the belief that the Peelites, gently handled, might be lured into a reunited Conservative party. From the fall of Peel to his own first accession to power, he could only play a waiting game, pending a settlement of the Protection issue. He knew Disraeli had already ratted, and had decided in his own mind that free trade must be given time to vindicate or discredit itself. All this confirmed him in his lifelong stance as opposition leader – vigorous if intermittent in attacking the government of the day, resigned and even timorous about the prospect of regaining office himself.

When his first real chance did come, with Lord John Russell's fall in February 1851, Stanley set out briskly enough to find allies. But the Peelites failed him, some of his own followers proved chicken-hearted, and he abruptly abandoned the enterprise. It looked at first as though the pattern might be repeated when the next summons to Buckingham Palace came just a year later (21 February 1852). Conservatives were in a paper-thin majority in the House of Commons, but forty or fifty of them were Peelites. Failing once more to get help from outside, Stanley – or rather Derby, as he had now become through the death of the thirteenth Earl – managed to put together a Cabinet from among his own faction. Pakington, Henley, Herries, Spencer Walpole . . . even today one senses the lack of resonant names. However, the Peelites undertook to keep Derby in office for the time being, subject to a decision over Protection and an autumn Budget. Derby himself lay

[3] In the course of the letter to Malmesbury quoted on p. 422.

very low about Protection, and even when a general election came on in July, merely reiterated that the voters must give their verdict. In fact, the issue was never put to them from the Government side – it was a common saying that a Derbyite was a Protectionist in the country, neutral in a small town and a Free Trader in the cities.

Finally, some twenty-five extra Derby supporters were returned – not enough to make their leader independent of the Peelites. So now he must rise to his feet and tell the House of Lords that the majority of the people were in favour of free trade and that the Corn Laws would not be revived. The old Anti-Corn Law Leaguers tried to insist on a more abject recantation, but a compromise motion by Palmerston in the Commons saved the day.

With this awkward corner turned, Derby attempted once again to broaden his base, and once again we find him in conclave with Peelites and with Palmerston. But the former would not swallow Disraeli and the Queen balked at Palmerston, under whose leadership in the Commons the Peelites might possibly have served. The next great obstacle, the Budget, had to be faced without allies.

Disraeli had been a doubtful choice as Chancellor of the Exchequer. He was no economic expert, as he admitted to his chief, who replied with a famous Derbyism – 'You know as much as Mr Canning – they give you the figures.' His task was to contrive a Budget which would appease the agricultural interest without infringing the sacred tenets of free trade. His devices to do this, the desperate straits into which he was subsequently driven, and the final foundering of his Budget before a Gladstonian typhoon which burst upon him in the early hours of 17 December 1852, belong essentially to Disraeli's own story. Derby, who knew, if anything, even less about finance, could do little to help him, and in any case was marooned in the wrong House of Parliament. The best he could offer was inspiriting noises at critical moments – 'Put a good face on it and we will pull through, *l'audace, l'audace, toujours l'audace!*'

And so the first Derby Government fell, amid more jeers than sympathy. Except that Lord Malmesbury proved a rather better Foreign Secretary than most people had expected, few of its members had time, or perhaps the capacity, to create a reputation. It is typical of the whole situation that though there were six Cabinet members in the Lords, the Prime Minister took charge of everything and answered for them all.

Derby went back into opposition still at the head of the strongest parliamentary group – certainly more united than Aberdeen's coalition of Whigs, Peelites and Radicals, which was wide open to disruption by an opposition leader out for blood. But Derby was in no hurry. Minority had scarred him, and while he realised that Aberdeen could be unseated, he did not give much for his own chances. This exasperated those who were keeping the party together in the Commons, particularly his own dour young son Edward Stanley, and of course Disraeli.

By now, certain uncomfortable traits in Derby's character were fully developed. As far back as the period after the fall of the 'Dilly', he had shown a tendency to retreat, at the more humdrum moments, to his great estate at Knowsley and to throw himself into sporting pursuits from which all but his most aristocratic cronies were necessarily excluded. Even Disraeli was not invited there until December 1853. To men for whom politics were their life – and in many cases their living – the spectacle of 'the Captain', as they called him, holed up for weeks or even months together in distant Lancashire, shooting pheasants when fit, or nursing his own agonising brand of gout, was only one better than hearing gossip of him at Newmarket or Doncaster, gambling and chaffing as though he had not a political care in the world. 'Boyish' was a pleasant enough epithet for that handsome young man in the Whig blue and buff; it did not sit so well on the middle-aged statesman who had grown a paunch.

The outbreak, and swift mismanagement, of the Crimean War brought Derby back into the arena, and in fact led to one of the most controversial episodes of his career. Aberdeen fell, and on 31 January 1855, Lord Derby drove once more to see the Queen. Overnight, Lord Ellenborough had warned him, *'Don't leave the room without kissing hands'*, but that is just what Derby did. He told the Queen that though public opinion was demanding Palmerston, the latter was too old, blind and deaf to be capable of carrying on the war, and that he himself must go away and talk to Peelites such as Gladstone and Sidney Herbert. Like all Derby's card houses, this one fell flat; the next day he informed the Queen that he could not go forward, and after further manoeuvres Palmerston came in.

Naturally, for the Conservative activists this was their worst disappointment yet; they believed, as many have since, that Derby threw away the finest prospect he ever had of taking office with the nation behind him, and in due course fighting and winning a general election. Yet it is impossible to feel much confidence in his chances as a war minister. The nation was not in fact behind him but behind Lord Palmerston, and that was the only thing that counted.

So – back to Knowsley, and more detachment than ever from day-to-day affairs at Westminster. Derby's reply to a despondent letter from Malmesbury (15 December 1856)[4] is the *locus classicus*. He has been, he says, too busy shooting to give time to politics (this may have been a mild tease) and appears surprised that the party has been able to keep together at all 'in the absence of any cry or leading question' to demarcate the two sides of the House. Palmerston has been 'a Conservative minister working with Radical tools'. For himself, he was never ambitious of office and is unlikely to become more so now, but will accept it if he sees a chance of not only gaining power but keeping it. That must depend on the Government committing a very gross blunder. The letter ends with a perfunctory reference to 'active exertions' at the forthcoming general election. Ice-cold cheer, this, from an opposition leader!

The 'gross blunder' came of course with Palmerston's ill-timed Conspiracy Bill. Pam resigned and Derby was sent for (20 February 1858). The Conservatives were in a heavier minority than ever, but this time Derby hardly hesitated. Within twenty-four hours he had kissed hands. Though Gladstone and Lord Grey refused their help, his Cabinet was strengthened by a couple of ex-Peelites, Sir Robert's brother General Peel (War Office) and Lord Ellenborough (Board of Control). The latter, as it turned out, was a doubtful asset.

In his ministerial statement to the Lords (1 March), Derby used a comparison which is the more significant since he was to repeat it almost word for word when taking office for the last time in 1866. This was to the effect that while it was easy enough to tell a High Tory from a Radical, the intermediate stages were as elusive as those between the various grades or ranks in society at large. 'There is a broad interval between the highest and the lowest, but the gradation whereby the one melts into the other is so impalpable that it is difficult . . . precisely to say where one commences and another ends.' There could be no greater mistake, he went on, than to suppose that 'a Conservative ministry means a stationary ministry'. Like those old country houses which successive generations had altered and improved, our institutions must be adapted to the needs of society. Finally, the Derby who in 1852

---

[4] Earl of Malmesbury, *Memoirs of an Ex-Minister* (London, 1885), p. 385.

was talking of 'stemming the tide of democracy' now revealed that he was ready for a further instalment of electoral reform.

The Government's immediate preoccupation, however, was with Indian and European affairs. They pushed forward the plan (already adumbrated under the previous regime) to transfer political power in India from the East India Company to a Secretary of State, assisted by a Council, and though Ellenborough nearly wrecked the whole thing by trying to saddle the Council with an absurdly complicated structure, a simplified scheme went through. Ellenborough was to have been the first Secretary of State, but before the change could take effect he got the Government into further hot water. In the aftermath of the Indian Mutiny he sent the Governor-General, Lord Canning, a severe 'rocket' for his alleged confiscatory policy in Oudh, and allowed this to get into general circulation before Canning had even received it. There was a terrific outcry, and the administration was only saved by Ellenborough resigning and the Queen reluctantly authorising Derby to use the threat of a dissolution.

Happier episodes in the Government's first session were its swift and amicable settlement with France over the 'conspiracy to murder' affair which originally brought it to power, and the ending of the long contention that had kept Jews from sitting in Parliament. As a young Whig, Derby had regularly voted to remove Jewish disabilities, but the parliamentary oath 'on the true faith of a Christian' still remained, and one of the 'churchiest' of our prime ministers hesitated to scrap it. Yet he wanted the question settled, and finally agreed to a compromise whereby the House of Commons should be allowed to frame its own rules of admission. Derby was also following his lifelong principles when he opposed suggestions to open the trusteeship of schools to Dissenters and to abolish compulsory church rates.

Next came the first essay at a Conservative Reform Bill. Today it is chiefly remembered for its 'fancy franchises', giving special voting rights to professional men such as lawyers, doctors and teachers and to persons with various levels of savings, government pensions, investments in the Funds, and so on. Even this low-key measure was too much for two Cabinet members, who resigned, and in the House of Commons a critical amendment was carried by a majority of 39. On 4 April 1859, Derby announced a dissolution, and in the subsequent general election had once more the maddening experience of gaining about twenty-five seats but being left in an overall minority.

For the last time, an attempt was made to recruit the help of Palmerston, and when that failed of Gladstone – Gladstone, who had accepted the Ionian Islands High Commissionership from Derby the year before, Gladstone, who after speaking up for Rotten Boroughs in the Reform Bill debate had gone into the lobby alongside Disraeli, and was to do so again in the final Division which turned Lord Derby out. But as usual he ducked out of reach, only to surface again almost immediately as Palmerston's Chancellor of the Exchequer. Apart from his personal position as inevitable successor to the aged Pam, he certainly regarded the latter as sounder than Derby on the question which was obsessing him just then and which sealed the Government's doom – support for Cavour and the Italian Nationalists against Austria.

The next five years can be passed over swiftly. There were several occasions on which Derby's compact forces in the Commons could have made things distinctly awkward for Palmerston, but he preferred to give support, in almost formal terms, to a minister whose home policy was no less conservative than his own. While he continued to deliver his slashing speeches in the Lords, Knowsley claimed him more and more – not merely as sportsman now, but as Lancashire magnate deploying all his old administrative drive to fight the 'Cotton famine' of 1862–4, and as amateur poet and scholar amusing his leisure, and ever-longer interludes of gout, in translating the *Iliad*. His version, though not very exciting, at least stands up to those of his great predecessors, Dryden, Pope and Cowper.

Foreign affairs aroused Derby to a more critical attitude, but not until the Danish imbroglio of 1864 did he seize the headlines by condemning the Government for its worldwide policy of 'meddle and muddle'. This still gave the Conservatives little leverage in the election of the following year, and by one more gentle tilt of the seesaw they lost about the same number of seats they had gained in 1859.

Their eventual return to office arose therefore in a more striking degree than in 1852 or 1858 from dissensions in the enemy ranks – this time the split over yet another Reform Bill and the withdrawal of the anti-Reform Whigs into their 'Adullamite' cave. Lord Derby, who had declared time and time again that he would never resume office 'on sufferance', kissed hands once more. Only two years earlier he had still been lamenting to Malmesbury the lack of suitable office-holders if (as he characteristically put it) they were *doomed* to come in. Yet his third

424

Cabinet was his most impressive, and in spite of fierce strains and some resignations, proved his most durable. Apart from Disraeli and himself, Malmesbury (now Privy Seal), Sir John Pakington and Lord John Manners were survivors from 1852; Stanley (Foreign Secretary) and Peel (War) represented the best of the 1858 intake, while there were notable newcomers in Lord Carnarvon (Colonies), Viscount Cranborne – the future Lord Salisbury (India), Sir Stafford Northcote (Board of Trade) and Gathorne Hardy (Poor Law Board). Spencer Walpole – unfortunately as it happened[5] – returned to office as Home Secretary. Northcote had been sponsored by Disraeli, who also exerted strong influence over other appointments – in truth, the 1866 ministry compels attention more as the overture to the drama of Benjamin Disraeli, Prime Minister, than as Lord Derby's farewell performance.

Yet there is little doubt about which of them took the lead in committing their party to the great and central measure of their administration, the second Reform Bill. In his ministerial statement to the Lords (9 July) Derby declared that nothing would give him greater pleasure than to see 'a very considerable portion of the class now excluded' admitted to the franchise, though he reserved complete liberty not to introduce a Bill unless he saw a fair chance of passing it. By 16 September he was telling Disraeli that he had come 'reluctantly' to the conclusion that they must deal with the subject. He enclosed a sketch for a Bill; Disraeli demurred, but Derby continued to press him. His idea was that they might begin with a series of Resolutions. If these were carried they would be 'on velvet', but the defeat of one or two of them would not be fatal. By 1 November he produced the further concept of a Parliamentary Commission, or study group.

All this was broadly accepted by the Cabinet, but if a Commission were appointed, how was it to be kept busy? Something 'really sticky' would be needed, and after listing a few alternatives Derby concluded 'of all possible hares to start I do not know a better than Household Suffrage, coupled with plurality of voting'. Disraeli might remain lukewarm, but here was the grand selling message – Household Suffrage, however counterweighted with extra votes for the more substantial classes.

Then came a fantastic sequence of events. After a threatened Cabinet

[5] He brought the Government into ridicule by bursting into tears when confronted by a deputation after the 'Hyde Park Riots' of July 1866. Whether these riots helped to panic Derby and Disraeli in the direction of Reform is still disputed.

revolt (the newer men such as Cranborne and Carnarvon were more hostile than the old stagers), the Resolutions were put before Parliament in a vague and sketchy form. Disraeli, on his own initiative, met the 'needling' of the Opposition with a promise to produce a Bill on the day that the Resolutions were due to be voted upon (25 February). There were critical Cabinets on the 16th and 19th, and on Saturday the 23rd a hurried meeting accepted the leadership's draft. But after a weekend of studying the figures, Cranborne realised that Disraeli had concealed the fact that they would probably give the working-class voters a two-to-one majority, and this he could not stomach. Carnarvon and Peel joined him in revolt and on the Monday morning a compromise Bill, ditching Household Suffrage, was flung together. The meeting ended ten minutes before Derby was due to attend a party meeting; two hours later Disraeli was to introduce the Bill into the Commons. It went down very badly. With an unexpectedly large section of his own party joining with the Opposition to demand a more sweeping measure, Derby took the last great decision of his political career. In the teeth of the resignations of Cranborne, Peel and Carnarvon, a Household Suffrage measure was substituted for the 'Ten Minute' Bill.

Thereafter, Derby's influence on events in the Commons naturally diminished. It was left to Disraeli, by artifice, audacity and the supreme command of parliamentary tactics, to win the vital divisions and send up a much amended measure in triumph to the Lords. Derby introduced it there, and two phrases used in the subsequent debates powerfully helped to complete his historical image – his own description of the Bill as 'taking a leap into the dark' and Lord Granville's story of him telling Disraeli, 'Don't you see how it has dished the Whigs?' On 9 August 1867, the second Reform Bill received the Royal Assent. Six months later Derby, pleading ill health, relinquished the seals of office, and Disraeli became Prime Minister.

What is the student of Derby's career to make of all this? To many, he figures as a sort of lifelong latent reformer, fascinated, as Dr Asa Briggs puts it,[6] with the thought of comprehensive Reform for its own sake and more consistently concerned with social justice than ever appeared on the surface. The evidence is not strong. We saw that even in 1832, in the days of his impetuous, eloquent youth, he was the sword-arm rather than the spontaneous champion of Reform, and as middle age

[6] *Victorian People* (London, 1954), p. 288.

advanced empiricism gained on him in everything except the defence of the Established Church. Later still there was some widening of sympathies, especially after his contacts with the cotton operatives during the Famine had taught him how little revolutionary they were, even under the cruellest pressure.

Genuine reformer or not, when Derby died within twenty months of resigning office (23 October 1869), the obituarists were almost unanimous in writing down his career as a failure. They attributed this to his lack of consistent political theory and steady political action. Yet it is hard to imagine any other statesman, with only the least able segment of a broken party behind him, making a much better job of three minority premierships. His reputation as a 'gambler' is certainly misleading. Malmesbury, who knew him best, speaks of 'much reflection and calmness' before action. People who wanted to talk politics when he was up to his neck in racing or shooting could be exasperated by his indifference, but his mind operated on a two-way switch – it is Malmesbury again who records how, returning from covert-side, he could 'sit down at once to write the longest and most important paper right off, in a delicate hand and without a single erasure'.[7]

A word needs to be said about the parliamentary oratory of 'The Rupert of Debate'. The *Annual Register*, commenting on his speech on the Paper Duties in 1861, remarked that it was 'a wonder in its own way', but could give little idea of his old style – its music, its fire, its rapidity, its irresistible dash. Yet earlier Hansards hardly convey these qualities either; not surprisingly, since they are all attributes of delivery rather than composition. On the printed page, Derby's speeches are very much in the ponderous idiom of their time – utterly unlike Disraeli's best in that respect.

This brief essay is not claimed as a final verdict on Lord Derby. The time for that will presumably come when, at long last, somebody gets down to a full-length biography. But even then he seems likely to remain a somewhat shadowy, somewhat equivocal figure, moving in and out of the limelight of nineteenth-century British politics.

[7] Malmesbury, *Memoirs*, p. 32.

NOTE

'*The Rupert of Debate.*' First applied to Stanley by Disraeli, with satirical intention, during a privilege debate (24 April 1844), when the two men were still on opposite sides of the House: 'The noble lord in this case, as in so many others, is the Prince

Rupert of parliamentary discussion; his charge is resistless; but when he returns from pursuit he always finds his camp in the possession of the enemy.' Put to unforgettable use by Bulwer Lytton in his *New Timon* of 1845:

> 'One after one the Lords of time advance,
> Here Stanley meets – how Stanley scorns the glance!
> The brilliant chief, irregularly great,
> Frank, haughty, rash, the Rupert of Debate!'

'*Scorpion Stanley.*' Not coined by O'Connell, as is often thought, but joyously stolen by him from a leading article in the *Examiner* of 29 March 1840.

'*The Derby Dilly.*' In Canning's 'Loves of the Triangles', a 'mathematical and philosophical poem' of 1798, all about things that go in threes, there is the couplet:

> 'So down thy hill, romantic Ashbourne, glides
> The Derby Dilly, carrying three insides.'

O'Connell in February 1835 jokingly applied it to Stanley's 'third party', though apparently substituting 'six' for 'three', which made no better sense. 'Dilly', slang for *diligence* – cf. the 'Brighton Dilly' of Regency days.

'*Dishing the Whigs.*' Whether or not Derby used the phrase, 'dishing the Whigs' was a time-honoured sport. 'The Whigs are dished – dead,' wrote Disraeli to Lord John Manners, 8 March 1848.

'*A Leap in the Dark.*' In even wider currency than the preceding, long before Derby's remark of 1867 attached it permanently to his name. As early as 1841 Lord John Russell applied it to the Dissolution of that year, and Palmerston used it about the Reform proposals of 1860.

BIBLIOGRAPHY

As indicated in the text, Derby still awaits his biographer, and there has been only fragmentary publication of his papers. Towards the end of the Victorian period, and within a year of each other, appeared two short studies, *The Earl of Derby*, by George Saintsbury (Sampson Low, 'The Queen's Prime Ministers' series, 1892) and *The Life of the Earl of Derby*, by T. E. Kebbel (W. H. Allen, 'The Statesmen' series, 1893). Both worked on the assumption that a biography on the grand scale must soon follow. Of the two, Kebbel took more trouble to obtain first-hand information; Saintsbury was of course the better writer, and his outspoken Toryism is frequently amusing. Some of Derby's more important speeches are reprinted in a Lancashire publication, *Historical Sketches of the House of Stanley*, by Thomas Aspden (Preston, for the author, 1877). Second only to Malmesbury as a contemporary witness is Charles Greville – the fact that he was hostile to Derby in politics and suspicious of him on the Turf adds a special flavour to the numerous and oft-quoted comments in his *Diaries*.

THE EARL OF ABERDEEN

BY

NORMAN McCORD

George Hamilton-Gordon, 4th Earl of Aberdeen. Born 28 January 1784 and succeeded his grandfather, the 3rd Earl, in 1801, his father having died in 1791. Educated at Harrow and St John's College, Cambridge. Travelled in southern Europe and the Levant 1802–04, and carried out excavations at Athens and Ephesus. Married 1805, Catherine, daughter of the 1st Marquess of Abercorn. She died 1812 and no children survived. Appointed special ambassador to Austria 1813. Signed treaty of Töplitz 1813; present at the battle of Leipzig, and signed the treaty of Paris 1814. Remarried 1815, Harriet, dowager Viscountess Hamilton; five children. Chancellor of the Duchy of Lancaster, 1828; Foreign Secretary 1828; resigned 1830. Secretary for War and the Colonies under Peel 1834–35; Foreign Secretary 1841–46; resigned (with Peel) over the Corn Laws; became leader of the Peelites 1850; formed coalition cabinet 1852; ordered the fleet to Constantinople 1853 and declared war (the Crimean War) in March 1854; driven from office January 1855; retired and created KG 1855. Died 14 December 1860.

George Hamilton Gordon, 4th Earl of Aberdeen, by J. Partridge

THE EARL OF ABERDEEN

George Hamilton Gordon, fourth Earl of Aberdeen, was born in 1784, five years before the outbreak of the French Revolution; he died in 1860, nine years after the Great Exhibition. His life therefore spanned a period of immense change in Britain. In 1784 Britain was still largely a decentralised rural society, even if industry was already embarked on its course of expansion. In 1860 an increasingly industrialised and urbanised society was justly proud of the role of 'workshop of the world'. In 1784 formal government played only a small role, but by 1860 rapid social and economic change, coupled with an unprecedentedly rapid increase of population, had necessitated considerable changes in the nature and activity of government. Aberdeen was one of the small ruling group who had to face the transformation of Britain in the space of a couple of generations. His part in this process was of less importance than that of Peel, for instance, yet his career was still one of considerable interest.

He was born into the landed aristocracy which continued to dominate Britain, as the eldest son of Lord Haddo, the heir to the third Earl of Aberdeen. The Gordon family was one of the most distinguished in the Scottish peerage, with a lineage traced, not without some doubt, to the man whose arrow had inflicted Richard I's fatal wound. The future Prime Minister's father died in 1791, his mother in 1795, and partly owing to friction with his grandfather the upbringing of the young orphan took him into the centre of late eighteenth-century political life, for the two men who played the most important parts in his guardianship in those years were Henry Dundas, Lord Melville, and William Pitt himself. He was therefore early attracted to the Tory side in politics. He succeeded his grandfather as the fourth Earl of Aberdeen in 1801, a few years before he came of age, and therefore never served a political apprenticeship in the House of Commons as so many young aristocrats did. In 1806 he became a Scottish representative peer, and remained a member of the House of Lords for the rest of his life. In the closing stages of the Napoleonic War he was employed in diplomatic tasks, mainly in helping to propel Austria into the Allied camp, and for his services here he received a United Kingdom viscountcy in 1814. He was present at some of the battles of the 1813–14 campaigns, and understandably derived from those experiences a sincere distaste for the bloodshed and waste of war.

Thereafter he was for some years engaged almost entirely in non-political activities. The estates he had inherited presented him with a considerable challenge, which he took up as a matter of duty, earning a place as an improving landlord. He spent a good deal of money and effort in such improvements as planting trees, and in providing better housing for those who lived on his property. As a territorial magnate he was much involved with the affairs of the Aberdeen district, and even when he was Prime Minister he did not relinquish his detailed concern with the local affairs of the district, finding time to attend not only to the business of his own estates, but also to the multifarious business of local societies and institutions in which his position had inevitably involved him.

In addition his intellectual interests were considerable. He had been educated at Harrow and Cambridge, and imbibed in those institutions a genuine interest in classical antiquity and art, which he retained throughout his life. Early visits to Greece stimulated these interests and turned him into an ardent philhellene. He was later to serve as an active trustee of the British Museum and the National Gallery, and he was for thirty-two years President of the Society of Antiquaries. He was not therefore a 'full-time' politician at any point, but, like many of his contemporaries active in public life, he combined a political career with the care of a substantial private estate and a variety of other non-political interests.

Aberdeen returned to active political life in 1828, on the formation of the Wellington Government. He entered that Cabinet at its inception as Chancellor of the Duchy of Lancaster, but with the departure of the Canningite ministers led by Huskisson a few months later he was promoted to the Foreign Secretaryship. This gave him a welcome opportunity to assist in the creation of the independent Greek kingdom in 1830. He was Secretary for War and Colonies in Peel's short-lived first Government of 1834–5. With Peel's triumph at the polls in 1841 Aberdeen returned to the Foreign Office, and at once inaugurated a more pacific policy than that which his predecessor, Palmerston, had introduced. A war with China was brought to an end, successive negotiations with the United States of America settled thorny boundary problems involving Canada's south-eastern and south-western frontiers, while in Europe Aberdeen brought about more friendly relations between Britain and France. Inevitably his official duties limited his interventions in domestic affairs, although he was a cordial supporter of Peel's general policies. The impending disruption in the Church of Scotland was the only domestic issue in which he took a major part, and here with the best will in the world he was unable to effect a peaceful solution to that tangled problem. During the Corn Law crisis Peel had his full support, and he left office with his leader in 1846. During the Russell Government which followed his interest in foreign affairs continued, and he pressed Peel to oppose Palmerston's aggressive policy towards Greece in the celebrated Don Pacifico crisis of 1850.

Peel's death later in 1850 left his followers in a difficult position. Peel himself had done little to preserve an independent political grouping, but many of the Peelites were anxious to retain their political cohesion, and Aberdeen emerged as the recognised head of this group, which included a formidable range of talent. Aberdeen and his associates courted unpopularity by their trenchant opposition to Russell's foolish, but immensely popular, Ecclesiastical Titles Act in 1851. That measure, designed to curb the Roman Catholic Church, was only one of a series of events which foreshadowed the fall of Russell's Government. Aberdeen was already spoken of as a possible premier at the head of a coalition of Whigs, Radicals and Peelites, and after the brief Conservative ministry which succeeded Russell in 1852 this coalition duly came into being, with Aberdeen at the head of a Cabinet which contained six Peelites, six Whigs and one very respectable Radical. The difficulties which accompanied the formation of the ministry were considerable, but largely confidential, so that at first sight the Aberdeen Government appeared strong and likely to enjoy a considerable tenure. Queen Victoria wrote of it as 'the realisation of the country's and our most ardent wishes . . . it deserves success, and will, I think command great support'.

Few Cabinets have seemed stronger in ministerial talent. The Peelites contributed Aberdeen himself, and men of acknowledged ability like Sir James Graham and Gladstone, whose first Budget in 1853 provided the new Government with a spectacular early success. Russell, Palmerston and Lansdowne were among the Whig ministers. If the nominal followings of the ministers could be relied on, the Government's majority seemed secure, while there seemed a very good chance of winning yet more support from Conservatives unhappy at the apparently arid politics of Derby and Disraeli. The session of 1853 saw a number of valuable if unspectacular reforms enacted, including a useful Factory Act, and if the deepening international crisis in the Near East was already worrying, it did not yet seem to threaten the security of the Government.

However, the way in which the Government drifted into the Crimean War seriously undermined its position in public opinion, and it was unable to withstand the mounting criticism that followed the revelations of mismanagement in the conduct of the war. The shift in public opinion was exemplified by *The Times*, then perhaps at the peak of its effective influence. That paper had given a general support to the Aberdeen Government in its early days, but in December 1854 it moved into a posture of vitriolic criticism of the shortcomings of the Government's administration of the campaign in the Crimea. However, the hostile public opinion was not something *The Times* created, but something it joined and encouraged. If the dispatches of its celebrated war correspondent, William Russell, were the most famous and among the most trenchant of the hostile reports, those reports were paralleled by scores of other scathing reports from members of the Army and visitors to the front. The mounting criticism out of doors was accompanied by a failing of the Government's parliamentary support. Early in 1855 the House of Commons inflicted on the Government one of the most stinging demonstrations of want of confidence by passing by 305 votes to 148 Roebuck's motion for a select committee to inquire into the condition of the Army in the Crimea, and the conduct of the government departments responsible for that condition. The Government at once resigned, and Aberdeen's career as a leading politician was over. For the remaining years of his life he played some part as an elder statesman, notably by trying his best by private urging to keep alive the Peelite/Whig coalition, which was not to be finally consolidated until the formation of Gladstone's first Government in 1868.

As prime minister Lord Aberdeen was not a great success. He was well aware of his own limitations, and at the formation of his Government regarded his appointment as something of a stop-gap. Events beyond his control, however, frustrated his intention to step down in Russell's favour at some convenient time, and he remained at the head of the Government until its fall. He was not a great leader of men, and failed to establish his authority and enforce his policies. It is possible that, but for the eruption of the Crimean War, the coalition he led might have established itself as a powerful ruling grouping, dedicated to 'free trade and moderate progress', concepts which could well have retained the support of the majority of politically influential elements in British society. This must remain, however, very much one of the 'ifs' of history, for the strains of the Crimean War shattered the Government's position and destroyed its hold on support in Parliament and in the country. For the Government's poor record in coping with this crisis in foreign affairs Aberdeen must bear much of the responsibility, and yet if some of the factors affecting his position are examined it may be possible to mitigate the condemnation.

Aberdeen's premiership took place in circumstances which would have posed difficulties to any executive. The period between the first and second Reform Acts was one in which the House of Commons enjoyed a greater independence than it had enjoyed in earlier periods or was to enjoy in future. The 1832 Reform Act had done something to clean up the electoral system, while leaving control of the constituencies in practice largely in the hands of minority ruling groups who could not easily be controlled by government. A man tended to sit in the mid-century House of Commons not so much because he was simply a good party man of ability, but because of his own status, wealth and influence. Increasingly the older methods by which governments had retained a hold on the Commons were being eroded; the use of government patronage as a cement of political support was increasingly limited and subject to criticism. Ironically enough, the Aberdeen Government itself, and especially its Peelite members like Gladstone and the Duke of Newcastle, played a part in the decline of the political use of patronage by their advocacy of open competition for Civil Service appointments.

If this older method of consolidating the Government's parliamentary influence was increasingly ineffective, the cohesion of party discipline was not yet strong enough to provide a government with a secure basis of parliamentary support. The Aberdeen Government held office at a period of especial uncertainty in party allegiances. Russell's failures of 1846–51 had greatly shaken his position as a leader of the Whig–Radical grouping, which had in any case never shown any very great unity. His conduct during the Aberdeen Government's tenure did nothing to strengthen the Whig ex-Premier's hold on his nominal following, and his resignation from Aberdeen's Government in face of Roebuck's hostile motion was widely, and not unjustifiably, interpreted as a disgraceful act of political desertion during a crisis. The aftermath of Aberdeen's resignation, when Russell could not find more than a handful of colleagues willing to serve under him, while Palmerston went on to form a government with relative ease, showed how far the nominal leader of the Whigs had sunk in influence. In these circumstances the Aberdeen Government was never in a position to rely confidently on the full support of the large Whig–Radical grouping in Parliament.

Since the split over the Corn Laws in 1846 the great Conservative party which Peel had led to victory in 1841 was irremediably broken. The Peelites certainly numbered in their ranks the majority of the very able ministerial group which had served in Peel's second Government, but their following in Parliament and in the country was smaller than their talents; they were to a large extent a notable group of political generals without an adequate army behind them. The Conservatives who had broken with Peel over the Corn Laws now followed Lord Derby with reasonably strong cohesion, but eyed their leader in the House of Commons, Disraeli, with markedly less cordial loyalty. On the whole the Peelites showed more capacity for union in these years than either Conservatives, Whigs or Radicals, but their basic numerical weakness in Parliament made this asset of limited value. Probably less than fifty Members of the House of Commons elected in 1852 could be counted as genuine Peelites, though from time to time their numbers were swelled by temporary support from other groupings.

In these confused and limited party situations the House of Commons itself was during the 1850s the principal agency in making and breaking governments. Party leaders and government ministers had no effective sanctions for bringing to heel recalcitrant followers, while the allegiance of many MPs was not at all clear – it was not unusual to find candidates describing themselves on the hustings in these years as Liberal Conservatives or Conservative Liberals. Members of Parliament enjoyed this independence and did not hesitate to use it with freedom. It was not a general election but the will of the House of Commons which brought down Russell's first Government and ejected its Conservative successor in favour of the Whig–Peelite–Radical Aberdeen coalition. It was the House of Commons which ignominiously ejected that coalition ministry, and installed Palmerston's first Government in its place. A fortuitous combination in the House of Commons defeated Palmerston over his

China policy in 1857, and if he returned triumphant from the general election of 1857 it was only to meet defeat in the House of Commons the following year on his policy towards France. A minority Conservative Government contrived to stay in office until 1859 when a further parliamentary combination ejected it. Governments were unable to rely on a solid basis of parliamentary support until the emergence of stronger party cohesion in the late 1860s improved matters for them. This basic political weakness of governments in the 1850s was one major factor behind the failure of the Aberdeen ministry.

There were other underlying factors too. The Aberdeen Government in its one way was undoubtedly a reforming administration in domestic affairs, and its ministers during the first peacetime months in office tackled a variety of reforming projects. Factory reform, Civil Service reform, law reform and even further parliamentary reform all had a place in the Government's programme. It might be thought that this should have won for that Government more support from Radical groups than it actually received. Yet the course of British Radicalism in the years after 1846 was not calculated to provide encouragement to a government trying to combine a policy of cautious improvement in domestic policies with a foreign policy which aimed at avoiding war. After the repeal of the Corn Laws Radicalism in Britain, which had never displayed any very high degree of unity, was very clearly divided. There were some prominent Radicals, such as Cobden and Bright, who strenuously advocated a pacific approach in foreign affairs, but there were other Radicals whose sympathy for oppressed nations abroad led them to advocate projects of intervention for purposes of liberation which far transcended anything Palmerston himself was ever prepared to contemplate seriously. The continental revolutions of 1848 had markedly accelerated that tendency, and the enthusiastic receptions accorded to refugees like Kossuth and Garibaldi emphasised the increased interest of British Radicalism in national crusades overseas. For Radicals of this school Russia was the arch-oppressor and the Crimean War a suitable occasion for the whole strength of Britain to be deployed in procuring the freedom of subject Poles, Hungarians or Italians. The moderation and vacillation of the Aberdeen Government in its relations with Russia, and then the woeful shortcomings in the management of the war, meant that the overwhelming bulk of Radical opinion in Britain moved to join the Opposition to Aberdeen's ministry. Up and down Britain Radicals denounced the Russian tyrant, and were even led to strange lengths of praise for the Government of Turkey. Aberdeen, more justly, thought that the Turkish system of government was 'vicious and abominable', but public opinion was so strongly anti-Russian that this kind of judicious assessment merely added to the Government's growing unpopularity. In these circumstances it is scarcely surprising that it was a Radical motion in the House of Commons that was to bring the Aberdeen Government down, and many Radical votes swelled the crushing majority by which Roebuck's motion was carried. If 102 Liberal votes of one kind or another supported Aberdeen in the crucial division another 84, including many Radicals, joined the official Conservative Opposition in ejecting the coalition Government which they had at first supported. The Aberdeen Government, however, could scarcely be blamed for failing to foresee how strong and determined the Radical swing to bellicose courses would be.

It is equally unreasonable that the Aberdeen Government should have borne all the obloquy derived from the patent shortcomings of British military administration in the Crimea. This was a situation they inherited, and many of the MPs who supported the Roebuck motion, and who joined in the anti-Russian outcry, had been adamant in the cause of cheap government in preceding decades. For most of the nineteenth century the armed forces of Britain were run on a financial shoe-string, and successive parliaments had shown themselves much more concerned at reducing defence estimates than in equipping the country with operationally effective armed forces. The responsibility for the weaknesses of Army and Navy during the Crimean War did not in reality lie at the door of a government which had only taken office early in 1853, but rather in a long course of neglect and cheese-paring which had taken place since 1815, and was indeed to continue for long after the Crimean War had ended. The fact that the British armed forces were inefficient and unready when war came in March 1854 was not the fault of one government, but the result of a prolonged course of economy for which a whole succession of governments and parliaments, and indeed the general public insistence on cheap government, were in reality responsible. The Aberdeen Government was blamed and condemned, but its share of responsibility for this basic element in the situation was relatively small.

Yet when all allowances have been made, the Aberdeen Government still bears considerable responsibility for its undoubted failure as a national administration. The Prime Minister himself was not well qualified to undertake the task of managing a ministerial team which posed serious difficulties of personalities from the beginning. The most difficult member of the team from the beginning was Lord John Russell, who throughout resented his supersession in the premiership by Aberdeen. He held a key position as the nominal leader of the grouping which provided the bulk of the Government's parliamentary support, but he behaved as a very unsatisfactory ministerial colleague, to such an extent that by the time of his resignation from the Government he had succeeded in alienating even the Whig colleagues with whom he had entered the coalition. Russell would have presented serious difficulties to a premier of even tougher calibre than Aberdeen; as it was throughout the life of that Government the Prime Minister was perennially plagued by Russell's erratic attempts to assert himself and force his will on the Government. Aberdeen tried again and again to bring Russell around by sweet reasonableness, succeeding repeatedly but at the cost of his own increasing disillusionment at the task he had embarked upon, as he told Bright, 'sensible of his deficiencies'. The recurrent difficulties with his disloyal subordinate played a part in the decline of Aberdeen's energy and grip. From the Government's inception, however, Aberdeen's authority over his colleagues had been uncertain. He was not a man who could dominate a Cabinet as a Peel or even a Liverpool could do. Aberdeen was much more a conciliator, more concerned at securing agreement than in securing the adoption of policies which he himself felt to be right. He was prone to second and third thoughts about decisions already reached, and altogether showed an inability to present incisive leadership to his Government. It is fair to point out, however, that he was not alone in this Cabinet in that kind of vacillation and lack of clarity of vision.

Aberdeen himself must bear much of the responsibility for the Crimean catastrophe which overwhelmed his Government. As an ex-Foreign Secretary of considerable experience, he knew something of the tangled problems of the Turkish empire. While Foreign Secretary in Peel's second Government he had discussed Russo–Turkish problems with the Tsar himself only ten years before. It is perhaps typical of Aberdeen's personality that he apparently left the Russians under the impression that the two countries were more agreed on Eastern matters than was in fact the case. The one man in the Aberdeen Government who should have been able to give a decided lead as the crisis developed, and that the Prime Minister himself, failed to display the authority on this issue to which his experience and his position could have entitled him. It is probable that Russia could have been deterred, and a peaceful solution arrived at, if it had been made clear much earlier that Britain and France were prepared to go to war on the issues involved. As it was, prolonged and tortuous negotiations were allowed to drag on in conditions of uncertainty, while at home Russophobia mounted. A prime minister, anxious to avoid the horrors of war, allowed his administration to drift towards war – a phrase used with disastrous frankness by the Foreign Secretary on 14 February 1854. The lack of decisiveness on the part of the British Government was one important factor in bringing the war about. Aberdeen himself, propelled reluctantly into a war which he had feared and opposed, did not make a good war leader, and he patently failed to provide any great inspiration during the remainder of his ministry. The minister principally concerned in Army matters, the Duke of Newcastle, was not a success; he worked hard, but possessed no great insight or ability to rise above detail. It was true that by the time the Government fell much had been done or inaugurated to remedy the deficiencies which had brought about the dreadful death-rolls of the winter of 1854-4 in the Crimea, but there had not been the sense of urgency and clear grasp of essentials which alone could have reacted in time to save the Army and with it the life of the Government. Even when the individual abilities of many of the ministers are admitted, and their modest achievements in domestic and financial matters are considered, the members of the Aberdeen Government cannot be acquitted of all responsibilitiy for the tragedy of the Crimea. They continued to employ unsatisfactory men in key positions, and the undoubted fact that they did not know where to turn to find better men does not absolve them from their failure to replace key officers in whom they themselves had lost confidence. Britain has at times produced war leaders who could do a great deal better than this, though Britain has not always done so, and the failures of the Aberdeen Cabinet as war directors are not unique in modern British history.

Lord Aberdeen himself must remain something of a pathetic figure in the gallery of British prime ministers. As Foreign Secretary under a strong prime minister in 1841-6 he had acquitted himself competently, and it was his tragedy that he was induced to accept responsibilities which were beyond his abilities. Imbued with a strong sense of public duty, he accepted in difficult circumstances the responsibilities of the premiership for which he knew himself to be ill fitted, because he believed, and was repeatedly assured by others, that his leadership, if only on a temporary basis, was a prerequisite to the creation of a stable administration. His Government set off under apparently favourable auspices, and in its first months achieved some notable successes. The deterioration of international relations, and the drift of war, faced him with greater responsibilities still, and his limited abilities as head of government, and war minister, involved him in a political catastrophe which a stronger and more determined premier might have avoided. If his personal failures did exist, and they certainly did, responsibility lies also with his ministerial colleagues, and with those at whose pleading he consented to form a government and undertake responsibilities for which he was not well equipped. His career illustrates only too clearly that amiability and goodwill are not by any means the only qualities required in a successful prime minister.

BIBLIOGRAPHY

The best biography of Lord Aberdeen remains that by his son Arthur (Lord Stanmore), *The Earl of Aberdeen* (London, 1893). In recent years a good deal of interesting work on the Peelites as a political grouping has been published by J. B. Conacher; a number of earlier articles led in 1968 to the publication of a major study of Aberdeen's Government, *The Aberdeen Coalition, 1852–5* (Cambridge).

VISCOUNT PALMERSTON

BY

JASPER RIDLEY

Henry John Temple, 3rd Viscount Palmerston. Born 20 October 1784, son of Henry, 2nd Viscount Palmerston. Succeeded 1802. Educated at Harrow, Edinburgh, and St John's College Cambridge. Elected MP for Newport, Isle of Wight, 1807. Junior Lord of the Admiralty under Portland, 1807; offered the exchequer by Perceval in 1809 but preferred the office of Secretary for War and held it until 1828 under five prime ministers. MP for Cambridge University 1811–31; Bletchingley 1831; South Hampshire 1832; Tiverton from 1835; Foreign Secretary 1830–41. Married 1839, the widow of the 5th Earl Cowper. Foreign Secretary 1846–51; Home Secretary under Aberdeen 1852–55; Prime Minister 1855–65 with one short interval in 1858–59. Died 18 October 1865.

Henry John Temple, 3rd Viscount Palmerston, by F. Cruickshank

VISCOUNT PALMERSTON

If public opinion polls had been invented in 1860, they would probably have shown that 85 per cent of the British public approved of Palmerston as Prime Minister, though when he first took office as Foreign Secretary, thirty years before, less than 10 per cent would have had a good word to say for him. In his last years 'Old Pam' was so popular that both his supporters and opponents knew that he would win every general election until he died, whether he fought it on a Radical or on a Tory policy. The people loved him for his vitality. He could ride to hounds, consume enormous meals and pursue women when he was nearly eighty; but he could also sit for hours on the government front bench, with no refreshment except an occasional cup of tea in the Members' dining room, and then, after walking home from the House of Commons to his house in Piccadilly, work half the night writing reports to the Queen – standing, not sitting, at his desk in order to stop himself from falling asleep. The people loved him for the stoutness with which he defended British interests abroad, and equally, perhaps, for his willingness to give way, and abandon unpopular measures, in response to the pressure of public opinion at home.

When he first became Prime Minister in 1855, at the age of seventy, he had already achieved some of the greatest triumphs of his career. Since his entry into politics forty-eight years before, when family influence procured him a position in the Government even before he obtained a seat in the House of Commons, he had spent forty years in office in either a Tory or a Whig Government, and sixteen years as Foreign Secretary. It is as a Foreign Secretary, even more than as a Prime Minister, that he is remembered today; and when he became Prime Minister he inspired the foreign policy of his Government, though he was scrupulous in not interfering with his Foreign Secretaries in the day-to-day conduct of foreign affairs. Britain, with its powerful Navy and its prosperous economy, was the most powerful nation in the world in Palmerston's time; and Palmerston, holding excellent cards, played the hand supremely well. He laid down his guiding principle in foreign policy in a speech in the House of Commons in March 1848:

445

that the furtherance of British interests should be the only object of a British Foreign Secretary, and that Britain had no permanent friends or permanent enemies. Sometimes his view of British interests led him to support the cause of constitutional freedom, and he was then denounced as a revolutionary by the Conservatives and applauded as a champion of freedom by the Radicals; but on other occasions he believed that it would be in Britain's interest to support dictators and enemies of constitutional freedom.

In Portugal he supported the moderate Liberals, both against the autocratic Conservatives whom Metternich favoured, and against the Radicals and Democrats, who at one time were supported by France; but in Spain, where the French supported the moderate Liberals, Palmerston backed the extreme Radicals, and justified his action by the surprising argument that Spain, unlike Britain and every other country in Europe, was ripe for democracy. In Serbia, where the landowners were supported by Russia, Palmerston supported the peasant revolutionary, Milosh, who had established a military dictatorship and was refusing to grant the demand of the large landowners that he should govern with the assistance of a constitutional Council of Boyars; and the Tsar, the great protector of European autocracy, thereupon instigated a constitutional revolution against Milosh. On the River Plate, Palmerston supported General Rosas, the dictator of Buenos Aires, against the Liberal Government of Uruguay, because he feared that the French were trying to establish a foothold in South America by supporting the Liberals of Montevideo; and he persisted in his support of Rosas even after Rosas' *gauchos* had murdered a number of British settlers in Uruguay and Argentina. Despite his long campaign to suppress the international slave trade, and his reputation as an opponent of slavery, he supported the South and the cause of slavery in the early stages of the American Civil War.

In 1851, Palmerston supported the *coup d'état* by which Napoleon III overthrew the Constitution of the French Republic. While English Liberals were expressing their indignation at Napoleon III's action in arresting his political opponents in their beds and suppressing the Republican Constitution, Palmerston congratulated Napoleon on his action, and said that if the Liberals 'meant to strike a sudden blow at him, he was quite right . . . to knock them down first'. Palmerston also supported Napoleon III in 1861, when Napoleon sent an expeditionary force to invade Mexico and set up the Austrian Archduke

Maximilian as Emperor of Mexico. Palmerston preferred Maximilian to the Liberal leader, Juarez, because he thought that strong autocratic government in Mexico would be more likely to preserve law and order and establish the necessary conditions in which British traders could carry on their affairs. He had previously supported the Government of the military dictator General Santa Anna in Mexico for the same reason.

Palmerston's reputation as a Radical in foreign policy was undeserved. He had been a junior minister in the Government that signed the Treaty of Vienna of 1815, and his original idea, when he went to the Foreign Office, was to continue the system by which the affairs of smaller nations were settled by the Great Powers at international conferences. His first achievement on taking office was the settlement of the Belgian problem; but though a Belgian historian has called him '*le père de la Belgique*', he accepted the idea of an independent Belgian state as a second-best solution, after the revolution of 1830 had convinced him that Belgium could no longer remain as a part of Holland. He never thought of Belgium as anything other than a factor in Great Power relationships.

Palmerston originally drifted almost by chance into the position of a champion of constitutional freedom in Europe. In 1832 an outbreak of student unrest at some German universities caused the powers of the German Confederation, at the instigation of Metternich, to introduce censorship and other regulations restricting constitutional liberties in the German states. William IV, as King of Hanover, was a member of the German Confederation, and his representative in the Diet voted in favour of the autocratic decrees. In order to appease the indignation that the vote of the Hanoverian delegate had caused in Liberal circles in Britain and abroad, Palmerston made a speech in the House of Commons – in a debate that only eleven MPs troubled to attend – in which he mildly criticised the decrees of the German Diet, and uttered some vague platitudes in support of the principles of constitutional government. His speech was applauded by the German Liberals, and 200,000 copies of it were circulated in Germany. Metternich and the absolutist powers thereupon denounced Palmerston as a dangerous Radical revolutionary, and the Austrian, Russian and Prussian Governments concluded the Treaty of Münchengrätz, by which they agreed to suppress revolutionary outbreaks wherever they occurred. This threw Palmerston closer to France and the Liberal forces in Britain and on the

Continent. He replied to the Treaty of Münchengrätz by the Quadruple Alliance with France and the Liberal Governments of Spain and Portugal, whom he supported in their civil wars, first in Portugal and then in Spain, against the Conservative and autocratic forces under Dom Miguel and Don Carlos. Thanks to Palmerston's support, Liberalism triumphed termporarily in both countries.

In allying himself with France – which still preserved a revolutionary reputation even under the bourgeois monarchy of Louis Philippe – Palmerston had alarmed King William IV and the British Tories, defied the deep-rooted anti-French prejudices of the British people, and won the support of the Radicals; but in 1839 he made a complete reversal of policy, and, to the delight of the Tories and the dismay of the Radicals, united with Austria and Russia against France during the Middle Eastern crisis. His solution of the long-standing conflict between the Sultan of Turkey and Mehemet Ali, the vassal Pasha of Egypt, shows his boldness of conception, his ruthlessness in execution, and his disregard of all other considerations when British interests were involved. Mehemet Ali had conquered Syria in 1833, and had governed it for six years by a brutal military dictatorship, which was more resented than the corrupt and equally tyrannical regime of the Sultan. France supported Mehemet Ali in the hopes of extending her influence eastwards from Tunisia on the North African shore of the Mediterranean; Russia supported the Sultan out of fear of French designs in the Levant, and from a desire to uphold the authority of a lawful sovereign against a rebel leader. Palmerston wished to prevent a clash between France and Russia in the Middle East and the disintegration of the Turkish Empire. He came to the conclusion that the only way to achieve this was to require Mehemet Ali to evacuate Syria and return to Egypt – 'by such means the Desert would be interposed between the two parties'.

He put this forward as a solution after the Sultan's armies had ended the six-year truce by crossing the Turco-Syrian border and attacking Mehemet Ali's troops, and had been routed at the Battle of Nezib. Neither the Sultan's aggression, and his military defeat and incompetence, nor the claim made by Mehemet Ali's sympathisers in France that the Pasha was a civilising influence in the Middle East, could deter Palmerston from inflicting this humiliation on Mehemet Ali, and restoring Syria to the rule of the Sultan. He was convinced that 'Egyptian civilization must come from Constantinople, and not from Paris, to be durable or consistent with British interests of a most important kind'.

In view of this, 'no ideas therefore of fairness towards Mehemet ought to stand in the way of such great and paramount interests'.

As France refused to join the other Great Powers in imposing this solution on Mehemet Ali, Palmerston went ahead without France, and signed the Treaty of London of 15 July 1840, by which Britain, Russia, Austria and Prussia agreed to use whatever force was necessary to expel Mehemet Ali from Syria. This aroused the greatest indignation in France, and it seemed that a major European war was inevitable. But Palmerston, almost alone among his Cabinet colleagues, did not worry. He believed that France would be prepared, if necessary, to go to war with Britain, Russia, Prussia and Austria 'if those Powers were to threaten to invade France, to insult her honour, or to attack her Possessions; but France will not go to war with the other Great Powers of Europe to help Mehemet Ali'. His policy was completely successful. Mehemet Ali was expelled from Syria, and France did nothing to help him.

When Palmerston, after five years in opposition, returned to the Foreign Office in 1846, a series of events identified him more closely than ever with the Radicals in Europe. The foreign autocrats believed that he was the arch-revolutionary who was responsible for all the trouble in Europe in 1848; and he was called a 'Red' by a Conservative MP in the House of Commons. In fact, Palmerston's attitude to the revolutions of 1848, which he described as a struggle 'between those who have no property and those who have and wish to keep it', was mixed. He gave moral support to the revolutionary Government of Lamartine, which was established after the February revolution in Paris, because he believed, like Karl Marx, that it was the only bulwark between France and a Communist revolution. In Spain he supported the extreme Radicals, and suffered a defeat. But in Germany he successfully opposed the revolutionary threat to the rule of the Danish monarchy in Schleswig-Holstein. In Hungary, though he had some sympathy with the revolutionary nationalist movement, he refused to give it any support, or to make any official protest when Russian troops intervened to help Austria suppress the revolt. 'Much as Her Majesty's Government regret this interference of Russia, the causes which have led to it, and the Effects which it may produce,' he wrote to the Chargé d'Affaires in St Petersburg, 'they nevertheless have not considered the occasion to be one which at present calls for any formal expression of the opinions of Great Britain on the matter.' It was only after the rebels had been defeated that Palmerston, in response to British public opinion, protested against the hangings and floggings by which the victors were punishing the Hungarian patriots. But by supporting Turkey in her refusal, under a Russian threat of war, to extradite the Hungarian refugees, he won the undying gratitude of Radicals throughout the world.

Palmerston did not give any assistance to the Polish struggle for independence from Russia, although the friends of Polish freedom, under the leadership of Lord Dudley Stuart, had established a vociferous lobby in the House of Commons. Palmerston gave no active support to Poland in 1831, 1836, 1846 or 1863; and he refused to take up the Polish cause in 1856, when the peace treaty was being imposed on a defeated Russia after the Crimean War, though this was probably the only occasion when he would have been able to do something practical to help the Poles. The Polish poet Niemcewicz, who had an interview with Palmerston, found him 'colder than ice'; and the leader of the Poles in exile, Prince Czartoryski, was quite unable to get him to go to war to liberate Poland. 'The English nation is able to make war,' said Palmerston, 'but it will only do so where its own interests are concerned. We are a simple and practical nation, a commercial nation; we do not go in for chivalrous enterprises, or fight for others as the French do.'

But in Italy, Palmerston modified his usual policy of ignoring everything except British interests, because here he was influenced by British public opinion, to which he was always responsive. The traditional British policy in Italy had been to support Austria against French expansion; but the British people, because of their hostility to the Pope and Roman Catholicism and their romantic adoration of Garibaldi, were enthusiastically in favour of Italian unification and liberation. So Palmerston, after pursuing the traditional pro-Austrian policy during the revolution of 1831, became pro-Italian in later years. 'North of the Alps,' he wrote in 1848, he wished Austria 'all the prosperity and success in the world'; but south of the Alps she must give up Lombardy, and perhaps Venetia also. In 1859 he won a general election in Britain on a pro-Italian policy; and he was able to reconcile British interests and British public opinion by working for an independent united kingdom of Italy, which would be as effective a barrier to French expansion as the presence of the Austrian army in a disunited Italy.

In the Far East, Palmerston's policy involved Britain in three wars with China and a bombardment of Japan. His object here, as in other parts of the world, was not to acquire territory – he took 'the desert island of Hong Kong' reluctantly – but to secure the Chinese market for the British trader. 'The rivalship of European manufactures,' he wrote in 1841, 'is fast excluding our productions from the markets of Europe, and we must unremittingly endeavour to find in other parts of the world new vents for the produce of our industry. The world is large enough and the wants of the human race ample enough to afford a demand for all we can manufacture; but it is the business of the Government to open and to secure the roads for the merchant.' As China resisted the British trader, Palmerston used force to overcome this resistance.

There was no feeling of racial superiority in Palmerston's attitude to China. He once called the Chinese Mandarin Governor, Yeh, 'an insolent barbarian wielding authority at Canton'; but this was in an address to his constituents when he was electioneering on a chauvinist policy and successfully smearing his Conservative opponents as pro-Chinese and anti-British. He thought the Chinese were no better or worse than other races. 'Depend upon it,' he wrote, 'that the best way of keeping any men quiet is to let them see that you are able and determined to repel force by force; and the Chinese are not in the least different, in this respect, from the rest of mankind.'

In 1851 Palmerston was dismissed from the Foreign Office at the insistence of Queen Victoria, who disapproved of his policy of supporting revolutionary movements in Europe. He returned to the Government after only a year in opposition; but it was as Home Secretary, and not in the office with which the whole nation associated him. During the Middle Eastern crisis of 1853, when the Great Powers slowly drifted into the first major European war for forty years, Palmerston was not directly in charge of British foreign policy, though his influence in the Cabinet forced the pacific Premier, Lord Aberdeen, to stiffen his attitude towards Russia, and ultimately to declare war. After the first disasters at Sevastopol and Balaclava, popular indignation with military incompetence in the Crimea forced the Government to resign, and public opinion demanded that Palmerston should become Prime Minister. His colleagues in the Cabinet knew that he had been as much responsible as the rest of them for the mistakes which had been made; but no one else had the confidence of the nation. 'I am, for the moment, *l'inévitable*,' he wrote on 15 February 1855, ten days after he had formed a government.

Palmerston's appointment as Prime Minister did not lead to much improvement in the efficiency of the military command in the Crimea; but the war was won, and thanks to Palmerston's intransigence Russia was forced to accept harsh terms at the Peace Congress, and to relinquish the right to maintain warships in the Black Sea. Palmerston was very popular in Britain after the end of the Crimean War, and he won a great victory at the general election of 1857 when he appealed to the country to support his aggressive policy in China. Next year he suddenly fell from power when the House of Commons rejected his Conspiracy to Murder Bill, which placed restrictions on the freedom of foreign political refugees in Britain; but after less than eighteen months in opposition, he was again Prime Minister, this time at the head of a Liberal Government with Radical support. He and his party had won the general election of 1859 on a pledge to introduce new measures of parliamentary reform, which would give the vote to the working classes in the towns. But Palmerston, who had always opposed this proposal, succeeded in holding up the measure until after his death, in office, six years later, and it was not until 1867 that the second Reform Bill was passed.

In home affairs, the story of Palmerston's second premiership is of a Prime Minister who, by relying on his great personal popularity, his jovial temperament, and his skilful handling of his supporters, succeeded in thwarting, as far as possible, the political and social reforms which were favoured by the majority of his Cabinet, and especially by his Chancellor of the Exchequer, Gladstone. But Palmerston was in perfect harmony with the 'silent majority' of the period, though not at all with the ideas of the advanced intellectuals. He remained largely unaffected by the humanism of the nineteenth century. He moved forward along the lines of reform that the pioneers had indicated, but only when the majority of his contemporaries did the same; as his friend, Henry Bulwer, put it, 'in the march of his epoch he was behind the eager but before the slow'. He fought his first election in 1806, when he was a young man of twenty-one, as a supporter of the slave trade; thirty years later, as Foreign Secretary, he played the leading part in suppressing the slave trade of foreign nations by the use of the British Navy. As a young junior minister at the War Office, he strongly defended flogging in the Army; and though, some years later, he recommended that the maximum number of lashes that could be administered for a 'small' offence should be reduced from 300 to 200, he remained a believer in flogging all his life. In 1820 he played an active part in tracking down a young poacher, who had wounded his gamekeeper in Hampshire, for which the poacher was hanged, despite an agitation for a reprieve; and Palmerston's conduct in the case caused him to be attacked by Cobbett and the Radicals as a prototype of the oppressive landlord. But he ended his career, in Disraeli's words, as the Tory chief of a Radical Cabinet, and presided at the foundation of the modern Liberal Party in 1859.

He was out of sympathy with the new morality of the mid-nineteenth century, with its campaigns to redeem prostitutes, and said that he thought prostitutes fulfilled a useful function in society, because the existence of prostitutes prevented men from pursuing respectable women – a statement that did not apply in his own case. As Home Secretary he introduced some measures of penal reform, and took the first steps to establish a system of special treatment for young offenders; but when an outburst of violent crime aroused public indignation in 1862, when he was Prime Minister, he urged his Home Secretary to abolish most of the reforms which he himself had introduced nine years before. He believed ardently in free trade and the principles of complete economic freedom which he had learnt as a student from his Whig teachers at Edinburgh University, and insisted on applying them even when they meant allowing the export of food, and the denial of Poor Relief, in time of famine. He supported the new Poor Law of 1834, in the face of criticism from both Tories and Chartists, and reacted only with a jovial laugh when his Chartist opponent in his constituency at Tiverton asked him how he would like it if he and Lady Palmerston were confined in separate quarters in a workhouse and forbidden to see each other. But he helped Lady Palmerston's son-in-law, Lord Shaftesbury, in his campaigns to introduce social reforms, and he won the gratitude of the trade union movement by his support for the Ten Hours Bill.

Palmerston has been described as a Conservative at home and a Liberal abroad; but there was no real contradiction between his internal and foreign policy. He believed, like most Englishmen of his generation, that the British Constitution and social system of the early nineteenth century were the best in the world, and as near to perfection as any merely human institution could ever be. He believed in constitutional monarchy, with a sovereign who was by no means politically powerless, but who was subject to the law, respected the privileges of

Parliament, and acted on the advice of his ministers. He believed in a Parliament in which one House was composed of the wealthiest land-owners, and the other was elected on a franchise which gave the vote to only 5 per cent of the adult males in the country. He believed in the rule of law; but when the State was in danger, the rule of law included the Six Acts, which Lord Liverpool's Tory Government, in which Palmerston was a minister, passed in 1819 at the time of Peterloo, and which severely restricted the political freedom of the opposition parties. He believed in the freedom of the press, but of a press whose circulation was restricted to the wealthier classes by the stamp duties and the paper tax. He was a Conservative at home because he wished to preserve this system and prevent any developments in the direction of democracy. He was a Liberal abroad because he wished to see this system replace the absolutist monarchies of the Continent. In 1863, during the Polish revolt against Russia and the American Civil War, he told the House of Commons that peaceful England stood half-way, politically as well as geographically, between the two hateful extremes of royal despotism and Republican democracy.

This firm belief in English superiority was the chief cause of Palmerston's popularity in his later years as Foreign Secretary and as Prime Minister. The ordinary Englishman loved him because he sent gun-boats to protect the rights of any British subject who was injured or insulted abroad. In the debate in the House of Commons on the case of Don Pacifico in 1850, Roebuck declared that though the Tsar of Russia could send any of his own subjects to Siberia when he pleased, Palmerston would never permit him to do the same to a British subject. This was the Palmerston myth; but the reality was a little different. Palmerston used the Navy to blockade Greece to vindicate the rights of Don Pacifico, and to bombard Canton and Kagoshima to avenge an insult to the British flag or the murder of a British subject. But when Russian officers arrested an Ionian islander, who was a British subject, in Bucharest, Palmerston merely sent a protest; and he did nothing at all when a negro seaman, who was also a British subject, was dragged off his ship by the authorities at Charleston under a law that made it an offence for a free negro to be at large in the state of South Carolina. Russia and the United States were too powerful to be treated like Greece or Portugal.

There were only two occasions when Palmerston came near to using force against a great power to uphold the rights of a British subject or the honour of the British flag. Both times it was against the United States. The first occasion was in 1841, when a Canadian militiaman was put on trial for murder in New York because he had shot a United States citizen on the United States side of the frontier in the course of his official duties during the suppression of a rebellion. The case aroused strong feelings in both Britain and the United States, and the pressure of British public opinion drove a reluctant Palmerston to the brink of war. The other occasion was the case of the *Trent*, during the peculiar circumstances of the American Civil War, when a Northern warship stopped a British vessel on the high seas and removed two envoys of the Southern Confederacy who were travelling to Europe. In both cases, Palmerston's threat of war induced the United States to back down; but in the closing years of the Civil War, Palmerston developed a healthy respect for the power of the United States, and tolerated affronts to the British flag which were as flagrant as the case of the *Trent*. In 1858, he had stated that there were only three nations in the world who were strong enough to challenge British naval superiority – France, Russia and the United States. In the last months of his life, in 1865, he believed that it was the United States from which the threat to British power would come in the future.

Palmerston's policy of threatening weaker states with British power, and of conciliating stronger nations as much as possible, outraged the Nonconformist conscience and the sense of sportsmanship of some of the British people. Many Englishman saw him, as the cartoonists of *Punch* did, as a plucky boy who fought big bullies twice his size; but his critics, including such varied personages as Prince Albert, Cobden, Lord Cardigan and Marx, agreed with the Radical MP, Attwood, that Palmerston was 'a bully to the weak and a coward to the strong'. Palmerston's Cabinet colleague, Sidney Herbert, wrote: 'Palmerston can never resist shaking his fist in the face of anyone whom he is not afraid of. If they show fight, he runs away.' Palmerston replied to this accusation by pointing out that no one should accuse him of capitulating to powerful states, because he had been in favour of going to war with Russia in defence of Turkey in 1853.

When Palmerston was conducting British foreign policy, he did not act in the sporting spirit of a boys' public school, but in accordance with the harsh realities of international politics. He used British power to the full, in Britain's interests, against weaker opponents, and prevented Britain from clashing with powerful states in contests in which Britain might suffer damage. To have done less would, in his opinion, have been failing in his duty as a British Foreign Secretary. He had no faith in Cobden's ideal of international arbitration, and usually refused to submit to the arbitration of a third power in international disputes. He did not believe that any power could be an impartial arbitrator where Britain was concerned, because there was no state that did not have a conflict of interests with Britain in some part of the world. He thought that such conflicts were inevitable, because though he believed that there were many spheres, especially in trade, in which nations could co-operate for their mutual benefit, there were other areas in which interests were irreconcilable – for example in the Middle East, where Britain and France were like two men in love with the same woman. 'It would be very delightful if your Utopia could be realised,' he told Cobden, 'and if the nations of the earth would think of nothing but peace and commerce, and would give up quarrelling and fighting altogether. But unfortunately man is a fighting and quarrelling animal; and that this is human nature is proved by the fact that republics, where the masses govern, are far more quarrelsome, and more addicted to fighting, than monarchies, which are governed by comparatively few persons.'

It was therefore necessary to preserve British military strength. To have a powerful army and navy was like carrying an umbrella on a showery day; if you took it, you were sure not to need it, but if you did not take it, you would regret it. Unless Britain maintained her military superiority, she was lost, because though the anger of a weaker power did not matter, the anger of a stronger power meant national humiliation. Palmerston applied this rule to other nations, and expected them to apply it to Britain. When Bismarck ignored his bluff and invaded Schleswig-Holstein in 1864, after Palmerston had promised that in this case he would go to the assistance of Denmark, he did nothing to help the Danes, and announced, with a cheerfulness that shocked his Foreign Secretary, Lord Russell, that there was nothing he could do against 200,000 soldiers. But the British people did not lose faith in him. In 1865 he won another general election, but died before he could meet the new Parliament.

His humiliation at the hands of Bismarck was one of the few defeats of his career. In general, his handling of foreign policy was brilliant and successful. Cobden accused him of what would today be called 'brinkmanship'. 'Palmerston likes to drive the wheel close to the edge,' he wrote, 'and show how dexterously he can avoid falling over the precipice.' Only once during Palmerston's lifetime did the carriage go over the precipice. This was in 1853, during the months before the outbreak of the Crimean War, when Palmerston was in the Government, but not at the Foreign Office. If he had been in charge of Britain's foreign policy at the time, the carriage would probably just have managed to stay on the road.

BIBLIOGRAPHY

Biographies of Palmerston

Bell, H. C. F., *Lord Palmerston* (2 vols, London, 1936)
Dalling, Lord (Sir Henry Lytton Bulwer) and Ashley, Evelyn, *The Life of Henry John Temple, Viscount Palmerston* (5 vols, London, 1870–6)
Pemberton, W. B., *Lord Palmerston* (London, 1954)
Ridley, Jasper, *Lord Palmerston* (London, 1970)

Studies of Palmerston's policy

Connell, B., *Regina v. Palmerston* (London, 1962)
Douglas, George, Eighth Duke of Argyll, *Autobiography and Memoirs* (2 vols, London, 1906)
Guedalla, Philip, *Gladstone and Palmerston: being the correspondence of Lord Palmerston with Mr Gladstone 1851–65* (London, 1928)
Martin, Kingsley, *The Triumph of Lord Palmerston* (London, 1924) (for the Eastern Question in 1853, and the Crimean War)
Southgate, D., *'The Most English Minister . . .': The Policies and Politics of Palmerston* (London, 1966)
Vincent, J., *The Formation of the Liberal Party 1857–68* (London, 1966)
Webster, Sir Charles, *The Foreign Policy of Palmerston 1830–41* (2 vols, London, 1951)

BENJAMIN DISRAELI
EARL OF BEACONSFIELD

BY

JOHN VINCENT

Benjamin Disraeli, created Earl of Beaconsfield 1876. Born 21 December 1804, first son of Isaac D'Israeli, author, and Maria, daughter of Naphtali Basevi, merchant. Baptised into the Church of England 1817. Educated at the schools of Miss Roper (in Islington), the Rev. Potticany (Blackheath) and the Rev. Eli Cogan (Walthamstow), ending in 1819. Married, 1839, Mary Anne, widow of Wyndham Lewis, MP; she was created Viscountess Beaconsfield in 1868 and died in 1872. MP for Maidstone, 1837–41, Shrewsbury, 1841–47; Buckinghamshire, 1847–76. Chancellor of the Exchequer, 1852, 1858–59, 1866–68; First Lord of the Treasury and Prime Minister 1868 and 1874–80; Lord Privy Seal 1876–78; PC 1852; Trustee of the National Portrait Gallery (1856) and British Museum (1863–81); DCL (Oxford) 1873, LLD (Glasgow) 1873, FRS 1876, KG 1878. Died 19 April 1881. No issue. Author of numerous novels, Coningsby, Tancred, Sybil, Lothair, Endymion, *among them.*

Benjamin Disraeli, Earl of Beaconsfield, by J. E. Millais

BENJAMIN DISRAELI

Mr Gladstone once said to his son that 'Mr Disraeli was in the centre of three rings – his party, which he understood perfectly and governed completely; the House of Commons, of which his knowledge was good; the country, of which he was very ignorant.'[1] This judgement contains a core of truth: Disraeli was greater as leader of a parliamentary party than as Prime Minister and head of a government. With Fox, he was the greatest leader of an opposition this country has known. For most of his career a single-minded parliamentarian, his knowledge of the country at large was highly selective, and much limited by the peculiar background of his early life.

The evidence for Disraeli's early years is inevitably slight.[2] Three points stand out. Firstly, Disraeli was born and bred a town boy, nurtured in Holborn and Bloomsbury, without any knowledge of the rural pursuits that made an English gentleman: riding a horse was always a problem for him. Secondly, though his parents had at heart rejected most of Judaism, he was brought up in many ways as a Jew by religion, received lessons in Hebrew, and was not received into the Church of England until he was twelve. Thirdly, for reasons unknown, he was not educated as befitted the son of a rich and distinguished man of letters. He left school at about fifteen, thereafter engaging in only desultory study. After some time reading at home, he entered a solicitor's office for three years, then gave it up as unsuited to his requirements. Disraeli, aged 20, was already in 1825 a very ambitious youth of distinctive character and no prospects.

Disraeli's first attempt to take the world by storm occurred in 1824–6. He took part in an attempt to create a great newspaper, the *Representative*, to rival *The Times*, by using the money of the publisher Murray and the mind of Lockhart. The paper failed, and Murray lost £26,000. A brilliant novel of politics and society then appeared, anonymously, caricaturing poor Murray. Its initial success turned to disaster as

---

[1] Viscount Gladstone, *After Thirty Years* (London, 1928), p. 162.
[2] For his home background, see James Ogden, *Isaac D'Israeli* (Oxford, 1969): for Disraeli in the 1820s and 1830s, see B. R. Jerman, *The Young Disraeli* (London, 1960).

Disraeli's authorship leaked out. By 1826, Disraeli was *persona non grata* in the smart literary circles around Murray, access to which had been his only silver spoon. A failure at 21, Disraeli retorted upon the world with a prolonged breakdown or nervous illness. In addition, he had acquired Stock Exchange debts, a millstone round his neck for most of his life. The family moved, in 1829, to Bradenham in rural Buckinghamshire, with their son's illness very much in mind. In 1830, however, Disraeli was still an unemployed invalid of 25, apolitically nursing his constitution in country quiet, outside society.

In 1830-1, however, the pattern of his life was changed decisively by a tour in the Mediterranean and Near East, during which his nervous troubles virtually disappeared. He found aspects of Turkish life profoundly congenial: yet he never returned. It was a curious time for a future politician to be abroad, but when he returned, he was determined to cut a figure. Early in 1832 he took up residence in the West End. In 1832-4 he took his bearings, a minor mistress, and an idiosyncratic Radical line in politics. In 1834 he met and committed himself to Lord Lyndhurst, an ageing intriguer who became his mentor, and to the Conservatives. The years 1834-7 were ones of political and financial struggle, and of a considerable affair with Henrietta Sykes, mother of four and wife of a baronet: she died in 1846. Her feelings for him were intense: for his part, he felt able to pass her on to Lyndhurst, an act that was held against him in later years. Political success came in 1837, with election for Maidstone, and relative financial security with his marriage to Mrs Wyndham Lewis, a widow twelve years his senior, in 1839. Out of all his early precocity, his years of ill health, and his rakish adventures of the 1830s, he carried forward into middle life nothing more useful than an indifferent marriage (in the world's eyes), a bad name, and large debts.

In 1837-41 Disraeli was a loyal follower of Peel. In 1841 he begged Peel for office. In 1842 he remained loyal, though bitterly disappointed, conspicuously rejecting the opportunity to join the faction of agricultural malcontents who were the true opposition to Peel within the Tory ranks. With this section he had virtually no contact (or sympathy) before 1846. His course, instead, was to try to form a third force, neither wholly for nor wholly against Peel, but simply, in ideology, far above his prosy level-headedness, and in numbers capable of holding the balance. The numbers were a dream, for 'Young England', not originated by Disraeli but taken over by him, centred on three young men just down from university: Smythe, a Byronic cynic, Manners, a knight errant, and Baillie Cochrane, a fop. Pilgrimages were made northwards, and in 1843 Disraeli, opening the Manchester Athenaeum in company with Dickens and Cobden, declared Manchester to be as great a human enterprise as Athens. The mood was one of Tory democracy, in the sense that note was taken of the poor: the remedies were paternalistic. 'Young England' was a talking-point in 1843–4, but not an influence upon events, and by 1845 it belonged to the past. In one way at least it was not impeccable, for Disraeli sought to attach to it a scheme by which he and his comrades would exert influence on behalf of the French Government.[3] The real importance of Young England was not that it led Disraeli to break with Peel: it may, by distracting him, even have deferred such a break. Young England did, however, stimulate Disraeli to write novels far more remarkable than anything of which he had hitherto appeared capable: *Coningsby* (1844), *Sybil* (1845), and *Tancred* (1847).

Up to the end of 1845 there was little sign of Disraeli turning into an active parliamentary figure. He did not speak frequently before the crisis of 1846.

1845 saw the break-up of Young England, with its members disagreeing over the Maynooth grant, and Smythe, his leading ally, accepting office in Peel's last ministry. Early in 1845, Disraeli compared the situation to 'the third year of the Walpole administration'.[4] He spent most of summer and autumn 1845 abroad and out of touch with affairs, reaching Paris in December to hear of the ministerial crisis in London. Far from hurrying home, the Disraelis remained in Paris. 'I do not think I shall be tempted to quit this agreeable residence – especially as the great object of my political career is now achieved,' Disraeli told Palmerston on 14 December 1845.[5]

Disraeli's attacks on Peel, beginning on the first night of the Corn Laws debate, were a supreme rhetorical achievement, and no one at the time was unaware of the fact. The real question was how many ordinary

[3] For Disraeli's memorandum for the King of the French, 1842, offering to use 'a party of the youth of England' to manipulate the House of Commons and the press in French interests, see W. F. Monypenny and G. E. Buckle, *The Life of Benjamin Disraeli, Earl of Beaconsfield* (6 vols, London, 1910–20), ii, 409–13.
[4] Disraeli to his sister, 6 Feb. 1845. (*Lord Beaconsfield's Letters 1830 to 1852*, ed. R. Disraeli (London, 1887), pp. 204–5.)
[5] Monypenny and Buckle, op. cit., ii, 340.

Conservative MPs, having made their protest, really wanted to bring Peel down, and to create a separate Protectionist party. The formation of this latter body, early in 1846, decided nothing: even the partial acquisition of Stanley as leader and Bentinck as lieutenant decided nothing. In the end, under seventy Tory MPs[6] were able to bring themselves to vote Peel out of office on the Irish Coercion Bill on 25 June 1846. It remained for succeeding years to decide whether the Corn Law crisis had produced anything more than one more ephemeral splinter group on the right wing of the Conservative party.

The years 1847–8 showed how much Disraeli remained an outsider in the Protectionist party, and how little his achievement in 1846 had done to give him a permanent status in politics. Lord George Bentinck, hitherto a racing man who was not active in politics, had emerged in 1846 as the most forcible personality among the Protectionists in the Commons. It was to him, not to Lord Stanley, the party leader, that Disraeli attached himself. Indeed, until 1849 Disraeli and Stanley had little contact even for business purposes. Bentinck wanted his party to be a party of uncompromising principle where Peel and Protection were concerned, but to be reasonably tolerant on Irish, Catholic, and Jewish questions. His backbenchers were simple bigots, and Stanley, and the Commons whips under his control, felt bound to give way to their views. At the end of 1847 Bentinck resigned, after he and Disraeli had set the teeth of their party on edge by supporting Jewish rights. Disraeli remained on the front bench, to which his friend never returned: but he had no official position in the party. In 1848, a new leader, Lord Granby, was appointed by Stanley. His sole merit was that he was not Disraeli: and he resigned after four weeks, leaving the party in the Commons leaderless for the rest of 1848. Bentinck's sudden death, in September 1848, released Disraeli from loyalty to an impossible politician, and was to that extent an advantage, but it did not mean that Disraeli inherited the leadership by natural succession.

Disraeli had been relying on Bentinck and his brothers for a massive sum of money to purchase the Hughenden estate in Buckinghamshire. In the event Bentinck's brothers continued to provide finance, and in 1848 Disraeli finally became a country gentleman, having also acquired a safe seat for the county at the 1847 general election. Stanley still opposed Disraeli's advancement, as did the Whips, and it was only

[6] Robert Stewart, *The Politics of Protection: Lord Derby and the Protectionist Party 1841–52* (Cambridge, 1971), p. 74.

after many months of manoeuvre and confrontation that, early in 1849, a triumvirate of Disraeli, Lord Granby, and Herries, an aged bureaucrat, was chosen by Stanley to lead in the Commons. The triumvirate lasted on paper till early in 1852, but never existed in practice. Disraeli was in brilliant form in the 1849 session: in the three sessions from 1849 to 1851 his attacking tactics made the acrimonious little groups of 1846-8 into an effective alternative government. In 1851 the Whigs were defeated, but Stanley either could not or would not take their place. From the day Disraeli took over, however, it was only a matter of time before the Derbyites took office. Russell resigned over a trifle in February 1852, and Derby formed a minority government.

The 1852 ministry appeared laughably weak. It was a purely Tory ministry, without any accession of strength from Palmerston or from individual Peelites, such as the Protectionists had hoped for in 1849-51. For all that, the ministry managed its business creditably. There were very few embarrassing moments, and the new ministers emerged as conscientious and honest, if limited. Disraeli himself was highly pleased with affairs until the last few months of the ministry. Abroad, the aftermath of Louis Napoleon's *coup de'état* was handled without incident. The business of the year, however, was of very little consequence save for the general election (July) and Disraeli's second Budget (December). The December Budget, designed essentially to compensate the landed interest by tax reductions for loss of protection, embodied Derbyite acceptance of the new situation. It came unstuck, partly for technical reasons, ultimately because the negotiations between Whigs and Peelites for coalition had been completed: but not before Disraeli had established himself as the indispensable leader of a united Derbyite party in the Commons.

The 1852 ministry, by abandoning Protection, left the Derbyites without a *raison d'être* for the rest of the 1850s, and out of office until 1858-9. Their prospects were at first felt to be grim, for Aberdeen's deep conservatism left little scope for providing what Derby wished, a party of resistance to Reform; while Disraeli's experiments with a Radical alliance, and his foundation of his own paper, *The Press*, in May 1853, excited much suspicion. In 1854, however, Russell's Reform Bill, widely regarded as an extreme measure, cheered Tory spirits and enabled them to look forward confidently to the break-up of the coalition. It is important to realise that the Tory leaders were very much not disheartened until the Crimean War. 'Disraeli is furious with the war, which he thinks keeps Government in,' Malmesbury wrote.[7] Despite a moment early in 1855 when a Derby government seemed possible, the Derbyites, unable to unite on a distinctive pro-war or anti-war policy, were completely overshadowed by Palmerston in 1855–8, years in which even Disraeli found little he could do.

The 1858–9 ministry was a success. Its Reform Bill, which did not pass, and its India Bill, which did, showed Tory ministers as capable of dealing with large schemes of legislation in a liberal spirit, in a way unknown in 1852. Ministers made no serious errors, though Malmesbury allowed himself to appear more opposed to Italian liberty than he was. Disraeli, now helped by the very able young Northcote, was able to appear a respectable, if not brilliant, Chancellor of the Exchequer. A start was also made on Tory social policy, with Disraeli carrying a major measure for the sewerage of London, and some legal reforms being carried. There were absurdities in Disraeli's Reform Bill, as in his Indian proposals, but the confidence of the Tory leaders and the unity of the party made a good impression compared with the discord amongst its opponents. This was reflected in the best election results for the Derbyites between 1841 and 1874. The 1858–9 ministry was very much a conscious preparation for an inevitable coming election. As such, it very nearly, but not quite, was a brilliant success, under its slogan of 'Conservative progress'.

The 1857 election was the first to bring into prominence the threat posed to the Church of England by an increasingly aggressive Dissent. Church Defence Associations sprang up in reply: and Disraeli was quick to spot the need to revive the rather latent connections of Church and Toryism. Disraeli also needed to take up a soundly reactionary policy on church questions for three reasons. Firstly, the line of 'Conservative progress' set out in 1858–9, while useful for making inroads into the Liberal consensus, needed balancing by a complementary traditionalist doctrine. Secondly, Disraeli wanted to commit his party to a reactionary line on church matters, so that it could remain flexible and uncommitted on Reform. Thirdly, Disraeli could and did win parliamentary victories on matters like Trelawny's Church Rates motions, without bringing the Government down (since they were Private Members' proposals). From the late 1850s, many senior Conservatives had plans for quietly conceding the main issues like church rates:

[7] Earl of Malmesbury, *Memoirs of an Ex-Minister: An Autobiography* (London, 1884), i, 434.

Disraeli, acting upon a higher strategy, saw to it that denominational controversy became the essence of party politics in the 1860s. From 1860 to 1868, Disraeli made defence of the Church the most conspicuous commitment of his party.

Between 1859 and 1865, a state of truce between the parties was a mixture of belief and fact. Disraeli, at least, accepted the party truce to the extent of being far less aggressive than in the 1850s. The truce meant different things at different times. In 1859-60, Tories wished to avoid a further election, although Palmerston's majority was only around a dozen. In 1861-2, the deaths, first of the Queen's mother, then of Prince Albert, were taken as grounds for subduing political strife. In 1863 and 1864, spirited challenges by the Opposition fell through partly because some Tory Dissidents preferred to keep Palmerston in power, partly because the Tory leaders' own strategy was to avoid coming to power until they could do so on their own terms, with a majority, and for a long period. In addition, Palmerston and the Tory squires were in real agreement on fundamentals, and this made the decade 1855-65 a period in which Disraeli could do little but mark time.

The Conservative position on Reform in the period 1850-66 was by no means one of simple dislike of a wide franchise. The party, and Disraeli, did at times take up a public posture of reaction, partly because (especially in Derby's case) they thought that the right role for the party, partly in order to lure away dissatisfied right-wing Whigs. This was most obviously the case in 1854 and 1866. In general, however, the Tories and Disraeli easily avoided any rigid commitment against Reform. Some leading Tories actually wanted Reform: young Lord Stanley wrote in 1853, 'It is the duty of statesmen . . . to bring within the pale of the Constitution everyone whose admission cannot be proved dangerous.'[8] Derby himself was not inclined to take the lowering of the franchise too seriously, provided that the political situation in the counties remained unaffected. As early as 1854, Disraeli and Derby had drawn up a Tory Reform Bill in case of need. Influenced by the conservatism of universal suffrage in France, important Conservatives came to believe that significant concessions could be made in the franchise without affecting the *status quo* in the counties, or the *status quo* in Parliament. In 1866, the general drift of Conservative opinion was towards compromise and a small reduction in the urban franchise, and but for Disraeli and Derby the question might well have been settled

[8] Monypenny and Buckle, op. cit., iii, 501.

quietly for a generation. Disraeli's tactics, however, were to split the Liberal party while also refusing coalition with Liberal anti-Reform Dissidents: thus, having wrecked Russell's Reform Bill of 1866, he and Derby again came to power, uncommitted to any policy, and unallied to any outside group, in June 1866.[9]

During the winter of 1866–7, a consensus emerged among Tory ministers in favour of action on the Reform question. Agitation out of doors may have determined this consensus: it did not decide whether such action was to be real or illusory, restrictive or inclusive. Disraeli naturally had many ideas, eventually coming out in favour of pure procrastination. In this respect he was decidedly less bold than his colleagues. Derby, however, was leader, and retained some of his rashness. The Tories decided to act, and Derby then fell ill. Throughout the 1867 session, the existence of both the party and the Bill rested on Disraeli's shoulders. He could not afford to fail. He tried, first, to create a restrictive measure designed to attract the support of all those who loathed Reform. Three right-wing ministers (Salisbury, Carnarvon, and General Peel) resigned over this, and the right-wing Whigs would not give support. This right-wing opposition to a moderate Bill made it certain that only an extremely Radical Bill could be passed. Unable to lure votes from the Whigs, Disraeli laid bait for the Radicals, who were happy to accept. The Bill eventually passed, altered out of all recognition from the Bill originally introduced: but this did not mar Disraeli's achievement. His party remained intact and in office, while the Liberals had disintegrated and Gladstone had been reduced to impotence. That, for Disraeli, was the meaning of the Bill.

The single provision of the Bill that really mattered was that the urban working class got the vote, subject to technical exceptions. It was not that this produced recognisable changes in political patterns in the short term: on the contrary, it simply gave existing middle-class Radical MPs in the big cities more constituents to canvass. On the other hand, omitting to enfranchise the politically conscious working class at such an early date might have led to a very different kind of politics. As it was, the 1868 election produced results little different from that of 1865: only in working-class Lancashire and suburban Middlesex

[9] See especially M. Cowling, 'Disraeli, Derby and Fusion, October 1865 to July 1866', *Historical Journal*, viii (1965): also F. B. Smith, *The Making of the Second Reform Bill* (Cambridge, 1966), and M. Cowling, *1867: Disraeli, Gladstone, and Revolution* (Cambridge, 1967).

did the Conservatives break new ground. The Conservatives probably benefited by controlling some of the details of the Bill, and also because the necessity of compiling a new register gave them grounds for remaining in office as long as possible. Finally, Disraeli benefited, by becoming the undisputed successor to Derby in February 1868, for a brief and unremarkable ministry of ten months.

Reform apart, Disraeli made no special mark in 1866–8. He conquered Abyssinia to rescue some missionaries, but gave it back to the Abyssinians. He allowed some progressive measures of social policy to pass, on subjects such as housing and London hospitals, but it was, after all, a Liberal majority that passed them. In his Budgets and in foreign and imperial policy, Disraeli maintained an economical, unadventurous, Little England approach, as befitted a Chancellor of the Exchequer. He did not take up the mantle of Palmerston by claiming to be the 'patriotic party': his choice of Stanley, a peaceful semi-Liberal, for the Foreign Office, stood in the way of that. The ministry was the youngest and ablest of the three Derby minority Governments. A new generation of politicians, including Northcote, Gathorne Hardy, Cranborne (Salisbury) and Carnarvon, sat in the Cabinet, and the Tories could no longer be called 'the stupid party' with any justice. In addition, Disraeli was, in 1868, beginning to form close ties with the Queen in a way that Derby never had.

For many traditional Tories, the one redeeming feature of the 1867 Reform Bill was that its enactment had reduced the Liberals to utter confusion. When confusion was speedily replaced, in 1868, by a Liberal electoral victory, the demand went up for Disraeli's head. Ineffective in office in 1868, Disraeli during the election campaign had created a mood of Anglican militancy, which found his pacific tactics over the Irish Church in 1869 distinctly feeble. In retrospect, he was simply waiting for the tide to turn: but in February 1872 his colleagues made their most serious attempt to ditch him. At a meeting of most Tory leaders, except for Salisbury and Derby, at Burghley House, the question of the leadership was talked over, and all except Manners and Northcote were against Disraeli. Nothing was done, but the danger was great, for there was always an unknown, but large, element of the Tory party that thought of Disraeli as 'that hellish Jew,'[10] as one senior backbencher put it. From 1867 onwards, Salisbury remained irreconcilable, and not on speaking terms with Disraeli, but was too obvious a focus for

[10] Sir R. Knightley, MP, to Lord Bath, 7 Mar. 1867 (Longleat MSS).

disaffection to be effective. There were, however, good grounds in 1867–72 for thinking that, as the leading Tory Duchess put it, 'We can never have a united party as long as Dizzy is the head of it.'[11]

What hold Disraeli had over his party was almost entirely due to his performance in Parliament. His speeches outside Parliament, 116 in all, only occasionally assumed general political significance. Some main themes can, however, be discerned. He took great pains to identify with the agricultural interest, and no fewer than twenty-five of his speeches are in some way related to this topic. There was no other body of interests that he cultivated assiduously, but whereas an appeal to the working class can be found at many points, any such appeal to the urban middle class is conspicuously absent. There were great gaps in his campaigning, too. He hardly spoke outside Parliament between the last of his Young England speeches in October 1844 and the 1847 election campaign: nor between the fall of the 1852 ministry and the 1857 election, save on local topics. (This latter period of repose was perhaps connected with his having *The Press* as mouthpiece.) It was not that he did not know how to 'stump', for in 1849 he had launched a Protectionist variant of the Midlothian campaign: but on the other hand, in the 1874 election campaign he made only two speeches. He had great talent for making the kind of speech that achieves a sweeping redefinition of the general situation, but he used it very sparingly.

The triumph of 1867 marked the beginning of a dark period in Disraeli's life. He lost the political initiative, and in 1872 nearly lost the Tory leadership. His health worsened. To complete the misery, his wife died, in December 1872. She had nearly died in 1868, and for some time before her death, though concealing her state and remaining socially active, she was in the grip of what both knew to be terminal illness. In 1872, the year of his greatest outdoor speeches, Disraeli was mainly concerned with cheering and nursing her. In the late summer of 1872, he took her 220 miles in drives around the suburbs of London. At her last party, at Hughenden a month before she died, Harcourt and Rosebery were guests. As the end approached, Disraeli wrote, 'I am totally unable to meet the catastrophe. . . .'[12] His losses were partly material, for his wife's income of £5,000 per annum, and their London home of half a lifetime, Grosvenor Gate, passed back to her first

[11] Duchess of Buccleuch to Lord Bath, 17 Dec. 1868 (Longleat MSS).
[12] Monypenny and Buckle, op. cit., v, 228.

husband's family, and Disraeli within weeks was living unhappily in a London hotel ('hotel life in the evening is a cave of despair').[13] This was a trifle, however, compared with the loss of the total devotion and approval which had sustained him throughout his political career.

The Conservatives in the years after 1867 were an unhappy party, and leading them was a thankless task. Nevertheless, as early as 1870 the light became visible at the end of the tunnel. A major conflict broke out within the Liberal ranks, with many of the Dissenters going into open opposition to the official party. In 1871 and 1872 the by-elections began to go seriously wrong. In 1873, Gladstone lost his major piece of legislation in the Commons (the Irish University Bill), while much of the rest was defeated in the Lords. After March 1873, when Disraeli refused to take office prematurely, the Liberals remained in office, but hardly in power: and the by-elections remained disastrous. In January 1874, with his hand forced by Cabinet and legal difficulties, Gladstone called a snap election. The only real issue was whether the country was tired of Gladstone, which it undoubtedly was. All that had to be done was for it to say so, which it did. The Tory majority in Britain was respectable, but it was enhanced by a landslide in Ireland, where the Home Rulers won nearly all the Liberal seats.

Of the innumerable reasons for the Liberal defeat, few had anything to do with Conservative merits. One cause for self-congratulation, however, lay in the field of party organisation. The Conservatives were much better organised in 1874 than before or later: and much better organised, again, than their opponents. Starting from scratch in 1846, the Conservatives had gradually built up a party machine. Up till 1852, the Chief Whip, Beresford, had done everything, with unhappy results. After his departure, the party in the fifties and sixties had relied on a large firm of London solicitors to manage its election business. In 1870 the agent, Spofforth, retired after a long career, and his work was transferred to a Conservative Central Office, with an ambitious young barrister called Gorst as Principal Agent.

Between 1870 and 1874, in very favourable circumstances, Gorst imparted zeal and system to the party machine. He was, however, not in close contact with Disraeli, who on the available evidence had not contemplated a new departure when Spofforth left. Gorst received no reward from the party for his services, and withdrew leaving Central Office to less able men. The Tory organisers in 1880 did nothing to

[13] Robert Blake, *Disraeli* (London, 1966), p. 527.

mitigate an unfavourable situation, but neither in 1874 nor in 1880 did the Tory chiefs see organisation as a matter of great concern.

Disraeli's new Cabinet was the smallest since 1832. It had twelve members, six of them peers, six commoners. The peers all went back to posts they had held during 1866–8, with the exception of Richmond, promoted to Lord President in recognition of his loyal leadership of the Lords, a position he continued to hold until Disraeli's ennoblement in 1876. None of the ministers of 1866–8 was obviously dropped, except for Marlborough, who later became Irish Viceroy, and Pakington, who lost his seat and was given a peerage and a lucrative Civil Service job. Disraeli, who consulted an inner group of Hardy, Northcote, Cairns, and Derby about appointments, clearly wished to heal old wounds, and attached much importance to wooing Salisbury and Carnarvon, whose return to the fold was in some doubt till the last moment. Salisbury, Carnarvon, Manners, Hardy, and to some extent Northcote, formed something of a High Church group within the Cabinet. The youngest minister was Carnarvon at 43. There were two weak appointments, Malmesbury, who was 67 and deaf, the oldest minister except Disraeli, and Ward Hunt, an archetypal country squire with an interest in subjects like cattle plague, who found the Admiralty heavy going. Malmesbury resigned in 1876, Disraeli taking his purely nominal office and, for a time, its £2,000 salary, while the unfortunate Hunt died in office in 1877, aged only 52. This led to a minor reshuffle, with Disraeli replacing Malmesbury in the Lords, Hicks Beach, the successful young Irish Secretary, staying at his post, but being admitted to the Cabinet, and W. H. Smith, the great newsagent in whose practical abilities Disraeli had complete confidence, replaced Hunt at the Admiralty, to the delight of Gilbert and Sullivan. This first reshuffle of 1876–7 had no political implications: that of 1878 had, for the resignations of Derby and Carnarvon were the product of eighteen months of tension. Salisbury took Derby's post; Gathorne Hardy replaced Salisbury at the India Office, with a peerage; Colonel F. A. Stanley, a quiet and homely country gentleman and Derby's brother, replaced Hardy at the War Office; the Duke of Northumberland took the Privy Seal; and Hicks Beach took over from Carnarvon. In addition, Lord Sandon was moved to the Board of Trade, previously outside the Cabinet. The front bench in the Lords gained Cranbrook, an ageing major figure, and Northumberland, a rich nonentity, in exchange for Carnarvon and Derby: while in the Commons Cranbrook's loss was hardly compensated by the gain of two minor figures like Stanley and Lord Sandon. The ministry was not getting stronger as time went by. Disraeli's only imaginative appointment, that of Derby's friend Cross to the Home Office without previous official experience, was to some extent balanced by his exclusion of Education, the Local Government Board, the Board of Trade (to 1878), and Ireland (except, for non-Irish reasons, in 1876–8) from the Cabinet.

The session of 1874 was a quiet one, partly through unpreparedness, partly because party and country alike wanted tranquillity. According to Cross, Disraeli had to rely entirely on the various suggestions of his colleagues,[14] contributing nothing definite of his own. A give-away budget was something of an anti-climax, and had little political effect. A political debt was paid to the publicans by a Licensing Act. Cross carried a Factory Act which the Liberals had in the pipeline. An Act was carried abolishing patronage in the Scottish Church, which awoke dormant church controversies in Scotland very much to the Government's future disadvantage. Foreign policy and imperial affairs were both conspicuously absent from the scene. The Ashanti war came neatly to an end, and the Tsar visited London for his daughter's wedding. The only strongly reactionary Bill, Sandon's Endowed Schools Bill, which sought to draw the grammar schools back to the Church, was dropped.

What excitement there was came from the Public Worship Regulation Bill, introduced not by the Government but by the Archbishop of Canterbury, in order to repress excessive ritualism among the clergy. The Bill was dangerous to Disraeli, for it divided the Cabinet and annoyed High Churchmen: it was also potentially advantageous, for it was broadly what the country wanted, and it divided Gladstone from the Liberal rank and file. Disraeli skilfully avoided most of the dangers, while gaining most of the advantages, and the Bill passed.

The session of 1875 opened with Gladstone's announcing his definite retirement, previously hinted at, from the Liberal leadership, though not from parliamentary life. Lord Hartington took his place, elected unanimously after Forster's withdrawal; Disraeli was more than ever master of the House. With neither the Irish, the Liberals, nor the foreign powers giving cause for anxiety, Disraeli embarked on the most impressive and attractive legislative programme of his career, though in few cases can his active involvement in any particular measure be shown. Cross carried an Artisans' Dwellings Bill, designed to allow local

[14] Richard, Viscount Cross, *A Political History* (priv. pr. Eccle Riggs, 1903), p. 25.

authorities to pull down slums: not being compulsory, and being rather costly to ratepayers, its practical value was limited. Quite different in scope were two Bills, carried by Cross, which settled the basis of labour law for a generation. They were the Magna Carta of British trade unionism. Disraeli claimed that he, with Cross, pushed them through a reluctant Cabinet. Whatever the details, Disraeli clearly wanted good relations with the unions, and his efforts were warmly appreciated.

The above measures, perhaps accidentally, gave a sense of a ministry committed to vigorous social reform. A number of useful minor reforms completed the picture. There was no trace of reaction in the air, except for a famous fracas involving the Radical reformer Plimsoll over the Merchant Shipping Bill. The government Bill on this subject was un-contentious, but on 22 July Disraeli himself announced its withdrawal to make way for a Bill benefiting farmers. Plimsoll, in a famous scene, declared that hundreds of seamen would die as a result. Public opinion supported Plimsoll's wild behaviour, Disraeli backed down, and a temporary Bill was rushed through. Apart from this incident, Disraeli's handling of the House was faultless, and his reputation never stood higher.

In 1876 the situation changed, in domestic as much as in foreign matters. By-elections began to go seriously wrong. Disraeli's age and poor health appeared at last to be wresting from him his hold over Parliament. The session, a quiet one, comparatively undisturbed by foreign affairs, contained only two notable pieces of legislation: the Royal Titles Bill, making the Queen Empress of India, which received a bad press, and Sandon's Education Bill, which introduced the principle of compulsion into primary education. A Merchant Shipping Bill was carried, of no very drastic character. The shipowner was left free to paint his Plimsoll line where he thought fit. The theme of social reform which stood out in 1875 had fallen back to a routine level in 1876, not because of Irish or Eastern distractions, but because ministers had nothing much in mind. In August 1876, with himself and his party in poor shape even before the Bulgarian atrocities crisis broke, Disraeli decided to lead the party from the Lords. His prospects of remaining leader at the next election cannot have seemed good.

Ireland, which Disraeli never visited, played little part in his plans. At various times from 1846 to 1878 he sought parliamentary advantage from intrigues with Irish Catholic groups in the House of Commons. At the 1868 election he played the Orange card, but there was no love lost between him and Protestant Ulster. The actual government of Ireland did not cause him any anxiety, especially in 1874–80, when there was no real need to do anything, and able subordinates like Hicks Beach (Irish Secretary 1874–8) looked after the petty business. Disraeli carried no major Irish legislation, though in 1868 and 1877–8 he toyed with the Irish Universities question. Responsible Tories might even welcome the advent of the Home Rulers: 'Their humbug has a good deal to do with keeping Ireland quiet,' Beach wrote.[15] By 1878 the main group of Home Rulers under Butt, himself an old friend of Disraeli's in the 1850s, had come to prefer Tory rule. Butt thought, 'There are men in the present Cabinet more likely to deal fairly with Ireland than any we would be likely to find in a Whig Cabinet.'[16] More important to ministers than Home Rule was the obstruction carried on by a small minority of Irish Members, sporadically in 1875–6, systematically in 1877 and thereafter, except for a lull in 1878. This did not prevent major legislation, for there was little to prevent, but it did throw routine business into confusion, and more important, it meant that House of Commons ministers were extremely tired men by 1880.

Once Disraeli had satisfied himself, during the session of 1874, that he had healed the long-standing divisions in his party, his mind turned decisively to foreign policy. He had always been interested in the subject, although he had been abroad only once since 1845–6. He approached the topic with an open mind, especially where Turkey was concerned. He was fundamentally in sympathy with the Turks, and had in youth volunteered to fight for them, yet at the time of the Crimean War he had shown no flicker of war fever, and in the 1850s and 1860s his approach to foreign affairs had usually been that of an economising Chancellor intriguing against Palmerston for the 'Little England' Radical vote. True, the bias of his rhetoric was naturally towards patriotic declamation, and after the 1874 election Disraeli had every reason to continue a line of argument that had proved successful, namely that his party stood for a firm, and the Liberals for a weak, foreign policy. So far, so good: but Disraeli did not wish to extend this stance into thorough-going imperialism or annexationism, if only because he did not believe the electorate was imperialist. Peace with honour the country might want, if the alternative was peace with dishonour: but it did not, Disraeli considered, want war with honour. The

[15] David Thornley, *Isaac Butt and Home Rule* (London, 1964), p. 355.
[16] ibid., p. 367.

aggressive, and expensive, tendencies branded by Gladstone as 'Beaconsfieldism' were a mild and backward-looking attempt to take up the mantle of Palmerston, not a foretaste of Joseph Chamberlain.

Disraeli entered the fray with two chance successes. In May 1875 he intervened to prevent impending war between Germany and France. In November 1875 he acquired, not the Suez Canal Company, but a large minority shareholding therein. The purchase certainly proved a fruitful investment, but its political consequences in getting the British into, or the French out of, Egypt, were slight. Still, these events suggested to Disraeli that he had flair, and in autumn 1875, when the first revolts in Balkan Turkey broke out, it naturally occurred to him that he might solve the Eastern question. It certainly did not occur to him that the high-minded Victorian public which had thrown its weight so effectively behind Plimsoll in July 1875, and against the Fugitive Slave Circular in the winter of 1875–6, might also turn excitedly to what appeared a classical problem of diplomacy. During most of 1876, the key question was whether the Powers should and could impose far-reaching reforms on the Christian provinces of Turkey. The Powers, other than Britain, were ready to do this, whereas both British parties were opposed to this approach, and reluctant to give up their traditional protection of Turkey. On 9 May 1876, Hartington gave support to Disraeli's policy. On 24 May, the British Fleet was sent to Besika Bay, giving the Turks every reason to think that in the last resort Britain would protect them against any demand, however reasonable. Traditional Liberal criticism has centred on the way British policy in 1876 aimed at frustrating a moderate and peaceful settlement, and made inevitable the outbreak of hostilities between Turkey and Russia in April 1877.

During the summer of 1876, however, the Bulgarian atrocities made the question a central issue in British domestic politics in a wholly unexpected way. The first reports were published in the *Daily News* on 23 June. They did in fact exaggerate the numbers, if not the horrors. On 26 June, 10 July, and 31 July, Disraeli denied, minimised, or spoke with apparent jest in reply to questions about the massacres. His answers, partly due to poor staff work at the Foreign Office, were fuel on the flames. In August and September, as first-hand reports came in, a massive grass-roots agitation grew up amongst all classes outside Parliament, with Christian leaders unusually prominent amongst them. The agitation convinced Disraeli of the need to back down. On 3 September

1876 he told Salisbury, 'We must now dictate to Turkey.' On 5 September Gladstone, who though not in retirement had previously kept in the background, produced his famous pamphlet, *The Bulgarian Horrors and the Question of the East*. For Disraeli, the focus of the problem then shifted, from placating popular disquiet to discountenancing the Liberal party. He had, in addition, a crucial by-election to face on 22 September, defeat in which might even cost him the leadership. He turned again to a hard line: but this time the hard line was for domestic as well as diplomatic consumption.

Between September 1876 and April 1877, as war became inevitable, Disraeli's chances of winning British public opinion increased as his chances of maintaining the integrity of Turkey disappeared. In 1876 Disraeli had refused a settlement which at least appeared to maintain existing frontiers. In 1877, after Russian successes in the war, he was trying to secure not much more than the security of Constantinople, a very different matter. The success of Russian arms had to have its reward – that Disraeli did not and could not challenge. His main problem in 1877 lay in controlling his Cabinet. As the Russians marched south, the Cabinet wrangled bitterly. Salisbury, Disraeli's chief opponent, could muster enough support to prevent a war policy (or the bluff of war), but not enough to carry out his own policy of a negotiated settlement with large concessions. Both 'hawks' and 'doves', therefore, had in practice to acquiesce in the inertia of Derby, the Foreign Secretary. Disraeli's game throughout 1877 was to detach Salisbury from Derby and Carnarvon, the other main opponents of confrontation.

This was not a quick or easy business: as late as 12 January 1878 there was a threat of joint resignation by Derby and Salisbury. From then on, however, it was downhill. Derby resigned a first time on 23 January, returned, and finally resigned on 27 March. Disraeli rejected the Russian terms calling for a big Bulgaria (the Treaty of San Stefano) and set out to force Russia to the conference table. On 4 April the House of Commons voted 310–64 in favour of calling up the Reserves. At the end of May, Indian troops arrived in Malta. While the stage was thus being publicly set for another Crimean War, the diplomatic basis fo the Treaty of Berlin was being laid in direct Anglo-Russian and Anglo-Turkish negotiations. Finally, Disraeli and Salisbury set off to the Congress of Berlin (4 June–4 July), at which Britain gained public recognition of its main objectives, a 'small' Bulgaria, and a secure frontier for Asian Turkey. On his return, a majority of 143 ratified the Treaty of Berlin (3 August 1878), every Tory voting with the Government. Disraeli's complete failure to protect Turkey, as intended in 1876–7, was lost sight of in face of his evident success as a firm defender of British interests in 1878, an impression which Gladstone's opposition greatly enhanced.

The moral of the Eastern crisis was that a war policy that did not involve actual warfare was a useful way of reducing Turkish losses, though they still remained at a level that two years earlier had seemed unacceptable to both British parties. It was also useful in consolidating Disraeli's hold on his Cabinet, his party, and the British public, and for inflicting serious wounds on the Liberals. Unfortunately for Disraeli, his paper war in the Balkans was soon followed by very real wars in Afghanistan and Zululand, both of them involving massacre of British forces. Though there was no connection in fact between the three situations in the mind of Disraeli and his Cabinet, the Liberals said there was, and were widely believed. Disraeli's success in 1878 had made it plausible to say that he was a man for such adventures.

In the last stages of the Eastern crisis, the Russians had sent a mission to Kabul. Lytton, the Viceroy, reacted by preparing an armed column which was to march on Kabul to secure the reception of a British mission, and the expulsion of the Russians. It was not obvious that a diplomatic solution was impossible: senior ministers in London wished to try this, but, being tired and on holiday, got no immediate results, and failed to control Lytton, who, tired of waiting, marched to the frontier in clear disobedience of orders. His force was turned back, and London, until then quite innocent of aggressive intent, was faced with a question of prestige, and therefore, on current assumptions, a deliberate war became necessary. The British invasion, in winter 1878–9, went smoothly, there was no trouble with Russia, and a British mission was installed at Kabul. On 3 September, all members of the mission were murdered, and Roberts entered Kabul a second time on 13 October 1879, in good time to provide ammunition for Gladstone's Midlothian campaign, which began on 25 November. Though the soldiering went well, there was little glory for Disraeli in a conquest which he had not initially wanted, which he had not effectively sought to avoid, but to which he had twice fully committed himself, for very little obvious benefit.

The Zulu war was like the Afghan in that disobedience by the man on the spot was crucial, but unlike it in that the soldiering was badly done. Sir Bartle Frere, the High Commissioner, a man of simple expansionist views, wished to break the Zulu state, which was certainly a threat, but was causing no immediate trouble. Worse, he wished to do this in the autumn of 1878, when Disraeli had an Afghan campaign on his hands, and needed all his troops in readiness to make the Russians live up to their promises in European Turkey. The Cabinet expressly forbade a Zulu war. Frere, knowing this, started one. Almost the first Disraeli knew of the matter was on 12 February 1879, when news of the destruction of a British force of 1,200 men at Isandhlwana (22 January) reached London. Despite a final victory over the Zulus at Ulundi in July 1879, it was the initial defeat that mattered in its general effect on public opinion, although Disraeli at the time was probably more concerned with the effect of a remote colonial war on his ability to put pressure on Russia. Disraeli's rage over the folly of the war knew no bounds: but he failed to communicate this effectively to the British public, and Liberals were able to imply that the episode was representative of government policy.

The success or failure of Disraeli's foreign policy was all-important in the latter years of his ministry, for he had virtually ceased to have any home policy. The three sessions of 1877, 1878, and 1879 were remarkably barren in their legislative output, not primarily because of Irish obstruction, which was only intermittent. No major social reform was passed, while the weak state of the economy did not permit any exciting Budgets. Northcote, Disraeli's successor in the Commons, was thought to lack firmness and, still more, magic, in his handling of the House. Disraeli was unable to do much to mend matters. Pressure of foreign affairs apart, his health throughout 1877 left him 'prostrate with pain and debility'. 'Whether I can go on . . . I hardly know,' he wrote in April, and in October 1877 he was letting it be known that it was quite impossible for him to continue. This was, of course, partly another move in the game, but he must have been extremely unfit. He made few speeches in 1877, but the occasion when he told the Lords that railway accidents were 'the greatest subject that can come under your consideration' did not suggest a mind closely involved with domestic topics.

The 1878 session lasted seven months, the longest for many years, but proved equally sterile. In the Queen's Speech, ten out of thirteen paragraphs were directly related to the Eastern question, and against the background of the last stages of the Russian advance towards Constantinople, the Commons had little to debate other than Scottish roads and bridges. With distress in many industries, the Budget raised income tax by twopence, and made loans for social purposes to local authorities more difficult. The ministry passed only one reform of consequence, that of Irish intermediate education. This made a mark on the Irish secondary school system, and was the only Irish measure of interest carried during 1874–80. Gladstone gave Ireland good legislation and political excitement in 1868–74: Disraeli (and Beach) gave Ireland no legislation, good administration, and political quiet, in 1874–80. That Irish rural society began to fall to pieces in 1879, owing to climatic and economic changes beyond human control, should not be taken to mean that Disraeli's Irish policy was inappropriate at the time, or less meritorious than that of Gladstone.

The session of 1879 might have provided a fresh start. With Cabinet conflicts resolved, and relations with Russia now firmly in the hands of Salisbury, Beaconsfield had a year, or perhaps two, in hand in which to win the confidence of the country before going to an election. True, economic conditions were bleak, with unemployment in particular at record levels, and a crisis of low prices in agriculture. There was no question of the Government's taking any unorthodox step, except in Ireland, to remedy the distress, and the general feeling that taxes were too high inhibited any new departures in budgetary or social policy. Nevertheless, the chance to impress existed.

In fact, the main item in the meagre bill of fare promised was an Army Bill, the discussion on which turned into a debate on flogging. Beaconsfield did not care either way about the 'cat', but believed that abolition would split his party. After vehement opposition, and some concessions, the Bill passed, flogging was retained, and the Conservatives found they had spent most of the session on a measure that provided ideal propaganda for their opponents. The only other measure of consequence to pass was an Irish University Bill, which set up an examining body for Irish higher education, without establishing any new seats of learning. A very large number of minor measures, of the type of the Irish Dogs Regulation Bill and the Metropolis Carriage Bill, were introduced by ministers and then dropped for lack of time, energy, support, or interest. There was no theme, no co-ordination, simply departmentalism run riot and ministers obstructing each other's progress. In August 1879 ministers bade *au revoir* for the session by requiring a vote of £3,000,000 for the Zulu war. With extraordinary absence of artistry, Beaconsfield set the stage for the Midlothian campaign by letting his ministry appear without any redeeming features.

By autumn 1879 the Liberals, perhaps for the first time since 1873, looked the more credible government of the two parties, though few were confident of victory at the next election. The Liberals had had good by-election results earlier, when the party was in a state of torpor and decomposition. Now, with the party in full cry, they ran into two chance by-election reverses (February 1880), and the Government, which had planned to continue throughout 1880, decided at very short notice to hold a spring election. As with Gladstone in 1874, they left themselves with no time to make any impression in the campaign, which found their organisation in a state of weakness, their leaders ill or engaged in routine business, and the party with nothing to say. Disraeli tried, and failed, to start a scare about Irish Home Rule, and the tone of the campaign was dominated by Liberal criticism of the Government's record (the Liberals being no less without any policies or programme of their own than the Conservatives).

The election was a more serious reverse in terms of seats than in terms of a real rejection by the public. A few thousand votes the other way would have returned Disraeli to power. Nevertheless, despite the apparent arbitrariness of the overall statistics, there were some clear influences at work. Some of these were beyond Disraeli's control. The most important single change compared with 1874, the return of Dissent to the Liberal fold, was only partly of Tory making. The economic depression, which Disraeli saw as the main cause of defeat, was simply a bolt from the blue. Long-term social change in Wales also brought a Liberal advantage which just happened. The Liberal landslide in Scotland owed more to a serious Tory mistake, over the Patronage Bill of 1874, which had stirred up religious passions. The majority of Conservative losses, however, were widely spread through the English counties, the English large cities, and the English small or medium boroughs, all groups which responded fairly readily to the political situation in Parliament and on the platform. The Tories lost the 1880 election, not because they were doomed by structural factors to lose it, but because they did not fight it seriously at the level of general political utterance.

The general election of April 1880 was not seen by Disraeli, or anyone else, as the end of the road. He did take the opportunity to honour or reward the intimates of a lifetime: Baillie Cochrane and Manners, both survivors of Young England, received honours, as did Monty Corry, his perfect private secretary since 1866, while Lord Henry Lennox, his infatuation of the 1850s, received financial reward. There was, however, no question of Disraeli's retiring from the party leadership. If anything, the party felt it needed him more in bad times than in good.

The attacking skills that Disraeli had let rust in office now revived. Though his way of life might be that of an old man, his political strategy was that of his younger days. While dissuading the House of Lords from premature confrontations, Disraeli did his best to split up the Liberal majority. He spoke luridly of the great destructive powers of Gladstone and Radicalism, as instanced in the rather puny Irish land measure brought in by Gladstone in 1880. He may, in fact, have believed his own propaganda, for there is probably no period of his life when his mood was so alarmist, and when he was so inclined to make the Tories a party of resistance to Radicalism, pure and simple. When Disraeli last took stock of the political situation, his assessment was that the dominant fact for the Tory party must be the general alarm and despondency among the landed class.

Up to December 1880 there was every reason to think that Disraeli could continue to lead the party for years to come, and with singular ability. He even acquired a house in London during the winter to enable him to do so. He also began to write a novel about Gladstone,[17] the initial chapters of which show no decline in his powers. During the spring of 1881 his health declined, but he remained politically and socially active till a month before his death, from bronchitis, in April 1881.

We shall never know Disraeli well. His intimates did not Boswellise him. His inner thoughts, on the Jewish people for instance, could hardly hope for a sympathetic hearing. The real degree of his enthusiasm for, or distaste for, the English aristocracy and gentry, and their way of living, is unknowable. There were few people he felt at home with, and his apparent moments of self-revelation to female correspondents were no doubt carefully composed. Little is known, too, of what the Tory squires really thought of him. Except in the 1830s, he kept no diary, and he left no memoirs. His papers, though copious, may give a quite inadequate idea of his relations with the Queen, with Palmerston, and with the Rothschilds. There is some mystery as to how he died a rich man. He remains, despite the shadowiness, a sympathetically un-

[17] Printed in Monypenny and Buckle, op. cit., v, 531–60.

orthodox figure: a man willing to sell his political position for use by a foreign power, an early advocate of a Zionist state, the first man to smoke 'pot' (for medical reasons) while Prime Minister, the only novelist to become a party leader, and a man who, though unusually chaste, was almost certainly attracted by both sexes. By any standards, past or present, he did not lack moral originality, conforming inwardly to no views but his own.

He left the Tory party very much as he found it. Below the surface, changes were taking place that were to turn the Tories from the 'country party' of the squires into the party of business, the residential suburbs, and the genteel south-east. Disraeli did little to hasten such changes, which gave him little pleasure, and in any case even by 1881 the process had not gone very far. So far as he looked for a new accession of support, it was (intermittently) in the direction of the working class that he hopefully turned his eyes. On the whole he preferred to keep the Tory party as it was, and to concentrate on the rearrangement of parliamentary factions. This, the technique of parliamentary opposition, was what he was superbly good at. As a Chancellor of the Exchequer he was entirely unremarkable, as a legislator negligible with the extraordinary exception of 1867. As a statesman, coming to foreign policy late, he faced a crisis partly of his own making, and came out of it better than could have been expected for a Power without allies or an army. His defeat in 1880 was a result of the short-term situation in 1879–80, and did not reflect generally on his hold on opinion after 1874. In particular, he was unlucky to be premier during seven lean years for the economy. The Conservative party he left behind was, as always, a not very competent body with an opposition mentality. In one respect – and this was perhaps his greatest achievement as a party leader – Disraeli had conferred a priceless and lasting advantage upon them. By an indefinable process, beginning about 1860, Disraeli made the Liberals look left-wing and dangerous to men of property, and thus ensured the future of his party.

BIBLIOGRAPHY

Blake, Robert (Lord Blake), *Disraeli* (London, 1966); *The Conservative Party from Peel to Churchill* (London, 1970)

Feuchtwanger, E. J., *Disraeli, Democracy, and the Tory Party* (1968)

Hanham, H. J., *Elections and Party Management; Politics in the Time of Disraeli and Gladstone* (London, 1959)

Monypenny, W. F., and Buckle, G. E., *The Life of Benjamin Disraeli, Earl of Beaconsfield* (6 vols, London, 1910–20)

Smith, Paul, *Disraelian Conservatism and Social Reform* (Cambridge, 1967)

W. E. GLADSTONE

BY

E. J. FEUCHTWANGER

William Ewart Gladstone, born 29 December 1809, youngest son of John Gladstone, a merchant of Liverpool, a supporter of Canning and member of Parliament from 1818–27. Educated at Eton and Christ Church, Oxford. Married Catherine, daughter of Sir Stephen Glynne, 1839; eight children. MP (Tory) for Newark 1832–45; under Peel held minor office 1834–35; was Vice-President, Board of Trade 1841, President 1843; resigned in 1845, but rejoined the same year as Secretary of State for the Colonies. MP for Oxford University 1847–65; Chancellor of the Exchequer in Aberdeen's Coalition 1853–55, under Palmerston briefly in 1855 and from 1859–65, under Russell 1865–66. MP for South Lancashire 1865–68; Leader of the House of Commons 1865–66. MP for Greenwich 1868–80; Prime Minister 1868–74. MP for Midlothian 1880–95; Prime Minister 1880–85 (1880–83 also Chancellor of the Exchequer), 1886 and 1892–94. Died 19 May 1898. Author of The State in its Relations with the Church, *1838;* Studies in Homer and the Homeric Age, *1858;* A Chapter of Autobiography, *1868;* The Bulgarian Horrors and the Question of the East, *1876; etc. Also editor of critical edition of the works of Bishop Butler, 1896.*

William Ewart Gladstone, by J. E. Millais

W. E. GLADSTONE

Gladstone's public life lasted sixty-one years and no other major political figure of the nineteenth century, except the Queen herself, equalled it in duration. During this time Gladstone traversed an exceptionally wide band of the political spectrum and developed from the Ultra-Conservative of the 1830s into the Liberal father-figure of the 1880s. Yet throughout his long life span he remained recognisably the same personality, of whom Balfour could say, after talking to him two years before his death, 'He is and always was, in everything except essentials, a tremendous Tory.' Gladstone's unusual political migration from right to left is the major theme of his career; and perhaps the most important clue to it is that to him politics always remained a second best to the priestly vocation which was his first love, and that his political path was a constant quest for God.

'Oxford on the surface, Liverpool underneath.' This was often said of Gladstone in Whig circles and it was true that he never lost the trace of a Lancashire accent. His father, John, was a Scotsman who made good in Liverpool and built up a fortune of three-quarters of a million pounds, a very large sum by early nineteenth-century standards. Much of the family wealth came from West Indian plantations and slaves; John Gladstone was a leading representative of the West Indian planter interest and opponent of the Abolitionists. This cast a shadow over his son's early political life, for filial piety and obedience were deeply ingrained in William. It was not without heart-searching and qualms of conscience that he detached himself from many of his father's convictions and causes. In politics John Gladstone was an ardent disciple of Canning and a prime mover in getting his mentor to represent Liverpool in Parliament for fifteen years. The Liberal Toryism of Canning was, therefore, the political tradition in which Gladstone was brought up and it remained alive in him throughout his long public life. Perhaps even more important than the Canningite heritage was the evangelicalism of his family background. Although Gladstone moved away from his evangelical roots in his early twenties they had left an indelible mark on his personality. Deep personal piety, an abiding sense of sin, a need to mortify and humble the self, an acute moral sensitivity, these were characteristics that remained an essential part of him throughout his life. They were transmitted to him by his mother, who spent much of her life being an invalid, and by his elder sister, Anne, who died at an early age of consumption. These two women also gave Gladstone a view of womanhood that was pure, saintly and idealised.

Gladstone passed through the traditional educational process of the upper class, Eton and Oxford. It was a big change to go from the self-contained, intensely religious middle-class life of Liverpool to the virtually pagan jungle of Eton. Already Gladstone had the self-control, the energy and ambition, the orderly habits and the great intellectual powers to enable him to survive. When he left Eton in 1827 his life there seemed to him to have been 'a time of very great and numerous delights'. Even deeper bonds of affection tied him to Oxford. He arrived there at a time of much intellectual vigour, but he had left before Keble's Assize Sermon of 1833 started the religious controversies of the Oxford Movement. The young Gladstone made his mark through his academic achievement and as a speaker in the recently established Union. His mind, supported by great energy and application, was a matchless instrument for the acquisition and marshalling of information, though perhaps the deepest levels of speculation were closed to him. His oratory, he soon found, gave him power over men; it was backed throughout his life by his fine physical presence and magnificent voice and as he grew older, by the increasing weight of his moral stature. Orator and statesman were indissoluble in him; he was fervent, zealous, a man of causes; but also impulsive and excitable. As he matured and amassed a vast store of political experience, he developed great powers of casuistry and an instinctive canniness which tempered and made viable his impetuous dynamism. While Gladstone was still at Oxford the great crisis over parliamentary reform swept the country. It was on the Reform Bill that he made the famous speech in the Union in May 1831, which first brought him to the notice of a wider public. By logical deduction from first principles, a mode of argument that always remained characteristic of him, but was as yet undisturbed by any trace of pragmatism, he had convinced himself that reform was the work of anti-Christ. It conjured up the spectre of revolution, Popery and utter ruin. From the Liberal Conservatism of Canning, Gladstone had now moved to an Ultra-Tory position; he had done so not by instinct, but by ratiocination, and he could by the same process move away from it again.

Towards the end of his time at Oxford Gladstone was much exercised by the choice of a career and strongly inclined towards the Church. His father persuaded him, after an intense and emotional correspondence, to go into politics. He left Oxford with a double first; completing his education with an Italian tour in 1832, he had the culminating experience that turned him from an evangelical into a High Anglican. The vision of Rome, renewed study of the Book of Common Prayer, these were some of the experiences that gave him an understanding of the Church as the community of believers and finally broke the narrow familial preoccupation with personal salvation. During the Italian tour the offer came to him of a parliamentary seat at Newark; the patron was the Ultra-Tory Duke of Newcastle whose son, Lord Lincoln, was Gladstone's friend at Eton and Oxford and for many years in later life his close political colleague. Thus Gladstone entered the House of Commons after the first election held on the reformed franchise, an earnest young man of 23, a High Anglican Tory with the most orthodox views on all major issues of the day. His main preoccupation was the future of the Church, at a moment when it was under attack as part of the established order in an era of reform.

Gladstone quickly established himself as a rising man on the Tory side of the House and held junior office in Peel's short-lived ministry of 1835. At this stage of his career, he was not so much an Ultra-Tory as a 'ministerial man'. Peel took him increasingly into the inner councils of the party and he was clearly marked out for promotion. He was well to the right of his master and of most Tories only in his view of the Church. He held that the Church was the spiritual aspect of the state and that, therefore, enjoyment of the full rights and duties of citizenship implied membership of the Church of England. Gladstone expressed these views, so much at variance with the tendencies of the age, in his first book, *The State in its Relations with the Church*, published in 1838. He wrote it in only two months under pressure of intense inner necessity. In reviewing it in the *Edinburgh Review* Macaulay used the phrase 'the rising hope of stern, unbending Tories,' which has clung to Gladstone ever since. The publication of such unfashionable opinions temporarily clouded the relations between the promising young politician and his leader; but when the Tories won the general election of 1841 Gladstone was again a strong candidate for office. He wanted to be Chief Secretary for Ireland, but Peel had the perspicacity to see that this impulsive and emotional young man, suspected of the 'romanising' tendencies of the Oxford Movement, would be disastrously out of place in Ireland. Instead he sent him 'to govern packages' at the Board of Trade, first as Vice-President and, from 1843, as President with a seat in the Cabinet. Here Gladstone's great industry, intellectual energy and capacity to learn found an ideal outlet.

Gladstone now learnt the lessons that established his economic liberalism. He was intimately associated with the economic and fiscal policies by which Peel's Government moved progressively towards free trade. Most of the detailed work on the revisions of the tariff carried out in 1842 and 1845 was done by him. He gained an unrivalled insight into the workings of commerce and industry, previously only known to him indirectly through his father, and into the operations of government departments. At the Board of Trade he received countless deputations from the multifarious interests affected by the tariff reform; he was closely involved in the consultations within the Government that led to Peel's reintroduction of the income tax in 1842. The regulation of the railways, which became an important issue in the 1840s, was another sphere in which he displayed his powers as a constructive administrator and statesman. His experiences at the Board of Trade convinced him that it was the duty of the State to create the conditions under which the economic initiative of the individual could flourish with the least possible interference; that the utmost economy of operation and the absence of any kind of corruption were the first pre-requisites of public administration. The removal of international barriers to trade would at the same time secure the greatest possible advance in wealth and well-being and make war and the waste of military expenditure increasingly impossible and unnecessary. To the end of his life Gladstone took great pride in the advance of prosperity of the ordinary people which his work as a public financier and administrator had made possible; but on the other hand he was never an egalitarian, nor was he ever interested in social change for its own sake. He firmly believed in the existing social order, in the beneficent role of aristocracy, and that it was the first duty of statesmanship to work for stability and social harmony. For those lowly in the social scale his prescription was self-help; he considered that no moral benefit would be derived from the State's doing for a man what he ought to do for himself.

Early in 1845 Gladstone resigned from Peel's Government over the Maynooth grant. The proposal to increase the government grant to this priests' seminary was meant as a gesture of peace towards Ireland.

Gladstone was in favour of it: even in the few years since the publication of his book his religious and ecclesiastical views had developed rapidly. The need for religious liberty had become much more real to him, not least because of the persecution at Oxford of Tractarians, with whom he had much in common. His acute sense of morality and justice had also made him much more aware of the wrongs and grievances under which the majority of the Irish population was suffering. Gladstone's sensitive conscience would not allow him to support the Maynooth grant as a member of the Government. The position he now took was so different from that with which he was associated in the public mind that he felt he could not give even the slightest appearance of clinging to office for its own sake. Thus he supported the Maynooth grant from the back benches; Cobden, after listening to his resignation speech, said that Gladstone's talent was marvellous but that after an hour of explanation he knew 'no more why he left the Government than before he began'.

Gladstone returned to Peel's Government as Colonial Secretary for the last six months of its existence, after the decision had been taken to repeal the Corn Laws. He went with Peel into the wilderness when the Government was defeated in the summer of 1846. Henceforth he was a Peelite, and the label Liberal-Conservative, often adopted by Peelites for electoral purposes, well describes his ideological position. From the point of view of practical politics, however, the situation of the Peelites was increasingly frustrating. Peel himself, until his death in 1850, refused to organise his followers; elections and the steady drift of back-benchers, mainly back to the Conservative fold, left only a small rump, mostly leaders and a few followers; and even the leading Peelites, of whom Gladstone was one, were not in the long run able to maintain their cohesion. Gladstone himself only held office for just over two years in the thirteen years between 1846 and 1859. His support for the repeal of the Corn Laws forced him to part company with the Duke of Newcastle and Newark, and he was without a seat in the House of Commons until the general election of 1847. Then he was elected as one of two Members for Oxford University, an honour he had greatly coveted. Politically it was a doubtful blessing because the Conservative High Anglicanism which was still predominant in the University and to which Gladstone owed his election tended to restrict his freedom of movement in national politics. Moreover, the complex political and religious cross-currents at Oxford forced Gladstone into a number of fiercely contested elections during the eighteen years in which he represented the University. Although Gladstone regarded Peel as his mentor in politics and was intensely loyal to him, he became increasingly irked by his leader's refusal to organise the Peelites as a parliamentary party and to use their bargaining power, which was much more formidable than their mere numbers would indicate.

It was perhaps fortunate for Gladstone that private preoccupations distracted him somewhat from politics during those years. Hawarden, the Flintshire estate of the Glynnes, his wife's family, was in dire financial straits and Gladstone had to use all his energy as well as the financial resources inherited from his father to prevent the loss of the estate. The experience was of great value to him when a few years later he came to deal with the nation's finances. Hawarden became his permanent country home, the backcloth to his public life and the scene of his happy family life. Catherine Glynne, whom he had married in 1839, thoroughly understood his intense, emotional, earnest nature and shared his fundamental simplicity; she was also the most discreet of political wives. Through her Gladstone was connected with many of the great Whig families, the Wyndhams, Grenvilles, Lytteltons, Spencers and many others. With her husband's support she was active in many charitable enterprises and the Gladstones knew at first hand something of the abject poverty of the Victorian age. William's own great charitable interest, in which he had his wife's support, was the rescue of prostitutes. From his idealised view of womanhood, which he shared with many Victorians, the fallen woman was seen as the ultimate in degradation and her rescue as a humbling office of piety. This work exposed Gladstone to countless rumours and calumnies and in his latter days as Prime Minister his entourage tried to persuade him to give up his 'night walks'. He did not do so until old age forced him to and it is a tribute to his radiant innocence that no scandal could ever touch him.

Soon after Peel's death in 1850 Gladstone and his family went on a prolonged visit to Naples. The first-hand experience of political oppression under the Bourbons, which he gained during this visit, forms another important milestone in his evolution towards political liberalism. Here was naked injustice, 'the negation of God erected into a system of government'; in the face of such evils Gladstone could not remain silent and the Conservative orthodoxies about the stability of Europe and the danger of revolution which he had hitherto taken for granted could not restrain him. His *Letters to Lord Aberdeen*, in which he publicly attacked the Neapolitan Government in 1851, caused an international sensation and clearly marked him out as a Liberal sympathiser, perhaps more so than he yet meant it.

In domestic politics there was still much talk of Conservative reunion and Lord Derby, the Tory leader, tried to bring Gladstone back into the fold when he attempted to form a government in 1851 and when he in fact formed a short-lived minority administration in 1852. The most obvious barrier to Gladstone's return to the Tory ranks was the continued inability of the Conservative leaders to turn their backs on Protection once and for all. Gladstone did not want to become separated from his closest Peelite colleagues, men like Sidney Herbert or Newcastle, and between him and the Tory squirearchy on the back benches there was mutual antagonism. Increasingly Disraeli's growing influence on the Tory side became perhaps the most important obstacle to Gladstone's return to his former moorings; to complete personal antipathy and mistrust there was added the calculation that a party had room for only one future leader. Gladstone played a leading part in the attack on Disraeli's Budget of 1852 which led to the fall of Derby's Government. The way was thus opened to a coalition of Whigs, Peelites and Radicals which foreshadowed the Liberal amalgamation a few years later. The Peelites, in spite of their small parliamentary following, had a large share of the offices, including the premiership in the person of Lord Aberdeen. Gladstone became Chancellor of the Exchequer. He held this office for two years in the Aberdeen Coalition and again for seven years from 1859 to 1866. During this time he established it as one of the key posts in any government and created new standards of financial policy and administration.

Gladstone's Budget of 1853 outlined a scheme by which the income tax was to be abolished gradually over the next seven years. Never before had a Chancellor looked ahead in this way, although in the event the heavy military expenditure of the Crimean War was to frustrate Gladstone's plan. Gladstone also introduced a general succession duty on all forms of property in this Budget, in place of the legacy duty up to then levied on personal property only. His Budget speech won him great acclaim, not only for the financial accomplishments it revealed but as an oratorical feat. The great power he had now attained as a parliamentarian made it impossible ever to disregard him in the shifting political combinations of the 1850s. Apart from his first Budget of 1853, that of 1860 was probably the most important he brought in.

In it he completed the establishment of free trade in conjunction with the Cobden Commercial Treaty with France; he also abolished the paper duties, for so long decried as 'taxes on knowledge' by all Radical movements. The obstruction of the House of Lords frustrated the abolition of the paper duties in 1860; in the following year Gladstone forced the peers to give way by putting all his proposals in one Finance Bill, which has become the modern custom. Gladstone's Budgets were based on the most rigid exercise of economy in the public service; in enforcing it the Treasury became the central department of state. Economy was a real passion with Gladstone and he carried his hatred of waste down to the paltriest detail. His work as a public financier did much to establish him in the minds of the middle classes of the mid-Victorian age as their champion, and in the 1860s the prosperous sections of the working classes also saw him as one of the chief architects of their well-being. This did much to pave the way for his assumption of the Liberal leadership in the future.

Militarism and war were forces plainly antagonistic to the policy of economy and peace which Gladstone had espoused as the disciple of Peel. Initially he supported the Crimean War, for it seemed to him that Russia had violated the code of conduct he felt should bind the nations of Europe together. The unity of European civilisation was very real to him, deepened by his extensive studies of the classics and the Christian religions and churches. By the beginning of 1855 he considered that the war was being carried on beyond the point where it was just and he resigned almost as soon as Palmerston took office as Prime Minister. The debonair jingoism of Palmerston became almost as repugnant to Gladstone as the brazen opportunism of Disraeli. His opposition to the war threw him into the political company of Cobden and Bright and this was significant for the future; but immediately it made him highly unpopular and for the next few years, in the prime of life, he was as isolated as he had ever been.

When in 1859, after the defeat of the second short-lived Derby–Disraeli Government, Palmerston returned to power, Gladstone at last found it possible to take office again. He approved of the support that Palmerston and Lord John Russell, his Foreign Secretary, intended to give to the Italian *risorgimento* while he had been affronted by the pro-Austrian policy of the Conservatives; in this way he found it compatible with his conscience to serve under Palmerston. The few remaining Peelite leaders, like Sidney Herbert, also joined, and cynics might say that a government led by two old men offered Gladstone the best chance of a rapid advance to the top. For the next six years he served under Palmerston, always carrying a letter of resignation in his pocket, as he put it. The two men clashed frequently, particularly on the recurring problem of military and naval expenditure. Palmerston, who did not know 'in theology Moses from Sydney Smith', was out of sympathy with Gladstone's High Anglicanism, while Gladstone had only contempt for Palmerston's aristocratic raffishness. There was, however, also an underlying respect, for Palmerston retained some liberal traits while his growing inclination to leave the *status quo* undisturbed did not unduly offend Gladstone's basically conservative attitude. Palmerston's Government, prodded by Russell, made a half-hearted effort to take up the question of electoral reform in 1860, but when this failed Gladstone was not perturbed. Four years later, however, he made the famous speech in which he said that 'every man who is not presumably incapacitated by some consideration of personal unfitness or of political danger is morally entitled to come within the pale of the Constitution.' What had changed in the meantime? Gladstone had become honestly convinced that the sober and prosperous working men of the 1860s could no longer be, in justice, excluded from the franchise. What had brought him among other things to this conviction was his own contact with the masses. He found that his great oratorical gifts were just as effective with the people at large as they were in the House of Commons. The high moral tone of his utterance struck a deep chord with the Victorian masses. The man in the street did not always understand Gladstone's meaning but he knew that he was on the side of the angels. Gladstone, in his turn, derived from this communion with the masses the certainty that he was walking in the path of righteousness. Among major political figures he more than any other bridged the gulf between the still aristocratic and exclusive parliamentary world and the great democracy waiting without. This process had only just begun in the early 1860s, but cynics might again say that by associating himself however cautiously with the cause of reform he was unmistakably staking out his claim to the succession to Palmerston and Russell.

In the general election of 1865 Gladstone was finally defeated at Oxford – his political and ecclesiastical views had become too Liberal. Instead he was returned for South Lancashire, whither he went 'unmuzzled' and amid scenes of great enthusiasm. After Palmerston's death in October 1865 he led the House of Commons under the premiership of Russell in the Whig attempt to pass a Reform Bill. It was a moderate Bill and indeed Gladstone's own views on the extension of the franchise were anything but radical, whatever the reform movement in the country at large had come to expect of him. Even the moderate Bill of 1866 frightened off a sufficient number of Whigs to bring about the fall of the Government, and Disraeli was given the chance of tackling the reform question from the Tory side. In the complex parliamentary situation of 1867 Gladstone was not at his best. He proved unable to bring together the Radical and moderate sections of the Liberal 'broad church' and Disraeli, with a party no less divided and in a minority, out-manoeuvred him. The management of men and of parliamentary groups was not Gladstone's forte.

It required a great moral cause to release Gladstone's dynamic energy and to make him fully effective as a leader. In 1868 he found his cause in the wrongs of Ireland, and the affairs of that unhappy country were henceforth to dominate most of his remaining career. The first Irish grievance to which he addressed himself was the anomaly that in a country three-quarters Roman Catholic the Established Church was Anglican. In moving his resolutions on the disestablishment of the Irish Church in May 1868 Gladstone welded the Liberal Coalition together again and paved the way for electoral victory and a Liberal Government led by himself. He had come a long way since the days when as the champion of the Established Church he had fought against the most meagre concessions on the temporalities of the Church of Ireland.

Gladstone's first Government was perhaps the greatest reforming administration of the nineteenth century. He did not dominate it in the way in which a modern prime minister would dominate his Cabinet and his party or even in the way in which Peel exercised a general control over the whole range of his administration. Gladstone took complete charge of the legislation connected with the cause that above all others he had at heart, Ireland. The other great reforms of this ministry, for example the Education Act of 1870, were in the main departmental measures, the concern of the relevant minister, in this case W. E. Forster. Gladstone played a full part in the preparation and Cabinet discussions of such proposals; but in the Cabinet he was no more than *primus inter pares*. It would have been repugnant to him to infringe the autonomy of departmental ministers. He lent to the agreed measures of his Government, such as the Education Act or Cardwell's Army re-forms, the full weight of his parliamentary authority, where this was required. He led his party from a position of detachment. He took little interest in the small change of party management and electioneering. He was in politics for great causes and as long as the heterogeneous following of the Liberal party was prepared to support him in these he could give leadership of unrivalled power. When in the latter years of this administration the support began to crumble he felt the bond was broken and contemplated retirement. Gladstone's closest confidant among his colleagues was Granville who had a wide knowledge of the political world and of Court circles. When Granville became Foreign Secretary in 1870 he worked closely with the Prime Minister on the day-to-day conduct of foreign policy. He also helped Gladstone in his relations with the Queen, which began to be strained in the later years of this ministry.

Gladstonian Liberalism can be defined largely in terms of the reforms accomplished during this period in office between 1868 and 1874. These reforms were almost entirely concerned with abolishing existing hindrances and restraints to full individual self-expression. Where interest groups, like the trade unions, made demands that would have required more positive intervention by the law, Gladstone's Government would not fully meet them; the trade union legislation of 1871, therefore, disappointed organised labour. Many of the other major measures of the Government also caused as much disillusionment as they gave satisfaction: many Nonconformists were deeply offended by the Education Act, because it failed to create a universal system of secular education and instead seemed to perpetuate the predominance of the Church of England in the voluntary system. Bruce's Licensing Act of 1872 did not satisfy the temperance interest while turning the brewing industry into the staunchest of Tory supporters. Gladstone's own formidable energies were concentrated on the Irish Land Act of 1870, his first attempt to deal with the grievances of the Irish peasantry caused by an alien form of land tenure. In spite of the great labour Gladstone expended on it the Act was not very effective; there was a limit beyond which even he was not prepared to go in attacking the sacred property rights of landowners. In 1873 Gladstone tried to complete his Irish trilogy with a Bill to set up an Irish university to remove the disabilities from which the Catholics suffered in higher education. It was acceptable neither to the Irish hierarchy, nor to much of English opinion, particularly not to many Nonconformists. Gladstone's Government was defeated and only the refusal of Disraeli to take office compelled it to carry on. In January

1874 Gladstone rather unexpectedly dissolved Parliament: he hoped to recover the popularity his Government had clearly lost by forecasting a Budget based on economy and reduction of income tax. But this prescription, through which Gladstone had two decades earlier made his great reputation as a public financier, was no longer to the same extent the key to electoral success. Instead the disaffection of many Liberal activists and general apathy produced the first clear Tory victory since the days of Peel. For Gladstone it was the culmination of growing disillusionment with his followers and fatigue with the burdens of leadership. He had talked much of retirement and now declared his intention of resigning the Liberal leadership as from 1875. Hartington succeeded him as Liberal leader in the Commons and Granville in the Lords. Gladstone did not, however, resign his seat in Parliament.

For two years he was immersed in theological, literary and scholarly work. When the Vatican published its decree on papal infallibility in 1870 Gladstone had felt himself unable to speak out, although he had been kept fully informed of what went on in Rome, particularly by his two close Catholic friends, Lord Acton and Döllinger, the German theologian, both of them leading opponents of the decree. Now he went into the attack with a pamphlet which sold many thousands of copies within days. Gladstone admired the Catholic Church though he was never tempted to join it; he felt it had now deliberately cut itself off from the main currents of the age. Many were unable to give Gladstone credit for the honesty of his views and felt that the pamphlet was an attempt to mend fences with the Nonconformists and Protestant opinion in general. Another view was that such excursions into theological controversy were hardly appropriate in a leading politician.

In the summer of 1876 the Eastern question and Disraeli's pro-Turkish stance began to become matters of major political controversy. Gladstone was at first slow to commit himself to the rising agitation; but it soon became impossible for him to hold back. He became convinced that here was a cause he had to take up – the attack on the immorality and cynical opportunism of the Government's foreign policy, 'Beaconsfieldism', as he came to call it. It was a cause that re-established the rapport between himself and the moral consciousness of the masses, particularly those sections that made up the rank and file of the Liberal party. On the other side of the great divide there were the 'classes', the upper ten thousand, who in Gladstone's view had been increasingly corrupted by wealth and greed. Gladstone now became 'the People's

William', the man who in countless speeches aroused the fervour of large multitudes, and who, felling trees at Hawarden, became the centre of many pilgrimages. Nowhere was the difference between Gladstonian Liberalism and Disraelian Conservatism more clear-cut than in foreign policy. Gladstone stood for international justice, self-determination of peoples, peace and retrenchment, Disraeli for national interest, power and prestige.

Gladstone was unable to modify Beaconsfield's policy on the Eastern question to any extent and his rival had his moment of triumph in 1878 at the Congress of Berlin. Thereafter 'Beaconsfieldism' rapidly ran into trouble: economic slump at home was paired with foreign fiascos in the Zulu and Afghan wars. Gladstone was adopted as Liberal candidate for Midlothian and in November 1879, when the next general election could no longer be far away, he went to campaign in his new constituency. For a leading statesman such an appeal to the ordinary people of the land was unprecedented. Gladstone was the centre of immense popular enthusiasm; but he was also execrated more than ever before in the drawing-rooms of London society. It was a matter of some embarrassment to him that his whirlwind re-entry into the political arena had in practice undercut the leadership of his colleagues, Granville and Hartington. When the Liberals won a resounding electoral victory in the spring of 1880 it was inevitable that the Queen had in the end to send for the GOM, much as she would have preferred to have either of his two Whig colleagues as her first minister. By this time she was convinced that he was a wild and dangerous old man.

Gladstone may have sounded more and more Radical to the Queen's conservative ears, but in fact he had little sympathy for the Radicalism of which Joseph Chamberlain and Sir Charles Dilke were now the leading representatives. He found room for them in his Government with some reluctance, only Chamberlain initially obtaining Cabinet rank. The dominant place in Gladstone's Government went to his long-established Whig and moderate Liberal colleagues, who in his view had a prescriptive right to the leading ministerial posts.

Gladstone's second ministry had no more of a prearranged programme of legislation than his first, nor was there, this time, a backlog of domestic reform held up by previous inertia. The Prime Minister thought his own tenure of office was temporary; his task was to reverse the policies of 'Beaconsfieldism' and then to return to the retirement he had reluctantly left. One major reform was generally expected of this

Government and considered a *sine qua non* by the Radicals: the extension of household suffrage to the counties. As such a change would have to be followed fairly rapidly by fresh elections, Gladstone decided to postpone it until later in the life of that Parliament. As it turned out, domestic legislation was largely crowded out by a series of foreign crises, by the running sore of the Bradlaugh case and, above all, by Ireland. In spite of what his opponents said about him Gladstone had a lively sense of national dignity and an even stronger feeling for Britain's obligations as an imperial and colonial power. In some cases, for example Afghanistan, he was able to reverse the policy of his predecessors and reap advantage and credit for the nation; in other instances, such as South Africa, he was unable to bring about a clear-cut change of policy. Egypt above all highlighted the dilemma of Gladstonian Liberalism in an age of growing imperialist rivalry. The Prime Minister took the steps that led to the Battle of Tel-el-Khebir and virtual British control of Egypt with the greatest reluctance. His failure to face up to the consequences put a burden on the conduct of British foreign policy which he never fully grasped. The same half-heartedness led to the involvement in the Sudan and eventually to the death of Gordon, an episode that discredited his Government more than anything else.

Ireland was an even greater distraction from domestic legislation. Parnell now led a tightly-knit group of Irish Nationalists at Westminster and was prepared to use the manifold opportunities for obstruction available under the parliamentary procedure of those days with complete ruthlessness. Gladstone wanted to deal with the grievances of Ireland constructively and in the Irish Land Act of 1881 offered a much more far-reaching remedy for the problems of the Irish peasantry than he had been able to do eleven years earlier. He could not, however, escape from the need to use repression to cope with the disturbed state of Ireland and much of the impact of his constructive intentions was lost. At Westminster Parnellite obstruction produced a revolution in parliamentary procedure which facilitated the gradual departure from the individualistic Liberalism for which Gladstone stood.

It was not until 1884 that the Government was able to turn to the further extension of the franchise. The third Reform Bill and the Redistribution Bill that accompanied it produced, in the form in which they finally reached the statute book, universal male household suffrage and a system of single-member constituencies broadly as we now know it. It was, along with the Corrupt Practices Act of 1883, the most thorough revision of the electoral system accomplished during the nine-teenth century. In the long-drawn-out reform battle of 1884, which involved a clash between the two Houses of Parliament, Gladstone showed that his domination of the House of Commons, of the political world and of public opinion at large was undiminished.

In 1885 Gladstone's Government, endlessly plagued by crises and internal dissensions, was defeated. It was, however, the very diversity and disunion of the Liberal party that convinced Gladstone that it was still his duty to remain as leader at least until the next election, to be held under the new franchise. The general election of 1885 returned over eighty more Liberals than Conservatives in Great Britain; but it also returned over eighty Nationalists in Ireland outside Ulster who under Parnell's leadership held the balance of power at Westminster. Gladstone had for some time recognised the force of Irish nationalism and the justice of its claims. It was the same generous and essentially liberal insight that had enabled him to sympathise with the national aspirations of the Balkan peoples. His diagnosis of the Irish problem was confirmed by the sweep of the Nationalists in Southern Ireland in November 1885, but he had refused to enter into an auction for Par-nell's support before the election and the Irish leader had in fact given his backing to the Tories. After the election Gladstone hoped that Salisbury's Government would grasp the Irish nettle and he was pre-pared to give them his help. These hopes were disappointed, partly because Salisbury refused to take on so thankless a task, partly because Gladstone's own conversion to Home Rule was prematurely announced in the famous *Hawarden Kite*.

To some he was now 'an old man in a hurry', as Lord Randolph Churchill described him; a man who for the sake of holding on to power a little longer and in the egotistical blindness that only he had the solu-tion was prepared to break the unity of the kingdom and Empire and of his own party. To others, and they included a majority of Liberals, he was the great and generous statesman who would replace the age-old Anglo-Irish feud with a 'union of hearts'. After the lapse of nearly a century Gladstone's scheme of Irish autonomy seems a conservative and balanced attempt to solve an intractable problem, perhaps one of the few opportunities to create a tolerable *modus vivendi* between England and Ireland. It required a man of Gladstone's greatness to recognise the problem, propose a solution and launch it into practical politics; but a much lesser man, more versed in the arts of political management, might have been able to get a Home Rule Bill of sorts through the House of Commons without too much damage to the cohesion of the Liberal party. The loss of Whigs and moderate Liberals had long been foreshadowed and might have mattered little in the longer run; but the loss of Chamberlain and his Radical Unionist followers was damaging. With the general election of 1886 the Liberal party, generally expected to be the majority party dedicated to reform, entered upon twenty years of virtual impotence. Gladstone, under whose mantle the divergent Liberal elements had gathered twenty years earlier, had come near to destroying the instrument he had once helped to create.

Gladstone, aged 76, was to remain Liberal leader for nearly eight years. He could still inspire popular enthusiasm, although others, for instance Chamberlain and Randolph Churchill, could now emulate him, though perhaps trading in a debased coinage. He was determined to keep Home Rule for Ireland in the forefront of the Liberal programme. There was in fact no other cause commanding sufficient support in the Liberal party to replace it. Gladstone had little interest in the many other reforms that were now proposed or in the preparation of elaborate reform programmes which he dismissed as 'constructionism'. What he called 'socialism' was repugnant to him; there seemed to him a growing danger that the moral sense of the masses, which had stood in such striking contrast to the selfishness of the classes, would itself be corrupted by the demand for material welfare. Gladstone was none the less prepared to support a list of reforms, such as were proposed in the Newcastle Programme of 1891, provided the cause of Irish Home Rule was kept alive.

The fall of Parnell in 1890, as a result of the divorce suit brought by Captain O'Shea, was a body blow to that cause and deprived Gladstone of an independent Liberal majority in the general election of 1892. Nevertheless he made a last heroic effort to do justice to Ireland. His second Home Rule Bill passed the House of Commons in 1893, but was rejected by the House of Lords. Even then he would have been prepared to continue the battle by going to the country over the powers of the Peers. His colleagues, however, were no longer prepared to support him. At heart he was still a Peelite Conservative committed to Peace, Retrenchment and Reform and he was increasingly at odds with his Cabinet over foreign and imperial policy and rising defence expenditure. He felt himself to be a 'survival' and in March 1894 he resigned for the last time, after over sixty years in the House of Commons. What hurt him most about his departure was the Queen's inability to disguise her relief. Often in his few remaining years he dreamt that she had invited him to breakfast, but the invitation never came.

Gladstone was a towering figure in the Victorian age. The shape and the content of politics would have been quite different without him. His range of interest and activity beyond politics was unusually wide and he wrote prolifically on religion, theology, the classics and literature. Only the natural sciences were a closed book to him. His Celtic ancestry was unmistakable and he was the greatest Scotsman who ever ruled England. Towards the end of his long public life there was a sense in which he had outlived himself, but the values he championed with such fervour have perennial validity.

BIBLIOGRAPHY

Biographies
Birrell, Francis, *Gladstone* (London, 1933)
Burdett, Osbert Henry, *W. E. Gladstone* (London, 1927)
Checkland, S. G., *The Gladstones: A Family Biography 1764–1851* (Cambridge, 1971)
Feuchtwanger, E. J., *Gladstone: A Political Biography* (London, in preparation for publication 1975)
Hamilton, Sir E. W., *Mr Gladstone* (London, 1898)
Magnus, Philip, *Gladstone: A Biography* (London, 1954)
Morley, John, *Life of William Ewart Gladstone* (3 vols, London, 1903)

Documents
Bahlman, Dudley W. R. (ed.), *The Diary of Sir Edward Hamilton* (2 vols, Oxford, 1972)
Bassett, A. T., *Gladstone's Speeches: Descriptive Index and Bibliography* (London, 1916); (ed.) *Gladstone to his Wife* (London, 1936)
Brooke, John and Sorensen, Mary (eds), *The Prime Ministers' Papers: W. E. Gladstone. I: Autobiographica. II: Autobiographical Memoranda* (London, 1971–2)
Foot, M. R. D. (ed.), *The Gladstone Diaries* (2 vols, Oxford, 1968)
Guedalla, P. (ed.), *Gladstone and Palmerston* (London, 1928); *The Queen and Mr Gladstone* (2 vols, London, 1933)
Lathbury, D. C. (ed.), *Correspondence on Church and Religion of W. E. Gladstone* (2 vols, London, 1910)
Ramm, Agatha (ed.), *The Political Correspondence of Mr Gladstone and Lord Granville 1868–76* (2 vols, London, 1952); *The Political Correspondence of Mr Gladstone and Lord Granville 1876–86* (2 vols, Oxford, 1962)

Other Works

Blake, R., *The Conservative Party from Peel to Churchill* (London, 1970)

Cooke, A. B. and Vincent, J. R., *The Governing Passion: Cabinet Government and Party Politics in Britain 1885–6* (Brighton, 1974)

Hamer, D. A., *Liberal Politics in the Age of Gladstone and Rosebery* (Oxford, 1972)

Hammond, J. L., *Gladstone and the Irish Nation*. New impression with an introduction by M. R. D. Foot (London, 1964)

Hammond, J. L. and Foot, M. R. D., *Gladstone and Liberalism* (London, 1952)

Hanham, H. J., *Elections and Party Management: Politics in the Time of Disraeli and Gladstone* (London, 1959)

Hirst, F. W., *Gladstone as Financier and Economist* (London, 1931)

Hyde, Francis Edwin, *Mr Gladstone at the Board of Trade* (London, 1934)

Schreuder, D. M., *Gladstone and Kruger. Liberal Government and Colonial 'Home Rule' 1880–5* (London, 1969)

Seton-Watson, R. W., *Disraeli, Gladstone and the Eastern Question* (London, 1935)

Shannon, R. T., *Gladstone and the Bulgarian Agitation 1876* (London, 1963)

Vincent, J. R., *The Formation of the Liberal Party, 1857–68* (London, 1966)

LORD SALISBURY

BY

ALAN PALMER

*Robert Arthur Talbot Gascoyne-Cecil, 3rd Marquis of Salisbury,
second son of the 2nd Marquis by his first wife. Born 3 February
1830. Educated at Eton and Christ Church, Oxford. Voyaged round
the world 1851–53. MP for Stamford (Lincs.) 1853 and elected
Fellow of All Souls. Married, 1857, the elder daughter of Sir
Edward Hall Alderson. Wrote for the* Saturday Review *and the*
Quarterly Review. *As Lord Cranborne entered Derby's cabinet in
1866 as Secretary of State for India; resigned February 1867.
Succeeded as Marquis 1868. Chancellor of Oxford University
1870; Secretary of State for India 1874–78; Foreign Secretary
1878–80; represented Britain at the Berlin Congress 1878; Leader
of the House of Lords 1881; Prime Minister 1885, 1886–92,
1895–1902, (also Foreign Secretary 1886–92, 1895–1900). Died
August 1903.*

Robert Arthur Talbot Gascoyne-Cecil, 3rd Marquis of Salisbury, by G. F. Watts

LORD SALISBURY

Lord Salisbury was born fifteen years after Waterloo and died fifteen years before the German Armistice. Although detesting all soldiering he was in a curious way a link between the Napoleonic struggles and the wars of the twentieth century. For as a boy, young Robert Cecil walked beside his godfather, the Duke of Wellington, at Walmer Castle, listening to tales of Bonaparte and Marshal Soult; while as 'Prime Minister since God knew when', he was host to Lord Randolph Churchill's red-headed son, who was already experienced in a somewhat different type of warfare. In the year of Salisbury's birth Stephenson's *Rocket* first thundered from Liverpool to Manchester and in the year he died the Wright Brothers' aeroplane made its first flight. Salisbury's working habits depended as much on railways and steamships as do those of a modern politician on aircraft. We find him, for example, ordering his secretaries to make certain his red dispatch boxes are placed on the 4.20 from King's Cross to Hatfield; we read of him catching the night sleeper to confer with his sovereign in Scotland or the packet boat from Newhaven to take a holiday at his villa near Dieppe; and we hear of his delight in dodging importunate journalists by hiding in a third-class carriage – not for him the hurried sanctuary of a VIP lounge. The influence of steampower went even further: to a large extent, Salisbury's world map – increasingly tinted a patriotic red during his premiership – was shaped by the coaling capacity of warships and the projected routes of railways across Asia and Africa. He was, in Britain, the pre-eminent statesman of the Age of Steam, a time when political life was slower than today but infinitely more comprehensive than anything that had gone before.

The Cecils had risen to prominence in another age of expansion, the reign of Elizabeth I, but since the days of the great Burghley and his son an unduly long hiatus filled the family annals. Successive generations concentrated their interest on the county politics of Hertfordshire and Middlesex. The second Marquis, Robert's father, was however an exception: he took an active part in national government, sitting as Lord Privy Seal alongside Disraeli for ten months in the Derby Cabinet of

1852. At that time there seemed little prospect that either of his sons would achieve even this limited distinction: the elder, Lord Cranborne, had a pathetically deficient mentality; and Robert himself, the younger, was a sad disappointment. When fourteen he had been able to throw off Latin verses at school with effortless ease, but twelve months later he complained that life at Eton was 'insupportable'. To save him from further bullying his father took him away, entrusting his education to a private tutor in the family home at Hatfield. Achievement, too, fell far short of promise at Oxford. Lord Robert went up to Christ Church in the first weeks of 1848, Europe's 'Year of Revolutions'. He worked diligently, interested himself in politics and religion, and held office in the Oxford Union, though the prestige prize of the presidency eluded him. Unfortunately the strain of academic study week by week over-taxed his strength. He began to walk in his sleep, and before the end of his second year at the University he suffered what his physician termed 'a complete breakdown of his nervous system'. To be placed in the fourth class Honours list for Mathematics sadly mocked his intelligence, and it did not help him to recover his health. It began to seem as if the future Lord Salisbury might even become as mentally afflicted as his brother.

In desperation the second Marquis accepted the advice of his doctor and sent Lord Robert on a voyage around the world. He sailed for Australia by way of southern Africa in July 1851, eventually visiting Tasmania and New Zealand as well and returning across the Pacific and round Cape Horn. Travel was good for his health; it was also of in-estimable value to him educationally. When he arrived home in 1853 he was fit enough to stand as Tory candidate for Stamford, where he was returned to Parliament unopposed. Already he had a field of specialist study and experience. At twenty-three he knew more about the problems of a growing empire than most Members of the Commons: he had seen for himself the frustrations facing British officials as they sought to reconcile Boers and Kaffirs; he had visited the new goldfields in South Australia, incongruous among the diggers in his frock-coat and white top-hat, but noting with surprise that instead of murders and lynch-laws 'there is less crime than in a large English town'; and he had ridden from settlement to settlement across more than 200 miles of New Zealand, jotting down in his journal what he heard and what he observed of the colonists' difficulties. Although in 1853 the colonial question still aroused little interest in the Commons the world was narrowing with every steamship launched from the slipways, and the Member for Stamford's knowledge of what lay over the horizons soon began to mark him off from the High Tory squires around him.

So, indeed, did other matters. He married at twenty-six, a far younger age than most aspiring politicians among his contemporaries; his wife was a woman of intellect as well as of charm, daughter to a judge rather than a member of one of the party dynasties. Unfortunately Lord Robert's financial situation did not accord with the position in society he was expected to maintain, and the young couple had at first to live in Fitzroy Square (where one fashionable hostess complained it was impossible to call on them as 'she never left cards north of Oxford Street'). But this particular domestic problem indirectly had an important effect on Lord Robert's political career: to earn money he turned to political journalism, writing regular articles for two weeklies and, from April 1860 onwards, contributing to the famous *Quarterly Review*. It was these articles, some of them forty pages long, that made his reputation.

They were, as in most periodicals of the time, unsigned. But their authorship soon became known and Lord Robert's literary style easily recognisable. It showed a feeling for the trenchant phrase, a sense of the past, and a precision of argument refreshingly distinct from the measured pomposity of most Victorian periodical journalism. He did not pull his punches. The very first article he wrote for the *Quarterly* attacks Disraeli's flexibility of principles and Gladstone's quest for social equality in taxation, a false and foolish ideal ensuring that 'the rich will pay all the taxes and the poor will make all the laws'. Lord Robert's writing on domestic politics reveals an almost Aristotelian fear of democracy as the embodiment of mob rule transmitted into action by an elected demagogue. He was never afraid of the 'people' as such, only of their collective political judgement. It was a nice distinction, but to a generation still overshadowed by the revolutions of 1789 and 1848 a valid one.

Far more impressive were his articles on diplomatic questions and his biographical essays. He studied the intricacies of the Schleswig–Holstein dispute and the background to the Polish revolt in astonishing depth and he was thus one of the first English commentators to comprehend the character of Bismarck's diplomacy. What he saw of Prussian policy he did not like, but he cared still less for the badinage and bluster of Russell and Palmerston. His ideal British statesman was the much maligned Castlereagh: here, he insisted, was a man who had known how to maintain a judicious balance between committing his country to continental action and avoiding entanglement in alien concerns. 'A nation may uphold its honour without being Quixotic,' he wrote in April 1864, 'but no reputation can survive a display of Quixotism which falters at the sight of a drawn sword.' This was a sound principle of conduct for a rising politician who was already showing more interest than anyone else on the opposition benches in the changing power pattern of Europe. Salisbury's sense of imperial responsibility may have sprung from his travels; but his instinct for statecraft he perfected by reading, writing and reflection among his books at Hatfield or in the study of the house he acquired in Arlington Street.

Exactly fourteen years elapsed between Lord Robert's comments on Quixotic diplomacy and his first appointment as Foreign Secretary. For much of that time it still seemed likely that, despite his massive intellectual authority, he would never attain high office. He consistently refused to compromise his own beliefs for party advantage, for this seemed to him to make nonsense of the purpose of politics, and he was too strong a personality to follow meekly the lead Disraeli was giving to the country squirarchy. In July 1866, a year after he succeeded his unfortunate brother as Lord Cranborne, he was offered the India Office by Lord Derby and he accepted the post. For seven months he showed remarkable mastery of Indian affairs, but he was not happy in the Cabinet. He did not see how he could remain a member of a government prepared to extend the franchise, even though the original Derby–Disraeli proposals for the second Reform Bill had built-in safeguards against a surfeit of democracy in the form of plurality voting. In February 1867 Cranborne informed Derby he would have to resign. Disraeli complained he had been stabbed in the back (although he showed no rancour towards the assassin) and Cranborne seriously considered giving up politics altogether. The mood, however, soon passed; though out of the Government, his pen remained active and the articles in the *Quarterly* lost none of their bite.

In the following spring the second Marquis died and Cranborne became Lord Salisbury, master of Hatfield House in his own right and a member of what he later termed 'the dullest assembly in the world'. It was, once again, tempting to live in Hertfordshire, indulge his scientific curiosity with experiments on a grand scale at Hatfield, and allow politics to go to the Devil and Mr Gladstone. He did indeed begin a serious study of farming technique, painstakingly assessing the problems of the estates he had inherited; he refurbished the chapel at Hatfield and constructed a laboratory for himself; and on one occasion he surprised the editor of the *Quarterly* with an article in praise of photography rather than his customary survey of what mattered in Church and State. But he was not a man to vegetate for long, nor did he see any reason why he should not continue to amuse himself with science while speaking and writing against political changes he detested. In Ireland, in the Universities and in the Army the Gladstonian broom seemed to him to be sweeping away indiscriminately the chaff of ages and the seeds of security. By 1874 he was even willing to contemplate 'the nightmare' of serving in a government under Disraeli, and when the Tories won the general election that year he agreed to return to the India Office.

But the affairs of the subcontinent occupied him far less than he anticipated. Within a year revolts in Turkish Bulgaria and Turkish Herzegovina led to conflict between Muslims and Christians, with Russia backing the Balkan Slavs against their Ottoman rulers. Salisbury was involved in decision-making from the very start of the crisis, for quite apart from its strategic and religious implications for India, his understanding of foreign politics made his advice invaluable to the Cabinet. In November 1876 he was sent as British delegate to Constantinople, where it was hoped an international conference could induce the Turks to reform their system of government. The conference failed and the crisis worsened, but Salisbury's experience broadened still further his insight into the problems of diplomacy. He had travelled by way of Paris, Berlin, Vienna and Rome meeting the leading statesmen of the Continent and thus acquiring a personal knowledge of the workings of Europe's chancelleries such as no British Cabinet minister had possessed for half a century. When in the spring of 1878 it looked as if war would break out between Britain and Russia Lord Beaconsfield (as Disraeli had become) transferred Salisbury to the Foreign Office in the belief that an incisive and resolute policy would keep the peace of Europe. He was right.

Even before moving into the Foreign Secretary's room, Salisbury shut himself up in his study at Arlington Street and wrote a circular message to the principal European governments. He was accustomed to analysing and reviewing on paper the diplomatic questions of the day and the circular reads like one of his *Quarterly* articles with the argument made impersonal and the taunting phrases held in check. In the circular he proposed a basic settlement of all the disputes in the Eastern question, with preliminary agreements between the Powers to be amplified and confirmed in an international congress. It was in fulfilment of this policy that Salisbury accompanied Beaconsfield to Berlin later that summer, subsequently sharing popular adulation for having brought back 'peace with honour'. In retrospect, of course, the Berlin Treaty looks less impressive than it did to contemporaries for it created more problems than it solved, but at the time it prevented Russian dominance of the Balkans and the Straits; there was no major war in Europe for over a third of a century. For this achievement the author of the circular message deserved, and received, some credit.

Salisbury found this second experience of conference diplomacy even more stimulating than the month he had spent in Constantinople. Characteristically, however, he deplored the fuss and publicity and had to be coaxed by Beaconsfield before he would accept the great honour of the Garter. Privately he let it be known that he considered that the happiest consequence of his journey to Berlin was his meeting with the distinguished German physicist, Hermann Helmholtz, with whom he exchanged views on electro-magnetism. But the Berlin Congress had a double significance in his career: he lost the old antipathy for Beaconsfield once he became his partner in the diplomatic game; and he emerged, for the first time, as a likely contestant for the Tory succession should the Prime Minister's health finally give way. These two developments were, of course, closely connected. Salisbury much admired his chief's tenacity and resilience, while the Prime Minister himself was impressed by his Foreign Secretary's vigour and verbal courage. Both these qualities were certainly lacking in Sir Stafford Northcote, who as Chancellor of the Exchequer and leader in the Commons, was Beaconsfield's heir apparent. On the other hand Salisbury's essentially negative attitude to domestic reform, his contempt for popular enthusiasm, his dislike of social functions, his apparent disregard of the new mass organisation of the party, all counted against him. It was difficult to envisage someone so independent and aloof as Prime Minister of Jingo England.

Beaconsfield died in April 1881, having lost the previous year's election as much from party muddle and confusion as any other single cause. Salisbury duly succeeded his lost leader in the Lords; but had it been necessary to form a Conservative Government the Queen was firmly resolved to send for 'her old and kind friend' Northcote, chief opposition spokesman in the Commons. Salisbury, though respecting the Crown as the supreme symbol of Empire, never flattered his sovereign, nor did he even bother to hide a positive distaste for life in the Scottish Highlands. Why should he? He was without ambition. Had Northcote formed a ministry, he would inevitably have offered Salisbury the Foreign Office, and that was all he wanted.

Yet when Gladstone was defeated on the Budget in 1885 it was to Salisbury rather than to Northcote that Victoria turned, summoning him to Balmoral by a telegram which reached Hatfield when he was engaged in a particularly interesting experiment with a primitive telephone. For in opposition Northcote had shown himself unable to stand up to Gladstone over Ireland or to Lord Randolph Churchill's pressure group of Tory Democrats within his own party. The Queen, alarmed by the growth of Radicalism at home and by protracted unrest in Ireland, believed she needed 'strong and able and safe men' in her Government, and looked to Salisbury to find them. And the Conservative party – especially what Salisbury himself called the 'Villa Tories' in the middle classes – agreed with her. But that winter the electorate, following Joe Chamberlain rather than Gladstone, thought otherwise; and Salisbury after seven months of minority government returned to his laboratory at Hatfield.

Not, however, for long. Within eight weeks of Gladstone's return to Downing Street the Liberal Government was split down the middle over Home Rule, and a fresh election in midsummer gave the Conservatives a convincing majority. Salisbury formed his second ministry in the last week of July 1886 confident that this time he would exercise the reality of power. Though the Liberals were once more in office from 1892 to 1895, his was the decisive voice in British politics for the next sixteen years.

It was a voice that more and more of the electorate were hearing. For although Salisbury distrusted democratic government, he took pains to master its skills. He grew to respect the party machine and to listen as attentively to national agents as to diplomatic envoys, if only because they too were in a sense bearers of news foreign to him. Even before the 1885 and 1886 election campaigns, Salisbury had begun to address mass meetings in big cities and market towns throughout England, determined to counter the powerful influence of Gladstone's rhetoric; once he accustomed himself to this strange practice he stumped the country, at times positively enjoying the experience. He spoke slowly, emphatically, showing now and again an almost absent-minded informality, with none of Gladstone's sustained oratory or Disraeli's flights of imagery. It was an honest style, lit occasionally by a mordant phrase, free from humbug and condescension. Somehow it conveyed the presence of a magisterial authority easily assumed and kindly exercised, inviting trust and respect if not affection. No one expected a voice so reasonably sensible to promise heaven on earth; and no one was disappointed. Opponents outside the Conservative party, and carping critics within, consistently underestimated Salisbury's effectiveness as a public speaker.

At first, too, they underestimated him as a political manager. It was tempting to see Salisbury as the spokesman of a vanishing world, a patrician who would soon be swept from office by the irresistible force of Tory Democracy. That Salisbury stayed while Tory Democracy was swallowed up by the older tradition of the party was a consequence of two events which no observer would have predicted at the start of his second ministry: the appalling error by which Lord Randolph Churchill, the leader of the Tory Democrats, offered his resignation as Chancellor of the Exchequer over a relatively minor issue; and the willingness of Salisbury to allow the cautiously progressive members of his Cabinet to filch many of Lord Randolph's ideas of reform, especially where they benefited the agricultural interest. The legislative record of the Salisbury ministry is slight in comparison with the achievements of both Liberal and Conservative administrations in the previous decade, but enough was done to prove that the Prime Minister had at least a passing interest in domestic reform.

Most of the changes helped the farming community. This is hardly surprising; the countryside was hit by an agricultural depression, and the Tories were traditionally spokesmen 'for the country gentlemen of England'. Some reforms did, however, benefit the rural working classes (who had been enfranchised by the Liberals in 1884). Bills were introduced which modified the agricultural rating system, assisted smallholders, simplified the transfer of land, helped combat disease in livestock, adjusted the burden of tithes, and established local elected councils in the counties with powers similar to those enjoyed for half a century by the municipal corporations. As if to emphasise the priority of farming matters in Conservative thought, Salisbury established a department of agriculture, with a government minister at its head. His views were changing, sometimes with devastating logic: since Parliament insisted on making primary education compulsory, it seemed iniquitous to him that the poor should be expected to pay for their children's schooling, and thus the old defender of exclusiveness in the ancient universities introduced free elementary education for the mass population. Eager to stir the House of Lords from its torpor, he even proposed a measure to create life peerages for fifty men of distinction. But this reform, which was seventy years ahead of public thinking, was never enacted, partly through the pressure of other business.

Under Salisbury, as under his predecessors, much debating time at Westminster was occupied by the seemingly intractable problems of Ireland. He had always believed that (as he once wrote in the *Quarterly*) Home Rule by its very nature threatened 'the highest interests of the Empire'. Once he was in power he sought to check the continued lawlessness in Ireland by firm government, with his nephew Balfour – the Chief Secretary for Ireland – meeting violence with a combination of arbitrary pugnacity and ameliorative legislation. This was ultimately a policy that postponed decisions rather than patching up a solution; but at least Balfour's skill in the Commons guaranteed support for his uncle from Joe Chamberlain and his Liberal Unionists. This combination, originally forged over Irish affairs, was to have its greatest significance a decade later.

Salisbury's most distinguished achievements were concerned, in the broadest sense, with the well-being of the Empire. It was under his leadership that Britain acquired Kenya, Uganda, Nigeria and Rhodesia, as well as establishing control over the upper waters of the Nile and countering the ambitious plans of the French in Africa and the Russians in the Far East. These successes, to which might be added advantageous settlements with Germany and Portugal over African boundaries, mark off the second and third Salisbury ministries as peak periods of empire building. Yet the Prime Minister himself was never a conventional imperialist: he did not bother to read the fashionable publicists of the age; he had no use for theories of expansion; and he assumed every new colonial responsibility with reluctance, always conscious that annexation of territory created problems for a government instead of solving them. At heart he preferred an Africa of coastal settlements backed by a huge undeveloped hinterland where missionaries and agents of chartered companies fended for themselves. But if there was a danger of other European Powers trespassing on what had been a preserve of British traders, then Salisbury was willing to act in defence of British commercial rights and traditional interests. The great imperialists of the age

– Rhodes, Mackinnon, Goldie – saw the acquisition of a particular sphere of Africa as an end in itself: for Salisbury the scramble for Africa was only one aspect of a challenge being offered to British overseas supremacy by the other Great Powers. He had always believed that colonies should as soon as possible develop their own institutions and remain free from Whitehall's bureaucratic control, but he was convinced they could never survive unless their leaders recognised that the Empire was, above all, 'a combination for purposes of self-defence'. Hence he preached again and again the need for a powerful Navy and a flexible foreign policy if the work of the empire builders was to be consolidated.

For almost fourteen years Salisbury was Prime Minister: for more than eleven of them he served as Foreign Secretary as well as heading the Government. None of his predecessors had combined these offices, while among his successors the task was attempted only by Ramsay MacDonald (and then for a mere ten months). Critics inside and outside his party complained that he held on too long to the Foreign Office, speaking with increasing disparagement of his 'masterly inactivity'. But Salisbury had an understanding of diplomatic technique equalled among British statesmen only by Castlereagh, Palmerston in his first spell at the Foreign Office, and perhaps Curzon. He had no preconceived methods for dealing with diplomatic problems, preferring to meet each fresh challenge with an answer dependent on local conditions and the general balance of world forces. Thus he favoured partitioning regions beyond the reach of British naval or military expeditions into spheres of influence, supporting the creation if possible of buffer states between great power rivals, but elsewhere he would follow an almost Palmerstonian forward policy. For Salisbury there were no natural allies and no natural foes: he was prepared to co-operate with Italy and Austria-Hungary in the Mediterranean in the late 1880s, to police the troubled island of Crete jointly with Russia and France a decade later, and to work with Germany over the problems of China at the end of the century. He disliked long-term commitments, partly because they imposed limits on his freedom of action but also because he believed no government liable to be overthrown by popular vote should assume responsibilities that its successor might find morally difficult to honour. Though doubting at times the wisdom of the democratic process, he respected its conventions more conscientiously than many of its champions.

Popular legend has identified Salisbury with a policy of isolation, especially in the closing years of the old century. It is true that while Europe was divided into two rival camps (Germany, Austria-Hungary and Italy facing the Dual Alliance of France and Russia) Britain was able, through her massive preponderance of naval power, to remain without an ally. But Salisbury did not favour isolation under all circumstances. He used the famous phrase 'splendid isolation' sardonically in the first instance, gently rebuking in a speech at the Guildhall the patriotic self-righteousness of some of his own colleagues, notably Chamberlain. Since he believed passionately in the need for constant diplomatic exchanges, a policy of total isolation seemed to him completely wrong-headed. One of the ablest state papers he ever wrote, the circular dispatch of 20 October 1896, was an appeal to the other European Powers to solve the latest problems of the Eastern question by joint consultation rather than by a dangerous unilateral action; and, just as the circular of April 1878 had facilitated the summoning of the Berlin Congress, so this parallel document paved the way for an ambassadorial conference in Constantinople (though, on this occasion, with little success). More than half the work of the foreign service in his third ministry was concerned with finding common ground between London and the European chancelleries so that disputes could be thrashed out in negotiations. This was especially true of the British ambassadors to St Petersburg: Salisbury would have liked a comprehensive Anglo-Russian settlement since he feared that the quarrels of the two empires in Turkey, Persia and the Far East were a potential menace to the peace of the whole world.

There were, however, strict limits to the concessions he was prepared to make in any negotiations. He broke off talks with Russia when it seemed to him that the Tsar's proconsuls in Asia wished to absorb the northern provinces of China, where the British had considerable economic interests. Similarly, though willing to discuss African frontier problems with the French, he worked consistently to consolidate British influence in Egypt, refusing to acknowledge any French rights to establish a protectorate over the basin of the Upper Nile. No episode is so dramatic in Salisbury's premiership as the confrontation at Fashoda in 1898 when Kitchener, fresh from his victorious conquest of the Sudan, faced Colonel Marchand's expedition which was seeking to blaze for France a tricolour trail from west to east across Africa. Salisbury prepared for a general war with France rather than concede Marchand's claim to hold the Fashoda region in the name of the Republic. When, in the following spring, the French gave way and signed an agreement renouncing all ambitions to control the Nile Valley, Salisbury achieved a remarkable diplomatic victory. His understanding of the French political scene, a knowledge gained from long familiarity with the strains and stresses of the Third Republic, enabled him to ride out the crisis with iron nerves. The notion of an Anglo-French war was totally repugnant to him; he was rightly convinced that firmness and resolution would rule out any such disaster.

Unfortunately Salisbury did not show a similar understanding of South African problems. Ever since his visit to Cape Colony nearly half a century previously, he had distrusted the Boers, seeing in their narrow Calvinism an obstacle to his own ideal of racial harmony. He was, however, prepared to seek better relations with the militant Transvaalers, especially after the folly of Jameson's ill-conceived raid of 1895. But Salisbury left such matters to the Colonial Secretary, Chamberlain, in the first instance, and both men were more dependent than they realised on Milner, the Governor of Cape Colony. Bad advice and divided counsels led Salisbury's Government to treat Kruger's Boers with an obstinacy as uncompromising as that shown by the Prime Minister towards the French at Fashoda. But Pretoria was not Paris; and to his dismay Salisbury found in the autumn of 1899 that it was impossible to prevent Kruger from appealing to arms. 'Joe's War', as Salisbury privately called the conflict in South Africa, may have rallied popular feeling around his Government, but it lost him his mastery of the Cabinet and destroyed the freedom of action on which he based his diplomatic system. The effort to recover his ascendancy cost him his health.

By the autumn of 1900 Salisbury was rapidly ageing and his colleagues found him no longer willing to act decisively. The Conservative triumph at the polls in October – and, to some extent, the actual timing of this 'khaki election' – owed more to the political instincts of Chamberlain than to the Prime Minister. At last the old man agreed to leave the Foreign Office, handing over responsibilities to Lord Lansdowne. He headed the Government for another twenty months. Occasionally he intervened effectively in policy-making, notably in May 1901, when one masterly final memorandum rejected proposals that Britain might join the Triple Alliance of Germany, Austria-Hungary and Italy. But in the summer of 1902, very tired and very frail, he resigned and retired to

Hatfield. When he died thirteen months later people mourned the passing of a patriarchal figure whom the voters respected rather than revered. His natural shyness and reserve, his self-effacement and loathing of publicity had never captured the imagination. He remains the least known of the great prime ministers.

BIBLIOGRAPHY

Blake, Robert, *The Conservative Party from Peel to Churchill* (London, 1970)

Cecil, David, *The Cecils of Hatfield* (London, 1973)

Cecil, Lady Gwendolen, *Life of Robert, Marquis of Salisbury* (4 vols, London, 1921–32)

Cecil, Robert, Marquis of Salisbury, *Essays*, vol. 1, biographical, vol. 2, foreign politics (London, 1905)

Grenville, J. A. S., *Lord Salisbury and Foreign Policy: The Close of the Nineteenth Century* (London, 1964)

Kennedy, A. L., *Salisbury, 1830–1903: Portrait of a Statesman* (London, 1953)

Penson, Lillian, *Foreign Affairs under the Third Marquis of Salisbury* (London, 1962)

Pinto-Duschinsky, M., *The Political Thought of Lord Salisbury 1854–68* (Oxford, 1967)

THE EARL OF ROSEBERY

BY

ROBERT RHODES JAMES

Archibald Philip Primrose, 5th Earl of Rosebery. Born 7 May 1847, the son of Archibald, Lord Dalmeny, and Wilhelmina, daughter of the 4th Earl Stanhope. Educated at Brighton, Eton and Christ Church, Oxford. Succeeded his grandfather 1868. Married 1878, Hannah, daughter of Baron Meyer Amschel de Rothschild; two sons, two daughters. Lord Rector of Aberdeen University, 1878; of Edinburgh University, 1880. Under-Secretary, Home Office 1881; resigned 1883; First Commissioner of Works 1884; Foreign Secretary 1886; member of the first London County Council and Chairman 1889; resigned the same year, but resumed the office in 1892. KG 1892, Foreign Secretary 1892–94; Prime Minister 1894–95; resigned the Liberal leadership 1896. Chancellor of the University of Glasgow 1908; Lord Rector of St Andrew's 1911. Died 21 May 1929. Author of Pitt, *1891;* Appreciations and Addresses, *1925,* Peel, *1899;* Napoleon the Last Phase, *1900,* Lord Randolph Churchill, *1906,* and Chatham—His Early Life and Connections, *1910.*

Archibald Philip Primrose, 5th Earl of Rosebery, by Sydney P. Hall

THE EARL OF ROSEBERY

Archibald Philip Primrose, fifth Earl of Rosebery, was Prime Minister for only fifteen months, between March 1894 and June 1895. It was, as Winston Churchill has commented, 'a strangely-lit episode', in which Rosebery had 'a bleak, precarious, wasting inheritance'. When he thankfully resigned in June 1895 he was only forty-eight years of age. 'There are two supreme pleasures in life,' he subsequently wrote. 'One is ideal, the other real. The ideal is when a man receives the seals of office from his Sovereign. The real pleasure comes when he hands them back.' A year later he relinquished the leadership of the Liberal party. Although he lived until 1929, he never held public office of any kind again. Yet he remains one of the most perplexing and profoundly interesting men who have held the highest political office.

He was the elder son of Lord Dalmeny and the former Lady Wilhelmina Stanhope, and it is perhaps to the Stanhopes rather than the Primroses that we look for some explanation of his outstanding ability and introspective personality. 'She spoke with an exquisite precision, both of utterance and of diction,' G. W. E. Russell wrote of Lady Dalmeny. 'She hardly uttered a sentence without giving it a turn which one remembered: and her inclination to sarcasm was not unduly restrained. She was born in a learned home, and had lived all her life with clever and educated people.' She was also headstrong, and her intellect was brisk rather than profound. Lord Dalmeny, the heir to the Rosebery title and estates, is more remembered for his devotion to physical fitness than for his contribution as Liberal MP for Stirling Burghs, and his sole literary production was a pamphlet entitled *An Address to the Middle Classes upon the Subject of Gymnastic Exercises*. In January 1851, when his elder son was three and a half years of age, Lord Dalmeny died from a sudden heart attack, and Archibald succeeded to his title.

His mother married, in 1854, Lord Harry Vane, the heir to the very considerable Cleveland fortunes. Dalmeny was a reserved but precocious child. By the age of ten he was engrossed by Macaulay and had read Thiers' *History of the Consulate and the Empire* in its entirety. At Eton, where he was one of the pupils of William Johnson (later Cory), one of the greatest of all Etonian teachers and a poet in his own right, he was not outstanding. 'He was not remarkable for scholarship,' a contemporary remarked of him, 'but he possessed plenty of cool assurance', and Johnson wrote of him – in words that were to haunt Rosebery's reputation in his lifetime and subsequently – that 'he is one of those who like the palm without the dust'. Impatience with Dalmeny's lack of performance commensurate with his abilities was a persistent theme of Johnson's reports, but he also wrote of him, 'he has the finest combination of qualities I have ever seen.' One passage in particular from a letter from Johnson to Dalmeny's mother should be noted: 'He has in himself wonderful delicacy of mind, penetration, sympathy, flexibility, capacity for friendship – all, but the tenacious resolution of one that is to be great.'

From Eton, Dalmeny proceeded to Christ Church, Oxford. Already he was attracting attention as a gifted but somewhat enigmatic young man – 'very intelligent and formed,' Disraeli noted – but his period at Oxford had a comical flavour. Together with Lord Randolph Churchill, he and a few friends formed a coterie which, as he later admitted, 'saw regrettably little of the rest of the University'. He travelled a great deal, and his enjoyment of what he once called 'the noise, stench and villainy' of the Turf grew. Indeed, it was this latter fascination that brought his Oxford career to an abrupt end in 1869 when the college authorities gave him the choice of selling his racehorse – entered for the Derby, where it finished last – or remaining to take his degree. To the horror of his family, the dismay of his tutor – who had anticipated a first for his pupil – and the admiration of the Bullingdon Set, he chose the racehorse. It was not a decision he later viewed with much satisfaction.

By this stage, he had succeeded his grandfather as the fifth Earl of Rosebery and inherited the family estates. These brought him an income in excess of £30,000 a year, which was in those days a not inconsiderable fortune. He was eagerly courted by the Conservatives and the Liberals, but although he did not commit himself at this stage, it was evident that his sympathies lay with the latter.

It is difficult to be precise about the origins of Rosebery's Liberalism, but it is significant that although he was invited as an undergraduate to contest Darlington for the Conservatives, Disraeli had immediately realised that Rosebery was in the opposing camp. Family tradition may have had something to do with it, and certainly Rosebery had a Whig distaste for Tories from an early age. Despite his mode of life, he involved himself in working-class amelioration movements soon after leaving Oxford, and, despite his personal affection for Disraeli, was increasingly more attracted to Gladstonian Liberalism. In November 1871, in a speech in Edinburgh, he attacked class divisions with a spirit and a strength that disconcerted both his audience and his family. In the Lords, he began to emerge as by far the most talented of the younger Peers on the Liberal benches. He travelled a great deal – including three visits to America and one to Russia – and both his speeches and his letters emphasised the serious nature of a personality many observers had doubted.

Much of this can be subsequently understood. What is more difficult to comprehend is the aura – what we would now describe as 'charisma' – that he now began to convey to his contemporaries. His wealth, intelligence and superb speaking voice do not provide the full answer, although they were undoubtedly major factors. His management of Gladstone's Midlothian campaigns of 1879 and 1880 made him a national figure, but even before this he was being spoken of as a probable front-rank political personality.

He was clearly ambitious, although he affected a lack of interest in his own career, and was intensely sensitive to any charge of personal ambition. His wife – Hannah Rothschild, whom he married in 1878 – was more open than he, but his speeches in the 1874–80 Parliament were clearly designed to promote his position, and he was not the organiser of the Midlothian campaigns for nothing. This celebrated event was a turning-point for Rosebery, and he was well repaid for the £50,000 he said he spent on it (an estimate this commentator regards with scepticism). The campaigns – and particularly the first, in December 1879 – may have won the 1880 general election for the Liberals, but they certainly established Rosebery's position as a major national political figure.

Rosebery's complex relationship with Gladstone holds the key to his political career. In the Midlothian campaigns Gladstone was over seventy, and it would have been difficult to anticipate that he would remain the dominant figure in British politics for the next fourteen years. J. M. Barrie wrote that 'during the first Midlothian campaign Mr Gladstone and Lord Rosebery were the father and son of the Scottish people', and there were many who viewed the relationship thus. But it was an uncomfortable relationship from the outset. Immediately after the Liberal triumph of 1880, and Gladstone's return to the premiership, Rosebery was offered a post in the Government, which he refused on the grounds, as Lord Granville told the Queen, that 'it would look as if Mr Gladstone had paid him for what he had done'. The offer was renewed shortly afterwards, and again rejected. Meanwhile, Rosebery had taken a keen interest in the situation whereby Scotland was administered, so far as the central government was concerned, by the Lord Advocate. Through a series of ludicruous but painful misunderstandings, Gladstone came to believe that Rosebery was thrusting himself forward and Rosebery became convinced that he was being neglected.

This pattern was destined to be repeated. Rosebery was always one of Gladstone's blind spots. At moments when a kind word or sympathetic understanding by the older man would have swept away all misunderstandings, Gladstone was silent. At moments when frankness by Rosebery would have been understood and appreciated, he sulked or despaired. The gulf between the two was never really closed. At the close of his life Gladstone regarded his promotion of Rosebery as one of his greatest mistakes; in his last recorded conversation Rosebery lamented that he had not followed Disraeli.

The gulf between Rosebery and Gladstone, opened by the latter's impatience with the performance of the younger man – first virtuously refusing office on two occasions and then apparently mortified by the absence of a third offer on his own terms – was perceptibly widened in 1881–2. An offer of the India Office under-secretaryship was declined in May, but an appointment to the Home Office with special responsibilities for Scotland was accepted in July. Rosebery was given to understand by Gladstone that the inferiority to the Lord Advocate would be purely temporary, but as the months passed and nothing happened his discontent grew. Gladstone was understandably obsessed by the Irish question, now in one of its most ugly and complex periods, and Scotland became discontented at her neglect. Rosebery contemplated resignation ('if I could find a pretext for leaving the Government without paining Mr Gladstone, I should go at once'), but when he received the news of the assassination in Dublin of the new Chief Secretary for Ireland, Lord Frederick Cavendish, it was a case of 'all hands are wanted at the pumps'. But within a few weeks he was discontented again, and in December 1882 the combination of lack of promotion and the continued neglect of Scotland resulted in a determination to resign which was only averted by intermediaries. 'The people who bother him at this moment more than all England are the Queen and Lord Rosebery.' Herbert Gladstone wrote of his father at this time. 'It is marvellous,' Gladstone wrote impatiently to Granville of Rosebery, 'how a man of such character and such gifts can be so silly.'

Rosebery did have solid grounds for grievance, but Gladstone's irritation is also comprehensible. The episode passed, but Rosebery was sore. 'It is incredible,' John Morley remarked, 'the want of *nous* which Mr Gladstone shows about Rosebery.' This comment was made in 1892, but has equal application to the earlier period. For his part, Rosebery had already demonstrated a weakness of character which has been accurately depicted by Winston Churchill:

'In times of crisis and responsibility his active, fertile mind and imagination preyed upon him. He was bereft of sleep. He magnified trifles. He failed to separate the awkward incidents of the hour from the long swing of events, which he so clearly understood. Toughness when nothing particular was happening was not the form of fortitude in which he excelled. He was unduly attracted by the dramatic, and by the pleasure of making a fine gesture.'

The issue on which Rosebery chose to resign was a statement in the Commons by the Home Secretary, Harcourt, which accepted the criticism that there was no under-secretary in the Commons. The real immediate cause was the continued failure to create a Scottish Department with Rosebery as its head, but the decisive element had been the collapse of Rosebery's relationship with Gladstone. Undoubtedly, Rosebery had expected special consideration; in the view of many of his colleagues and contemporaries, he had deserved it. This had been an ominous opening to Rosebery's ministerial relationship with Gladstone, and as a beginning to an official career represented something approaching a fiasco.

In several of Rosebery's earliest speeches he had emphasised the role of the British Empire, and his world voyage in the winter of 1883–4 was to have a profound impact upon Rosebery himself and upon the history of the Liberal party.

At this stage, the Liberals found themselves in a predicament that was to become increasingly serious. The 'imperial issue' had had hardly any domestic political significance in Britain until the 1870s, when its effects appeared to be negative. But the new interest in imperial questions in the 1860s, which Disraeli had discerned – perhaps prematurely – in the 1870s, became a major political factor in the early 1880s. The unexpected recrudescence of the Irish question and the bombardment of Alexandria, the Battle of Tel-el-Kebir, and the consequent 'temporary' British movement into Egypt had further aroused interest in, and high feelings on, these questions. Liberal thinking on the subject was confused and contradictory, whereas the Conservatives were increasingly regarding themselves as the Imperial party. The dichotomy within the Liberal party on this dilemma was to do more than any other single factor to lead to its impotence in the period 1886–1906.

Rosebery's interest in, and commitment to, what he subsequently called 'Imperialism, sane Imperialism, as distinguished from what I might call "wild cat" Imperialism' was greatly enlarged by his travels. In Adelaide, on 18 January 1883, he made the declaration that 'there is no need for any nation, however great, leaving the Empire, because the Empire is a Commonwealth of Nations', and on his return he publicly advocated the cause of Liberal imperialism, and became a strong supporter of the Imperial Federation League. His attitudes further separated him from Gladstone, who viewed the new movement with distaste and dismay. When offers were made to Rosebery to return to the Government, now in deep difficulties, he declined on the grounds of his opposition to its colonial policies.

The Gladstone Government, forced on by popular demand, had reluctantly dispatched a relieving force to Khartoum, where the adulated General Gordon was beleaguered. The enterprise was too little and too late, and a storm of obloquy descended upon ministers. The Government survived a motion of censure by only fourteen votes, and it was characteristic of Rosebery to use this hour of disaster to offer to rejoin the Government. It was a moment to 'swallow all my scruples and put my shoulder to the wheel'. Rosebery entered the Cabinet in February 1885 as First Commissioner of Works and Lord Privy Seal.

By this stage the much vaunted Liberal majority of 1880 had crumbled, and the Government Rosebery had dramatically joined perished quickly. Rosebery was disillusioned with his brief membership of the Cabinet. 'My experience of the present Cabinet,' he wrote in a personal memorandum, 'has convinced me that it cannot properly conduct the affairs of this country.'

The Liberal Government fell in June 1885, and was replaced by a Salisbury administration derided by Joseph Chamberlain as 'the Ministry of Caretakers'. The general election, held in November, gave Parnell's eighty-six Irish Nationalists the balance of power between the Liberals and Conservatives, and heralded the tumultous events of the next nine months. In this period, Gladstone committed himself to Irish Home Rule, Lord Randolph Churchill aroused Ulster, Lord Hartington and Joseph Chamberlain left the Liberals, and domestic politics were flung into total confusion. This extraordinary situation gave Rosebery his opportunity.

At the end of January 1886 the Salisbury Government, eagerly courting its own defeat on the Home Rule issue, was defeated in the House of Commons, and thankfully resigned. In the short-lived and grievously torn Liberal Government Gladstone then formed, Rosebery became Foreign Secretary. Granville was by now clearly unfitted for heavy official responsibilities, Sir Charles Dilke was involved in an unpleasant divorce case, and the Queen was hostile to the proposal for Lord Kimberley. It was already evident that it would be difficult to retain Hartington, Chamberlain, Sir Henry James and other Liberal leaders committed against Home Rule. Gladstone agreed to Rosebery's appointment without enthusiasm, on a *faute de mieux* basis.

The third Gladstone Government was short-lived and was dominated by Home Rule. The Bill was introduced in April, fervently debated throughout May, and was defeated on second reading on 8 June. The Government at once resigned, and was heavily defeated in the subsequent general election. The great Liberal majority of 1880 was now a shaken and disheartened minority. The combination of the defection of seventy-eight Liberal Unionists and the loss of so many of the major personalities in the party had been traumatic, and the party faced long years of Conservative rule in low morale.

In this crisis, Rosebery's star had risen remarkably. Almost alone among the Whigs, he had stood by Gladstone. 'The spectacle of this eloquent, magnificent personage separating himself from the bulk of his class, "biding by the Buff and the Blue", excited the hostility of the Unionist Party, and filled the Liberals in the shade with a sense of hope and expectancy for the future', as Churchill has written. His tenure of the Foreign Office, although brief, was principally characterised by his determination to maintain the continuity of foreign policy and his evident competence and knowledge. In particular, his calm handling of a potentially serious crisis in the Balkans won golden opinions, and impressed both the Queen and Gladstone – a formidable achievement. Speaking at Manchester on 25 June, Gladstone singled out Rosebery for special mention, describing him as 'the man of the future'. His reputation reached new heights when he was elected for the newly created London County Council in 1889, and then elected its first – and probably most distinguished – Chairman. His appeal to Londoners to 'do something for the people' and determination to achieve practical social improvement particularly attracted younger Liberals who were irritated by Gladstone's preoccupation with Home Rule and his neglect of domestic social reform.

By this stage, Rosebery was to many of his contemporaries the most fascinating man in public life. He was exceptionally well read, and his books – particularly his studies of Pitt and Lord Randolph Churchill – were characterised by wit, insight, and elegance. He was an ardent and knowledgeable bibliophile, and he created one of the great private collections in the country. John Buchan noted of the library at The Durdans that it was 'so full of rarities that the casual visitor could scarcely believe them genuine'.

The hospitality at his houses was always generous, although rarely lavish. His conversation, when he was in the mood, was memorable. After a dinner-table discussion on contemporary fiction a friend noted of Rosebery that 'one might think that he had never studied any other subject'. The young Winston Churchill later wrote that 'his voice was melodious and deep, and often, when listening, one felt in living contact with the centuries which are gone'.

His moods varied greatly, and already he was afflicted with the insomnia that was to plague him for the rest of his life. When out of humour his face would become a cold slab of boredom and distaste, and the chill of his displeasure could freeze the company. He constantly sought solitude, particularly in Barnbougle Castle, which he rebuilt in the early 1880s to house his treasures and where he could read, work, and meditate. Even his beloved sister Lady Leconfield never entered the Castle in Rosebery's lifetime, and it is in this strange building – and particularly in Rosebery's tiny bedroom at the top – that one feels closer to him than anywhere else.

As a public speaker he attracted and held the largest audiences in the country apart from Gladstone. His voice had a special quality that could stir and enthrall an audience, and every speech was meticulously prepared. 'Whenever there was a crowd in the streets or at the station, in either Glasgow or Edinburgh,' Margot Asquith wrote, 'and I inquired what it was all about, I always received the same reply: "Rozbury!"' Augustine Birrell later recorded of him that

'his melodious voice . . . his underlying strain of humour, his choice of words, never either staled by vulgar usage or tainted with foreign idiom, and above all his "out of the way" personality, and a certain nervousness of manner that suggested at times the possibility of a breakdown, kept his audience in a flutter of enjoyment and excitement. He was certainly the most "interesting" speaker I have ever heard.'

His passion for racing was an addiction that puzzled his more serious friends. His pleasure was centred on the peripheral delights, the friendship and *camaraderie* of the Turf, the excitements and frustrations of owning racehorses, the early morning matches on Epsom Downs, the gay dinner-parties, and the clatter, colour, and spirit of the meetings. He was a successful owner; between 1875 and 1925 his horses won every great race with the exception of the Ascot Gold Cup, and the Mentmore Stud was justly celebrated. 'Let not ambition mock these homely joys', as he himself once remarked.

Rosebery lived in a style that awed even Gladstone. Dalmeny, although beautifully situated on the Firth of Forth, is not a particularly large house, and at one point Rosebery commissioned plans for a much more imposing mansion. The Rothschild mansion, Mentmore, in contrast, is a very large house indeed, and was filled with treasures. The Rosebery house in Berkeley Square was not insignificant, and The Durdans was a large and imposing house hard by Epsom Downs. The Villa Rosebery near Naples was large, beautiful, and luxurious. Rosebery travelled a great deal, and never in discomfort. It was not surprising that the public regarded this Radical–grandee–scholar with such fascination. In Scotland he was revered, and in any company he stood out.

At this moment, with Rosebery's fortunes so high and his prospects so glittering, his wife died after a distressing and prolonged illness in 1890. The effect on Rosebery was devastating. He was plunged into a profound depression from which he was slow to recover. The melancholy aspect of his personality was greatly increased, and emphasised his need for solitude. His insomnia became much worse, and was to remain with him all his life. He took no part at all in politics in 1891, and gave broad hints that he had abandoned public life. When the Liberals won a precarious victory in the 1892 general election it took all the energies of his colleagues and the intervention of the Prince of Wales to persuade him to become Foreign Secretary, and there is no doubt in the mind of this commentator that his reluctance was genuine. But the episode marked a sharp decline in Gladstone's estimation of him, and was an ominous beginning to the last Gladstone administration.

Rosebery became Foreign Secretary for the second time on his own terms, and he quickly made it clear what those terms were. 'He is absolute at the FO,' Reginald Brett noted. 'He informs his colleagues of very little and does as he pleases. If it offends them, he retires. We shall remain in Egypt and the continuity of Lord S[alisbury]'s policy will not be disturbed.'

The first difficulty arose over Uganda, and it emphasised the acute division on imperial and colonial issues between Rosebery and Edward Grey on the one side and Gladstone, Morley and Harcourt on the other. In the Liberal party as a whole there was a majority against further commitments in Africa, and particularly against a Liberal Government assuming responsibility for Uganda in place of the bankrupt East Africa Company. This was exactly Rosebery's objective, and a major Cabinet crisis was only averted by a compromise whereby the East Africa Company was given an interim subsidy. This enabled Rosebery to prepare opinion for his policy of annexation, which was eventually achieved in 1894.

This crisis emphasised that the ill feeling between Harcourt and Morley could be exploited by Rosebery on imperial issues, and also that the Government could hardly survive Rosebery's defection. When the issue of the British presence in Egypt erupted in January 1893, Rosebery – vehemently supported by the Queen – won the day with little difficulty. But the episode marked another dismal stage in the Gladstone–Rosebery relationship. A speech by Rosebery at the Royal Colonial Institute on 1 March, in which he said, 'We are engaged at the present moment, in the language of the mining camps, in "pegging out claims for the future,"' did not improve matters. Indeed, from this point the relationship moved from coolness to painful antipathy.

It is pointless to attempt to apportion blame for this situation. The division was as much ideological as it was personal, and it is understandable why Gladstone determined not to recommend Rosebery as his successor when, with deep reluctance, he resigned in March 1894. By this stage, however, Harcourt's overbearing manner had made him intolerable to his colleagues, and the Queen's selection of Rosebery – Gladstone not having been consulted – had the support of the majority of the Cabinet.

But the succession crisis was a bitter, rancorous affair. Harcourt eagerly sought the premiership, propelled forward by his devoted son Lewis (generally known by the unlovely nickname of 'Loulou'). When it was clear that their chance had gone, the Harcourts pressed severe conditions on Rosebery, of which the most important concerned foreign policy. He resisted strongly, and insisted that Lord Kimberley should succeed him at the Foreign Office. Rosebery believed that he had won his point. The Harcourts were convinced that Rosebery had bowed to their pressure to be consulted on all foreign policy matters.

Rosebery's position as a Liberal Prime Minister in the House of Lords would have been difficult in any event. In the circumstances of his accession it was virtually impossible. The third Home Rule Bill had been contemptuously rejected by the Lords, with hardly a ripple in the country. By-elections were sombre. The Government held office only with the support of the Irish. The Radical element in the Liberal party was impatient and hostile. The Cabinet itself was deeply riven on personal and political lines, with the Harcourts determined to cause trouble. The Queen exercised vigilant attention for any signs of 'flattering useless Radicals'. A poisoned chalice indeed!

The most serious aspect of all was that the Government had no policy at all. Home Rule had been so dominant that the collapse of the measure had exposed the barrenness of the Liberal planning. Gladstone's 'Newcastle Programme' of 1890 had contained virtually every proposal dear to every section of the party, but it could hardly be categorised as a coherent programme, and its all-embracing character contained its own destruction.

The Irish and the Radicals swiftly showed their hand. In his very first speech in the Lords as Prime Minister, Rosebery gave the clear impression that Home Rule would have to be held in abeyance until there was an English majority to support it. That evening an amendment to the Address moved by Labouchère, which virtually abolished the powers of the Lords, was carried by two votes. The vote was rescinded, and Rosebery's apologia averted a major crisis, but as a beginning to a premiership it could hardly have been worse. Rosebery's position never really recovered, and from this moment he was constantly under fire until he seized his opportunity for resignation in June 1895.

The relationship with Harcourt worsened over the 'death duties' Budget of 1894 and as a result of a series of battles over foreign policy. 'The fate of the present Government,' Harcourt wrote to the Prime Minister, 'and the issue of the next Election are temporary incidents which I view with philosophic indifference.' The rift was widely broadcast by the Harcourts, as was that over the abortive Anglo-Belgian Treaty relating to the Upper Nile. As Asquith subsequently wrote, Harcourt's 'lack of any sense of proportion, his incapacity for self-restraint, and his perverse delight in inflaming and embittering every controversy, made co-operation with him always difficult and often impossible. Cabinet life under such conditions was a weariness both to the flesh and the spirit.'

The impression was gradually being gained that Rosebery was a lightweight. The Queen urged him to take 'a more serious tone' in his speeches, 'and be, if she may say so, less *jocular* which is hardly befitting a Prime Minister.' Some of his public appointments – notably Professor Yorke Powell as Regius Professor of Modern History at Oxford – were so lamentable as to arouse widespread derision. When his horse *Ladas II* won the Derby in June[1] the Nonconformist conscience professed itself outraged. A close friend, Edward Hamilton, complained that Rosebery's speeches 'have been a little too flippant and make people think that, for a Prime Minister, he is not serious enough or sufficiently in earnest'. His colleagues found him difficult to see, and one described him as 'shy, huffy, and giving himself the airs of a little German king'.

The fact was that, faced with this situation, Rosebery – now plagued by persistent and debilitating insomnia – retreated into an isolation in which elements of self-pity were not entirely absent. The leadership a prime minister must give to a Cabinet was not forthcoming, and his obsession with reform of the House of Lords was not shared by his colleagues, who in effect disavowed him. His conduct, in short, illuminated his principal political defects of impatience, lack of proportion, excessive sensitiveness to criticism, and indecision which had been apparent since he had first held office.

[1] *Sir Visto* won in the following year, thus giving Rosebery the unique distinction of winning the Derby twice while Prime Minister.

On 19 February, after vehement attacks on him in the Commons which Harcourt had flagrantly ignored, Rosebery delivered an ultimatum to his Cabinet in a desperate attempt to restore his authority. The device succeeded, temporarily, but almost immediately afterwards he suffered what appears to have been a nervous breakdown. The immediate cause was severe influenza, but behind this lay the insomnia, and beyond that lay causes that cannot be precisely defined. 'I cannot forget 1895,' he subsequently wrote. 'To lie night after night, staring wide awake, hopeless of sleep, tormented in nerves, and to realise all that was going on, at which I was present, so to speak, like a disembodied spirit; to watch one's corpse, as it were, day after day, is an experience which no sane man with a conscience would repeat.' On 8 May, while making a short speech in London, he lost the thread of his remarks, and recovered himself with difficulty in a shocked silence.

The Government drifted dismally towards inevitable disaster, its councils acrimonious, its leaders divided, its supporters dispirited or violently disillusioned, its stature at home and abroad visibly disintegrating. On 21 June, in a snap vote, the Government was defeated on the issue of the supply of cordite to the Army. Rosebery eagerly argued for resignation, and for once was supported by Harcourt. The urgings of the party officials, that a sudden resignation with no comprehensible electoral policy would be suicidal, were overruled by a Cabinet sick of office.

The subsequent general election exposed these schisms cruelly. No coherent Liberal policy was presented, and in the Unionist triumph – the most considerable victory won by any political party since 1832 – Harcourt and Morley were in the ranks of the defeated. 'I do not need consolation with regard to this election,' Rosebery wrote on the morrow of the Liberal disaster. 'It was inevitable, and can scarcely fail to do good. The Liberal Party had become all legs and wings, a daddy-long-legs fluttering among a thousand flames; it had to be consumed in order that something more sane, more consistent, and more coherent could take its place.'

Although this marked the end of Rosebery's ministerial career – at the age of forty-seven – he remained a major political figure for another decade. For more than a year after the fall of his Government he was leader of the Liberal party in name – but in name alone. 'There was nothing very definite in the position taken up by Lord Rosebery,' the

Annual Register commented with tartness but with truth. He was, in fact, seeking an opportunity to escape from this last thraldom, and the occasion came when Gladstone emerged from his retirement for the last time to declaim against the Turks for the Armenian massacres and to urge a European crusade against 'the great assassin'. Rosebery's public line had been more cautious, and he eagerly seized his opportunity. On 8 October 1896 he announced his resignation from the leadership. To Gladstone he wrote, characteristically, 'I wish you to know from myself that I have resigned the leadership of the Liberal Party – that is, if I ever held it, of which I am not quite sure.'

But in spite of everything, his followers remained devout. As E. T. Raymond wrote, 'Dalmeny became a St Germain, and it was long before the dream of a Rosebery restoration was quite banished.' The Harcourt–Morley combination proved flaccid, and the feeling that Rosebery had been grossly ill used gained ground. His independent aloofness became attractive, and as the reputations of Harcourt and Morley declined, the party began to regard its former leader with greater enthusiasm. When the obscure Campbell-Bannerman succeeded Harcourt at the beginning of 1899 there were many who regarded him as a *locum tenens*. H. W. Massingham described Rosebery as 'the veiled prophet'; Morley compared him to 'a dark horse in a loose box'; his rare speeches commanded more attention and interest than any he had made as Prime Minister. Such are the swings of public interest.

What were Rosebery's intentions? His own statements are so contradictory that it would be possible to prove either that he was intent upon a serious return to the Liberal leadership on his own terms, or that he had lost all taste for politics. Perhaps the correct estimate is that of Edward Hamilton: 'What he likes (at least this is my belief) is to figure largely in the mind of the public, and at the same time to be independent and thus not over-weighted with responsibility.'

In the South African war Rosebery vehemently and with high eloquence supported the policies of the Unionist Government. In this he was supported by Asquith, Grey, Haldane, and other rising young Liberals, but found himself opposed by the bulk of the Parliamentary party. When the underestimated Campbell-Bannerman joined the ranks of those Liberals opposed to the war, the battle was joined. The Liberal League was the open forum of the Liberal imperialists, and as long as the war lasted it had a potent influence. But when Chamberlain raised the flag of Imperial Preference in May 1903 the situation was transformed. The war was over, and general Liberal sentiment was now markedly in favour of those who had opposed it; now, the magic banner of free trade could cover all the warring elements in the party. Furthermore, the Liberal Leaguers were becoming exasperated by Rosebery's vagueness and refusal to lead. His position was, accordingly, weak before he dramatically cut himself off from Campbell-Bannerman on the issue of Home Rule just before the resignation of the Balfour Government in December 1905 – and the subsequent Liberal triumph. He was offered the post of Ambassador to Washington, but curtly refused. This was the end.

The last years were melancholy. Rosebery's political attitudes became more markedly Conservative, and his alienation from the Liberals became most evident in his violent opposition to Lloyd George's 'People's Budget' of 1909, which he attacked as 'the end of all, the negation of faith, of family, of property, of monarchy, of Empire'. This last foray was the final death knell of the Liberal League.

As the First World War approached, Rosebery viewed politics and international affairs with increasing dismay and revulsion. He had opposed the *entente* with France, and had been universally derided. He had no political position. He wrote in 1910,

'The secret of my life, which seems to me sufficiently obvious, is that I always detested politics. I had been landed in them accidentally by the Midlothian election, which was nothing but a chivalrous adventure. When I found myself in this evil-smelling bog I was always trying to extricate myself. That is the secret of what people used to call my lost opportunities, and so forth.'

No doubt, he believed it.

His hopes for the future were concentrated on his younger son, Neil Primrose, whose political career was prospering greatly. Neil's death in action in Palestine in 1917 was a virtually mortal blow to his father. Early in November 1918 Rosebery was prostrated by a stroke, and although he lived for another ten years it was a forlorn, sad, and lonely aftermath. 'It was a melancholy experience for me,' John Buchan wrote, 'to see this former Prime Minister of Britain crushed by bodily weakness, sorrowing over the departing world, and contemptuous of the new. . . . I went for a drive with him, I remember, at The Durdans on an April day in 1929. I had never seen Surrey more green and flowery, but he was unconscious of the spring glories, and was sunk in sad and silent meditations.'

He died in the early hours of the morning of 21 May 1929, and was buried at Dalmeny. It was thirty-four years since he had relinquished the premiership.

Of course, those who regard politics in swift and simplistic terms can easily dismiss Rosebery. It is not difficult to categorise his deficiencies and describe his failures. But of all modern prime ministers since Disraeli, he remains one of the most fascinating and remarkable. Intellectually, he was at least the equal of Salisbury, and superior to Balfour or Asquith. As a public speaker, he was comparable to Gladstone in his prime. But fortune, which had smiled on him so long, withdrew her favours abruptly in 1890. One is presented with the sad picture of a prime minister who was acutely intelligent, but politically and personally utterly alone, ravaged by insomnia and by indecision. But so strong was the impact of his personality, and so high were his talents, that for another decade he was eagerly courted by his admirers and feared by his opponents. As Churchill wrote of his adherents: 'At first they said "He will come." Then for years "If only he could come." And finally, long after he had renounced politics for ever, "If only he would come back"'.

Tragedy and high political attainment are often closely linked. But there have been few prime ministers who aroused comparable emotions of admiration and sympathy as Rosebery did and still does. The tragedy of his career was not simply a personal one. It involved the division of the Liberal party, and the loss to the service of the nation of a man of the most exceptional calibre. It is not the task of the historian to apportion blame. He may be permitted, however, to lament the perverse Fate which raises men to the highest posts and then casts them brutally down, to be replaced – as in Rosebery's case – by inferiors.

BIBLIOGRAPHY

Buchan, John, *Lord Rosebery* (London, 1930)
Crewe, 1st Marquis of, *Lord Rosebery*, 2 vols. (London, 1931)
James, R. Rhodes, *Rosebery* (London, 1963)

ARTHUR JAMES BALFOUR

BY

KENNETH YOUNG

Arthur James Balfour, created 1st Earl of Balfour 1922. Born 25 July 1848, son of James Maitland Balfour and Lady Blanche Gascoigne Cecil, sister of the 3rd Marquess of Salisbury. Educated at Eton and Trinity College, Cambridge. Elected MP for Hertford 1874 (retained the same seat until 1885). Private secretary to Lord Salisbury (Foreign Minister) in 1878; President of the Local Government Board under Salisbury 1885–86: Secretary for Scotland 1886; Chief Secretary for Ireland 1887–91; FRS 1888; First Lord of the Treasury and leader of the House of Commons 1891; Leader of the Opposition 1892–95; MP for East Manchester 1895–1905; Leader of the House 1895–1902. During Salisbury's absence abroad and from illness in charge of the Foreign office, 1898–1902. Succeeded Salisbury as Prime Minister 1902; President of the British Association 1904; defeated in the election of 1906; elected MP for the City of London (1906–22) and leader of the Conservative Party until 1911; joined the first Coalition ministry of May 1915 as First Lord of the Admiralty; OM 1916; Foreign Minister (1916–19); second British plenipotentiary at the Paris Peace Conference 1919 and signed the Treaty of Versailles; Lord President of the Council (1919–22 and 1925–29); chief representative at the League of Nations 1920, and the Washington Conference 1921–22. KG 1922. Died 19 March 1930. Author of A Defence of Philosophic Doubt, *1889;* Essays and Addresses, *1893;* The Foundations of Belief, *1895;* Theism and Thought, *1923; etc.*

Arthur James, 1st Earl Balfour, by P. A. De Lazlo

ARTHUR JAMES BALFOUR

The political world fell about laughing in January 1887 when Prime Minister Salisbury announced that the new Chief Secretary for Ireland was to be Arthur James Balfour. After a moment of utter disbelief the Irish MPs chortled with anticipatory glee: 'We have killed Forster, we have blinded Beach.[1] What shall we do with Balfour?' And one paper justified its incredulity by asserting that Balfour was 'a silk-skinned sybarite whose rest a crumpled rose-leaf would disturb'.

In this less than flattering way Balfour, the future Prime Minister, came to the notice of the public at large. He had been in the House for thirteen years, since 1874 but had not even exerted himself sufficiently to venture upon his maiden speech until two years later when he spoke on, of all subjects, Indian silver currency. Subsequently he somewhat desultorily joined with Randolph Churchill and two others (the 'Fourth Party') in sniping at his own leaders; then held minor offices in Salisbury's Governments in the 1880s.

The 'great' Lord Salisbury was his uncle. Balfour's father, a rich Scottish laird and MP, died when he was six; and Arthur Balfour was brought up by a clever but tyrannical mother, becoming in the process what was called 'delicate'.[2] But he survived Eton and enjoyed Trinity College, Cambridge, where he was known as 'Pretty Fanny', not, it seems, because of any dubious sexual proclivities but because he collected blue porcelain rather than riding to hounds, preferred listening to music to shooting birds, royal tennis (later golf) to rowing, and intellectual conversation to almost anything else. Hunting, shooting, drinking and whoring he despised.

At Cambridge he became a professionally adept philosopher, though caring 'not a jot' for the history of philosophy but only about 'the clash of benefits held by modern men about the universe'. Henry Sidgwick was his philosophical mentor; John Strutt, the brilliant physicist,

---

[1] Former Chief Secretaries for Ireland, one Liberal, one Tory.
[2] The psychological aspects of this are well brought out in Lucille Iremonger's *The Fiery Chariot: a study of British Prime Ministers and the search for Love* (London, 1970), pp. 159–174.

gave him an insight into the practicalities of science and its ramifi-cations; and the don F. W. H. Myers inspired an interest in psychical research. These matters kindled his ardent intellect throughout his life.

He was certainly the only British prime minister to have a genuine reputation among philosophers as a philosopher, based on such works as *A Defence of Philosophic Doubt* (1879), *The Foundations of Belief* (1895) and the Gifford lectures on 'Theism and Humanism'. He desired in his early manhood to become a professional philosopher, but his mother gave him 'a tremendous rating' for, as she saw it, seeking to shirk the responsibilities of his position in society; shrewdly, she insisted: 'Do it and you will find that you have nothing to write about by the time you are forty.' He did not do it. Philosophy became a hobby only.

All his days he loved Society – not the rough-and-tumble, hard-drinking, horsey society of many of his contemporaries but the graceful, sometimes intellectual, sometimes frivolous, often speculative conversa-tion of the so-called 'Souls', a group of beautiful, usually aristocratic women, and clever men such as Oliver Lodge and H. G. Wells, who met in London drawing-rooms and country houses. Here his distinction of mind, his discriminating judgement, his wit and his bachelordom made him the cynosure of all eyes, the adored of many women.

The Duchess of Marlborough (Consuelo Vanderbilt) saw him as 'some fine and disembodied spirit. . . . When he spoke in philosophic vein it was like listening to Bach. His way of holding his head gave him the appearance of searching the heavens and his blue eyes were absent, and yet intent, as if busy in some abstract world. Both mentally and physically he gave the impression of immense distinction and of a transcendent spirituality.'

So in 1887 the public was right: what on earth could this pampered exquisite, this charming idler, this sceptical-seeming logician, this dilettante, drifting as the young Asquith saw him 'with lazy grace in a metaphysical cloud land',[3] do with an Ireland half aflame as usual with planned resistance to law and order, dark murders and famine?

Salisbury knew his nephew better. True, he had not been greatly impressed by some of Balfour's parliamentary performances, causing his nephew disconsolately to confide that 'he had quite come to the

---

[3] J. A. Spender and C. Asquith, *Life of Lord Oxford and Asquith* (London, 1932), pp. 102–3.

conclusion that he had no aptitude for politics and that as a public man he was a failure'.[4] But Salisbury guessed that behind the soft paw was a feline claw – when for example Balfour, referring to Gladstone's *volte face* over Irish Home Rule, sneered at the GOM: 'Mr Gladstone was formerly as ready to blacken the Irish Members' characters, as he is now ready to blacken their boots.' And in Balfour his uncle discerned something of his own younger self – deep interest in science, a sense of humour, an ability to write excellent English, a distaste for crude sports, a gift for shrewd if often undetectable management of politicians: Balfour, as someone later said, could tread across snow without leaving any tracks. Both kept the vulgar at arm's length. Both, too, had a profound belief in God – and this, Margot Asquith believed, was the deepest moving force in Balfour's life.

In 1887 politics was Ireland. Ireland, which had broken so many, built Balfour. Cool, utterly unafraid for his personal safety, he travelled his willowy way, offering a policy of stick-and-carrot, through that unhappy country; and the only mishap he had there was when his brougham was run into from behind by the jaunting-car of escorting detectives. He not only pacified the country ('bloody Balfour', the *enragés* called him) but gave it the means to attain prosperity through development schemes, drainage, Land Purchase and Congested Districts Acts. He settled Ireland for almost twenty years. He was as successful when he visited the precincts of St Stephen's from his headquarters in Dublin Castle. Accurately did Lord George Hamilton state in his memoirs: 'The history of the House of Commons for the next four years [i.e. from 1887] is really a record of Balfour's marvellous Parliamentary performances.'[5] The former Commons understrapper became the Cabinet kingpin, a power feared by his less agile opponents for his polished raillery and intellectual satire, for he could sting as well as cajole.

Balfour was on the way up. His love affair with Mary Elcho (later Lady Wemyss) was at its height. Salisbury appointed him Leader of the House and in 1895 (after the collapse of the Rosebery Government) First Lord of the Treasury, in short the spokesman, as well as the confidant, of Prime Minister Salisbury in the Lords. Such was his prestige that cartoonists and gossip writers made him a 'personality'.

The public fancy was caught by the contrast between langour and

[4] op. cit., pp. 102–3.
[5] *Parliamentary Reminiscences and Reflections, 1886–1906.*

toughness; they saw him as a sort of Sir Percy Blakeney.[6] They rejoiced in the long-legged, tennis-playing, golfer aristocrat who cycled – a habit that greatly shocked Gladstone – to Downing Street wearing pince-nez. They savoured his celebrated forgetfulness, his *insouciant* muddling of regiments with corps, thousands with hundreds, one Member with another. Newspapers he professed not to read and when Winston Churchill suggested that press comments were sometimes of value, he remarked (or so the story went): 'I have never put myself to the trouble of rummaging through an immense rubbish heap on the problematical chance of discovering a cigar end.'[7]

This was the *persona* – with its apocrypha – the public enjoyed. In private he was rather different. He could be haughtily cold to women who loved him and of whom he tired, and the intimacies of marriage he avoided. He spoke of himself as a self-indulgent bachelor with expensive tastes. Yet his nephews and nieces loved him dearly and he indulged them like a fond parent. He was soft-hearted, too, which he mostly concealed. Yet on at least three occasions – on the death of his first love, May Lyttelton, of his brilliant young brother Frank and of his dearest friend Alfred Lyttelton – he burst into tears in public.

Neither public nor private *persona* was allowed to interfere with the pursuit of politics, in which he could be ruthless, abandoning both causes and personalities when it seemed expedient,[8] nor with his conduct of ministerial business which was severely practical. 'In [political] business,' wrote John Morley, 'he is absolutely without atmosphere.' To Balfour, as to his uncle, politics was always 'the art of the possible'. True that, when in doubt, he was capable of treating a Cabinet meeting as a seminar[9] – no bad way of eliciting opinion, at least from those as mentally dexterous as himself – and at the end taking no decision at all.

Such in essence was his attitude to the hysterically debated topic of tariff reform. Of its practicality and value he was as sceptical as in *A Defence of Philosophic Doubt* he was of the excessive claims of science. But Balfour's boredom with the protectionist doctrine in the face of

---

[6] The apparently effete Englishman who rescued French aristocrats from the guillotine in Baroness Orczy's 'Scarlet Pimpernel' novels.

[7] Cynthia Asquith, *Remember and Be Glad* (London, 1952), p. 31.

[8] On his own initiative as acting Prime Minister he telegraphed Buller: 'If you cannot relieve Ladysmith, hand your command over to Sir Francis Clery and return home.'

[9] Denis Judd's phrase in *Balfour and the British Empire* (London, 1965).

Joseph Chamberlain's tenacity in propagating it smashed the Cabinet over which Balfour presided from 1902–5 into diffractive smithereens affecting many issues with which he was profoundly concerned.

Balfour in reality was effectively Prime Minister for longer than the official three and a half years. Salisbury was often ill. So Balfour often found himself in charge, and as until 1900 Salisbury was also his own Foreign Minister he gained great experience in that then most important office which he took over for lengthy periods. Between uncle and nephew there were but 'rare and occasional differences'.[10] From Salisbury, one of the greatest Foreign Secretaries, Balfour learnt never to be precipitate, never to expect too much, to play his cards close to the chest, above all never to be self-deceiving whoever else had to be deceived. In short, to be diplomatic.

The tutelage prepared him for dealing with matters about which his colleague, Joseph Chamberlain, showed the fervid enthusiasm that would have been approved by the Nonconformist preachers at whose feet he and his family sat – but not by Lord Salisbury. One was the question of a formal alliance with Germany. Since the Crimean war Britain had remained splendidly isolated: what did her Imperial Majesty need with allies? However, in the latter years of the century there had been ominous signs of ganging up against her. Chamberlain believed that the proper response was a treaty with Germany. Balfour was not totally opposed to this and indeed took part in some of the tortuous negotiations. Salisbury, however, regarded the Kaiser as unstable, thought his one object was to lure Britain into war with France and was unwilling to be connected with the decaying Austro-Hungarian Empire. Balfour, learning fast, wrote his uncle on 14 April 1898, 'Of this loving couple I should wish to be the one that lent the cheek, not that imprinted the kiss.' From Germany neither cheek nor kiss was forthcoming; and by 1900 negotiations tailed off – for ever. The wisdom of allowing this to happen has been much debated. The truth is that the Kaiser, aware of the new-found industrial strength of his country, simply lost interest, turning not the cheek but a rather less dignified part of the anatomy to his grandmother's country.[11]

---

[10] As Balfour said in his sorrowing letter to King Edward VII after Salisbury's death. See Kenneth Young, *Arthur James Balfour* (London, 1963), p. 195.
[11] A detailed study, using French and German as well as British official papers, is Steven C. Hause's as yet unpublished *The Realignment of European Alliances, 1898–1901.*

Chamberlain's other great passion was for a closer knitting of the Empire – an Imperial Parliament and an Imperial *zollverein* with the motherland. A vision indeed and one that, after the embarrassments of the South African war, appealed to many not only on the Tory side.

Balfour thought the scheme, as elaborated by Chamberlain, to be impracticable. The Empire was too diverse, too heterogeneous, too unequal in the capabilities of its several parts and too centrifugal in its ambitions. He saw little natural harmony in it. As for the Dominions, they were big boys now and must be allowed to go their own way. He hoped – and worked hard – for their co-operation but it could, he believed, come about only by their free will. Imperial evolution would happen, was happening, and could not be prevented. It was Balfour himself, many years later, who presided over the Empire's legal emancipation – or dissolution – enshrined in the Statute of Westminster which was ratified in 1932 after his death.

Balfour, like Salisbury, was happy with the Empire as it was; certainly they did not want it bigger. Salisbury had criticised Disraeli for allowing officials to take over Transvaal in 1877; he was furious with Lord Randolph Churchill for annexing Upper Burma. As grasping imperialists intent on painting ever more bits of territory red on the map, the Tories generally were far less credible than such Liberals as Rosebery. It was an expense in both men and money from which the material return was almost as speculative as the South Sea Bubble. 'For my part,' said Balfour in 1906, 'the last thing I want to see is an extension of the British Empire. I want to see its strengthening and consolidation.'

Exactly. We must hold what we have. Expansion could be permitted only where it clearly served existing British interests, for instance safeguarding the route to India, that biggest jewel in the British crown, belief in whose supreme importance was axiomatic with Tories – perhaps, it occurs to me, because, like Balfour himself, whose grandfather in the early nineteenth century had returned thence a millionaire, their fortunes came from that country. So on this principle Balfour was ready to blockade Algeciras in 1898 unless Britain was allowed to inspect naval works there, such works being a potential threat to Gibraltar,[12] the keyhole to the Mediterranean, to Suez, to India.

It followed that, if what was had must be held, some organisation for co-ordinating the military defence of the Empire in case of war was

[12] British Museum Additional MS. 49706.

essential. There must, too, be systematised preparation to defend the Empire's heart, Britain herself. Balfour saw that, ally-less, she was more vulnerable to invasion than she had been even during the Napoleonic wars. From the mid-1890s Balfour did not doubt that war, igniting one country after another, was a distinct possibility.

The incompetence of British military leadership during the war against the Boers had startled him. He, as a senior minister, knew in full the incompetence, even though he could not admit it in public. The cunning of the Boer fighters had come as a surprise. Salisbury (backed by the Treasury) had always been lukewarm about military precautions. 'His mind didn't work on those questions, they didn't bite on it,' Balfour told his niece.[13] Not so Balfour who in the 1890s had backed the raising of twelve new battalions for the Army, an increase in artillery and £5 million for military works and stores. Still, he was dismayed when the Royal Commission on the South African war revealed: 'No plan of campaign ever existed for operations in South Africa.' Privately he complained that 'the mistakes that have occurred are entirely due to the advice of experts respecting matters on which experts alone have the right to form an authoritative opinion.' 'The chief blunders have been made, in my private opinion, by our generals in the field.' Nor was he much better pleased with the Navy; in fact, 'I am extremely indignant with the Admiralty for their want of foresight in connection with the detention of neutral vessels', that is German ships suspected of gun-running to the Boers.[14] And in addition, as Balfour saw, 'there was no co-ordination, no co-operation between the people in charge of land and sea war and defence'.[15] Not only that: Navy and Army were at loggerheads over their division of responsibility for defence, even of the British islands. The Navy maintained that its function was to seek out and destroy the enemy's navy; the Army, disbelieving in the Navy's invincibility, urged that large garrisons be maintained in Britain as well as throughout the Empire. 'Our safety against invasion was a subject of bitter controversy between the Services,' he told Mrs Dugdale.

Balfour could not tolerate either his own dismay or the perilous situation of his country. When in July 1902 he succeeded his uncle as Prime Minister, he set about remedying matters. Remedy them he did and I do not doubt that this was his greatest achievement. St John

[13] Blanche E. C. Dugdale, *Arthur James Balfour* (London, 1936), i, 365.
[14] Young, *A. J. Balfour*, pp. 107–8.
[15] Dugdale, op. cit., i, 365.

Brodrick (later the Earl of Midleton) wrote to Curzon: 'Arthur Balfour is the first Prime Minister who has given real consideration to national defence.'[16]

First of all, within weeks of becoming Prime Minister in July 1902, Balfour reconstituted the old Defence Committee of the Cabinet. He had every right to claim many years later (talking to his niece and biographer), 'I had the idea, which was really original. I don't say that out of conceit – I mean simply that the Defence Committee had no precedent.'[17] Its originality lay in the fact that the old Defence Committee, which met infrequently, could merely take up points referred to it by the Cabinet, which seldom did so because it forgot the Committee's existence. Balfour's creation could independently survey in detail all the strategical military needs of the Empire. The Prime Minister himself would normally take the chair; defence chiefs, as well as the appropriate Cabinet ministers, would form a permanent nucleus with others called in as required. Additionally, the CID, as it came to be known, had a permanent secretariat, modestly staffed, so that for the first time its transactions were fully recorded. The Committee was flexible enough to include on occasion Dominions defence ministers: 'A new precedent of great imperial significance,' Balfour informed King Edward.[18]

Under Balfour's powerful urging, the War Office agreed that all important defence papers should reach the Cabinet only via the CID, and the fiery black-a-vised Admiral Fisher agreed on close co-operation between Navy and Army and even suggested an amalgamation into one service.

The CID, Balfour emphasised, remained a consultative not an executive body; but once the Prime Minister and the War and Navy ministers had agreed in committee, the 'advice' would usually be activated. Balfour 'deserves every credit not only for devising this scheme [the CID] but also for giving his time and energy to it after calling it into being.' So said the Liberal Haldane, later to be Secretary of State for War. Indeed not only did Balfour chair all the CID meetings – which were fortnightly – but himself submitted numbers of papers for its consideration. Defence of Britain, defence of India (against Russia) were his main themes. This led among other things to the crea-

[16] Quoted Judd, *Balfour and the British Empire*, p. 73.
[17] Dugdale, op. cit., p. 365.
[18] Young, *A. J. Balfour*, pp. 224-5.

tion of the Territorial Army in 1907; but little escaped the attentions of the CID.[19]

Parallel with the re-creation of the CID was the War Office (Re-constitution) Committee set up by Balfour in November 1903. Lord Esher was its chairman. He had a passion for military affairs and his recommendations – for an Army Council and a general staff system, among others, were accepted. Balfour, fearful of what a Liberal regime might do when his Government fell (he had little doubt it would), placed Esher on the CID as a permanent member to ensure that even out of office he would know what was afoot. Happily the succeeding Liberal Governments made full use of the CID, and Asquith went so far as to put his fallen opponent back on it before the outbreak of war, so that Austen Chamberlain would write thirty years later:

'It is impossible to overrate the service thus rendered by Balfour to the Country and Empire. Without this Committee and the work done by it under him and his successors, the outbreak of the Great War would have found us wholly unprepared for the problems with which it at once confronted the Government and, humanly speaking, victory would have been impossible.'

Just how fervidly Balfour felt about defence may be judged by the fact that, with his Cabinet shot, as it were, from under him, and resignation politically desirable, he hung on to office to ensure that, of all things, the Field Artillery should be rearmed with eighteen-pounders. A small matter? He did not so regard it and told his niece that he delayed resigning because of this matter of which none of his colleagues were aware. 'The rearming of the Field Artillery I considered vital for the safety of the Empire and worth risking a *débacle* in the Unionist party and I was determined not to go out of office until we were so far committed to the expenditure that no Liberal Government could withdraw from the position.'[20] These eighteen-pounders were fired with effect in Flanders in 1914.

Nor, it should be added, did Balfour neglect the Navy. Fisher, the

[19] See F. A. Johnson, *Defence by Committee: The British Committee of Imperial Defence, 1885–1959* (Princeton, 1960).
[20] Young, op. cit., p. 232. Mrs Dugdale made this note but did not use it in her biography.

bluff First Sea Lord, scrapped obsolescent ships, built the Dreadnoughts,[21] expanded from two fleets to three and established a Navy
War Council. Estimates rocketed and the Liberals howled in close
harmony with the Treasury. Unperturbed, Balfour backed Fisher to the
hilt. When in 1912 Churchill gave Asquith's First Lord (McKenna) the
credit, Fisher wrote, 'He ought to have gone further back than
McKenna for the credit. *It was Balfour!* He saw me through – no one
else would allow 160 ships to be scrapped, etc. etc. etc.'[22] In this case,
Balfour's misgivings about the Liberals were justified. The Campbell-
Bannerman Government, which succeeded Balfour's, abandoned the
naval programme and so encouraged Germany to draw level again.

Let us be quite clear what Balfour was about: with measured tread
and a logician's ingenuity he was preparing for war, diplomatically as
well as militarily. But against whom? As late as 1904 the secret war
plans envisaged the enemy as France plus Russia. In that same year,
however, Balfour's trusty and perceptive friend, Lord Esher, wrote that
because Germany contemplated the absorption of Holland 'there must
come a day when France and England will have to fight Germany in
order to neutralise the Dutch Kingdom, and this day may not be very
far off'. Esher did no more than formulate what Balfour had for some
time felt in his bones.

He had worked hard for the Anglo-French Convention, which was
signed in 1904. Lansdowne did most of the negotiation; but the driving
force was Balfour's. The Convention – *entente cordiale* – ended Britain's
long policy of isolation and gave her serious commitments in Europe.
Militarily, at first, it meant little. Though secret staff talks with the
French began, France's military deficiencies were glaring, and the
French were terrified by Germany, which had forced the resignation of
Foreign Minister Delcassé, negotiator of the Convention with Britain.

Balfour next turned his attention to neutralising France's ally,
Russia, which had advanced into Manchuria and China and was regarded as the prime potential threat to India. Fortunately, Russia was
also a certain threat to Japan, as the Japanese well knew. British and
Japanese interests coincided. They signed a limited alliance for five

[21] Unfortunately the war when it came was not one where such battleships could be
deployed. The only line-of-battle contest was Jutland (when Balfour was First
Lord). Hindsight makes clear that Fisher should have spent on convoy vessels, not
Dreadnoughts, many of which never fired a shot in action.
[22] Fisher to Esher. See Young, *A. J. Balfour*, p. 233.

years in 1902 – limited because Britain pledged to go to Japan's help only if she were to be attacked simultaneously by two countries. Balfour decided to go further – and for excellent reasons. 'A war between Japan and Russia, in which we were not actively concerned and in which Japan did not suffer serious defeat, would not be an unmixed curse,'[23] he suggested to the King (December 1903). If Russia won she would be seriously weakened because she would have to maintain long lines of communication and financially burdensome forces in the area.

The following year (1904) Russia fought Japan and lost. Her rebuff in the Far East she took as final. She also made known her desire for an understanding with Britain, which was concluded in 1907. During the Russo-Japanese war the British public, with whom the Russians were unpopular, and who applauded every Japanese success, thought their Prime Minister acted timidly. It was, however, tightrope-walking not timidity. A Russian fleet fired on some Hull trawlers (believing them to be disguised Japanese torpedo boats); there was uproar in the British press and demands for reprisals which would have meant war. War, military and naval involvement, were no part of Balfour's plans. He made some threatening noises, a little diplomatic blackmail. It worked. As Admiral Fisher told his wife: 'It has nearly been war again. *Very near indeed*, but the Russians have climbed down. Balfour is a splendid man to work with.' In August 1905 Balfour, encouraged by Japanese military prowess, concluded a firmer treaty with her. Now Britain was to go to her aid if only one enemy assailed her. In return Japan was to help Britain defend her interests on the Indian Frontier.[24]

So the dogs of war ambled to the kennels prepared for them. It was nine years yet to Armageddon. As yet, no arrangement was irreversible. The Kaiser, though by now he could scarcely be blamed for feeling encircled, could still have broken the circle if he had sought to do so. But he had appreciatively tasted the nectar of power – and Germany *was* powerful, even merely counting heads. She had a population of 80 million, compared with France's 40 million and Britain's 40 million.

How far can we ascribe these new diplomatic dispositions to Balfour himself? According to Austen Chamberlain, totally:

'No Prime Minister ever took a closer interest or . . . more active part

[23] Young, op. cit., p. 234.
[24] Balfour saw the snag here. As he told the King, this might provide an excuse for a 'Radical government' to reduce our Army in India on the grounds that there would be an unlimited supply of men from Japan.

in the conduct of foreign policy. . . . It does not detract from Lansdowne's services as Foreign Secretary to say that his chief accomplishments would never have been achieved but for the constructive mind of Balfour and the constant support he gave him, not only in executing his foreign policy, but in conceiving and shaping it.'[25]

British statesmen by tradition looked eastward. Prophetically Balfour looked to the West as well. At first he found the westward land far less bright than did A. H. Clough in his famous hymn.[26] In 1895 United States President Grover Cleveland took it upon himself to warn Britain that his country would resist 'by every means' any appropriation of Venezuelan territory Such would be 'wilful aggression'. He referred to the dispute between British Guiana and Venezuela, which had recently seized British territory and fired on a British gun-boat.

The dispute came to nothing – or rather to arbitration. But Balfour declared, against the tut-tutting of most Tories, 'The time will come, the time must come, when some statesman of authority will lay down the doctrine that between English-speaking people war is impossible.'[27] From this moment he pressed for close co-operation between Britain and America and foresaw, hopefully, that such co-operation would become the cornerstone in a new international balance of power. This is why, among other reasons, he supported the United States in its war against Spain in 1898.

His aspiration was not dashed. Gradually American politicians forgot to think about 'Britain, our historical foe'. By 1905 Choate, United States ambassador in London, did not demur when Balfour asserted his belief that 'the two great co-heirs of Anglo-Saxon freedom and civilisation have a common mission'. This aim Balfour himself did much to encourage during visits to the United States in the First World War – even afterwards, to the point of undoing the Japanese treaty because of American fears, subsequently justified, of rivalry across the Pacific, upon which they stared 'with eagle eyes'.

Of course Balfour was not affected by any English-speaking union sentimentality. He dealt only (in politics) with the realm of realities. He knew that by the turn of the century, perhaps before, Britain was falling behind industrially. Her steel production, for example, was al-

[25] Quoted Young, *A. J. Balfour*, p. 236.
[26] 'Say not the struggle naught availeth.'
[27] Quoted Young, op. cit., p. 172.

ready third to that of Germany and the United States, textiles stagnated, and she was becoming ever more dependent on imports to feed her people: Britain's wheatfields were diminished by another half million acres between 1890 and 1900, which meant trouble in case of war and in fact – because German submarines sank so many supply ships in the Atlantic – almost caused Britain to surrender in the first world war. Warm friendship with the future all-powerful Uncle Sam was, therefore, a *sine qua non*.

It was not just industry and wheat. Britain, once the leader in technological invention, was lagging there too. Yet Balfour was sure, long before most politicians, that while the future doubtless should be left to Providence, progress – whatever that implied – would depend on the faster, ever faster, application of science to industry. Technology! He had not in his youth mixed with scientists such as Strutt (later Lord Rayleigh, his brother-in-law) for nothing. As Prime Minister, he was intellectually stimulated by contact, official and social, with J. J. Thomson, Ernest Rutherford, John Larmor, Oliver Lodge. It is noteworthy, says Professor A. S. Eve, that Balfour, the philosopher, quickly understood the work of the physicist. Did he hear and if so did he ponder Rutherford's apparently jesting remark of 1904 that 'some fool in a laboratory might blow up the universe unawares'? Certainly in the 1920s, as an elder statesman and Baldwin's Lord President of the Council, he used his influence to see that public money went into the Department of Scientific and Industrial Research, into atomic experiments at Cambridge and elsewhere. As Prime Minister he gave the presidential address in 1904 to the British Association for the Advancement of Science and received the rare praise of Rutherford himself.

The future, Balfour was sure, lay in 'the modern alliance between pure science and industry', and he said in his lecture on 'Decadence' in 1908:

'On this we must mainly rely for the improvement of the material conditions under which societies live . . . although no one would conjecture it from a historic survey of political controversy . . . science is the great instrument of social change . . . the most vital of all revolutions which have marked the development of modern civilisation.'

There lay the hope for the poor, not in the levelling down preached by Lloyd George and the Socialists.

Dark thoughts, however, broke through, for he knew that in technical education and training Britain had fallen far behind Germany and even France.

'Turning scientific discoveries to practical account – technical instruction – there is nothing of which England is at this moment in greater need. There is nothing which, if she in her folly determines to neglect, will more conduce to the success of her rivals in the markets of the world, and to her inevitable abdication of the position of commercial supremacy which she has hitherto held.'[28]

Polytechnics existed, but too few.

Education in general preoccupied Balfour. 'There is probably no more serious waste in the world than the waste of brains, of intellect', . . . and the wastage in Britain was horrifying.[29] This is why he persisted, in the teeth of every kind of discouragement and at the risk, as Chamberlain repeatedly warned him, of bringing down the Government, in pushing forward the Education Bill in 1902. It differed little from the failed Bill of 1896: it proposed to unify primary education, then composed partly of rate-aided Board Schools and partly of voluntary schools, managed by the Church of England or other denominations, which often had little money for teachers or equipment. The proposal was to give them state aid and at once the Nonconformists – who were mainly Liberal voters – raised an outcry against the State's subsidising Anglican schools. The 1896 Bill was then withdrawn.

Balfour's second attempt was no less a tussle and he himself drafted every line of the Bill with the able assistance of Robert Morant, an official in the Education Office. Eventually it was passed: both secondary and elementary education were placed on the rates and brought firmly under county and county borough councils. The Act ensured that teachers should be properly paid and that all children should have an equal standard of education wherever they might live. Grants (that is state aid) to secondary schools – grammar and the like – resulted in an increase in pupils; and there was a spate of university foundations – Manchester, Liverpool, Leeds and Sheffield. Thus Balfour built the

[28] Speech to Chemical Society, London, 27 March 1895 (*The Times*).
[29] In 1885 there were, proportionately to population, two and a half times more students in the German states than in Britain.

substructure of an educational system which proved its worth over and over and lasted almost unchanged into recent times.

There is no doubt that when Balfour was determined, he would fight for his progeny like a cornered animal. Usually his causes were good. Certainly it was so in education; and in this case his Liberal and Non-conformist opponents were revealed as putting petty sectarian issues before better education for all – about which some of them had often prated. Ironically, some Conservatives have dubbed Balfour's Act 'state Socialism' (whatever that means), and have claimed that in after years Balfour himself said, 'I did not realise that this Act would have as its consequence more expense and more bureaucracy.'[30]

Balfour's outlook on education was not narrowly practical: 'Industrial work unbalanced by literary work, literary and industrial work unbalanced by speculative work are unfit to form the mental sustenance and substance of academic training,' he told the Convocation of Victoria University,[31] Manchester, in 1891. 'Science knows no country and is moved by no passion – not even the noblest passion of patriotism.'

Balfour had more than a little of the Radical in him. He was not Radical in the contemporary authoritarian sense: neo-Rousseauian generalisations never influenced him and usually bored him. Consider, however, his attitude to King Edward VII. That monarch he constantly, and with *insouciance*, baulked, not, as some have said, because he was Whiggish towards the monarchy or Tory towards the 'upstart' Hanoverians, and certainly not because he disapproved of the monarch's private life if he bothered even to listen to the gossip. Of course he would not belong to the raffish circle around the throne; where Edward was gross, Balfour was discriminating. But censoriousness was not in his nature.

No, it was simply that from time to time Edward wanted to do things that cut across Balfour's policies; and Balfour blandly, politely, would not have it. True, on the death of Queen Victoria he had written to his mistress, Lady Elcho: 'The King will take up a good deal more of his Ministers' time than did the Queen . . . I think he is in the

---

[30] The remark is quoted in Elie Halévy's *A History of the British People*, vol. i, Epilogue, p. 207; but contrary to his custom, Halévy gives no source for the quotation.

[31] This was a collection of university colleges that preceded the grant of charters to the constituent colleges.

right.'[32] Well, perhaps; but even when Edward was still Prince of Wales and Balfour merely First Lord of the Treasury he had vetoed the Prince's proposed contribution to a newspaper: the Prince was known to be an intimate of such Liberals as Campbell-Bannerman.

He insisted in 1901, against the King's express interdiction, that the Duke and Duchess of Cornwall – later King George V and Queen Mary – should tour Australia, New Zealand, South Africa and Canada. He had his way. In 1902 Balfour's Foreign Secretary, Lansdowne, desired that the Shah of Persia be given the Garter in return for certain benefits to Britain. The King disliked the Shah and refused. Balfour insisted and Balfour won.

He refused to allow the King to see Cabinet papers 'as of right' before decisions were taken. He prevailed; as usually he did when the King wished to give peerages to persons Balfour thought unworthy; and he contradicted those who credited Edward with the *entente cordiale*: 'We must not think of him as a dexterous diplomatist,' he said, though graciously granting that the King, 'by his personality alone', impressed the French with 'the friendly feeling'[33] of Britons towards them. Privately he wrote to Lansdowne: 'So far as I can remember, during the years which you and I were his Ministers, he never made an important suggestion of any sort as to large questions of policy.'

After the catastrophic defeat of his party and himself in January 1906, Balfour returned to lead the Opposition. Not all Tories were happy with this leadership; their dissatisfaction came to a head when Balfour and a majority of the shadow Cabinet decided not to oppose the Liberal Government's Bill to reduce the Lords power of veto, particularly over finance Bills. If the Lords, the bulk of whom were Tories, refused to pass the veto-reducing Bill, Asquith threatened to create some 400 Liberal peers to ensure its passage. This would have caused a tremendous constitutional crisis; it might even have shaken the throne. Balfour and Lansdowne, the Tory leader in the Lords, refused to take the risk. Some of the Tories accused them of cowardice, of giving way on a matter of principle. A slogan was invented: 'Balfour must go.' Balfour, though he thought himself ill used, did not wait long. He resigned the leadership on 8 November 1911.

That – and a peerage – should have been the end. Instead it was a new beginning. When the war was about to breakout, Asquith sought

[32] Young, *A. J. Balfour*, p. 201.
[33] Young, op. cit., p. 247.

Balfour's advice. He made him a permanent member of the Committee of Imperial Defence. When Asquith was forced to form a coalition, the only Conservative to get a key post was Balfour, who succeeded Churchill as First Lord of the Admiralty, an office in which he did not shine. His subsequent role as Foreign Secretary was much more his *métier*.

Today Balfour's name, if mentioned in non-political company, evokes the 'Balfour Declaration'. The Declaration, made on 2 November 1917, was, of course, a Cabinet decision; as Foreign Secretary Balfour happened to sign it. Not that he disagreed with 'the establishment in Palestine of a national home for the Jews'; indeed, after his meeting and subsequent friendship with Chaim Weizmann in 1905, he was strongly in favour of it. Thus Balfour's death in 1930 was lamented by Jews all over the world.

Strangely enough, Balfour was no Semitophile; he once said, after a long talk with Cosima Wagner at Bayreuth, that he 'shared many of her anti-Semitic postulates'. As Prime Minister he had spoken strongly against alien (in those days almost entirely Jewish) immigration into Britain. And the Aliens Bill, restricting immigration, passed into law in the last year of his premiership. As long ago as 1899 he had remarked in a private letter: 'I believe the Hebrews were in an actual majority – and tho' I have no prejudices against the race (quite the contrary) I began to understand the point of view of those who object to alien immigration!'

These attitudes would not, of course, preclude his support for a Jewish national home; on the contrary it was a natural if somewhat cynical corollary. Better the Jews in Palestine than in Britain. At the same time he was fascinated by the uniqueness of the Jewish race and its history and by such paradoxes as the fact that the founder of Christendom, himself a Jew, had been rejected by his own people. He appreciated the enormous Jewish contribution to science, the arts and civilisation in general.

What he helped to do for the Jews, Balfour pondered late in life, was the most worth-while thing in his political career. He was almost certainly wrong. Although the Declaration specifically stated that 'nothing shall be done which may prejudice the civil and religious rights of existing non-Jewish communities in Palestine' (90 per cent then of the population), it was clear that this could never be assured. Balfour either knew and ignored it or had been rendered so starry-eyed (a most

557

unusual condition for him) by wizard Weizmann that he allowed his optimism too free a rein. He should perhaps have listened more carefully to the sole Jew in the Cabinet, Edwin Montagu, who in a memorandum to his colleagues forecast that Zionism would cause suffering by encouraging anti-Semitic countries to expel their Jews and would then put the Jews in a position where they in turn would expel the present inhabitants from Palestine and take all the best lands.

Gradually during and after the war, Balfour drifted from *moyen âge* into *doyen âge*, from politician to statesman, from 'Mr' (via Sir Arthur) to the first Earl. He remained almost continuously in high office until a year before his death at eighty in 1930. He liked office – even to the point of switching allegiance from Asquith to Lloyd George during the war, and then from the Conservative party to the post-war Coalition; and when the Coalition collapsed he was soon back as a Conservative minister. As Churchill once said, he was 'like a powerful cat walking delicately and unsoiled across a rather muddy street'. This liking for office was not, however, quite as one contemporary commentator saw it: 'A man who would make almost any sacrifice to remain in office. He loves office more than anything this world can offer. . . . So restless, so dissatisfied, even in old age, outside the doors of public life.'[34] This is too naive a view of a maze-like character. He was not ambitious in the vulgar sense. He gave a clue to his attitude to politics when he remarked to John Morley: 'When I am at work on politics I long to be in literature and vice versa.' In him the desire for action and the desire for contemplation were mixed about fifty-fifty. Or, put another way, he wanted to avoid the tedium inseparable from unrelieved politics and no less, as every writer knows, from unrelieved 'literature'. Desmond MacCarthy puts it exactly: 'There were moments throughout his career when it was apparently with relief that he felt again beneath him the firm ground of abstraction. . . . Then again he would throw off the robe of the philosopher . . . and put on his ruffles and rapier to fight for his side.'[35]

In politics he followed Sydney Smith's terse maxim, 'Take short views', because, as Balfour said in a Rectorial address at Glasgow, the wise man will have 'a full consciousness of his feeble powers of foresight. He will be content to deal as they arise with the problems of his own generation.' Visions of 'some millennial paradise' were no substitute for 'the private virtues of citizens, their love of knowledge, the

---

[34] Harold Begbie, *The Mirrors of Downing Street* (London, 1917).
[35] *Portraits* (London, 1931), p. 24.

energy and disinterestedness of their civil life, their reverence for the past, their caution, their capacity for safely working free institutions. . . .' There indeed he spoke with the voice of true Conservatism. At the same time he knew that change was inevitable and that the best safeguard against too rapid change was to preserve the flexibility of Britain's political customs and institutions.

In philosophy, it is true, his speculations – and without doubt his intuitive, almost mystical nature – opened up to him curious immeasurable vistas: 'Metaphysicians,' he wrote, 'are poets who deal with the abstract and the super-sensible instead of the concrete and the sensuous.' Yet in philosophy, too, short views prevailed. As he told his biographer-niece, 'Don't worry your head about what need be said about my philosophy. . . . All that any man's thought is, is a contribution greater or lesser to the stream of thought of his own time which flows on and turns into the thought of the next generation.' (He was latterly much affected by Henri Bergson's 'flux' philosophy.)

He continued to believe in God – 'a personal God to whom men may pray'. As for death he said once, 'I do not think, so far as I can judge in the absence of actual experience, that I am at all afraid of dying.' He did not doubt personal survival beyond the grave whatever his final conclusions about communication between the living and the dead.

His own death on 19 March 1930 was undramatic and at eighty-two in the fullness of time. But it had an ironical prelude. As though to strengthen his thesis of man's feeble powers of foresight, he had long ignored the warnings given by his accountants of his diminishing fortune. With a recklessness elsewhere foreign to him he had since before the war poured thousands upon hundreds of thousands of pounds into schemes for making powdered peat into an industrial fuel. On his deathbed he asked his nephew, later the third Earl, whether there would be enough left for him to live on. It was not quite as bad as that. Nevertheless after his death his magnificent library was broken up and sold; Whittingehame House was let and the house in Carlton Gardens sold. Balfour died a comparatively poor man.

BIBLIOGRAPHY

Dugdale, Blanche E., *A. J. Balfour*, vols i and ii (London, 1936)

Esher, Viscount, *Journals and Letters of Viscount Esher*, edited M. V. Brett (London, 1934)

Gollin, A., *Balfour's Burden* (London, 1965)

Johnson, F. A., *Defence by Committee* (London, 1960)

Judd, Denis, *Balfour and the British Empire* (London, 1968)

Young, Kenneth, *Arthur James Balfour* (London, 1963)

SIR HENRY
CAMPBELL-BANNERMAN

BY

JOHN WILSON

Sir Henry Campbell-Bannerman, born Glasgow 1836, younger son of Sir James Campbell, business man and Lord Provost. Educated Glasgow High School, Glasgow University and Trinity College, Cambridge. Joined the firm of J. & W. Campbell in 1858; married, 1860, Charlotte, daughter of Major-General Sir Charles Bruce. MP for Stirling Burghs, 1868, and represented this constituency for forty years. Assumed the additional surname of Bannerman in 1871. Financial Secretary, War Office 1871–74 and 1880–82; Parliamentary Secretary, Admiralty 1882–84; Chief Secretary for Ireland, 1884–85; Secretary of State for War 1886. Member of the Hartington Commission, 1888–90. Again Secretary of State for War 1892–95; secured the resignation of the Duke of Cambridge as C.-in-C. 1895. Resigned office same year, when the Rosebery government was defeated on a motion to reduce his salary. GCB 1895. Leader of the Liberal Party in the House of Commons 1899; leader of the Opposition, 1900; Prime Minister 1905–08. Resigned owing to illness, 3 April 1908. Died at No. 10 Downing Street on 22 April 1908.

Sir Henry Campbell-Bannerman

SIR HENRY CAMPBELL-BANNERMAN

Henry Campbell-Bannerman, the first man to be given the official title of Prime Minister, was an unusual sort of man to hold that office. He was easy-going, indolent, devoid of great ambition and devoted to his own comfort. He put the interests of his ailing wife before those of public affairs and nothing was allowed to interfere with his annual autumn holiday at the spa of Marienbad in Bohemia. Yet his period at 10 Downing Street – a mere two years – was one of the most successful of any modern Prime Minister.

He was in politics all his life, and was MP for the Stirling Burghs for forty years, but it took him a long time to reach the top, and until the splendid sunset of his last two years he was consistently underrated.

He was a lowland Scot, a Presbyterian, son of a self-made businessman who had become a Knight, a Tory and Lord Provost of Glasgow. His elder brother, who inherited the running of the family business, became a Tory MP. Although he had a conventional education at the High School and University of Glasgow and at Trinity College, Cambridge, his father sent him as a boy to the Continent, and he grew up speaking fluent French, good German (which he spoke with a 'smart Viennese accent') and some Italian. He was not in the least insular and was thoroughly at home in Europe, but he never visited the United States, India or other parts of the British Empire. His wife Charlotte, another Scot, shared his tastes and also spoke fluent French. She was a diabetic, for which there was then no cure, so she became enormously fat and suffered dreadful pain in her last years. But they were extraordinarily devoted to each other.

Henry Campbell (the Bannerman was added, reluctantly, in 1871 when he inherited property from an uncle) was a Liberal MP from 1868. He and his wife lived a comfortable, spacious life in enormous London houses during the session. That in which they spent most of their time, 6 Grosvenor Place, still stands and was sold in 1972 for more than £2½ million. They had a large country house called Belmont near Meigle in Forfarshire (Angus) which they loved. Both of them were thorough Scots and much preferred living on 'the best side of the Tweed'. They entertained a great deal and kept a fine table. Every autumn they went off for six weeks or so to Marienbad, which became in their time a social mecca. Campbell-Bannerman's colleagues, indeed, often tried, and usually failed, to get him back from Marienbad or down from Scotland. He liked an unhurried way of life and said once, 'Personally I am an immense believer in bed, in constantly keeping horizontal', an unusual sentiment for an active politician.

Campbell-Bannerman, or C.B. as he was always called, spent a good deal of his official career at the War Office in the first years under Edward Cardwell, a reforming minister whom he greatly admired and made his pattern in life. He was twice Financial Secretary and twice Secretary of State for War, and was much concerned all his life with Army affairs and War Office reform. He was opposed to the conception of a general staff as leading to foreign entanglements and consisting of officers who would 'sit apart and cogitate' and thus get up to mischief. His most notable achievement was bringing about the resignation of the Duke of Cambridge, a portly Hanoverian who was resolutely opposed to what he called 'pwogwess', after thirty-eight years as Commander-in-Chief; a task that needed all his resources of tact, patience and ingenuity. He achieved it with the help of Queen Victoria, with whom his relations were invariably sunny. At the War Office he was much liked by both soldiers and civilians, but detail bored him and he was sometimes found in his office reading a French novel.

In the House of Commons he was universally popular but for most of his career he made no great mark. He was not a brilliant speaker, though his speeches were always lucid and well written, and he did not have the quickness needed to deal with unexpected attacks, though he answered questions with gaiety and sparkle. His qualities were not those that make the best show in a noisy debate. They were those that caused Mr Gladstone to describe him as 'cantie' and 'couthie'.

Early in his career he had had a short spell as Chief Secretary for Ireland, and his imperturbability in the face of the furious assaults of Irish Members in the House greatly increased his reputation. It was said of him that he treated the Irish party 'like one of the mists of his native land – a tiresome phenomenon, but not one to be overcome by indignation or denunciation', and that he had 'unfathomable, unreachable depths of imperturbability'. When the Liberals split over Gladstone's conversion to Home Rule for Ireland in 1886, C.B., after some agonising doubts, stuck to his leader. He had come to believe that there was no alternative to a separate Irish Parliament and to self-government for Ireland, and he remained a Home Ruler for the rest of his life. He thought that Home Rule all round – for Scotland, England and Wales as well as for Ireland – would be a good solution, but realised that it was politically unattainable at that time.

He became leader of the Liberals almost by accident: because Rosebery, Harcourt and Morley had successively eliminated themselves from what seemed a thankless task and because Asquith, at forty-six, was regarded as too young and doubted if he could afford to take on a full-time job.

C.B. was regarded by many Liberals as a mere *locum tenens*, who would keep the seat warm until Rosebery elected to return. He himself had only modest ambitions, and when he was a member of the Rosebery Government in 1895 he had made a determined effort to have himself nominated for the Speakership, an aim that was frustrated by Rosebery and Harcourt, who regarded him as an indispensable member of that most unhappy of administrations. In the party he was looked on by the brighter spirits as an amiable but undistinguished old war horse who could not hold a candle to the brilliant and dashing Rosebery. The contrast could not have been greater – Rosebery a patrician, a glamorous public figure, the darling of the press; C.B. plain, predictable, unexciting. Yet Rosebery failed because he lacked common sense and was so aloof and enigmatic that people became exasperated. C.B. succeeded precisely because he had common sense in ample measure.

No sooner had C.B. become leader of the Opposition than his party faced the crisis of the Boer War. Rosebery, Asquith, Haldane and Grey – the Liberal Imperialists – supported the war. Other Liberals like Lloyd George, Bryce, Courtney and C. P. Scott strongly opposed it. The party seemed certain to split and then disintegrate. But, vilified and abused by both sides, C.B. held his party together, though in big debates, with only lukewarm support or open mutiny behind him, he was often worsted by Balfour, who led the Conservatives, and who mocked him unmercifully. He himself took a middle position. He voted supplies to the Government, but from the first disliked Chamberlain's policy of bluff, which failed, and the subsequent ineffectual efforts to force the Boers to submit. He also regarded Milner's policy in South Africa as disastrous. In June 1901, influenced by what he had been told by Miss Emily Hobhouse, just back from South Africa, he defied the whole weight of patriotic emotion when he spoke out against farm-burning and the herding of Boer women and children into concentration camps and described these as 'methods of barbarism'. He was denounced with unparalleled fury – a clergyman wrote to him saying, 'Sir, you are a cad, a coward & a murderer, & I hope you will meet a traitor's or a murderer's doom' – but in the end he was seen to be a man of courage, absolute integrity and unwavering principles, and the British public came to respect a man who had been right and had refused to trim his sails to the storm.

The end of the Boer War and Chamberlain's call for protectionist policies in May 1903 helped C.B. to reunite the Liberals. On the issue raised by Chamberlain he had no doubts. 'To dispute free trade, after fifty years' experience of it,' he said, 'is like disputing the law of gravitation.' Chamberlain's proposals he described as wild and reckless. Politically they helped him greatly, for not only did the Liberals unite in opposing them, but the Conservatives were split. C.B., therefore, was able, by patience and skill, to put together a political coalition of the left, the greatest ever constructed in this country. It included Free Trade defectors from the Conservative benches, of whom the most notable was Winston Churchill, the Liberal Imperialists like Asquith and Grey, the radicals like Lloyd George, and the new Labour party. Soon after Balfour had resigned in December 1905 and C.B. was asked to form the first Liberal Government for ten years, Asquith, Grey and Haldane, acting on a plan worked out three months earlier with the connivance of King Edward's private secretary, tried to force C.B. into the Lords, where he would have been Prime Minister in name only. But, supported by Charlotte, he stood firm, and the conspiracy collapsed. All shades of Liberals were represented in the new Government, one of exceptional ability, and in January 1906 C.B. led the Liberals to their greatest electoral triumph, a landslide victory. They won 229 seats from their opponents – Balfour and many of his colleagues lost their seats – and ended with a majority of 222 over the Conservatives and 88 over all other parties combined.

C.B. was in power at last. W. T. Stead now wrote of him:

'He is the hub of the Cabinet. All the spokes centre in him . . . he is the solidest, most seasoned, best balanced of all the Liberals. Sir Henry Campbell-Bannerman is not a flighty rhetorician, neither is he an artful dodger. Still less is he a haughty patrician. He is a plain, honest, respectable, good-humoured Scot, wary and canny beyond most of his countrymen . . . with a cool head and a warm heart. . . .'

But he was sixty-nine, and he was an ailing man with only two years to live. Charlotte, too, was at the end of the road, and after many sufferings she died in 1906. Nevertheless, as Prime Minister C.B. achieved more than many who have been much longer in No. 10. He it was who held his party together when it had achieved power. When Balfour returned to the House he began speaking in the same ironic, supercilious style he had employed so successfully before, but C.B. angrily rebuked him with the words, 'Enough of this foolery', in a four-minute speech which crushed Balfour and was described by Balfour's own sister-in-law as the greatest parliamentary triumph she had ever witnessed. Balfour never baited him again. C.B.'s authority became immense, and it was said of him that 'his premiership was common sense enthroned'.

But it was more than this. As Sir Robert Ensor wrote:

'Radicalism and socialism alike . . . were radiant with sudden hopes of a new heaven and a new earth. No leader not alive to that morning glory could have carried the house with him: and that was where Campbell-Bannerman in his kindly and generous old age gave the parliament an incomparably better start than the efficient but earth-bound Asquith could have done.'

In his Cabinet, made up of Imperialists and anti-Imperialists, Home-Rulers and anti-Home-Rulers, Feminists and anti-Feminists, moderate Liberals and extreme Radicals, differences melted away under his benign influence, and he controlled it very effectively. He was much better than his successor, Asquith, at preventing differences between colleagues from getting out of hand. And it was the same story in the House of Commons, where his ascendancy was unchallenged. Grey, who had been one of his fiercest critics, and had despised C.B. as second-rate and intellectually inferior, admitted later that he had not realised that the House of Commons needed to be 'grasped by the heart, and not by the head'. It was said of C.B. that when he got up in the House 'the discontented became reconciled; the rancorous were transformed into geniality; the rebels came back to the fold'.

C.B.'s greatest achievement was the settlement with South Africa, under which the defeated Boer states – the Transvaal and the Orange

Free State – were given full self-government and allowed to elect Boer governments. This was a wise, large-minded and imaginative solution which turned Botha and Smuts into lifelong friends of Britain and resulted in South Africa's coming to Britain's help in two world wars. It also undid the harm done to British standing by the Jameson Raid and the hectoring, aggressive policies of Milner and Joseph Chamberlain in South Africa. It won for Britain a reputation for generosity and magnanimity. Winston Churchill and Lloyd George testified that the inspiration for this settlement came from C.B. himself. He also put an end to Milner's scheme for bringing in Chinese coolie labour to work in the Transvaal mines.

As Prime Minister, C.B. did not hesitate to take his own line, even against his chief colleagues, as he did when he accepted the Labour version of the Trades Disputes Bill, giving trade unions immunity from legal damages, and over the inclusion of domestic servants in the Workmen's Compensation Bill. He helped the first working-class MP's to find their place in the House of Commons. For him, Labour held no terrors.

He was, as Prime Minister, under pressure from his supporters, who had suffered for long years in the wilderness of opposition, to push through with the greatest possible speed a massive programme of social reform. But it soon became apparent that this could not be done while the House of Lords, in which the Conservatives had an overwhelming majority, retained intact its power to block legislation. The clash came when C.B.'s Government introduced an Education Bill designed to rectify the clerical bias of Balfour's 1902 Act, and to abolish religious tests. This was strongly supported by the Nonconformists and as strongly opposed by the Church of England and by Roman Catholics. Balfour, powerless in the House of Commons in face of the great Liberal majority there, said bluntly, when this came to be debated in the House of Commons, that the real discussion must be elsewhere – meaning in the Lords – and did not hesitate to use Conservative power in the Lords to destroy C.B.'s Bill and other Liberal legislation. C.B. described this as 'the treachery of openly calling in the other House to override this House', and said of Balfour's tactics:

'There is one thing I have learned in my parliamentary experience . . . it is not cleverness that pays in the long run. The people of this country are a straightforward people. They like honesty and straightforwardness of purpose. They may laugh at it and they may be amused by it, and they may in a sense admire it, but they do not like cleverness. You may be too clever by half. . . .'

Inevitably the two Houses came into conflict. Though it was to be left to Asquith to tackle this constitutional issue, it was C.B. who suggested the way out – a version of the suspensory veto.

As Prime Minister C.B. introduced four Land Bills and was active in the cause of land reform, seeking to arrest the depopulation of the countryside and to increase the number of smallholdings. But on this economics were against him.

In foreign affairs he agreed, though with some apprehension, to the opening of staff talks with the French. He spoke out for parliamentary democracy in Russia after the dissolution of the Duma by the Tsar, approved a tough line against Turkish pretensions in Sinai but supported efforts to achieve international disarmament. Sir Charles Hardinge, Permanent Under-Secretary at the Foreign Office, described him as 'the best Prime Minister that this Office has ever had to deal with'.

He was one of the first to concern himself with the problems of the quality of life, particularly in large cities like his native Glasgow. 'What', he said, 'is all our wealth and learning and the fine flowers of our civilisation and our Constitution and our political theories – what are all these but dust and ashes, if the men and women, on whose labour the whole social fabric is maintained, are doomed to live and die in darkness and misery in the recesses of our great cities?'

C.B. held to the principles of Cobden and Gladstone. He himself defined Liberalism as

'the acknowledgement in practical life of the truth that men are best governed who govern themselves; that the general sense of mankind, if left alone, will make for righteousness; that artificial privileges and restraints upon freedom . . . are hurtful; and that the laws . . . ought to have for their object the securing to every man the best chance he can have of a good and useful life.'

He believed absolutely in free trade and in self-government for those who wanted it, whether they were the Irish or the Boers in South Africa. He had a sure touch when dealing with the difficult problems of relationships between different peoples. He was a moderate on social reform and disliked too much state interference, but he greatly preferred small yeomen proprietors to big landowners and he worked all his life to improve the lot of humble people.

Above all, he was one of the nicest and most sensible men ever to lead a political party or to be prime minister. No prime minister was ever more loved by his followers. He was a modest man, who disliked fuss and over-exertion, but he had the wisdom and sagacity of a good family solicitor or of an old shepherd, and he was afraid of no one and nothing.

BIBLIOGRAPHY

Harris, Jose F. and Hazelhurst, Cameron, 'Campbell-Bannerman as Prime Minister', *History* (October, 1970), 360–83

Mackie, J. B., *The Model Member. Sir Henry Campbell-Bannerman, Fifty Years Representative of the Stirling Burghs* (1914)

O'Connor, T. P., *Sir Henry Campbell-Bannerman* (London, 1908)

Spender, J. A., *Life of Rt Hon Sir Henry Campbell-Bannerman G.C.B.* (London, 1923)

Wilson, John, *C.B.: A Life of Sir Henry Campbell-Bannerman* (London, 1973) (contains a full bibliography)

H. H. ASQUITH

BY

JOSEPH GRIMOND

Herbert Henry Asquith, 1st Earl of Oxford and Asquith (created 1924), son of Joseph Dixon Asquith, cloth manufacturer of Morley, Yorks. Born 12 September 1852. Educated at the City of London School and Balliol College, Oxford. Married 1887, Helen, who died 1892; four sons and one daughter. Called to the Bar. Entered Parliament as member for East Fife in 1886 and appointed Home Secretary in Gladstone's Government 1892. Married 1894, Margot Tennant, daughter of Sir Charles Tennant, one son and one daughter. Chancellor of the Exchequer under Campbell-Bannerman 1905; Prime Minister on Campbell-Bannerman's resignation 1908. Continued as Prime Minister until 1916, when succeeded by Lloyd George. Leader of the Opposition 1916–18. Defeated in election of 1918, but returned as MP for Paisley 1920, till defeated in 1924, when he accepted an earldom. KG, FRS 1924. Retired from party politics 1926. Died 15 February 1928. Author of The Genesis of War, *1923;* Fifty Years of Parliament, *1926;* Memoirs and Reflection, 1852–1927, *1928;* Occasional Addresses 1893–1916, *1918;* Speeches, *1927.*

Herbert Henry Asquith, 1st Earl of Oxford and Asquith, by A. Cluysenaar

H. H. ASQUITH

Asquith was a comparatively poor member of the northern middle class. He was in some measure the leader in a shift of political power from the aristocratic or upper-middle, rather rich, classes to a new stratum. Campbell-Bannerman was from a similar stable but richer. Disraeli was a joker in the prime ministerial pack. Mr Gladstone was Eton. But Mr Asquith was at the City of London School.

If there is any truth in the conventional view of northern Englishmen as hard-headed, hard-working, stalwart and somewhat unimaginative, Mr Asquith was typical. Overlaid with the supposed graces of London and Oxford, yoked to the extravagances of the Scottish Miss Tennant, Asquith's Yorkshireness was apt to be forgotten. He never had much contact with the county of his birth but there must have been some residue of Morley left in the family when D. H. Lawrence after his only meeting with his daughter, Violet, could remark, 'You could see at once she is a Yorkshire lass.'

Equipped with an excellent mind, undistracted by too much curiosity, he sailed from school to Balliol and from Balliol to the Bar, collecting first classes and prizes as he went. The ease with which he dominated the House of Commons, his social life with Margot, the fact that he was Prime Minister longer than anyone in the last 200 years and his disdain of publicity and gimmicks have given him a certain aloof, self-sufficient air in the history books – 'The Last of the Romans', proud, cold and cautious. This seems far from true. He never shrank from risks. He had a difficult start at the Bar. He did not in fact earn much of an income until after his cross-examination of the Manager of *The Times*, before the Parnell inquiry, an incident full of drama in the classical legal tradition. It was indeed a risk to stand for Parliament for a Scottish seat in 1886 when MPs got no salary or expenses. And in later life it was he who sometimes kept Lloyd George's head to the wind when Lloyd George showed signs of quavering before attack. Nor was he cold. He formed deep friendships which were of much importance to him. In his early days he saw much of Haldane, already looking like a character out of Lear, and Grey. Later he had a varied social life and his attachment to Miss Venetia Stanley has attracted a good deal of comment. He was certainly no calculating politician. From his early days his intellect was governed by a warm conviction of the importance of reform, improvement and the maintenance of political standards.

When he first entered Parliament Mr Gladstone was engaged in his titanic struggle to achieve Home Rule for Ireland. The folly and selfishness of his Unionist opponents are almost unbelievable. And the cost of denying Home Rule to Ireland has been heavy. A terrible responsibility lies upon the Tory party. Mr Asquith, as one would expect, was a Home Ruler. He was indeed a deep admirer of Gladstone. And he held his first Cabinet appointment as Home Secretary in Mr Gladstone's Cabinet of 1892. If we are to assess Asquith's place in political history it is worth considering his early days in office. For his political life was all of one piece. He held the view of the conduct of politics with which he started until he finished, and that view owed a considerable amount to Mr Gladstone. But Mr Gladstone was a passionate man, absorbed in various designs from theology to Home Rule. Mr Asquith was never quite so absorbed. Mr Gladstone, however, also had a wide view of the many sides of politics. He had political imagination. He believed in the power and responsibility of politicians. He held to the tradition that politics is more than administration: more than office: more than a career: that it is an education as well as the management of life in all its aspects. The public service is a service to the public and not an opportunity to manipulate their affairs. He certainly believed that politics was about the quality of life – that phrase which has become hackneyed and indeed rather odious by being mouthed by all sorts of publicists who never seek to put it into practice. He was a meticulous administrator. These were also Asquith's qualities. What is not always realised about Mr Gladstone was his astringency. The stories of his final Cabinet when tears flowed freely illustrate this side of his character. He looked round with much disdain and ever afterwards referred to it as the 'blubbering' Cabinet. Asquith too lacked the superficial emotions. Asquith regarded Gladstone as a survivor of the heroic age in English politics. And no summing up of Asquith should forget that he carried on the Gladstone tradition of politics as a heroic and endless engagement in trying to translate moral attitude into practice and raise the standards of aesthetic and intellectual as well as economic life.

The Home Secretary's position in any government is fraught with danger. The House of Commons quickly latches on to personal cases. The issues of the Home Office too are avidly seized on by the press. They are often of genuine difficulty: the Home Secretary is the minister who has to face at first hand moral claims and counter claims. Cases blow up from a clear sky. Further, the Home Secretary now has to temper adherence to the dogma of his party with a regard for what is generally acceptable. Asquith can claim some credit for this development. Politics is an art of complexity and many facets. The reconciliation of claims by reference to some system of values is the essence of the politician's task and in no office is it more difficult or more necessary than in the Home Office. Sometimes a Home Secretary must risk putting his colleagues in political jeopardy. Sometimes he has to ensure that he does not seem to browbeat the public against its own judgement. Asquith was adept in finding the right course. He has left behind a tradition which persists to this day.

The political events of the decade between the fall of Lord Rosebery's Government in 1894 and his accession to office again as Chancellor of the Exchequer in Campbell-Bannerman's Government of 1905 – Ireland, the House of Lords, the South African war – helped to form the statesman from the politician in Asquith. Were this a biography, Asquith's attitude to these problems would need to be dealt with at some length. But as the main theme of this book is the contribution of our prime ministers to British political history these topics can largely be discussed in relation to his tenure of office. A non-political event that took place while Rosebery was still Prime Minister on 10 May 1894 must however be mentioned. In a scene of some splendour Asquith married Margot Tennant. The register was signed by four prime ministers, past, present or to be. The streets were crowded. Whether one thinks that Asquith's advent to Downing Street opened a new age or was the crowning achievement of the old regime – I myself will argue that he was one of the crucial links in our history ensuring continuity but sowing the seeds which are still flowering today – certainly Margot was a new type of prime minister's wife. Lady Melbourne had glamour, Lady Campbell-Bannerman had influence. Margot contributed new extrovert qualities. Above all, she had vitality which had a streak of Edwardian vulgarity but was felt directly and pervasively by everyone she met. Hunting, smart Edwardian life, its corollary of fundamental religion (had she not prayed in a railway carriage with General Booth?) and an originality of mind which made her a successful hostess to all sorts of writers, painters and playwrights, combined to make her a personality of her own. Downing Street under the Asquiths was the centre of a blend of official and personal entertaining hardly seen again until the White House under Kennedy. How much Margot affected Asquith's political judgement I find it difficult to tell. Little, I think. I doubt if she had fixed political opinions. Her likes and dislikes were strong and strikingly expressed – of Lloyd George, 'cannot see a belt without hitting below it'; or, in a less biting moment, 'I saw Linky Cecil in the Park this morning riding his horse like a string of opinions'. But she was mercurial and generous and whether the wounds their repetition must have inflicted went on to fester I do not know.

Her style of life cannot have made relations with some wings of the Liberal tradition at all easy. On the other hand, warm and appreciative letters from her to Lloyd George exist. However, there she was to remain, extravagant ('I hope to leave nothing but debts'), exhausting (appalling accounts have come down of the deafening noise in the dining-room of the Wharf at Sutton Courtney), uninhibited, not beautiful ('I have no face, only two profiles clapped together'), but tigerishly loyal and a powerful influence on all near her.

It is a great temptation to write about Campbell-Bannerman, one of the most attractive British politicians. Nor indeed would it be wholly irrelevant to an assessment of Asquith, for though they were never close friends, indeed had serious political disagreements and differed in social and political style, yet it was Campbell-Bannerman who started the great Liberal era of 1905–14 which must be associated for ever with Asquith's name.

Asquith became Chancellor in Campbell-Bannerman's Government of 1905. In Asquith's case the importance of the Chancellorship was enhanced as he was deputy leader to a prime minister who was ill, idolent, and in any case had no Oxford Union inclination to make speeches in the House of Commons.

Asquith's Budgets are important in fiscal history. He first differentiated between earned and unearned income. And it was under him that super-tax was first accepted in principle though implemented when Lloyd George was Chancellor. I have said that I regard Asquith as a crucial and seminal link in political history. As Home Secretary this had been more in changing the style of that office than in legislation (though he introduced a moderately important Factory Act), but as Chancellor he started a substantive move forward. He took an initiative that projected the State into what was for Britain an entirely new role. I refer of course to the foundation of the social services. Never again after Asquith could any government disclaim responsibility for the troubles of the poor or unfortunate. The notion that the business of the State was to hold the ring so that individuals would make their own way and provide for their old age by their own exertions was killed. So was the belief that the *laissez-faire* system could meet all economic needs except for a small area such as refuse collection where the profit motive was hardly enough. And indeed a great breach was made in the intellectual boundaries that surrounded the nineteenth-century State. This took many forms. It led to a new conception of the State as a positive instrument changing society and going far beyond law and order, defence and the pursuit of national interests. It led to a new view of the wealth and capabilities of the State. It challenged the rights of the upper classes. And it stimulated a new type of democracy. As the State became more and more involved in their pensions, unemployment pay, the support of their constituency industries and the provision of funds for their local authorities, MPs could no longer even pretend with J. S. Mill that constituency or private interests were not their affair. In the long term Asquith's initiative changed the focus of government. It slanted it away from foreign affairs and the aggrandisement of the state in the eighteenth-century sense. It slanted it away even from personal liberty, the maintenance of the Constitution and the extension of the franchise which had occupied the nineteenth century.

Asquith started these moves. I am not saying that this leap forward was unique to Britain. Bismarck might well claim to be the world founder of the Welfare State. But in Britain it was started not as an extension of a paternalist or collectivist philosophy, but within the democratic framework by someone who never doubted that framework. Asquith gave this new development its particularly British qualities. The legitimacy of British democratic progress was never questioned or broken by Asquith. No political changes can be pinpointed to one year, one event, or one man. The Factory Acts had already breached the doctrine of *laissez-faire*. They imposed state intervention in new fields. But they were negative. In a sense they were still 'holding the ring' – an extension of the legal framework. The whole conception of the joint stock company was an interference in economic affairs, but again not a positive use of the State's wealth and power to help certain individuals. Nor, finally, am I saying that the changes for which Asquith was primarily responsible happened all at once. Far from it. They have been continued by the Health Service, by the family incomes supplement. They are still happening, that is what makes them so important.

As with many great reforms the actual change now seems very small. It was a non-contributory old age pension of 5 shillings a week for those over seventy whose total income did not exceed 10 shillings. Even allowing for the fact that the pound was perhaps ten times as valuable as it is today, it does not seem now an act of cataclysmic extravagance. But it did to Asquith's conservative contemporaries. And it is one of the few legislative changes long remembered with gratitude by several generations of recipients. Even now someone occasionally remembers that the Liberals brought in the old age pension.

This first step towards the Welfare State was to be followed by unemployment insurance and the employment exchanges when Lloyd George was Chancellor and Asquith Prime Minister.

The next great matter with which Asquith had to deal was the constitutional question of the relationship between the Commons and the Lords. Here too so accustomed have we grown to a surviving but impotent House of Lords, so astonishingly indefensible and indeed disastrous does the behaviour of the Tories of Asquith's day now appear, that perhaps we fail to appreciate what a difficult matter it was at the time. We also fail to appreciate how well Asquith handled it. Great damage was done to Ireland and to Britain by the rejection of useful Bills such as the Education Bill of 1906 and the Licensing Bill of 1908. But if the Lords had had their way the situation might have been much worse. Or if more radical solutions had been found, though I personally believe they would have been justified, we might have lost both a second chamber and that 'legitimacy' which alone of major European governments the government of Britain can now claim. On balance I believe Asquith was too tolerant. But I do not underestimate the dangers and threats of active treason which he faced. Nor do I believe that the majority even of liberal opinion would then or now have welcomed the more drastic solution of abolition of the second chamber.

The obstruction of the House of Lords had started long before Asquith became Prime Minister. As has been said, the Lords had thrown out Gladstone's Home Rule Bills. Their motives were a mixture of obscurantism, selfishness and political expediency. For anxiety about the general good there was little evidence. They threw out the Education Bill, but not the Trades Disputes Bill because to have done so might have harmed the Tory party. The bigoted stupidity of the Tory Lords reached its apex when they threw out Lloyd George's Budget of 1909.

Britain has no written Constitution. But her wisest statesmen have had a strong constitutional sense. The strongest element in this sense has been that British government is an affair of limits and balances. The minister as well as the subject is under an impartial law. Not only must the Government respect the law as it stands at any moment; in changing it they must have regard to prescriptive rights and the organic nature of British society as well as natural justice or moral imperatives. Further, British parliamentary government is not a fully-fledged system of positive participatory democracy. Indeed it is now and was more so in Asquith's day a system dependent upon the leadership of an executive, not directly elected but subject to criticism and control by a House of Commons and a House of Lords with a largely negative but important role. These Houses had to be argued with and convinced. In Asquith's day they contained many more men of independence with a position of their own in politics not dependent on the party machine. More MPs were less concerned to achieve some office. Ministers remained much longer in the Commons listening to debates than they do now. Roy Jenkins quotes Harcourt as saying, 'When I am ill I am in bed, when I am well I am in the House of Commons.' The constitutional doctrine was strong: stronger and more pervasive perhaps than in a country where it is laid down in a document and protected only by a court of law or a two-thirds majority. It was imbedded in the hearts and heads of the best of those who ran the system. Asquith knew that populism was not the British type of democracy. And he consciously approved of the British way of doing things as giving stability and guaranteeing change with protection of personal freedom and the rights of minorities.

The breaking-point came over the Budget of 1909. It was against every constitutional convention for the peers to reject the Finance Bill. But they did. Parliament, or rather the non-elected wing of Parliament, refused the Government the financial means to run the country. The Government could not carry on in these circumstances. Parliament was dissolved. At the general election the Liberals gained a small majority over the Tories alone and a large one counting Labour and the Irish Nationalists. The issue was now threefold. The need to pass the Budget. The need to curb the House of Lords. The possibility of reforming it.

All these issues concerned the position of the Crown. It is not my business to write a history of this matter. Asquith, showing consummate diplomacy both towards the King and the Irish, who were in some respects restive, forced the Tories to accept the Budget. But the need to curb the Lords remained. Democratic government could not continue so long as the Lords behaved as they had behaved for the last twenty years. But at this point Edward VII died and these most trying constitutional matters came before a new and inexperienced king. Again Asquith showed almost too much forbearance. He negotiated with the Tory leaders. He made every effort to keep the King out of the controversy. But in the last resort he was firm. The creation of peers was promised and the House of Lords lost its powers to frustrate a Commons majority.

Not only was this a constitutional crisis important in itself in the history of our country; it established the powers of the Lords for fifty years. And it set a precedent in how in Britain constitutional crises should be tackled. It was not a precedent always followed. It was not followed by Lloyd George's Government over Ireland. But it has to some extent, and allowing for different circumstances, been followed by Baldwin over the Abdication and Mr Whitelaw over Ulster. Both showed a reluctance to use the steam-roller of a Commons majority: both negotiated patiently: each had a clear purpose to which he adhered.

It may be convenient at this point to look at Asquith's treatment of the Labour party. The Liberal party in the early years of the century deliberately made room for the Labour party. An attitude very different from that of late taken by the present Labour party to the Liberals. The small and insecure Labour party of the first decade of the century could probably have been strangled at birth by the Liberals. But Liberals such as Asquith believed that all shades of opinion had their rights to representation. The Labour vote represented a part, be it a small part, of the electorate. It should be represented in the House of Commons. His own son, Raymond, was running in harness with a Labour candidate for the double member constituency of Derby when he was killed. It is interesting to compare Asquith's attitude with that of Lloyd George. From 1910 Lloyd George from time to time toyed with the idea of a coalition with the Tories – and of course never achieved office without seeking most of his support from the Tories. There was nothing particularly secret in his moves. But it is interesting that he never seems to have sensed the value of close co-operation with Labour or the value of close Liberal-Labour co-operation.

It was Asquith who in 1923 decided that there should be the first Labour Government. He held the balance of power with the considerable number of 158 Liberal seats as against 191 Labour and 285 Tories. He could have kept the Tories in office, taken office himself or forced some sort of coalition. But to him it seemed clear that once the Tories retired the next call must go to Labour. Their advent was viewed with horror by many people who appealed to Asquith for succour. As usual he was neither frightened nor unsure. He saw all too well that constitutional propriety demanded that the King should call upon Ramsay MacDonald. He believed too that nothing would be more likely to embitter Labour supporters and do irremediable damage to the Constitution and the nation than the feeling that they had been excluded from office by a coalition of the old guard. Asquith had seen Ireland lost by the fear and short-sightedness of the Tories, he was not to repeat their mistake.

Ireland was indeed another of the great issues of the 1910 Parliament. It was an issue that Asquith failed to bring to a successful conclusion owing to the outbreak of war. But again he showed his patience, his firmness and his determination to stick to the rational and radical course. Howled down by the Tories led by Hugh Cecil, faced with treason in the Army, encouraged by the ineffably treacherous Sir Henry Wilson and rebellion in Ulster, he drove steadily to the conclusion he reached in 1914, which could have saved Ireland from the disasters and tragedies that continue to this day.

By 1914 Asquith and Redmond had a firm agreement which would have given Ireland all she wanted including in the longer term unity with Ulster. The Tories and the IRA, the two evil geniuses of Irish history, made that impossible. When the Treaty came the Irish got less than Asquith had won for them. And they got it in circumstances that have left a fatal residue to this day.

The other activity in Asquith's political career which I have left to the last, for it is the one aim upon which his reputation has largely suffered, is the 1914–18 war. His conduct of military affairs has not the seminal importance of the founding of the Welfare State which, as I have claimed, along with other developments of policy led to long-term results in the conduct of British affairs. But it was of course of immense importance in the history of Britain.

The reputation of wartime leaders is always subject to prejudice. Ultimate success ensures praise. Reputations are founded on the most curious premises. Some people seem to believe that we should have surrendered in the last war had it not been for Churchill. To me it is inconceivable that Britain would have folded up without a fight in 1940 whoever led us. It is even more inconceivable that once America and Russia were in the war the allies could have lost. This does not mean that Churchill was not a great war leader. But it does mean that we should not have lost the war without him.

Churchill started with the advantage of clean hands. He was not responsible for the lack of preparation for a war. In Asquith's case the curious thing is that he was not driven from office because he took the country into war unprepared as Chamberlain did. On the contrary, it has never gone better prepared into a war. If the direct credit for this belongs to Haldane, Asquith is certainly entitled to some share in it and the ultimate responsibility for it was his.

Asquith was not guilty of bad timing and indecision as Chamberlain was over Norway. Nor indeed was he forced into coalition and then out of office through conspicuous military failings or lack of munitions. The Dardanelles failure certainly was a main cause of the coalition. But the prime author was of course Churchill.

As for the aftermath of his resignation, the great mistakes and disasters of the war such as the appointment of Nivelle and the disaster of the Chemin des Dames and Passchendaele took place when Lloyd George was Prime Minister. The evidence shows that Asquith was a competent, steadfast war Prime Minister who on many occasions showed his qualities of loyalty, good judgement and determination. Why was he evicted?

Perhaps whoever is in the saddle at the beginning of a war is unlikely to last it out. But to me the qualities that led to his undoing had little to do with the war. He was intellectually somewhat arrogant. He neither appreciated such men as Bonar Law nor made much effort to understand them. He had curious flaws in his judgements about people. Though he sometimes realised his superficiality, to the end he liked and admired Balfour, a disastrous politician and frequently devious in his dealings with Asquith. However dedicated he was to his duties as Prime Minister, Asquith seems to have given the impression of not being sufficiently involved. This impression crops up again and again in letters. His own letters to Venetia Stanley show by modern standards a curious commentary on his outlook. He was no hypocrite and no showman. He despised the despicable press that hounded him. No doubt too he was tired. It is difficult for anyone today to appreciate the appalling strain of the First World War. Asquith lost one son and had one badly wounded. Bonar Law lost two sons.

Asquith was at once a link and a new departure. He carried in his respect for reason, the Constitution and Parliament the great nineteenth-century traditions of Gladstone. He had a traditional distrust of demagogy. He loathed the type of administration made up of political adventurers and 'hard-faced men who had done well out of the war', such as Lloyd George was content to lead. Had he been there, the peace treaty would have been more far-sighted. He would never have engaged in Lloyd George's Eastern Mediterranean goings-on. Yet, as I have said, he started a major new political departure which set Britain on a new course into the twentieth century. That our parliamentary system survived the aftermath of the First World War and absorbed the rise of the Labour party, that Liberal values still dominate us and discussions, however distorted by appeals to self-interest and the mass media, are still guides of the political system, is largely due to the Asquith tradition.

I have mentioned that under the Asquiths 10 Downing Street became a centre for official and unofficial entertaining of artists and all sorts of people distinguished outside politics. It is true that most of these came from one social set. But it was a wide and talented set. Asquith was subjected to a campaign of vilification and slander unequalled in our history. The main protagonists were such Tories as the Duchess of Sutherland, the top of the so-called aristocracy and the press. He was also accused of all manner of perversion by Lord Alfred Douglas because he befriended the friends of Oscar Wilde. This should be recalled not only to show the incredible behaviour of the British Conservative upper classes and the difficulties under which the left operates in this country (a far higher standard is expected of it than of the right) but also because an important part of Asquith's style as Prime Minister was his contact with circles outside politics. He continued the Gladstonian tradition of addressing public meetings. In his constituency he would explain government policies to meetings in towns as small as Ladybank. And, as he himself said, he found his audiences of railwaymen and farm labourers well informed, appreciative and critical. (A good point would be greeted with murmurs of 'Weel turned, Asquith, weel turned'.)

As Prime Minister he continued to see people who were neither in search of favours, nor his hosts nor guests in an official capacity. He never, I think, had a government car. He could, therefore, at least see the taximeter ticking up the cost. Part of the present yawning gap between politicians and the public is due to the insulation of ministers from ordinary life. They do not notice rising prices or the breakdown of public services as they are wafted in their official cars from their official residences to their well-appointed offices. They lunch and dine in the company of their kind or their clients. It is no matter for wonder, therefore, that the gap between the government and the governed is a major feature of our time. One cannot imagine Asquith tape-recording conversations or employing a personal bodyguard of public relations officers like a renaissance bravo. Nor would he have tolerated the bureaucratic outlook. Too many of those in charge of our affairs seem primarily concerned with their professional advancement. More and more is the public service associated with the reduction of individuality to a uniformity of methods and outlook. Bureaucracy aims at the lowest common denominator. Asquith viewed politics as essentially bound up with some pursuit of individuality and excellence. Democracy to him was not the grey imposition of bureaucratic fashion from above.

For eight and a half years Asquith presided with complete authority over the most brilliant Cabinet of all time. He was an accomplished chairman, a masterly expositor and loyal to the point of rashness. In all this, in his contact with a fairly large slice of ordinary life, in his loyalty and steadfastness and his respect for the proprieties of the Constitution, the seeds sown by his premiership did not immediately bear fruit. But in the long run they have done. We face new dangers today from faceless men and the worship of technology but the endurance of our standards of public life for half a century is a continuing reminder of Asquith's service to the British people.

BIBLIOGRAPHY

Asquith, H. H., *Memories and Reflections*, 1852–1927, 2 vols. (London, 1928); *Speeches*, 1887–1926 (London, 1927)
Jenkins, Roy, *Asquith* (London, 1964)
Spender, J. A., and Asquith, C., *Life of Lord Oxford & Asquith*, 2 vols. (London, 1932)

DAVID LLOYD GEORGE

BY

PETER LOWE

*David Lloyd George, created (1945) Earl Lloyd-George of Dwyfor
and Viscount Gwynedd of Dwyfor. Born 17 January 1863.
Educated Llanystumdwy, near Criccieth, by his uncle. Articled to a
solicitor at Portmadoc, 1879. Married (1) 1888 Margaret Owen;
two sons, three daughters, (2) 1943 Frances Louise Stevenson.
MP (Caernarvon Boroughs) 1890–1945. Identified with Welsh
nationalism 1894–96. Opposed Joseph Chamberlain and Unionist
Government 1899–1902. President of the Board of Trade under
Campbell-Bannerman 1905; Chancellor of the Exchequer under
Asquith 1908; introduced the 'Peoples Budget' 1909; introduced
the National Insurance Act 1911; Minister of Munitions 1915;
Secretary of State for War 1916; Prime Minister, Coalition
Government 1916–18 and 1918–22; Representation of the People
Act 1918; Fisher Education Act 1918; participated in the Paris
Peace Conference 1919; Irish settlement 1921; resigned the
Premiership 1922 and rejoined the Liberal Party 1923; Liberal
leader 1926 (resigned 1931); leader of the Independent Liberals
1931–45; resigned as MP 1945 and died 26 March same year.
Author of* War Memoirs *(6 vols), 1933–36;* The Truth about
the Peace Treaties, *1938.*

David Lloyd George, 1st Earl of Dwyfor, by W. Orpen

DAVID LLOYD GEORGE

David Lloyd George was perhaps the most unconventional of all British prime ministers in his background, character, outlook and policies. There was a highly adventurous, buccaneering quality about his six years in the premiership, between December 1916 and October 1922. Contemporaries were entranced, dazzled, astounded, impressed, alarmed and shocked by his behaviour and attitudes. One feature was certain: Lloyd George could never be ignored. He had emerged as a prominent and vociferous politician at the time of the South African war and continued to be respected or feared until the Second World War. Although he was born in Manchester, Lloyd George was brought up in rural Wales in humble circumstances and his Welsh background was vitally important in his life; he always spoke Welsh in his family circle and would even discuss high policy in Welsh on occasion, as with the deputy secretary of the Cabinet, Thomas Jones. Lloyd George was devoted to Wales; while he rose to become a statesman of world stature, he never forgot his homeland and frequently returned there for relaxation. The deep influence of his early years in rural, Nonconformist Wales was revealed in his radicalism, which was conditioned by his dislike of landowners and inherited wealth; he did not fully comprehend urban radicalism and the more extreme manifestations of socialism. As a young man, he was ruthlessly determined to advance his career. His attitude is illustrated in one of his early letters to his future wife:

'My supreme idea is to get on. To this idea I shall sacrifice everything – except I trust honesty. I am prepared to thrust even love itself under the wheels of my Juggernaut, if it obstructs the way. . . . Believe me – & may Heaven attest the truth of my statement – my love for you is sincere & strong. In this I never waver. But I must not forget that I have a purpose in life. And however painful the sacrifice I may have to make to attain this ambition I must not flinch – otherwise success will be remote indeed. . . .'[1]

[1] K. O. Morgan (ed.), *Lloyd George: Family Letters 1885–1936* (Cardiff and London, 1973), p. 14, undated letter, probably 1885, Lloyd George to Margaret Owen.

He was elected to Parliament in 1890 as Liberal Member for Caernarvon Boroughs, the constituency he represented continuously until shortly before his death in 1945. As a politician Lloyd George was motivated by a fierce concern for ordinary people and a determination to do all he could to assist them in improving the conditions of their lives. He emerged as the leader of the Radical wing of the Liberal party before 1914 and gave a powerful stimulus to the social policies of the Liberal governments. In the practice of politics, Lloyd George was mercurial, vocal, tenacious and flexible. While he believed that confrontation was sometimes necessary, he was concerned with making tangible progress and would exploit any opportunity to secure a realistic compromise.[2] He earned a reputation for brilliance as a political tactician including an extreme deviousness; he was undeniably devious but the extent was often exaggerated.

Lloyd George's personal life was as complex as his political career. He married Margaret Owen, daughter of a Welsh farmer, in 1888; they had five children and remained married until her death in 1941. Publicly he preserved the image of the respectable family man; he had numerous affairs with women, however, and from 1912 a permanent mistress, his attractive and intelligent private secretary, Frances Stevenson, with whom he lived whenever he could and by whom he had a daughter. Yet he regarded his wife with genuine affection and she helped him in his political campaigns, on occasion undertaking a heavy programme of speeches, as in the 1918 general election and in the important Cardiganshire by-election in 1921. Understandably she resented his affairs but Lloyd George wrote to his wife, in a revealing passage, that this was a facet of his nature which had to be accepted:

You say I have my weakness. So has anyone that ever lived & the greater the man the greater the weakness. It is only insipid, wishy washy fellows that have no weaknesses. . . .

You must make allowances for the waywardness & wildness of a man of my type. What if I were drunk as well? I can give you two samples you know of both the weaknesses in one man & the wives do their best under those conditions. What about Asquith & Birkenhead? I

[2] Two examples before 1914 being his attempts to settle the conflict involving the Welsh Church in 1895 and his proposal for a coalition government with the Unionists during the constitutional crisis in 1910, as noted by K. O. Morgan, 'Lloyd George's Premiership: A Study in Prime Ministerial Government', *Historical Journal* xiii, 1 (1970), 131–2.

could tell you stories of both – women & wine. Believe me hen gariad [old darling]. I am at bottom as fond of you as ever. . . .[3]

Frances Stevenson's deep feeling for Lloyd George is revealed in the following extract from her diary:

'We went down to Walton H. on Saturday afternoon (21 April) & had a perfect weekend. I do not think that we have ever loved each other so much. D. says that ours is a love that comes to very few people and I wonder more & more at the beauty & happiness of it. It is a thing that nothing but death can harm, and even death has no terrors for me now, for D. asked me yesterday if I would come with him when he went. He begged me not to stay behind, but for both of us to go together, and I promised him to do so, unless I have any children of his to claim me. So, I am not afraid now of the misery if D. is taken away, for then I shall go too & his end will be my end, and until then everything is happiness, if our love stays. I hope by any chance I shall not go first, for I know his misery would be great, and he could not leave his work, which is a great one. I am so happy now that we have decided this, for sometimes my heart would stop beating with terror at the thought of life without D.'[4]

It is in some respects surprising that his personal life did not result in a major scandal, given the number of his enemies and the extent to which the British public expected moral rectitude in its leaders.

Lloyd George became Prime Minister at the end of 1916 owing to the lack of success in Britain's war effort and to the bankruptcy of the Asquith Coalition. While Asquith had some achievements to his credit, notably in helping to create the relative unity with which Great Britain entered the war in 1914, he had failed in all essentials as a war leader. He did not inspire confidence or provide decisive leadership; by the latter months of 1916 it was widely felt in Parliament and in the country that change was necessary. Lloyd George was the one member of the Coalition whose standing in the country had risen steadily, principally because of his outstanding success in developing the ministry of munitions in 1915-16. As Frances Stevenson noted in her diary in early

[3] Morgan, p. 203, Lloyd George to his wife, 24 July 1924.
[4] A. J. P. Taylor (ed.), *Lloyd George: A Diary by Frances Stevenson* (London, 1971), p. 153, diary entry for 23 April 1917.

December 1916, there was a widespread faith in Lloyd George throughout the country and the nation would accept him as a virtual dictator.[5] Many politicians disliked and distrusted him but they, too, were forced to admit that the Government could not continue as it was. Lloyd George challenged Asquith directly by demanding a drastic reform of the Government's war-making machinery so as to eliminate the unwieldy large Cabinet, substituting a small committee in its place, and aiming to relegate Asquith to a subordinate position, although he would remain Prime Minister. After initial vacillation, Asquith declined to accept Lloyd George's conditions and resigned as Prime Minister; he most probably but mistakenly believed that Lloyd George would be unable to form a government.[6]

The major political difficulty facing Lloyd George when he assumed office was that he did not lead a political party. It is true that MacDonald in 1931 and Churchill in 1940 were in a similar position but MacDonald had led the Labour party for a considerable period and Churchill soon inherited the Conservative leadership after Neville Chamberlain's resignation. Throughout his premiership, Lloyd George lacked the support of a powerful political party of his own; he possessed the allegiance of the amorphous Coalition Liberals but depended for survival on the loyalty of the Unionists (Conservatives), as was made brutally clear by the circumstances of his fall from power in 1922. He appealed to many Unionist backbenchers, if not their leaders, in 1916 because he exemplified a ruthless, determined approach to waging war, in itself a recognition of the importance of mobilising all the resources of the country regardless of the infringements on individual liberty. Of the situation when he formed his Government he wrote in his memoirs:

'Had there been a united party behind me which, with dependable allies, would have commanded in the House of Commons a majority solid and large enough to carry me through the inevitable vicissitudes of evil as well as good tidings for a period of two years and more, I should have had a freer, a wider and a more promising choice. I could then have secured a more homogeneous form of Government and a Government

[5] Taylor, op. cit., p. 132, diary entry of 5 December 1916.
[6] For a discussion of Lloyd George's record in the war before he became Prime Minister, including an assessment of the complicated events in November–December 1916, see P. Lowe, 'The Rise to the Premiership, 1914–16', in A. J. P. Taylor (ed.), *Lloyd George: Twelve Essays* (London, 1971), pp. 95–133.

more sympathetic to the War policy in which I believed. I was anxious to change the men and methods which were too much associated with old war direction.'[7]

He at once abolished the old full Cabinet and set up a small War Cabinet of five members, which met almost daily and continued to function until late in 1919. In addition, he established a Cabinet secretariat to service the numerous requirements of the War Cabinet. This was a development of fundamental importance constitutionally and, more immediately, it achieved much improved efficiency in the political organisation of war. Previously there had been no official minutes of Cabinet meetings, the only record being the prime minister's frequently cursory letters to the monarch. The haphazard growth of the Committee of Imperial Defence provided the nucleus of a secretariat. The secretary of the CID, Sir Maurice Hankey, who kept the minutes of the War Committee which had functioned under Asquith, took command of the Cabinet secretariat and built it into a formidable body.[8] Lloyd George set up a complementary personal secretariat of his own, known or derided as the 'Garden suburb'. Unlike the Cabinet secretariat, which survived as an autonomous body as a result of Hankey's strenuous efforts after Lloyd George's resignation, the 'Garden suburb' disappeared in 1922. The value of the War Cabinet and the Cabinet secretariat was that they constituted an efficient means of formulating high policy; sub-committees of the War Cabinet were often formed to examine various issues. The Prime Minister was not particularly consistent or predictable in his handling of the War Cabinet. He summoned meetings whenever he desired them, sometimes with inadequate notice, or arbitrarily altered the schedule; this annoyed Hankey, who disliked having to change his meticulous arrangements.[9] Lloyd George also held meetings at breakfast, which did not suit some who attended. His actions reflected his dislike of convention and his preference for discussing issues verbally rather than in writing. Despite Lloyd George's erratic

[7] D. Lloyd George, *War Memoirs of David Lloyd George* (2 vols, London, 1938), i, 620.

[8] For the development of the secretariat and Hankey's role see the admirable biography by S. Roskill, *Hankey: Man of Secrets*, vols i–ii (London, 1970–2).

[9] For the views of Lloyd George's colleagues and officials on the functioning of the War Cabinet, see T. Wilson (ed.), *The Political Diaries of C. P. Scott, 1911–28* (London, 1971), pp. 277–9; K. Middlemas (ed.), *Thomas Jones: Whitehall Diary* (3 vols, 1969–71), i, 31; and Roskill, op. cit., i, 371, 618, 621 and ii, 32–4, 148.

behaviour, there was no doubt that the Government was infinitely more dynamic and efficient. Business was conducted more thoroughly and information reached the War Cabinet more rapidly. Lloyd George possessed immense energy and stimulated the entire governmental machine. Unlike Asquith, he was not afraid to take decisions; the calibre of leadership was radically different. After the war, the pressure from his colleagues eventually brought about a reversion to the traditional Cabinet in October 1919; Lloyd George pondered the possibility of having a medium-size Cabinet of twelve members but Hankey emphasised the need to retain the loyalty of all his colleagues, which could only be attained through a large Cabinet.[10] The full Cabinet returned but brief minutes, essentially comprising conclusions, were kept.[11] Lloyd George's premiership was, therefore, of fundamental significance in constitutional terms for the adoption of new methods of organising the central conduct of government business. As in other respects, he gave the powerful impetus that led British politics and government away from the lingering connections with the nineteenth century into the twentieth century.

When it came to the wider issue of waging the war, Lloyd George's achievements are best revealed in his innovatory policy of bringing new blood into Whitehall and in the reform of the Navy; he was conspicuously unsuccessful at gaining effective control of the Army. As Minister of Munitions, he had persuaded various businessmen to enter Whitehall and contribute their specialised knowledge to improving production; as Prime Minister, he extended this trend to other areas. The appointment of Sir Joseph Maclay as Shipping Controller was the earliest example, Maclay being appointed before his ministry had been created.[12] The appointment of Sir Eric Geddes as Controller of the Navy (and later First Lord of the Admiralty) and of Lord Rhondda as Food Controller were other examples.[13] These appointments were sometimes resented, not least by military and naval personnel, but were usually successful, the one notable disappointment being Neville Chamberlain in the admittedly difficult role of Director of National Service.[14]

[10] Roskill, ii, 127.
[11] Roskill, ii, 106.
[12] Lloyd George, *War Memoirs*, i, 726.
[13] ibid., i, 734, 791. Rhondda (D. A. Thomas) was a former politician and colleague of the Prime Minister.
[14] ibid., i, 809–12.

Within the armed forces, Lloyd George's difficulties in securing changes in strategy stemmed from the independent authority enjoyed by the commanders and from his own tenuous position as Prime Minister. He had long been critical of the British military leaders in particular and of their obstinate belief in a breakthrough on the Western Front, despite the futility of their previous tactics. In 1915–16 he had advocated a campaign in the East, designed to help Russia and eliminate Austria-Hungary or Turkey. While the concept was not simple to implement successfully, as the misfortunes in the Dardanelles demonstrated, the generals were not in the least inclined to favour such ideas: they felt that civilian politicians were not properly equipped to assess strategical matters and regarded the more vociferous of them, such as Lloyd George, with thinly disguised contempt. Lloyd George believed that it was essential to attain improved co-ordination between the allied armies and to avoid further huge casualties in pointless bloody offensives. It was tragically ironic that his chief failure lay in this sphere and that the horrors of the offensive in Flanders in 1917 occurred while he was Prime Minister. He disliked Sir Douglas Haig, the Commander-in-Chief in France, but could not remove him. Haig was popular with King George V: more significantly, he was popular with the Unionists, so that it was politically impossible to remove him provided Haig kept his political nerve and continued to resist Lloyd George's attempts to undermine his power. Sir William Robertson, Chief of the Imperial General Staff, was another implacable opponent of the Prime Minister. While Lloyd George would dearly have liked to replace Haig, he ruefully conceded in his memoirs that there was probably no one who was superior to Haig.[15] He was, however, successful in removing Robertson in February 1918 and replaced him with Sir Henry Wilson. The alternative to replacing Haig was to improve co-operation with the French and subordinate him to the French generals, whom Lloyd George believed to be more capable. This was the policy he pursued, with limited success, in 1917 and 1918. Lloyd George was captivated by General Nivelle early in 1917 and thought he had the solution that would produce a victorious offensive in France. Nivelle's offensive proved a miserable failure and allowed Haig the opportunity to urge his own ideas for an attack in Flanders in consequence. Haig was extraordinarily optimistic on the chances of success; Lloyd George reluctantly

[15] *War Memoirs*, ii, 1366. On reflection, he thought that the Australian, Sir John Monash, might have been superior (ibid., ii, 2016).

assented, since he was unable to enforce an alternative strategy.[16] The campaign to which the name 'Passchendaele' is attached became a nightmare of carnage and mud, ending as a battle of attrition that failed at tremendous cost. To a large extent, Lloyd George was a prisoner of the military. There were no dramatic new initiatives in military policy. His most concrete advance was in securing the appointment of Foch as Supreme Allied Commander in April 1918 but Foch's power was limited; Haig survived as British Commander until the end of the war. Lloyd George did not seemingly possess any profound strategical insight but had he possessed a freer hand he would certainly have terminated the policy of attrition, for he was never one to adhere to policies that had manifestly failed.

With the Navy, Lloyd George imposed his authority to greater effect. The gravest problem at sea was the extent of merchant shipping losses in 1916–17 resulting from the German submarine onslaught in the Atlantic. Neither the Admiralty nor the Board of Trade had any solution to the problem. Unless the situation was speedily remedied in 1917, Britain would be driven to surrender by starvation and shortage of raw materials. The First Lord of the Admiralty, Sir Edward Carson, had been a close political ally of Lloyd George in 1916; once in office, he became extremely negative and supported the Admirals without question. The obvious solutions to the vast shipping losses were to organise shipping more tightly, so as to eliminate the carrying of commodities that were not urgently required, and arrange for ships to travel in convoys. Sir Joseph Maclay worked to secure the former objective. The Admiralty was at first hostile to convoys, holding that they would multiply and not reduce losses owing to the difficulty of ensuring necessary co-operation from merchant captains and because of the volume of shipping involved. Lloyd George descended on the Admiralty in person in April 1917 and, according to his own account, insisted on the adoption of convoys. This account has been challenged as too colourful and exaggerated: the Admiralty had reluctantly come round to the view that convoys were necessary and were apparently prepared to adopt them before Lloyd George's famous visit.[17] However, it can-

[16] ibid., ii, 1247–1364 for Lloyd George's acrid discussion of the Flanders offensive and his mordant criticisms of the British commanders in France.

[17] For Lloyd George's account, see *War Memoirs*, i, 691–2. For the revisionist view, see A. J. Marder, *From the Dreadnought to Scapa Flow* (5 vols, London, 1961–70), iv, 152–66.

not be doubted that his deep concern and sympathy for the younger, more imaginative naval officers galvanised the Admiralty into more vigorous action than it would otherwise have adopted. The use of convoys soon proved the answer to the submarine depredations. Lloyd George was very critical of the naval chiefs, particularly of Jellicoe who seemed too defensively minded as First Sea Lord. It was first necessary to remove the obdurate Carson, which was achieved by promoting him to membership of the War Cabinet; Geddes replaced him as First Lord and in December 1917 Jellicoe was replaced by Wemyss. By this time the worst of the naval crisis was over. Lloyd George had contributed forcefully to the reforms within the Admiralty and he possessed effective control over the Navy by the end of 1917. One of the outstanding successes of his administration by 1918 was the war at sea. To cite his own words:

'The great Allied triumph of 1917 was the gradual beating off of the submarine attack. This was the real decision of the War, for the sea turned out to be the decisive flank in the gigantic battlefield. Here victory rested with the Allies, or rather with Britain. The moment the War became a struggle, not to beat the foe in a fight, but first to exhaust his strength and then to beat his defences down, the sea became inevitably the determining factor.'[18]

While Lloyd George has gone down in history as 'the man who won the war', as the extreme advocate of complete victory and maximum mobilisation of resources, he did not always think in terms of fighting on until Germany and her allies surrendered. Late in 1917 and early in 1918, he seriously considered making a compromise peace with Germany at the expense of Russia. The two revolutions of 1917 crippled and then terminated Russia's active role in the war. Milner, a member of the War Cabinet, was an enthusiastic advocate of encouraging German expansion in eastern Europe at Russia's expense.[19] Lloyd George's position is still shadowy but it appears certain that he did contemplate such a compromise peace.[20] There was no likelihood of such a peace materialising, however, for the simple reason that Germany

[18] *War Memoirs*, i, 711.
[19] See A. M. Gollin, *Proconsul in Politics: A Study of Lord Milner in Opposition and in Power* (London, 1964), chap. 20.
[20] Wilson, *The Political Diaries of C. P. Scott*, pp. 303-4, 329.

did not desire it. The matter is of interest primarily since it illustrates again the flexibility of Lloyd George's thinking and his desire to utilise the opportunity of escaping from a situation of stalemate.

The general election of December 1918 was an astonishing personal victory for Lloyd George. He had decided several months in advance that he would fight an election under the auspices of the Coalition as soon as the war ended. Sidney Webb, and perhaps others, had reflected on the possibility of Lloyd George's becoming leader of the Labour party, but the Prime Minister felt that his fortunes, at any rate for the foreseeable future, were linked with the Unionist party of which he might become leader.[21] As soon as Germany sought an armistice, Lloyd George determined to hold the election and campaign on the dual platform of the victorious war leader of the past and the man who would guide the nation through the reconstruction of 'normalcy' afterwards. Hankey, the secretary of the Cabinet, described him as he appeared immediately after the election campaign and before the votes had been counted:

'Ll.G. has brought the country through the war, but is very anxious lest he should not get the big majority in the election on which his supporters count. Consequently he is in a nervous, irritable and difficult frame of mind. The mistake he is making is to try and absorb too much into his hands. He seems to have a sort of lust for power; ignores his colleagues, or tolerates them in an almost dictatorial way, and seems more and more to assume the attitude of a dictator. . . .'[22]

When the results came in, the extent of his triumph was clear: candidates pledged to support the Coalition secured 478 seats and the rest 229 seats. The latter figure included some who supported Lloyd George, although they had not received the 'coupon', and the 73 Sinn Fein Members who refused to take their seats. The Opposition in the House of Commons was reduced to a weakly led Labour party dominated by worthy trade union stalwarts and to the Asquithian Liberal rump.[23] Hankey observed that Lloyd George was 'almost stunned' by

[21] Wilson, p. 320, diary entry of 16–19 December 1917, and Taylor (ed.), *Lloyd George: A Diary by Frances Stevenson*, p. 144, diary entry of 14 February 1917.
[22] Roskill, *Hankey*, ii, 39.
[23] Asquith lost his seat but was returned in a by-election at Paisley in February 1920. In the intervening period, the Independent Liberals were led by Sir Donald Maclean.

the magnitude of his victory.[24] The general election of 1918 was the most personalised of any election in the twentieth century and the victor did not lead a strong political party of his own. While the huge victory was encouraging in one respect, it was alarming in another: Lloyd George was the prisoner of the Unionist masses who were opposed to conciliatory policies at home and abroad. He hoped to persuade his Coalition Liberals and the Unionists to agree to fusion in a new Centre party under his leadership, which he made strenuous efforts to secure in 1920. Neither party was prepared to assent: the Coalition Liberals prided themselves on their Liberalism and they were indeed an appreciably larger band than the Independent Liberals, while the Unionist rank and file as distinct from their leaders now distrusted Lloyd George.[25]

The issue of making peace and of dealing with the numerous concomitants occupied the largest proportion of Lloyd George's time between the end of the war and his resignation: his international activities brought some praise but more criticism. As a generalisation, it might be said that the law of diminishing returns operated and that his role in foreign affairs resulted in steadily fewer benefits: in the end it contributed significantly to his fall. In the 1918 election, he had promised appropriate punishment for Germany's misdeeds. He neither supported nor favoured a lenient peace for Germany. Equally he did not wish to punish her too severely and obviate any possibility of reconciling her to the peace terms. The tasks facing Lloyd George, Clemenceau and Wilson were immense and complex. Given all the relevant circumstances – chronic instability in Europe, the looming menace of Bolshevism, the clamour for harsh treatment of Germany, the pressures of time, apart from clashes of personality – it was sanguine in the extreme to expect a lasting settlement to emerge in Paris.[26] Lloyd George's achievement was that the Treaty of Versailles was less severe as a result of his efforts than it would have been otherwise. He showed a

[24] Roskill, ii, 40.

[25] On the Coalition Liberals, see the cogent survey by K. O. Morgan, 'Lloyd George's Stage Army: The Coalition Liberals', in Taylor (ed.), *Lloyd George: Twelve Essays*, pp. 225–54. For the Unionists, see Lord Beaverbrook, *The Decline and Fall of Lloyd George* (London, 1963), *passim*.

[26] For a full discussion of the background to the Paris peace conference, see A. J. Mayer, *Politics and Diplomacy of Peacemaking: Revolution and Counter-Revolution in Europe* (London, 1968).

willingness to stand up to Clemenceau, Foch and Wilson and, in particular, warned them of the danger of Bolshevism spreading to Germany in his Fontainebleau memorandum. Simultaneously he had to out-manoeuvre both his own Secretary of State for War, Winston Churchill, and the French in their desire to intervene more actively in Russia.[27] He shrewdly realised that large-scale intervention in Russia against Bolshevism would be the most effective way of encouraging revolution in western Europe itself, which was war-weary. In addition, the labour movement in Britain was becoming more bellicose and disliked the Government's anti-Bolshevik policy. The Treaty of Versailles was accepted with extreme reluctance by Germany in June 1919. Lloyd George bore his share of responsibility for the unwise features of the treaty, especially reparations and the attempt, about which he was curiously enthusiastic, to try the ex-Kaiser.[28] Yet it has to be remembered that, harsh as it was, Germany was left virtually intact with the resources to become a formidable power again in the near future. The aspect of the treaty most distasteful to Lloyd George was the eastern frontier assigned to Germany and the existence of the Polish corridor: it seems all the more ironic that the occasion of Great Britain's entry into the Second World War in 1939 was to defend Poland.

His role on the diplomatic stage at Paris had filled Lloyd George with a desire to extend his participation in international diplomacy. His Foreign Secretary, Curzon, was willing to submit to Lloyd George's outrageously arrogant behaviour towards him and to accept the Prime Minister and the 'Garden suburb' assuming many of the functions of the Foreign Office. Lloyd George believed that personal diplomacy at the summit was the answer to pressing problems; it was preferable to the 'old diplomacy' which had culminated in the war of 1914. It was a mistaken and unfortunate conclusion. Summit diplomacy requires careful preparation if it is to succeed: frequent meetings of leaders endeavouring to resolve thorny issues in a hurried atmosphere cannot succeed. Unfortunately Lloyd George had succumbed to the meretricious glamour of foreign travel. His preoccupation with foreign policy distracted him from the domestic scene in Britain and meant that he failed to give the consistently decisive leadership in the reconstruction

[27] Roskill, ii, 45, 47, 62, 69, 70–1.
[28] D. Lloyd George, *The Truth About the Peace Treaties* (2 vols, London, 1938), i, 142.

of the country which was required and expected when he was so triumphantly re-elected. This is not to maintain that his domestic record was one of failure but rather to emphasise that he did not achieve all he could have done had he not been so preoccupied abroad. Towards the Russo-Polish war of 1919–20 his policy was muddled and uncertain but implemented with his customary tactical astuteness. Lloyd George detested the Poles and had a sneaking admiration for the Bolsheviks, which was however combined with suspicion. His policy was saved from ruins by the obstinacy and determination of Pilsudski in the battle of Warsaw, for which Lloyd George and the French claimed the credit subsequently.[29] One of the principal short-term successes of his Government lay in its contribution to the Washington conference of 1921–2; the conference agreed on the termination of the Anglo-Japanese alliance and on the adoption of ratios for capital ships to minimise dangerous naval rivalry in the Pacific. Lloyd George had originally hoped to attend the conference but the gravity of the Irish crisis precluded it. Instead the British delegation was ably led by the veteran Lord Balfour, aided by the ubiquitous Hankey.[30]

Of the domestic problems Lloyd George faced, the growing belligerence of the labour movement and the deteriorating situation in Ireland were the most serious. A new feeling of unity and common identity with an accompanying resolution to assert the latent power of the working class had swept through the labour movement in the years immediately preceding the First World War. It was in part diverted by the coming of the war, since much of the labour movement responded to the appeal of patriotism. However, in certain industries and geographical areas, notably in industrial Clydeside and in the mining valleys of south Wales, industrial discontent manifested itself in a number of conflicts. Lloyd George did not properly understand the mood of militance; he was impatient with industrial discontent during the war and tended to attribute it to pacifist or subversive elements. The war was a profound stimulus to change in every respect within British society, as in Europe as a whole. The trade unions expanded greatly in size during the war and after down to 1920. The new generation of union leaders, such as Ernest Bevin, were adamant that the conditions

[29] N. Davies, *White Eagle, Red Star: the Polish-Soviet War 1919–20* (London, 1972), pp. 167–77, 224.
[30] See I. H. Nish, *Alliance In Decline: a Study in Anglo-Japanese Relations, 1908–1923* (London, 1972), chs. xix–xxii.

of work and the wages of their members must be improved.[31] Between the spring of 1919 and the spring of 1921 the industrial situation was extremely dangerous, more so fundamentally than at the time of the General Strike in 1926. The desire for sweeping reform, the inspiration of the Russian Revolution before the ideals had begun to turn sour and the atmosphere of instability throughout Europe coalesced to confront Lloyd George with a series of crises that tested his skill and deviousness to the full. Thomas Jones, the deputy secretary of the Cabinet, wrote to him early in 1919:

'Bolshevik propaganda in this country is only dangerous in so far as it can lodge itself in the soil of genuine grievances. There is no doubt that large numbers of work-people are expecting a big and rapid improvement in their social and industrial conditions. . . .'

A definite reiteration by yourself of the Government's determination to push forward with an advanced social programme is the best antidote, and this should be followed up by instructions from you to the Departments concerned to get on with the necessary Bills at top speed. . . .[32]

Lloyd George was preoccupied with the deliberations in Paris but when he visited London was, according to Jones, 'full of schemes of dealing with the miners and the railwaymen should they come out during the next week or two'.[33] Lloyd George had promised, in his election campaign, a vigorous administration which would implement a thorough, imaginative programme of reconstruction. His promises were by no means broken: his Government extended unemployment insurance to all industries and made progress with educational and housing reforms. Nevertheless, there was no carefully directed, ambitious policy of social reform.

The major industrial confrontations occurred with the unions comprising the so-called 'Triple Alliance' of miners, railwaymen and transport workers. The triple alliance was far less formidable in practice than

[31] For a useful discussion of Bevin's attitude and of the post-war Labour movement, see A. Bullock, *The Life and Times of Ernest Bevin* (2 vols, London, 1960–7), i, 98–179. Trade union membership totalled more than 8 million in 1920, of which nearly $6\frac{1}{2}$ million were affiliated to the TUC (Bullock, i, 100, n.).

[32] Middlemas, *Thomas Jones: Whitehall Diary*, i, 73–4, Jones to Lloyd George, 8 February 1919.

[33] ibid., i, 76, Jones to Hankey, 10 February 1919.

it was on paper because there was no machinery for prior discussion and unified co-ordination between the three unions concerned; each put its own interests first and the miners in particular were truculent. However, the failure of the triple alliance did not become obvious until 1921. The miners demanded nationalisation of the coalmines in 1919 and improved wages: they declared their willingness to strike to secure their objectives. Lloyd George shrewdly offered a Commission of Inquiry, headed by a progressive judge, Sir John Sankey, and stated that the Government would be bound by the report. The miners accepted the inquiry. Evidence was given by the coal owners and miners; the miners emerged creditably. The Commission was divided in its ultimate report: Sankey favoured nationalisation but Lloyd George used the lack of unanimity as a pretext to postpone action, appreciating that his political position would not allow him to contemplate nationalisation. One victory had been won by Lloyd George. The railwaymen were also belligerent, if less so than the miners. The Government was helped by the personality of J. H. Thomas, General Secretary of the National Union of Railwaymen, who was an astute moderate disinclined to embark on conflict if he could avoid it or to maintain it once it had started. Periodic crises continued in 1920-1 and the Cabinet was most alarmed at the trend.[34] Planning developed to meet the contingency of a general strike but time was needed to prepare adequately. The most serious industrial challenge came in April 1921, when the miners decided to strike to defend the principle of national, as opposed to local, wage agreements and to prevent reductions in wages. The railwaymen and transport workers agreed to support them. Just as the strike appeared inevitable, Lloyd George cleverly exploited an equivocal statement made by the General Secretary of the Miners Federation, Frank Hodges, to open a rift within the miners' Executive and between the miners and the other two unions. Faced with a situation where the miners did not seem to know whether to accept Lloyd George's compromise proposal, the railwaymen and the transport workers reluctantly withdrew their support. 'Black Friday', as 21 April 1921 was mordantly referred to in militant labour circles, was, in the words of Thomas Jones, 'the most exciting day since the Armistice'.[35] Thereafter, the self-confidence of the unions was undermined, although militance was still pronounced

[34] Middlemas, op. cit., i, 99–103.
[35] ibid., i, 153, Jones to Bonar Law, 24 April 1921. For Bevin's view, see Bullock, *The Life and Times of Ernest Bevin*, i, 173–4.

until 1926. Equally important was the fact that economic depression had set in after the post-war boom and trade union membership declined, as the unemployment figures rose to the high level that persisted for the rest of the inter-war years. Lloyd George's achievement was that he succeeded in manoeuvring between those who wanted a confrontation: the reactionaries in his Cabinet and in the Unionist party, on the one hand, and the vociferous trade union militants, on the other. He discerned the revolutionary potential and defused the situation on critical occasions through his consummate tactical ability.

Of all the post-war problems Lloyd George handled, the one in which he faced the most bitter censure, and paradoxically also enjoyed outstanding ultimate success, was Ireland. During his premiership, he had to grapple with the climax to the long struggle for self-government in Ireland. He had striven hard to reach a settlement after the Easter Rising in 1916, when Asquith had entrusted him with the task of negotiating a solution: the attempt had foundered, as previous and subsequent attempts were to founder, over the difficulty of reconciling Ulster to Irish independence. As Prime Minister, between 1916 and 1921, Lloyd George was too preoccupied with the urgent demands of war and peace to give Ireland the concentrated attention it merited. Conditions in Ireland steadily worsened in 1916–18 as a result of the growing popularity of Sinn Fein and hostility towards England stemming from the drastic military suppression of the Easter Rising. John Redmond had courageously staked the future of the Irish parliamentary party on English sympathy for Irish Home Rule in return for his generous support of the war. The gamble had failed and the parliamentary party's authority was progressively diminished.[36] In 1917 the Government sponsored the gathering of the Irish Convention, modelled on the earlier body in South Africa which had produced the Union. The Convention fully indulged the Irish love of interminable debate but sadly failed in its mission. In March–April 1918 the war was causing such grave anxiety that Lloyd George proposed an understanding whereby the Home Rule Bill would be applied, except in Ulster, in return for the enforcement of conscription in Ireland. This was logical in view of the pressure on Lloyd George from the Unionists but was politically maladroit: it caused profound indignation and temporarily united the rising star of Sinn Fein with the declining force of the Irish

[36] For a lucid discussion of the Irish question during Lloyd George's premiership see F. S. L. Lyons, *Ireland Since the Famine* (London, 1971), pp. 380–463.

parliamentary party in a concerted campaign against the proposal.[37] It was not pursued further but the damage had been done.

In the general election of 1918 the Government pledged itself to do all possible to obtain a just and equitable solution. The prospects of attaining it were not enhanced by the return of the seventy-three Sinn Fein Members who refused to attend Westminster and of a dismal rump of six Members representing the vanished supremacy of the parliamentary party. Sinn Fein already constituted an embryo administration: in 1919–20 power increasingly fell into its hands and the grip of Dublin Castle correspondingly slackened. Opinion in England had advanced during the war: as *The Times* remarked, 'We are all Home Rulers today.'[38] Even right-wing Unionists who had trenchantly opposed Home Rule in 1912–14 were prepared to envisage its appearance so long as Ulster was not compelled to be a part of a united Ireland against its wishes. The bulk of Irish opinion was, however, no longer satisfied with Home Rule and desired full independence. Lloyd George's policy in 1919–21 was designed to persuade and then coerce Ireland into accepting a settlement. When this failed, he adroitly switched to a conciliatory policy, pursued with brilliant tactical astuteness in the negotiations with the Sinn Fein representatives between October and December 1921.

In 1920 the Government introduced the Government of Ireland Act, which set up two parliaments in Dublin and Belfast: the latter was intended to reduce the Ulster fear of subjugation to Dublin, although it was hoped that Ulster might later agree to accept unity provided reasonable autonomy was permitted. It was, ironically enough in the light of developments after 1969, accepted reluctantly by Northern Ireland; Sinn Fein contemptuously rejected it. Thereafter followed the rapid collapse of law and order in 1920–1 and the use of extreme violence by both sides in enforcing their respective policies. Lloyd George was entirely willing to envisage the use of force in Ireland. By so doing he exposed himself to severe criticism from a variety of opponents which contributed to the decline in his personal standing.[39] The rise in mutual atrocities and the sanctioning of the activities of the notorious 'Black

[37] See F. S. L. Lyons, *John Dillon: A Biography* (London, 1968), chap. 15.
[38] *The Times*, 26 March 1919, cited in D. G. Boyce, *Englishmen and Irish Troubles: British Public Opinion and the Making of Irish Policy, 1918–22* (London, 1972), p. 25.
[39] See Boyce, chapters 2–8, for a discussion of English reactions and of the activities of the Peace with Ireland Council, formed in the summer of 1920.

and Tans' offered no remedy and accentuated the weariness of British public opinion. While Lloyd George publicly defended his policy, his shrewd grasp of reality is shown by his private warning to the commander of the 'Black and Tans', General Tudor, against unnecessary coercion and by his encouragement of Archbishop Clune's unofficial mediation in 1920–1.[40] By the summer of 1921 Lloyd George recognised that the policy of coercion was bankrupt but, for political reasons, he could not proceed too swiftly in the other direction. He was dependent on the Unionists for survival and, while they were certainly more progressive than formerly, it would be impossible to expect them to accept Sinn Fein's terms. For its part, Sinn Fein was ready to negotiate: unknown to the Government, the IRA's resources were gravely depleted and Michael Collins was not optimistic about the chances of continuing the struggle.

In the new conciliatory chapter opening in July 1921, following the first discussions with de Valera, Lloyd George relied heavily on Thomas Jones and on Alfred Cope, a progressive official at Dublin Castle, to foster contacts with Sinn Fein. He revealed the whole range of his negotiating skills in the talks held in London between October and December 1921. He was conciliatory or tenacious, as the moment required, but always flexible and dynamic: the Irish delegates were no match for him. The crux of the problem was, as always, Irish unity. Sinn Fein was committed to independence for the whole of Ireland; Northern Ireland was vehemently opposed to the idea. Lloyd George had to discover some means of bridging the gap. He soon discerned that there were differences among the Sinn Fein leaders, particularly between Arthur Griffith and Michael Collins in London and de Valera in Ireland: he put pressure on Griffith especially to adhere to an undertaking he had given accepting a boundary commission to determine the frontier between the rest of Ireland and the newly defined Ulster. The alternative was a resumption of the struggle. James Craig, the Prime Minister of Northern Ireland, was intensely suspicious of the negotiations and inspired much anxiety. Lloyd George spoke of resignation if the Ulster Unionists prevented a settlement. Austen Chamberlain and his colleagues stood firm in support of Lloyd George. After heated debates among themselves, the Sinn Fein representatives signed the agreement with Lloyd George on 6 December 1921: the Irish Free State came into existence, within the British Empire as Lloyd George

[40] Boyce, pp. 55–6 and Middlemas, *Thomas Jones* . . ., iii, 44.

had insisted and contrary to the wishes of much Irish opinion. By any criteria, it was an outstanding triumph for Lloyd George.[41] However, it had come after a singularly unpleasant and distasteful period for which he bore a large share of responsibility. The stark memory of the events of 1920–1 robbed him of comprehensive appreciation of his success. It is currently and understandably fashionable to look more critically at the settlement of 1921 in the light of the breakdown of the Stormont regime in 1969–72 and of the British Government's recognition in 1972 of the need for a lasting solution to the Irish question. However, settlements should be appraised ultimately by the exigencies of the contemporary situation: there can be little doubt that Lloyd George in 1921 achieved the most satisfactory settlement feasible at that time. The failure of Stormont was arguably not inevitable; it was ensured nevertheless by the reactionary character of Ulster Unionism.[42]

Lloyd George was brought to power as a result of a major crisis in wartime necessitating new leadership; his fall from office was occasioned by fear of his leading Britain into war in the Middle East against the resurgent Turkey of Kemal Ataturk. Lloyd George had proved surprisingly successful in attracting the leaders of the Unionist party and in preserving their loyalty. Indeed attitudes within the Unionist party by 1922 were the reverse of 1916: in 1916 mass support for Lloyd George had come from the backbenchers longing for dynamic leadership and the leaders had been hesitant – in 1922 the backbenchers had had enough of dynamism but the leaders were under the magician's spell. The famous Carlton Club meeting, on 19 October 1922, reflected the extent of the disenchantment with Lloyd George; the success of the meeting was guaranteed by the contributions of two prominent Unionists who changed sides, one former colleague, Bonar Law, and one member of the Cabinet, the relatively insignificant Stanley Baldwin. The Chanak crisis symbolised rather than explained Lloyd George's fall. The decline in his standing and the growth of opposition stemmed from a combination of circumstances. He had based his appeal on vigorous,

[41] In the words of a recent historian, 'Only a negotiator as wily and indefatigable as David Lloyd George could have turned the unfavourable situation which had arisen by early November 1921 to his advantage' (Boyce, *Englishmen and Irish Troubles . . .*, pp. 167–8).

[42] See Lyons, *Ireland Since the Famine*, pp. 682–755, for an account of Northern Ireland between 1921 and 1970. For a personal view by a reforming leader, see Lord O'Neill of the Maine, *The Autobiography of Terence O'Neill* (London, 1972), pp. 40–3, 110–54.

efficient government and on the successful solution of complex problems. To many people, by 1922, the record of the Government did not
seem impressive. The Paris peace conference was a disappointment
and had not produced the stable Europe which had been hoped for. The
concatenation of other conferences engendered cynicism. When the
post-war boom broke, the economy declined with large-scale unemployment. There was chronic discontent among labour. The Irish
crisis had considerably damaged the Government. It was unfair to
blame Lloyd George personally for the disappointments and, as has
been seen, there was a positive side to most of the above issues. But
Lloyd George's record was tarnished. In addition, there was the sale of
honours and the formation of the Lloyd George political fund. Previous
governments, whether Conservative or Liberal, had sold honours for
political purposes. Lloyd George did so on a more blatant scale and
established his own fund to finance his future campaigns. In a conversation with J. C. C. Davidson, after he had left office, Lloyd George
defended his actions. According to Davidson:

I dropped the remark that Mr Lloyd George was fortunate in being
much better situated than the Conservative Party. He laughed at the
remark and, which [sic] his characteristic flair for altering his ground,
burst into an enthusiastic defence of the system of raising Party funds
by the sale of honours. 'You and I,' he said, 'know perfectly well it is a
far cleaner method of filling the Party chest than the methods used in
the United States or the Socialist Party.' He complained that the
Socialist Party was a trade union party solely because of the power of
the trade unions to withhold funds. 'In America the steel trusts supported one political party, and the cotton people supported another.
This placed political parties under the domination of great financial
interests and trusts.' 'Here,' said Mr Lloyd George, 'a man gives
£40,000 to the Party and gets a baronetcy. If he comes to the Leader
of the Party and says I subscribe largely to the Party funds, you must
do this or that, you can tell him to go to the devil.' 'The attachment of
the brewers to the Conservative Party was the closest approach.' said
Mr Lloyd George, 'to political corruption in this country. The worst
of it is you cannot defend it in public but it keeps politics far cleaner
than any other method of raising funds.'[43]

[43] R. Rhodes James, *Memoirs of a Conservative: J. C. C. Davidson's Memoirs and
Papers, 1910–37* (London, 1969), p. 279.

There was a certain robust frankness in Lloyd George's attitude, but while in office he had failed to give adequate consideration to the feeling of many people that the distribution of honours should not be abused.

Lloyd George's caution rapidly deserted him after the 1918 election. As both Hankey and Lloyd George's newspaper friend, Lord Riddell, noted he had become more arrogant, dictatorial and complacent after several years as Prime Minister and a total of seventeen years continuously as a Cabinet minister between 1905 and 1922.[44] Lloyd George had to some extent succumbed to the occupational hazard of all politicians – a belief in his own indispensability. When he surrendered the seals of office to King George V, he left Downing Street and the world of high politics for ever. He could not engineer a return to office because he did not possess a strong party of his own; he was a great leader with a dwindling band of supporters. After the Unionists rejected him, the logical answer was to join the Labour party and aim, within a short time, to become its leader. Lloyd George was undoubtedly a Radical by temperament and belonged naturally to the left rather than the right. However, he was disliked and distrusted by the most prominent Labour politicians and trade union leaders, not least by Ramsay MacDonald. The Lloyd George political fund was a further obstacle. So he remained a Liberal, nominally at any rate, until his death. Throughout the middle and later 1920s and 1930s he remained out of office, amidst all the setbacks at home and abroad, to his country's immense loss.

David Lloyd George was the most independently minded prime minister of modern times. Handicapped by the absence of a powerful party to support him, he more than made the most of the opportunities fate allowed him. This is the paradox of his leadership. It has rightly been said of him that he was a 'presidential' prime minister, 'the nearest thing England has known to a Napoleon'.[45] When his policies succeeded, he took the credit and reaped the reward, as in 1918. By 1922 the policies appeared in a more murky light; the credit balance had been used up. The future down to 1940 lay with Baldwin, MacDonald and Neville Chamberlain, men of a very different outlook.

[44] Roskill, *Hankey*, ii, 148, 215, and Lord Riddell, *Lord Riddell's Intimate Diary of the Peace Conference and After 1918–23* (London, 1933), pp. 48–9, 67.
[45] A. J. P. Taylor, *English History 1914–45* (Oxford, 1965), p. 73.

BIBLIOGRAPHY

There is no satisfactory biography of Lloyd George at present but the following works are helpful to varying degrees.

Grigg, J., *The Young Lloyd George* (London, 1973)

Jones, T., *Lloyd George* (London, 1951)

Morgan, K. O., *Lloyd George – Welsh Radical as World Statesman* (Cardiff, 1963)

Owen, F., *Tempestuous Journey: Lloyd George, his Life and Times* (London, 1954)

The diaries and memoirs of Frances Stevenson, later the Countess Lloyd-George, are valuable, particularly the former.

Lloyd George, F., *The Years That Are Past* (London, 1967)

Taylor, A. J. P. (ed.), *Lloyd George: A Diary by Frances Stevenson* (London, 1971)

On Lloyd George's premiership the following should be noted.

Blake, R., *The Unknown Prime Minister: The Life and Times of Andrew Bonar Law 1858-1923* (London, 1955); (ed.), *The Private Papers of Douglas Haig, 1914-19* (London, 1952)

Beaverbrook, Lord, *Men and Power* (London, 1956); *The Decline and Fall of Lloyd George* (London, 1963)

Boyce, D. G., *Englishmen and Irish Troubles* (London, 1972)

Bullock, A., *The Life and Times of Ernest Bevin*, vol. i (London, 1960)

Davies, N., *White Eagle, Red Star: The Polish-Soviet War, 1917-20* (London, 1972)

Kinnear, M., *The Fall of Lloyd George: The Political Crisis of 1922* (London, 1973)

Lloyd George, D. *War Memoirs* (either 6 vols, London, 1933-6 or 2 vols, London, 1938); *The Truth About the Peace Treaties* (2 vols, London, 1938)

Lyons, F. S. L., *Ireland Since the Famine* (London, 1971)

Lyons, F. S. L., *John Dillon: A Biography* (London, 1968)

Marder, A. J., *From the Dreadnought to Scapa Flow*, vols iv-v (London, 1969–70)

Mayer, A. J., *Politics and Diplomacy of Peacemaking* (London, 1968)

Middlemas, K. (ed.) *Thomas Jones: Whitehall Diary*, vols i, iii (London, 1969–71)

Morgan, K. O., *Wales in British Politics 1868-1922* (Cardiff, 1963); (ed.) *Lloyd George: Family Letters 1885-1936* (Cardiff, 1973); 'Lloyd George's Premiership: A Study in "Prime Ministerial" Government', *Historical Journal* xiii, 1 (1970), 130–57

Nish, I. H., *Alliance in Decline: Anglo-Japanese Relations 1908-23* (London, 1972)

Pakenham, F., *Peace By Ordeal* (London, 1935)

Taylor, A. J. P., *English History 1914-45* (Oxford, 1965); *Beaverbroork* (London, 1972); (ed.) *Lloyd George: Twelve Essays* (London, 1971)

Ullman, R., *Anglo-Soviet Relations 1917-21* (3 vols, London, 1961–73)

Wilson, T., *The Downfall of the Liberal Party 1914-35* (London, 1966); (ed.) *The Political Diaries of C. P. Scott 1911-28* (London, 1970)

ANDREW BONAR LAW

BY

JOHN RAMSDEN

Andrew Bonar Law. PC (1911), LLD (Glasgow). Born in Canada 16 September 1858 and later moved to Glasgow. Educated in Canada, then at Gilbertsfield School (Hamilton) and Glasgow High School. In business in Glasgow 1885–1900. Married 1891 Annie Pitcairn Robley; two sons, two daughters. MP for Glasgow (Blackfriars) 1900–06; Parliamentary Secretary to the Board of Trade 1902; MP for Dulwich 1906–10, Bootle 1911–18; PC and leader of the Conservative Party 1911; Colonial Secretary under Asquith 1915–16; Chancellor of the Exchequer and Leader of the Commons under Lloyd George 1916–18; MP for Glasgow Central 1918–23; Lord Privy Seal 1919; resigned for reasons of ill-health 1921; Prime Minister 1922; resigned and died 1923. Member of the War Cabinet 1916–19; Leader of the Unionist Party 1912–21.

Andrew Bonar Law

ANDREW BONAR LAW

Bonar Law was Prime Minister for a shorter term than any other modern premier: becoming Prime Minister on 23 October 1922, he was obliged to retire through ill health on 20 May 1923, and died in October 1923. However, before this he had been leader of the Conservative party for ten years and had been Leader of the House of Commons and *de facto* deputy Prime Minister to Lloyd George from 1916 to 1921. Thus, although Prime Minister for such a short time, Law had already been at the summit of British politics for a decade. Moreover, his seven months as Prime Minister were filled with serious problems and decisions, the importance of which were only grasped later. It was during this period that British politics returned to 'normalcy' after the hot house years of Lloyd George's rule. It was therefore necessary for the new Government to decide how far to proceed with the dismantling of the coalition system of government, both in terms of institutions and policies, and in terms of political style. An equivalent tidying-up problem in foreign affairs concerned the settlement of debts incurred during the World War. In all of these affairs, Law exerted an important influence; it was perhaps only because of the shortness of his premiership that he was able to make such a small impact on the popular mind, but a further explanation of his political obscurity must be found.

When leaving Law's funeral service at Westminster Abbey, Herbert Asquith is reputed to have remarked, 'It is fitting that we should have buried the Unknown Prime Minister by the side of the Unknown Soldier'. The anecdote circulated widely and became the title of Robert Blake's biography of Law.[1] As a book, *The Unknown Prime Minister* did a great deal to rescue Law from oblivion, but its title perhaps did even more to bury him. Many who know nothing else about Law, now know that he was unknown; but this is to miss the real point of Asquith's remark, which contained a certain element of truth as well as an intention to denigrate. Law was in fact no less well known than any other Prime Minister in the sense of being known to be Prime Minister.

[1] Robert Blake, *The Unknown Prime Minister* (London, 1955), p. 13 and *passim*.

Where Law differed from a man like Asquith himself was in the depth of knowledge the public was allowed to share, the depth of personal and private feelings that was exposed. In this more limited sense, it cannot be denied that Law always remained a shadowy figure to those outside his immediate circle of colleagues. Famous he may have been but familiar he never was, and this is perhaps the most interesting aspect of his entire career. He was the first *ordinary* man to hold the highest political office in Britain – the first Prime Minister who asked the public to identify with him as an equal rather than to admire him as a hero figure.

Law was in no sense a brilliant man and, like Baldwin after him, he was able to make a virtue out of his lack of brilliance. In so far as Law had a public image at all it must have been as a rather pedestrian figure, a man with no warmth of character, with a narrow mind, and with no small-talk. Politically, he was seen as near the extreme right of his party and tinged with a reactionary bigotry. Very little of this public image had any foundation in fact and to those few who knew him well, Law gave an exactly opposite impression. The men who became personal friends were not men likely to enjoy the company of a narrow-minded boor, and both Lloyd George and Beaverbrook relied heavily on him.[2] His greatest advantage, which explains his attraction to the brilliant men of his day, was his ability to listen and then to make sound commonsense criticisms of the high-flown schemes suggested to him. Outsiders saw him as hard and brutal but his friends saw him as all too indecisive and unassuming. As for his reputation for bigotry, this can be explained entirely in terms of what he did for political advantage. In 1913 and 1914, Law had encouraged Protestant Ulster to the point of civil war against the British Government, but behind the scenes he had been working strenuously for a compromise settlement.[3] Without Law's inflammatory speeches, the Unionists could never have got such a good deal out of Asquith's Liberal Government as they were getting by 1914. In effect, Law was tough-minded enough to risk more than the Government over Ireland and because of this he gained more. To a liberal intellectual like Asquith, Law's tough but realistic Irish policy was not only repugnant but also incomprehensible. Law defied political conventions further by the direct and unaffected style of his public speeches and by his refusal to get involved in the normal Westminster round of

[2] A. J. P. Taylor, *Beaverbrook* (London, 1972), pp. 46-7 and p. 211.
[3] Blake, op. cit., p. 149.

dinners, parties and receptions.[4] In this sense too, Asquith was speaking truly when he said that he did not know Law. However, by 1922, Law's past career had furnished him with considerable experience of power politics, and the way in which he finally achieved the premiership provided a further lesson.

Law had retired because of his health in 1921 and remained on the touchline of politics for the last eighteen months of the Lloyd George Coalition. As that Government sank deeper into crisis in 1922, it was to Law that the dissident Conservatives turned for a lead.[5] Normally loyal, Conservatives found it difficult to justify a rebellion and so the presence of an ex-leader in the wings provided an important legitimating factor for rebellion against Austen Chamberlain, Law's successor in the party leadership. At this supreme crisis of his career, with the highest prize his for the taking, Law was tortured by doubts. He was being dragged back into politics despite continued bad health and he could only return over the political corpse of Austen Chamberlain, for many years his loyal supporter. Torn by loyalty and duty on one side and friendship on the other, Law wrote a letter to his constituency chairman, announcing his retirement from politics; he then showed the letter to Beaverbrook, who converted him, as he was probably intended to do.[6] As so often at moments of crisis, Law needed reassurance before taking crucial decisions, but he was incapable of refusing his party's call. He therefore attended the Carlton Club meeting to vote against a continuance of the Coalition and his very presence helped to secure the Coalition's fall. Law thus became Conservative leader again and was almost automatically asked to form a government, for the Conservatives already had an overall majority. Here Law demonstrated his weakness by refusing the King's commission until he had been formally elected as leader of his party.[7] He was elected unanimously – for his coalitionist rivals were not prepared to push the disagreement so far as actually to permit a contested election for the party leadership. Once elected, Law immediately accepted the King's invitation and was able to draw on all the reserves of party loyalty to the leader in forming his Government. It was thus that Law became Prime Minister by a sort of legal rebellion, legal in that it was quite obviously the right of the Conservative party

---

[4] Blake, op. cit., p. 87.
[5] Maurice Cowling, *The Impact of Labour* (Cambridge, 1971), p. 206.
[6] Taylor, *Beaverbrook*, p. 197.
[7] Blake, *The Unknown Prime Minister*, p. 459.

to change its leader if it wished to do so, and yet still a rebellion which left a legacy of mistrust and opposition.

Law's great problem in forming his Government was the refusal of most of the late Cabinet to join the new one; Austen Chamberlain had suggested that if the party had no confidence in its leaders then they must find new leaders, and it was to Law that the task fell. Success was made more likely by the fact that not all of the late ministers shared Austen Chamberlain's views: Lord Curzon, Stanley Baldwin and Sir Arthur Griffith-Boscawen from the Lloyd George Cabinet agreed to serve with Law, and most of the junior ministers agreed to serve. What was lacking was the whole group of experienced coalitionist ministers – Austen Chamberlain, Lord Birkenhead, Arthur Balfour, Winston Churchill, Sir Robert Horne and Sir Laming Worthington-Evans.[8] No government could ignore such men and there is no doubt that they were missed, for what the new Government lacked was not so much ability as experience. Into the Cabinet for the first time in 1922–3 came Neville Chamberlain, Sir Philip Lloyd-Graeme, L. S. Amery, Edward Wood; Sir Douglas Hogg and Sir Samuel Hoare became junior ministers and Stanley Baldwin became Chancellor of the Exchequer after little over a year in the Cabinet. Like Pitt's first Government in 1783, the Law Cabinet had to stagger on with a surfeit of peers, shunned by most big political names, but finally vindicated by the electorate. The new ministry was dismissed contemptuously by Birkenhead as 'a government of the second eleven', but if the first team were all sulking in the pavilion, where else was Law to find his players? From the talent available to him, Law chose wisely, although the care lavished on the senior posts was not always repeated at the next level, as Sir Robert Sanders noted:

Yesterday I was offered & accepted Ministry of Agriculture. The manner of it was quaint. Stanley Baldwin dashed in about 7 p.m. 'Peter will you take Agriculture?' 'Yes, love to' I said. 'All right that's settled' and off he went. Went to the Palace this morning & kissed hands as PC & then took oath as Minister . . .. So far it is a real old Tory Cabinet. Of the H. of C. members most of us are intimate friends. It is curious that Peel, Baldwin & I were all in the Upper Sixth at Harrow together.[9]

[8] Cowling, *The Impact of Labour*, p. 214.
[9] Diary of Sir Robert Sanders, 25 October 1922. I am grateful to Hon. Mrs V. E. Butler for permission to quote from the diary.

This description includes almost all of the characteristics of the Law Cabinet, its easy informality, its 'real Old Tory' complexion, and the importance of Baldwin. The Carlton Club meeting, called not by the rebels but by the then leader Austen Chamberlain, had been attacked as a 'reactionary intrigue', and so by extension the new Government was soon labelled as 'reactionary'. If it was reactionary at all, it was only in its composition and this of course was forced on Law; it did in any case include several members like Hoare and Wood who were well to the left of the party. The only other problem of composition occurred when Griffith-Boscawen lost his seat at the general election; after a frenzied search, Griffith-Boscawen fought a by-election at Mitcham but when that too was lost he retired from politics. This further loss of experience was partially mitigated by the promotion of Neville Chamberlain to the Cabinet.

It might have been expected, in view of the Cabinet's lack of political experience and its dependence on Law for its very existence, that it would have been under his close control. That would be to misjudge Law, who preferred not to dominate his Cabinet but to leave ministers free to run their own departments. This policy was to be subjected to severe strain with Baldwin's settlement of war debts, but it also resulted in Chamberlain's 1923 Housing Act, a major piece of social reforming legislation. It was in the Cabinet itself that the Law Government made its most important decision, when it decided to prune but not to abolish the apparatus of Cabinet secretarial assistance which it had inherited from the Coalition Government. No secretariat had existed before the First World War, and only military necessity had changed the practice, but in the years after the war the whole system became tied up with Lloyd George's personal style of government. The teams of policy- and press-advisers who were imported into Downing Street by Lloyd George were regarded as a serious constitutional impropriety and this 'garden suburb' was further discredited by its connection with the honours scandals of 1921 and 1922. As usual, Law took a realistic line and decided to retain the secretariat itself while removing most of the rest of the apparatus.[10]

However, before the Government could begin its term, it was plunged into an immediate general election. Law decided on a general election in order to establish the new Government, and it was announced three days after his appointment as Prime Minister. An election victory

[10] H. Daalder, *Cabinet Reform in Great Britain* (London, 1964), p. 60.

would not only give a full five years of office, but it would also discredit those Conservatives who had stayed outside the Government and who would be greatly embarrassed by an election campaign. The keynote of Law's election campaign was therefore the apostolic line of Conservative succession whereby he himself was the practising heir of Disraeli and Lord Salisbury. Law also made a clear distinction between his new Government and the last one; in speeches and in his manifesto, he defined his policy as 'tranquillity', and his picture appeared on pamphlets with the slogan 'Safety First'. A contrast was to be made between the 'dynamic force' of the Lloyd George Government and the peaceful tranquillity of Law's Conservatism. Taunts about the new Government's 'second-class brains' can only have helped, for the reputation of clever politicians stood rather low after the Lloyd George Government. Law reaffirmed pre-war Conservative policy in its negative as well as its positive forms.[11] Thus he gave a pledge that tariffs would not be introduced without a further general election – identical to the pledge he had given in 1913. He also reaffirmed the determination of the Conservatives to get on with the reform of the House of Lords, left unfinished by the Liberals in 1911 and shirked by all subsequent governments. (In the event, the Law Government too failed to grasp this nettle.) The most important issue of all, Ireland, had been implicitly settled by the decision to call an election in November 1922; such urgency was only necessary if Parliament was to meet again before the end of 1922 in order to pass legislation within the time-table of the Government of Ireland Act. Despite pressure from extremists in his own party, Law refused to go back on the Irish Treaty negotiated by Lloyd George in 1921; Ulster had won a good bargain from the prolonged struggle over Home Rule and it was not in Law's nature to fight for abstract principles. In this as in all other areas, Law sought to present a picture of a party that would avoid confrontations and antagonisms. Above all, his Government would return politics to the conditions of peace which had not prevailed since 1914. Law's personal message to the electors concluded:

There are many measures of legislative and administrative importance which, in themselves, would be desirable . . . but I do not feel that they can, at this moment, claim precedence over the nation's first need,

[11] F. W. S. Craig (ed), *British General Election Manifestos* (Chichester, 1970), pp. 10–12.

which is, in every walk of life, to get on with its own work with the minimum of interference at home and of disturbance abroad.[12]

Law seems to have grasped intuitively the electorate's deep feeling of nostalgia for the years before the war; more than anything, what was wanted was a period of rest and recovery, of no crises and no great changes. Perhaps that was merely what Law himself wanted, but apparently his view was shared by those who voted in 1922.

The Conservative party won in 1922 its first election victory since 1900 and secured the overall parliamentary majority that Law and his party managers had expected. In fact, the victory was based heavily on the splitting of the anti-Conservative vote in many constituencies, but surprise at the result itself gave the Government a good deal of new confidence. Law now seemed set for five years of Conservative government in the traditional style. This moment of triumph would perhaps have come, but for the war, in 1916, but now it was too late, for Law himself had less than a year to live.

The one major Cabinet crisis that occurred between the election victory of November 1922 and Law's resignation in May 1923 found Law in conflict with the whole of his Cabinet. In January, Baldwin returned from Washington, where he had been seeking a final settlement of all outstanding loans.[13] In relation to the United States, Britain was a net debtor to a considerable extent and the only argument was about the rate of repayment and the rate of interest. It was felt that a quick settlement would help to steady the international credit system and would encourage other countries to settle outstanding debts. However, Baldwin unfortunately leaked details of his proposals to the press on his return and thereby precipitated an international political crisis. Once the proposals were known in the United States, it became impossible to expect any further improvement in what many regarded as a highly disadvantageous settlement. Instead of considering proposals to which it was in no way committed, the Cabinet found itself instead faced with a choice between the proposals and the Chancellor of the Exchequer. Many of the Cabinet disliked the proposals, but only Law wished to turn them down and thereby to challenge the American Government to a showdown. Isolated in his own Cabinet, Law considered resignation, but great pressure was exerted on him and he

[12] Craig, op. cit., p. 12.
[13] K. Middlemas and J. Barnes, *Baldwin* (London, 1969), p. 143.

finally agreed to stay on and accept the majority decision. It was unprecedented for a Prime Minister to take up an issue, find it rejected by
his own Cabinet and yet not resign. There was however at least one
exact precedent in the past career of Law himself, when he had
announced a change in the party's tariff policy in 1912. After much
pressure he had finally given way, and after further persuasion he had
agreed to stay on as leader.[14] As Prime Minister, Law continued to place
the unity of the party as of higher value than any matter of policy. 'I
must follow them, I am their leader,' he is reputed to have said. There
is no better case than the US debt settlement of 1923 to illustrate the
weakness of a prime minister who is concerned to preserve party unity.
On the merits of the case, however, Law was probably right; other
countries which were not so keen to settle their debts quickly were able
to secure much better terms later. At the time though, Law was in a
minority of one, and he was not assertive enough to press his views
against such odds.[15]

At the end of April, Law was advised to go on a sea voyage because
of a further illness, and in May he collapsed and resigned. He was then
found to be suffering from an incurable throat cancer, which can only
have been worsened by the strains of the previous six months. His last
political action was a curiously ambiguous one, concerning the choice
of Baldwin as his successor.[16] Law certainly refused to give formal
advice to the King but equally certainly he favoured Baldwin for the
succession. Eventually, a memorandum by his former secretary, J. C. C.
Davidson, was shown to the King as if it did represent Law's view and
this document was an important influence towards the selection of
Baldwin rather than Curzon. Perhaps Law could simply not bring himself to face the prospect of thwarting the hopes of Curzon, the only one
of the party's old guard who had stood by him in the last six months. It
was not so surprising, however, that Law really favoured Baldwin, for
after all Baldwin was his protégé and was a politician made in his own
image. Law had been Conservative leader during most of Baldwin's
career in politics, and Baldwin was PPS to Law in 1916; in many ways,
Baldwin's public image as a politician was made up of Law's private
virtues, and like Law he prized honesty more than brilliance. However,
as well as a political style, Law also handed on to Baldwin a whole new

[14] Blake, *The Unknown Prime Minister*, p. 115.
[15] Blake, op. cit., p. 494.
[16] R. Rhodes James, *Memoirs of a Conservative* (London, 1969), p. 154.

generation of party leaders. The men promoted ahead of their time into Law's Cabinet of 1922 were, with very few exceptions, to remain at the head of British politics for the rest of the inter-war years.

Law died on 30 October 1923, and typically his will asked that he should be buried quietly. His friends and colleagues refused this last request and so Law became the first Prime Minister to be buried in Westminster Abbey since Gladstone in 1898. Appropriately, Baldwin spoke about the death of Law to the House of Commons; he spoke of the personal and national loss which had been sustained, but most of all he spoke of the gentle and considerate man that the public and even many politicians had never known.[17]

BIBLIOGRAPHY

Blake, R., *The Unknown Prime Minister: The Life and Times of Andrew Bonar Law 1858-1923* (London, 1955); *The Conservative Party from Peel to Churchill* (London, 1970)

Cowling, M., *The Impact of Labour, 1920-24* (London, 1971)

James, R. Rhodes (ed.), *Memoirs of a Conservative: J. C. C. Davidson's Letters and Papers* (London, 1969)

Taylor, A. J. P., *Beaverbrook* (London, 1972)

Taylor, H. A., *The Strange Case of Andrew Bonar Law* (London, 1932)

[17] Stanley Baldwin, *On England* (London, 1926), p. 169.

STANLEY BALDWIN

BY

KEITH MIDDLEMAS

*Stanley Baldwin, created Earl Baldwin of Bewdley, 1937. Born
3 August 1867, son of Alfred Baldwin, ironmaster, and Louise
Macdonald, one of four sisters, the others marrying Edward Burne-
Jones, Lockwood Kipling and Edward Poynter. Educated at Harrow
and Trinity College, Cambridge. Joined the family business.
Married Lucy Ridsdale 1892; two sons and four daughters. MP
for Bewdley 1908 in succession to his father; private secretary to
Bonar Law and Financial Secretary to the Treasury under the Lloyd
George Coalition Government. President of the Board of Trade
1921; took the initiative in the revolt of junior ministers which
resulted in the fall of the Government. Chancellor of the Exchequer
1922–23; Prime Minister in preference to Curzon 1923; leader of
the Opposition 1924; Prime Minister 1924–29; consented to serve
in MacDonald's 'National' Government of 1931; Prime Minister
1935–1937 (retired). Died December 1947.*

Stanley Baldwin, 1st Earl of Bewdley, by R. G. Eves

STANLEY BALDWIN

A well-tried story of the early 1920s had Churchill, playing chess with Asquith, urge his opponent to open up the field – 'Get out your Baldwins' (pawns). Yet, twenty-five years later, when Baldwin's Worcestershire memorial was dedicated at a dismal, sparsely attended ceremony in 1948, Churchill, alone of the ministers of the inter-war years, came down and spoke: 'He was the most formidable politician I have ever known in public life.' Rarely has the reputation of a prime minister in modern history fluctuated so violently as did Baldwin's, between public ignorance after the First World War and extravagant vituperation in the middle of the Second, adulation on his retirement in 1937 and cautious reappraisal in more recent years.

To many of those who in May 1923 queried why the self-effacing Chancellor of the Exchequer should have been preferred as Prime Minister to Lord Curzon, glittering ex-Viceroy of India and ex-Foreign Secretary, it seemed that Baldwin was indeed Churchill's 'pawn' and that Curzon's failings were alone responsible – his notorious antipathy to the nascent Labour party, and the fact that he could never take a seat in the House of Commons. Until the beginning of his longest term of office, in 1925, Baldwin's public presence, and the observations of many of his Cabinet colleagues, still echoed Curzon's disdain at being rejected for such a man. As Thomas Jones wrote, in friendly disparagement, after his first acquaintance with the family in 1923, 'I am never sure whether the PM is thinking at all or simply wool-gathering. Here in his rural home one feels the old England of the villages is getting a bit of its own back in the person of S.B.'[1]

Political observers found it more than strange that a man who had spent his first eight years in the House of Commons as an orthodox backbencher should after another seven take the highest office. It was a shorter parliamentary career than that of any politician since the growth of national parties in the nineteenth century, but, in sharp contrast to the youthful leaders such as Rosebery and Gaitskell, Baldwin did not

[1] R. K. Middlemas (ed.), *Thomas Jones: Whitehall Diary* (3 vols, London, 1969–71), i, 256.

even become an MP until he was forty-one. The nearest parallel is Campbell-Bannerman, Prime Minister at sixty-nine; but he died two years after, whereas Baldwin's three terms spanned nearly the whole inter-war period.

The view of him as a compromise candidate put up by the Conservative managers to calm the rough tides of opinion in the party after the fall of Lloyd George's Coalition drew some colour from Baldwin's resemblance to familiar Tory stereotypes: the successful businessman turned politician, expert in a narrow field, like the men Lloyd George had relied on in the war, such as Lords Weir and Cowdray; or the magnate with wide influence in the countryside and on the 1900 Committee, such as Baldwin's real political friends, William Bridgeman and Edward Wood (Lord Halifax). For his achievements appeared modest. His successful industrial experience, at work, first for his ironmaster father, and then after 1908 as financial director of Baldwin & Sons, was recognised by Bonar Law, and then by Lloyd George who made him Financial Secretary to the Treasury in 1916. Here, in what was one of the more important posts outside the Cabinet, and as deputy to Bonar Law, Leader of the House, he acquired the political standing he had lacked and significant acquaintance with Whitehall and the mandarins of the Treasury. But he accepted the prevailing financial orthodoxy and he could be found, as the war ended, urging the need for retrenchment and economy in order to face what he, like most ministers, feared would be a peacetime slump. His famous gesture after the Armistice, in which he donated one-fifth of his total fortune (£120,000) to the nation 'as a thank-offering in the firm conviction that never again shall we have such a chance of giving our country that form of help which is so vital at the present time',[2] was made anonymously, and signed simply 'F.S.T.'. In the post-war euphoria scarcely anyone emulated his example.

Later, as President of the Board of Trade, he was responsible for such undramatic but useful measures as the Safeguarding of Industries Act, and for the extension of government authority in the fields of statistical information, standardisation and merchandise marks. In a still unprofessional age, his influence, like that of A. J. Balfour and Lord Haldane, was directed towards making the sphere of government administration, vastly extended as a result of the war, both effective and efficient.

[2] The Times, 24 June 1919.

There was nothing here, except a notable Cabinet dispute over tariffs, under the Safeguarding Act (of all things, centred on the duty on fabric gloves), to turn Baldwin against the leadership of Lloyd George, which the chiefs of the Conservative party, Law, Birkenhead and Austen Chamberlain, seemed likely to endorse in perpetuity. His reasons were private, though only partly personal. He believed in what he called 'the morally disintegrating effect of Lloyd George on all whom he had to deal with', whether MPs, Civil Servants, trade unionists or the public; and he regarded Lloyd George's relations with the press barons, Lords Northcliffe, Beaverbrook and Rothermere, as a close conspiracy alien to the proprieties of Cabinet government. Like his close friend, J. C. C. Davidson, he knew enough of the world of Maundy Gregory, where honours were traded, like groceries, with the prices clearly marked, to feel that 'the system was poisoning the whole atmosphere of public life'.

He felt the political decay of the Coalition even more keenly. Lloyd George was a parliamentary middleman, a broker who, in order to contain a 'ministry of all the talents', could destroy the two-party system by eviscerating both Liberals and Conservatives. Baldwin might have used Disraeli's words on Peel to describe him: 'He is so vain that he wants to figure in history as the settler of all the great questions; but a parliamentary constitution is not favourable to such ambitions; things must be done by parties, not by persons using parties as tools.'[3] Wedded unquestioningly to party politics, Baldwin was to see a supreme need after 1922 'to restore and maintain the unity of the party' – not least because, looking across the Channel, he saw only the weakness of the Weimar Constitution, and the shifting, corrupt alliances of the Fourth Republic in France. These feelings sustained a hostility to Lloyd George which lasted into the 1930s.

Of course when Baldwin, appalled at the Chanak affair and at the bellicose stand against Turkey made in defence of his pro-Greek policy by Lloyd George, decided in October 1922 to resign from the Cabinet in protest and stand as a free Conservative, he did not break up the Coalition single-handed. That needed a majority of junior ministers, who had watched anxiously Lloyd George's manoeuvrings for a general election on the Coalition platform, dissident Cabinet ministers, Sir George Younger, the party Chairman, and the Chief Whip, as well as the cumulative pressure of party agents and the press; and finally,

[3] Robert Blake, *Disraeli* (London, 1966), p. 223.

decisively, the presence of Bonar Law at the Carlton Club meeting on 19 October. It needed the external decay of the Coalition, the ruin of Lloyd George's European policy after the break-up of the Genoa Conference, the grave estrangement of the Dominions after Chanak, and the spectre of mass unemployment at home.

Yet the role of catalyst is not insignificant. Baldwin saw clearly what he was doing and he carried weight, though not in terms of public affiliations. His speech at the Carlton Club, with its mordant phrases – 'The Prime Minister is a dynamic force and it is from that very fact that our troubles arise. . . . It is owing to that dynamic force that the Liberal party has been smashed to pieces. . . . I think that, if the present association is continued, you will see the process go on inevitably until the old Conservative party is lost in ruins' – was second in effect only to Bonar Law's. He lacked, of course, the political birthright of a Chamberlain or a Churchill and at that time he lacked Cabinet presence. Tom Jones wrote in 1921 of 'the long silences of S.B.'. But he represented the party, pillaged of its leaders by Lloyd George and vulnerable in the constituencies to the threat of a politically mature Labour party. He also had won the high esteem of powerful Civil Servants, Sir Norman Warren Fisher, the Head of the Treasury, Sir Maurice Hankey, Secretary of the Cabinet, and Treasury officials such as Bradbury, Leith-Ross, Niemeyer; even of Maynard Keynes, who looked to him to help solve the intricate problems of the post-war European economy. His party political base, built up during the war, when he played host to the Tory opponents of Asquith, was only enhanced by the break from Lloyd George. He was respected in the City and in business circles and, as Chancellor, was favoured by Montagu Norman, Governor of the Bank of England.

A man for the post-war Establishment, then, and a fit heir for Bonar Law, since his record on the crucial post-war issues was impeccable, in the party sense. Baldwin had stood to the right over the Irish Treaty, though not with the diehards against it. He had advocated economy and retrenchment in 1919, yet dissociated himself (in his own famous phrase) from 'the hard-faced men who looked as if they had done well out of the war'. His speeches on social policy since 1908 had been humane and liberal, his record as an employer was outstanding by pre-war standards, and (unlike Lloyd George) he was respected by trade unionist MPs and by the Labour party as a whole. He believed, as did most men in government, in the need to restore the international trading network, and the Gold Standard at the pre-war parity. Unlike many of his colleagues, he was familiar with the Continent from pre-war experience. He spoke French fluently, and a little German, and, like Mac-Donald in 1924, found no difficult in casting his policy in a European mould.

Above all, Baldwin claimed to stand for well-tried things and traditional remedies, at a time of intense Conservative sensitivity to the dangers threatening the social framework. Revolution in Russia and Germany, inflation across Europe, war in Ireland, thunderous discontent at home, had left even the Cabinet unsure whether peace could ever wholly be restored. Beside the paladins surrounding Lloyd George, he seemed mundane; a sound family man, a good churchman, a lover of the country, a speaker who could distil the quintessence of English history into words and talk openly about 'the things that strike down into the very depths of our nature, and touch chords that go back to the beginning of time and the human race'. The public picture of affable sympathy, as it became known through columnists and cartoonists, ignored both his classical literacy and the high degree of nervous tension which enjoined frequent rest and travel abroad, but it was not unrecognisable. When Baldwin explained the results of the election that returned Bonar Law as Prime Minister, he quoted Lloyd George's disparaging phrase that Law was 'honest to the point of simplicity'; 'By God,' he went on, 'that is what we have been looking for.'[4] He might have been speaking of himself.

Law made him Chancellor of the Exchequer. In the six months at the Treasury, he had to cope principally with the intractable problem of the British war debt to the United States which, four years after the Armistice, had become a festering sore. The Americans contended that Britain was wholly responsible, while the terms of the Balfour Note, suggesting the general trading-off of all inter-allied debts, amounted, as Baldwin told a City friend, to the jibe, 'We will pay you if we must, but you will be cads if you ask us to do so'. Baldwin went to Washington in January 1923 and after tough but amicable talks with the American Treasury, the Commission on the Debt, and East Coast bankers, reached an agreement which provided for annual payments of $161m for ten years and $184m for a further fifty-two, harsh in comparison with British aspirations but generous in relation to American. Law objected and was furious when discussion was effectively pre-empted

[4] *Whitehall Diary*, i, 241.

by the unguarded remarks Baldwin made to journalists on his arrival at Southampton. In Cabinet, however, the Prime Minister was isolated, and upset so greatly that his close friend Lord Beaverbrook believed the episode hastened his premature death.

That he risked such political conflict with his leader, and a public outcry in the press, can be explained by Baldwin's synoptic approach to the problem not only of inter-allied debts, especially those of France to Britain, but of German reparations, unpaid since the end of 1921, the spiralling inflation of both German and French currencies, and the disastrous outcome of the French military occupation of the Ruhr (the attempt 'to dig out coal with bayonets') early in 1923. As Chancellor and later Prime Minister, Baldwin saw the absolute need to re-establish the European exchange rates and normal trading relations, if British industry were to be able to recover. Thus the results of the debt settlement – an improvement of the pound against the dollar, and a warmer American attitude towards Europe's financial troubles – must be seen together with the long, tortuous bargaining to get France out of the Ruhr, and the personal confrontation between Baldwin and the French premier Raymond Poincaré, in September 1923. The lines came together with the *entente* between the two new Prime Ministers, Herriot and MacDonald, in 1924 and the first sensible settlement of reparations by the committee headed by an American, General Dawes. For this and the changed climate, for the brief golden years after Locarno, Baldwin deserves some credit.

During the intricate king-making of May 1923, at least four participants could claim to have influenced the choice, yet in the end, with his accustomed shrewd common sense (and against the urging of Lord Stamfordham, his private secretary) King George V made his own choice. Baldwin took his elevation with a mixture of wry humour, humility and religious dedication. Meanwhile the Central Office set the press to make him more widely known; the story of F.S.T. was leaked, and one sardonic observer wrote: 'All of us are astonished at the swiftness of his ascent. . . . A plain man, domesticated like B.L., fond of books and music and walks in the country. Nothing like B.L.'s brain – much slower, and always eager to consult one or two others; but stands by his decisions, once taken.'[5]

Passive expectation was belied. Baldwin had been a protectionist since 1903 when his father followed Joseph Chamberlain's original

[5] *Whitehall Diary*, i, 237.

Tariff Campaign. He became convinced, during his summer holiday at Aix-les-Bains, that protection was the only remaining cure for unemployment, then totalling $1\frac{1}{2}$ million, or 10 per cent of the (insured) working population. There were also other reasons; strong pressure had built up in the Cabinet in preceding months, much of it the result of clamour by interested groups of industrialists. The Prime Ministers of South Africa, Australia and New Zealand made keen bids for quotas and tariff agreements at the Imperial Conference in October; and there was a chance of splitting off the remaining Tory coalitionists, Austen Chamberlain, Birkenhead and their followers, and perhaps even the Liberal, Churchill, from Lloyd George.

Unfortunately, Bonar Law had left the damaging heritage of a promise of no major fiscal change without a general election. The 1923 tariff policy did not touch corn, but it did represent the reversal of a century of British policy. Although Baldwin, in an exercise of almost presidential power, pushed it through Cabinet in a single meeting, he was constrained by party divisions, chiefly between the Cecils and the Chamberlains, and by the fear that Lloyd George himself might switch from free trade, to exempt food and call a general election. At its best, his policy stood for help to the declining staple industries where unemployment was heaviest, and for the development of reciprocal trade with the Empire; but during the campaign the message bore all the signs of the confusion that was still endemic in the party. Against the old cry of 'dear food' raised by the Liberals, who united under Lloyd George and Asquith for the first time since 1916, it was not enough. Against the Conservatives' 257 seats, the Liberals held 158, Labour 191, and by courtesy of Asquith, the first Labour Government took office.

The *cognoscenti* expected Baldwin to fall and be forgotten. He had indeed to eat humble pie: the Lancashire interest and Austen Chamberlain exacted a pledge not to reintroduce a tariff without clear proof of a change in public opinion. There were attempts to enforce his resignation. But they failed; and as 1924 passed, sweeping MacDonald away on a tide of anti-Russian sentiment, Baldwin and the party were strengthened precisely because of the way party politics had been polarised. The Coalition Conservatives came into the fold; and Churchill also – though not without a storm which led Baldwin to write, 'Leading the party is like driving pigs to market'. Meanwhile Lloyd George, by his own choice shackled to the increasingly obsolete doctrine of free trade, and cut off again from Asquith, was reduced over the next decade

to offering himself, his brilliant schemes, and his fund, to the highest
bidder in what had become again, and despite his efforts, a two-party
system.

During his time in opposition, Baldwin began the long process of
party reform. With Neville Chamberlain as his instrument, a new
manifesto, *Aims and Principles*, was published; the Shadow Cabinet was
formalised for the first time, and a series of party committees set up,
responsible to the leader rather than to Central Office. In the summer
of 1924, in a series of major speeches, Baldwin launched what came to
be called the 'New Conservatism'. It was his only populist experiment,
but it was successful in the hardest task of an opposition, which is to
capture attention in the teeth of the reigning government. Many of the
themes of the next decade were already evident: the needs of Imperial
defence, despite arms limitation; independence for India; peace in
industry, and schemes for housing and social welfare. Out of 1923
Baldwin had also learnt the value of political education. In future, over
industrial strife, India and rearmament, he was to wait, some thought
too long, until the electorate had been taught to accept what his governments proposed. Deductions from one episode reinforced his natural
caution and became a cardinal rule of democracy. So, as Lord Haldane
wrote, 'Baldwin has established himself. He is out to develop a democratic Conservatism – and he has a great deal of sympathy with the
aspirations of Labour'.[6]

Before the election of 1929, Baldwin chose not to issue a manifesto
but to fight on his Government's record and to attack the manifestos of
his opponents. Conservative spokesmen claimed that record could
stand beside the Governments of Disraeli or Gladstone or of 1906.
Although historians, counting the total of the unemployed, have on the
whole been less flattering, by most political standards it was a great reforming ministry.

The Conservatives began with one of their two absolute majorities
in this century, with over 50 per cent of the vote in contested seats, and
415 MPs against 152 Labour and only 42 Liberals. Whatever the effect
of the 'red scare' and the Zinoviev letter, this result suggested that 1923
had been only a momentary revival in the prolonged death of Liberal
England. The Cabinet Baldwin chose was as formidable as the majority
in the House of Commons, for it included Curzon, Balfour, Churchill,
Hailsham, Salisbury, Austen and Neville Chamberlain, Birkenhead,

[6] Baldwin papers.

Steel-Maitland, Hoare, Amery and Cunliffe-Lister. It was more difficult, however, to lead than to choose such a *galerie* of talent. Many of them, in their letters and memoirs, suggested that Baldwin, like a Disraeli in carpet slippers, had led from behind, and that successes accrued to them as individuals – particularly the Chamberlains and the Chancellor of the Exchequer, Churchill. Yet most contemporaries had to conclude that, despite their achievements, it was a *Baldwin* Cabinet.

Baldwin had a great capacity for taking advice, from Civil Servants, private secretaries, party officials, journalists and friends; but since he was a competent broker of ideas, as well as a ruminant and original thinker, few others branded him with theirs. The secret of his style of leadership lay in the creation of a supportive environment in which others could work. To the creative minds, Chamberlain with his long list of Bills and Churchill with his 'hundred horsepower brain', he gave freedom from irksome restraints and petty control; to others, like Austen Chamberlain before Locarno, he gave private help and asked no credit. Lord Eustace Percy, Minister of Education, saw that 'his support contributed more to their very solid achievements than any attempt he could have made to alloy their policies with bright ideas of his own in the Lloyd George manner'.[7] Again, the contrast with his predecessor was marked. Unlike Lloyd George or Neville Chamberlain, Baldwin never tried to be senior partner in each department as well as president of the Cabinet. His style was similar to Disraeli's, and Churchill commented, 'He was singularly adroit in letting events work for him and capable of seizing the right moment when it came.'[8] Birkenhead used to say, wisely, 'He takes a leap in the dark; looks round – and takes another'.

To those obsessed with the paraphernalia of red boxes, he appeared idle; but rather he was a reflective, indulgent chairman of Cabinets. Davidson saw that 'he intervened rarely with a definite conclusion of his own, yet when he did so, his mastery was complete'.[9] Thus he spoke out, decisively, against the Tory attempt to change the basis of the trade union political levy by McQuisten's Private Members Bill in 1925, in a famous speech which ended with the appeal; 'Give us peace in our time, O Lord.' A year later he forced through a reluctant party the

[7] Lord Eustace Percy, *Some Memories* (London, 1952), p. 128.
[8] Winston Churchill, *The Second World War*, i, 'The Gathering Storm' (London, 1959), p. 202.
[9] Viscount Davidson, Draft Memoirs (Davidson papers).

reorganisation of the electricity supply in the first Conservative essay in state capitalism. Above all, he made it possible for his ministers to speak out freely in Cabinet and yet listen to each other; and he created an environment in which men whose stature and wills could not easily be contained around a table found easy access, a sense of place, and a corporate aim. Samuel Hoare noted the contrast after Baldwin retired in 1937; 'Chamberlain seemed at once to crystallise all the fluid forces in the Cabinet. His clear-cut mind and concrete outlook had an astringent effect upon opinions and preferences that had hitherto been only sentiments and impressions. As soon as he succeeded Baldwin, I became increasingly conscious of two distinct points of view in the Cabinet.'[10] With this talent went a rare mastery of the House of Commons and of his backbenchers which rested on patience, infinite tact, and the acceptance of the art of the possible. As he once told a dinner of Royal Academicians; 'Your instruments, by which you work, are dumb – pencils and paints. Ours are neither dumb nor inert. I often think we rather resemble Alice in Wonderland, who tried to play croquet with a flamingo instead of a mallet.'

Between 1925 and 1929 Baldwin's direct influence is to be found principally in economic and foreign policy, rather than in social reform. In that sphere, given his head, Chamberlain ran remorselessly through a tide of legislation culminating in the Local Government Act of 1929 and the administrative foundations of the Welfare State. Meanwhile, Baldwin broke slowly through the carapace of his years at the Treasury. In his only Budget speech, in 1923, he had called for 'an avowed and sustained programme of debt reduction from revenue'. Such orthodoxy underlay his own and the Labour Government's approaches to what the Treasury called 'the Departmental Problem' until interest rates finally fell in 1932. His essay in Protection can, however, be seen as an attempt to escape from the remorseless logic of deflation and return, at the old parity, to the Gold Standard as the only cure for the overriding questions of unemployment and industrial stagnation. After the loss of that hope in the 1923 election, Baldwin had reluctantly to accept the consequences, and take over where the Labour Government and Snowden had left off. Despite the fulminations of Keynes, he supported Churchill in returning to gold in 1925. It was not then clear that the pre-war standard had worked, not of its own momentum, but because the Bank of England made it work. But in the later 1920s it proved impossible to

[10] Lord Templewood, *Nine Troubled Years* (London, 1954), p. 257.

build up strong enough reserves, in relation to Paris and New York, to support such a role again, while high interest rates made the conversion of the wartime National Debt impossible and impeded the flow of capital for industrial investment.

For these reasons, and despite his pledge against tariffs, Baldwin was tempted to use the Safeguarding procedure as a means to help industries threatened by excessive competition and dumping. Sadly, he allowed himself to be restrained by Churchill's threat to resign over the test case of iron and steel. Some ways *were* found to help industry; Baldwin was instrumental in the formation of the Lancashire Cotton and English Steel Corporations, and he urged the Bank of England to take the first steps in what became in 1929 the Bankers Industrial Development Corporation. Some government facilities were provided via the Industrial Transference Board for unemployed men to change jobs; and industry was relieved of the burden of rates. These were not insignificant measures in the 'rationalisation' period after 1927, which saw the creation of great combines such as ICI and British Oxygen. But, like all his ministers, Baldwin accepted the Treasury arguments against the use of government funds on any large scale to propagate employment by public works. Retrenchment was still valued as the classic remedy, while deficit financing was repelled, together with Lloyd George's brilliant programmes set out in the Yellow Book and *We can conquer unemployment*. In a dubious precedent, Baldwin asked the Treasury to prepare an antidote to the latter, for public consumption – and this negative response proved to be the only real Conservative manifesto for 1929.

Industrial discontent and the General Strike were seen through a similarly clouded glass. Baldwin stood for a world of free bargaining, in which a government's duty was to hold the ring and protect the weak, without going so far as to coerce the strong. It was not an easy line to maintain in the 1920s, given the rapid decline of the coal industry, working-class insecurity in the face of unemployment, and the desperate struggles of employers' organisations to recapture markets and profits which led to the widespread attempts to lower wages in 1925–6. Since 1910, and particularly under Lloyd George, governments had committed themselves further and further to intervention in major strikes. However Conservatives might deplore the trade union expectations to which this gave rise, they could not easily ignore them. Each special circumstance thus became a test case.

Baldwin intervened, personally, on 'Red Friday' in July 1925, to extend the government subsidy to the coal industry, despite warnings of Conservative economists and mine-owners, because he believed that the public was not then ready for a showdown over the issue of reducing wages. Yet he believed wages were generally too high in the declining staple industries for Britain to recapture her export markets in coal, iron and steel, cotton and the rest. In his view, rationalisation of the mines, as expressed in the Samuel Report, was the correct approach; streamlining would make them profitable, and profitability would, in time, restore wages. Nationalisation was not an answer nor (and here there was a good deal of ambivalence) was state capitalism, even though that had already been acceptable when applied in the case of the Central Electricity Board.

The Government prepared for the General Strike with considerably more resolution than the TUC, and its organisation included not only the civilian volunteer brigade but a highly efficient deployment of paramilitary strength. The evidence of the negotiations in the fortnight before the Strike shows that Baldwin went well beyond the majority of his Cabinet in his attempts to agree on a formula with the trade union negotiating committee; but he would not use government authority to coerce the mine-owners, and when the talks broke down he took a high 'constitutional' stand – against the day when government would become, irrevocably, third party to any major dispute. The Government won, but for the last time; and as the coal strike dragged on, in desperate misery, into the winter, Baldwin and Churchill attempted to pick up the pieces. They were only partly successful. Despite Baldwin's broadcast 'our business is not to triumph over those who have failed in a mistaken attempt', he was unable to prevent widespread victimisation of strikers, many of whom lost seniority and pension rights.

Baldwin had been known as an unusually humane, if paternalistic, employer. He knew well and valued what he regarded as the moderate trade union leaders, Pugh, Hodges, Hicks, Bevin or Citrine, but he eschewed the Communist party and the Minority Movement. Hence his support for the 1927 Trades Disputes Act, intended as an occasion to define picketing, bring in a secret ballot and restore what Conservatives considered the imbalance of 1906 Act. Even when it was distorted by violent pressures from the party Conference into a vindictive and legally absurd reprisal, he did not dissent. Conservative policy towards industry was still inchoate. Without the aid of Protection or state control, there was perhaps no way to create a 'national' coal industry to satisfy both owners and miners. Instead, after the men returned, beaten, to district agreements and longer hours, Baldwin, working through Lord Weir, discreetly set the stage for the Mond-Turner 'peace in industry' talks which took place in 1928. As the number of strikes fell sharply, and as real wages for those in work rose slowly, the methods of round table bargaining came to appear successful and desirable in contrast to the open warfare of the 1920s. By the 1930s, what had been only tentative ideas of state interference and regulation had become, in Baldwin's third term of office, acceptable and even rooted in Conservative dogma. Against the charge that these years were wasted in sterile strife, it is fair to say that the period 1921-6 was exceptional: militancy and working-class solidarity were a response to the last major assault by employers' associations against trade union rights and established wage levels. Without the strife, Baldwin might not have been able after the General Strike to forecast a new *entente* between government and TUC, and certainly not one that lasted for forty years.

In foreign affairs, Baldwin's policy was in the long term equally definitive for his party and for the National Government of the 1930s. He took the chair at the Committee of Imperial Defence regularly after Curzon's death in 1925, believing (as he said when he opposed the creation of a separate Ministry of Defence) that the Prime Minister himself must have full knowledge of grand strategy and the means to control it. As Chairman, he instituted the Joint Planning Committee and the Chiefs of Staff annual review of defence, and did much to whittle down inter-service rivalry. But in defining the balance between defence requirements and the claims of the peacetime Budget, he had to contend with Churchill's restless search for economy, the assault on the naval estimates, and the 'cruiser crisis' of 1925 – perhaps the nearest his Government came to breaking up, and on lines of the old division between Coalition and Baldwin devotees.

Towards the League of Nations Baldwin showed a sympathetic scepticism. While he mortified League supporters by abandoning the Geneva Protocol, he gave Lord Robert Cecil (and, by association, the League of Nations Union) a place in the Cabinet and put up with his harangues because he represented to the public all the emotional and political capital vested in the concept of collective security. Nevertheless, Baldwin gave priority to old-style diplomacy and to the balance of power in Europe. Sensitive to the economic strength of Stresemann's

Germany, he was in the 1920s isolationist in the sense that Lord Salisbury had been – so long as the winds across the Channel were fair. Mistrustful of Russia and the subversive work of the Comintern, he also turned against the United States because of the aggressive role of the 'big Navyites' and the American attack on British cruiser ratios at the Geneva Disarmament Conference in 1927. Chamberlain noted: 'S.B. says he has got to loathe Americans so much he hates meeting them.'[11] This sharp contrast with 1923 reflected his disappointment at the American failure to live up to role of arbiter in European affairs. The mood did not last and amity was restored in Roosevelt's day, but by then, after the Depression, American isolationism was firmly anchored in public policy. This was the price of Baldwin's perception of the incompatibility of American ambitions and British Imperial defence.

No prime minister can emerge from a five-year term with his old vitality intact. Baldwin, once a competent skier and still a prodigious walker, had been exceptionally fit, but by 1929 he was suffering from diminishing returns even from his lengthy holidays abroad. The nervous weakness of his childhood returned, especially in the months after the General Strike. Family discontents dogged him: his eldest son lived with another man, and for a while, until their reconciliation, as a Labour MP taunted his father from the opposite benches of the House of Commons. Steel shares plummeted in the 1920s and diminished income brought Baldwin a series of debilitating worries. Astley was run on a pittance and the house in Eaton Square had to be sold. Much of his former lightness vanished, and his quips – about Lloyd George ('he who lies in the bosom of the Goat spends his remaining days plucking out the fleas'), or Curzon ('I met Curzon in Downing Street, from whom I got the sort of greeting a corpse would give to an undertaker') – were heard more rarely. His acquaintances noted an increasing deafness. He was, after all, 62.

There is no need to look to the leader alone for the loss of the 1929 election. Abroad, the Depression was gathering; at home, rising unemployment. The memory of the slack years 1927–8, the fitful attacks of the press, and the behaviour of the lunatic fringe of the party, all contributed, while Labour and Liberals made steady gains in local politics and by-elections. But against the vivid promises of the Liberal programme and *Labour and the Nation*, both of which urged vast

[11] Neville Chamberlain papers.

extension of state authority, Baldwin could only proclaim bleakly that there was no easy substitute for the long road of economic reconstruction, by what now seemed a scarcely credible private enterprise.

For this reason, the attacks on his leadership revived when the results (Conservatives 261, Labour 287, Liberal 59) were known. His failure was doubly exposed because many had predicted astonishing success for Lloyd George, and when that too was denied, they blamed Baldwin's torpor for the Labour gains. In 1924, reprisals had come chiefly from the press lords, Beaverbrook and Rothermere, but in the two years after 1929, it was more broadly based and the rebels found two great causes, Empire free trade and the 'defence' of India against independence. In retrospect, given Baldwin's experience of Dominion protectionism at the Ottawa Economic Conference in 1932, Empire free trade was a decade late and slightly absurd. But both causes appealed to deeply felt Tory traditions, the more so since this time the dissidents had a Crown Prince in Neville Chamberlain. Against what Bridgeman called 'a display of the worst qualities of the Party under the effects of defeat',[12] Baldwin retreated steadily. The campaign enforced the resignation of his close friend J. C. C. Davidson as chairman of the party, and over India Churchill, 'once more the subaltern of Hussars of '96', retired to the back benches. Yet it was only when the Principal Agent defected, in February 1931, that Baldwin seriously considered resignation. He was instead induced to test his popularity at the by-election at St George's, Westminster, where Duff Cooper agreed to act as his champion. During the campaign, which Cooper won spectacularly, Baldwin worked off a lifetime's anger against irresponsible Fleet Street political demands: 'What the proprietorship of these papers is aiming at is power, and power without responsibility – the prerogative of the harlot throughout the ages.'

Beaverbrook said afterwards: 'He always won – the toughest and most unscrupulous politician you could find – cold, merciless in his dislikes.'[13] For once in his lifetime this was true of Baldwin; and his fury was enhanced by a sense of time slipping by. His recapture of the political limelight was overdue, for the Labour Government was manifestly tottering. In the subsequent months, some of the ground of attack against MacDonald was fair – the failure even to contain unemployment after the promises of 1929, and the refusal to consider a

[12] Lord Bridgeman, Political Notes II (Bridgeman papers).
[13] Sir John Elliott papers.

tariff (now firm Conservative policy); but some was less so, for it was questionable for an ex-Prime Minister, who in his own time had accepted the bankruptcy of the Unemployment Insurance Fund, to damn Labour's borrowing from future taxation as 'unsound finance'. Overtures from MacDonald in the summer of 1931 were rejected: and when the storm broke in August, Baldwin held firmly that if the Government resigned, the Conservatives should reign instead. Sympathy for the Labour party did not extend as far as support for its incompetence. He resisted Neville Chamberlain's blandishments to join a National Government and wrote to him: 'I think in the long view it is all to the good that the Government have to look after their own chickens as they come home to roost, and get a lot of the dirt cleared up before we come in. To have the consequence of their finances exposed – and acknowledged to the world – within four months of their budget, would be a wonderful lesson.'[14]

Nevertheless, Baldwin obeyed when the King asked him, as Conservative leader, to join the National Government under MacDonald. He did respect the Labour leader, and he accepted the need, then and later, to contain Liberal support in face of the world crisis. Party duty was served by ensuring fair shares in the election of 1931 – an often vindictive affair in which Baldwin, more than most, restrained himself from throwing mud at the Labour party MacDonald had left. He contented himself with talk of 'sound, clean, honourable finance' and 'the acid test of democracy', and many who had voted Labour for a generation abstained or even swelled the massive National gains, like Thomas Jones, who 'voted Conservative for the first time in my life . . . we had to do it. . . . we could not trust them with the Bank of England – just yet. But that too will come.'[15] In the aftermath, with his sense of the absolute need for a two-party system, and his fear of what Jones called 'parliamentary dictatorship,' Baldwin may have helped to accomplish the latter. He never denied the moral challenge of socialism. He admired Lansbury's courageous leadership of the denuded Labour party in the 1930s, and in ways both open and obscure he tried to keep open the parliamentary stage for its revival after 1935. What he despised were 'economic dons who were using the working man as a tool for trying their intellectual experiments on England', and he deplored the attempts of the ILP, the Communist party and the Socialist League to drag

[14] Neville Chamberlain papers.
[15] Thomas Jones, *Diary with Letters* (London, 1953), p. 20.

politics out of the House of Commons onto the platform of populist revolution.

The fact that Baldwin was only Prime Minister again between June 1935 and June 1937 is significant: he allowed the compact with Mac-Donald to run for four years, despite the enormous preponderence of Conservatives in the Coalition. As Lord President of the Council, Baldwin had a brief to interest himself in whatever issues he chose. Others took the great offices – Neville Chamberlain the Exchequer, Simon the Foreign Office. Like Balfour after 1904, Baldwin became an elder statesman above the ordinary rut of party warfare. To a large extent as a result of his work, the Conservatives had emerged from their half-way house of 1929 into acceptance of the tariff, low interest rates, a managed currency and abandonment of the fixed parity with the dollar. They would not yet face up to the problem of the depressed areas, nor Keynesian economics, but these were not the issues Baldwin chose in the 1930s. Instead he took India, his preoccupation since his choice of Edward Wood (Lord Irwin, later Lord Halifax) as Viceroy in 1926. To bring the subcontinent nearer to independent status seemed the climax of his career, an achievement for which he would have been happy even to split his party. Discord was inevitable, whether the rebels were led by Churchill or not. After the Irwin Declaration which he supported, though doubtful about the specific promise of Dominion status, Baldwin was unable to smooth over the jagged conflicts of Conservative opinion. During what he called 'the year my party tried to get rid of me', he identified his opponents and sought instead to smash them. In the debate on the Round Table Conference in 1931, he said of Churchill's intemperate language: 'I felt that if George III had been endowed with the tongue of Edmund Burke, he might have made such a speech.' Uneasy parallels with the tragic dealings with Irish nationalism recurred, through four years of strife, through the next Conference, the Commissions of Inquiry, and the elephantine progress of the Government of India Act, until its conclusion in 1935. As Party leader, he sustained the filibustering of the diehards of the India Defence League which reached its climax at the 1934 Party Conference when the platform survived by a meagre 17 votes – 540 to 523 – the nearest a Conservative leader has come to public defeat in recent times.

Baldwin made India an issue of confidence in his own leadership, and although it is arguable that he knew little of the real India and could not hope to see it through Indian eyes, he saw clearly that the debate lay with the British Parliament, which alone could grant political freedom. In one of his finest speeches he graduated from his traditional concept of Empire to a truly modern stance: 'There is a wind of nationalism and freedom blowing round the world, and blowing as strongly in Asia as anywhere. . . . What have we taught India for a century? We have preached English institutions and democracy and all the rest of it. We have taught her the lesson and she wants us to pay the bill. . . . And are we less true Conservatives because we say: "The time has now come"?'[16]

Many of his arguments for Indian independence were strategic. Just as with India, so with Egypt and the Suez Canal: it was time to settle before Britain's standing in the world was challenged too sharply. Since his first concentration on European problems in 1923, Baldwin had brooded on the terms for British survival in a world in which she was no longer more than one great power amongst five others – the United States, Russia, Japan, Germany and France. Unlike these, as he found from bitter experience, Britain had permanent commitments and liabilities across a world Empire, from which she drew little practical support. Hence his opposition to the scaling down of the cruiser ratio at the London Naval Conference in 1931 and his sensibility to the aggressive designs of Japan in the Far East. During the Shanghai crisis, in January 1932, Baldwin foresaw the depth of Britain's weakness and her inability to defend her interests in China, Singapore, even Australia and New Zealand. He threw his weight behind the demands of the Chiefs of Staff for abrogation of the Ten Year Rule, but the point at which he finally abandoned the MacDonald Government's quest for disarmament came when the report of the Defence Requirements Committee of the CID, in February 1934, defined Japan as the immediate but lesser threat; 'We take Germany as the ultimate potential enemy, against whom our "long range" defence policy must be directed.'[17]

During 1934, and at the heart of government policy-making committees, Baldwin strove to put that warning into practice, through new priorities of allocation within the defence budget, and by radically revised forward planning In March 1934 he defined his argument in the House of Commons: 'In air strength and air power, this country shall no longer be in a position inferior to any country within striking distance

[16] Speech to the Conservative Central Council, 4 December 1934.
[17] CAB 50/51.

of our shores'.[18] But this policy led to a sharp division in the Cabinet. It took shape in a confrontation with Neville Chamberlain over the defence estimates in June 1934, but personal differences only masked the contrast between two views of overall foreign policy, both of which superseded the search for disarmament. Chamberlain stood for limited liability, for a withdrawal from European commitments, in particular the promise of a field force to France, for concentration on air defence rather than on offensive bomber capacity, and for an accommodation with Japan in the Far East. Against this, Baldwin advocated the view that whatever the white Dominions might demand, it was impossible to withdraw Britain from the European context. Because Baldwin won, overall, the field force was retained as a pledge to the defence of northwestern France and Belgium; and the Locarno provisions were tacitly extended to Holland. The Navy was set to maintain the ratio of its lead over Germany – a policy that gave rise to the bitterly disputed Anglo-German Naval Treaty – and the mammoth base at Singapore was begun as a counter to Japanese expansion. The prime aim was the creation of a bomber deterrent, backed up by fast fighters and radar, to restrain Germany from aggression (much as the atomic bomb has been used in diplomacy since 1945) and to bring the Nazi regime to terms before it was too late.

Baldwin's standpoint was Eurocentric; and risked grave Dominion fears of exposure, because he declined to come to terms with Japan at the price of alienating the United States, for whose aid, in a European conflict, he still hoped. Over the next three years this policy encouraged a remarkable improvement in the Air Force: Scheme F, adopted in January 1936, added over three years 8,000 new aircraft of the latest types, including Hurricanes, Spitfires and Blenheims. Great risks were taken, the Hampdens and Wellingtons were ordered before prototypes had been tested, and the Bristol Beaufort went into production straight off the drawing-board. They were successful and Baldwin has a good claim to the Air Force that contained the German attacks in 1940. But rearmament conflicted with the popular mood – and it had only mixed results abroad.

In spite of his many speeches on rearmament in the 1930s, Baldwin found the process of public political education as hard to achieve as Churchill did in a hostile House of Commons. One of his potent warnings, 'The bomber will always get through', aimed at the unpreparedness

18 Hansard 286 co. 2078.

641

of 1932, proved a two-edged phrase, and in later years was used to defend appeasement, while his pledge to the pacifists of 'no great armaments', rather than rebutting accusations of a renewed arms race, stuck in the public memory as pledge against any rearmament. The tide of pacifism ran high, and not merely in the millions of signatures on the Peace Ballot. Sensitive to electoral vagaries, Baldwin watched swings of 20–25 per cent against the National Government in nearly every by-election from summer 1933 to summer 1935, of which Fulham East was only one amongst fifteen seats lost to a Labour party wedded blindly to disarmament. When he became Prime Minister, he was able to redress the balance by the cautious timing of the general election in November 1935 where he won a guarded mandate to rearm. This he preferred to Churchill's autocratic advice: 'There need be no talk of working up public opinion – you must not go and ask the public what they think about this'.[19]

Considering the broad support for war in 1939 it is likely that Baldwin was right. But the rearmament programme ran into severe difficulties in 1936, into bottlenecks of production, shortages of skilled labour, factory space, machine tools, and above all, into a debate in which the National Government and the parties refused to accept the logic of war demands on peacetime 'normal' economy. Worse, in 1935–6 the deterrent failed to deter. If Baldwin had been Prime Minister, or if he had gone to Stresa in April 1935, to try to ram home the disadvantage of Germany when faced by the other Locarno powers, there might perhaps have been hope for a European *détente*. In the event, Hitler refused to be tied to arms limitation, used the British Defence White Paper of 1935 as justification, and claimed 'absolute equality of status'. Anglo-French accord dissolved, over the Franco-Soviet Treaty and the Anglo-German Naval Treaty, even before the Italian invasion of Abyssinia. The attempts of Laval and Hoare to settle Mussolini's demands at the expense of Abyssinia and the League brought particular personal shame for Baldwin who, though largely ignorant of his Foreign Secretary's commitment, was forced by public clamour to sack him, and then stand penitent before an angry House of Commons. In the wake, Germany reoccupied the Rhineland and Britain proved militarily, and France politically, incapable of enforcing the Treaty of Versailles. The 'Subterranean Stage' of German recovery was complete.

Baldwin was urged by such powerful friends as Geoffrey Dawson,

[19] Hansard, 8 Nov. 1934.

Editor of *The Times*, to take advantage of Hitler's promises which accompanied the militarisation of the Rhineland in April 1936. Then, as in 1933, he refused to meet Hitler personally, fearing to commit the country as Chamberlain was later to do before Munich. Instead, Baldwin hung, doggedly, to the French *entente*; and it can be argued that, until the end of 1936, the Baldwin-Eden line of 'keeping Germany guessing' (what Vansittart called 'cunctation') while catching up in armaments had been, in terms of relative strength, a success. But in 1937 Belgium withdrew into neutrality and the Spanish Civil War focused attention on the growing weaknesses of France.

Supporters of the deterrent policy wavered, even before Chamberlain came to power bearing fixed ideas of limited liability. Some saw Britain's role in a form of Atlanticism, or as part of an Imperial aggregate; others looked to a more direct deal with Germany over African colonies; and this wave swept away the restraints, into the full flood of appeasement in 1938. Baldwin could not withstand it. He had already collapsed from overstrain in the summer of 1936, leaving Eden to cope with the Spanish Civil War – and he would almost certainly have retired that year if it had not been for the Abdication crisis.

Much of the attention focused on that dramatic and romantic episode has detracted from the reasons why Baldwin judged it so seriously. Long before the King's attachment to Mrs Simpson was known in Whitehall, he had been worried by what he had seen of the King's cursory attitude to his duties as monarch, and his pro-German sympathies. Baldwin hoped that the former might, with time, approximate more to the dignified version demanded by an Empire opinion which was in many ways decades behind British attitudes. The latter was more serious, given the Government's conclusion that Germany was the enemy against whom Britain should rearm. But Baldwin did not submit to the demands of several ministers and senior Civil Servants that the King's desire to marry Mrs Simpson should be used as a pretext to replace him. Only Edward VIII's firm will, and the Dominion reactions to it, made abdication inevitable.

Baldwin's handling of the crisis – his tact and the manner in which he ensured a dignified conclusion – was greatly praised at the time, as the supreme act of his political career. He himself attached more importance to the warnings he gave, after he had begun to hand over defence policy to Neville Chamberlain, and before his actual retirement in June 1937: such as that to the House of Commons in February 1937: 'We shall neither assure our safety and that of the Empire, nor play our part in securing the peace of the world, unless we bring our forces up to the necessary standard. Deterrence is our object . . . ineffective deterrence is worse than useless.'

Within weeks of that speech, Chamberlain had begun to recast defence priorities to the exclusion of deterrence. The new order led directly into the appeasement policy which culminated in the Munich 'settlement' of 1938. With that, Baldwin disagreed, and for a while he became the focus of the Tory opposition to Chamberlain. But he was nearly seventy then, and he preferred to abstain from active politics, propagating instead, in lecture tours in Britain and America, his distilled opinions about the value of democracy and the evils of totalitarian authority. The hyperbolic praise showered on him in 1937 soon dissolved, and the war brought obloquy and splenetic denunciation for his alleged failure to rearm. A sustained assault against his reputation was mounted, by sections of the press, the authors of *Guilty Men*, and a number of private individuals whose letters penetrated, unfailingly, to Astley, where he spent his retirement. He bore them in public silence. Privately he came near to despair and found pleasure only in his friends, and in his honorific duties as Chancellor of Cambridge University. Restricted by ill health, he walked with difficulty; afflicted by the public clamour over the requisitioning of his garden gates for scrap, he seems to have accepted the role of scapegoat and sought comfort in his High Anglican faith. His wife died first, leaving him bewildered and lonely: he followed in 1947.

It was not a time for praising the great men of the inter-war years, and Baldwin suffered posthumously in the account of his unwilling first biographer. Criticism was directed, ironically, to rearmament, an issue where his record was impeccable, and the equally important work of the 1920s was ignored. Now, half a century has passed since he became Prime Minister and his achievements can be seen in the mainstream of British Conservatism, which he did more than most twentieth-century party leaders to shape. His public persona, remembered through his mastery of the political platform, the House of Commons, and broadcasting, coloured two decades – the Baldwin Age. His phrases and images became clichés from constant repetition. By giving illustration and substance to the concepts of party, democracy, freedom, he welded his own particular vision into a public consciousness and ensured that the result reflected a wholly 'English' tint. In this he fulfilled Hegel's dictum: 'The great man of the age is the one who can put into words the will of his age, tell his age what its will is, and accomplish it.'[20] His definition of politics lay midway between nineteenth-century paternalism and the as yet unsolved search for popular participation. As he told Halifax in 1928, 'Democracy has arrived at a gallop in England and I feel all the time that it is a race for life; can we educate them before the crash comes?'[21]

The 'civilisation' he spoke of frequently, defended, and feared to see destroyed in war with Germany, was, properly, European from before the 1914 deluge; it was restricted by certain standards but was not exclusive, nor wholly class-based. He would quote approvingly the words of Colonel Rainboro, who put the case for the Army in the Putney debates of 1647: 'Really, I think the poorest he that is in England hath a life to live as the richest he.' Baldwin's creed was that of individual responsibility through political commitment. Hard as it was for him to understand the dictators, he did not make the mistake of underestimating them or the ideology they represented. He defended democracy to a Canadian audience in 1927: 'How often has mankind travelled on the circumference of a wheel, working its way to a point that you could call democracy. Go but a little further, and democracy becomes licence, licence becomes anarchy, and the wheel goes full circle and anarchy comes back to tyranny, and man has to fight his way back out of tyranny once again.'

BIBLIOGRAPHY

Baldwin, A. W., *My Father: The True Story* (London, 1955); *The Macdonald Sisters* (London, 1960)
Hyde, H. Montgomery, *Baldwin, the Unexpected Prime Minister* (London, 1973)
Middlemas, R. K. and Barnes, A. J., *Baldwin: A Political Biography* (London, 1969)
Young, G. M., *Stanley Baldwin* (London, 1952)

[20] Hegel, *Philosophy of Right* (London, 1942), p. 295.
[21] Halifax papers.

JAMES RAMSAY MACDONALD

BY

KEITH ROBBINS

James Ramsay MacDonald, PC (1924), FRS (1930); Hon LLD (Wales, Glasgow, Edinburgh, Oxford, McGill), JP. Born 12 October 1866, son of J. MacDonald of Lossiemouth, and educated at a board school. Secretary, Labour Party 1900–12; Treasurer 1912–24; Chairman, Independent Labour Party 1906–09; Leader of the Labour Party 1911–14; member LLC 1901–04. Sometime editor of Socialist Library *and the* Socialist Review. *Contested (Lab.) Southampton (1895), Leicester (1900), W. Leicester (1918), E. Woolwich (1921). MP (Lab.) Leicester 1906–18, Aberavon 1922–29, Seaham 1929–31, Seaham (Nat. Lab.) 1931–35, Scottish Universities 1936–37. Chairman of Parliamentary Labour Party and Leader of the Opposition 1922; Prime Minister and First Lord of the Treasury, Foreign Secretary 1924; Leader of the Opposition 1925–29; Prime Minister and First Lord of the Treasury 1929–35; Lord President of the Council 1935–37. Married 1896 Margaret Ethel, daughter of Dr J. H. Gladstone, FRS; two sons, three daughters. Died 9 November 1937. Author of* Socialism and Society, Labour and the Empire, Socialism and Government, Margaret Ethel MacDonald – a Memoir, Social Unrest, The Government of India, Parliament and Revolution, *etc.*

James Ramsay MacDonald, by J. Lavery

JAMES RAMSAY MACDONALD

The early twenties in Britain witnessed a glut of prime ministers. Lloyd George, the man who had won the war, struggled in vain to keep his peacetime Coalition together. When it collapsed, in October 1922, few supposed that he would not be back. Bonar Law then formed a 'pure' Conservative administration. Within six months cancer was diagnosed and he died shortly afterwards. Then came the amiable ordinary Stanley Baldwin and it seemed that the country was about to settle down. Nevertheless, before the end of the year, despite his parliamentary majority, Baldwin declared that he could not fight unemployment unless he had a free hand to introduce Protection. That free hand was not vouchsafed. Both opposition parties gained ground but Labour was the larger. Free trade prevented a Conservative-Liberal coalition. Since prime ministers were on short service commission, Asquith may have supposed that soon, when Labour had failed, he would be called upon once more.

It was, therefore, a novel group of politicians who visited their rather puzzled monarch at Buckingham Palace in January 1924. For the most part quaintly attired, and looking somewhat embarrassed, they kissed hands on appointment as Ministers of the Crown. Having resumed their normal dress, the new Cabinet posed for a photograph. With one exception, the social origins of the members stood out – gentlemen and players rubbed shoulders uneasily on the road to Jerusalem. The exception was the new Prime Minister. Ramsay MacDonald faced the camera with resolute assurance, his features displaying neither humour nor amazement. He contrived to make the occasion seem perfectly natural. Nothing in his manner or appearance betrayed the fact that at his birth, fifty-seven years earlier, the suggestion that he would be a future Prime Minister would have been deservedly derided, for he was the product of a passing liaison between a ploughman and a serving-girl, both living in the north of Scotland.

At this juncture, MacDonald was the most remarkable man in British public life. He had not been to public school or university. He had not distinguished himself in commerce or in a profession. Yet he had broken through from obscurity to the highest office in the land. Lloyd George apart, he was unique among prime ministers. He knew in his own life the reality of deprivation and poverty. Mindful of this fact, there were those who believed that his first act would be to drag the mighty from their seats. Few could have predicted the course MacDonald did follow over the next decade.

The fears gained strength from the fact that it was Labour that was in office for the first time. In January 1924 new man and new party came together. The King could not recall an occasion when his first minister had to be sworn of the Privy Council before accepting office. Nevertheless, he thought the Socialists ought to be treated fairly and given a chance. The coincidence was indeed highly significant, though the relationship between leader and party was more complex than it would appear to indicate. Neither gloating over his origins nor denying them, MacDonald had changed in the course of his long journey from Lossiemouth. He did not forget the past, indeed he regularly returned to the scenes of his upbringing, yet its inheritance was ambiguous. He wanted the circumstances of the masses to change, as his had changed, but at the same time was there not something striking about his own achievement which marked him off from the masses?

MacDonald's strict Scottish education gave him a taste for reading and study. His matriarchal home encouraged the belief that he was rather out of the ordinary. Perhaps taunts about his illegitimacy spurred him to outstrip those who taunted. He came to England, first in 1884 and then, in 1886, to stay. He took clerical jobs, working hard and studying in the evenings. He did some occasional journalism. Politics already attracted him – he had latterly become private secretary to a Liberal candidate. MacDonald was sober, industrious, intelligent and eloquent. If he could wait, some Liberal association might adopt him as a candidate.

About this time, 1893, the Independent Labour Party was formed in Bradford. Its leading light was Keir Hardie. MacDonald had already corresponded with him, but delayed a year before applying for membership. He stated that he had hitherto placed his trust in Liberalism but he now encountered a disturbing hostility to Labour. MacDonald's decision was a bold one. The future of the new party was very uncertain and metropolitan intellectual circles tended to look down on this provincial creation. Undeterred, he campaigned up and down the country and became a member of the ILP's national council. His marriage, in

1895, to Margaret Gladstone, daughter of a distinguished scientific family, did not impede this activity. She shared his interests and their home became a place where Socialists visiting London frequently called. His wife's private income helped him to fit into the intellectual middle class. He may have lacked an extensive formal education but he gave the appearance of being thoroughly at ease in discussing the scientific and social questions of the day.

The Labour Representation Committee was formed in 1900 and MacDonald became its unpaid secretary. Its purpose was to co-ordinate the activities of the existing Socialist societies and the trade unions. An independent Labour group in Parliament was the aim. He excelled in this post. He negotiated a secret agreement with the Liberals whereby the two bodies agreed to give each other a clear run in certain constituencies. Under this arrangement, MacDonald himself entered the House of Commons in 1906. There were those who saw the twenty-nine 'Labour' MPs so returned as the advance guard of what would prove in a short time to be a mighty army. Looking at his colleagues, MacDonald was more sceptical.

The basic problem that confronted the Labour party, as it now called itself, was one of ideology. How wide should its net be thrown? Should it embrace all supporters of 'Labour', confine itself to trade unionists or restrict membership to Socialists? MacDonald's role in these debates was of fundamental importance. In a series of books, *Socialism and Society* (1905), *Socialism* (1907), *Socialism and Government* (1909), *The Socialist Movement* (1911), *Syndicalism* (1912) and *The Social Unrest* (1913), he made a decisive contribution to the party's thinking. In this decade his own outlook was settled. His prose style may not excite universal admiration. He is both pretentious and, at times, vague, yet the basic argument he presented was serious and his ability to interest his readers cannot be disputed. He was neither a Marxist nor a Utopian but he believed, nevertheless, that he was a Socialist. His critique of the existing capitalist system was a moral one. 'In every workman's heart,' he wrote 'there is a dim perception of a social order based upon the instinct of human equality and justice.' In time, expediency and business advantage would yield before this perception. The resulting 'society of human order' was what he called Socialism, and until it came there would be 'an agitating ferment in all other social forms'. The Co-operative movement, social welfare measures and agencies, profit-sharing, were all good in themselves but they only represented stations along the road to freedom. The time had now come to nationalise the land, the mines and the railways.

MacDonald did not doubt that it would be difficult to achieve this new order. Society could not be magically transformed overnight. However, he claimed that the Socialist method was the Darwinian method. Socialism was the logical culmination of Liberalism, not its antithesis. It wanted to extend not to restrict human liberty, but only where there was proper organisation and control could individual liberty flourish. He therefore worked for what he called 'organic transformation'. He despised what he termed the 'wild ravings' of Syndicalists and others who thought that they had found a short-cut to the future, by-passing Parliament. In his view, the nation was not a mere abstraction but rather a real community which transformed itself in the light of its past. The clamour in some quarters for a 'thorough' Socialist party was a mere apeing of methods proper to countries not endowed with a functioning parliamentary system. He went even further. Socialism was more likely to come about through a 'socialistic' party than through a Socialist one. A pure Socialist party would be tempted to believe that it could ignore the methods by which a society evolved, but that would be a profound mistake. It was also wishful thinking to believe that the assumption of governing authority by the people would make the State redundant. The object of government, he concluded, was not to enlighten the individual to do without government, but to enlighten him so as to co-operate with it.

MacDonald was Chairman of the ILP from 1906–1909, and it is not difficult to understand why he did not have an easy time keeping the party together. When he became Chairman of the Labour party in 1911 his problems were even greater. There was little parliamentary discipline and on a number of important occasions members opposed each other in the lobbies. The idea of a distinct Labour party did indeed make some progress but, in a period of social and industrial unrest, many felt that it should have been faster. Since MacDonald was, for most of the time, in one or other position of leadership, the criticism fell upon him. Personal relations with his colleagues deteriorated, particularly with Henderson and Snowden. MacDonald became introspective and acerbic. His wife died at the end of 1911 and he brooded long over his loss. For a time he talked of giving up politics altogether. His colleagues did not seem to realise how fortunate they were to have him.

The proper course for Labour to follow was still being debated when war broke out in 1914. The conflict split the party on new lines. Mac-Donald condemned British intervention, but after the invasion of Belgium most of his colleagues supported it. Probably with relief, he resigned the chairmanship, though he retained the post of Treasurer. His personal attitude towards the war was very complex, not to say contradictory. His statements are carefully qualified, if not deliberately ambiguous, and this has prompted the supposition that he hoped to emerge at a later stage in the conflict as the man to negotiate peace. He associated with dissident Liberals in the newly formed Union of Democratic Control though he was sceptical of some of its leading ideas. Yet, whatever the subtlety of his views, he was branded as a pacifist and the full welter of patriotic fury fell upon him. The personal slights he believed he received during these years left a permanent mark.

Throughout the war MacDonald firmly denied that he wanted a German victory, but he considered that it would be possible to arrange a reasonable negotiated peace. A penal settlement imposed as a result of outright victory would have disastrous consequences. He hoped that the growing confidence of international Socialism would mean that there would be a much greater sense of community among nations. He welcomed the revolutions in Russia in 1917 and his commitment to peaceful evolution seemed momentarily to waver. His popularity in the ILP reached levels never attained in the past. Yet this reputation for Radicalism did not mean that MacDonald was losing touch with the solid centre of the party. After Henderson resigned from the Cabinet in 1917, the way was open for a reconciliation between 'pro-war' and 'anti-war' factions. In any case disagreement on the war had not impaired co-operation on other issues. The days of a 'progressive alliance' with the Liberals were over. Labour was increasing in confidence and it was time to consolidate the party organisation and prepare for peace.

In the general election of December 1918, MacDonald's lonely wartime stand brought him scant reward. He lost his seat at Leicester and other 'pacifists' also fared badly. Labour emerged with a mere sixty-three seats, an improvement on 1910, but a figure that seemed insignificant beside the massive support for the Coalition. The idea that five years later Labour would take office and that the spurned candidate for Leicester would be Prime Minister seemed far-fetched. Labour's position was in fact stronger than its meagre representation seemed to suggest. It was equipped with a new constitution and a new programme. The wartime split in the Liberal party provided an opportunity for advance. Even in 1918, Labour was stronger than the non-Coalition Liberals and was, in effect, the Opposition. This status would be lost if the Liberals succeeded in coming together again as a united political force, but it was questionable whether this would happen. The leaders of the other parties were more worried by the advance of Labour than they allowed to appear.

MacDonald was bitter about his defeat at Leicester. He raged against the 'unregenerated villadom' and the 'darkened slumdom' to whom he attributed his defeat. His strength lay with 'the intelligent artisan and the intellectual well-to-do', but that had not been sufficient. Despite his anger with the obtuse democracy he refused to abandon his faith in open elections and the parliamentary process. Many around him were doing so. The post-war world hardly offered the peace and security that had been promised. Labour condemned the treatment of Germany in the peace settlement. Domestically, there was disillusion and industrial unrest. The example of the Soviet Union was contagious in some circles. 'Direct action' was in the air. MacDonald sharpened his criticism of government policy but he did not change his fundamental standpoint. In *Parliament and Revolution* (1919), he deprecated slavish imitation of the Soviet Union. Revolution would only create more problems in Britain than it would solve. Parliament was still essential and what was needed to make it more effective was better political education of the people. He was anxious to make it clear that opposition to intervention in the Soviet Union did not mean acceptance of Communism. His influence was critical in preventing the ILP from joining the Communist International and he worked hard to revive the Second International. In *Socialism: Critical and Constructive* (1921), he again stressed that Socialism could only move men 'by education and moral idealism . . . it takes no part in a purely horizontal tug of war between the working and the capitalist class, but is a Plutonic force beneath both heaving them upwards'.

The verdict of the general election in November 1922 seemed to show that Pluto was pushing to some effect. The Conservatives gained a clear majority but Labour had more seats than the still divided Liberals. MacDonald had tried to return to the House of Commons in the Woolwich by-election in 1921. Will Crooks's old seat was won by a VC who made free use of MacDonald's wartime position. In the general election he came back as member for Aberavon and within a few weeks was once again elected Chairman of the Labour party. The circumstances in which, a year later, he became Prime Minister, have already been described.

The mature MacDonald of 1924 was Labour's greatest asset. In the ten years since he had last been Chairman of the party there were a number of occasions when his career had seemed in ruins. The experiences toughened him but they also accentuated his tendency to rely exclusively on his own judgement. His stature both as a speaker and as a writer was invaluable. The poor performance of the Labour party in the post-war House of Commons in his absence seemed to show that his ability as a tactician was sorely needed. Henderson may have been a better organiser, Snowden a more electric orator, Clynes a solider worker, but in sum their qualities could not compete with the new Prime Minister. In this respect, the narrowness of the majority by which he had been elected leader was no real reflection of his stature in the party. There were the usual mutterings from Lansbury and others that MacDonald's Socialism was not their idea of Socialism, but they were discounted. MacDonald seemed to have sufficient support from all sections of the party to see him through.

Loneliness in high office is inescapable. It brought no new terror to MacDonald. From the very beginning, from the way in which the Cabinet was chosen, it was made clear that authority rested with the Prime Minister. He had no hesitation about appointing men who had little connection with Labour if their services were needed, though there were more working men than in any previous Cabinet. He made himself Foreign Secretary, believing, rightly, that no one else had a superior claim. He ruled the Cabinet firmly from the outset as if he had been sitting in the Cabinet room all his life. His less confident colleagues were both impressed and alarmed. They were pleased that MacDonald could hold his own with his predecessors, yet this very success meant that he would be unlikely to inaugurate a new style of government. A Labour prime minister seemed to be like any other prime minister. It also began to look as though a Labour government was like any other government.

MacDonald was not worried by these criticisms. He had early decided that it would be better if Labour did very little. It was in office, not in power. The Liberals were watching and waiting. Once they sensed that the Government was conducting itself incompetently, or that it was stepping ahead of what would be electorally popular, they would bring it down. Since there was a good chance that his colleagues would prove incompetent, it was best not to allow them to parade this publicly. Only in two areas, housing and education, did Labour strike a new note. The Housing Minister, Wheatley, was the only newcomer to make a name for himself. Local authorities were encouraged to increase their house-building for rent by an increased subsidy. The building industry was encouraged to gear itself for higher levels of activity by the prospect that this would continue for many years.

MacDonald himself was chiefly occupied with foreign affairs. The situation in the Ruhr, following the French occupation in 1923, had reached the stage where both France and Germany might be prepared to accept a settlement. He persuaded both countries to agree to fresh proposals for settling the reparations question drawn up by a committee under the American General Dawes. The result pleased the Prime Minister. He had demonstrated to France and Germany that Britain would act as a detached conciliator in Europe. The French connection, which he had so much disliked before 1914, was undermined and the Germans were encouraged.

In other respects, MacDonald was less 'successful'. Although personally not very enthusiastic about the League of Nations, it was expected that he should support it. He even appeared at Geneva. The great project of the time was the 'Protocol' which was supposed to strengthen and clarify the founding Covenant of the League. However, the employment of 'sanctions' – which could include the use of force – divided the Labour party. MacDonald gave his blessing to the plan, but in so qualified a form that it is likely that Labour would have rejected it in the end. That task was bequeathed to its successors.

The Prime Minister was also cautious in his dealings with the Soviet Union. On coming into office, he recognised the Soviet Government but the slogan 'friendship on the Left' had little appeal for him. He took a firm line in the negotiations with the Russians on questions of war debts, loans and trade. It was probably pressure from the back benches, led by E. D. Morel, that eased the path to the agreement. The fact that a treaty was eventually concluded led to criticism from the Conservatives and the Liberals. It seemed that the Cabinet was susceptible to 'pro-Communist' activity. When, shortly afterwards, the Government decided not to prefer charges against the Communist J. R. Campbell, accused of incitement to mutiny, the opposition parties saw their opportunity. MacDonald refused to accept a Liberal amendment – calling for a select committee investigation – to a Conservative motion of censure. The Conservatives then voted for the amendment and the first Labour Government was over. It had lasted less than a year.

In the general election of 1924 the Conservatives gained a comfortable majority over both opposition parties. It was a vigorous contest, made sensational by the release of the 'Zinoviev' letter purporting to urge British Communists to embark on a campaign of disruption. Labour lost seats but increased its vote substantially. The Liberals slumped badly. Inevitably, the record of the Labour Government was criticised within the party. Some now believed that Labour should never have accepted office in circumstances in which it could not carry out Socialist policies. There were over a million unemployed and the Government had made little contribution to solving the problem.

MacDonald seemed unperturbed. He had demonstrated to the country that Labour could be trusted to govern. Patience was needed and in due course the party would be given power, not merely office. The left growled angrily and the ILP went off in search of 'Socialism in our Time'. MacDonald refused to follow. Even though the general Strike in 1926 could have provided an opportunity to sharpen the class-consciousness of the Labour party, he would not be drawn. MacDonald reverted to his earlier conviction that Socialism was more likely to be achieved by a party that was not 'pure' in its Socialism. There was no evidence that the nation as a whole wanted Socialism and it was, to him, a contradiction in terms to talk of imposing it on the people. Socialism was a matter of intellectual and moral conviction which the community as a whole had to be persuaded to adopt. Time had to pass so that the appeal to 'Labour and the Nation' could be consolidated.

MacDonald never had enough time. At the general election in May 1929 Labour became the largest single party in the House of Commons. Nearly as many voted Labour as voted Conservative. The Liberal vote increased substantially but it was not reflected in additional seats. Nevertheless, the Liberals still held the balance, though they were in a weaker position than in 1924. MacDonald was at last near to that moral consensus of the nation which he so much prized. He anticipated that the Government would have a long life since the Liberals would be unwilling to expose themselves to a fresh election. This time the situation seemed much more propitious for Labour.

The Prime Minister seemed in a confident mood. He was even prepared to allow Arthur Henderson to become Foreign Secretary. George Lansbury became First Commissioner of Works. Philip Snowden resumed as Chancellor of the Exchequer. A million workers were still unemployed, but the industrial outlook seemed brighter and Labour was confident that the figure could be reduced. A modest degree of public expenditure would suffice, if the Chancellor could be persuaded to agree. As far as international policy was concerned, it was hoped that Henderson could settle the outstanding German grievances, mollify French anxieties, strengthen the League of Nations and bring about general peace and disarmament.

It is conceivable that all of these desirable ends could have been accomplished had it not been for the Great Depression which began in the United States in October 1929. Within a year the number unemployed had doubled and there were fears that the total would go on rising inexorably. The crisis was of a proportion beyond all calculation in May 1929. It was, at last, the crisis of capitalism, so long expected and so eagerly anticipated in Socialist circles. Eager anticipation did not characterise the reactions of the Labour Government. The Prime Minister told the Labour Party Conference in 1930 that 'the system' had broken down everywhere, as it was bound to do. The difficulty for MacDonald, however, was that it had apparently broken down under a Labour government. Labour would have relished the collapse if it had occurred under a Conservative government, but now it had an unwelcome degree of responsibility. MacDonald found himself entangled in the vagueness of his own rhetoric. What exactly was this 'system' that had broken down? Was it really 'capitalism' that was on trial?

The simplest solution to the difficulties was apparently to move directly to Socialism. There would not even be any need for a revolution. The Prime Minister could carry through the necessary changes under the rubric of his beloved 'organic transformation'. Yet, with the road so unexpectedly open, the Prime Minister suddenly found that he could not see the details of the Socialist city ahead. Twenty years earlier he had written of the seaman who steered by certain marks and then, as appropriate, altered course and followed new marks when the old could lead him no further. 'So', he had concluded, 'with Socialism.' The Socialist method was the 'organic and experimental one of relieving immediate and pressing difficulties on a certain plan, and in accordance with a certain scheme of organisation.' In the second Labour Government, MacDonald had no 'certain plan', though the difficulties were immediate and pressing. He had run out of metaphors and the limita-

tions of his economic judgement were exposed. There was little openness towards new ideas and policies.

The Prime Minister no longer even seemed efficient and confident.
He could derive no encouragement from his colleagues and could not
share his own problems with them. Only in matters of foreign policy did
he show any of his old vigour and spark. His visit to the United States
in October 1929 was regarded as a personal triumph and put an end to
a period of Anglo-American tension. It paved the way for the London
Naval Conference of 1930–1 at which again MacDonald played a leading role. He seemed to revel in these occasions and foreigners still
found his personality impressive. It was understood that the Prime
Minister would deal personally with Anglo-American relations but in
fact he did not confine himself to this sphere. He constantly expressed
views on relations with France and Germany, on the League, on disarmament and on the Soviet Union which frequently clashed with those
of Henderson, the Foreign Secretary. Their personal relations deteriorated and on several occasions it seemed possible that Henderson
would resign. MacDonald's views deserve respect, but the extent of his
supervision and intervention was inevitably irksome. It was sympto-
matic of his loss of confidence in other matters that he turned to the one
field of policy where he felt at home.

It was, however, impossible to ignore the effects of the Great Crash.
All sorts of unorthodox ideas for dealing with the crisis were being
canvassed. The Liberals under Lloyd George had fought the election
with ambitious schemes of public works – roads, houses, telephones,
power stations – which would mop up unemployment. MacDonald was
suspicious both of Lloyd George and the scale of the programme. However, he did appoint J. H. Thomas as minister with special responsibility for employment, assisted by Lansbury, Mosley and Johnston. It
did not take long for the limits of Thomas's understanding and energy
to be revealed. In January 1930 the Prime Minister announced the creation of the Economic Advisory Council composed of economists,
businessmen and trade unionists. He chaired these sessions but little
seemed to emerge from them. The energetic young Mosley became
impatient and drew up a memorandum urging action over a wide front.
His proposals included public control of industry, increased pensions
and allowances and the public control of banking to finance development. However, he also proposed Protection for the home market. The
Chancellor of the Exchequer was not moved. He adhered rigidly to

free trade and to the balanced budget. MacDonald may have had some sympathy for Mosley's proposals but he had no stomach for a struggle with Snowden. Mosley resigned and Thomas went to the Dominions Office. MacDonald announced that he was taking personal responsibility for the fight against unemployment.

This announcement made little difference. The number out of work reached $2\frac{1}{2}$ million in December 1930 and the future of the Government began to look uncertain. It was unlikely that the Liberals, internally divided as they were, would continue to support it. The Prime Minister's hold on the party was not in danger – Mosley had made little impression – but the crisis only deepened. The Conservatives criticised the wasteful policies of the administration. A committee was appointed to investigate the position and reported at the end of July. It drew a most gloomy picture and recommended increased taxation and economies, particularly in unemployment expenditure. Three weeks later, the Labour Government was over. What began as a financial crisis turned into a political battle. In the end the figure of a 10 per cent cut in the dole proved the stumbling-block. Although the Cabinet contained a majority of one in favour of the proposal, the size and stature of the minority made the continuance of the Government impossible. MacDonald asked his colleagues for their resignations and they were offered.

Next day he returned to tell them that he had accepted the King's commission to head a 'National' Government and that Baldwin and Samuel had agreed to serve. He invited their co-operation in what would be a temporary expedient to resolve the financial crisis but only Snowden, Thomas and Sankey gave him their support. In due course the political parties involved would resume their respective positions.

In the event, something rather different happened. Despite its protestations to the contrary, the new Government took Britain off the Gold Standard. Shortly afterwards, MacDonald received his 'doctor's mandate' from the electorate with a massive majority. He remained Prime Minister until 1935 when he exchanged places with Baldwin and became Lord President. He resigned with Baldwin in 1937 and later the same year died at sea on a cruise to South Africa.

It was a quiet end to a stormy career. It would be a slight exaggeration to describe MacDonald as a mere figurehead in his final term as Prime Minister. For good or ill he maintained an interest in defence and foreign policy. Yet he was inevitably isolated, surrounded by the Conservatives and ultimately powerless to resist their wishes. 'National

Labour' never amounted to anything substantial. He had made his decision in 1931 and for the remainder of his life could never escape from its consequences. The Labour party expelled him, attacked him and did its best to humiliate him. It had not occurred to MacDonald that men who would have been prepared to accept the cuts would round on him so fiercely. On the other hand, it was alleged that MacDonald had betrayed the party and had been plotting this course for some time. A great deal was made of MacDonald's supposed weakness for aristocratic company. Historians since have agreed that the most satisfactory explanation for his conduct is that he was the outsider who longed to be inside. There is always room for theories of this kind. Yet, with justice, MacDonald did not see himself as being inconsistent in his actions. He had been committed to the remoulding of the nation, not the emancipation of one particular class. He had failed. Even in his failure, however, he remains the most remarkable Labour Prime Minister, the only one to have come from the working class, the only one to have learnt his lessons in the 'school of life'. It is, no doubt, a sad commentary on this experience that Labour has since come to expect its salvation from the University of Oxford.

BIBLIOGRAPHY

Barker, B., *Ramsay MacDonald's Political Writings* (London, 1972)

Bassett, R., *1931: Political Crisis* (London, 1958)

Elton, Lord, *Life of James Ramsay MacDonald (1866–1919)* (London, 1939)

Mowat, C. L., 'Ramsay MacDonald and the Labour Party', in A. Briggs and J. Saville (eds), *Essays in Labour History 1886–1927* (London, 1971)

Skidelsky, R., *Politicians and the Slump: The Labour Government of 1929–31* (London, 1967)

NEVILLE CHAMBERLAIN

BY

CHRISTOPHER COOK

Arthur Neville Chamberlain, PC (1922), FRS (1938). Born 18 March 1869, second son of the Rt Hon Joseph Chamberlain, and educated at Rugby and Mason College, Birmingham. Hon LLD (Birmingham, Cambridge, Bristol, and Leeds); Hon DCL (Oxford); Hon DLitt (Reading). Resided in the West Indies 1890–97. Birmingham City Council 1911; Alderman 1914; Lord Mayor of Birmingham 1915–16; Director-General of National Service 1916–17; MP (Unionist) Birmingham (Ladywood) 1918–29, Edgbaston 1929–40; Postmaster-General 1922–28; Paymaster-General 1928; Minister of Health 1923, 1924–29, 1931; Chancellor of the Exchequer 1923–24, 1931–37; Prime Minister and First Lord of the Treasury 1937–40. Married 1911 Annie Vere, daughter of Major W. V. Cole; one son, one daughter. Died 9 November 1940. Author of The Struggle for Peace, *1939.*

(Arthur) Neville Chamberlain, by H. Lamb

NEVILLE CHAMBERLAIN

Despite the fact that Neville Chamberlain was Prime Minister for only three years, from May 1937 to May 1940, his premiership has proved to be one of the most controversial in modern British history. Perhaps in compensation for Chamberlain's failure to 'sell himself' while he was alive, he was very fortunate to have as his official biographer Sir Keith Feiling. Feiling published a large and judicious defence of his subject six years after the latter's death in 1940; but, apart from this 'Academy portrait' and one or two apologias from his ministerial colleagues, Chamberlain found few writers in the post-war decade who would defend his policy of appeasement, which had so manifestly failed. For a long time, it was virtually historical orthodoxy that Neville Chamberlain was probably the most naive, vain and pusillanimous Prime Minister Britain had ever suffered; not only had he repeatedly given way in the face of the armed might of the dictators, but he had wantonly obstructed measures to augment British strength to face further confrontations. It is only really since the arrival of the horrible possibility of a nuclear holocaust and the failure of the British venture in Suez in 1956, which made clear the dangers of the cavalier alternative to the kind of policy Chamberlain and others were pursuing during the 1930s, that there has been a serious revision of the over-facile condemnation of the 'appeasers'.[1] With the opening of the relevant Cabinet papers after 1967, the whole controversy has been rekindled, and it is, perhaps, ironical that the first scholarly book to appear on Chamberlain's premiership, using the new Cabinet material, is written by an anti-appeaser of the late 1930s, Ian Colvin, and published by Victor Gollancz, arch-critic of appeasement.[2] Colvin's book attempts a real body-blow to the revisionist school because it argues that the Cabinet documents do not, in fact, vindicate Chamberlain's policy, but make it even more certain that Chamberlain even undermined democratic government by making certain vital decisions without first consulting

[1] See Donald C. Watt, 'Appeasement: The Rise of a Revisionist School', *Political Quarterly*, vol. 36, no. 2 (April–June 1965).
[2] Ian Colvin, *The Chamberlain Cabinet* (London, 1971).

the Cabinet. Colvin's indictment of Chamberlain has been somewhat tempered by his reviewers and subsequent narrative accounts, but a full-length reply to Colvin's charges is still awaited.

Despite Chamberlain's predictable and easy succession to Stanley Baldwin in May 1937, there was a touch of controversy about even in the early phase of the new Government. Chamberlain had been a most orthodox Chancellor since the formation of the National Government in November 1931, and had religiously maintained Birmingham's eleventh commandment, that one should balance one's books. However, he somewhat departed from peacetime orthodoxy in his last Budget (April 1937), in which he levied a special tax, the National Defence Contribution, on those who were making a profit from manufacturing arms. There was such an outcry against the new tax on the privately owned arms industry (which the Chamberlain family had been so involved with), that Chamberlain was forced to withdraw the tax and replace it with a straight 5 per cent tax on all profits. Although this return to financial orthodoxy was typical of the future Chamberlain policy (until March 1938), it was a very rare example of Chamberlain giving way to outside pressure and admitting that he was wrong. Stubborness and righteousness were the key-notes of Chamberlain's character.

Neville Chamberlain, despite his age (he was sixty-eight), was the obvious successor to Stanley Baldwin, for whom he had already deputised during the latter's illness. Churchill later admitted that 'there was no doubt who his [Baldwin's] successor should be. Mr Neville Chamberlain had, as Chancellor of the Exchequer, not only done the main work of the Government for the five years past, but was the ablest and most forceful Minister, with high abilities and an historic name.'[3]

Three days after being made Prime Minister, Chamberlain was elected Tory leader, and with a wider electoral basis than the party had previously been used to. Chamberlain received particular support from those Conservatives who desired a more active leadership than Baldwin had provided. In so many ways, Baldwin and Chamberlain, though loyal to each other, were complete opposites. A. J. P. Taylor has pithily described the differences between the two men: 'The two were yoke-fellows rather than partners, bound together by dislike of Lloyd George and by little else. Chamberlain was harsher than Baldwin, more im-

[3] Winston Churchill, *The Second World War*, i, 172. Quoted in Robert McKenzie, *British Political Parties* 2nd edn (London, 1963), p. 45.

patient with criticism and with events. He antagonised where Baldwin conciliated. He was also more practical and eager to get things done. He had a zest for administrative reform.'[4] Chamberlain, like Baldwin, was a Midlands businessman, though not a very successful one; he had spent seven years vainly trying to make a profitable venture out of his father's sisal plantation in the Bahamas. On his return to England, Neville went into the copper-brass business but found his real niche in Birmingham city politics, where he became Mayor in 1915 and founded the first and only municipal bank in England. In December 1916, Lloyd George made him Director-General of National Service, giving him responsibility but insufficient powers to fulfil the job properly. The appointment was disastrous and lasted only seven months, but it left Neville Chamberlain with a hatred of Lloyd George that lasted a life-time. Chamberlain was a most energetic administrator but an inexper-ienced politician, who compensated with a stubborn, self-righteous integrity. All his life he mistrusted the flamboyant rhetoricians – men like Disraeli, Lloyd George and Churchill.

Chamberlain made his reputation as Minister of Health during the second half of the 1920s. Keith Feiling describes the Chamberlain achievement in stark statistics: 'He was free from the elections [of 1924] on October 30th; on November 7th he set his office to work on a four-year plan, and on the 19th laid before the Cabinet a list of twenty-five measures which he desired to pass. Of these, twenty-one became law before he left the ministry, the remainder were incorporated in later legislation. . . .'[5] This same penchant for detailed planning and forceful execution marked Chamberlain's chancellorship and his prime ministership.

It was Chamberlain's great misfortune that during his tenure of the premiership, foreign affairs and not domestic issues overwhelmingly occupied the Cabinet's attention; for Chamberlain's forte was in domestic concerns and in peacetime preoccupations, such as recovery from the slump and rehousing. He was not the ignoramus in foreign affairs that some historians have made him out to be, by taking seriously a joke that Austen Chamberlain aimed at his brother. However, he approached foreign policy with too many mental blank spots. For instance he mistrusted Russia and had the same dislike of Eastern European affairs that had marked his brother's regime at the Foreign

[4] A. J. P. Taylor, *English History, 1914–45* (Oxford, 1965), pp. 205–6.
[5] Keith Feiling, *The Life of Neville Chamberlain* (London, 1946), p. 129.

Office. Chamberlain did not trust the diplomats, whose methods he found cumbersome and contorted, and decided to undertake his own personal brand of diplomacy, which would bypass the Foreign Office. Unfortunately, he did not possess the subtlety or the mental agility or the skilled subterfuge required of the successful diplomat. Because of his integrity he could not hide his knowledge, and as his biographer admitted, 'His mental definitions were black or white, he distrusted neutral greys'.[6] Furthermore, Chamberlain decided on a dual policy of appeasement of the dictators and rearmament, which required more tact and subtlety than he possessed.

Such was the strength of Chamberlain's character and will that he managed affairs so that Treasury thinking dominated the issue of re-armament and in consequence, to some extent, foreign policy; while the Home Civil Service, in the guise of Sir Horace Wilson and Sir Warren Fisher, provided much of his advice on foreign policy. Anthony Eden, at the Foreign Office, had initially welcomed Chamberlain as Prime Minister, expecting to benefit from a man who was interested in and would support his foreign policy. It was not long, however, before the two men clashed over the direction of foreign policy. In September 1937 Eden learnt that the Prime Minister wished to speak in public on foreign policy the following month but was embarrassed that Eden had arranged to make one of his rare speeches only three days later. If this was a disconcerting omen of the dominant role the Prime Minister wished to play in foreign affairs, there were other more solid issues on which the two men disagreed. In January 1938, while Eden was abroad, Chamberlain personally replied to an American 'feeler' for a plan to launch a world discussion on the underlying causes of present dis-contents. Roosevelt required a swift reply and received it in the form of a chilly communiqué that American plans were cutting across British plans to discuss the *de jure* recognition of Abyssinia with the French and the Italians. Eden favoured outright acceptance of Roosevelt's pro-posals but returned home too late to participate in drafting the reply. Eden could not agree with Chamberlain's efforts to override the dictators by making terms with Italy, especially as the Prime Minister conducted this particular piece of overseas wooing through his sister-in-law, Lady Austen Chamberlain, who happened to be wintering in Rome. It is important to note that Chamberlain did, in fact, agree to stop using Lady Chamberlain as his contact with Mussolini when Eden

[6] Feiling, op. cit., p. 122.

objected, and that he almost reversed his policy in the Cabinet on the matter of the Roosevelt plan in order to pacify Eden. As it happened, the President's plan came to nothing, whereas the issue of *de jure* recognition to Abyssinia was to provide the immediate cause of Eden's resignation in February 1938. It is not true that Eden resigned over Central European appeasement, or because he objected to the Prime Minister's dictatorial takeover of foreign policy; the two men differed about the method of dealing with the dictators, but the important fact is that Eden failed to convince the majority of the Cabinet that his was the correct policy. Eden's private secretary, Oliver Harvey, realised this fact in his diary entry for 3 November 1937: 'His [Eden's] supporters in the Cabinet are flabby or unassertive, i.e. Stanley, MacDonald, Elliot, De La Warr; his opponents, Simon, Sam Hoare, Kingsley Wood, Swinton, Hailsham, are important and effective.'[7]

Eden was replaced by Halifax as surely as the fashionable Edenesque Homburg hat was replaced in government circles by the more traditional bowler. The 'Glamour Boys' were defeated and the 'Old Gang' were surely entrenched. Sir Robert Vansittart, Permanent Under-Secretary at the Foreign Office and a staunch opponent of Germany, had already been 'kicked upstairs' to become the rarely consulted (and never listened to) Chief Diplomatic Adviser to the Government. There is much truth in the accusation that Chamberlain surrounded himself with advisers who already agreed with his line of thought, but there is no truth in Colvin's allegation that he undermined democratic government by making important decisions without consulting the Cabinet. Several critics of Chamberlain have accused him of using an 'inner Cabinet' of four, which included himself, Halifax and two former Foreign Secretaries, Hoare and Simon, to make major foreign policy decisions. Colvin itemises the shifts of personnel that took place in the Chamberlain Cabinet and concludes that

'the Cabinet composition in May 1937 contained a wider range of minds than the Cabinet that faced the war crisis of 1939 . . . of the twenty-three Ministers whose opinions and responsibility were necessary to the decisions on war and peace in August 1939, eighteen Ministers were so like-minded with the Prime Minister as to preclude a real sifting of policy. Only MacDonald, Elliot, Oliver Stanley, Hore-Belisha provided

[7] John Harvey (ed.), *The Diplomatic Diaries of Oliver Harvey* (London, 1970), p. 56.

a little leaven to the debate. This had become a Cabinet of nonentities, presided by one magisterial personality.'[8]

Colvin exaggerates the measure of agreement within the Cabinet and understimates the divergency of the opinions that were put forward by the Foreign Office and the Defence ministries. If Chamberlain had his way in the Cabinet, it was because of the sharp rationality of his arguments, not because he browbeat the opposition. Chamberlain reflected the pessimism of the Chiefs of Staff about the ability of Britain and France to face the military strength of the Dictators; his policy of negotiation with the Dictators received overwhelming public support.[9]

Chamberlain based his policy on an utter hatred of war, a deep desire for social reform (which excessive arms expenditure would have made impossible), a mistrust of diplomatic entanglements, a realisation of the military weakness of Britain, the unlikelihood of Dominion support in a European war, a belief in personal diplomacy, and a feeling that the Dictators had genuine grievances, which, if met, would re-establish peace in Europe. The so-called 'inner Cabinet' was basically in complete agreement with Chamberlain over his policy. Samuel Hoare was much keener on a Soviet alliance than his colleagues, and Halifax had serious qualms about Munich, but these differences were subsumed and the inner Cabinet had a unanimity that allowed the Prime Minister to achieve speedy assent for most of his plans in full Cabinet session. The Cabinet was always consulted on major issues, though sometimes only after an urgent decision had already been taken. There was nothing unusual in this – Lloyd George had relied on a much smaller group of confidants, while each Labour government of this century has had its own informal inner Cabinet.

Chamberlain's mistakes in foreign policy stem not from a lack of good advice, but from his own belief in rationality. A. J. P. Taylor has written of Chamberlain's agreement with Southern Ireland that 'he [Chamberlain] did not appreciate that practical grievances, though real, were often the cover for deeper sentiment, which could not be so easily satisfied'.[10] De Valera would ultimately be content with nothing less

---

[8] Colvin, *The Chamberlain Cabinet*, pp. 261–2.

[9] A Mass Observation survey of September 1938 showed that 70 per cent of those questioned favoured Chamberlain's decision to go to Germany and to try to negotiate a settlement of the Czech crisis.

[10] Taylor, *English History* . . ., p. 406.